MEDICINE AND HEALTH IN NORTH AMERICA

COLOUR AND CULTURE IN SOUTH AFRICA

INTERNATIONAL LIBRARY OF SOCIOLOGY
AND SOCIAL RECONSTRUCTION

Founded by Karl Mannheim

Editor W. J. H. Sprott

COLOUR AND CULTURE IN SOUTH AFRICA

A STUDY OF THE STATUS

OF THE CAPE COLOURED PEOPLE

WITHIN THE SOCIAL STRUCTURE

OF

THE UNION OF SOUTH AFRICA

by

SHEILA PATTERSON

ROUTLEDGE AND KEGAN PAUL LIMITED

Broadway House, 68–74 Carter Lane

London

KRAUS REPRINT CO.
New York
1969

First published in 1953
by Routledge & Kegan Paul Ltd
Broadway House, 68–74 Carter Lane
London E.C.4

LC 53-24278

CONTENTS

PART I—INTRODUCTION

PART II—PATTERNS OF DIFFERENTIATION AND DISCRIMINATION

v

PART III—THE PRESENT SITUATION

ACKNOWLEDGEMENTS

It is unfortunately not possible to list individually the scores of people who have helped me so generously over the three and a half years during which this study was made and written up. I hope, however, that they will all accept this assurance of my sincere gratitude, for without their unstinted bestowing of time, interest and advice the work would never have been accomplished.

In particular I should like to express my appreciation to my husband, Bruce Tyrrell Patterson, who bore with me patiently during the whole period, Professor Raymond Firth, Professor Isaac Schapera, Dr. Kenneth Little, Dr. H. J. Simons, Professor J. S. Marais and Professor I. D. MacCrone, all of whom have read through the draft at various stages of its production, and have contributed invaluable suggestions and criticism.

SHEILA PATTERSON

Johannesburg

PART ONE

INTRODUCTION

CHAPTER ONE

THE APPROACH

If any body shall reprove me, and shall make it apparent unto me, that in any either opinion or action of mine I doe erre, I will most gladly retract. For it is the truth that I seeke after, by which I am sure that never any man was hurt; and as sure, that he is hurt that continueth in any error, or ignorance whatsoever.—MARCUS AURELIUS.

GUNNAR Myrdal, in the preface to *An American Dilemma*, gives his general terms of reference in the following passage:
'The study, thus conceived, should aim at determining the social, political, educational and economic status of the Negro in the United States, as well as defining opinions held by different groups of Negroes and whites as to his "right status". It must, further, be concerned with both recent changes and current trends with respect to the Negro's position in American society. Attention must also be given to the total American picture with particular emphasis on relations between the two races. Finally it must consider what changes are being or can be induced by education, legislation, inter-racial efforts, concerted action by Negro groups, etc.'[1]
The execution of such a work required the co-operation of a large number of specialists in various branches of the social sciences over a considerable period of time. Any single-handed attempt to follow similar terms of reference, even in the smaller South African context, must therefore seem unduly ambitious. In the absence, however, of any large body of sociological literature on, or indeed of a general sociological survey of, the Cape Coloured People, it seemed advisable to make as wide a study as possible of this group within the framework of the larger society, even at the risk of superficiality.
After a brief historical sketch of the origins and formation of the Coloured People, the study does in fact follow the general pattern outlined by Myrdal,[2] except that the final practical stipulation has not been followed out in comparable detail. The Negro problem presents itself to many American sociologists as one of applied science, i.e., how to bring the Southern 'caste-system' into line with the egalitarian,

3

open-class system advocated by the 'American ideal', a system which is practised in the North and backed by the federal authorities.

In South Africa, there is no such internal disparity amongst various sections of the white community, all of whom, unlike Americans, live in close contact with coloured groups.[3] There is a similar democratic ideal, but it is, in practice, reserved 'for Europeans only'.

The vast majority of white South Africans, whether private citizens or public servants, would agree without demur that the major function of their social structure is to preserve 'white' or 'European' supremacy. There is therefore no question of bringing the social structure of one part of the country into line with a more liberal ideal structure, as constitutionally laid down.[4] In addition, the Cape Coloured problem is now only a part of the overall colour problem in South Africa, and suggested solutions, even if welcome, would have to take into account the whole picture, which presents many radically different features.

In this chapter we shall define more closely the groups with which this study is concerned, and the type of structural relationships which exist within or between them. In the first place, the larger society, that of the Union of South Africa, is not coextensive with a 'community'. Following MacIver, we take a 'society' to be 'the system of social relationships in and through which we live', and a 'community' to be a group of individuals living 'together in such a way that they share, not this or that particular interest but the basic conditions of a common life'.[5] While it is true that South Africa has a single political and economic structure, and its citizens constitute a unified group politically and legally in relation to the outside world, internal social relationships are not 'shared' in a reciprocal manner. Instead some relationships are imposed by one constituent group upon other groups, while other relationships are withheld.[6] In fact, this dominant group actively opposes the extension of a wider community or 'we' sentiment to the subordinate groups,[7] and seeks to perpetuate its own exclusiveness and domination by every possible means.

Although the larger society could not exist, as at present constituted, without the presence and participation of the subordinate groups, its forms, nevertheless, have been and still are largely dictated by the interests and attitudes of the dominant group. In describing and analysing the status of one particular subordinate group, we are therefore concerned more with the relations between the latter and the dominant group than with its relations with other subordinate groups, except in so far as these are a product of the former relationship.

This is particularly true in the case of a 'marginal' group such as the Cape Coloured, whose status within the general structure varies according to the attitudes of the dominant group. Stonequist[8] ranked the Cape Coloured People as 'racially marginal.' The greater part of this group is not, however, the product of hybridisation between the two major existing ethnic groups in South Africa, the Europeans and the Bantu.[9] It is, on the contrary, the product of past miscegenation between Europeans and Non-European groups which have largely ceased to exist as such, in an area of the Union in which the Bantu only arrived a century ago.[10]

The Cape Coloured People are intermediate between white and Bantu in the pigmentation scale, but they are not racially marginal.[11] Nor are they culturally marginal, since they have no roots in, and few contacts with, Bantu tribal life.[12] The alien cultures to which their non-white ancestors belonged have died out, with the exception of the Moslem sub-culture preserved in the Cape Peninsula. As Professor Marais writes:

'. . . the Coloured do not appear to differ from us to-day in anything except their poverty . . . A Coloured community as distinct from the European does not exist in any realistic interpretation of the term.'[13]

The Cape Coloured group is therefore neither racially nor culturally marginal in the strict sense.[14] It is, however, socially marginal, in that the status ascribed to it by the dominant group, or various sections of the dominant group, has, at least since the Act of Union between the four provinces in 1909, hovered between those of the sharply dichotomised white in-group and black out-group. In Part II of this study we shall show how the Coloured group has been and is classed with the European group in some respects, and with other Non-European groups in others, and try to trace some trends in this apparently haphazard process.

In brief, we are studying what has ceased to be a culture-conflict situation, but remains in essence a 'race' or, more specifically, a colour-conflict situation. In view of the number of 'white' genes within the Coloured group, and of 'coloured' genes within the white group, one might have expected the conflict to resolve itself by gradual stages. Any such prospect was, however, checked by the arrival upon the scene of a new and formidable group, the Bantu, alien to the European both biologically and culturally. The attitudes evoked in the European group by this contact resulted in a re-stressing of colour distinctions, thereby adversely and permanently affecting the status of the Cape Coloured group.

We have spoken of groups within South African society. These groups are classified on a basis of ethnic, or putatively ethnic, divisions. They are customarily, and perhaps somewhat loosely, referred to as 'communities'—the 'European (or white) community', the 'Coloured community', the 'Indian community', and even the 'Bantu community'. Historically, there is little justification for the term, although the different formal status accorded to each group within the social structure has undoubtedly succeeded in evoking some kind of 'we-sentiment' within each division *vis-à-vis* the others. The extent to which this has occurred amongst the various smaller communities within the Coloured group will be discussed in Chapter VIII.

From time to time we shall also have occasion to note the imperfect coincidence of attitudes towards other ethnic groups amongst various communities or sub-groups within the European group, as for instance the English-speaking, Afrikaans-speaking and Jewish communities, or various rural and urban groups. These sub-groups are given only for the sake of illustration; other possible classifications could be based on occupation, provincial or religious affiliation, or social class.

It may be that in these variations within the wider European group lurk the seeds of some future settlement of the race-situation. At present, however, it must be admitted that colour-situations evoke the maximum community response of which the European group is apparently capable, and there are few European individuals who would dare to go against their own group on such occasions.[15]

Before attempting to describe and analyse the status of a group within a larger society, we must give our definition of status, whether of groups or individuals, and describe the principal types and determinants of status-hierarchy which arise in more complex societies.

Status is understood to be the position of an individual or a group, relative to other individuals or groups, within a larger social grouping or society.[16] This relationship is evaluated both by the larger grouping and the individual or group concerned. In its widest social context, status is a relative, subjective and fluctuating concept. It both acts upon and is acted upon by the more restricted forms of status, economic, religious, legal and so on. The latter forms have both a subjective and a formal aspect, which do not always coincide.

In the case of individuals within a group status would necessarily involve some form of ranking. In the case of groups within a larger group, status involves social stratification, which may range from an open-class system to a caste-hierarchy, according to the bases on which status-evaluation rests in the given society. These bases or determinants may be acquirable or unacquirable. In the latter category comes the determinant of birth, either linked with distinctive physical traits such as skin-colour or not; in either case, 'passing' and the practice of adoption break the rigid rule without affecting the principle. In the category of acquirable status-determinants come wealth, occupation, religious or cultural affiliation, education, and so on. All determinants operate either singly, or more often in various combinations. The bases on which status rests in a particular society are derived from the system of values evolved by that society as a result of its functional needs and the specific historical processes through which it has passed. The type of status-hierarchy which arises, and the type of group on which it is based, depend upon the relative emphasis which a particular society lays upon these status-determinants.

Where the main stress is placed above all on birth, individual inequality and hereditary specialisation, a rigid hierarchy of castes on the Indian model may result. Wealth and appearance are said to have no significance except in so far as they may advance the individual member within his own caste.[17] Birth and property taken in conjunction may produce a somewhat less rigid social hierarchy, such as the patrician-knight-plebe stratification of the Roman Republic, or the later stages of the English feudal estates. In both, adequate wealth was required to support the claim of birth as a status-determinant. On the other hand, the acquisition of sufficient property might cause the absence of suitable birth to be overlooked. In either case, a small degree of social mobility existed.

Since the rise of the bourgeoisie, and the passing-over of estates into classes, the trend in Western societies has been towards an increased inter-class mobility, and a closer approximation to an open-class system, with its emphasis least of all on birth, and most of all on the fundamental, or at least potential, equality of the individual.

In such societies there must always be individual striving, uncertainty and tension. Professor Cox has contrasted this situation[18] with the static and peaceful order of a rigid caste-system, in which each individual is said to know and accept his place, whilst the rivalry for position is not between individuals but between castes in the hierarchy, a rivalry which does not undermine, but strengthens the hierarchy. He contrasts it too with another type of status-hierarchy, based not on culture or occupation, but on colour, a qualification quite as immutable as that of birth within a given caste. In this situation, however, skin-colour by itself will not be permanently regarded as a sufficient status-determinant by the inferior groups at least, and the resulting conflicts will weaken and ultimately destroy the hierarchy.

There has recently been a trend amongst American sociologists to interpret colour-status hierarchies in terms of castes, and classes within castes.[19] The antithesis of class and caste is tempting in its simplicity, and several features of a caste-system, such as the prohibition of exogamy, and emphasis on birth and hereditary inequality, are common to both types of hierarchy. On the other hand, it is uncertain whether the Indian caste-system was ever based on racial distinctions,[20] and it would be difficult to account for the existence of not several but thousands of castes on this basis. Moreover, present-day recruitment to castes from tribes on the periphery of the system apparently takes place on an occupational basis, each individual craftsman or worker entering the caste whose hereditary specialisation coincides with his former occupation. In addition, endogamy in the caste system is maintained for religious and cultural reasons, and not in order to preserve certain distinctive physical traits.

In a colour-hierarchy, on the other hand, certain members of the subordinate groups may have attained cultural and occupational parity with members of the dominant group, as no caste-member could have done outside his own caste. The majority of these outstanding persons of colour are, however, still ascribed status according to distinguishable physical traits. The few who are not so distinguishable, and who have attained cultural and occupational parity, pass easily into the dominant group, and are lost to their own.

In justification of the 'caste' interpretation of colour-hierarchies, it must be said that in the period which followed the initial contact, in the simple agricultural society of the seventeenth-century Cape, the correlation between colour, culture and vocation was more complete than it now is. At that time, however, there was no 'caste-like' hierarchy and little colour feeling. Nor was there much attempt to preserve separate cultures or to restrict the haphazard extension of European culture to indigenous groups. It would, in fact, be equally apt to seek an analogy in the mediaeval European system of estates, which were functional and legally differentiated on a broad basis.

In neither case, however, is the analogy valid. Although the fundamental basis of caste affiliation is birth, it is not linked with physical traits.[21] In the case of estates, and still more of modern social classes, the status-determinants are acquirable to a greater or lesser extent. A colour-hierarchy, however, lacks the homogeneity and, after a period of acculturation, the stability of caste- and estate-systems. Again, in the major existing colour-hierarchies, those of South Africa and the American South, there is considerable variation and inconsistency in the formal and customary patterns of relationships between colour-groups, and evidence of great fluidity and change over a comparatively short period.

It therefore seems better, for the sake of clarity, to avoid the use of the term 'caste', even qualified as 'colour-caste', in referring to groups of this nature. For want of a better name, I shall call them ethnic or colour-groups. It seems advisable also to avoid the term 'class', since such situations can clearly not be described in terms of the vague, subjective shadings of modern, non-functional, social-class distinctions,[22] despite the nineteenth-century tendency of Cape Colony officials to refer to 'the coloured classes'.

A true colour-hierarchy is one in which religious, cultural and occupational differences have disappeared or been modified, while colour remains firmly ensconced as the ultimate status-determinant. This is an attribute which permits of little ambiguity. A person may be more or less coloured, but he is still a coloured person, and remains so whatever his class.[23] A complex, internal class-system has grown up amongst the Coloured people, but there is as yet little evidence for inter-class action or feeling between various colour-groups, even though the classes on either side of the colour-bar are based on similar determinants, and produced by similar causes.

There are various kinds of status which an individual or a group may hold within a larger group, such as legal status, political status, economic status and so on. A man or group may have formally equal legal and political status within a society and yet have very low social status. It is the latter kind of status with which this study is primarily concerned, the widest kind of social status, which is usually based not on one but on a combination of determinants. In the South African situation, the principal determinant is that of pigmentation, with cultural and economic determinants supporting and partially obscuring it.

Social status is, as has been said, a subjective and relative concept. It depends not only on the evaluation of a group by other groups within the society, but on the acceptance of this evaluation by the group concerned. In conquest-situations, the dominant group usually imposes a status-hierarchy based on its own values-system, which must be accepted by the conquered and subordinate group or groups. In colonial situations, where the dominant and subordinate groups are widely different in culture and physical traits, the status-hierarchy, once established, tends to perpetuate itself over a considerable period.[24]

In such situations, the values-system of the subordinate group actually breaks down in the course of culture-contact and change, or is broken down deliberately by the dominant group for its own purposes. The void is then filled by the modified values-system of the dominant group, a values-system according to which inferior status is ascribed to the subordinate group. In accepting the dominant values-system, the subordinate group, for a time at least, ascribes to itself and accepts inferior status. This close coincidence of status ascription by both groups produces a stable and static society and status-hierarchy.

Since no societies are permanently stable, dynamic forces sooner or later begin to act upon the status-hierarchy. Such forces may be of many kinds. They may arise within either of the groups concerned, or come from outside. They may spring from new political ideologies, from industrial revolutions or similar shifts in economic structure, from new or revived religions, such as Christianity or Islam, from increased acculturation in the subordinate group,[25] from large-scale miscegenation leading to a blurring of group distinctions, from a cultural deterioration of the dominant group, and so on. Any or all of these factors may disturb or unbalance the status-hierarchy, which should ideally be a structure accepted by all groups within it, whatever their status and rôle, rights, privileges and duties.

A disturbance of the status-hierarchy is particularly likely when the operation of one or more factors of the kind mentioned introduces inconsistencies into the values-system of the dominant group, which are ultimately communicated to the subordinate group. For instance, the spread of egalitarian doctrines and practice amongst members of the dominant group in recent years is incompatible with the status-hierarchy as at present conceived,[26] particularly in the case of acculturated individuals and groups who are forced to accept inferior status on the grounds of colour-distinction alone.

When a subordinate group, or a section of its individual members, begins to feel dissatisfied with its ascribed status, and when it achieves sufficient economic, political and military strength to support its demands for a higher status *vis-à-vis* the dominant group, the latter can react in one of two ways. It can submit to a reassessment of status on a different basis, or it can attempt to maintain the existing colour-hierarchy, and ultimately to restore the original status-hierarchy where colour and culture coincided, by means of discriminatory legislation and the use of force.

The overt grounds of status-determination in colonial societies are usually cultural or racial. In societies where status is based primarily on culture, there is a greater willingness to concede a higher status to those individual members of a subordinate group who have become sufficiently acculturated, and even to admit them formally to the dominant in-group.[27]

In societies, however, where status has come to be associated with race or colour, any demand from a subordinate group for higher status on the same grounds as those on which status is based within the dominant group is likely to evoke, not concession, but hostility and counter-aggression. Though such reactions may appear to succeed in their object of maintaining the status quo, the dynamic forces nevertheless continue to act until a new equilibrium is reached, by whatever means.

As has been stated earlier, a stable social structure tends to be associated with an agreement by all groups as to their relative status, while any major disturbance in this status-hierarchy, or refusal by a sufficient number of members within a subordinate group to accept the status previously ascribed to this group, is to be associated with social unrest and change.[28] When the higher status of the dominant group has lost all other bases than that of ethnic distinction, the status-hierarchy ceases to be indefinitely defensible, and the whole social structure is endangered.

This process must be particularly acute in societies which have ceased to be 'colonial', in the sense that they have become the only home of the dominant group. In such situations, a dominant group has much more difficulty in readjusting its own values. This is particularly so in the Union of South Africa, where a small and permanent white population rules over more than three times its own number of Africans, a large mixed-blood group and a smaller Indian minority. A small but increasing number of acculturated Non-Europeans have begun to question the status automatically ascribed to them as members of 'inferior' ethnic groups, often basing their objections on the values-system accepted by the Europeans within their own group. The European group has intensified its attempts to enforce the existing status-hierarchy. This intensified pressure has in turn affected the status-balance, and caused many more members of the subordinate groups to become dissatisfied with their status, and even to unite together, ignoring the status-levels which formerly divided them.

In such cases the dissatisfaction with ascribed status may spread deep into the as yet unacculturated masses, far beyond the reach or control of those individuals who initiated the demand for higher status. The larger society may then face the possibility of violent overthrow rather than a peaceable reorganisation of its status-hierarchy. Signs of such an eventuality are not altogether lacking in South Africa to-day.

This study may be of some little use in estimating possible developments in South Africa, since it is an attempt to analyse the various stages in the relationship between the dominant Europeans and the mixed-blood group which is so culturally and biologically close to it. Undoubtedly European-Bantu relationships now occupy the major place on the racial scene. Nevertheless, the situation as between Europeans and Coloureds is not characterised by certain factors which complicate the other relationship, such as the difference in cultures and the fear of ethnic and cultural swamping. It is not, perhaps, altogether too late to hope for the possibility of a peaceful settlement of the lesser problem, which might serve as a guide to the other.[29]

*   *   *   *   *

The methods of investigation adopted in this study were largely dictated by the great size and geographical dispersal of the community studied, which made intensive fieldwork difficult, by the limited period of the writer's stay in the Western Cape,[30] where alone the major part of the literature was available, and by the often-expressed demand for a general sociological reference book about the Cape Coloured group, which might serve as a starting-point for more intensive and detailed studies of this group.

All these factors conditioned the method of work, limiting it for the most part to library research,[31] and the writer's own field-work to a series of attempts to check, through personal contacts in the Cape Town and Western Cape Coloured communities, on the accuracy of facts and situations disclosed by the literature, and to get an idea of the reactions of the Coloured community to these facts and situations.

European attitudes were more easily available in the course of everyday life over a period of fifteen months, and such observation was supplemented in the course of interviews with civil servants, clergymen, trade union officials, teachers, farmers, industrialists and others, the majority of whom were extremely helpful. Difficulties were, however, sometimes encountered in such interviews, from individuals who appeared to detect or expect criticism of their 'way of living', and it was then difficult to phrase questions in a form that would seem innocuous. Occasionally, the mere fact of showing interest in the condition of the Coloured People was sufficient to arouse a wary hostility.

Allowance was made for probable bias, conscious or unconscious, in

B

all statements of fact or opinion made by informants, and in all newspaper articles and other written sources, including government publications. An attempt was also made to offset the writer's own personal bias,[32] and the preconceptions from which no student who has had any previous contact, particularly of a purely theoretical kind, with race problems can really be free.[33]

A further difficulty arose which does not usually trouble anthropologists in conventional primitive-culture situations. They may enter fully into the life of their group, or they may continue in the rôle of outside observer. They are not, however, compelled to fill two simultaneous rôles, those of 'European' and of 'investigator', vis-à-vis two separate groups of similar culture but different status within the same terrain. The student of a race or colour-situation is, however, usually accepted as a member of the dominant group by both dominant and subordinate groups, if he is white. As a resident member of the dominant group, he is expected to conform to the existing and approved mores in his relations with the group studied,[34] although a certain amount of 'academic licence' is permitted. Members of the group studied may be visited in their own homes or places of work, but convention frowns on visits by Non-Europeans to European houses on equal social terms, and forbids social meetings between members of the two groups in all but a handful of public places. The situation is further complicated for women investigators by the 'unwritten law' which forbids social contacts with male members of the subordinate group.[35]

These conventions are usually observed with punctiliousness by members of the subordinate group, whether from pride, cautiousness, habit or for other reasons. This formal observation of the conventions did not, however, seem to prevent Coloured people from talking freely when interviewed, though probably not so freely as they would have talked amongst themselves. I gained the impression that they talked more readily to me because I was an outsider, and in some cases because I was English, as many Coloured people seem still to feel some emotional link with Britain.[36]

Even those individuals who were as much opposed to the British system as to the South African structure showed a willingness to discuss the most controversial subjects, which suggested that a certain relief from tensions was obtained by the mere expression of resentment at white domination to a white person.[37]

As a consequence of the limiting factors mentioned earlier, the major part of this study (Part II) has been restricted to a detailed account of the various patterns of differentiation and discrimination, (if indeed differentiation in such a sphere can be other than discriminatory), whereby the dominant European group has, in custom and law, achieved and maintained for itself a superior status, and allocated an inferior status to all other groups in the society, with particular reference to the status of the Cape Coloured group.

In Part III it is proposed to examine the extent to which the action of the patterns outlined in Part II have produced and conditioned a recognisably separate Cape Coloured community, and to discuss the dynamics of the prevailing status-hierarchy, and the possible directions of development for the Coloured community. Dynamic factors in the situation include past and present white colour-attitudes, and Coloured reactions both to European attitudes and to the differentiatory patterns in which these attitudes find expression.

CHAPTER TWO

THE CAPE COLOURED PEOPLE

He arose and he exists in our midst; he knows no other civilization than that of the white man; whatever his shortcomings may often be in respect of it, his 'lewensbeskouing' is fundamentally that of the European and not that of the Native, and he uses the language of the white man as his mother tongue. In his case there can thus be no question of segregation . . . Economically, industrially and politically the Coloured man must be incorporated with us.[1]

F OR statistical[2] and administrative purposes, the population of the Union is usually divided into four groups: European, Native (or African), Asiatic (mostly Indian), and 'Coloured and other Mixed Races'.[3] About 75 per cent of the latter are 'Cape Coloured', with whom this study will be mainly concerned. The term 'Cape Coloured' has primarily a cultural and territorial content. It applies to those persons of mixed race who are born into, regard themselves as and are accepted as members of the Cape Coloured group, which has its focus in the Western Cape. A Coloured person living outside the Cape may have originated in this way and retain these links, or he may be the product of another kind of cross, for instance between a white and an African or Indian, or between an Indian and an African.[4] In such cases he is simply a Coloured person, with no claim to the designation of 'Cape Coloured'. Even in the Cape itself, there have arisen separate communities of mixed blood (usually white and Hottentot) whose members have not wished to be regarded as part of the Cape Coloured group, despite a similar ancestry. Such groups have always laid stress on their 'white blood' and have proudly claimed the name of 'Bastards'.[5]

Throughout the twentieth century, the Coloured group as a whole has remained in approximately the same relationship (c. 8 per cent) to the total population.[6] Nearly 90 per cent of the Coloured population lives in the Cape.[7] Over one-quarter of the Coloured population of the Cape is concentrated in the Cape Peninsula districts of Cape Town,[8] Simonstown, Wynberg and Bellville. A considerable number of Coloured people in the Transvaal originated in the Cape, moving to the urban districts of the Rand for economic reasons. In Natal the concentration of Coloured people is highest near the Cape border.

Since 1921 the changing distribution of the Coloured population between rural and urban areas has followed the general South African tendency towards urbanisation.[9] In contrast to the African figures, there was in 1946 a slight preponderance of Coloured women over men in the urban areas, while the position was reversed in the rural areas. This may be due to the comparatively large number of Coloured women doing domestic or other work in the towns, whereas African men tend to leave their families in the reserves when they seek work.[10]

Except in some isolated cases, the languages spoken by the Coloured people are and have for generations been European.[11] Over 90 per cent of the Coloured people in the Cape Province speak Afrikaans in their homes, but nearly 35 per cent of this Cape group are bilingual in Afrikaans and English, the latter language having been acquired to an increasing extent at school in the last few decades. In the urban areas of Cape Town, more Coloured people speak English as their home language than in the Province as a whole.

In English-speaking Natal, two-thirds of the Coloured population speak English at home, and one-quarter Afrikaans. Unlike the other Provinces, Natal has a sizeable group of Euro-Bantu Coloured, some of whom speak a Bantu language at home.

In the predominantly Afrikaans-speaking Northern provinces, the numbers of Coloured people speaking this language are high. The Transvaal percentage (c. 80 per cent) is decreased by the numbers of English-speaking Coloureds in the urban areas, English being still the chief language of industry and commerce in the Union.

The religious affiliations of the Coloured population have long been predominantly European.[12] About 90 per cent of Coloured people belong to some Christian denomination, while nearly half the remainder are Moslems or Cape Malays, who form a separate religious and social community within the Coloured group.

Such comparative vital statistics as are available for the Coloured group are not altogether satisfactory,[13] but certain facts do emerge from them. The Coloured birth-rate is one of the highest in the world, but is offset by a high infantile mortality rate and a high death-rate. The complete expectation of life for a Coloured man is nearly twenty-three years less than that of a European man, while the figures for Coloured and European women respectively are 44 and 68.31 years. The figures for deaths amongst Coloured people from specific types of disease vary from city to city, but with the exception of cancer, cardiac diseases and others not connected with poverty, overcrowding and malnutrition, exceed the European figures many times over. In recent years all types of mortality rates have decreased for all racial groups, but there has been little if any narrowing of the gap between European and Non-European rates.

* * * * *

In view of the official custom of classifying the population according to ethnic affiliation for all administrative purposes,[14] one might suppose that no particular difficulty would be encountered in defining and distinguishing each group. That this is not so, in the case of the Coloured group at least, is suggested by the considerable number of attempts made to define a 'coloured person' in various acts of legislation and in the courts over the past fifty years. (See Appendix I for some of these definitions.)

In general, definitions have been somewhat negative, the Coloured group being described by the exclusion of other races or tribes. When forced to be more positive, legislators have introduced visible physical traits and habitual associations, both of which criteria can lead to awkward situations in practice. The main problem of definition seems to have been not between Coloureds and Africans, but between Coloureds and Europeans. An attempt at final definition is being made in the 1950 Population Registration Act, under the terms of which it is ultimately proposed to issue registration cards recording various statistics, race and electoral qualifications to the entire population.[15]

The vague and negative content of most definitions becomes quite explicable when we turn to examine the origins and history of the Cape Coloured People. In this examination we are not concerned with the same problems as the physical anthropologist or historian. We must rather attempt to indicate the lasting social consequences which followed the mingling of such diverse ingredients in a racial and cultural melting-pot for three hundred years.

Without this brief account of Coloured origins and history, many aspects of the present situation in South Africa, as for instance the lack of cohesion amongst the Coloured people themselves and the differing colour-attitudes still evident amongst whites in the Western Cape and Transvaal, might appear quite inexplicable.

Probably the main ingredient in the Cape Coloured People of to-day were the slaves, who seem to have outnumbered the Hottentot group.[16] In cultural advancement some were perhaps closer to the whites who brought them in than to these Hottentots, who formed the aboriginal population and the second element in the Cape Coloured group. Originally the slaves were brought in to perform agricultural and other work in the growing colony, for which the backward, easy-going, pastoral Hottentots had been found unsuitable.

There were two main sources of slaves—Asia, and East Africa.[17] Slaves from the latter area were in the majority,[18] and 'the vast majority came from Madagascar, i.e., they were Negroid by race with an infiltration of Indonesian blood, and spoke an Indonesian language (Malagasy) with remnants of a few Bantu words.'[19] Shiploads of these slaves came in regularly to the Cape during the seventeenth and eighteenth centuries. They were usually employed as agricultural labourers on the colonists' wine, grain, fruit and vegetable farms.

The Asiatic slaves, though fewer in number,[20] were the élite of the slave group. They came from various parts of the Malay Archipelago, Ceylon and India, from areas either under or in contact with the Dutch East India Company. Some were convicted criminals who, after serving their sentences, became 'Free Blacks', settling in Cape Town, where they later came to form the nucleus of the small class of skilled Coloured artisans. Others were political exiles of considerable eminence and culture,[21] with their attendants. Many were Moslems, and the term 'Malay' came in the Cape to denote a religious rather than an ethnic group.[22] Many again were skilled craftsmen, builders, cabinet-makers and so on, and in general they remained as house-slaves in the larger urban centres. Here the level of culture amongst their white masters made their own skills and talents more appreciated, while they themselves had easier access than the field-slaves and Hottentot herdsmen to the better elements of white colonial culture.

The second constituent of the future Cape Coloured People were the Hottentot aborigines encountered by the first Dutch traders, who set up an entrepôt at the Cape for ships *en route* for the East. The Hottentots were a primitive, nomadic, pastoral and hunting people, with a combination of Bushman and Hamitic cultural and physical traits. Except in a few inaccessible mountain areas, they had displaced their more primitive cousins, the Bushmen, from the Cape coastal belt, and their wandering, loose-knit tribes were to be found scattered from the Kei River in the east to the Orange River in the north. Unlike the Bantu at a later date, they put up little effective resistance to the colonists.

The third element in the Cape Coloured group were the Bushmen.[23] Professor Marais considers that 'their contribution, though a minor one, is. more important than is generally realised'.[24] The frontier-colonists seem to have thought them worth acquiring as herdsmen, when the shortage of even Hottentot labour became acute towards the end of the eighteenth century; their methods of recruitment were usually violent, as in general they seem not to have regarded the Bushmen as human beings like themselves.

During these commando-raids the major proportion of those encountered were killed: some children and adults were however taken prisoner and distributed to farmers as apprentices.[25] In addition, numbers of Bushmen along the frontier seem to have offered their services voluntarily as herdsmen for at least part of the year. The extent to which Bushmen had become domesticated is shown by the 1824 return for the sub-district of Cradock alone, which referred to 547 adult and 388 child apprentices, and 405 adults and 437 children living on European farms without being apprenticed.[26]

While some of these Bushmen may finally have returned to their own people and territories, many others remained as apprenticed labour on the same terms as the Hottentots, and must finally have been merged in the latter group, which was already heavily diluted with white and slave blood.[27]

The final group which has made a major contribution to the composition of the Coloured group, and without which there would indeed have been no Cape Coloured People, was the European group. The majority of officials and colonists were Protestant by religion and North-West European by origin.[28] Most of the original colonists were farmers or artisans, probably of no great refinement, so that the cultural gap between them and the élite of the Eastern slaves and exiles was possibly not very great.[29] There were in addition the uncounted seamen of all nations who passed through the Cape down the centuries.[30]

In the original contact-situation, the most important crosses were those between European men and slave or Hottentot women, and between slave men and Hottentot or Hottentot-Bushmen women, that is to say, between the men of the socially superior and the women of the socially inferior groups. In both the European and the slave groups men far outnumbered women for a long period,[31] and the relatively few European women were not so likely to risk their higher social status and economic position for the sake of casual, much less of permanent, intercourse with slaves or the despised Hottentots. Even to-day, when the sex-ratio in all ethnic groups is more or less equal, it is usually the European man and the Coloured woman who seek intercourse outside their group.[32]

Undoubtedly the Coloured People of to-day are to a far greater extent the product of irregular than of regular intercourse, in as far as white-coloured crosses are concerned. In the earlier colonial period, when intermarriage took place between a European man and a slave or mixed-breed woman, the children were usually absorbed in the European group.[33]

More recently, there has been a continuous and legalised infiltration of Coloured blood into the European group, particularly the urban artisan class in Cape Town. In some cases the European partner might be aware of his or her spouse's antecedents;[34] in others, the second partner might have severed all family connections and be passing as white. Thereafter, such a conjugal family would pass as European; the woman would be registered as a European voter and the children would attend European schools, thus getting better economic opportunities in after life.

It is almost impossible to estimate the true incidence of these covert mixed marriages, as they were often neither recognised nor registered as such.[35] That there have been a considerable number in recent times is suggested by the large number of objections lodged by the Nationalist Party in Cape constituencies against women registered on the European voters' roll, on the grounds that they were Coloured, and therefore not entitled to a vote.[36]

On the other hand, the children of irregular or casual unions have, as colour-prejudice increased, tended to remain in their mother's group. In the early colonial period this was not so, as the half-breeds were considered, by the authorities at least, as belonging to the European community in the right of their father.[37] They were entitled to their freedom as a right (males at the age of 25, females at the age of 22), after having been instructed in Christian doctrines and baptised.[38] Three-quarters of the children born to slave mothers at the Cape by 1671 were found to be half-breeds.[39] Many of these and later half-breeds, quarter-breeds and so on, may not have been the ancestors of the present Coloured people, but rather of European South Africans. However, their existence points to the beginning of a process which no legislation or colour-bar has so far been able to stamp out.[40]

Each European group in South Africa is anxious to disclaim at least part of the responsibility for the Coloured group. The English-speaking South African blames the Afrikaner, while the Afrikaner blames the British.[41] Both unite to blame transient visitors or attempt to disprove the presence of a considerable European strain in the Coloured people.

The second cross, that between Hottentot and European, had a different social context. The only case on record of such a marriage in early colonial days is that between the Hottentot woman Eva, sister-in-law of the Cochoqua chief. She had been brought up in the household of van Riebeeck himself, and was used as an interpreter and intermediary in dealing with the Hottentot clans. In 1663 she was married to the surgeon-explorer, Pieter van Meerhoff, her marriage feast being provided by the Commander and Council. Her legitimate children were educated at the Company's expense and a daughter married a prosperous Cape farmer.[42]

About a century and a half later, when race attitudes had crystallised, far greater indignation was caused amongst the frontier Boers by the earliest leader of the London Missionary Society, Dr. van der Kemp, who married a freed slave woman, and his successor, James Read, who took a Hottentot to wife.[43]

The main reason for the comparative infrequency of regular European-Hottentot unions, even at a time when Christianity rather than skin-colour was the test, is probably to be sought in the immense cultural gap between the two groups. From the beginning the Europeans seem to have felt nothing but contempt and dislike for this *botte, plompe ende luye stinckende natie* (dull, stupid, lazy, stinking people), as van Riebeeck described them.[44] The stereotype soon evolved by officials, travellers and colonists who came into contact with them is perpetuated only mildly in the Concise Oxford Dictionary's figurative sense of 'person of inferior intellect or culture'.

Nevertheless, as the colonists trekked farther away from the civilised Cape, their very way of life compelled them to shed many of the little niceties of European culture.[45] The layout of their homes shrank to a couple of rooms, their personal belongings to what they could carry in their wagons, their libraries to a single Bible. Due to their incomplete control of their environment and resentment of any authority, they were compelled to adopt a semi-nomadic, pastoral way of life, which was not so entirely different from that of the Hottentots whom they displaced and reduced to a landless, rural proletariat. In these circumstances, to which was added a chronic shortage of European women, many frontier colonists contracted informal unions, sometimes of a permanent nature, with Hottentot women.[46]

In such cases, however, the hybrids were not received into Boer frontier society, but became groups on their own, perpetuating their existence and multiplying by intermarriage where they could not marry white. Such were the Bastards who pioneered the North-West Cape,[47] and were already a sizeable group by the second half of the eighteenth century.[48] Their function seems to have been that of second-class Europeans, useful as pioneers and frontier-defence forces against Bushmen, Hottentots, and later Bantu, but always losing their lands and rights when Europeans made a determined advance.

Another important cross which contributed to the present Cape Coloured group was that between slaves and Hottentots. Here again, it was possibly due to the high ratio of slave men to women, and also to the effects of propinquity, as many farmers employed both slaves and Hottentots on their farms.[49]

These were the principal original strains and crosses which produced the Coloured people of to-day. By the beginning of the nineteenth century, the position had altered in that the pure Hottentots had practically ceased to exist in the Colony, and the second, third, and fourth generations of mixed-breeds were breeding amongst themselves and increasing in numbers. Although colour-prejudice had hardened, the European contribution seems not to have diminished greatly. Indeed a further mixed breed was later added to the South African Coloured group, in its widest definition, by European-Bantu miscegenation, particularly in the Eastern Cape and Natal. The Cape Coloured people do not regard the majority of Natal Coloureds as an integral part of their group, although the latter are reckoned as such for census and administrative purposes. This may be due as much to geographical as to cultural distance, for where Cape Coloureds, Griquas and other Coloureds live together, there seems to be a feeling of community, possibly enhanced by the presence of Africans in the same area.[50]

The European-Bantu hybrids do not concern us so greatly for the purposes of this study. There is, however, another recent cross which may have a growing significance, that between Coloureds and Africans. It seems to be on the increase,[51] particularly in the Eastern Province and African reserves, where contact is greater, and occurs even in the Western Cape, as the cultural gap narrows between the detribalised African and the Coloured unskilled worker.[52] It has been suggested[53] that the increasing number of regular unions of this type, combined with the drop in European-Coloured marriages over the same period, is an index of the declining status of the Coloured group *vis-à-vis* the European group.[54] This increase may, on the other hand, be rather an index of the ascending status of the Europeanised African *vis-à-vis* the Coloured group.[55]

No attempt has so far been made to estimate the incidence of informal Bantu-Coloured unions. The Negroid features sometimes noticeable in Coloured people in urban districts, particularly in the Western Cape, may be attributable to their slave ancestry, which included a considerable Negroid strain from Madagascar and Mozambique. In the Eastern Cape, on the other hand, such Negroid features are probably due to a more recent mingling of Coloured and Bantu. Here again, however, we should not overlook the fact that the eastern Hottentot tribes were broken and engulfed by the downward surge of the Bantu in the eighteenth century, so that we find certain 'Hottentot' physical (and linguistic) traits in the westernmost Bantu, and might expect to find some Negroid traits in the hybridised remnants of these Hottentot groups.

The only other cross of any importance is that between Coloureds and Indians. In a sense this is only a reinforcement of the Asiatic slave element in the Coloured people. The Indians, who form a large ethnic minority in South Africa to-day, are, however, for the most part, the immediate descendants of Indian labourers imported for work on the Natal sugar-plantations. For many purposes they are accorded the same status as the Coloured people by the authorities. Mixed marriages usually take place between Indian men and Coloured women, as the Indian group has a preponderance of men.[56] Coloured women seem to favour Indian husbands for economic reasons, as the latter are believed to have more ambition and commercial aptitude than is found amongst Coloured men.[57] The same considerations may be said to apply to the comparatively small numbers of coloured St. Helenans and Mauritians, who are classed as part of the Cape Coloured community.

To sum up, then, the Cape Coloured people of to-day are the product of an early series of mixed unions, mainly irregular, between Europeans and slaves, Europeans and Hottentots, slaves and Hottentots. The original hybrid groups have been perpetuated, increased and further intermingled by endogamy and cross-breeding, and by additions from the original strains.[58] More recently, the group has been further augmented and diversified by European-Bantu, Coloured-Bantu and Coloured-Indian crosses, and in addition by innumerable casual sexual contacts with Europeans of all nations.

* * * * *

In this section it is necessary only to indicate those historical factors which directly determined the evolution and development of the Cape

Coloured group in its present form. In the early contact period, the Cape Coloured People did not exist as such; there existed only its component parts, the slaves, the Colonial Hottentots, the Free Blacks,[59] the Bastards and so on. It was not until after Emancipation in 1834 that all these elements began to be grouped under a general term, and regarded as a single entity.

In the earliest days of European-Hottentot contact, the fact that the Cape settlement was originally intended as an entrepôt for ships on the way to the East, and not as a colony, undoubtedly had a moderating effect on official attitudes to the aborigines. The latter were in a position to make available or cut off supplies of cattle, and had, therefore, to be handled with kid gloves for a considerable period, in order to avoid expensive hostilities.[60]

The inevitable result was, however, only delayed, for as colonisation proceeded the Hottentots lost their lands and herds as easily as they would have done at the beginning. By that time, however, certain conventions were accepted by the authorities, so the Hottentots were always legally free, although customary discrimination had reduced them to near-serfdom by the beginning of the nineteenth century.

The official policy did not prevent the rapid growth of dislike and contempt for the Hottentots amongst Europeans at the Cape. These emotions were largely inspired by the Hottentot way of life, so alien and primitive to European minds, by their frequent abuse of official friendliness (as it must have seemed to the Europeans), sly and thieving ways, and refusal to trade in cattle on a sufficient scale. The Hottentot case would probably have been that they had a special claim to the use of the lands on which the Europeans had settled (exclusive private land-ownership not being a part of their system). No doubt the provocative behaviour was not entirely one-sided, since the European garrison was by 1654, only two years after the settlement, in a high state of tension[61] which augured ill for future inter-racial relations.[62]

The decision to experiment with colonisation was put into force in 1657. A small number of freemen were settled by the Liesbeek River to cultivate the ground and rear livestock, while other freemen began to practice various skilled crafts. This new policy was inspired by the Company's desire to cut expenditure, and to make the supply of meat and agricultural products for passing ships more reliable. In fact, it was the beginning of a process which the Company may not have foreseen, and did not have in mind, a process which was to lead to the colonisation of a whole country, and the destruction or absorption of the aboriginal peoples of the Cape.

The next important development was the deliberate and large-scale introduction of slaves. This had not been practicable before, despite requests from van Riebeeck, as none could be spared from other Company territories. In 1658, however, two consignments of West African slaves arrived, and 226 were retained to balance the 134 Europeans.

For the sake of economy, the Company proposed to use slaves for its own work, but could hardly, in view of the plentiful supply, refuse to allow the freemen to do likewise.

The future consequences of this policy were foreseen by the Council of India, in a dispatch to the Cape in 1658:

'In our opinion, the Colony should be worked and established by Europeans and not by slaves, as our nation is so constituted that as soon as they have the convenience of slaves they become lazy and unwilling to put forward their hands to work.'[63]

It has already been recorded how the number of slaves grew until at the time of Emancipation they numbered 39,000 in the Cape Colony.[64] This, of course, does not include those who had gained their freedom, or who had passed into the European community by intermarriage.

As the habit of slave-owning grew on the colonists, the attitudes thereby engendered were undoubtedly extended to the Hottentots,[65] who, although technically free, were culturally far less advanced than the slaves. The story of the expropriation of the Hottentots is soon told. Unlike the Bantu, they put up little effective resistance to European settlement, and seem to have been incapable of inter-tribal action on a scale sufficient to contain the advancing colonists. With the establishment of a permanent European settlement of stock farmers, they had lost their initial importance as the major source of such products. As the colonists moved outwards from Cape Town, they settled on lands on which various Hottentot tribes had from time immemorial possessed grazing and water rights, paying no compensation to the latter, who were usually too ignorant to put in counter-claims on the grounds of prior occupation.[66]

After the first few years, no determined efforts to convert them to Christianity or train them for any other way of life seem to have been made. Their tribes had been broken and their numbers drastically decreased by three smallpox epidemics. In the Eastern Province, whole tribes had been conquered and absorbed by the Bantu vanguard. By the end of the eighteenth century there were only a few Hottentot kraals remaining in the Western Province, some of which were soon to become mission stations. Other Hottentot tribes such as the Nama and Koranna had early withdrawn northward from the vicinity of the European settlement.

Such was the condition of the Hottentots when the British first occupied the Cape in 1795. Although there were signs of a determination on the part of the Company's officials to regulate European-Hottentot relations, and to curb the injustices all too frequently committed against the latter group, the power to enforce these legal checks was lacking. Attempts to do so in the district of Graaff-Reinet helped to cause a Boer revolt in 1795.[67] In a later insurrection against the British in 1799, Boer attitudes must have been further inflamed by the fact that Hottentot troops were used against them.[68] More will be said later about the use of Hottentot and Coloured troops against Europeans, and its consequences.[69]

The nineteenth century saw the beginning of a determined effort on the part of the authorities (British, Batavian, then British again) to extend the effective rule of law to the frontier and to regulate the status of the Hottentots. The Hottentot-Xhosa rising (Third Kaffir War) of 1799 drew attention to their grievances as no more peaceable means could have done. To meet these grievances, the authorities made provisions for the official attestation of labour contracts (on printed forms) for periods of three months or over. In practice these regulations were little more than gestures of good-will, as the short-lived Batavian administration had not the means to enforce them. A beginning had however been made.

Following the second British occupation in 1806, a more determined and forceful attempt was made to regulate the Hottentot problem. The labour laws of 1809–19 went side by side with a policy of providing land for Hottentot settlement under missionary auspices, a policy to which we shall return later in this chapter. In brief, the labour laws[70] regulated Hottentot life from the cradle to the grave: they provided that every Hottentot must have a fixed and registered place of abode, from which he was not to move without a pass, and that all labour contracts of one month and upwards must be registered; laid down certain provisions designed to protect Hottentots against any abuse on the part of their masters;[71] and dealt with apprenticeship, children who had been maintained by their parents' employer to the age of eight years being apprenticed to the latter for ten further years[72] and orphans being apprenticed till their eighteenth year to Europeans.[73]

Most important were the official efforts to ensure that legislation was enforced, and also made known to local officials, colonists and Hottentots. In addition, the number of local courts was increased, and circuit courts (with administrative as well as judiciary powers) were introduced in 1811. Whatever the position before, the Hottentots were now subject to the normal administration of the law and, in addition to duties, had rights which were enforceable by the courts.[74] The effects of this body of legislation were diverse. On the one hand, it curbed the lawless capriciousness with which many masters were apt to treat their Hottentot servants,[75] and encouraged the latter to look to the law for their protection. On the other hand, it officially allotted an inferior status to the Hottentots by singling them out as such, and it served the interests of the colonists by making available to them a supply of Hottentot labour, and perpetuating this through the apprenticeship regulations.[76]

Whether any government could have done otherwise than recognise and attempt to regulate what was in fact a *fait accompli* is doubtful. The weakness of these laws was that the major part of their administration depended on local officials, who were also farmers. Thus, while the 'pass' and 'apprenticeship' provisions were rigidly enforced, the clauses designed to protect the Hottentots were sometimes evaded.[77] In addition, Hottentot labour was virtually immobilised[78] by the need to obtain permission to seek another master from the same local official (veld cornet), and the Hottentots were thereby deprived of the opportunity of selling their labour in the best market.[79]

The aim was, of course, to prevent vagrancy, as the former way of life of the Hottentot was now termed.[80] Considerable numbers of such vagrants seem to have existed well into the nineteenth century. They preferred to live by hunting and gathering and occasionally by stealing stock, rather than sell their labour to the farmers, even though they risked, when caught, being contracted to an employer by the local authorities, on the employer's own terms.

About the time of this low ebb in Hottentot affairs, a new and powerful force was entering the field, one which was to establish a partial sanctuary for the Hottentots, and to exert a strong influence on the course of British colonial policy and the development of the Cape Colony itself.[81]

The first missionary station had been established in the first half of the eighteenth century by the Moravian, George Schmidt, in an isolated part of the colony (Genadendal) not far from Caledon.[82] He left the station, however, after six years, and no further missionary work amongst the Hottentots was undertaken for about fifty years. It would appear that the colonists were not too anxious that the Hottentots be allowed the benefits of a Christian education, 'Christian' and 'European' being now more nearly equated concepts. There were also, and perhaps more important, local sectarian jealousies, the Dutch Reformed Church having the practical monopoly of religious practice in the Colony.[83]

The Moravians returned to Genadendal in 1792, to face renewed hostility from the local Boers. As the Moravians studiously avoided political action and did not advocate social equality between Europeans and Hottentots, it seems that the mere fact of their working on behalf of the Hottentots was sufficient to arouse the colonists' anger. Genadendal rapidly became a centre for Hottentots for miles around, and as such threatened the Boers' labour supply, since residence there offered a third and legal alternative to farm-labour or vagrancy.[84] In addition, missionary efforts to educate the Hottentots aroused the jealousy of the Boers, whose own children were often illiterate.

The initial resentment aroused by the work of the Moravians was, however, nothing in comparison with the odium which settled around the London Missionary Society, which owed its foundation to the Evangelical Revival. While the Moravians and other missionary groups, such as the Berlin and Rhenish societies, concentrated, not unsuccessfully, on the social and economic improvement of their charges, the London Missionary Society devoted its major energies to raising the general status of the Hottentots by political action.

A few words must be said about these mission stations or 'institutions', before outlining the results in the Cape of the London Missionary Society or 'Exeter Hall' policy, which was inspired by the wider religious and philanthropic movement in early nineteenth century Britain. All the institutions seem to have had great success in their primary objective, which was to bring the gospel to the Hottentots. In the secondary objective of teaching their charges a more settled and civilised way of life, the London Missionary Society is, however, often adversely compared with the Moravians.[85]

Mention has already been made of the authorities' endeavour to meet Hottentot grievances by a dual policy of regulating their conditions of labour and providing land for them under missionary auspices. The latter policy had to be modified owing to the lack of suitable land, most of which had by now been taken up by European colonists.[86] The institutions were never in a position to support themselves and their inhabitants fully, but they did provide 'cities of refuge' for the Hottentots, from which the able-bodied were able to sell their labour, in which the aged and ill could find shelter and their children some education.[87]

By the late 1820s they sheltered about 6,000 Hottentots, and after Emancipation in 1824 these numbers were further swollen by an influx of freed slaves. Overcrowding, poverty, the low standard of living of their inmates, and, at times, their faulty administration,[88] prevented the mission stations from going ahead as originally planned. Nevertheless, they exerted a rapid civilising influence, and without them the plight of the Hottentots would have been infinitely worse, and their future black indeed.

Whatever the shortcomings of the London Missionary Society in its purely institutional work, there can be no doubt that this organisation, through its leader Dr. John Philip, was primarily responsible for the repeal of the Hottentot legislation of 1809–19. The instrument of this reform was the famous Ordinance 50 of 1828.[89] As it referred specifically to 'Hottentots and other free persons of colour' and contained improved provisions for apprenticeship and relations between masters and Coloured servants, it was not strictly a colour-blind measure. Nevertheless, it opened the way for the colour-blind franchise conferred on the Cape in 1853,[90] following which no legislation affecting the Coloured people as such was passed in the Cape Colony.

The Ordinance evoked resentment and opposition amongst the majority of colonists. Exaggerated claims of increased vagrancy and crime were current,[91] and intensified land settlement and agricultural training were required to give the Ordinance a constructive turn. Such positive action was, however, lacking. Instead, the next years were taken up with determined attempts by the colonists[92] to render

Ordinance 50 abortive by introducing a Vagrant Law,[93] and with personal attacks on Dr. John Philip,[94] on whose person all their resentment seemed to be concentrated. In the meantime, many Hottentots left the farms and those who could not find room on the institutions moved to the towns and villages, to form the nucleus of the unskilled urban Coloured proletariat of to-day. The lot of those who stayed on the farms seems to have improved slightly, in that a small cash wage became the rule, in addition to payment in kind.[95] On the other hand, Ordinance 49 of 1828 had brought Bantu labour with its even lower standard of living and wage demands into the Eastern Cape.

One section of the Coloured people had now been formally freed. Within five years the Emancipation Act, which unlike Ordinance 50 had a wider than Colonial significance, did the same for the slaves.[96] By 1833, the latter were mostly Colonial-born, and because of their greater degree of acculturation, were probably in a better position to live up to their improved formal status than were the Hottentots. Some skilled urban slaves had since the beginning of the nineteenth century been allowed to ply their trades away from their masters on payment of a stipulated fee and to earn what they could;[97] while both urban and rural slaves might cultivate plots and sell the produce for their own profit. Emancipation was not fully accomplished until 1836. After this date slaves seem to have left their masters, some for the towns and villages, some to the frontier settlements. Others became vagrants, while a considerable number flocked to the missionary institutions, thereby putting an extra burden on the latter's already strained resources.[98]

Two further events were to exert a considerable influence upon the subsequent history of the Coloured people. These were the Great Trek of 1836, and the arrival of the Bantu upon the eastern frontier of the Cape Colony.

The Great Trek was the reaction of several thousand (mainly Boer) farmers to official policy, which had since the beginnings of the century been encroaching on their freedom as employers of labour, whether slave or free. Most of those who trekked were not in fact slave owners, but their mentality was similar.[99] In addition, they resented the growing 'interference' of the state in matters such as the administration of the law.

The removal of those most irreconcilably opposed to the new philanthropic policy (which came presently to be called 'Cape liberalism') could only be beneficial to the Coloured people in the short run, for those Europeans who remained realised that they must accept both the policy and the principle of stronger government controls. Thus it came about that for the next seventy years or so the Coloured people in the Cape had nominal equality, and an opportunity of converting it into a genuine equality.

The long-term effects of the Great Trek were in fact anything but

C

beneficial for the Coloured people.[100] The irreconcilable settlers took their prejudices and grievances with them to the new Republics which they finally established in the North.[101] In these Republics there was to be no equality between people of colour and the white inhabitants, either in Church or State.[102] At the time of Union these two conflicting principles again confronted each other, and this time it was the liberal one which retreated, as the Trekkers came home to the Cape.

By this time the Bantu peoples had come to constitute South Africa's major colour-problem. Their fighting qualities and their overwhelming numbers had increased the element of fear in European colour-attitudes.[103] As fear and prejudice grew, the status of the Cape Coloured group could not fail to suffer in European eyes,[104] and it remained only to be seen whether the Coloured people had, in the period of theoretical equality, acquired sufficient political and economic power to counteract this colour prejudice by their own efforts.

PART TWO

PATTERNS OF DIFFERENTIATION
AND DISCRIMINATION

CHAPTER THREE

POLITICS

Classes excluded from a share in power have always been classes excluded from a share in benefits.[1]

POLITICAL differentiation and discrimination do not always have so immediate and harmful an impact upon the masses of a subordinate group or class as do the differentiatory and discriminatory forms encountered in the economic sphere, or the often petty but wounding slights encountered so frequently in everyday life. They are nevertheless of paramount importance in achieving and perpetuating a status-hierarchy upon whatever basis the dominant group may desire. Political differentiation is in fact the formal means by which a particular group may retain for itself the major share of economic and social benefits available in that particular society.

In the Union of South Africa a dominant minority is endeavouring to preserve, by every device of law and custom, a conquest- and slavery-situation; this situation is nevertheless gradually breaking down, under the impact of such ideologies as liberal humanitarianism and nationalism, and before the rise of industrial capitalism.

Politically, South Africa somewhat resembles the ancestor of Western democracies—the Greek city-state.[2] That is to say, it consists of a ruling minority group whose members enjoy full and equal civic rights, superimposed upon a considerably larger group, ethnically and often culturally different, whose members, while subject to many civic duties such as the payment of taxes, have little or no share in political rights. The resemblance ends, however, when we turn to the basis of differentiation. Barbarians might become Hellenised, but there is no appeal from a judgment determined by skin colour.

To such an extent is this division still a part of South African life that comparatively few white South Africans find any incongruity in their references to South African democracy. Democratic forms of government have so far been the prerogative of the European group, except for their partial and reluctant extension to the Coloured community in the Cape. Although few debates in the South African

31

Parliament proceed for any length of time without some mention of Non-European affairs, the context of most references to 'the South African people' is confined exclusively to the European 'we-group'.[3]

This limitation of context, and the approximate agreement as to ends[4] between the major European parties, gives South African political life a somewhat unreal and sterile atmosphere, enlivened by personalities rather than by policies.[5]

South Africa's parliamentary forms are similar to those of Great Britain, with supreme executive power formally vested in the King by the South Africa Act, the King being represented by the Governor-General. Side by side, however, with this democratic form of government for one section of the population, there is a system of extra-parliamentary government for another and larger group. The executive is empowered under the Native Administration Act (1927) to legislate for Africans in African areas by proclamation.

Certain Coloured groups living in African areas come under the administration of the Native Affairs Department, and this fact is a source of grievance to the Coloured people as a whole. Up to 1951, however, the majority of the Coloured people occupied an uneasy place in South African political life, as in most other spheres; midway between the European community, whose political institutions they have shared for nearly a century, and the eight million Africans, who are ruled by proclamation and the relics of tribal authority.

Parliament in South Africa consists of a Senate and House of Assembly, to both of which, since Union in 1909, only Europeans may be elected or nominated. The Senate has forty-eight members (forty-four until the incorporation of South-West Africa in 1950), of whom four are elected by African electoral colleges throughout the Union, while eight are nominated by the Governor-General in Council. Four out of these eight are, under the requirements of the South Africa Act of 1909, to be nominated 'on the ground mainly of their thorough acquaintance, by reason of their official experience or otherwise, with the reasonable wants and wishes of the coloured[6] races in South Africa.'

These Senators, where they represent 'coloured' interests at all, tend to concentrate on African affairs. Coloured voters have until now been on the common roll in the Cape, and their interests have in theory been represented by the Cape Senators and the members of those constituencies in which they voted, along with those of European voters. Pending their transfer to a separate roll, Coloured voters form over 25 per cent of the electorate in only one constituency,[7] 20–25 per cent in three, 15–20 per cent in two, 10–15 per cent in twelve, 5–10 per cent in fourteen, and under 5 per cent in twenty-three constituencies.

They have usually been faced either with no choice of candidate at all, some urban seats being United Party strongholds, or with a choice between the United Party and the Nationalist Party.[8] This has been no choice at all since the Nationalists announced their intention of

removing the Coloured people to a separate communal roll, a change
which is not acceptable to the great majority of Coloured voters.

The effectiveness of the Coloured vote,[9] which had dwindled until
it could be decisive only in a few evenly-balanced constituencies,[10]
had therefore shrunk still further, since a vote against the United Party,
or even an abstention, was a vote against the pre-1951 Coloured
franchise. In such circumstances, one would not expect to find most
Cape M.P.s over-zealous on behalf of their comparatively few Coloured
constituents, in cases where the specific interests of the latter were
considered to run counter to those of the white population.[11]

Before Union in 1909, the four constituent provinces had very
different franchise arrangements for their Non-European populations.
Some of these arrangements are still extant to-day, although any
disparities in the European franchise have now been removed. All
Europeans, male or female, over the age of twenty-one are entitled
to vote and stand for office, unless otherwise disqualified.

The position of the Coloured franchise in the Cape Province before
the Separate Representation of Voters Act (No. 46 of 1951) was that
any Coloured male over 21 years might be registered as a voter on the
common roll who was:

'a Union national;[12] can sign his name and write his address; and
either has, in any part of the Union or South-West Africa, for twelve
months prior to his application for registration, been in actual occupation of a shop, house, or other premises of the value of not less than
£75 or earned a salary of not less than £50 a year,[13] or has for six
months prior to his application for registration been a registered
holder of a licence to dig for diamonds in the province (with a proviso
in certain instances of being certified by a magistrate as of good
character) . . .'[14]

The pre-1951 Cape Coloured franchise was all that remained of the
officially 'colour-blind' political institutions of the Cape Colony prior
to Union in 1909; the African voters were removed from the general
Cape electoral lists to a communal roll under the terms of the Representation of Natives Act (No. 12 of 1936).[15] After the granting of the
first Constitution in 1853, the Cape franchise was available to all adult
males, irrespective of colour or race, who fulfilled certain property
qualifications. This non-racial franchise was mainly the result of insistence by the British Government, which would not have sanctioned
a franchise which drew a colour or race distinction; it was, however,
accepted by the Colony, though not without some opposition.[16]

Even the incorporation of the mainly Bantu Transkei in 1892 only
resulted in a stiffening of the qualification by a simple educational
test and a raising of the financial qualification.[17] The purpose of this
was to exclude the 'raw' tribal African, or 'Blanket Kaffir', with his
completely alien cultural background, at least until he should have

become acculturated.[18] From that time, however, until the passing of the South Africa Act in 1909, the theoretical equality of the Coloured people in the Cape remained unchanged.

There were three distinct political rights involved at this time. They were: firstly, the right to vote; secondly, the right to stand and serve as an elected or nominated representative;[19] and thirdly, the right to be counted as an elector in the event of a reallocation of seats. By the South Africa Act of 1909 (sections 25 and 44c), the last two rights were taken from the Coloured voters of the Cape,[20] and colour-conscious legislation was thereby resumed.

The sacrifice of these two rights represented a concession on the part of the Cape delegates at the discussions which preceded Union.[21] It was a concession to the two former Boer Republics, the Orange Free State and Transvaal, and to Natal, whose representatives flatly refused to countenance any extension of 'colour-blind' legislation to their own territories, or to sit in the same council-chambers with Non-European delegates.[22]

Thus in 1909 the Coloured and other Non-European voters of the Cape were left with one political right only—the vote. This was safe-guarded by an entrenched clause of the South Africa Act, which laid down that this franchise could be altered only by a two-thirds majority vote of all members of both Houses of Parliament sitting together.[23]

At the time leading Cape delegates hoped that a more liberal policy would prevail when the North became sufficiently mature.[24] In the Cape Parliament in 1909, Dr. Jameson, speaking on the Draft Act, said:

'We who believe in no colour line and equal rights feel that it should not be forced upon the people of other colonies before they are ripe for it—it must be a slow and gradual process, and this doctrine will ultimately prevail, for they will come to see that it is good for the country.'

It cannot be said that subsequent events have justified such opti-mism.[25] Since 1909, whenever the Cape Coloured vote seemed likely to become powerful, its importance has been whittled away by succes-sive Acts which have prevented it from rising above a certain ratio in relation to European numbers.[26] The enactment of this legislation has also demonstrated the growing indifference amongst Cape whites, under the influence of Northern colour-attitudes, to the principle of an equal cultural franchise for all men, whatever their race or colour.

The Women's Enfranchisement Act (No. 18 of 1930)[27] was the first measure so to decrease the importance of the Cape Non-European franchise.[28] This gave European women throughout the Union the right to be registered as voters for the House of Assembly and the Provincial Councils, and to be nominated, elected and to sit and vote as Senators, Members of the House of Assembly or Provincial Councils.

It was shortly before this that Dr. D. F. Malan, then Minister of the
Interior in General Hertzog's Cabinet, made a statement in favour of
the extension of the franchise to Coloured as well as to European
women, which is often quoted by his present opponents.[29] The Coloured
vote was still divided between the two major parties in the nineteen-
twenties, and Nationalist utterances struck a note entirely different
from that prevalent to-day, whether or not they were motivated by
other considerations than expediency. It may be that Cape members
of the Nationalist Party, such as Dr. Malan, were still unconsciously
bound by the traditions of over a half-century of colour-blind government. It is difficult to imagine a Nationalist speaker uttering or a
Nationalist audience listening to such sentiments to-day.

Dr. Malan's leader, General Hertzog, who was not from the Cape,
nevertheless held firmly from the mid-1920s until the end of his career
that, while the Africans should be segregated, the Coloured people
belonged culturally with the European group, and should be treated
'on an equality with Europeans—economically, industrially and
politically.'[30] He saw the danger of a Coloured-African political
alliance, and preferred to retain the Coloured group as allies of the
Europeans by giving them a vested interest in continued European
supremacy.

The fear of driving the Coloured people 'to rest in the arms of the
Native'[31] lost temporarily in intensity[32] as successive measures diminished
the relative importance of the Coloured vote.[33] In June 1934 a section
of the Nationalist Party (known as the 'Purified Nationalist Party')
split off under the leadership of Dr. Malan from the main party, after
the latter's fusion with the South African Party (S.A.P.) under General
Smuts.[34] By this time Dr. Malan's attitude to the Coloured vote had
changed sufficiently for him to announce a platform of political,
economic and social separation for the Coloured people in an election
speech made at Porterville on 4th April, 1938.[35] This change of attitude
was sharply criticised by General Hertzog, who called it 'falsity and
infidelity';[36] in this he anticipated the main argument of the defenders
of the Coloured franchise over a decade later, few of whom take their
stand on the wider issue of human rights.

The Women's Enfranchisement Act had at one blow halved the
importance of the Coloured vote in the Cape itself. It was further
diminished by the Franchise Laws Amendment Act (No. 41) of 1931,
which brought the European male franchise in the Cape into line with
the rest of the Union, by abolishing the property qualification and
extending the franchise to every white male person over twenty-one
years.

Further legislative measures with the same trend were Act 35 of
1931, the Representation of Natives Act (No. 12 of 1936), the Electoral
Consolidation Act (No. 46 of 1946), and the Electoral Laws Amendment Act (No. 50 of 1948). The first made it possible to challenge

Non-Europeans on the Provisional Voters' List to appear (in person if the educational qualifications were challenged, otherwise by proxy), to establish their qualifications at the Magistrate's Court, under pain of being struck off the roll.

In practice certain abuses seem to have crept into the administration of this law, resulting in the removal from the roll of properly qualified Coloured persons, sometimes without their knowledge. The electoral officer is supposed to notify the person concerned before removing his name, but the registered letter may or may not reach the addressee. If it does, it may not do so in time to enable the latter to report to the Magistrate's Court within the specified period. Such appearance is rendered more difficult by the considerable distances involved, particularly in country constituencies, and by the fact that few Coloured men are easily able to afford the travelling expenses. Moreover, few are their own masters and European employers may not look with favour upon a request for leave on such grounds.

In recent years the Nationalist Party has lost any hope of large-scale Coloured support, and after 1948 its campaign to decrease the United Party vote[37] was extended to a 'witch-hunt' or 'colour-purge' designed to unmask Coloured women who were 'passing' as white,[38] and were registered on the European women's voters' roll.[39] If any such women could be proved to be Coloured, they were automatically disfranchised, as Coloured women have no vote.[40]

A determined attempt was also made to prove that certain male voters registered as Europeans were in fact Coloured; the man in question would only be transferred to the Coloured voters' roll if he could satisfy the necessary qualifications. Several informants claimed that some men who were proved to be 'Coloured' had refused to re-register on the Coloured list, preferring to lose their vote rather than to publish their ethnic affiliation.[41] This process has more far-reaching effects than disfranchisement. It may mean loss of a job or demotion to Non-European wage-levels, change of school and consequently poorer education for the children, and social ostracism.[42] The only escape for the persons involved has been to move to another area and endeavour to 'pass' there.[43]

The main tests according to which such investigations have been carried out are those of appearance, associations, and descent, in that order. In late 1949, a great deal of indignation was aroused in the Western Cape following reports that electoral officials were placing too much insistence on investigations into descent. In answer to a telegram of protest from the M.P. for Cape Town Castle,[44] the Minister of the Interior replied that appearance and 'predominant habitual associations' should be sufficient to enable the electoral authorities to make their decision. Only if 'specific contrary allegations' were made might the officials have to go further.[45]

The Representation of Natives Act (1936), while not directly affecting the Coloured people's formal rights, carried the process of discriminatory and race-conscious legislation further by removing African voters in the Cape from the common roll. For the future Africans in the Union were to be represented by three members of the House of Assembly and four elected Senators, and by the Native Representative Council, a purely advisory body. The Act was passed by the necessary two-thirds majority laid down by Sections 35 and 152 of the South Africa Act, a majority which had seemed unattainable to the Cape representatives and the British Government in 1909. It was an intimation to those Coloured people whose ears were attuned to future developments that no group's rights were necessarily inviolate.[46] The Act also effectively disposed of the possibility of any eventual Coloured-African electoral bloc.[47]

Since the Electoral Amendment Act of 1948, Coloured men applying for registration in the Cape have been compelled to fill in their applications before a magistrate, police officer or electoral officer. Where the literacy qualification is concerned, there is alleged to be considerable variation between the examinations conducted by the competent individuals, many of whom, particularly in the country districts, share the racial views of most whites around them.

The necessity of going through this procedure has probably served to discourage a considerable number of potential Coloured registrations.[48] Reliable European informants have claimed that Coloured persons going to register are sometimes intimidated and refused registration by the responsible official, particularly when the latter is a police officer, as is often the case.[49] Party officials are entitled to go with applicants for registration, in order to see that the regulations are observed. In the more remote districts, however, this is not always practicable.

The measures enacted from 1924 to 1933 were the work of a Nationalist Government. The two acts of 1946 and 1948 dealing with electoral matters were put through by a United Party Government under General Smuts. In addition Act No. 40 of 1945 provided for the preparation of rolls for each electoral division for white men, white women and Non-Europeans respectively, for compulsory registration of European voters, and compulsory notification of changes of address (non-notification being punishable by a maximum fine of £10). No such provisions were to apply to Coloured voters, who, as has already been mentioned, had also to reapply for registration on the new voters' lists started in 1946.[50]

These were the major acts of legislation which, while adhering to the letter of the Constitution, gradually scaled down the importance of the Coloured vote. The penultimate step is the pending transfer of Coloured voters to a separate roll, which has necessitated a breach or at least a legal reinterpretation of the 'entrenched' two-thirds majority clause in the South Africa Act, as Nationalist support in both Houses, even with the new South-West African seats, was not sufficient to do more than pass the measure by a bare majority.

Coloured political rights and status were basically defended by Sections 35 and 152 of the South Africa Act. At the time, a Coloured deputation, assisted by W. P. Schreiner, an ex-Prime Minister of the Cape Colony, told the Colonial Secretary, Lord Crewe, that it was not satisfied with this safeguard. The Under-Secretary of State, Colonel Seely, said in the House of Commons that the matter was 'purely academic', as it was provided in the Royal Instructions that such a Bill should be reserved.[51] The attainment by the Union of sovereign independence following the report of the Imperial Conference in 1926[52] and the Statute of Westminster in 1931 disposed of this safeguard.

Thereafter the Coloured franchise was in the hands of the Union Parliament, representing a predominantly white electorate. As the prescribed two thirds majority was not available in 1951, it was necessary to find legal authority for removing this 'dead hand of the past', so that the legislation transferring Coloured voters from the common roll might be put through Parliament as an ordinary Bill, on a simple majority. The new Speaker, Mr. J. H. Conradie, whose views on the validity of the entrenched clauses were well known before his appointment,[53] ruled that the Union Parliament had the unfettered right to legislate according to any procedure which it thought fit.[54] The Opposition opposed the introduction of the Bill on a point of order, and its subsequent passage (to which the guillotine was applied), largely on legalistic grounds,[55] leaving the wider moral issues to be raised by a comparative handful of churchmen and liberals on the one side, and a combination of ex-Communists and leaders of formerly moderate Coloured and other Non-European groups, on the other.[56]

The extent to which colour-attitudes had hardened by 1951 was evident in the defensive attitude now adopted even by the latter groups. Their rallying-cries were 'Defend the Franchise' and 'Save the Constitution'. There has arisen no European leader of the calibre of W. P. Schreiner in the early years of the century, and the possible extension of the Cape Coloured franchise to the Northern provinces,[57] as proposed even in the Hertzog period, has now ceased to be a political issue at all.[58]

The Separate Representation of Voters Act[59] provides for the transfer of Non-European voters from the Cape common roll to a separate Coloured roll, upon which all Non-Europeans in the Cape who are not registered on the present common roll, but who are or become qualified to be so registered, may also be enrolled, and for the division of this Coloured voters' list into four parts corresponding to four electoral divisions, to be fixed by a commission of three Supreme Court judges, for the purpose of electing four members of the House of Assembly (the qualifications for these members to be the same as for all others, i.e., they must be Europeans), and into two divisions for the purpose of electing two members of the Cape Provincial Council (in this case they may be Non-Europeans). The first election of such members of the House of Assembly or Provincial Councils is to take place only after the next dissolution of the House, or expiry of the Council's term of office, and after a new Union delimitation of seats.

In neither Assembly nor Provincial Council will these members have the right to vote at the election of senators under the provisions of section 25 of the South Africa Act. The number of Coloured electoral divisions may be increased or decreased, not according to the number of Coloured voters, but in relation to an increase or decrease in the number of European members, in the ratio of 4 to 150.

An additional Senator, who must have resided for five years in the Cape Province, is to be nominated by the Governor-General 'on the ground of his thorough acquaintance, by reason of his official experience or otherwise, with the reasonable wants and wishes of the non-European population in the province of the Cape of Good Hope', to represent these Non-Europeans in the Upper House. Non-Europeans or Natives in Natal who were registered as voters on the common roll when the Act came into force will remain so registered if they retain their qualifications for registration and remain resident in Natal, but no further registrations will be made. The Natal Coloured vote will, in fact, die out with the present voters; opposition to these provisions was made more difficult by the fact that Non-European political rights outside the Cape were not entrenched in the South Africa Act.

The Separate Representation of Voters Act also provides for the establishment of a Board for Coloured Affairs, to consist of three Non-European members nominated by the Governor-General to represent Natal, the Transvaal and the Orange Free State, and eight elected Non-European members who must be qualified to be registered on the Cape Coloured voters' list, two to be elected by the Cape Coloured voters in each Union electoral division. The Commissioner for Coloured Affairs in the new sub-department to be set up under the Department of the Interior is to be Chairman of the Board, with a casting vote in the event of a parity of votes. Non-European members of the Board are to hold office for five years. The Board's functions will be mainly, if not entirely, advisory and consultative.

The provisions of this Act speak eloquently enough for themselves, but attention may be drawn to the unequal pegging of the ratio of representation of the Coloured people (numbering over a million) and of the European group (numbering over $2\frac{1}{2}$ million) at 4 to 150; to the lack of provision for any future representation of the Coloured people in the three Northern provinces in either national or provincial legislatures, or of Coloured women anywhere in the Union; to the admission by the Prime Minister that this legislation constitutes a 'relative diminution' in the power of the Coloured vote;[60] and to the threat uttered by the Minister of the Interior during the debate on the Bill that the future Coloured Representatives would have to go 'if they do not see things in the broader interests of the country.'[61]Most important of all considerations, however, is the fact that at no stage were the Cape Coloured people, either as a whole or through any adequate representative body, consulted about their views on the question of their own franchise rights, while their opposition to these proposals has been made quite clear in their press, in group protests and in mass demonstrations.

*   *   *   *   *

This brief history of the Coloured franchise was included in our account of the formal political status of the Coloured people in the Cape Province, since it is there that the Coloured question overshadows the African problem as it does nowhere else in the Union. We must now outline the pre-1951 position in the other provinces.

In Natal at the time of Union there was, as in the Cape, no constitutional discrimination between white and Coloured persons from the time of the Charter of 1856. There was, however, evidence of hardening attitudes towards Non-European groups even before Union. Law No. 11 of 1865 and Act No. 8 of 1896 excluded Africans and Indians respectively from the enjoyment of political rights and privileges.[62]

The Franchise Amendment Law of 1883 gave the vote to every male inhabitant of three years' residence whose income was equal to £96 per year.[63] This qualification has remained unchanged for the Coloured people of Natal, but their right to stand and serve as elected or nominated representatives in both Houses of Parliament was, as with the Cape Coloured, removed by the South Africa Act in 1909. The 1937 Government Commission on the Coloured people note one anomaly in Natal, where St. Helenans and Mauritians might be enrolled in the voters' list as 'Europeans',[64] although many of them are listed in the Census returns under 'Mixed and other Coloureds'.

In the Orange Free State and the Transvaal Republics the Coloured people had not enjoyed political rights from the setting-up of these republics, in 1854 and 1849 respectively, to the time of Union. In the Orange Free State, 'Coloured persons' were clearly differentiated from other ethnic groups and were given certain property rights, but 'burgher rights' were restricted to 'white persons' by the Constitution.[65]

The Transvaal Republic was even more explicit as to the political status of the Coloured people. Article 6 of the 'Thirty-Three Articles' referred to above (drawn up at Potchefstroom in 1844 and ratified by the Volksraad in 1849) laid down that no ' "bastard" may sit in our meetings as a member or judge up to the tenth generation.' In June 1855 the Volksraad, debating upon a proposal to extend burgher rights to all European strangers, laid down that 'all persons of colour are excluded from this provision and the Burgher rights may never be granted or allowed to them.' The Grondwet of 1858 drove the final nail into the coffin of equal rights (Article 9): 'The People[66] will permit of no equality between the White and the Coloured inhabitants, neither in Church nor in State.'[67]

Finally, when constitutional government was extended to South West Africa political rights were confined to European males only.[68] The franchise was extended to European women under the provisions of the South-West African Constitution Amendment Proclamation No. 103 of 1939. This arrangement was retained when the territory was incorporated in the Union in 1950.

*   *   *   *   *

Turning to the Provincial Administrations, we find the general pre-1951 franchise position in the various provinces more or less duplicated. In other words, Coloured people in the Transvaal and Orange Free State had no provincial franchise, while in the Cape and Natal they had to satisfy the same qualifications as were required for the parliamentary franchise. In the Cape, however, they might also sit as councillors, and two Coloured men actually did so.[69]

*   *   *   *   *

There remains the municipal franchise, where some variations from the parliamentary and provincial patterns are to be observed. Nowhere in the Union are Non-European groups as such specially or separately represented on municipal councils.[70] Either they are not represented at all, or their interests are presumably held to be the same as those of fellow-townsmen.[71]

In the Cape, the Municipal Franchise Ordinances[72] do not disqualify Non-Europeans by reason of race, colour or sex from voting for or being elected to municipal councils.[73] In Cape Town and the Cape Division particularly there have been and still are Coloured and Indian councillors sitting as full members.[74] The qualification set for both Europeans and Non-Europeans by Ordinance 22 of 1925 is either ownership of property liable to be rated at £100 value or occupation of property of the rateable value of £200.[75]

In Natal Coloured males (but not Indians) are eligible for the municipal franchise on the same qualifications as Europeans. These consist of ownership of rateable property of an assessed value of £50 or occupation of rateable property of the gross annual value of at least £10. These and other property qualifications elsewhere in the Union do, of course, indirectly discriminate against Coloured voters, as the latter are less frequently in a position to fulfil them than are Europeans.[76]

According to the 1937 Cape Coloured Commission there is a further restriction on the Natal municipal franchise, in that only parliamentary voters may vote for borough councillors, and borough councillors must be parliamentary voters. It is to be presumed that, as a result of the Separate Representation of Voters Act, such Non-European voters will gradually cease to exist.

In the Transvaal, Ordinance No. 4 of 1927 laid down that only Europeans might vote in the election of municipal and village councillors.[77] In 1944 the Coloured Advisory Council asked the Johannesburg City Council to extend the municipal franchise and the right to serve on the City Council to its Coloured community. The City Council replied that the question involved a general principle beyond the Council's jurisdiction, and should be addressed to the Provincial Council. As the request had already been referred to the Provincial Authority, and rejected by the Administrator in Executive Committee, the matter thereupon lapsed.[78]

In the Orange Free State also, Coloured people have no municipal franchise, with the exception of those persons who are of European parentage on one side and are therefore entitled to own or occupy land.[79]

*   *   *   *   *

A political institution regarded by radical Coloured groups as discriminatory, in implication if not in immediate effect, was the Coloured Advisory Council (C.A.C.), a body set up in 1943 under the wing of the Department of Social Welfare to serve as 'machinery' for 'developing and maintaining closer contacts between the Government and public bodies on the one hand and the Coloured people on the other, and for the purpose of obtaining first-hand information regarding the problems and needs peculiar to this section of the community.'[80]

The C.A.C. had originally been a Coloured Affairs Department (C.A.D.) under the Minister of the Interior. The name and constitution were, however, changed, apparently in an attempt to mollify the considerable hostility and resentment which were immediately displayed by considerable sections of the Coloured people.[81] The term 'Coloured Affairs Department' was too reminiscent of the Native Affairs Department. It suggested to many Coloured people that the authorities intended to treat Coloured interests as different from those of the white community, thereby slowing down the extension of fuller rights, and to use the separate department to apply total segregation.[82]

The question of the C.A.C. split politically-conscious Coloured people into sharply opposed parties. The C.A.C. functioned for nearly seven years, visiting Coloured communities all over the country, making representations on Coloured problems to the departments concerned, and submitting annual reports of its activities. It seems to have fulfilled a useful function in drawing attention to and sometimes obtaining remedies for minor abuses.

From what has been said earlier in this chapter it will be clear that the interests of Coloured South Africans are not fully or even adequately represented through the normal legislative bodies. Given good will on both sides there might have been some purpose in the existence of such a body, as a preliminary to greater equality of representation.[83] It is, however, open to question whether such good will is possible in a political structure in which white interests are intended to remain paramount.

As far as the Coloured Advisory Council is concerned, the question is an academic one. It continued to function[84] for nearly two years after the Nationalist Government's accession to power in May, 1948, in the face of intensified attacks from its Coloured political opponents. By 1949 Nationalist intentions towards the Coloured people were clear; in the political sphere they included a separate roll, a limited number of representatives in both Houses (possibly with limited rights) and a separate Coloured Affairs Department. In January, 1950, all but four members of the C.A.C. resigned,[85] their position in relation to their own community having apparently become untenable.[86]

The new Sub-department of Coloured Affairs, at present under the Department of the Interior, was initiated on 5th March, 1951. Dr. I. D. du Plessis, formerly a lecturer in Nederlands and Afrikaans at the University of Cape Town, who had concentrated on studies of the Cape Malay community, was appointed as head of this Sub-department, with a salary of £1,750 a year (the annual salary of a departmental secretary is £2,100). The Minister of the Interior announced that the Sub-department's function would be to co-ordinate all matters affecting the Coloured people, which are at present spread over the other different departments. As with the Native Affairs Department, such co-ordination will make it easier to administer differentiatory laws and regulations, and to deprive Coloured people of even the formal equality which they still possess in a few fields. To make the new department more palatable, the Commissioner has announced that it will 'open up new avenues of employment' to them in the shape of senior civil service posts serving their own people. So far, this prospect has evoked little enthusiasm amongst most Coloured people; the former C.A.C. supporters have united with the Anti-C.A.D. group to denounce any Coloured person who might take up such a post as a 'quisling'.

* * * * *

In democratic states it is commonly considered that every citizen has the right to public employment in all grades, subject only to his competence and qualifications. This question has both a political and an economic aspect and will be dealt with in more detail in Chapter V. In the Union, this right is very far from being realised as far as the Coloured people are concerned. In a period of increasing colour-prejudice, this constitutes a further differentiation against the Coloured group, who cannot always expect the same consideration of their interests from European officials, particularly if those interests happen to be in collision with those of a European.

D

In the Cape Colony prior to Union there was no legal or administrative bar to the employment of Coloured people in public service. In fact few were so employed in graded posts, except in the Departments of Railways and of Posts and Telegraphs, both of which employed several hundred Coloured people in lower-grade positions. The main reason for this was probably the low standard of education which prevailed amongst the Coloured population.

Since Union educational facilities have improved, but administrative orders have almost deprived the Coloured people of the possibility of employment in graded posts.[87] Since the Nationalist Government's latest term of office began, this process has been justified under the *apartheid* principle,[88] although promises have been made that the number of openings will ultimately be increased by staffing Coloured areas with Coloured officials.[89] Such *apartheid* appointments are not, however, equivalent to throwing open all public posts to any citizen on a basis of merit.

Apartheid (or racial separation in all spheres)[90] has been advocated as a high political ideal by eminent members of the Dutch Reformed Churches and the Afrikaans-speaking universities. Ideally applied, it would, it is claimed, benefit all racial groups. The time for such application passed, however, with the frontier period.

In practice, the Coloured people, Indians, and large numbers of detribalised Africans are so bound up with the European population economically, and, in the case of Coloureds, spatially, that the practical applications of *apartheid* has meant only deprivation for the Non-European groups.[91] It has become 'an instrument of domination . . . which retains the segregated in the social and political structure with the dominant white group, but subjects them to the denial of important rights.'[92]

The corner-stone of this modified and one-sided *apartheid* is to be the Population Registration Act (Act No. 30 of 1950). The original intention was to have a complete register of the entire population, but the present Act, probably for reasons of economy, does not apply to South-West Africa, and excludes all African women, and all African males under 18 years. It will therefore affect little more than one half of the population, and may be regarded as primarily an attempt to draw a final line between Europeans and Coloured people.[93] When the Register is complete,[94] identity cards giving vital statistics, ethnic group, and electoral qualifications will be issued, to be produced on demand.[95] The Government will then be able to proceed at full speed with its plans for segregation in all spheres of life, and in particular residential segregation as envisaged in the Group Areas Act.[96]

*   *   *   *   *

As Coloured people are on the whole excluded from public service within the country, it is perhaps superfluous to point out that no

Coloured person or other Non-European has the opportunity of serving or representing his country abroad, either as a permanent diplomat, or even as a delegate to any international conference.[97] In the trades union sphere at least, suitable candidates are available, but the authorities have never given the necessary formal permission for such journeys.[98]

Such formal permission to leave the country is apparently necessary in the case of Non-Europeans, and the procedure for obtaining a passport is said to be more stringent in practice where they are concerned.[99]

*   *   *   *   *

Another civic right or duty from which Coloured people and other Non-Europeans are now excluded is that of serving in the armed forces in a combatant capacity. Reference has already been made to the prevalent European fear of arming Non-Europeans,[100] particularly Africans. Memories are long in South Africa, and the activities of the 786 Bastards enrolled by the British[101] in the N.W. Cape at the beginning of the Anglo-Boer War, which caused a pro-Boer rising amongst the European farmers, have not been forgotten.[102]

In the early nineteenth century Cape Colony Coloured troops played a considerable rôle, and one historian of Afrikaner stock declares:

'Indeed it is no exaggeration to say that in the Xosa wars of 1846–7 and 1850–3 the Coloured people played a greater part in the defence of their country than the European burghers, who responded badly to the calls for service.'[103]

Even before Union, however, 'the strong prejudice that exists against the organisation and arming of the Coloured classes' had led to the Burgher Force and Levies Act of 1878, which relegated Coloured persons to the category of 'levies'. The Cape Mounted Rifles, by then a mixed Coloured-European unit, had already been disbanded in 1870.[104]

In 1912 Coloured people were definitely excluded from military service by Union legislation. By the end of 1915, a Cape Corps of Coloured volunteers was being raised for active combatant duties under the Imperial Army Council. About 25,000 volunteers enlisted in the Corps, which saw action in Africa, Palestine and France, and acquitted itself most creditably.[105] It was, however, disbanded on its return from the war, the band alone being allowed, as a gesture, to continue its existence.[106]

During the 1939–45 war, the Union Government decided to use Non-Europeans in a non-combatant capacity only, to release European troops for front-line service. Five motor transport companies were raised for the Cape Corps by May, 1940. Over 45,000 men served with the Cape Corps during the war, not to mention the Cape Malays who served with the Indian and Malay Corps and the 800 Coloured men with the S.A. Navy.[107] Some home units were armed for guard duties, and others carrying out duties at the front were given arms to enable them to defend themselves against enemy patrols.[108] Cape Corps casualties were: dead and presumed dead—1,091; wounded—472; prisoners-of-war—627.[109]

Public feeling against having Non-Europeans in the armed forces even in a national emergency was apparently responsible for the 'dilution' policy. By its application, Non-European units were split up into small sections, attached to European units as drivers, dispatch riders, stretcher-bearers and hygiene assistants.[110] This policy 'resulted in breaking up their own respective organisation' and 'in preventing the Cape Corps or the Native Military Corps being listed amongst the "units" in any engagement.'[111]

The highest rank open to Coloured volunteers was Warrant Officer I, and the rates of pay, allowances, leave gratuities, pensions and so on showed the usual differentiation between Europeans, Coloureds and Africans.[112] Annual leave was thirty days for Europeans, twenty-four days for Coloureds and eighteen days for Africans. Even the Governor-General's National War Fund, a voluntary fund started after 1939 to assist servicemen and their dependents, limited assistance for Coloureds to three-fifths of the upper European limit. It is, however, claimed that this limit was not rigidly observed.

After the war the decision as to whether the Cape Corps should remain a part of the permanent force hung fire until the Nationalist Government took office in 1948. In early 1949, the Minister of Defence stated in Parliament that the Coloured Corps would be disbanded, adding that Coloured persons would never again be called upon to go on active service in uniform, but would only be asked to act as servants to European soldiers.[113]

*   *   *   *   *

In the less formal sphere of party politics there is the same story of differentiation. In discussing the Coloured franchise, it has been shown how the attitudes of the major European parties have varied according to political expediency and their prospects of winning the Coloured vote in certain evenly-balanced constituencies.[114] In the Nationalist Party, such policies of expediency have at times, and particularly in the Nationalist Party ranks, been modified or nullified by the uncompromising race attitudes of individual members.[115]

Racialist outbursts have become more frequent over the last few years, even in high places. An often-quoted instance is that of the Minister of Labour, Mr. Ben Schoeman, who referred to the Non-European section of the South African people as 'Hottentots, Kaffirs and Coolies'.[116] Some weeks later, at the Transvaal Nationalist Party Congress, there was, in addition to a series of resolutions showing a high degree of racial feeling,[117] an outburst by one delegate who shouted, on the entry of an African messenger with a report: 'Kick the Kaffir out.'

Needless to say, the Nationalist Party does not allow Coloureds or other Non-Europeans into party membership,[118] although in earlier days it did work through purely Coloured political organisations such as the African National Bond (A.N.B.). One of the most effective Nationalist propaganda charges against the United Party has been to accuse its leaders and officials of being 'kaffir-lovers',[119] and the party itself of being 'a Coloured party'.[120] Just before the Provincial Elections of 1949, *Die Burger* told its readers how the United Party so relied on Coloured and Indian support that its Port Elizabeth district office was in a house owned by two Indian teachers, with an Indian school being taught in a neighbouring room and 'the same entrance for everybody'.[121]

It cannot be said that the United Party has a strongly opposed racial policy.[122] This party is usually at pains to refute charges that it is dominated by 'liberals', seeks 'social equality',[123] or denies the necessity for permanent white leadership.[124] Did it not do so, it might lose large sections of its own supporters, particularly Afrikaans-speaking voters in the country districts, whose attitudes to Coloured people are often barely distinguishable from those of Nationalist supporters.

A recent statement of United Party policy reads:

'The policy of the United Party in relation to the Cape Coloured People is based on the recognition of the special position which the Coloured people occupy in our multi-racial society and of the desirability of raising the standards and improving the living conditions of the Coloured people. In regard to political rights, the United Party reaffirms the principle laid down by General Hertzog that the Coloured people are not to be deprived of their existing political rights and (the United Party) will resist any proposals to change their franchise in a manner that would diminish these rights.

'In regard to economic status, the United Party will continue to foster wider opportunities for employment, and stands for the principle that Coloured people at the Cape shall not by reason of their race or colour be debarred from engaging in any form of industrial occupation or employment, and for the provision of facilities for their vocational training . . .

'In regard to social status, the United Party, recognising that the maintenance of social separation is in accordance with the desire of both Coloureds and Europeans, stands for the improved and increased provision of housing, educational, social and health amenities for the Coloured people in such a manner as to stimulate, on a voluntary basis, the development of separate Coloured residential areas, with powers of local self-government for such areas and conduct of the various administrative, civic and other services in such areas by Coloured people themselves.'[125]

The attitudes of white United Party organisers seem to range from friendly patronage to the view that Coloured voters are a necessary evil. In constituencies with a heavy Coloured vote, Coloured organisers have played a considerable part in pre-election and election activities. At such times they are in evidence in urban party headquarters, and seem to be on easy terms with European party officials and helpers.[126]

Coloured supporters of the United Party are usually organised by separate Coloured committees,[127] and special local meetings are held for Coloured constituents only. This is presumably in order to avoid outraging the susceptibilities of race-conscious European supporters, by compelling them to sit unsegregated in the same hall with Coloured people. In general, it would appear that the United Party does not at present regard Coloured voters as much more than second-class citizens, an interpretation which is further borne out by the tendency referred to earlier for United Party M.P.s to defend their majorities by claiming that they would have been elected on European votes only.[128]

Now that the Coloured voters have been removed to a separate roll and can therefore play no direct part in determining future election results in difficult constituencies, latent colour prejudice amongst United Party officials and rank and file may become even more evident. On the other hand, the United Party, faced with the loss of the seats in which the Coloured vote was decisive, will definitely need the support of the four Coloured Representatives, and is in any case pledged to restore the *status quo ante* in the event of its being returned to power.

If such a change of government takes place there may, however, be dynamic possibilities in the divergent political views and the very lack of a single and rigid guiding principle within the United Party, and above all in this party's connection with industrial and even with mining interests, both of which have at times shown themselves less interested in the preservation of the old colour-hierarchy than with attaining a balance between plentiful, cheap labour and maximum efficiency, considerations which take little account of skin-colour.

It is, however, doubtful whether such factors are strong enough to balance the rising demand for political rights from sections of the subordinate groups. It would seem that as individual members of the subordinate groups become more fully acculturated and acquire educational and economic status which would make them valuable citizens in a society not based on pigmentation, so the dominant group feels itself more definitely threatened and passes on to the defensive. In the present South African situation, European attitudes towards Coloured political rights have been influenced by their fear of the much larger problem of African political rights,[129] and their conditioned inability to believe that persons of another colour should or could ever become sufficiently acculturated for political equality.[130]

The old Cape franchise was based on cultural and economic qualifications which few Africans had yet had the time to acquire. Even in the pre-Union Cape, there were signs of a growing tendency to restrict African political influence, but this took the form of exclusion by increasing the qualifications for all groups, irrespective of colour.[131]

In this situation, the presence of a large and acculturated Coloured lower class provided a valuable buffer, and resulted in a more elaborate status-hierarchy than the simple white-black dichotomy prevailing in the North.

After Union came the victory of 'Northern' ideas, the transition from a qualified universal franchise to an unqualified white franchise, with its concomitant of increased colour differentiation and prejudice.[132] The Coloured vote has lingered on as an anomaly deplored by most white voters,[133] but retained by the Cape for both sentimental and tactical reasons. It had, however, lost its major function once the differential basis for white and Coloured voters was accepted, and could no longer serve as a means for broadening the basis of the electorate along unified lines. Politically, the Coloured group had ceased to act as a buffer group, nor after Union was it geographically in a position to do so.[134]

*　　*　　*　　*　　*

Throughout this study comparisons with the American Negro question spring to mind. It must be emphasised that the two situations, while similar in many ways, are by no means parallel. The American Negro is essentially a part of American society, retaining few, if any, separate culture traits. This is true of the Coloured community in the Cape, but not as yet of the majority of Africans within the Union. The entry of the latter upon the scene has had a definitely depressing effect on Coloured political status, in a society where the principle of 'equal rights for every civilised man' was but insecurely grafted on to a centuries-old belief in colour distinctions, supported by every sanction of God and man.

It is the weakness of the 'Cape liberal tradition', as compared with the strength of 'the American Creed',[135] and in the relative numerical strength of the various groups that the major differences between the two situations are to be found.[136] In the United States, the prospects of an ultimate and peaceable solution seem more likely. In South Africa, where the largest subordinate group, which far outnumbers all other ethnic groups in the country, is still barely acculturated, and is not really accepted as a part of the society, there exists the possibility of a fundamental and violent disturbance of the present status-hierarchy.[137]

This prospect is only brought nearer by the denial of equal rights, rewards and opportunities in the political sphere to those individuals who have thoroughly accepted the European values-system, only to find themselves rejected on the irrelevant but unalterable ground of skin-colour.[138] The psychological consequences of such rejection are reinforced by the inadequate facilities and general discrimination which are their lot in every aspect of social life, as members of a group which lacks adequate political representation.

CHAPTER FOUR

THE LAW AND ITS ADMINISTRATION

Rules of law must be impartial . . . impartiality is in fact one of the main elements of reasonableness. There is a presumption that all the inhabitants of this country enjoy civil rights under the law. The rules of law must consequently provide equality of treatment for all persons, irrespective of wealth, colour, race, religion or any other characteristic. Thus, for the enjoyment or protection of rights, 'it makes no difference whether the individual occupies a hut or a palace': whether he be white or coloured, a European or a non-European. It follows that rules of law must make no difference depending on differences of class in the treatment of persons. Hence 'class legislation which presses unduly on certain sections of the community, by oppressing them or interfering with their rights, is invalid'.[1]

I N 1838, the Coloured people in the Cape were raised to equal formal legal status with the European community. Since then, they and other Non-Europeans have been theoretically subject to the Rule of Law in South Africa. The act of conferring formal equality, which was inspired by the Colonial Government in London, could not, however, change the attitude of the colonists towards their former slaves and servants.

In the Cape Colony, 'class' legislation was forbidden.[2] The liquor laws were in fact the only legislation which differentiated between the Coloured and other sections of the community.[3] After Union, however, well over fifty Acts were passed enabling Ministers to differentiate on grounds of race or colour, even before the present Government began to implement its *apartheid* policy. These for the most part affected Africans, in respect of whom the Rule of Law has been virtually abrogated since 1927.[4] A considerable number of laws have, however, differentiated with regard to the Coloured people, particularly since 1948, and even in 1937 the Cape Coloured Commission found their legal position 'complicated' and 'hampering'.[5]

There is no charter of civil liberties in South Africa, like that of the United States, to afford formal protection to under-privileged minorities. The supreme legislature is therefore not bound by similar restrictions,[6] and has since Union occupied itself with 'colour bar' legislation aimed at one or more Non-European groups in every sphere in which these groups seemed to be overstepping the boundaries of their ascribed rôle and status.[7]

A large part of this discriminatory legislation, particularly as it affects Africans, is not directly promulgated by Parliament, but through the delegation of powers to government departments.[8] Many of the discriminatory regulations which affect Coloured people in such matters as residence, recreation, education and municipal franchise are the result of enabling powers conferred on the various Provincial Councils. It must be left to legal experts to decide how far this body of differentiatory laws and regulations does abrogate the Rule of Law in its application to the Coloured community.

The practical application of these various laws will be discussed under their separate headings. Here we are more concerned with the attitudes of the dominant community, as reflected in the law and its administration. It is doubtful whether the majority of South African whites have ever felt that non-whites are their equals before the law; they have rather tended to regard the law as their own law[9] and the main instrument for social control and the maintenance of the desired colour-hierarchy.[10] This attitude probably accounts for the absence of institutionalised lynching in the Union.[11]

In these circumstances it would seem that discrimination is determined less by the law than by differential administration, and by inequalities in the meting out of justice.

The direct administration of the law and of justice is almost exclusively in the hands of Europeans,[12] with the exception of a few police and prison officers in the lowest grades. The comprehensive powers of the South African Police with regard to the enforcement of the innumerable statutory restrictions imposed on Non-Europeans, particularly Africans, make its methods of recruitment and training of particular importance.[13]

European recruitment appears to have been a major problem up till very recently, and recruits have been increasingly drawn from one section of the white community, the Afrikaans-speaking rural element.[14] This preponderance of officers, particularly at the bottom grades, from the lower economic levels of a group noted even in South Africa for its uncompromising racial attitudes[15] does not augur well for an objective administration of the law in practice.

Amongst the Coloured community incidents of police discourtesy and physical mishandling are a commonplace of conversation,[16] and the Lansdown Commission found it necessary to issue an admonition in this matter.[17]

The relevant passage mentioned the many complaints made to the Commission about such treatment, and the difficulties of obtaining evidence of specific cases.[18] The Commission did not distinguish between the treatment given to different Non-European groups in this context, and it seems unlikely that any considerable distinctions exist in the handling of prisoners, particularly as many police officers in the larger Coloured centres may come from rural areas where Africans predominate.

In fairness, however, to the police force in general,[19] it should be said here that such incidents are not officially countenanced at a high level, and could possibly be reduced by administrative reforms within the police itself. Even so, the police force would still reflect the unequal social environment in which it functions,[20] and be called upon to administer the increasing number of differentiatory statutes.

Although the greater part of law administration is in European hands, the non-commissioned establishment of the South African Police makes provision for Coloured, Indian and African police officers, in both the uniformed and the plain-clothes branches, for work in Non-European districts.[21] In theory, the law does not limit a policeman's power according to his colour, but many powers are reserved to higher ranks, to which Non-Europeans are not appointed. In practice, therefore, they have authority only over other Non-Europeans,[22] and their conditions of recruitment, training and pay scales are inferior. (See Appendix E.)

When one considers that the cost of living is the same for Europeans and Coloureds, and that many of the latter attempt to maintain reasonable European living standards, it becomes obvious that the better-educated type of Coloured man is not attracted to this service,[23] with its maximum salary of £300 per annum (exclusive of non-pensionable allowance) in the highest achievable rank of first-class sergeant.[24] There is no formal educational qualification as with Europeans.[25]

In status, remuneration, training[26] and conditions of service generally the Coloured police officer occupies a marginal position between his European and African colleagues, though somewhat closer to the latter. His opportunities for promotion are limited.[27] The small Coloured establishment sometimes means that Coloured areas are policed by African constables.[28] This arrangement is said to be a source of humiliation to many middle-class Coloured people.[29]

The pattern of discrimination is reflected throughout the financial provisions made for European and Non-European officers. In the case of uniform allowances the distinction is made between the two groups only. Nor are Non-European N.C.O.s given a correspondingly larger allowance than constables. Free medical services have long been available for the wives and children of European police officers, but the extension of such services to specified Non-Europeans was only recommended by the Centlivres Commission in 1946.[30]

Enough has been said of the status of Coloured police-officers to indicate considerable discrimination, not only against them as individual state employees, but against the Coloured community whose special needs they are supposed to serve, if the policy of 'separation' or *apartheid* is to be justly followed out.

In theory, these principles should postulate the institution of equal services and facilities for all groups. In practice, the interests of one are subordinated to those of the other. The under-privileged racial groups in the Union undoubtedly regard the police force as the protector of European rights and privileges as against their own.[31] This is borne out even by the Police Commission of Inquiry.[32] It is a view of their functions which seems to be shared by many police officers, particularly at lower levels, despite some high-level attempts[33] to bring about a better relationship between the police and Non-Europeans.[34]

The police are entrusted with the maintenance and enforcement of law amongst the general public. When a citizen is accused of transgressing that law,[35] he comes into contact with another instrument of its administration, the courts.[36] These have their personal and procedural aspect, the Bar and Bench on the one hand, the awaiting-trial and court regulations on the other.

In a country where the seeming impartiality of the common law is at variance with discriminatory statutes reflecting the prejudices of the dominant white group, the extent to which the civil liberties recognised in this common law are enforced (and respected by the subordinate groups) is in the highest instance dependent on the judiciary.

As in Britain, the South African higher judiciary is traditionally independent of the executive, and has on a number of occasions upheld the rights of Non-Europeans, often reducing or even reversing the decisions of lower courts. Complete impartiality is, however, hardly to be expected, as both judges and magistrates are drawn exclusively from the European group,[37] and must, consciously or unconsciously, reflect some part of the race attitudes by which they have been surrounded all their lives.

The writer has gained the impression from some (though not all) Coloured people interviewed that, while they expect a reasonably fair trial for people of their own group before a judge,[38] they have no such certainty when facing a magistrate.[39] This belief in magisterial prejudice is undoubtedly widespread amongst Coloureds as well as Africans.

The reasons for its existence, if justified, may perhaps be sought in the mode of appointing magistrates,[40] and in the vastly overloaded case-lists of their courts, which handle the great bulk of the Union's legal work.[41] A magistrate's[42] practical experience is admirably summed up by Dr. H. J. Simons:[43]

'Much of the magistrate's practical experience is gained before his elevation to the bench, as a clerk of the court and as public prosecutor. In these capacities he develops a tendency to view the machinery of justice from the standpoint of the prosecution, and, through an intimate association with the police, to acquire a dangerous confidence in their infallibility. To accept the evidence of a police witness against the uncorroborated version of the accused is very nearly a principle in the magistrates' courts. The bias, however, is not only acquired through earlier training; it is also a product of the conditions under which the courts function. Overwhelmed in the larger centres by a great mass of petty cases, most of them undefended, the courts are constrained to adopt the most expeditious methods for completing the roll. Unable for want of time to investigate cases thoroughly, they assume tacitly that the police would not have laid a charge if the accused were not guilty of some offence.'[44]

If judges are in fact more impartial in their administration of the law where Non-Europeans are concerned, the reason may be sought in a combination of the following factors. Their legal studies are wider, their bar practice has enabled them to preserve independence of the executive or the police, they do not have to cope with the vast numbers of petty offenders, mainly Non-European, who face the magistrates, they are not so dependent upon local opinion, and the traditions of their office are drawn from a philosophy and a *milieu* outside their own social environment, with its sources in Western Europe.

On the other hand, they are still as individuals a part of this South African social environment, and unable always or wholly to resist its demands.[45] The apparent hardening of judicial attitudes over recent decades might be the reflection only of the increasing number of discriminatory statutes which have appeared since Union, for even the most liberal Bench would only have a ceitain flexibility in interpreting existing laws. It seems, however, more likely that the Bench itself is not immune from the general waning of 'liberal' attitudes.[46]

We have considered the major agents of the law, the police force and the judiciary, and noted the possibilities of discrimination which must necessarily arise where such agents are, for the most part, drawn from the dominant white group. Such discrimination must necessarily outweigh high-level attempts at objective administration of the law, particularly in a country where the vast majority of Europeans consider that the interests and aims of the Non-Europeans necessarily run counter to their own. The social pressure on all sections of the police force and judiciary from their own group is therefore overwhelming in controversial issues, and the case of the Non-Europeans must necessarily suffer.

Apart from European attitudes, official and otherwise, poverty and their own ignorance[47] would appear to be important factors which discriminate against the Coloured people in their contacts with the procedural aspect of the law, and sometimes produce a feeling of injustice which they ascribe to colour prejudice on the part of the officers of the law. They are often unaware of their rights either as awaiting trial prisoners or in the courts.[48] Poverty makes the granting of bail less likely,[49] and forces a person given the option of a fine to serve his sentence, while those better off go free.[50]

For the same reason the vast majority of Coloured offenders are undefended.[51] This is a great drawback to an accused person in any court, and the responsibility which rests on the judge or magistrate to look after his interests cannot, even with the best of intentions, be carried out fully.[52] In addition, persons charged with more serious offences and unable to raise bail may be imprisoned for months awaiting trial, due to congestion of the courts and other reasons.[53]

Where the police are concerned, it is difficult to avoid the impression that officers, particularly in the lowest grade, are not always so careful to inform Non-European prisoners of their rights as they should be.[54] Undoubtedly the African suffers more from such discrimination than the Coloured, owing to his different cultural background, and unfamiliarity with both the language and the European legal system. However, the poorer and less educated Coloured people, who constitute the bulk of Coloured offenders, also suffer in this respect.[55]

The question of legal aid is another sphere in which the Coloured accused suffers indirect indiscrimination on account of his lower economic status.[56] The State provides this service *pro Deo* only in murder, rape and treason cases, where an accused is on trial for his life, but no provision is made for an attorney's assistance in such cases.[57]

Some legal aid is now available to indigent accused persons of all races at the Legal Aid Bureaux[58] recently established through the initiative of the South African Institute of Race Relations[59] in the larger urban centres of Cape Town, Johannesburg, Durban, Bloemfontein, Pretoria and Port Elizabeth. As yet this does not affect the rural districts, where the most ignorant and poverty-stricken Coloured communities are to be found.

Although the present system is still in its infancy, and suffers from lack of funds, it would appear preferable in the South African context to direct Government control.[60] Similar work, combined with prison visiting and other social work, is carried out by the Social Services of South Africa. Again, however, the work is limited by lack of funds.

Before leaving the question of legal aid, it should be pointed out that Coloureds or other Non-Europeans must almost invariably seek the services of a European attorney or advocate, since the number of men of their own groups who have entered the legal profession is infinitesimal.[61] In present circumstances, this has one advantage, in that a European advocate can probably get a better hearing in a European court than could a Coloured man. On the other hand, the Coloured accused cannot always count on the same interest, particularly in cases where a European is involved.

This type of case always affords the greatest opportunities for discrimination, particularly where the case is one on which a jury would normally sit.[62] This was recognised by the legislature in an Act enabling the Minister of Justice to remove trials to other districts and to direct trial by judge without jury in a varied series of offences, including those where the accused is a Non-European and the complainant a European, or vice versa.[63]

The Lansdown Report mentioned 'a strong suspicion that a European jury is not a satisfactory tribunal for the trial of a case in which a European is charged with an offence against the person of a Non-European or vice versa;'[64] it also estimated that 75 per cent of Supreme Court criminal trials are now held without jury,[65] thanks to the option given by the Act referred to above.[66]

In societies with a more homogeneous population, a strong argument for the retention of the jury system might be based on the advisability of admitting human values in the administration of justice.[67] In South Africa, however, the trial of cases involving Europeans and Non-Europeans by an all-European jury can only serve to permit the expression of European race-prejudices,[68] and to increase the undoubted tendency of the courts to give more value to the testimony of European than to that of Non-European witnesses.[69]

The final aspect of legal procedure in which differentiation or discrimination against Non-Europeans might be expected is in the passing of sentence. Where a dominant minority is apprehensive as to the safety of both person and property, this may be to some extent reflected by the judiciary's choice of penalty, where the law permits such choice.

In South Africa the customary forms of punishment are: death, imprisonment,[70] corporal punishment, fines and non-punitive measures such as suspended sentences.[71] As in other spheres of Union public life, full and up-to-date statistics are not available, but it is hoped to indicate certain discriminatory trends in the application of these sanctions.

There is a widespread belief in South Africa, amongst both those who approve of such discrimination and those who deplore it, that Non-Europeans are in fact given more severe sentences for all forms of offence.[72] The same belief is widely current amongst Non-Europeans themselves. There is certainly a marked discrepancy between the percentages of recent convictions to prosecutions on a murder charge, when the figures are broken down according to the race of the accused and the deceased.

Table A[73] shows a marked variation in the conviction prosecution ratio, according to racial affiliation. Where a European is accused of killing another European, the probability of a conviction is high. Where a Coloured or African is the accused and the victim a European, a conviction is even more likely. Where a European is accused of killing a Non-European,[74] the ratio drops to 13.5 per cent. Where only Non-Europeans are involved on both sides, the ratio is intermediate. In other words, where the deceased is a European, the accused is more likely to be convicted, whatever his racial affiliation. Where a Non-European is the victim, the accused is more likely to go free.[75]

This supports the impression which one gains in the sphere of health ⅰ social welfare, that a Non-European life is held much cheaper than their own by the dominant Europeans.[76] It would be difficult to find a jury or judicial officer to convict a European of murder where a Non-European is the victim.[77] Wherever possible, the charge is modified to one of culpable homicide or assault.[78] The same rule applies in rape cases, which may also involve the death sentence.[79] No European has gone to the gallows for such a crime against a Non-European.[80]

At the other end of the scale of sanctions comes the imposition of fines, usually with an alternative of prison for non-payment. We have already cited the relevant passages in the Lansdown Report, which make it clear that large numbers of petty offenders, particularly Non-Europeans, are serving prison sentences simply because they were unable through poverty to take advantage of the option of a fine. Table B[81] shows this trend very clearly for a recent period.

The report then refers to the disproportion of fines imposed upon Africans as compared to their earnings. The same comment would apply to Coloureds too, though to a somewhat lesser extent. Magistrates, although they can hardly fail to be aware of the poverty of most Non-Europeans, do not always seem to take this into account in fixing the amount of the fine. Such a fine with the alternative of prison would in fact be equivalent to a sentence of prison without the option.[82]

Coloured informants consulted on this point expressed views which, whilst not necessarily objective or unbiased, more than corroborated the Lansdown Report findings. In two cases, informants suggested that certain magistrates deliberately imposed maximum fines on Coloured people, in many cases higher than on Europeans convicted of the same types of offence, but rarely lower. This was correlated by the informants with the demand from white farmers for Non-European convict labour.[83]

Statements of this type are almost impossible to check in detail, and may often be greatly exaggerated. It would indeed be difficult to expect objectivity from members of a minority group on which legal and other institutions press so heavily. However, the widespread expectation of discrimination on the part of such a group is as much an undermining of the concept of the Rule of Law as are the bias of the judiciary and the increasing list of discriminatory statutes.

It is at least certain that the Coloured offender has less chance than the European of avoiding prison, with its consequent ill-effects for himself, his family, which is deprived of its breadwinner, and the community, which in up to 38 per cent of cases gains a recidivist[84] with an added criminal knowledge acquired in prison.[85]

The next sanction to be considered is that of corporal punishment. In the Union this is supported by both British and Afrikaner tradition. From its persistence until recently in the British penal code and until now in British public schools, one must assume that the British have faith in its deterrent and educational value. In South Africa, where the purpose of sanctions, at least as far as Non-Europeans are concerned, seems to be almost entirely deterrent[86] and even retributive, many country farmers are still said to prefer the *sjambok* to the courts for disciplining their Non-European labourers.[87]

It is not therefore surprising to find that even the fairly liberal European viewpoint represented in the Lansdown Report, while stressing the need for greater consideration of the reformative purpose of punishment, found it necessary to accept the probably deterrent value, 'in the present state of South African society', of corporal punishment for adult offenders of all races,[88] and to recommend its retention in cases of sexual and other assaults, wilful cruelty to children and animals, repeated stocktheft and housebreaking.[89]

The retention of whipping in the latter two cases would mainly affect Non-Europeans, who constitute the majority of such offenders.[90] It is also a concession to the demands of European property-owners.[91]

The Lansdown Commission's recommendations are in advance of practical administration, and one might expect to find that the judiciary tends to impose sentences of corporal punishment more frequently on Non-Europeans than on Europeans. This expectation is borne out by the following table:

TABLE C[92]

SHOWING OFFENDERS ADMITTED TO PENAL INSTITUTIONS WITH
SENTENCES OF CORPORAL PUNISHMENT OVER THE PERIOD 1923–44

| Year | Europeans | | | | | Non-Europeans | | | |
	Adults	Young Offenders	Total	Percentage of 'Serious' Convictions	Adults	Young Offenders	Total	Percentage of 'Serious' Convictions
1923	24	47	71	2.7	2,083	184	2,267	13.6
1928	27	73	100	3.2	2,285	112	2,397	10.0
1933	26	95	121	5.7	2,091	1,590	3,681	16.0
1938	12	3	15	0.7	1,707	410	2,117	8.8
1944	17	2	19	0.9	1,918	189	2,107	6.6
1948	16	2	18	0.2	2,722	235	2,957	5.4

The figures in Table C show a decrease in the proportion of sentences with corporal punishment to the total convictions, reflecting the gradual introduction of more progressive ideas into the administration of justice. However, they also show a consistent and considerable bias in favour of the European.[93] It is impossible to determine from the figures available just how far Coloured offenders are affected by this severity, but from the other evidence considered there is no reason to suppose that they would be untouched by it.

South African magistrates are also empowered[94] to order spare diet,[95] solitary confinement and hard labour,[96] in addition to a sentence of imprisonment. Spare diet and solitary confinement are also part of prison discipline, but will be considered later under that aspect. Such additional punishments are, however, infrequently imposed;[97] in such cases as occur they are often deleted on appeal or review.

In South Africa, as elsewhere, the treatment of juvenile delinquency is considered as a separate problem. The Children's Act (No. 31) of 1937[98] was both progressive and constructive, but its effect has not so far been fully felt, particularly by the Non-European communities, owing to lack of trained personnel for its implementation. No doubt the intervening war period has been partly to blame for this, but some responsibility for the neglect of Non-European juveniles must be placed on the shoulders of indifferent officialdom.[99]

The type of sentence passed by the courts in such cases must of necessity depend on the available means of dealing with young offenders.[100] It seems that, in practice, Non-European juveniles have often been sent to a reformatory or even prison, or sentenced to corporal punishment and returned to unsuitable homes, simply because there was no more suitable accommodation available.[101]

The position has improved in the last few years, but the number of institutions other than reformatories available to Coloured and other Non-European children 'in need of care' and young delinquents is far lower than the need.[102] In 1950 the first industrial school for Coloured youths was opened at Ottery in the Cape Peninsula, but this compares very badly with the provision for Europeans.

The large, though still inadequate, provision of reformatory accommodation for Coloured children suggests that the idea of deterrence has been uppermost in the minds of the authorities, and that their first concern has been to provide treatment which competent authorities regard as the last resort, apart from imprisonment, in dealing with delinquent children.[103]

The lack of other accommodation of a less drastic type, and of trained probation officers[104] to supervise young offenders in approved custody, must often mean that a Coloured juvenile convicted of a petty first offence arising out of environmental influences must take his first steps into a life-time of crime, whereas his rehabilitation would in other circumstances have been feasible.

The evils of the reformatory system[105] are further complicated by the lack of classification or segregation of various types of inmate, and by the inability of the staff, due to overcrowding, to give each case the full consideration which it deserves. For Coloured girls, the position was further complicated until recently, in that only one reformatory existed for all Non-Europeans, whatever their background.[106]

One further practice should be mentioned which is regarded as discriminatory by Coloured people, and which is disconcertingly reminiscent of the old Hottentot 'apprenticeship' regulations, of which

E

it is in fact a survival. This is the custom of apprenticing children declared 'in need of care', or punished as offenders under various acts, to unskilled or semi-skilled work on farms. Some years ago the C.A.C. requested that this system should be replaced by one of committing the children to suitable institutions to be provided by the Department of Social Welfare.[107] In the 1951 session, a Children's Act Amendment Bill was passed, one clause of which provides for the discontinuation of this practice for children under sixteen.

*   *   *   *   *

In considering the prison system, we shall again have to draw largely on the Lansdown Report, the only official review made of prisons and their organisation since the Prisons and Reformatories Act (No. 13) of 1911. The relevant section of the Report[108] stresses the shortage of funds for new buildings and staff, serious overcrowding and excessive militarisation and restraint.

Where overall inadequacies are so considerable, one might expect to find that provisions for Coloureds and other Non-Europeans will be the first to suffer.[109] The Union has a large territory with a small population distributed sparsely over it, except in the larger urban centres. Reasons of economy therefore often make it difficult, if not impossible, to introduce more than the primary segregation between sexes,[110] and between Europeans and Non-Europeans, despite the official policy of *apartheid* for all major groups.[111] This meets the basic demands of the politically vocal section of the community, while Coloureds and Indians have less possibility of making similar objections heard effectively, should they wish to do so.[112]

The prison regulations affecting such items as diet, separate sleeping facilities and so on, do follow the principle that the Coloured community has a mode of life intermediate between that of the European and African groups,[113] but in practice the Coloured prisoner shares many of the same facilities as the African.[114] European and Non-European prisoners are issued with different prison clothing,[115] that issued to the latter being much more conspicuous.

The almost invariable sleeping accommodation provided for all Non-Europeans[116] consists of communal cells housing from six to forty men, with cement or stone-flagged floors,[117] often vermin-infested, and usually with one or more open pails as the only sanitary system.[118] Beds are provided only for certain privileged classes, mainly European.[119] Other prisoners, European and Non-European, sleep on the floor,[120] a mat and two blankets (three in winter) being issued to all, a pillow only to Europeans. Thus although most Coloured people use European-type beds where they can afford it, no beds are provided for them except in prison hospitals.

Three separate diet scales are in operation in South African prisons, one for each major ethnic group.[121] These scales are an improvement on the system in force prior to the Lansdown Report, in that the totally inadequate short-term scales have been abolished.[122] Both short and long-term diets were drawn up before modern developments in dietetics.

Many Europeans consider that Non-European prisoners are better off in prison than they would be as free men,[123] and advocate harsher rather than improved conditions lest prison should come to seem a better place than the outside world.[124] This argument from lesser eligibility, familiar in England in the nineteenth century, indicates that its advocates have not even begun to accept the reformative function of penal sanctions.[125]

The highly inadequate provisions for educational and vocational training show the same spirit.[126] The position as regards general education is unsatisfactory for all prisoners, but particularly so in the case of Coloureds and other Non-Europeans, most of whom are illiterate, and for whom practically no instruction is available.[127] Even for those educated Coloured prisoners who might wish to study, there are no prison libraries worth the name except at Pretoria.[128] This is one of the only gaols with a schoolmaster on the staff, his work being, however, confined to Europeans. The possibilities of study are further limited by the fact that few Coloured prisoners have separate cells.

The Lansdown Report recommended the teaching of reading, writing, arithmetic, elementary hygiene and simple civics for both men and women, first aid training for men, child care, simple dietetics and home nursing for women.[129] Such recommendations could not be put into practice without the creation of further staff posts, as staff for the elementary general teaching of Non-Europeans is simply not available.

The facilities for vocational training are not much better. For European men a beginning at least has been made at Pretoria Central Prison.[130] Non-Europeans, including Coloureds, are still regarded mainly as a source of manual labour. There is some instruction in agriculture and gardening,[131] stone dressing, rope manufacture and brick making, but the emphasis seems to be rather on the work than on the instruction. Women receive no vocational training, except incidentally in the laundry work done by them in the prisons.

Differential treatment of the Coloured or African prisoner is also shown in the gratuity scales payable to prisoners for good conduct and industry.[132] Payment of gratuities to Non-Europeans was introduced only in June, 1935. While this is evidence of a more liberal attitude on the part of the authorities, neither the present nor the recommended scales can be said to do justice to the Non-European. A further gratuity payable on discharge is authorised by Prison Regulation No. 474 to well-conducted prisoners, otherwise ineligible for gratuities. This had for many years been confined to Europeans, but was extended to Non-Europeans in April, 1944.[133]

Non-European convict labour is employed on a large scale in South Africa. Prison standing orders forbid the hiring out or placing of

European prisoners to work on public roads where they would be constantly seen by the public,[134] while female prisoners of any race may not be employed outside the prison boundaries.

Non-European prisoners with sentences of between six and twenty-four months are hired out for a payment to the Prisons Department of 2s. per head per day. At the time of the Lansdown Report, about 2,600 prisoners were supplied to the South Africa Railways and Harbours Administration for navvy work, others to various provincial and local authorities for road-making, about 1,400 for surface work to the gold mines, many to private persons by the day, and others to farmers under contract, or (this was applicable to first offenders serving sentences of three months or less, and was known as the 'sixpenny scheme') to farmers at a wage of 6d. a day, plus food and quarters.[135]

In its final recommendation[136] the Commission advocated a policy of exclusive State employment for all prisoners, but recognised that this might not be immediately feasible. Indeed, any such step would meet with vigorous opposition from the private interests affected.[137] This was shown when the Prisons Department followed the Lansdown Commission's recommendation to terminate the 'sixpenny scheme' referred to above. Farmers immediately complained that they were being deprived of urgently needed labour, and a somewhat improved 'ninepenny scheme' was introduced as a temporary measure. The scheme is still in operation for those prisoners who volunteer, and has in fact been extended, although the Lansdown Commission was unable to approve of it except as a purely emergency one.[138]

The methods of punishment employed by the courts have already been described. Within the penal institutions themselves there is a further system of punishments and privileges contingent upon the prisoner's behaviour while serving his term. Here, while the general regulations[139] as to conduct classification apply to all races, there is some differentiation as to privileges.[140] For instance, smoking, which is regarded as a 'supreme indulgence',[141] is limited to Europeans, except for the Non-European indeterminate prisoners in Barberton Prison.[142] The recommended extension would, it was estimated, have cost in the neighbourhood of £10,000 per annum; it was therefore not carried out.

Of the other privileges, such a one as letter-writing is of little value to the majority of Coloureds and Africans, the majority of whom cannot read or write. Amongst the other privileges whose institution was recommended[143] were recreational facilities, extra furniture and bedding, special clothing, walks, and transfer to smaller or individual cells. The Prisons Department would hardly be in a position to carry out any recommendation involving extra expenditure, as we have seen in the account of prison accommodation and facilities generally.[144]

It was suggested that a wider list of privileges might obviate the necessity for applying the more drastic penalties at present in use, since their withdrawal would constitute a penalty in itself. The present penalties include the imposition of extra labour, solitary confinement, reduced diet and corporal punishment not exceeding six strokes.[145]

The general aims of a penal system depend ultimately for their realisation on the personnel employed to put them into practice.[146] At the highest levels there have, over the last decade or so, been signs of a reformative approach. At the point of impact with the prisoner, however,[147] it is doubtful whether such attitudes retain much force. As with the police, the social background and economic status of the average white prison-official make it unlikely that he will accord better treatment to the convicted Non-European under his charge than he would to the free Non-European in the street outside.[148]

Non-Europeans are of course frequently put in the charge of Non-European warders, and one might suppose that this would at least eliminate racial discrimination. In the case of African warders, however, these are often Zulus from the country districts, with no formal education. They are excellent at maintaining rough and ready discipline, but not disposed to deal tenderly with members of other tribes which they despise. Still worse may be the position of the Coloured prisoner who comes under such authority,[149] in the event of there being no Coloured warder available, or because he has opted for the African diet-scale and so been classed as an African in the prison records.[150]

Where Coloured warders are actually employed,[151] they are not necessarily the most suitable persons for such work. No formal educational qualification is required,[152] and their salary-scales, as compared with those for European warders, are discriminatory both for the recipients themselves and for the prisoners, put into the charge of persons whose economic status is rated so low by authority, and whose avenue of promotion is completely blocked.[153]

* * * * *

In his contacts with the law and its administration, the Coloured person is faced with laws, ordinances and regulations passed in a white parliament or white-dominated lower councils and local authorities, by members representing a body of voters of whom the great majority are white. These laws and regulations are administered by a white bureaucracy and a mainly white police force. If he comes into the courts, he must seek justice from a white judiciary, and if he is represented at all he must almost invariably be represented by a white counsel.

From the evidence that has been given earlier in this chapter, it should by now be clear that the Coloured community does not receive equal treatment in the administration of the law. This has the further consequence that the group differentiated against ceases to expect equal treatment and comes to regard the law as the 'white man's law'.[154] The result of this process can only be the undermining of the whole framework of law and order in the larger society. This development has been envisaged with some foreboding by more thoughtful South Africans, who have advocated the elimination of colour diffentiation in the administration of justice.[155] It is, however, open to doubt whether equal administration of justice can be achieved in a society in which certain classes or groups are singled out for legal differentiation, in which in fact the law is in process of establishing a separate status for each racial group.[156]

CHAPTER FIVE

ECONOMIC LIFE

A complete citizen should be both producer and consumer. The idea lives on that it has pleased God to call the larger part of mankind to learn and labour truly—not to get their own living but to toil in the service of their betters.[1]

THOUGH slavery was abolished in the British Empire in 1833, it has proved difficult to eradicate from the minds of most white South Africans the idea that the main function of the non-white[2] is to provide cheap, docile labour for the European. This idea was hardly questioned until the London Missionary Society began its work in 1798, and even to-day can still claim a large number of adherents.[3]

The slave-owning or serf-holding mentality was built up long before the Bantu became a source of labour for the European. The distinction between work that was proper for a European (i.e., farming) and what subsequently came to be known as 'Kaffir work' (i.e., manual labour) was thereby drawn for centuries to come. The majority of the slaves were unskilled, and worked on the land or in the home.[4] A considerable minority of the slaves were, however, highly skilled craftsmen, so that the concept of 'slave' or 'kaffir' work at first included both skilled and unskilled manual labour. Most of these skilled slaves remained in Cape Town, where they gradually came to monopolise many of the skilled trades; their monopoly was only gradually undermined by the arrival of skilled British artisans in the late nineteenth century, and in the 1920s by deliberate government action.

Compared with the slaves, the Hottentots played a less important rôle in the Cape Colony's economic life until the beginning of the nineteenth century. By this period, as has been said, there was a large body of 'free people of colour', mainly Hottentots, living more or less on the same level of existence as when the aborigines were encountered by the original settlers nearly two centuries before. In fact the Hottentots were considerably worse off. Their numbers had been decimated by successive smallpox epidemics, their pastoral tribal life had been shattered, their herds, lands and water-rights were gone, and their traditional way of life was branded and usually penalised as 'idleness', 'vagrancy' and 'thieving'.

With the exception of a few groups still living in kraals under their own chiefs or captains, and isolated 'vagrants', the great majority were reduced to complete though somewhat precarious dependence upon the white farmers, without the corresponding security for themselves and their families possessed by the slave, who was at least a valuable piece of property.

With the abolition of the slave trade, however, this abject, landless, rural proletariat acquired an increased value as a source of farm labour. This, however, brought them no benefits, for their theoretical freedom of contract was hedged around with pass laws, vagrancy acts and 'apprenticeship' regulations, which virtually immobilised the labour force.

Naturally, this immobilising of labour had its effect on agricultural wages, which were very low both before and after the legislation of 1809,[5] although the increasing labour shortage after the abolition of the slave-trade in 1807 might have been expected to produce a rise in wages. On the other hand, the Boer farmers dealt little in cash themselves, and were, therefore, in no position to pay in cash rather than in kind. It would seem that the best method of payment from the labourer's point of view was in cattle, which would, however, immobilise the labourer still further, stock being a perishable commodity and grazing rights essential.[6] In addition, the Hottentots were notoriously improvident, and seldom made the best bargain when selling their labour.

Earlier in this study we described the development of colour-blind political and legal institutions in the Cape. Progress in the economic sphere unfortunately did not keep pace with that elsewhere. In the last half of the nineteenth century most of the Coloured people remained as farm-labourers with barely-increased remuneration, and that largely in kind. The missionary institutions, which had provided a few thousands with some agricultural training, slightly better living conditions and a basis for existence, tended to decline with the fading influence of their parent-societies. These were the only bodies which might have tried to raise Coloured economic status, and apparently the only agencies to consider the Coloured people as potential consumers[7] as well as producers.

Other trends to be noted during the latter part of the nineteenth century were: the increasing pressure of African labour in the Eastern Province, which had the effect of undercutting even the low Coloured standard of wages: the beginnings of a drift to the *dorps* (villages) and towns and the formation of an unskilled urban proletariat: and the transformation of the former skilled slaves into a reasonably well-to-do, urban artisan class in Cape Town, with a practical mono-poly of most of the skilled trades.

The latter group was the only one in which fairly satisfactory progress was made under laissez-faire conditions, probably because of the higher general level of culture and skill of the imported slave element, and because for a long period few locally-born whites regarded the skilled trades as offering a possible opening for themselves. At-tempts to create a similar rural middle class of small-holders on lands formerly owned by the missions proved disastrous for those concerned, and resulted in the majority of such holdings being alienated to Euro-peans before 1921.[8]

The tumult and shouting over political rights died down about the middle of the century, and the Coloured people, as they were now called, were left to find their own economic and social level for over fifty years. The majority were apparently unable to help themselves, and the economic beliefs of the age did not favour outside or official assistance. Thus the Coloureds were on the whole unable to make sufficient use of the time at their disposal before Union to entrench themselves in an unassailable economic position, as property-owners, employers, consumers and skilled workers.

By the nineteen-twenties the African influx to rural and urban areas outside the reserves had assumed formidable proportions.[9] In addition to this pressure from an even lower economic group, the Coloured people had to face a new threat from above. The repeated subdivision of farm-holdings (under the Roman-Dutch inheritance laws), and the prevalent highly uneconomic methods of farming, had by the end of the nineteenth century created a làrge and increasing group of impoverished whites.[10]

The latter, unable to survive any longer on the land, were flooding into the *dorps* and towns to offer themselves as unskilled labourers on the open market. The skilled trades were practically monopolised by urban artisans more recently arrived from Europe than the Afrikaner, and holding other ideas on the dignity of labour for a wage and for a master. In the Western Cape there were also the skilled Malay and Coloured craftsmen.[11]

The Poor White, as he now came to be called, was thus compelled and indeed was only equipped to enter the unskilled labour market, which was the almost exclusive preserve of Africans and Coloured people throughout the country. For many years the European had left no other field available for Non-Europeans, and had been happy to employ their labour at the lowest possible remuneration. Now that a considerable proportion[12] of the European community had been driven out of its privileged position, the attitude changed. There was even a tendency to blame the Non-Europeans for Poor Whiteism, and for the low level of wages[13] which made it impossible for the Poor White to rehabilitate himself as a white without outside protection.

This rural exodus of the early decades of the twentieth century caused a change in attitude amongst those affected to what they had formerly despised as 'Kaffir work'.[14] In order to survive at all, the Poor White had no alternative but to accept any work he could get, usually for a master, but he was not generally prepared to accept 'Kaffir wages'.[15]

The idea that skin-colour and not skill should be the determining factor in the economic hierarchy and wage-levels was developed quite naturally by the former pastoralists as a defence against the levelling tendencies of industrialisation.[16] When it became apparent, however, that not all the Poor Whites were mindful of the superiority of their pigmentation,[17] and that some, as a result of proximity and a shared low standard of living, were even 'going Kaffir',[18] the European authorities found it necessary to take administrative action on their behalf.

This official action was directed mainly against the Africans, but in those areas of the Cape[19] where Coloureds constituted the bulk of the unskilled labour force it was natural that they should suffer too. The comparative few in the skilled trades were not for the time being endangered, as few Poor Whites had sufficient skill to enter this field.

The Nationalist-Labour coalition of the early 1920s, urged on by the fallacious belief that there was only a limited amount of prosperity in the country,[20] which must be redistributed with a greater emphasis on lightness of skin, instituted what was officially called the 'Civilised Labour Policy',[21] but was more often administered as a 'White Labour Policy'.[22] The ambiguity does not seem to have been fully resolved even in 1936, when the Cape Coloured Inquiry Commissioners were taking evidence,[23] and there is little doubt that this confusion had a more or less adverse effect on the employment of Coloured people in certain areas.

The Coloured people were not directly affected by the 'Colour Bar' (Mines and Works Amendment) Act of 1926. This was passed largely at the insistence of the white mine-workers of the Rand, who struck in 1922 as a protest against a Chamber of Mines decision to modify the conventional colour-bar by employing Non-Europeans on skilled work, and to increase the ratio of Africans to Europeans employed. This measure in fact classified Coloureds, Mauritians and St. Helenans with Europeans, while it excluded Africans from skilled and better-paid work on the mines. It was, however, an indication of a trend which was likely to increase, that of reserving the cream of available work and wages on a basis of skin-colour only.[24]

We have now to consider this discriminatory trend as it has affected the Coloured person in various economic fields in recent times. A distinction should be drawn between the official methods adopted to protect skilled white labour from Non-European competition, and the 'sheltering' of unskilled white labour at uneconomic subsidised rates, mainly in state undertakings.[25]

In the sphere of public employment,[26] the most important example of the application of the 'civilised labour policy' is to be found in the South African Railways and Harbours Administration, the largest official employer of unskilled and semi-skilled labour. As Dr. van der Horst has pointed out,[27] this is to-day one of the few large-scale undertakings where European employees outnumber Non-Europeans. Although the Coloureds have not suffered from the S.A.R.'s policy as have the Africans,[28] they are nevertheless at a disadvantage as compared with Europeans. In the Cape prior to Union they were able to rise to graded positions, although not in any great numbers.[29] Northern race-attitudes[30] put a stop to this possibility when the Provincial railways were united after Union, though Coloured officials actually holding graded posts were allowed to retain their positions, with equal pension and sick fund rights. Apparently this was a concession to Cape sentiment, as these men could not be employed in more than a few areas, where race feeling was least.

At present there is further discrimination in the wage scales, which do not differ greatly from those obtaining for the Africans.[31] In addition no Non-Europeans may belong to the sick fund, with the exception of the few remaining employees from pre-Union Cape times.

The position in other branches of the public administration is similar. There is no legal bar to the employment of Coloureds or other Non-Europeans in graded posts, but in practice they are employed only as unskilled labour, and here too they have to face European competition. There are a small number of Coloured interpreters, clerks and messengers in the Department of Justice, and the Department of Social Welfare has an establishment for a few Coloured social welfare officers (none of which posts were filled at the time of the Lansdown Commission's Report in 1946).[32]

In 1944, under the Smuts Government, an attempt seems to have been made to implement the recommendations of the 1937 Cape Coloured Commission.[33] A circular was sent round to all departments and provincial administrations[34] asking (a) if more Coloured people could be employed; and (b) if they could be employed in higher graded and more responsible positions.[35]

The response to this circular was not encouraging. Only thirteen out of thirty replies received to question 'a' were in the affirmative, and, with the exception of the Department of Social Welfare, all these affirmative replies were qualified by various conditions or contingencies. Question 'b' elicited nineteen negative and eleven positive replies, all but two of the latter being also qualified.[36]

On 20th September, 1945, a further circular was issued by the Prime Minister's Office,[37] stating that not enough had been done to implement the 1937 Commission's recommendation ; the Government had therefore decided to lay down a firm policy to ensure parallel social development and opportunities of advancement for the European and Coloured communities. This policy would where possible extend opportunities for Coloured people to serve their own community.[38]

Between 18th October, 1945, and 31st March, 1947, 507 new posts in government service were created for Coloured people, and 164 more posts were filled which had been previously held by 'other races', presumably Africans for the most part.[39]

In mid-September, 1949 (after the Nationalist Government had taken over), a directive was again issued from the Prime Minister's Office that Africans should be replaced by Europeans in the public service. An official of the Department of Labour, interviewed by the *Cape Argus* on 15th September, 1949, said that the policy dated back to the régime of General Hertzog (i.e., to the 'civilised labour policy'). He added that 'there were numbers of Europeans who could not compete with Natives for unskilled jobs in private enterprise, in which the Native was regarded as the labourer. These Europeans had to be given employment so that they would not become a burden on the state through a dole.'

This statement suggests that there is still a certain Poor White problem.[40] It is said that Coloured workers have also benefited by this new directive. On the other hand, there is no evidence that the implementation of *apartheid* in the railways and post offices has been accompanied by the appointment of Coloureds to more responsible posts in predominantly Coloured areas, although this prospect has always been held out to all Non-European groups as an inducement to accept the *apartheid* policy. In the Post Office, after nearly eighteen months of segregated counters, seats and telephone booths, the salary scales had only just been settled by early 1951, and the first training scheme for about twelve Coloured clerks had not yet begun.[41] On the railways, even less progress had been made, owing to the determined opposition of the white staff.[42] Such opposition was probably the determining factor in the Post Office delay too.[43]

The wages of Coloureds and other Non-Europeans in public employment tend to be somewhat lower than those obtaining in private industry, while the reverse tends to be true of European wages. Figures taken from the latest Industrial Census show a small disparity (greater when one takes into account the far smaller numbers employed in government establishments)[44] between the average wages (exclusive of salaries) paid to the various racial groups in 1944–5.[45]

The Cape Provincial Administration employs a large number of Coloured people as teachers and nurses. Apart from this, however, it has always followed a policy of employing Europeans and Non-Europeans on different work, the latter at lower wage-levels and mainly as unskilled labour. The highest post which may be held by a Coloured is that of messenger,[46] at a salary of £84 rising by £12 annually to £156. Coloured employees do not contribute to the pension fund but are paid a small pension if they have served for a certain period. Unskilled

Non-European labour on the roads is paid at local wages; here Africans have largely displaced Coloureds.

The Cape Divisional Council[47] also follows the same policy of not employing Coloureds and Europeans on the same level. In early 1951 there were 154 Europeans and 10 Coloureds in the head office, the latter employed as messengers at a salary of £96, rising to £204. The lowest European clerical grade starts at £180, matriculation being a necessary qualification. The qualification for Coloured employees is Junior Certificate, but some have matriculated, although they cannot hope to rise any further on this account.

The Cape Town Municipal Council has the most liberal employment policy of all public administrative bodies, a fact which is no doubt to be correlated with the existence of a large number of Coloured rate-payers, and with the presence on the Council of several Coloured Councillors.[48] The attitude of many municipal employees to Coloured people and Coloured affairs is noticeably different from that of most white government employees. It is paternalistic at base, but the more overt and brutal evidences of race-prejudice so frequently displayed by the police, white railway officials, labour bureaux and the like are generally absent.

In theory, all posts and grades in Cape Town municipal employment are open to members of all races, and there is no differentiation in wage-scales, pensions and so on. In practice few if any Coloured employees are employed above the lower grades, as this might put them in a position of authority over European employees. Cape liberal sentiment usually stops short of accepting such a situation. Coloureds are employed in fairly senior clerical posts in departments which are willing to accept them; the highest post to which Coloureds have so far risen is that of senior clerk, with a salary of £408 rising to £552. The minimum unskilled labour rate of 1s. an hour plus cost-of-living allowance is higher than the government or wage-determination rates. In early 1951 the Municipality employed 2,758 Europeans and 6,532 Non-Europeans, and paid out approximately £1½ million on the wages and salaries of each group.

*   *   *   *   *

The position of the Coloured people employed in private industry and commerce is better than in other major economic fields. Nevertheless, certain officially 'colour-blind' measures, two of them inaugurated during the period of the 'civilised labour policy', have acted as a barrier to their economic progress. They are the Apprenticeship Act of 1922,[49] which we shall consider later in connection with the trade unions, the Industrial Conciliation Act of 1924[50] and the Wage Act of 1925.[51]

The 'civilised labour' policy was also extended to private industry by means of the granting or withdrawing of import permits, and lowering of customs tariffs, contingent upon existing establishments increasing the ratio of Europeans to their total labour force, and in the case of new applicants, upon their agreeing to employ a certain percentage of Europeans.[52]

The Industrial Conciliation Act did not apply to farming, domestic service, government and provincial employment, and certain educational and charitable institutions.[53] The industrial councils set up under its provisions (representing employers and unions) have the power to make agreements on wages, hours and conditions of work, agreements which when gazetted gain the force of law, and may be extended by the Minister to employers and areas not represented on the Council.[54] As few employers are Coloured[55] and the trade unions concerned do not all admit Coloured workers, one would not expect to find Coloured interests fully represented on industrial councils,[56] particularly where they differ from those of Europeans.[57] The Cape Coloured Commission pointed out that a council might sanction a 'closed shop' arrangement.[58] This could, in the event of employment being restricted to an all-white trade union, constitute obvious discrimination.

In considering the effect on employment generally of the Industrial Conciliation Act, the Industrial Legislation Commission noted the agreement of various Divisional Inspectors of Labour that:

'the operation of agreements, as well of determinations, resulted in the less efficient employees being discharged, and in changes in the racial composition of the labour employed and in the proportion of males to females and of adults to juveniles.'[59]

The Industrial Conciliation Act was intended to provide a voluntary system of wage-fixing for organised industries and trades, while the Wage Act was to fill in the gaps for the majority of European workers, by setting up a compulsory system, primarily for the unorganised industries and trades.[60] It should be noted that neither measure applied to agriculture or domestic service, the major and least-organised fields of Non-European employment.

Until the enactment of the amending 1937 Wage Act, Wage Boards were not allowed to recommend 'uncivilised' wages, unless these were specially sanctioned by the Minister.[61] Several determinations were not made because this sanction was withheld, and prior to this date unskilled wages received no great attention. Between 1937 and 1948, however, increased numbers of determinations brought the total of employees covered by wage determinations up to 348,258. By the end of 1948, determinations under the Industrial Conciliation Act applied to 278,932 employees.[62] The possibility of an appreciable number of Coloured or African industrial employees offsetting their inferior skill or physique or the prejudice against their employment[63] by undercutting European wages had therefore become remote.[64]

In a country not inhabited by clearly defined groups of widely differing economic levels, the legislative protection afforded by these two Acts would have been spread rather more evenly over the working community, instead of being limited to industry. In South Africa, however, the legislation originated with a Nationalist-Labour coalition, that is to say, a combination of the representatives of the old, master-servant, patriarchal relationship, the unskilled urban Poor Whites, and the highly-paid[65] skilled white artisans in the North, who were just beginning to feel the threat of undercutting by Non-Europeans who had acquired sufficient skill. It originated in the years immediately following the 1920 slump, when the voters' demand for a 'civilised labour policy' was at its height.

In these circumstances, it is difficult to accept the view of the Industrial Legislation Commission, that any adverse consequences which may have ensued for the Coloured people in industry were due, not so much to the legislation itself,[66] as to race-prejudice on the part of employers and trade unions, although undoubtedly such prejudice was not absent. It is of course debatable whether, given the race-attitudes prevalent in the Union in the nineteen-twenties and now, any legislation could be drafted in such a way as not to become discriminatory in its administration.[67]

In the short run, the two wage-fixing acts seem to have caused a definite increase in wages paid for skilled and, to a lesser extent, for semi-skilled work. This increase was, with few exceptions, shared by all Coloured employees concerned.[68] The objection raised before the Industrial Legislation and Cape Coloured Commissions was, however, that wage regulation was causing a permanent decline in the numbers of Coloured people employed, as most of the latter were not at the present time equipped as to physique, education or vocational training to compete with Europeans at the high wage-levels laid down under this legislation.[69] In addition, they had to face growing colour prejudice from white fellow-workers, trade unions and employers.[70]

Witnesses before both Commissions attested to a widespread feeling amongst the Coloured people that wage legislation was discriminatory,[71] but it was found difficult to obtain precise information of the workings of such discrimination. The Cape Coloured Commission cited figures from Industrial Censuses over the period 1924 to 1934, to show the percentage drop in the number of Coloured wage-earners in all establishments in the Western Cape, from 54 per cent to 46 per cent of the total number employed.[72] Appendix N brings these figures up to 1946, and shows that the fall had been arrested,[73] probably due to increased opportunities for employment and the absence of more Europeans in the armed forces during the war.[74]

If, thanks to a shift in attitudes and circumstances during the war years, the Coloured people have been (at least until 1946) just holding their own as far as percentage industrial employment is concerned, there is still the possibility that they are gradually being ousted from the higher levels of skilled work. This was said to be the case in 1940,[75] even in such strongholds as the clothing and building industries.[76] It is possible that the war and the expansion of industry have arrested these trends for a period, but their fundamental causes remain: lack of education and training, inferior physique and environment on the Coloured side, and amongst Europeans, even in the Cape, fear of losing their privileged economic status, and growing colour prejudice.[77]

The present situation is a highly fluid one. More openings are undoubtedly becoming available to Coloureds in semi-skilled work in the expanding secondary industries,[78] semi-skilled rates being closer to unskilled than to skilled rates and therefore unattractive to many Europeans.[79] Both European and Coloured male workers are here threatened by the increasing number of women in industry.[80] It is possible that in addition to its direct influence on Coloured male employment this influx has had an indirectly adverse effect on European-Coloured industrial relations, by aggravating the demand for segregation lest the 'purity of white womanhood' be smirched.[81]

In skilled work Coloured males are most vulnerable in times of recession, when white employers will lay them off in preference to white employees.[82] In unskilled labour, particularly of the hard manual type, the Coloured is being forced out by African pressure, which, as a result of his inferior physique and higher standard of living, he is unable to withstand.[83]

This colour prejudice in industry, whether amongst European fellow-employees or European employers, has resulted in one major customary discrimination in private industry which of necessity harms the more ambitious and efficient Coloured workers. Further, by depriving all Coloureds of any major incentive,[84] it helps to perpetuate the very traits of indolence, inefficiency and lack of initiative which provide the rationalisation for continued belief in 'innate' Coloured inferiority. This discrimination consists in the absence of any major avenues of promotion beyond the rank of foreman; even the latter position is available in any case only to a very small minority. In establishments which employ mixed European and Non-European labour, this possibility is further qualified by the convention that Coloured persons must not have Europeans directly under them. Higher avenues of promotion are almost entirely closed, except in the few modest establishments owned by Coloured employers.[85]

Colour prejudice also found expression in the revised Factories, Machinery and Building Works Act (No. 22) of 1941, under a section of which the Governor-General was empowered to:

'make different regulations for different classes of persons on the basis of race or colour in respect of the accommodation facilities and conveniences to be provided in factories for employees while they are working, resting or eating therein, as to conditions of work of employees in any factories where, in the opinion of the Minister of

Labour, special provision is necessary to safeguard the physical, moral or social welfare of such employees.'[86]

This legislation is said to have affected Coloured employment adversely, in that some employers who formerly employed persons of different ethnic groups dismissed their Coloured workers rather than incur the extra expense of installing duplicate toilets, canteens and so on. On the other hand this could and did operate to the advantage of Coloured labour, and in several cases is said to have led employers in the Cape to accept European workers only if they signed on as Coloureds, thereby evading the necessity for installing expensive dual facilities.[87] In the Transvaal, on the other hand, Coloured workers are not accepted in some establishments which already employ both white and African labour. Where employers continue to employ workers of different ethnic groups, it is possible that this legislation has helped to keep Coloured workers in the lower wage-grades, in industries with a series of processes requiring different grades of skill.[88]

The industrial legislation which covers unemployment and workmen's compensation[89] is formally colour-blind for Coloured and Asiatic industrial workers, though not for Africans. The Unemployment Insurance Act (53/1946) has, however, been amended so as to provide that workers in the lower-income groups, which include most Coloureds,[90] may be deprived of their allowances if they refuse to accept suitable employment, which may include farm work.[91] Benefits are calculated according to earnings. The Registration for Employment Act (No. 34 of 1945) has led to the establishment of Juvenile Affairs Boards for Coloureds and Asiatics in the main urban areas, with the same status and functions as the European Boards. Nation-wide departmental labour exchanges, at which registration is compulsory in the main industrial areas, are maintained by the Department of Labour. Coloureds have also shared to some extent in the subsidies paid by the Department of Labour to semi-fit workers, and in the Central Organisation of Technical Training (C.O.T.T.) scheme for ex-volunteers of the recent war.[92]

The Workmen's Compensation Act (No. 30 of 1941), like other industrial legislation, does not apply to domestic and farm-workers; employers of such labour have, however, been able to register voluntarily since the amending Act of 1945.[93] Benefits are related to wages according to a formula laid down in the Act, which applies to all but African workers, who in general receive lump sum awards.

*　　*　　*　　*　　*

Over the last two years a Commission has been examining the whole field of existing industrial legislation, and its report is expected in early 1952. Witnesses before the Commission have suggested that this Commission's questionnaire and terms of reference show a political bias in favour of the Government's *apartheid* policy,[94] and an attempt to

F

interfere both with trade union autonomy, and with the principles of inter-racial unions and union organisation for Africans.[95] An exchange between the Chairman, Dr. J. H. Botha, and Mr. Frank Gallant, President of the Western Province Federation of Labour Unions, illustrates this point:

DR. J. H. BOTHA: 'Are European employees in this area race-conscious or not?'

MR. FRANK GALLANT: 'Only in isolated instances. In the majority of cases they are quite willing to work with non-Europeans.'

DR. BOTHA: 'Have Europeans and non-Europeans ever had the opportunity of belonging to 100 per cent European or non-European unions?'—'No.'

A DELEGATE: 'The Europeans seem to be emphatic on the point that they want one union irrespective of colour, for practical reasons.'

DR. BOTHA: 'Would Europeans be happier in unions for them only, in which they had the control and made the decisions, or would they prefer to belong to a union of which the majority were Coloured?'

MR. GALLANT: 'The outlook of the non-European is no different from the European in regard to wages and conditions.'

DR. BOTHA: 'Leaving out the past, and if it were practicable, and economic risks were eliminated, I want a clear statement on whether Europeans, non-Europeans and Asiatics would wish to associate with their own races or not in industry as in social life.'[96]

MR. GALLANT: 'In economic life I find that Europeans do not mind mixing with non-Europeans.'

DR. BOTHA: 'Their race consciousness in social life disappears on entering the factory?'

MR. GALLANT: 'I have found that Afrikaans-speaking people coming from up-country gradually lose that consciousness.'

DR. BOTHA: 'And I have known cases very much the opposite.'[97]

* * * * *

We now come to the third of the three acts said to have had the most adverse effect on Coloured employment, the Apprenticeship Act of 1922, and to apprenticeship and trades unionism in general.

Coloured apprenticeship scarcely exists outside the Cape,[98] where it is mainly confined to the traditional centre of Coloured skilled trades, Cape Town. Even here, however, the position is deteriorating. Although Coloured apprentices are holding their own in the building and furniture trades, they have been left right behind in the vastly expanded engineering industry,[99] and are being frozen out of the printing industry, traditionally a Cape Coloured occupation. In addition, their numbers are decreasing in proportion to those of European apprentices.

This discrimination arises out of both law and custom. In the first category come the apprenticeship regulations, which, though they contain no colour bar, set an educational standard too high for many Coloured boys,[100] whose schooldays begin later and are shorter than those of the European group. The regulations also lay down a period of training which various Commissions have described as over long for modern conditions in many cases,[101] and therefore exerting a restrictive effect on skilled labour.[102]

Customary factors which discriminate against the Coloured boy are his comparative poverty and the educational difficulties already mentioned. Above all, however, ranks the difficulty of finding a firm which will accept him as an apprentice.[103] This is attributed to hardening colour prejudice amongst both employers and employees.[104] In addition to all these obstacles, there is differentiation in the provision of technical education;[105] this will be described in more detail in Chapter VIa.

In one important sector of skilled work, there is not only partial but total exclusion of Coloureds. In this case the employer is the Government, which, according to the 1944-5 Industrial Census, had 3,334 indentured European apprentices, or nearly one-third of the Union's total of indentured apprentices.[106]

* * * * *

The history and development of South African trade-unionism[107] has been complicated, and its influence weakened, by the presence of large masses of unskilled, barely acculturated Non-European workers, and by the traditional status-hierarchy surviving from the eras of conquest, slavery and pastoralism.

Even the European workers who came to South Africa half a century ago could not altogether avoid the consequences of finding themselves privileged not only because of their skill but because of their skin-colour.[108] They saw the Non-Europeans as a future danger to their own monopoly of skill and high wages. An exception was made only in the case of the relatively few Coloured skilled workers in the Western Cape, into whose traditional sphere they encroached. With these Coloured artisans they made common cause, their interests being similar.

Colour-discrimination between workers was further accentuated when the Poor Whites and rural Afrikaners began to flood into the towns and industry. Unlike the European artisan immigrants, they lacked skill or any ideas of working-class solidarity, but brought their rural race-attitudes, sharpened by fear and poverty, into the industrial field.

Here they found themselves obliged to compete with equally un-skilled Non-Europeans at wages related to the latter's actual standard of living. In the circumstances, it is perhaps not surprising that they found no community of interests between themselves and Non-European fellow workers.[109] Such lack of working-class unity was not of course displeasing either to employers or successive governments.

It is not proposed to record the complicated history of South African trade union organisation from its beginnings.[110] A consistent slogan throughout has been 'equal pay for equal work'. This has served both to maintain the high wages of the white skilled worker and to keep most non-whites out of the more highly-paid jobs. At the present time, orthodox trade unionism is passing through a critical period in South Africa. It is rent by internal disputes on policy, particularly in relation to the unionisation of Non-European labour, and threatened with political infiltration both from the left and from the right. In addition to the 'black' and 'red' bogies, dissension between Afrikaans and English-speaking workers has been exploited with partial success, and there are forces at work to destroy independent trade unionism altogether, and to set up in its place a series of state-dominated, nationalist-minded workers' unions similar to those existing in the U.S.S.R. and the Argentine.

At present there are four major groups of unions: the localised Cape body, the Western Province Federation of Labour Unions (W.P.F.L.U.); the left-wing and centre rump of the Trades and Labour Council (T.L.C.); the right-wing unions which broke away from the T.L.C. in November 1950; and the 'Afrikaans-minded' Pretoria Co-ordinating Council of South African Trade Unions (C.C.S.A.T.U.), consisting of colour-bar unions which broke away from the T.L.C. in 1947 and 1948.

These groups do not, however, represent as many attitudes towards Non-European workers. The major aim in all cases is the maintenance of the privileged position of the white worker, or, in the Cape group, of the skilled worker. Differences of policy arise mainly as to the best methods of achieving this end; whether by exclusion of the Non-European worker from unions altogether, by his admission on a subordinate level, in a parallel organisation, or on terms of theoretical equality. The choice of method depends on such factors as the type of industry and the degree of acculturation and standard of living achieved by the Non-European in a particular area.

The W.P.F.L.U. is in spirit at least a survival of the old type of craft-union organisation. It was controlled, until his death in November 1950, by the late Mr. Robert Stuart, a veteran trade union organiser, who came to the Cape from Aberdeen nearly half a century ago. The W.P.F.L.U. was formed by a large breakaway group of unions which left the Cape Federation of Labour Unions (C.F.L.U.), also built up by Mr. Stuart, when the latter organisation was 'captured' by militant leftist unionists from Johannesburg.[111] It is based primarily on the garment and leather workers, and may have about 25,000 members.

In membership the W.P.F.L.U. reflects the labour situation peculiar to the Western Cape. It has what is probably a majority of Coloured members and a number of Coloured officials, declares that it has no colour prejudice,[112] and has consistently refused to affiliate to the S.A.T.L.C. on the grounds that the latter tacitly countenances Northern unionists' colour-bar policies; it has in the past been mainly interested in the skilled worker, fearing the masses of poor and unskilled whites as well as of non-whites. It has also pursued an unswervingly anti-Communist policy. Other trade unionists regard the W.P.F.L.U. as right-wing or centre in trade union matters.[113]

It is sometimes said that, like Cape political liberalism, the colour-blind policy of the Cape unions has ceased to be militant.[114] If this is so, the Coloured workers who in some cases form the majority of members in individual unions must be blamed for apathy and failure to defend their own status with sufficient energy.[115] To account for this apathy, it may perhaps be argued that until comparatively recently Coloured skilled workers considered their interests identical with those of Europeans, and therefore saw no reason to demand proportionate representation on executives, or to indulge in race-politics in union affairs. In addition, many of the semi-skilled workers who have recently entered the industrial field are women who regard their work not as a vocation but as a means of implementing the family income, and are not particularly interested in union activities.[116]

The second and much larger group of trade unions is of an 'industrial' as opposed to a 'craft' type, and is not confined to a single area of the Union, like the W.P.F.L.U. Ever since its formation in 1925, it has been under fire from both within and without,[117] either as being too leftist (some of its leaders have been Communists), or as tacitly countenancing the colour-bar policies of some of its affiliated unions, or again because it allowed purely Non-European (including unregistered African) unions to affiliate.[118]

Those leaders and members who saw the danger to white workers' interests of ignoring or discriminating against the growing masses of Non-European workers[119] did not succeed in converting all dissident unions within their group.[120] On the contrary, a number of unions left the T.L.C. between 1947 and 1949 on racial and other issues,[121] thereby weakening its position and impairing its claim to represent the majority of organised South African workers at the I.L.O. and elsewhere.[122]

This exodus caused a shift in the internal balance of power. At a special conference in Durban in November 1949 the 'centre' unions, which previously supported the militant 'left wing', voted with the 'right wing' on a proposal to investigate the desirability of changing the Council's policy on the affiliation of African trade unions.[123] This change of direction was probably dictated by the desire to prevent the further break-up of the T.L.C. and possibly to lure the departed 'right wing' unions back into the fold.[124]

One year later, however, a further breakaway occurred of eight 'right-wing' unions (consisting of seven artisan unions and the S.A. Society of Bank Officials, with a total membership of nearly 20,000). The T.L.C. was left with 127,000 members, largely representing the secondary industries. On this occasion the principal motive is said to have been fear of being involved with alleged Communists as a result of a resolution passed by the Executive.[125] Attempts to form a new central co-ordinating body out of these unions have so far failed, and two Cape Unions, the Brewery Employees and the Hotel, Bar and Catering Employees (both with a large Coloured membership) have since returned to the fold, while the powerful Amalgamated Engineering Union is said to be considering reaffiliation.

The fourth group is on the extreme right wing, with a membership mainly of nationalistic[126] white workers, most of them Afrikaans-speaking,[127] many only recently urbanised. The Pretoria Co-ordinating Council was formed in 1948 by unions which broke away from the T.L.C.[128] A memorandum submitted by this body to the last Industrial Legislation Commission urged the total separation of European and Non-European workers in industry, dwelling places and organisations, stated that further integration of African industries should stop, and recommended that:

'European trade unions should have a guardianship over the Natives in each industry, and that, in instances of mixed trade unions, the Coloured and Asiatic workers should be placed in separate branches with their own committees, which would serve in an advisory capacity. They should not, however, have representation on the controlling body of the European trade unions.'[129]

The Mineworkers' Union, is one of the main pillars of the Co-ordinating Council, is said to have fallen recently into the hands of the *Broederbond*-dominated Reform Movement.[130] The *Broederbond* is a secretive, ultra-Nationalist organisation to which several Nationalist ministers and a number of M.P.s belong. The Reform Movement is one of several Nationalist-minded organisations whose main task is to wean the white Afrikaner worker away from the 'Communistic', 'Kaffir-loving' and 'Jew-dominated' unions, thereby undermining the power of orthodox trade unionism in South Africa.

Other such organisations are the *Blankewerkersbeskermingsbond* (White Workers' Protection Association) and the *Federasie van Blanke Werkers* (Federation of White Workers). The latter group submitted a memorandum to the recent Industrial Legislation Commission in which it advocated the replacement of the present industrial councils by a permanent Reconciliation Council (*Versoeningsraad*), presumably under direct or closer state control, the introduction of a quota-system for the various races in skilled work, and separate wage scales for workers of different races. It also declared that Africans, being the responsibility of the State, should be permitted no labour organisations of any kind. Various Afrikaans-language groups not directly connected with labour, such as the Dutch Reformed Churches, the *Reddingsdaadbond* (an organisation aimed at furthering Afrikaner commercial and industrial interests), and the Federation of Afrikaans

Cultural Societies (F.A.K.), have also brought influence to bear over recent years in an attempt to win Afrikaner workers away from the trade unions, or to infiltrate and gain control of these unions from within.

The still close correspondence between colour-groups and levels of skill and culture[131] has not only provided white skilled workers with a valuable weapon in their attempts to protect their monopoly of the best jobs and the highest wages,[132] but has also served the purposes of outside groups concerned with preventing union between white and non-white workers, by showing that their interests are at variance. The disparity between skilled and unskilled wages is in fact so great that any attempt to improve the lot of the unskilled worker may in the short run affect the privileged status of the skilled worker.[133] The unduly high wages of the latter are bound up with the unduly low wages of the former, and a change in one might involve a corresponding adjustment in the other, as industry can only support a certain wage charge.

In this labour conflict, which is principally between the white and African workers of the North, the Coloured skilled worker suffers because his presence in the ranks of skilled workers is regarded as the thin end of the wedge by those whites, whether workers or not, who see their own position endangered, and wish to maintain, or rather re-introduce, a simple colour-dichotomy into the labour market.[134]

* * * * *

We have described the industrial situation in considerable detail, because it is there that a section of the Coloured workers has come nearest to status parity with whites, and the greatest degree of formal or legal counter-action has developed. Industry is not, however, the major sphere of Coloured employment. This is still agriculture, which in 1946 claimed 30.9 per cent of all Coloured men gainfully employed.[135] Their status as agriculturists is strikingly different from that of the Europeans, as the following table shows:

TABLE D.[136]

Race	Farmers	Farmers' Sons Assisting on Farms	Farm Labourers (Male)
E	106,780 (139,000)	22,051 (16,000)	2,551 (6,000)
C	4,471 (5,000)	1,558 (900)	74,644 (80,000)

The period of slavery and Hottentot serfdom has already been described. Although formal status differences have been absent for over a century in the Cape, the economic conditions of the Coloured rural worker have changed but little in that period. The old status-hierarchy has been perpetuated with little need for formal sanctions,[137] save the Masters' and Servants' Acts.[138] It has been perpetuated through the determination and unity of white rural society, often supported by the spiritual authority of the Dutch Reformed Church.[139]

On the Coloured side, it has been perpetuated through apathy, isolation, ignorance,[140] poverty, disease and drunkenness. Control of these factors is to a great extent in the hands of the white dominant group, which makes little attempt to alter conditions. One gets the impression that it is preferable and 'more natural' for a Coloured person to be stupid, dirty, lazy, dishonest, drunken and diseased, but above all docile, than for him to be intelligent, clean, energetic and ambitious. The former traits are accepted as a necessary evil, the latter regarded as an attack upon the colour-hierarchy.

It might be thought that, in view of the frequent complaints of a Coloured labour shortage heard from European farmers over the last century, Coloured agricultural wages would have risen accordingly. The laws of supply and demand do not, however, operate freely in a labour market where the labour force is tied by conservatism, ignorance of conditions elsewhere, and, frequently, by the possession of livestock which cannot easily be taken along in a search for work.[141] In addition, labour shortages may not always be as acute as farmers like to claim, and Coloured wages have been kept down by a constant stream of Africans from the reserves, into areas where Coloured labour formerly predominated.

Some idea of farm wages over the last decade[142] is given in Appendix P. These wages differ greatly from district to district, and between different types of farming. There are also great differences in the ratio of cash payment[143] to payment in kind, which may take various forms, such as rations,[144] grazing rights,[145] land or accommodation.[146] Wages, both total and in cash, seem to rise according to their proximity to the intensively-farmed Western Cape and the district immediately round Cape Town. On the other hand, cash wages tend to decrease to a level of as little as 10s. per month in the Eastern Province, where there is a greater supply of African labour, and are little higher in the far North and North-West Cape.[147]

In the wine-growing districts of the Cape Province, it has long[148] been the custom to give Coloured labourers a tot of wine at prescribed intervals during the day. The tot is also given seasonally by sheep and grain-farmers, in districts as far afield as Namaqualand, in order to attract extra labour. About 15,000 to 20,000 labourers are said to receive it annually.[149]

This 'tot system' enables wine-farmers to dispose of their cheap surplus wine. Wine-farming interests are apparently so strong that nothing has been done to abolish this system, long condemned by many European and Coloured leaders, by the Churches (including the Dutch Reformed Church of the Cape, which is the Church of most wine-farmers),[150] by the Cape Coloured Commission,[151] and by the Cape Coloured Liquor Commission.[152]

The Liquor Act (No. 30) of 1928 limited the daily amount of unfortified wine to be given to any Coloured labourer to one and a half pints. Prior to the Act two quart bottles or more were frequently given.[153] The arguments for and against the system were summed up by the Baxter Committee in 1918:

'On the one hand, it is contended that it does the labourers no harm when confined to adults, that they are used to it, and labouring hard "sweat it out"; the wine given is pure grape juice, and not canteen wine fortified with spirits; that the men will not work without it,[154] and that it is impossible to break down an immemorial custom. On the other hand it is alleged that the custom engenders a taste for alcohol at an early age; that on many farms boys of 16 and over get their "tots"; that five or six "tots" of wine is more than is good for anyone;[155] that the wine is of an inferior quality, and that it is given in most cases as part payment for work done.[156] The evidence of farmers who do not give wine seems to show that they have no difficulty in getting labour, and that good has resulted from the stoppage of wine. Your Committee is of the opinion that the "tot" system is a fruitful source of drunkenness amongst the Coloured people, and against the interests of the farmers whose great need is efficient labour, but to break it down will be no simple matter without the willing co-operation of the farmers.'[157]

This willing co-operation of the farmers is conspicuously lacking.[158] Major motives for its retention are the desire to maintain a permanent avenue for the disposal of about 700,000 gallons of wine in the year,[159] and to keep the cash wages bill low.[160] Possibly it is also hoped by wine-growers that the taste for wine thereby acquired will stimulate canteen and bottle-store sales, as indeed it does.

Behind both the tot-system and the system of part-payment in kind customary on farms throughout the country, there may, however, lurk the feeling, conscious or unconscious, that the established status-hierarchy is more easily maintained if the labourer is kept on a low economic level, without the independence (and franchise rights) that a higher cash wage would bring, or the incentive to better his lot by hard work.[161]

* * * * *

Domestic service is still the greatest single field of employment for Coloured women. The 1936 Census listed 59,255 Coloured women (81.4 per cent of all Coloured women gainfully employed) under this heading, as compared with only 11,647 Coloured men (or 5.6 per cent) of the total of employed Coloured men. By 1946, only 3.4 per cent (8,385) of gainfully occupied Coloured males and 50 per cent (60,010) of gainfully occupied Coloured females were employed in domestic service in houses and farms (exclusive of hotel and restaurant service). As in agriculture, wages, hours and conditions of work are still almost entirely regulated by custom, the Masters' and Servants' Acts being the major formal instrument of regulation.[162]

Both agriculture and domestic service are regarded by most white South Africans in the Cape as the traditional spheres of employment for Coloured people.[163] Any attempt to disturb the traditional relationship and conditions, whether it takes the form of demands for higher wages, better food and shorter hours from the employee herself, or of the introduction of a European employer-servant relationship and the payment of higher wages by recent immigrants,[164] is usually resented.

The relatively high wages mentioned in Footnote 164 are typical only of wealthy urban or peri-urban homes in Cape Town. In the country districts wages are unlikely to be any better than those for agricultural labour.[165] Wages in urban middle-class districts apparently rose very considerably during the war years.[166] This may be attributed in part to the rival attractions of factory work, with its higher cash wages, shorter hours and comparative freedom, and to the growing tendency amongst politically-conscious Coloured people to regard such 'service' as humiliating.

Conditions of service vary as much as wages. Servants' quarters consist almost invariably of a separate building or of rooms built on at the back of the main house, with a separate entrance.[167] Coloured servants prepare the food, make the beds,[168] bathe the children, and in general perform all the most intimate services about the house. There is, however, no question of their being allowed to share the same toilet conveniences. The better modern urban houses are usually built with a separate toilet and shower or bathroom in the servants' quarters. The more old-fashioned houses probably have a toilet only, and perhaps a tap. A tin bath is sometimes provided for the maid. On the poorer farms, the facilities for all races dwindle to little ramshackle sentry-boxes set up some distance from the living quarters and from each other, one marked 'Slegs Blankes' or 'Europeans Only', the other 'Nie-Blankes' or 'Non-Europeans'.

The furniture and equipment provided for most Coloured servants is usually of the cheapest and plainest.[169] In justification of this, one often hears the comment: 'It's no good giving them anything better. They don't appreciate it, and everything gets broken or spoiled or stolen.'

In the same way Coloured servants are usually provided with inferior food, because it is 'what they are used to'.[170] The conventional stereotype also lays down that Coloured servants are dishonest, so store-cupboards are provided with keys, food is often measured and given out every day, a close check is kept on the household bills, and drinks are usually kept in a locked cupboard. Coloured people are also considered to be immoral and oversexed, so that the great severity regarding stores and hours is often combined with an indifferent tolerance regarding a servant's personal behaviour: 'You can't expect to keep a maid these days unless you let her have men visitors.'

Signs of a shift in the traditional master-servant relationship are evident in the recent increase in urban domestic wages, in the reluctant provision of better accommodation and working conditions, and even in the worsening stereotype of the Coloured servant as formulated by European employers, and the tendency of the latter to refer nostalgically to the 'old days when servants knew their place and enjoyed their work.'

$$* \quad * \quad * \quad * \quad *$$

In view of the general pattern of Coloured employment, it is not surprising to find the Coloured community unable to support a considerable professional class.[171] Nor, in view of the increasing European demand for segregation of the Coloured people in all spheres of social and economic life, can a Coloured professional class be expected to derive much livelihood from the European community. Indeed, many Europeans are almost unaware of the existence of such a class, and when this is brought to their notice they are often unable to consider this fact or the persons concerned seriously. By becoming a professional man, the Coloured person has stepped outside his ascribed rôle as an unskilled or semi-skilled worker on the farm, in the town or in the home.

Nevertheless, when one considers the poverty, prejudice, and inadequate educational facilities which a Coloured person aspiring to enter the professions has to surmount, one must admire the few who have achieved their goal.[172] They are, however, all too few. In the 1946 census, of the 246,892 Coloured men and 102,008 Coloured women over 15 years old listed as economically active, 179 were either doctors (13),[173] clergymen (151), lawyers,[174] chemists or dispensers (14),[175] architects or engineers (1),[176] several of them having been trained overseas. The only appreciable fields open to a Coloured 'intelligentsia' are teaching[177] and nursing, which will be discussed in later chapters, and, to a lesser extent, the religious ministries.

Many Coloured people show a special aptitude for the arts, particularly music, dancing, acting and painting. Here again, however, the poverty of the community and the difficulty and expense of obtaining adequate training tend to frustrate talent. These arts in addition require a wider audience than the Coloured community can itself supply, and the majority of Europeans take little interest in such efforts.[178] The few dancers and painters who struggle to general notice usually end by going overseas for further study and fuller recognition.[179]

The Coloured community has produced very few writers.[180] This is only what one might expect of a poverty-stricken and largely illiterate community with no common traditions,[181] and until recently not even the nucleus of a cultured upper class.[182] The Coloured newspapers have never provided their contributors with a livelihood, and the European press is largely closed to Non-European writers.[183]

*   *   *   *   *

Of Coloured people as employers of labour, there is little to say. The 1944–5 Industrial Census listed 178 working proprietors,[184] almost all of whom are in a small way of business. There were 527 Coloured market gardeners and about 4,500 Coloured farmers in 1946, some of whom may have employed a few labourers. A few upper-middle-class families are able to afford a servant. There are a few Coloured welfare societies which employ Coloured persons. There is one Coloured hotel and one Coloured bus service in the Peninsula, and a number of co-operative, building and burial societies in the Cape Province. The Occupational Census of 1946 gave a total of 869 Coloured managers and proprietors of both sexes in wholesale, retail, manufacturing and other businesses. In the same occupations there were 47 (uncertified) Coloured book-keepers, 497 clerks, 47 typists and 2,148 shop assistants. Coloured persons rarely occupy these positions in European-owned establishments, so it seems likely that the majority were employed by Coloured employers. The Census also listed 2,436 hawkers, few of whom would, however, employ labour; 54 photographers; 10 stock-brokers; 2 quantity surveyors; 2 land surveyors; 4 theatre lessees and managers; 190 hairdressers and 'beauticians'; 21 hotel and licensed premises keepers; and 71 owners of restaurants and cafés.[185]

The major factor behind this state of affairs has been, not formal discrimination, but a combination of Coloured lack of means or enterprise and of European prejudice, which limits the clientele of a Coloured establishment to the Coloured community. In addition, allegations were made before the Cape Coloured Commission that the bodies which issue trading licences discriminate against Colured persons as such.[186] Formal discrimination is, however, introduced in the Group Areas Act, which provides for the compulsory transfer of disqualified companies within a certain period of time, without compensation, and for the non-renewal of trading licences to disqualified persons within areas proclaimed for group occupation or ownership. These measures are aimed primarily at the Indians in Natal, but will also cause great loss and hardship to Coloureds in the Western Cape.

*   *   *   *   *

Until 1951, no legislative restrictions discriminated against the Coloured person as owner or occupier of land in the Cape Province as they did in the Orange Free State and parts of the Transvaal.[187] Immovable property in certain desirable areas was sometimes bound by privately-made restricting covenants or clauses which forbade its sale to Non-Europeans.[188] On the whole, however, Coloured land-ownership has until now been influenced mainly by such factors as European prejudice, which would prevent a European from selling land or property in a particularly exclusive district to a Coloured person, and by Coloured poverty.[189]

While the number of Coloured urban house-owners may be on the increase,[190] that of rural land-owners has been declining for the last century, the land in most cases having passed into European hands.[191] This large-scale alienation of land has been attributed to such factors as lack of business experience and aptitude in general, ignorance of the value of the land owned, lack of industry or enterprise, inexperience of modern farming methods, mortgaging and debt.[192] In this case it would seem that formal equality has been detrimental to Coloured interests, the great majority of the remaining owner-farmers being those whose land is held on a restricted tenure, under government or church supervision.

*   *   *   *   *

White South Africans have long regarded the Cape Coloured people as producers only, and not as consumers.[193] That this largely remains the case to-day is probably due to Coloured poverty and lack of unity. Although the majority of Coloured people are wretchedly poor, they nevertheless constitute quite a powerful purchasing group, and potentially a much greater one.[194] In the United States, the Negro has already begun to influence the attitudes of white shop-keepers by his 'don't buy where you can't work' campaign.[195] In South Africa too, some Coloured groups have reached the point of considering such boycotting action.[196]

In the meantime, however, Coloured clients in European stores must usually buy clothes without trying them on.[197] The attitude of many European shop-assistants to Coloured customers leaves much to be desired,[198] and some Coloured informants complain that discourtesy and insults are on the increase.[199] If Coloured purchasing power increases, however, the fear of loss of custom may have a powerful modifying effect on such discriminatory treatment in private commercial establishments.[200] Other informants have said that the position to-day is a great advance on that of a decade or so ago.

European cafés, restaurants and hairdressers do not serve Coloureds or other Non-Europeans at all, although some snack-bars have a counter from which Coloureds may purchase food or minerals, which must be consumed off the premises, and are usually taken in the street outside.

Such establishments as banks and insurance companies make no apparent discrimination between Europeans and Coloured customers, particularly if the latter are well-dressed. This is the case in Cape Town, but may not apply to local branches in the rural areas.

*   *   *   *   *

Coloured people are subject to the same taxes, direct and indirect, as Europeans,[201] although very few of them pay income tax.[202] As has been shown, they do not as citizens have the same facilities and rights as do Europeans. As customers of the State, that is to say, as purchasers of stamps, wireless licences,[203] railway tickets, savings certificates and so on, they receive discriminatory treatment in post offices and on railway stations and trains, although they pay exactly the same as Europeans.[204]

It is difficult for the Coloured community to demand better treatment by threats of a boycott in the case of such state monopolies as the railways and postal services. Nevertheless, various Coloured political leaders have recently been advocating the mass withdrawal of Post Office savings, and cashing of Union Loan Certificates, in an attempt to make Coloured resentment felt by the Government.[205] In view of the present Government's general attitude and policy, however, it seems unlikely that such action will achieve any result.

*   *   *   *   *

We have described the general picture of economic discrimination in some detail, as the preservation of the economic colour-hierarchy would appear to be the real objective of the dominant white group in South Africa. The entire economic structure is based on cheap Non-European labour, unlike the over-all structure of the United States.[206] This is one of the factors which make the colour-problem in South Africa so much more difficult of solution.

As in other spheres, the Coloured people occupy an uneasy position between the upper and the nether millstones in the economic structure. Their position in the skilled trades is menaced by Europeans with all the backing that custom and legislation can provide, while their former monopoly of unskilled labour is threatened by an influx of barely acculturated African workers, whose fewer needs enable them to undercut even the lowest-paid Coloured.[207]

Because of his colour, the Coloured man is being increasingly forced by prejudice and *apartheid* legislation away from the white group with which he has always identified himself, into the black group of the economically exploited. As Coloureds and Africans have begun to show themselves capable of equalling European efficiency, the need for legislation to enforce the original economic hierarchy has increased. The legislation has been accompanied by an intensification of customary discrimination in all spheres, and a whipping-up of racial prejudice[208] by all possible devices and myths.[209]

The increased discrimination of the last quarter-century in South Africa should be viewed as a determined but Canute-like attempt to defend a traditional pre-industrial economic structure against the gradual advance of the former slaves and serfs. The growing demand by producers in secondary industry for semi-skilled Non-European labour,[210] combined with the insistence of the more enlightened sections of white workers on 'equal pay for equal work',[211] may both be discriminatory in isolation, but through interaction are facilitating this advance. The major resistance comes from the politically powerful employers of cheap agricultural labour and from some groups of white workers. There is, however, one principle upon which all employers of labour in South Africa can agree; that is, upon the undesirability and impracticability of true vertical *apartheid*, as advocated by some idealists in the Dutch Reformed Church.

CHAPTER SIX

SOCIAL SERVICES

A. EDUCATION

Education shall be directed to the full development of the human personality, and to the strengthening of respect for human rights and fundamental freedoms. It shall promote understanding, tolerance and friendship among all nations, racial or religious groups, and shall further the activities of the United Nations for the maintenance of peace.[1]

IN societies where certain classes or groups are excluded from political and economic power, their lower status will be reflected in the quality and extent of the social services provided for them by the dominant class or group. Conversely, inferior social services make it difficult, if not impossible, for the subordinate classes or groups to improve their status within the existing social structure. The original political and economic inequalities are thereby perpetuated in a vicious circle.

Of the social services, education is surely the most important for both the ruler and the ruled.[2] It enables the latter to raise his own status within his group and to help others do the same; so that in time a conscious and socially-awakened class of intellectuals will come into being, which may be able to organise its own group and thereby exert greater pressure upon the ruling group.[3]

The ruling class, on the other hand, uses education as a means for supplying itself with a docile labour force,[4] sufficiently instructed and trained to perform its allotted tasks, but not to hanker after further knowledge or intellectual speculation. Where there is more than one subordinate class or group, the ruling group may use education and other devices to perpetuate the difference between those groups, and to allocate a different, though always subordinate, status to each. In its own group it is able, by means of segregated education, to inculcate the principles of superiority and separateness from an early age, and thereby to perpetuate its own existence as a ruling group.

The ruler is obviously in a stronger position than the ruled, as he provides or sanctions the education and can dictate its nature. The hope for the subordinate group lies in the fact that, until recent times, state control has rarely been so complete that inconsistencies and loop-holes could not enter into the system. Of these, the subordinate group has been able to take advantage. For instance, the Cape Coloured people have greatly benefited from the diversity of views as to the aims of education held by the various groups and individuals concerned with their affairs.

The first plan for the education of the aborigines was presented as early as 1649, in a memorial to the Council of Seventeen. It was hoped that Hottentot children might be trained as servants, and edu-cated in the Christian religion, 'by which means . . . many souls will be brought to the Christian Reformed Religion and to God'.[5] The propagation of Christianity was then, as now, subordinate to the economic purpose.

When it was realised that the Hottentots preferred their own pre-carious and backward way of life to labour in the service of the Christians, no more was heard of Christian education for the indigenes for nearly a century. In 1737, the Moravian Father, George Schmidt, made an abortive attempt to establish a mission. After his departure six years later, there was again a gap until the Moravians returned to Genadendal in greater strength in 1792.

By this time, however, the frontier Boers, who were the chief employers of Hottentot labour, had so far departed from the aims of the original settlement as to resent attempts to Christianise and educate the heathen at all,[6] particularly as the missionaries were concerned with them not only as a labour-force but as individuals with souls to be saved. 'Christian', 'European' and 'white man' had by now become synonymous, as a result of the introduction of slaves and the conse-quent association of colour and heathendom with inferior status.

The only education which the colonists seem to have favoured for their servants was instruction in 'the rudimentary pastoralism which their employers practised',[7] a smattering of the Dutch language, and an inculcation of the habit of regular work. Instruction in farmwork and the Christian religion were amongst the provisos of the Hottentot apprenticeship law of 1812, but a Commission of Inquiry found most colonists 'averse to their receiving moral or religious instruction of any kind.'[8]

In some quarters at least, this functional view of Coloured education has persisted unchanged to the present time.

The first school founded in the Cape was not for Hottentots, nor for Europeans,[9] but for the younger slaves of the Company in 1658. The slaves were, of course, valuable property, and to leave them in complete ignorance impaired their value. The purpose of the school was to teach the slaves Dutch (for practical purposes, as their own diverse languages must have constituted a miniature Tower of Babel), and to give some religious instruction. This school does not seem to have prospered, but in 1663 the first mixed school was started, with

G

eighteen Europeans, four slaves and one Hottentot. To this, girl slaves were admitted in 1665.

The beginnings of segregation are to be seen in Commissioner van Rheede's instructions in 1695 that no Europeans were to be taken in the Company's slave lodge school,[10] nor slaves in the public schools which had by then been opened. These instructions were not apparently followed, for the Report of the Council of Student Wardens for 1779 shows that privately-owned slaves were admitted to all eight public schools in Cape Town (82 children out of a total school population of 696), while the lodge school had as pupils 44 Company-owned and 40 privately-owned slaves.[11]

By 1823 it was estimated that 1,551 slaves were attending school in Cape Town, 372 of them at a Moslem school.[12] The British administration seems to have made a determined attempt to extend slave education, as part of the legislation of the 1820s designed to improve slave conditions in general. For instance, Christian slave-owners near free schools were compelled by the slave proclamation of 1823 to send slave children between 3 and 10 years of age to the nearest school for at least three days a week.

The beginnings of Hottentot education had been delayed, but thanks to the intense missionary[13] activity of the early 1800s there were twelve institutions by 1820, and, ten years later, twenty-two within the boundaries of the present Cape Province, and five more in South-West Africa.[14]

That the change-over from pastoralism to even an inefficient agriculturalism was finally effected for the Hottentots must be attributed largely to missionary efforts. The Moravians in particular, with their special emphasis on the dignity of work, had considerable success in their institutions, while they and other societies even succeeded in setting up various local industries.[15] In addition, further practical vocational training was afforded by the necessity for erecting mission buildings with only small resources.

In the narrower educational sphere, the societies seem to have laboured under considerable difficulties. For example, in 1805 Governor Janssens ordered the missionaries to teach only reading and the scriptures, and prohibited them from teaching the Hottentots to write. In 1808 the General School Committee gave Lord Caledon the same advice. Even in 1826 the regulations drawn up for Erasmus Smit made no mention of writing.[16] In addition, the practical educational work of the institutions was hampered by their small size, which made economic self-sufficiency impossible, and forced all able-bodied inmates, young or old, to spend most of the year working for farmers in the neighbourhood.

After emancipation, the slave schools were superseded by mission schools, which were also attended by European children. In general, Coloured education passed into the hands of the Churches, where it has largely remained ever since. As many missionaries followed the

Coloured migration to the towns in 1828–48, the education of the rural Coloured has been neglected up to the present time.[17]

From the time of emancipation, the tendency to segregation in schools as in other spheres grew more marked, despite the official policy of non-discrimination.[18] In fact, this policy seems to have stimulated rather than soothed private class or colour-consciousness.

In the early 1830s there had already been a successful European demonstration against the attendance of Coloured children at the government school at Stellenbosch.[19] After the middle of the century European public opinion had prevailed, and thereafter Coloured education remained largely denominational, while European education became almost entirely secular, although there was no mention of colour in the 1865 regulations.[20] Poorer European children nevertheless continued to attend the mission schools until Union,[21] despite the legislative provision made by Dr. Muir, Superintendent-General of Education in 1893, for 'white mission schools' with higher salary scales. This was in effect a colour-conscious measure.

Although the Coloured people owe a vast debt to the churches for laying the foundations of their education, their confinement to these schools at a later stage, when European secular education was advancing rapidly, has been greatly to their disadvantage.[22] Where there is segregation or dual provision of facilities, it is rare to find the facilities equal, even if a 'separate but equal' policy like that of the United States Government be formally adopted. Even in the 'liberal' Cape, the Superintendent-General of Education, Sir Langham Dale, declared in 1889:

'The first duty of the Government has been assumed to be to recognise the position of the European Colonists as holding the paramount influence, social and political, and to see that the sons and daughters of the Colonists should have at least such education as their peers in Europe enjoy, with such local modifications as will fit them to maintain their unquestioned superiority and supremacy in this land.'[23]

In this historical introduction we have tried to indicate the main trends which can still be traced in Coloured education to-day. They include the belief that all education of a subordinate group is dangerous, or the somewhat more enlightened self-interest which holds that a servant with some education, preferably practical, is a better servant. There is also the great contribution of religious bodies to Coloured education, and the increasing tendency to segregation of educational facilities, with the state assuming direct responsibility for the education of the group which it represents, and only indirect responsibility for that of subordinate groups. Lastly there are the beginnings of detailed differentiation, and consequently of discrimination, between facilities and conditions of work in the various segregated systems of education.[24]

*   *   *   *   *

Since Union, primary and secondary education[25] have remained under the provincial administrations, while higher, vocational and special education come under the Union Department.

In considering primary and secondary education, we shall be mainly concerned with the Cape, where live the great majority of Coloured school-children. As has been shown, the European demand for segregation was present before Union, although the administration remained officially 'colour-blind' until 1893. With Union came open legal sanction for the principle of segregation. In the famous case of Moller v. Keimoes School Committee,[26] the verdict upheld the principle of segregation in schools where separate provision was available. Practice and prejudice received full recognition in the Cape Consolidated Education Ordinance No. 5 of 1921, which dealt with European and Coloured education in separate chapters.[27]

Since then, Coloured education has made considerable progress, but has never come near to overhauling European education. It is, however, closer to the latter than to African education, for historical reasons and as a result of the continued influence of 'liberal' attitudes in the Cape Administration. Here, as in other chapters, reasons of space make it impossible to compare in detail the provisions for Coloured and African education.[28] This account must be confined to the divergencies between Coloured and European education, which have historically run along parallel tracks, with the former always a bad second.

One of the major differentiations in Cape educational provisions for the two ethnic groups is that, while primary schooling is free for both European and Coloured children up to Standard VI,[29] it was not made even theoretically compulsory for the Coloureds until 1945.[30]

The Coloured Education Ordinance of that year provided for the gradual introduction of compulsory education for Coloured children between the ages of 7 and 14, or Standard VI,[31] wherever a request to this effect was made by a school board or committee.[32] This was to apply to undenominational schools only, of which there were 99 by the end of 1947, with an enrolment of 22,031 pupils, as opposed to 999 schools not under boards (almost all mission schools), with an enrolment of 140,982.

Only a few such areas of compulsory education have in fact been proclaimed in the five years since the Ordinance was passed.[33] Nor is it even possible that much more should be done in this direction, when the churches and provincial administration working together can hardly keep pace with the present annual increase in voluntary enrolments.[34] The universal introduction of compulsory education, which would involve finding funds, buildings and extra teachers for about 30,000 more children,[35] most of them living in the most remote rural areas, would probably overload the already strained system to breaking point. In addition, it would cause a further deterioration in the standard of education available, whereas the greatest needs of the present time are probably more post-primary facilities and a general improvement in quality.

Coloured education, particularly denominational, continues to lag behind European education. The continuation of denominational control may be a contributory factor to this inferiority. The great majority of managers[36] are European ministers, who may be expected to share to a greater or lesser degree the attitudes of the local white community, and to be concerned with the maintenance of the existing social order.[37] The Coloured teachers in these schools are appointed by the manager,[38] and their future may be endangered by any determined opposition to his policies.[39]

In the mid-1930s the Cape Coloured Commission asked school managers for their opinions on the efficacy of denominational control of Coloured education.[40] A large number, though not the majority, of managers favoured state control,[40] and elsewhere in the Report a Commissioner stated that the Dutch Reformed Church favoured such control.

A further disadvantage of denominational control is that education suffers through sectarian competition, rivalry and hostility.[41] In recent decades, Coloured education has become increasingly concentrated in the hands of a few large Churches.[42] The older Churches and missionary societies are gradually dropping out or passing on to other fields, their main task of conversion being completed.[43] In such cases the Dutch Reformed Church has often taken over.[44] The major hostility of this Church is directed towards the Roman Catholic Church, which has in a comparatively short space of time reached fourth place in the field of Coloured education.[45] Being a minority church in the Union, it has nothing to lose and many converts to gain by preaching and practising a more 'colour-blind' Christianity than would find favour with most white Christians in South Africa.

It would be of interest to inquire in more detail into the influence of the various Churches on their pupils. Inquiry should also be made into the connection between the Churches and secular educational authorities, and the motives of either or both in keeping Coloured education largely denominational.[46]

As far as the provincial authorities are concerned, financial considerations probably outweigh all others. South African political and economic measures are notably short-term, and the colossal sum required to take over the buildings, and the total, instead of partial, financing of Coloured schools, cannot fail to daunt successive Cape administrations. It is, however, argued that as a long-term policy, the Province might not lose financially by taking over the church schools, since under the present system it makes annual grants towards the purchase or hire of mission school buildings, which at the end remain the property of the churches.[47]

The system of financing Coloured (and Indian) education is now based on Act 38 of 1945,[48] which provides for a Union subsidy on a fifty-fifty basis, equalling the net expenditure of the province. Appendix T shows the net expenditure and net cost per enrolled pupil in the Cape Province over the period 1937–49. It shows that in 1949 over £6 million was spent on nearly 164,000 European children, just over £2½ million on rather more than that number of Coloured children and just over £1½ million on nearly 270,000 African children.[49] Although the position of Coloured education has improved, there is still a long way to go before educational segregation ceases to mean discrimination.

The major effect of this financial differentiation is to discriminate against the Coloured child *vis-à-vis* the European child in every respect and at every stage of his school life. Building cannot keep pace with the increased annual intake,[50] existing buildings are often unsuitable or inadequate,[51] and may consist of a single room. There is rarely any provision for gymnastics or physical training,[52] and often no adequate playground. Such essential class-room equipment as desks and chairs are in short supply, so the position with regard to scientific and other specialised equipment can be imagined.[53] There is a great scarcity of textbooks,[54] and school libraries are inadequate or totally absent.[55] It should be added that European schools have since the war suffered in a lesser degree from similar shortages, from overcrowding and from unsuitable buildings.

The Coloured child starts his or her school life with an initial handicap. Owing to overcrowding, he must usually wait a year longer than the European child to enter the pre-primary standards.[56] Owing to the scarcity of teachers trained in kindergarten methods and the enormous classes in which he must be taught, he does not make up this leeway.[57]

As he proceeds into the primary classes, his retardation increases rather than diminishes. For this there are several major reasons: continued overcrowding; the presence of backward and defective children who should be in special schools of one kind or another, were there special schools for them to attend;[58] inferior teaching[59] and organisation; the inferior buildings and equipment already mentioned; and poor home environment, physical ill-health,[60] under-nourishment,[61] and lack of economic incentive to scholastic achievement, as later opportunities for anything but unskilled labour are so meagre.[62]

In addition, free primary education ceases with Standard VI, while the minimum standard necessary for further training for the professions or skilled work is normally Standard VII or VIII.[63] The Provincial Education Department remits up to 40 per cent of the total fees payable at each secondary school and pays small boarding and travel bursaries.[64] Parents must find the remainder of the money necessary to keep their children at secondary school until they reach the required standard.[65] In addition, there were in 1947 only 9 Coloured high schools and 8 secondary schools, as opposed to 174 high schools and 66 secondary schools for Europeans (see Appendix V). Many parts of the Province are almost out of range of any Coloured secondary or high school.[66]

A projected change based on the Scottish system and recommended by the De Villiers Commission is the transfer of Standard VI from the primary to the secondary stage. Although this transfer is in line with practice in other countries, and in the Transvaal, some Coloured teachers regard it as a discriminatory measure aimed at their group in particular.[67] It is true that if the plan were put into immediate operation it would result in numbers of Coloured children being pushed on to the labour market after passing Standard V, as there is insufficient secondary accommodation for all those who would normally have gone from Standard V to Standard VI. The Cape Education Department does not, however, propose to make the change in any area until sufficient secondary school accommodation is available, and as education remains free until the Coloured child's fifteenth year, there is no reason why he should suffer from the plan.[68]

In the country districts, and particularly in the farm schools, the progress of the pupil may be hampered by the attitude of local European employers,[69] whose main interest is a continued supply of cheap labour.[70] This interest is often sanctioned by a literal interpretation of those parts of the Old Testament which refer to the divinely appointed destiny of certain peoples to be hewers of wood and drawers of water in perpetuity.

There is less differentiation in the Cape primary syllabus provisions for Coloured and European schools than in most other aspects of schooling, and such differentiation as there is was probably not overtly discriminatory in intention.[71] It involves a simplification of courses in geography, history, nature study[72] and domestic science; the two former are made simpler on the grounds that the Coloured child is at school for a shorter time than the European, in most cases only till Standard III or IV, and that it is best to give him a simplified but wider acquaintance with these subjects during the short time of his availability.[73]

Detailed study of the divergencies in the syllabuses[74] suggests that there are certain parts of South African history which require different emphasis for pupils of different ethnic groups.[75] In other subjects there are similar divergencies corresponding to prevailing socio-economic conditions.[76] It is perhaps in the case of domestic science that the differentiated syllabus faces up to the economic facts of South African life most squarely.[77] Most Coloured girls are destined to be domestic workers either for themselves and their families, or in European employment, or both, while Europeans are traditionally employers and supervisors of labour, domestic and otherwise.[78]

The syllabus contains some divergencies, but the text books used by both Coloured and European pupils are the same. Although laudable in principle, this duplication sometimes proves wounding to Coloured susceptibilities, as most, if not all, text books are written by whites, and at times reflect current race-attitudes all too faithfully.[79]

For the comparatively few Coloured children at present receiving a secondary education, the syllabus becomes colour-blind. Coloured secondary education is probably better in quality than Coloured primary education, though quantitatively facilities compare very badly with those for Europeans.[80] The schools are all under school boards, the teaching is of a higher standard, and the number of pupils per teacher is about the same as in European secondary schools. Nevertheless, it is affected by other than educational factors. First of all, many of the male teachers are there only because there is no other professional occupation available to them,[81] while the majority of pupils have a similar lack of vocational choice.[82]

The question of a completely different syllabus for Coloured primary pupils (there has been one for African children in the Cape since 1922) has sometimes been raised by persons and bodies whose aim is not necessarily to 'keep the Hottentot in his place', but rather to ensure that Coloured children should get the most out of their few years of schooling, to enable them to live a fuller life under economic and social conditions as they are at present.

It has, for example, been suggested that the curriculum, at least in Coloured rural primary schools, is too academic, and not adapted to local needs.[83] Conceivably, a Coloured man or woman who has received an education beyond his economic prospects may find the 'short, nasty and brutish' life of a Non-European unskilled labourer in South Africa even less tolerable than does his illiterate or semi-literate co-worker. Nevertheless, any departure from the principle, however theoretical, of equality, is regarded as a step back, and as likely to be exploited by those whose motives are far from altruistic. No Coloured representatives or groups have therefore been willing to support a separate syllabus.[84]

When all the discriminatory factors outlined so far in this chapter are taken into account, it is not surprising that scholastic results show considerable disparity. In the year 1946-7, 10,526 Europeans, 1,129 Coloured and 1,389 Africans took the Junior Certificate examination. Of the Europeans, 22 per cent passed first grade, 68 per cent second grade, and 10 per cent failed. Corresponding figures for the Coloured and African groups were, respectively, 5 per cent, 64 per cent, 31 per cent (Coloured), and 5 per cent, 68 per cent and 27 per cent (African).[85]

These and similar differences in performance are frequently cited as evidence of the 'innate' intellectual inferiority of Non-Europeans. Nevertheless, when to the educational disadvantages already mentioned are added inferior material conditions, which may have a deteriorating effect on intellectual as well as physical capacity,[86] the lack of incentive[87] already mentioned, and other forms of social discrimination, there is no real need to look elsewhere for explanations of such examination results.

In as far as purely educational factors are concerned, the Cape Coloured Commission came to the conclusion that the almost uniformly poorer performance (in nine cases out of ten) given by selected Coloured children, as compared with European children of almost identical I.Q.s, in a series of subjects tested by the Commission, might be sought, not so much in the uninteresting nature of the work, nor in unsatisfactory home environment, but in the lower standards and poorer methods of Coloured teaching.[88]

Coloured would-be teachers start with an initial disadvantage, in that most of them have much greater difficulty in reaching the necessary standard than do Europeans.[89] In quantity, training facilities available to them compare not too badly with those for Europeans. The latest available figures (1946–7)[90] showed nine Coloured training establishments, with 763 enrolments, and nine European schools and colleges with 873 enrolments.[91] The European establishments, however, have ninety-one teachers, while the Coloured establishments are staffed by only sixty-five. The training is said to have deteriorated in four of the nine Coloured establishments, owing to the loss of European assistants who requested transfers following the appointment of Coloured principals.[92] More specialised courses are available for Europeans, and more profit by them.[93]

For economic reasons, Coloured teachers are often unable to continue their training beyond the minimum two-year Coloured Primary Lower Certificate. In 1947, only sixty-seven Coloured students were taking any third-year specialised course, whereas the corresponding European total was 209. A further seventeen Coloured teachers only were taking the fourth-year diploma.[94] The majority (585) were taking the Coloured Teachers' Primary Lower Certificate (qualification, Junior Certificate), and the remaining 111 students were taking the Coloured Primary Higher Certificate (qualification, Senior Certificate) at the only college at which the course is available.[95]

Although the present position leaves much to be desired, it is nevertheless a considerable improvement on the past. In 1922, of 1,129 Coloured teachers, only 80 per cent were certificated, even with the lower qualification then required. In 1935, 93.1 per cent of the 2,488 teachers were certificated, and by 1946, 97.1 per cent out of 4,101.[96]

The Coloured teacher's salary, which is uniform whether the school is a state school or merely state-aided, is determined by his qualifications and position. The lower qualifications of the Coloured teacher are sometimes cited to justify the lower salary, increment and pensions which he receives, compared to the European.[97]

In the Cape this disparity in salaries has, in theory, existed since 1893.[98] In 1918, Ordinance 12 laid down differential salary scales for the two ethnic groups, that for Coloured teachers being, on the average, seven-tenths of current European scales, with increment and pensions correspondingly lower. In 1944 the Cape Provincial Council accepted the principle that Coloured salaries should be 80 per cent of the European scales,[99] while women's salaries were to be 80 per cent of men's salaries throughout. As European teachers' salaries are by no means high, even the new scales do not ensure a life of ease for the Coloured teacher, whose cost-of-living is identical, and who must maintain an even higher status in his own community.[100]

The 1944 Ordinance also extended European leave-privileges to Coloured teachers. In 1935 they had received the same sick-leave rights, and the pension scheme was improved in 1934 and again amended in the 1944 Ordinance. In 1944, too, the Cape Educational Department began to classify Coloured and European teachers according to the same system, a step forward which was made possible by the rapid progress of Coloured education.[101]

The Coloured teacher's task is made more difficult by the unwieldy classes which he has to teach. In 1947, there was an average of 35.6 enrolled pupils to each teacher.[102] Corresponding figures for European and African classes were 21.1 and 42.5. The theoretical staffing arrangements for both European and Coloured schools, based not on enrolment but on average attendance, are: in primary schools, two teachers to thirty pupils, thereafter one additional teacher for each additional thirty-five pupils; in secondary schools, two teachers to twenty pupils, thereafter one for each additional thirty pupils; in high schools, three teachers for twenty-five students, thereafter one for each additional twenty-five.[103]

In addition, living conditions are not always satisfactory. Successive commissions have stressed the difficulty of boarding teachers, particularly women, in poor and remote country districts.[104] As we have seen, teachers at denominational schools are often expected to do work not directly connected with teaching on Sundays. There are other cases similar to that of Carelse which suggest that the teachers' opinions are also strictly censured.[105] There are sometimes difficulties over the use of public libraries, not all of which pursue the colour-blind policy of the Cape Town Library.[106]

Relations between the Coloured teachers and pupils and the comparatively few European teachers (mostly female, because of the shortage of Coloured women teachers) still employed in Coloured schools in the Cape are said to be good;[107] the Europeans have usually remained in such schools by preference, despite the current shortage of teachers in European schools. There is nevertheless complete ethnic segregation in the teachers' organisations; the South African Teachers' Association (S.A.T.A.) and the *Suid-Afrikaanse Onderwysers Unie* (S.A.O.U.)[108] are 'for Europeans only', while Coloured teachers are divided between the Teachers' League of South Africa (T.L.S.A.) and the Teachers' Educational and Professional Association (T.E.P.A.).[109]

The foregoing account has been primarily concerned with Coloured primary and secondary education in the Cape. In conclusion, it must be said that the Cape educational authorities, while by no means observing strict equality between the various groups, appear to be making a considerable effort to improve matters, in the face of perpetually inadequate funds, and indifferent or sometimes hostile European public opinion.

The position differs in each of the other provinces, according to the local status customarily assigned to the various Coloured groups. In both the Transvaal and Natal, Coloured primary and secondary education fall under the same administration as does European education. In the Orange Free State,[110] it was until a few years ago administered by the chief inspector for African education, but is now under the European department. In all three provinces, the number of Coloured children is very small in comparison with those of other ethnic groups,[111] so that the manner of their preparation for adult life is not of great economic or social importance to the authorities. In Natal, alone of the three Northern provinces, education has been compulsory in undenominational primary schools for European and Coloured children since 1942. In all three Northern provinces, the majority of the schools are undenominational (all in the O.F.S., all but one in the Transvaal, nineteen out of thirty-four in Natal). Education is free for Europeans and Coloureds up to Standard X in these Provinces.[112]

* * * * *

Turning to vocational education, we find similar differentiation[113] in provisions made for the various ethnic groups. Vocational education may be subdivided into technical, agricultural and commercial training, apart from the higher professional education provided by the universities, of which an account will be given later.

For Europeans, facilities for technical education are fairly adequate. In 1946–7, 38,403 students were attending technical colleges (9,639 full-time, 28,764 part-time), 3,620 were in vocational schools, and 2,600 attending continuation classes.[114] By contrast, the number of Coloured students receiving all types and levels of technical education cannot be more than a couple of thousand. [115] The great majority of the 1950 total of Coloured technical college students were at the Cape Town Technical College, which had 827 Coloured students and 11,524 European students registered in that year. Of these 412 and 2,765 respectively were apprentices. European students attend classes in the main building, Non-Europeans at a separate and much inferior building in Roeland Street. Lectures are duplicated for both groups by the same teachers, all of whom, including the head of the Non-European section, are European.

The North Cape Technical College at Kimberley is 'for Europeans only', but conducts part-time classes for Coloured and African students in specially hired buildings. Coloured students, it was stated, 'do not like having to share classes with Natives, generally speaking', so separate classes are held. There is an average of 700 European students (day and evening) and sixty Non-Europeans (evenings only). Students can take any course provided that a minimum class of eight is obtained. A number of part-time classes in shorthand, typing and book-keeping have just been started for Coloured girls aged 16–17 years.

At the Natal Technical College in Durban, there were in 1949 thirty-four Coloured apprentices, thirty-seven women taking dress-making and eighteen cookery. There were about 6,000 European students. Coloured classes are conducted in separate buildings and with separate teachers, but they work to the European syllabus. The same is true of the Witwatersrand Technical College, Johannesburg, which had about 20,000 European students (full and part-time) and 400 Non-Europeans, of whom the majority were African or Indian, in 1949.

There are no facilities available to Coloureds for formal agricultural and commercial education, except for the commercial classes available at Cape Town Technical College and Newtown Coloured School, Johannesburg, and the rudimentary instruction which may be given *en passant* in primary or secondary schools. For the very few Coloured students who reach a University, commercial and agricultural degrees are also available.[116] Here again, other than educational factors come into operation, as the small Coloured stake in commerce and agriculture (except as landless, unskilled labour) limits the economic openings available to potential graduates in these fields.

For Europeans, on the other hand, there are both openings and adequate training facilities.[117] In 1925 the Union Government assumed responsibility for vocational education. There were then two departmental schools, seven single-teacher industrial departments, and nine state-aided institutions.[118] By the year 1946–7, apart from the technical colleges mentioned earlier, there were ten technical high schools, forty-three commercial high schools and nine housecraft high schools under the Union Department, with 5,820 pupils and a further 2,600 in continuation classes.[119]

There are also a number of commercial schools and business colleges under private management. In addition, the provincial secondary and high schools have tended increasingly to provide vocational instruction, limited in the case of the Coloureds, as we have already said, by the lack of necessary equipment.[120]

Agricultural education for Europeans is available at five colleges under the Department of Agriculture, a small forestry training school, three university faculties of agriculture, and seven agricultural high schools. Mainly theoretical agricultural instruction is also given in forty-four Cape high schools, all high and secondary schools in Natal, eleven schools in the Free State, and twenty-two Transvaal schools.[121]

There are about 1,200 full-time students and pupils taking vocational or professional courses at agricultural institutions. The De Villiers Commission found this position unsatisfactory for European farming.[122] The lack of even such training for Coloureds, a number of whom still own small-holdings, is therefore all the more glaring.

* * * * *

University education is also state-subsidised, although the universities are self-governing bodies. In this financial dependence on state aid may lurk the seeds of increased political intervention in university policy, particularly in racial matters.[123] There have been frequent attacks by Nationalist ministers on racial 'fraternisation' in some universities.[124]

In South Africa one can classify the various universities under three heads from the point of view of racial policy. Firstly, there are institutions which observe complete racial segregation, and therefore admit no Non-Europeans. They are: Pretoria, Stellenbosch, the O.F.S. College, Potchefstroom and, until 1951, Rhodes (all but the last named being Afrikaans-medium). The converse of this type is the completely Non-European university college at Fort Hare, until 1951 a constituent part of the South African University, but now affiliated non-spatially to the new Rhodes University,[125] from which Fort Hare students will receive their degrees.

Secondly, there is the 'mixed' type, Cape Town and the Witwatersrand, and thirdly the 'parallel' type of structure found in the University of Natal. The principal of Natal University, Dr. E. G. Malherbe, recently wrote an article emphasising the advantages of the latter type of structure in the present stage of European race attitudes in South Africa.[126] The examinations and degrees are the same, as are the lectures and teaching staff.[127] There is a separate library attached to the main one. Residential and recreational facilities are separate, and would not so far appear to be on a par with those provided for Europeans. As Non-Europeans (most of whom are Indians) pay much lower fees, perhaps this is only to be expected. Student activities are managed through a separate Students' Representative Council.[128]

Dr. Malherbe opposes the idea of a completely segregated and independent Non-European university, advocated by the apostles of *apartheid*, on the grounds that such a university might incur the same stigma as the 'nigger universities' of the United States.[129] Of the 'mixed' universities he suggests that as a result of the attitude of many European students, Non-Europeans are more likely to develop an inferiority complex and sense of resentment than to benefit from the contact.[130]

It is true that despite official university policy, and the scrupulous courtesy and frequent friendliness of the teaching staff,[131] Coloured and other Non-European students at the University of Cape Town do not have an altogether easy time.[132] While they attend the same lectures and classes, use the same libraries, pay the same high fees, and take the same degrees, they usually avoid other contact situations in which unpleasantness might arise. They do not participate in sports or social functions,[133] and tend to sit alone or with members of their own ethnic group even in lecture-rooms.[134] There are no residential facilities for them, and by reason of their small numbers[135] their voice has not always been heard in student representative activities.[136]

At Cape Town too, Coloured and Africans are not free to enrol for every course. They are not accepted for Engineering or Art, the former because practical work in an industrial establishment is an integral part of the course, and the union concerned will not permit this in their case, the latter apparently because it involves life classes, attended by both sexes and with a nude European model. In addition, the University does not guarantee completion of the medical course, which includes practical hospital work, to Non-European medical students.[137]

With all these drawbacks, however, this type of university is preferred by the majority of educated Coloured people, to whom any form of segregation has come to be synonymous with discrimination.[138] The principle of 'colour-blind' university education is also accepted by large numbers, possibly even the majority of those most concerned, the European students of such institutions, and by the National Union of South African Students, formed to look after the interests of students, regardless of colour, race or creed. The main resistance comes from the 'all-white' and segregated universities, and from the Afrikaans-speaking student association.[139]

*   *   *   *   *

It is perhaps in the educational field more than any other that signs of Coloured progress can be detected. The great increase over the last twenty years in the number of children receiving at least primary education, despite the lack of compulsion; the rise in the number of secondary and high schools; and the improved qualifications of Coloured teachers: all these are part of a process which is proceeding under its own momentum and can hardly now be checked. Thanks to the conflicting aims of those charged with its administration at various periods, Coloured education in South Africa has gone beyond the stage of 'training for helotry'[140] to a point where efforts to halt, divert or reverse it by the dominant group will be of no avail. The missionary from overseas with his evangelical fervour, the Cape administrator, traditionally though unbelligerently liberal, the Coloured teacher, fiercely egalitarian, and the industrialist, with his demand for 'literate instruments of labour',[141] have all contributed to this progress.

A major danger for the ruling group lies in the fact that its failure to provide adequate vocational training and the corresponding vocational opportunities, irrespective of colour or race, is producing an increasing number of frustrated and embittered secondary and high-school graduates. Most of these take up teaching for want of another outlet,[142] and thereby pass on their own bitterness and frustration to others.

For the Coloured group, due to the lack of scientific facilities and the virtual colour-bar prevailing in most professions, particularly those of engineering, the natural sciences and architecture, there is the possibility of over-concentration on the humanities, important as these should be in a modern society.

B. HEALTH AND SOCIAL WELFARE SERVICES

It hurts me indeed to see one group served first and the other waiting in darkness and silence. God was never for any special group among the unfortunate.[1]

The inadequacy of health and social welfare service in the Union to meet the needs of the Coloured people is in large part due to the immensity of these needs; such inadequacy also helps to perpetuate the vicious circle of disease and want in which most members of this group have lived for so long.

The Gluckman Report on the National Health Services, upon which the first part of this chapter will be based,[2] adopted a non-racial approach to its task, concerning itself with the requirements of the people of South Africa as a whole. Nevertheless, it has yet to be fully realised by many white South Africans that disease has no ethnic boundaries, and that the appalling prevalence of infectious and contagious diseases amongst Non-Europeans cannot be entirely without effect on the Europeans with whom so many of them come in contact, in homes, factories, offices, public buildings and the streets. On the other hand, a certain indifference and callousness may be engendered by the thought that improved health services can only serve to swell the 'black hordes', which may, it is feared by so many, one day overwhelm 'white civilisation'.[3]

This admirable report on the Union health services divided the latter into four categories: (i) promotive, (ii) preventive, (iii) curative, and (iv) rehabilitative services. The first and last shade over into the social welfare services, which will be described in the second part of this section.

Promotive health services have a very wide range, which covers recreation, physical education, housing, nutrition, eugenics, education and mental health. In this study most of these aspects[4] are covered in other chapters, or under the heading of social welfare later in this chapter, so we need only recapitulate their inadequacy and inferiority to similar services provided for the dominant white group. We should also mention the grave consequences of Non-European ignorance and superstition and what Professor Batson has called the 'Social Disservices', i.e., socio-economic activities which work against the promotion of health and social well-being, by reducing the standard of living of the poorer sections of the community, by reducing the demand for the labour of the poor, by excluding them from well-paid occupations, and by raising the cost of food, housing, clothing and other necessities, either by direct price control, by an increase in costs at the source of production, or by non-progressive direct taxation.[5]

* * * * *

Preventive health services include periodic medical examination, maternal and child health, school health, occupational hygiene, and immunisation from infectious[6] and non-infectious diseases. As there is no national health service in the Union,[7] the main preventive agency is usually the individual himself, although urban local authorities and some private firms supply such services for a comparative few, and education departments endeavour, as yet with only moderate success, to inculcate their importance amongst the children under their care.

Since the publication of the Gluckman Report, the central Health Department has established about thirty health centres, several of which cater for Coloureds,[8] while some urban local authorities have extended the curative services of previously established clinics to include such personal preventive services. The family rather than the individual is the clinical unit of such services.

In most urban centres, maternity and child-welfare services are available to all races, segregated as always; some clinics also give advice on family limitation. While there are ante-natal clinics for all expectant mothers who care to attend (a routine V.D. examination being provided at most), only abnormal or emergency cases can usually be accommodated in maternity hospitals or wards. Others may be admitted to the few private maternity homes which the Coloured community can support.[9] The majority of parturient Coloured women are left to their own devices, or to the services of midwives. There are not, however, enough of these to meet existing needs,[10] while the quality of their training is not in general very high, and some are actually unqualified.[11]

Child welfare services are available in most urban centres for Coloured and other children up to the age of two,[12] and medical and dental inspection is carried out in the comparatively small number of schools under School Boards. Even there, however, shortage of medical staff has in previous years meant that most children were not actually examined.[13] Indigent children may be treated in the case of certain kinds of defect. For most Coloured children over the age of two there is therefore little in the way of personal preventive health services. Comment has already been made upon the shortage of crèches and nursery schools for this group. The few that are in existence are the result of private or municipal enterprise, usually subsidised by the State. At these institutions medical inspection is provided, often on a voluntary basis.

The majority of Coloured people over the school-leaving age are not medically examined unless their health has already broken down. In a few cases, medical inspection is available at a worker's factory, or to would-be entrants into government or local service, while individual employers of domestic labour may send their servants to a doctor for a routine check, often to ensure that the servants have no communicable disease such as tuberculosis or a venereal infection.[14] Routine medical examinations are also available at the recently established health centres, which, however, could not yet cope with any appreciable proportion of the Coloured population.

At urban places of work, hygienic conditions are more or less enforced by industrial inspectors, and it is in their homes that the Coloured people suffer most from the lack or inadequacy of such non-personal preventive services as a pure water supply, adequate disposal of wastes, the hygienic handling of food, and the isolation of disease-carriers. In the urban slum-areas, the services provided by the local authority are usually insufficient for the excessive number of inhabitants, while in many locations they may be almost totally lacking. In the rural areas and in squatters' camps in the peri-urban areas, the inhabitants are usually left to their own and Nature's devices.[15] The inadequacy of services is made worse by the total ignorance about hygiene of the great majority of Coloured people, and by the prevalence amongst them of alcoholism, which lowers the physical resistance of the addict and the available income of his family, and of sexual promiscuity, which aids the spread of venereal diseases.

There are two state-aided, internationally-affiliated organisations which play a considerable part in the promotive and preventive health-services of the Union[16] and particularly in the provision of instruction in first-aid, hygiene and elementary nursing. These are the St. John Ambulance Association (and Ambulance Brigade), and the South African Red Cross Society.

In the former association, Europeans and Non-Europeans are organised into separate divisions, serving their own areas. Non-Europeans may be N.C.O.s, but higher officers are European. Examinations are on the same level for whites and non-whites, but in some cases the latter are excused theory. The Association falls under the Union Defence Force regulations, especially in times of national emergency, although its overall body is situated in London. A recent U.D.F. ruling that

H

separate parades should be held for European and Non-European divisions caused considerable resentment amongst the latter.

The S.A. Red Cross, which is affiliated to the International Red Cross, is also linked with the military authorities as an auxiliary to the nursing division of the Union Defence Force. Europeans only are trained for military work. In recent years training of Non-Europeans as V.A.D.s and Ambulance personnel has been carried out, with classes in first-aid, hygiene, home nursing and infant welfare in schools, community centres and factories. Non-European Red Cross detachments work among their own people, and some have their own officers. They have the same instruction and training as Europeans, but no written examination. Uniforms are said to be the same, with assisted purchase for those who need it; Non-European complaints about inferior uniforms apparently result from the fact that dress uniforms are not always supplied to them. In September 1949, the Surgeon-General instructed the National Council that Europeans and Non-Europeans should be inspected separately, despite a protest from the Vice-President of the Natal Region, on the grounds that the Red Cross was a world-wide organisation. As a result of this segregation in both associations, it is said that Non-European enthusiasm has somewhat diminished, and in isolated cases Coloured groups have set up their own autonomous ambulance and first-aid associations.[17]

*   *   *   *   *

Curative services represent an older concept of health services than do the other three categories, and the great majority of Coloured people would probably still define health as the absence of illness sufficient to prevent one from working. It is due to this attitude as well as to the complete inadequacy of both promotive and preventive services that Coloured wards and hospitals are quite unable to accommodate the seriously ill.

Curative services may be institutional or extra-institutional. The latter are provided by registered medical practitioners, dentists, nurses and so on, and by unregistered practitioners such as osteopaths, herbalists, and even witch-doctors. Urbanised Coloured people also make considerable use of the proprietary medicines available in chemists' shops. The availability of private medical and dental attention is conditioned by the economic status and the degree of civilisation reached by the population in a given area, and not by its health needs.[18] Consequently there are few doctors or dentists practising in urban slums, peri-urban shanty-towns[19] or rural areas.[20]

The needs of 'indigent' sufferers in the country districts are catered for by the district surgeons, employed, except in Natal, by the Department of Health, and by the subsidised nursing services. In the early years of the war the Gluckman Report estimated that while 2,000 doctors served the needs of the more financially fortunate part of the population (some 1½ million), the 381 district surgeons paid by the Department of Health (most of them part-time) had to serve the remaining 8 million.[21] There is no definition of a 'pauper', the decision being left in each case to the local magistrate, who is instructed to inquire whether the patient has relatives who could pay for the services of a private practitioner for him.

Doctors who have a Non-European practice have separate surgery hours and waiting-rooms for such patients, in deference to ordinary South African custom. A few middle-income group Coloured families get private medical attention through friendly societies, which cover part of the cost,[22] while many Coloured industrial workers get curative services from sick funds established as a result of Industrial Council agreements. Public servants (e.g., police and prison officers) and employers of the larger municipalities are usually provided with free medical attention, at least of the out-patient type. A great deal of specialised work in connection with all categories of health services is also done by voluntary associations and councils; this will be described in the section on rehabilitative health services.

The clinics conducted by various local authorities, to which we referred when outlining preventive health services, provide full curative treatment only for indigent patients, except in respect of venereal diseases and tuberculosis, where curative treatment has also the function of preventing further spread of the diseases. The reason for their limitation of curative services is to avoid encroachment upon the private interests of the medical profession.[23] In addition, all the larger provincial hospitals provide general out-patient services free or at a low cost, sometimes at clinics away from the main building itself.[24]

In the Union, institutional curative services are administered by a number of authorities, whose spheres often overlap.[25] Hospitals and charitable institutions were originally under the Provincial Councils. In practice, these bodies now control only public general hospitals and chronic sick homes; leprosy, mental and some tuberculosis and venereal diseases hospitals come under the central authority, while infectious diseases hospitals are the responsibility of the local authorities.[26]

The accommodation in all types of hospital is inadequate for the requirements of the population, and in the case of the Coloureds and other Non-Europeans, grossly so. Two of the factors which should determine the ratio of hospital beds to the population are the poverty and housing conditions of the community. In the case of the Coloured group these are so bad that it is often impossible to treat cases adequately at home. None the less, in 1946 there were only 23,593 hospital beds available for over 9 million Non-Europeans,[27] while 32,889 beds were provided for under 2½ million Europeans.[28] Only in the case of infectious diseases is a somewhat more liberal allowance of beds made, for obvious reasons.[29]

The provincially-financed general hospitals in the Cape are quite unable to cope with the increasing Coloured population and the growing demand for hospitalisation. It is said that six or seven babies, many of them suffering from gastro-enteritis, are turned away daily from the Groote Schuur Hospital in Cape Town.[30] This and other hospitals are permanently overcrowded, with overflowing casualty and gynæcological wards, and staff working to the limit of overtime. The wards are so filled with urgent and emergency cases that non-urgent surgical cases often wait several years for admission,[31] while convalescent patients have to be discharged long before they are fully recovered.[32]

As we have said, the Department of Health is in charge of various types of specialised hospital. There are ten hospitals for mentally disordered persons of all ethnic groups, with a total capacity of about 17,000; 2,000 patients in these hospitals are Coloured and over 7,000 are Europeans,[33] but the two institutions for mentally defective persons have no provision for Non-Europeans except for a few who are employed there as workers.[34] The consequence is that mentally defective Coloured adults and children live at home, often in appalling conditions.[35] Institutional treatment, when available, is free to those who cannot afford to pay.

There are five leper institutions in the Union, four for Africans only, the fifth, at Westfort, for all races. Although the disease scourged the Hottentot and slave population in earlier years, it is now most prevalent amongst the Africans, who provided 1,953 of the 2,114 inmates of these institutions in June 1948.[36]

Tuberculosis, although fairly frequent amongst the Hottentots in early days, did not apparently develop to its present alarming proportions amongst the Coloured and other Non-European groups until the last few decades.[37] In the last years of the nineteenth century consumptive patients began to come out from Europe for a cure in the dry highlands of the interior of the Union, thus helping to spread the infection in the rural areas.[38] Later the growth of overcrowded urban slums and shanty towns provided an ideal forcing-ground for the disease amongst the poorer sections of the urban population.

The institutional treatment of tuberculosis in its communicable forms is shared by the Department of Health and local authorities. In all hospitals, the cost of treatment is met in the following proportions: one-eighth by the local authority from whose area the patient comes, one-quarter by the province, and five-eighths by the Union Government.[39] Hospital facilities are inadequate even for European tuberculotics, tragically so for Non-Europeans.[40] In Cape Town it was recently estimated that about 4 per cent of the Non-European (mainly Coloured) population are sufferers from and carriers of tuberculosis (calculating an average of nine open cases to every death from tuberculosis). As Cape Town had, until very recently, only fifty instead of the optimum 100–200 beds to every 100 deaths,[41] the vast majority of these tuberculotics are at large to spread the disease still further, while many who could be cured if they were isolated and treated in the primary stages are incurable by the time they obtain admission to the hospitals.

Venereal diseases are treated in clinics and out-patient wards, and also in hospitals administered by the Department or the local authorities; in the latter case institutional facilities often take the form of blocks or wards attached to general hospitals. The Department refunds 100 per cent of the net cost.[42] The incidence of venereal disease amongst the various Non-European groups is not known, as the disease is not notifiable. The attendance figures for treatment give a far from adequate picture of the present position.[43] In 1948, 19,947 Non-European cases of syphilis and 2,931 of gonorrhœa were treated in hospitals (corresponding European figures 110 and 71), while there were 368,196 attendances for syphilis and 29,580 for gonorrhœa at clinics and out-patient wards (European figures 20,548 and 5,483).

About the curative services in general, the Gluckman Commission pointed out that it was unreasonable and unsound to expect the State forever to make good the deficiencies of the socio-economic system, as this would be tantamount to a perpetual system of poor relief.[44]

* * * * *

The aim of rehabilitation is to restore individuals to 'as complete functional activity as is possible'.[45] In the rehabilitative, as in the promotive and preventive, health services, it is difficult to draw a firm line between health and social welfare services proper. This is particularly true of the rehabilitative services, which are often accompanied by grants from the Department of Social Welfare. Rehabilitative services, which have both a medical and an educational aspect, may be subdivided into the following four categories: (a) occupational therapy and vocational training;[46] (b) follow-up and after-care; (c) invalidity grants and compensation; (d) re-employment. In none of these categories is the provision adequate, and for Non-Europeans it is, except for category (c), almost totally lacking, save for the services available to ex-servicemen,[47] and the efforts of voluntary associations. The tendency is rather to permit those in need of rehabilitation to eke out an empty and profitless existence on a disability grant or pension, than to spend the money on rehabilitative services which might restore the individual concerned to useful and perhaps unsubsidised membership of the community.

Persons in need of rehabilitative health services range from those who are convalescing from a temporary and remediable illness to those who are permanently disabled, the blind, deaf and dumb, epileptics and cripples. In its widest sense the former category includes the maladjusted and anti-social, who in the Union, particularly if they are Non-Europeans, usually end in prison. As we have seen in Chapter IV, there is little in the present penal system, even as it affects juveniles, to exert a rehabilitative effect on its inmates.

The care of the permanently disabled has so far been left mainly to voluntary associations, usually subsidised to some extent by the State.[48] The S.A. National Council for the Blind is the statutory co-ordinating body for the care of blind persons in the Union, with two affiliated schools and twenty societies with workshops, training centres and hostels. Of the two schools, one is for Non-Europeans. This is the Athlone School for the Blind at Faure, near Cape Town, which has a capacity of 190 pupils only. On 31st March, 1950, there were 32,701 registered blind[49] persons in the Union: 2,428 Europeans, 2,196 Coloureds, 201 Asiatics and 28,876 Africans. The workshops referred to above could, however, accommodate only 397 in all, 235 of them being Non-Europeans. Hostel accommodation was even less, with 221 places, 126 of them for Non-Europeans. There were, however, no Non-European hostels in the Cape, so that the Coloured blind were ill-served.[50] Apart from the lack of such facilities, the blind person's rehabilitation is impeded by the unwillingness of private employers to employ him, mainly because of training difficulties.[51]

The care of the deaf (including deaf-mutes and the hard-of-hearing) is largely in the hands of the S.A. National Council for the Care of the Deaf. As in the case of blind and epileptic children, the State gives financial aid to special schools for the deaf.[52] Of these there are two for Europeans only, with a capacity of 409, two for Non-Europeans only (at Worcester, Cape and Roodepoort, Transvaal), with a capacity of 101 and twenty-eight respectively, and the Dominican School for the Deaf in Cape Town, which is for all races, with segregated accommodation for 195 pupils in all.[53] *Per caput* maintenance grants are also available for children whose parents cannot pay. No specific pensions are available for the deaf, but those who are in poverty and are unable to support themselves on the open labour market are eligible for disability pensions. Like the blind, deaf persons suffer from the unwillingness of private employers to engage them, and from the scarcity of homes where those who are unable to adjust themselves to normal living may find sanctuary.

Epileptics who are certifiable are the charge of the Commissioner for Mental Hygiene. The shortage of accommodation and trained nurses in mental hospitals has already been mentioned. The incidence of non-certifiable epileptics who need special care in settlements, sheltered employment or invalidity grants, is unknown. The National Council for Mental Hygiene conducts clinics for all races, but the only colonies and schools so far available are for Europeans.[54]

The care of crippled persons is similarly left to the National Council for the Care of Cripples in South Africa, except for disabled soldiers and those employees who are covered by the Workmen's Compensation Act. Thanks to a gift of £100,000 from Lord Nuffield in 1937, this Council has been able to subsidise clinics, vocational training and special nursing courses[55] to a larger extent than have the Councils concerned with other types of disability. Most large hospitals have an orthopædic section for all races, while in the Cape Province there are a number of homes catering for Coloured people,[56] although the available accommodation is not adequate to meet the demand.

*   *   *   *   *

The present inadequate health services of the Union are accompanied by a shortage of trained personnel. In addition, the available medical practitioners, dentists and nurses tend to gravitate to the more well-to-do urban areas, leaving the most needy sections of the population practically unattended. Owing to the tardiness with which the principle of training Non-Europeans in medicine was accepted even by the 'liberal' Universities,[57] the present inadequacy of such facilities, and the prejudice with which such Non-Europeans are regarded by many of their colleagues[58] and the general European public, there are as yet very few Non-European doctors and an insufficient number of Non-European nurses.

As Non-European and European nurses are placed on the same register,[59] the precise number of Coloured and other Non-European nurses cannot be ascertained. It has, however, been estimated at about one-sixth of the total,[60] which in 1948 consisted of 11,573 trained nurses of all types, 7,565 midwives, 4,935 student nurses, and 567 student midwives.[61] There are also thirty-eight trained Coloured T.B. nurse aides in the Cape, with a further eighty undergoing training;[62] this scheme was evolved by the Cape Divisional Council in an effort to make up the shortage of fully trained nurses for T.B. institutions. In all cases, although their training and qualifications are identical, the salaries of Coloured nurses are much below those for Europeans,[63] and unlikely to appeal to Coloured girls who have achieved the necessary educational standard, and who can easily get more remunerative and less arduous work in a factory.[64]

Most senior positions in Non-European hospitals and wards are still held by white nurses, so that the opportunities for promotion are limited for Coloured nurses.

*   *   *   *   *

Like the health services, the social welfare services are faced with the impossible task of trying to relieve the injustices and inequalities of the existing socio-economic system. Their function is, in fact, palliative rather than rehabilitative. In particular is this true of the so-called social security measures at present in force, which, as far as the Non-European ethnic groups are concerned, fail almost completely to alleviate the grave social insecurity in which the vast majority are born, exist and die.[65]

During the last war a Committee was set up to investigate the existing social security arrangements, and to formulate a comprehensive social security scheme. Any such scheme, to be workable, had of course to be correlated with the existing socio-economic structure, and it was found impossible to put forward a scheme which would give all its beneficiaries economic security, in view of the low total earnings of the Union. The Committee therefore confined its scheme to cover allowances to assist beneficiaries during certain contingencies or periods, such as age, childhood, pregnancy, unemployment, disablement, illness, birth and death. The scheme was to be nation-wide, centralised, semi-contributory (according to income and benefit levels), related to ruling ethnic unskilled living standards, and adjustable at three-year intervals. An effort was made to base differentiation in benefits and contributions on differences in socio-economic status rather than on differences in race.

A Parliamentary Select Committee cut the scheme from an estimated initial cost of £30 million (of which £18 million was to be found from general revenue) to £19.5 million; its modifications were largely at the expense of the Non-European groups, particularly Coloureds and Asiatics. An Inter-Departmental Committee then sat to co-ordinate the proposed social security and national health schemes, and in 1945 the Government issued a White Paper, in which it announced its intention to extend and improve existing social security and health services; it was, however, decided that the country could not afford a contributory, comprehensive social security scheme.[66]

Before 1928 social assistance was available in the Union only in the form of poor relief, some medical treatment, and support for mothers and children under the Children's Protection Act; the costs were borne by the Provinces, private welfare organisations and the churches.

In 1928 non-contributory old age pensions were instituted (Act No. 22) for white and Coloured men over 65 and women over 60 years of age.[67] The original pension was £42 for Europeans, and half that sum for Coloureds, with a means limitation of £30 plus £12 for each minor child for Europeans, and £18 for Coloureds. The pension rate has been raised several times, and the maximum means plus pension allowance is now £120 per annum (£72 pension with free income of up to £48) for Europeans, £60 for Coloureds (£36 and £24), £48 (£30 and £18) for Indians, and £30 (£12 and £18) for Africans.[68]

Reference has already been made in Chapter III to war pensions, but not to the war veterans' pensions established under Act No. 45 of 1941. This Act applies to European, Coloured and Indian veterans[69] who served in the Anglo-Boer War or the two Great Wars, and who were not disabled, but are unable to work, and are not entitled to receive other forms of grant or pension. The means plus pension limitation is the same as that for old age pensions, except that Europeans are entitled to an extra grant of £48 per annum.[70] In 1950, 20,432 Europeans and 578 Coloureds and Indians received veterans' pensions.[71]

Disability grants were established in 1937 for Europeans over 16 years of age, and were extended by Act No. 36 of 1946 to persons of all races who suffer from permanent mental or physical disabilities which make it impossible for them to support themselves, and who are not in receipt of other pensions or grants. At the end of 1950, 11,966 Europeans, 5,540 Coloureds, 1,058 Indians and 33,391 Africans were in receipt of such grants, the average sum received by members of each group being slightly higher in each case than the average old age pension figure;[72] a similar means test is applied as to applicants for old age pensions. In cases where an individual is suffering from a communicable disease such as tuberculosis, payment of the grant is made contingent upon his accepting treatment.[73]

Pensions for blind persons over 19 years were inaugurated under Act No. 11 of 1936 (as amended by Acts 33/1943 and 48/1944). The scales are said to be identical with those for old age pensions,[74] but only one-half of a blind person's earnings are taken into account for the means test.[75] In 1950, 1,158 Europeans, 1,587 Coloureds, 138 Indians and 21,638 Africans were receiving this pension.

Family allowances were introduced in 1947 for all races except Africans, despite the Social Security Committee's recommendation that they should be made available for urbanised Africans.[76] These allowances presuppose that the beneficiary is employed,[77] and endeavour to make up in part for the fact that the Union's general wage structure is not correlated with family responsibilities.[78] Allowances are paid, to the mother as a general rule, for every third and subsequent child. The original maximum monthly allowances of £1 10s. per European child, and 15s. per Coloured or Indian child, were in April 1948 raised to £2 for Europeans and £1 for Coloureds, while the Indian allowance remained at 15s., and was discontinued altogether at the end of 1948.[79] The maximum monthly means plus allowance figure was raised from £17 to £23 for Europeans, and from £9 to £11 10s. for Coloureds, while the minimum monthly income necessary to qualify for an allowance was decreased from £7 to £5 in the case of Europeans, and raised from £3 10s. to £4 5s. for Coloureds; this was apparently done following European complaints that Coloureds and Indians in some cases could, under more or less similar conditions, obtain allowances equalling or exceeding those for Europeans.[80]

As a result of these adjustments, only 637 Coloured families were receiving grants on 31st March, 1948, a total of £5,197 being paid out on them. On the other hand, 943 European families divided a total of £18,622, while 1,603 Indian families received a total of £17,812 during the same period. Despite the finding of the Cape Town Social Survey, that 67 per cent of Coloured children of 15 years and under in Cape Town started life in households of poverty, and that households containing dependent children were more susceptible to poverty,[81] the overwhelming majority of Coloured families receiving family allowances were resident in rural areas in 1948.[82]

Maintenance grants in respect of children placed with foster-parents were instituted under the Children's Act of 1921. In 1937[83] these grants were extended to provide for the maintenance of destitute or nearly destitute children in the care of their own parents or guardians, in order that family life might not be broken up through poverty. These allowances are paid in respect of children of all racial groups except rural Africans, where it is regarded as the natural duty of the kraal head to support any minor under his care. The original rates, based on a means test, were increased in April 1947 and April 1948. They reflect the prevailing inequality; the maximum means plus monthly grants after the 1948 increase were £23, £11 10s., £9 and £4 respectively for Europeans, Coloureds, Indians and Africans, and the monthly maximum grants per first child were £3, £1 10s., £1 5s. and 12s. 6d. for the same ethnic groups.[84] Grants were payable for European children up to the age of 16, and for Coloureds up to the age of 14 (15 after 1944). On 31st March, 1949, the number of families in receipt of maintenance grants and the amounts expended on each group were as follows: Europeans—7,237 (£656,758); Coloureds—7,196 (£330,864); Indians—3,132 (£138,721); Africans—2,341 (£43,816). Since 1942 the scheme has been augmented by making allowances to the parents or guardians of such children, if they are not in receipt of other pensions or grants, to enable them to stay at home to care for the children, instead of being forced to go out to work.

The allowances paid to foster-parents appear to be somewhat higher than the rates given above. After two increases the maximum monthly allowances in 1945 for physically and mentally normal children[85] were £4 for Europeans, £2 for Coloureds and Indians, and £1 2s. 6d. for Africans. In March 1948, 522 European, 123 Indian, and 1,174 Coloured families were receiving such allowances in respect of 746, 227 and 1,904 children in each group.[86]

The oldest form of social service in the Union, as in most other countries, is that of poor relief. After 1940, the distribution of poor relief was removed from all provinces except Natal, after having been in their hands since 1919. It consists of rations, which are the same for Coloureds and Europeans[87] (as is the means test), additional poor relief in the form of clothes, blankets, coal and so on, allowance for rent in special circumstances (20s. for a single European per month, 10s. for a single Non-European, in Cape Town), and railway transport on occasions. The main principles of poor relief in the Union are that it should not be regarded as a right, should be temporary, should not be made attractive, and should aim at rehabilitation.[88] The persons for whom it is intended are those who are temporarily stranded, those unable to earn their own living by reason of illness,[89] for whom there is no other maintenance, pension or grant, and those who are unemployed, and not work-shy but genuinely unable to find work.[90]

In the last year for which complete figures are available, the number of beneficiaries in the various ethnic groups and the total amount spent on each group were as follows: 13,524 Europeans (£26,029); 7,914 Coloureds (£14,361); 728 Indians (£1,456).[91] Like other grants and pensions, poor relief for Africans is administered by the Department of Native Affairs, £35,000 being allotted for this purpose. The proportionate sums spent on poor relief for the different groups are approximately equal in this one alone of the social services; European beneficiaries profit only on rent allowances (£4,109, as opposed to £590 for Coloureds, and £72 for Indians in 1945). In other social security measures, assistance is apparently based on unskilled wage-levels, which are artificially propped in the case of Europeans, and on a somewhat arbitrary assessment of the relative standards of the four ethnic groups. This assessment seems to be based less on actual living standards—for a poor white lives no better than a poor Coloured—than on an estimation of what they should be if white superiority is to be maintained. In this way, social security, as administered by the State, becomes yet another instrument for perpetuating and reinforcing the existing colour-hierarchy.

Other social welfare services in which the State, through its Department of Social Welfare, has a share are: child welfare; the maintenance or subsidising of children's institutions and hostels, of homes for convalescents, inebriates and drug addicts, aged or infirm persons, shelters, and almshouses;[92] legal aid bureaux; rent control and emergency housing;[93] workers' hostels; work colonies; the administration of Coloured mission stations and communal reserves; vocational training and sheltered employment; work centres for needy women (European only); free school meals and food supplies at reduced prices for lower-income groups;[94] and the subsidising of social workers' salaries.[95]

In all these services ethnic differentiation is maintained, as it is in the welfare work carried out by the various local authorities, and by the voluntary associations. In the case of the latter, the differentiation may be less in the financial than in the organisational sphere. That is to say, associations which serve more than one ethnic group usually do so through separate committees and sub-associations, in deference to established custom and the attitudes of some European voluntary workers.[96]

Until thirty years ago private social welfare associations, including those attached to the churches, were responsible for almost all social welfare work in the various provinces. Even now, there are great gaps in the Union's social services which the State looks to them, and in many cases subsidises them, to fill. These gaps are the more marked in the case of the Non-European groups, whose needs are so much the greater. A 1938 departmental survey showed that 75 per cent of the 400 associations investigated confined their work to Europeans, and only 8 per cent to work amongst Non-Europeans only.[97] Nine years later, although the position had improved, it could still be said of the 1,000 known social welfare organisations in the Union that 'in the main they do not serve the small town, the rural areas, or the non-Europeans'.[98]

Until recently, in fact, the main aim of private social welfare work has been to assist, and to rehabilitate, those Europeans who have, through incapacity or misfortune, sunk below the social and economic level at which all members of a dominant group should live. A secondary trend in most cases has been the mitigation of the most acute instances of misery and insecurity amongst the subordinate groups, but only within the limits of the existing social structure.[99] The 'lady bountiful' complex has long been prevalent amongst white voluntary social workers, and has evoked a corresponding 'soup-kitchen' mentality amongst many Coloured and other Non-European recipients. It is against both these attitudes that those social workers who believe in encouraging lower-income groups to share in the organisation and responsibility of club and social welfare work have now to struggle.

The value of the past and present services of the private associations must not, however, be underestimated. During the present crisis in inter-group relations in the Union, one of their most important functions is, perhaps, the opportunity which they afford for personal contacts, solicitude and knowledge of one another between the white and non-white groups.

C. SPATIAL SERVICES—HOUSING, PUBLIC BUILDINGS AND TRANSPORT

Equal facilities, if separate, are rarely equal.[1]

Spatial segregation is perhaps the most obvious form of racial discrimination, and one that in an urban setting impinges on the life of the subordinate group at almost every turn. It may therefore evoke sharper reactions in this group than the greater but more dimly perceived discriminations of political and economic life.

Spatial segregation has so far not been applied to the Coloured people to the same degree as to the Africans, although the forms which it has taken in various parts of the Union have varied considerably.

Prior to March 1951 there was no legislation to prevent Coloured people in Cape urban or rural areas from living where they liked, although special legislation provided for the establishment of Coloured land-settlements within limited areas.[2] In practice most Coloured people have tended to concentrate in certain areas, either because of poverty,[3] or because private restricting clauses on recently developed estates have made it difficult for them to purchase or rent property in predominantly European areas.[4] Nevertheless Coloured people and lower-income whites live side by side in such Cape Town districts as Wynberg, Parow, and Salt River.[5] In the old-established suburbs of Newlands and Claremont, the classes and ethnic groups are still further jumbled; upper and middle class whites may live only a few hundred yards from lower-middle or upper-lower class Coloureds. Even the comparatively new development on the Walmer Estate has sections, separated only by a road, in which live upper-class Coloureds and middle-class whites.

On the other hand, municipal housing schemes in Cape Town as in other areas have clearly aimed at increasing residential segregation between Europeans, Coloureds and Africans.[6] The majority of these schemes are sub-economic,[7] and the type of accommodation provided is graded according to the financial resources of and the average level of material culture attained by tenants from the three ethnic groups.

In Cape Town there are one European municipal housing scheme and three African townships, but the major work of the municipal housing authorities is concerned with the Coloured group, for whom 5,000 units, most of them sub-economic, have so far been built.[8] In East London most of the Coloured population of about 4,000 live in the African locations, where some own houses; there is one Coloured sub-economic scheme with 200 houses, a further eighty-six units being under construction. In Port Elizabeth there are about 2,000 sub-economic and 200 economic units for Coloureds; the municipal housing schemes in this city have been held up as a South African model. In Kimberley there are over 500 sub-economic units available for Coloureds, and another 300 projected.[9] Durban has eighty-eight such units, with a further twenty-five under construction and twenty-five economic houses for purchase.

The preponderance of sub-economic housing schemes reflects the low economic status of the majority of Coloured people, for whom home-ownership or decent economic housing will remain a chimera as long as the economic colour-bar operates. The remedy for this is not in the hands of the municipal housing authorities, but the small number of home-ownership schemes does suggest that not all authorities are fully alive to the wider social possibilities of re-housing. A further consequence of this lack is that such townships as Kew Town (Cape Town) and Coronationville (Johannesburg) contain comparatively well-to-do tenants who are unable to move elsewhere and are consequently occupying houses which should go to the lower-income tenants for whom these areas were originally intended.

Amongst Coloured people it is a great grievance that while they live in a *pondokkie* on their own plot of land they may qualify for the municipal franchise, but once ejected and rehoused on a sub-economic housing estate they lose this franchise (to which only tenants who pay a monthly rent are entitled), and are subjected to humiliating controls and interference in their private affairs.[10]

In the smaller urban areas of the Cape, Coloureds have tended by reason of their poverty and the existence of private servitudes on land to be confined to the locations with other Non-Europeans. In these they are subject to the ordinary location regulations,[11] which exert a rigid control over the lives of their inhabitants.[12]

Even prior to the Group Areas Act, Coloureds in the other Provinces, who are everywhere a minority group, were more restricted as to residence, both urban and rural, than in the Cape. In Bloemfontein (O.F.S.), they live in a special Coloured area or in the African location, with the exception of a few exempted owners or occupiers of land.[13] Throughout the Orange Free State Coloureds were forbidden to buy or lease land unless they were either the offspring of a legal marriage with one white parent, or were classed as 'Bastards'.[14]

In the Transvaal and Natal there were no restrictions on Coloured rural land tenure, with the exception of mining land in the former province.[15] In the Transvaal capital of Pretoria, almost the whole small Coloured group lives in the locations. In Johannesburg, Coloureds were debarred from owning land in many areas under the Gold Law or by private servitudes.[16] Many of the Coloured population of about 32,000 live either in rented lodgings in central slum properties scheduled for industrialisation (Denver, Booysens, Ophirton, New Doornfontein, Fordsburg), in European back-yards in Doornfontein and Jeppe, and Indian-owned slums in Vrededorp; others own or rent accommodation in the predominantly African slums of the Western Areas (Newclare and Sophiatown),[17] or in the peri-urban African sections of Kliptown, Jacksonsdrift and Alexandra Township; the fortunate few rent houses in the sub-economic townships of Coronationville and Noordgesig, which contain 1,100 units between them,[18] or, if they are sufficiently well-to-do, own houses in the privately sponsored townships of Albertville and Protea.[19]

The trend towards increased residential segregation found formal expression in the Group Areas Amendment Act (No. 41 of 1950). This Act empowered the Minister of the Interior to enforce residential and trading segregation by stages, by proclaiming areas for the exclusive occupation or ownership, or both, of either white, native or coloured groups, or other sub-groups such as Indians, Chinese or Malays. A person who occupies property in an area set aside for occupation by another race will have to leave it one year after the area is proclaimed, unless he has been granted a permit, is a state employee, visitor or hotel guest, hospital or institution patient, *bona-fide* employee, domestic servant or member of the occupier's family. In areas proclaimed for group ownership, no disqualified person (including an heir) or company may acquire any immovable property except under the authority of a permit; in the case of a private person, the executors of his estate will be allowed one year in which to realise the property; a disqualified company will be given ten years in which to wind up its affairs or move elsewhere. Finally, persons who trade in areas set aside for another group will not have their licences renewed.

On 30th March, 1951,[20] the Act came into formal operation in all Provinces but the Orange Free State, the Cape only being excluded from the occupation clause for two years,[21] which means that inter-racial property transfers and occupation of premises are not yet affected. So far nobody's residential or trading rights are immediately affected, but local administrative bodies have been setting up local advisory boards to complete plans for group areas in their districts. Interested groups such as ratepayers' or tradesmen's associations may request that a certain area should be reserved for a particular ethnic group.[22]

The provisions of this Act, and the almost unfettered discretion allowed to the Minister and his body of inspectors, obviously afford great opportunities for racial discrimination. The initial stage, in which the *status quo* is pegged, confirms the white group in its present advantageous position, and the Act imposes no binding obligation on the administration to make adequate provision for the relative needs of other groups. The permit-system affords an opportunity for pro-longing the occupational and trading rights of Europeans in Non-European areas, on the grounds that Non-Europeans cannot yet provide sufficient professional and commercial services; there is little reason to suppose that similar latitude will be given to Indian, Coloured and Chinese traders in European areas. Although the Minister has to obtain Parliamentary sanction before proclaiming a group area, he need not do so during the first five years of the Act's operation, as far as the Cape and Natal are concerned. A degree of self-government in Non-European areas may be permitted but is not made obligatory by the Act.

Once an area is reserved for ownership, disqualified individuals and companies will necessarily suffer through the compulsion to sell their property to a member of the qualified group within the scheduled time. The Act makes no provision for compensation, and the decision whether the person or company is to be permitted to remain in the area, or is to be granted an extension of time, is left to the Land Tenure Board, whose members are appointed by the Minister, and are unlikely to come from non-white groups. In addition, the Act makes no attempt to correlate residential restrictions with available housing, an omission which could cause far greater hardship to the Non-European than to the European group. Nor is there any direction to the Minister and others concerned with the administration of the Act that segregation should be equitable; nor any mention of the general principles on which they should base their administration.[23] Although the execution of the Act will have to be spread over a considerable number of years, it is already difficult to envisage the wider social consequences with anything but the gravest misgivings.

* * * * *

Only in the last year or so has a definite attempt been made to introduce uniform spatial *apartheid* or segregation. In Cape Town and the Western Cape generally, there was until recently no formal differentiation between Europeans and Non-Europeans in public buildings. All comers were served in their turn by the official concerned, though the latter may not always have been as cordial and courteous to Coloureds as to Europeans. On July 31st, 1949, however, Dr. Dönges, then Minister of Posts and Telegraphs, announced that *apartheid* would be applied in all post offices,[24] with 'separate but equal' treatment for all.[25] Little protest was made by Cape whites,[26] with the exception of the Communist Party, which organised a demonstration denouncing *apartheid* outside the G.P.O. on two successive days in September 1949.

In the Cape Peninsula and Western Cape most municipal authorities do not have segregated counters. *Apartheid* was introduced at Bellville in late 1949, but most other municipalities near Cape Town have not so far followed suit; the Town Clerk of Cape Town has stated that there is no question of *apartheid* in Cape Town municipal offices.[27]

In general, the absence of provisions for spatial segregation may be correlated with the presence of a large number of Coloured municipal voters, but there is undoubtedly a growing demand for segregation by Europeans even in the 'liberal' Western Cape.[28] In Malmesbury, only forty miles from Cape Town, and with a considerable number of Coloured ratepayers, the Council has declared its Town Hall to be reserved for Europeans only, and has decided to build a separate hall for the Coloured community.[29]

Segregation in museums, parks, zoological gardens, public baths, camping sites and beaches will be described in Chapter VII. Separate public conveniences are provided in most cities, with the exception of Cape Town, where those in the centre of the town at least are used by all ethnic groups. Lifts are reserved for Europeans only in some public and privately-owned buildings in the Transvaal.[30] The arrangements for segregation in the House of Assembly have already been described. * * * * *

Similar variations in degree of segregation occur in the provision of transport facilities. The greatest degree of discrimination occurs in government-controlled, the least in privately-owned transport. Those Coloured people who are prosperous enough to possess their own cars, or the less well-to-do who own motor-cycles, horse-drawn carts or even bicycles, are in a position to avoid using transport in which such discrimination may occur.[31]

On the state-owned railways there has long been segregated accommodation for Europeans and Non-Europeans,[32] officially in all classes.[33] The accommodation allotted to first and second-class Non-European travellers is inadequate,[34] and on country lines is often not available at all. There are few, if any, buffet coaches for Non-Europeans, though some trains have Coloured or African waiters to serve Non-European passengers in their seats. It is apparently the practice to place Non-European coaches at the front and rear of mixed trains, positions where they in practice act as buffers to other coaches in the event of an accident.[35]

An exception to the segregation rule was found on the Cape suburban line until September 1948, when *apartheid* was partially introduced. Certain first-class carriages were set aside for Europeans only, while the remainder of the train in all classes was open to all races.[36] This arrangement was tested by Mr. A. E. Abdurahman, a member of the Trains Apartheid Resistance Committee, whose case was finally upheld by the Appellate Division in May 1950. In the meantime, however, the position had been regularised by the promulgation of the Railways and Harbours Amendment Act (No. 49 of 1949).[37]

As far as the Union railway lines are concerned, segregation has long been in force in waiting-rooms in some country districts in the Cape, as well as in the other provinces.[38] Over the last year or so, however, it has been extended. Separate ticket-offices, platform seats, entrances, exits and waiting-rooms (where possible) have been provided, even in the main Cape Town station.

Although facilities are in theory 'separate but equal', Coloureds and other Non-Europeans do not get the same value for their money as railway passengers.[39] Apart from the material inadequacy of the facilities provided for them, they are also exposed to the frequent arrogance and discourtesy of lower railway officials, porters (almost all of whom are white) and railway police. Discrimination of all kinds would appear to be intensified outside the larger urban areas.

Under the existing Act,[40] local Road Transportation Boards may stipulate the class of people to be conveyed when a motor-carrier certificate is issued. These powers have not been used to the same extent by all local boards. Bus and tram services in Cape Town are used by members of all groups,[41] although here again there is a good deal of European resentment, some of it based not so much on racial as on hygienic objections. The same is true of Paarl (Western Cape) and Kimberley (Northern Cape). In East London (Eastern Cape) no Non-European may use a European bus on a route served by a Non-European bus service during peak periods. In Port Elizabeth, Non-Europeans are not allowed to sit downstairs in certain buses.[42] In Johannesburg, Coloureds may use the back seats on the top decks of European buses if seats are available, or the African buses. In Pretoria and Bloemfontein all Coloureds use the African bus-services.[43]

I

In August 1949 Dr. Malan announced the Government's intention of enforcing *apartheid* in road transportation, and in October the National Transport Commission was instructed to investigate the possibility of securing separation of Non-European and European passengers, where it was not already in force. The Commission was also to inquire into the 'existing state of road passenger services, and whether these services are adequate, efficient and economical'.[44] The two terms of reference would seem scarcely compatible in view of the necessity for duplicating or curtailing services, increasing operational costs and fares,[45] and of the general dislocation envisaged by Cape Peninsula transport officials if *apartheid* were to be enforced as stated.[46]

This Commission has now reported, and a Bill to amend the existing Transportation Act was to come before Parliament in the 1951 session, but was subsequently postponed until 1952. It is said to contain provisions for enforcing complete *apartheid* in motor-carrier transportation throughout the Union, and for removing the control of road transportation from the municipalities. Another clause will enable local Boards to set aside seats in a vehicle for certain groups, thereby regularising the arrangements which already exist in such areas as Port Elizabeth and Durban.[47]

This legislation will also affect taxis, licensing arrangements for which vary according to the area at present. In Cape Town, owner-drivers may be white or Coloured, and usually drive passengers of all races.[48] The same applies in Port Elizabeth, but in Northern cities such as Johannesburg, licences are issued to Europeans for the conveyance of Europeans only, and to Non-Europeans for the conveyance of Non-Europeans only.

There is as yet no absolute segregation in air travel, probably because it would be uneconomic, and this means of locomotion is used only by foreign non-whites, usually prominent people, or a comparatively few well-to-do Coloureds and other Non-Europeans, to whose behaviour even the most fanatical racialist could raise no objection.[49] The air-crews and staff do not appear to differentiate in their treatment of passengers. Non-Europeans seem to avoid waiting-rooms and buffets, although there is, with one exception, no segregation as yet in force.

This exception is the international airport at Palmietfontein, Johannesburg, where a separate lounge-restaurant with toilet-room has been built for use by Non-Europeans on domestic routes. A similar lounge-restaurant is to be built adjoining the overseas section for Non-Europeans flying on international services. This is likely to give rise to a great deal of unpleasantness, particularly in the case of dark-skinned foreign diplomats.

Even more unpleasantness was recently generated by a set of '*apartheid* instructions' issued to S.A.A. staff. Hostesses have been told to tag all linen and blankets used by Non-Europeans with a special red tag;

such tagged articles will not be washed or cleaned with the rest, but will be sent for 'special hygienic processing and dry cleaning'. Linen towels in washrooms have now been replaced by paper towels to obviate the risk of European and Non-European passengers using the same towel. Cutlery, glass and china are also given 'special attention' when they are washed.[50]

Segregation for Coloureds and other Non-Europeans travelling by sea is confined to sleeping accommodation and table accommodation, as far as the Union-Castle Line (the main passenger carrier) is concerned. The staff, crew and many passengers are from the United Kingdom, and, while many are not free of colour-prejudice, do not adopt the same rigid attitudes in contacts with coloured passengers as do most South Africans.[51]

White demands for spatial segregation do not end with the grave. Cemeteries too are segregated,[52] while whites and non-whites may not everywhere travel to their ultimate resting-place in the same hearses.[53] It is outside the scope of the social scientist to inquire into events beyond that point, but there seems little doubt that many South African whites would be greatly put out to find no colour-bar in Heaven.[54]

CHAPTER SEVEN

SOCIAL LIFE AND RELATIONSHIPS

That it is so hard to keep oneself really humane, and so to be a standard-bearer of civilisation, that is the tragic element in the problem of the relations between white and coloured men . . .[1]

T HIS chapter is concerned with the sphere in which the social colour-bar operates. This sphere includes not only social life in the popular and more limited sense, but also the nexus of activities centring around the churches and other inter-racial associations whose ends are less restricted than those of the political, economic, educational and welfare associations already described.

It is the sphere in which white South Africans demand segregation most vehemently, and in which, rightly or wrongly, they regard the threat to their dominance as greatest. All other forms of segregation, in schools, places of work, transport and elsewhere, are conceived of as means of avoiding the greatest danger of all, social equality, which, it is held, would lead inevitably to amalgamation and the extinction of the white race.[2]

In the static society based on slavery there was little need for formal sanctions to uphold the social colour-bar, as the social distance between master and slave, white and non-white, was so great. In the late nineteenth century, there were signs of a weakening of the colour-bar in Cape Town itself, usually between Coloured and white artisans of approximately the same social status. Recently, the continued status rise of individual Coloureds and the spread of Northern colour-attitudes to the Cape have resulted in an increased imposition of formal sanctions aimed at social segregation. Nevertheless, custom still plays a very large part in maintaining the inviolability of white social life.

This chapter is sub-divided into three sections, concerned with differentiation and discrimination in recreation, religious life and social relationships.

Recreation includes cultural, spatial, sports and spectator facilities. In the cultural field, facilities are being increasingly restricted, where they were formerly available. In practice, this applies mainly to Cape

126

Town, as such facilities have rarely if ever been open to Non-Europeans elsewhere.

Privately-owned theatres in Cape Town are now reserved for Europeans only,[3] with the result that Coloured people have no opportunity of attending plays or concerts, unless these are held in the University or the City Hall. Here the Municipality does not permit exclusion, but Non-Europeans are usually seated in special blocks.

Recently a considerable controversy broke out in Cape Town over the decision by the Board of Trustees to ban Non-Europeans from the Labia Theatre, a newly-built theatre in which the various Cape Town repertory and amateur companies stage their performances. A number of Coloured and European individuals, and such bodies as the Cape Town Repertory Company (part owner of the building) and the Institute of Race Relations, protested against this whittling-down of rights.

On the other hand, the Afrikaans-speaking theatre group, the *Kaapstadse Afrikaanse Toneelvereniging* (K.A.T.), favoured the establishment of a separate Coloured theatre, while the chairman of the Board justified the colour-bar on box-office grounds, claiming that to admit Non-Europeans might cause a falling-off in European audiences. The dispute was aggravated by the fact that the theatre had been built with the proceeds of a public appeal for funds, to which a number of Coloured supporters had contributed, there being no mention of a possible colour-bar at the time.[4] By the end of 1950 the Cape Town Repertory Company had been forced to capitulate, by the threat that its annual Government grant of £250 would be withdrawn if it permitted mixed audiences.[5]

The Company therefore tried the experiment of having a weekly Non-European night with specially reduced prices. Response was very poor, both for this performance and for one organised by the K.A.T. in the Town Hall, as a result of a boycott campaign conducted by the Non-European weekly *Torch*,[6] and possibly also because only a fairly small number of Coloureds have acquired the play-going habit as yet.

At the same time suggestions began to appear in the Cape Town press as to the desirability of a separate Coloured theatre building where the Coloured community might 'develop its own talent', on a site 'within walking distance of their homes'.[7] The Repertory Company had already, at the request of the Coloured cultural organisation, the Eoan Group, agreed to train Coloured producers free for 'work amongst their own people'.[8]

Coloureds and other Non-Europeans are excluded from European theatres not only as audience but as performers. There is no opportunity for Coloured actors to join European companies, or for Coloured companies to perform before mixed or European audiences, save in occasional charity or amateur shows. The same rule of exclusion applies in the case of Coloured singers, musicians and dancers. This colour-bar in art has had a stunting effect on the growth of a native South African drama. The real life of the country is indissolubly bound up with its coloured peoples, whose presence on the stage with white actors is forbidden by convention.[9]

Separate cinemas (or bioscopes, as they are often called by South Africans) exist in all major towns, while a few of the older cinemas in smaller towns have segregated seating arrangements. Most of the Non-European cinemas in Cape Town are greatly inferior in material facilities, probably because they cater for largely poor and lower-class audiences. The films shown are usually serials, 'Westerns' and others of a similarly naïve type. Occasionally 'improving' films such as 'Hamlet' or 'Oliver Twist' are put on. Films dealing with colour problems or showing any form of social contact between white and non-white are of course taboo, but this restriction usually applies to European audiences also.[10]

Coloured people of the upper and upper-middle classes are thus deprived of the opportunity to see most of the better films. In addition, they sometimes complain that Non-European cinemas are the resort of the rowdier lower-class elements, who drink, smoke *dagga*, fight with knives or bicycle chains, and generally make conditions unpleasant for the rest of the audience.

There is no segregation in the South African Art Gallery in Cape Town. An official stated that 'there was no demand for it as yet'.[11] He added that large numbers of Non-Europeans (mostly Coloureds) came in on Sunday afternoons, while Europeans appeared to him to stay away at that time.[12] There are no toilet facilities at the Gallery, an arrangement which reflects a somewhat typical Capetonian tendency to evade the issue rather than proceed to open segregation or the reverse.[13] Private shows of painting, sculpture and so on are usually arranged in the galleries of local book-shops, and are open to members of all races who patronise the shops.

The South African Museum at Cape Town is open to members of all races at all times. This is also the case in Port Elizabeth, Kimberley, East London, and Pretoria.[14] In Bloemfontein, special days are set aside for all Non-Europeans, while in Johannesburg no Non-Europeans may visit the museum. The South African Library in Cape Town has no colour-bar, despite the *apartheid* provisions of the 1949 Provincial Ordinance dealing with libraries. This decision has resulted in financial loss to the Municipality, which is thereby debarred from receiving more than its present subsidy.[15] The Provincial scheme applies mainly in rural areas, where facilities are supposed to be 'separate but equal'.

Spatial facilities for recreation include bathing-beaches, camping-sites, baths, parks, gardens, zoos, cafés, restaurants and hotels. The provision of bathing-beaches is regulated by most municipalities under the enabling clauses of the Seashore Act.[16] Cape Town and the Cape Division have, however, no regulations on the subject. Officials declare that voluntary segregation has always been maintained by common consent, or what is sometimes referred to as a 'gentleman's agreement', based on custom and tradition. The areas traditionally frequented by the Coloured group are by no means so extensive or attractive as those appropriated by Europeans for their own use.[17] They are further endangered by the development of European townships on former camping-sites, resulting in objections by the new residents to continued camping; also by the increase in the Peninsula's tourist-trade, and consequent encroachment on formerly neutral or Coloured beaches and camping-areas.[18]

The spread of the bathing and camping habit has given rise to demands for increased facilities such as water, sanitary conveniences and so on; here again Coloured people feel that they are not receiving equal treatment.[19] Undoubtedly the trend is towards increased and ultimately formal segregation. In recent years there has been talk of developing Strandfontein, a rather barren stretch of sand-dunes about twelve miles from the city centre, with very poor communications, into a Coloured sea-resort. Coloured people regard this as an attempt to deprive them of nearer and more pleasant areas which they now use, and the scheme was turned down by a meeting of European and Non-European ratepayers in August 1950.

Other recreational facilities vary according to the municipality concerned.[20] Cape Town provides bath-houses and swimming-baths for Non-Europeans only, while its gardens, parks[21] and Zoo are open to all-comers, and there are no benches 'for Europeans only', except on railway platforms, which are under State jurisdiction. Kimberley has a special Coloured swimming-pool and no *apartheid* in gardens or parks. There are no municipal baths for Non-Europeans in East London, Port Elizabeth, Pretoria or Johannesburg.[22] In Bloemfontein Coloureds may use the bath in the African location, which provides separate showers for the two groups.

There is no *apartheid* in parks, gardens or zoos in Johannesburg,[23] Paarl, Port Elizabeth, East London and Pretoria, although the last three have special benches for Europeans only. In Bloemfontein parks and zoos are open to Non-Europeans only on certain days, and benches are marked 'Non-Europeans' and 'Europeans' respectively.[24]

The prejudice against bathing with Coloureds seems to be equalled by that against eating or even staying in the same establishment with them. With a very few exceptions, no café, restaurant or hotel[25] will accept Coloured clients, unless they are able to pass as white.[26] The only exception encountered was the open-air café-restaurant in Cape Town's Municipal Gardens, which is theoretically colour-blind.[27] This discrimination falls most harshly on upper and upper-middle-class Coloureds, who must usually make arrangements to stay in a private house if they visit another town.[28]

Dance-halls and private or public subscription dances are all for

Europeans only, although Cape Town municipal halls may be hired by any group for dances and other occasions. These dances were, until the passing of the 1950 Immorality Act, sometimes attended by white men, usually of the lower class.

European social clubs have of course a strictly segregated membership, which in the case of some of the more exclusive English men's clubs excludes Afrikaners and Jews. In one such Cape Town club, however, it is said that eminent Non-Europeans are occasionally entertained as guests by individual members, in both the club proper and the Ladies' Annexe.

There is an almost complete absence[29] of inter-racial participation in organised sport in South Africa. This does not mean that the Coloured people and other Non-Europeans are completely excluded from the physical propinquity and contact which is inevitably involved in most sports. They are, however, as in domestic and other social contacts, involved in physical contact only in a capacity involving the master-servant relationship, as changing-room attendants, groundsmen and so on.

This inferiority of status appears to mitigate if not to cancel out the otherwise unbearable implications of physical contact on an equal basis. Perhaps the best known instance of such a relationship is Gamat, the Malay attendant to the Rugby teams at the Western Province Sports Ground at Newlands, Cape Town, who also carries out the function of a masseur, and is said to pronounce certain good-luck charms[30] before every match, for the benefit of his home team.

The reason for this segregation in sport, a sphere in which group barriers are commonly supposed to become blurred,[31] may be partly due to such factors as educational segregation,[32] the schools being the major initiators of organised sports, to economic class differences and to residential distance. Above all, however, it is a reflection of the general colour-hierarchy, in which it is unthinkable that Coloured or African boxers or all-in wrestlers should fight and possibly defeat white opponents before mixed audiences, or audiences consisting of either Europeans or Non-Europeans.[33]

This ban is not confined to Non-Europeans within the Union. Prior to the 1949 visit of the New Zealand Rugby side, negotiations practically broke down because the South Africans requested that the Maori members of the team (nearly half of the total) should be left behind. The reason given officially was that they might be taken for local Non-Europeans and unpleasant incidents might occur in hotels and restaurants. The 'All Blacks' finally sent over an all-white team.[34]

The Union is by this attitude deprived of the possibility of including the most talented Non-Europeans in international sporting events. A recent case in point was that of the 21-year-old Coloured tennis champion, David Samaai of Paarl, who was sent to England on money raised by the Coloured community, and qualified for Wimbledon, although he was knocked out in the first round. The Cape Town press wrote him up quite fully at the time, but did not class him even as an unofficial 'Springbok'. Conversely, Coloured sportsmen are deprived of the wider competition and expert instruction which are essential to any player if he is to reach the highest class.

It is possible that this attitude of exclusiveness on the part of European sporting associations may be relaxed as more Non-European players of the first grade emerge. Such a process has occurred in the United States, which is frequently represented at international events by coloured runners, boxers and so on, while coloured baseball-players seem to have become quite a feature of local American teams, at least in the northern States.[35] In the Union at present, however, the absence of Non-European participants in teams representing South Africa against overseas teams is giving rise to a certain number of demonstrations hostile to the home team by Coloured spectators.[36]

There are no colour-blind European sports associations, and the European associations show little if any interest in their Non-European opposite numbers.[37] Nevertheless, sports-participation, whether active or spectator, plays a very considerable part in the life of Coloured people, especially in the urban areas, where facilities are better.[38] The *Torch* and *Sun* both run a sports page, giving Coloured sports news and reports of major European sporting encounters such as Test matches and racing results.

There is a certain amount of segregation in the provision of spectator facilities. Most large sports-grounds all over the Union, including Cape Town, have separate blocks of seats for Non-Europeans, usually those giving the worst view or most exposed to the sun or wind. While it is true that many Coloured spectators would in any case find themselves in such places because they could afford nothing better, such segregation is particularly hard on the minority who are able to pay for better facilities.[39]

The Kenilworth Race Course is an exception, as the various stands are open to all-comers according to their purse, with the exception of the enclosure reserved for members of the Turf Club.[40] Race-going is a favourite Saturday afternoon pastime for the Cape Town Coloureds, and there are occasions when up to a quarter of the Grand Stand's patrons appear to be Coloured or Malay.[41] Certain leading boxing promoters have not so far introduced segregated seating at any of their fights.[42]

*   *   *   *   *

In the United States, we are told, the churches and religion are 'on the whole a force strengthening the American creed'.[43] In South Africa, the functions which the various churches fulfil cannot be described so straightforwardly. In the past, the educational and social work of the missionaries played the major rôle in the acculturation of the Coloured People. To-day, one major group of churches actively

supports existing colour-divisions, while the majority of the others
have failed to modify the paternalistic attitudes of their white congregations, to which even their ministers have for the most part succumbed.
Indeed, it may be claimed that the propagation of true Christianity
in South Africa has met with more success amongst the Coloured
people than amongst the whites.

The principal religious affiliations amongst the Coloured group in
1946 are given in Appendix F. Ninety per cent of all Coloureds are
Christians, while 4.7 per cent of the remainder are Moslems (Cape
Malays).[44] The Dutch Reformed Churches had the largest percentage
(31.5 per cent) of Coloured Christians, and showed a gain on the 1936
figure of 29.2 per cent. Several informants have claimed that this
denomination has lost large numbers of Coloured and African members
since it accepted the policy of total *apartheid* early in 1950.[45] Such
a trend would only become evident in the 1951 Census figures, which
will not be available for several years.[46]

The Coloured membership of the Anglican Church shows a slight
drop from 21.2 per cent to 20 per cent of the total Coloured group,
and so, somewhat surprisingly, does the Congregational Union (11.3
per cent to 10.8 per cent).[47] The number of Coloured Roman Catholics
has increased from 4.7 per cent to 6.1 per cent of the total in the decade
after 1936. The Methodists show a moderate drop (10.6 per cent to
9.7 per cent), the Lutherans a larger one (7.7 per cent to 5.2 per cent),
while the Presbyterians and Baptists have remained static at .8 per cent
and .4 per cent respectively.

Amongst the factors which have produced these and similar changes
in Coloured denominational adherence are the racial attitudes of the
various religious bodies, the extent of their proselytising activities, and
the amount of educational work undertaken by them[48] amongst
Coloured children, as a reasonable proportion of their pupils may be
reckoned as converts.[49]

The Dutch Reformed Church[50] is the church of almost all Afrikaners,
that is to say, of over half the white population. It plays a far more
important rôle in Afrikaner life and thought than any denomination
other than the Roman Catholic Church does elsewhere to-day.[51] In
the rural districts the minister or *predikant* occupies a position of high
authority, while a former minister, Dr. D. F. Malan, is now Prime
Minister of the Union.

The attitudes of the D.R.C. to the Coloured People have varied
from time to time. This Church did little or no work amongst slaves
or Hottentots until evangelical influences began to be felt in the early
nineteenth century. However, the prospect of a large accession of
Coloured members caused the Synod of 1857, albeit unwillingly, and
as a concession to 'the weakness of some members', to make provision
for the 'congregation assembled or to be assembled from among the
Heathen to enjoy its religious privileges in a separate building.'[52]

Since its establishment in 1881, the great majority of Coloured members have belonged to the Dutch Reformed Mission Church,[53] which has separate ministers[54] (with a much lower stipend), separate congregations, buildings and church organisations.[55] It has the right to form its own synods,[56] but owing to the poverty of its congregations is financially dependent to a considerable degree on its Mother-Church.

While the great majority of D.R.C. ministers and congregations believe firmly in *apartheid* and white *baasskap* or supremacy,[57] there is not complete unanimity on this point in the Church.[58] This is even more true of some (though not all) ministers in the D.R.M.C., particularly those whose congregations are able to support them without assistance from the Mother-Church, and who can therefore choose their minister. An informant estimated that about 10 per cent of all Coloured *platteland* (rural) congregations are now self-supporting. In such cases, local rings and Church councils may, and often do, adopt attitudes quite opposed to those of the Mother-Church.

Two recent examples of such independent action were the publication of the report on the living conditions of the rural Coloured by the Oudtshoorn Ring (referred to in Chapter V), and the condemnation of *apartheid* by the Rev. I. D. Morkel, until late 1950 the Coloured manager of the D.R.M. School at Crawford, Cape Town, and chairman of the Wynberg Ring, who declared that Coloured people were coming to Cape Town or going overseas to escape persecution in the rural areas.[59]

At a meeting of the Cape D.R.C. Synod in October 1949,[60] it was stated by Mr. J. C. du Toit (a member of the Provincial Council and an elder of the D.R.C.) that Coloured missionaries might have to be put under permanent control instead of the three-year probationary period which they now had to serve.[61] On 15th November, 1949, the Synod also issued an official statement on race relations, advocating 'separate vertical development for each group', according to its own character and needs, and in accordance with its past history and future development.[62]

This concept of vertical *apartheid* was intended to supply a moral basis for the Nationalist Party's programme. It might indeed have done so, had there been any possibility of carrying out such a programme at this stage of South African development, or any genuine intention on the part of white legislators and voters to make the necessary sacrifice of land and non-white labour involved. The genuine idealism of some D.R.C. advocates of *apartheid* should not be overlooked. It does not, however, reflect the views of the majority of their congregations, to whom *apartheid* means rather that non-whites should live under white control in segregated areas which are unable to supply them with a living, from which they emerge to work at a low wage when required, and to which they return when they are not needed, or when they are too ill or too old to work. The reaction of the administration to the D.R.C's. alarming 'blue-print for *apartheid*' was therefore in effect to repudiate it,[63] by pointing out that many years would be needed to achieve *apartheid*, and that the non-white groups were too undeveloped to manage their own affairs and would always need white guidance and supervision.

In early 1951 a special commission submitted a report to the D.R.C. Synod on the Biblical basis of racial *apartheid*, which, it was claimed, meant in South Africa 'the separate development along their own lines of non-European races in political, economic, social and church spheres, so that each race maintains its identity'. An attempt by a delegate to substitute the phrase 'parallel development' for 'racial *apartheid*' was defeated, as was another proposal to add a rider to the effect that *apartheid* was in the interest of self-preservation and of white civilisation in future generations.[64]

While the D.R.C. is strongest in the rural districts, the Anglican Church finds most of its support in the urban areas and the coastal districts. Although most members of its white congregations share prevalent race-attitudes, the Church has on the whole adopted a remarkably liberal attitude on colour questions,[65] and has carried out a great deal of social and educational work.

Like other churches, however, it has been unable to function totally unaffected by local conditions, and the ignorance and poverty of many of its Coloured members have inevitably given rise to a paternalistic attitude in most of its ministers.[66] Moreover, the Anglican Church, despite the good works of its ministers and some laymen, has had less success in modifying the race-attitudes of most of the upper-class English-speaking South Africans who form the backbone of its white congregations.[67] Because of these attitudes, a number of churches, some in the country, others in Cape Town itself, have instituted separate Sunday-school and confirmation classes, and have reserved blocks of seats at the side or back for Non-European worshippers.[68] At times there have been difficulties over the sharing of the communion cup, although these are not tolerated by the ministry in general.[69]

These attitudes and practices were roundly denounced in November 1950 by the Anglican Synod, which associated itself with a resolution passed at the 1948 Lambeth Conference that no one should be ineligible for any position in the Church by reason of his race or colour. The resolution denounced the tendency of present legislation to decrease the rights of the individual and to relegate Non-Europeans to a position of permanent inferiority.[70]

As elsewhere, the Roman Catholic Church in South Africa is concerned less with distinctions of colour than with those of creed and culture,[71] despite the fact that many of its white adherents (usually of Irish, Portuguese or English extraction) share the attitudes of the local white group.[72] There are no separate church buildings or segregated seats in church. European and Coloured priests are trained in Ireland or Rome, where there is no colour-bar.

There is only one Coloured priest at present, in a Coloured district in Cape Town.[73] There is no distinction as to stipends. On the question of intermarriage, an informant stated that priests, being civil officers, must abide by the legal ban, but as priests cannot object. If the occasion were to arise, the priest would explain that there could be no civil consequences, and that the couple by living together would be committing an offence under the Immorality Amendment Act. If they still insisted, he would have to marry them in the Church. No such case has so far arisen.[74] The great increase in the number of Roman Catholic schools for Non-Europeans,[75] and the general spread of Roman Catholicism, has of late been worrying the Dutch Reformed Church. The Cape D.R.C. has a 'Committee for Vigilance against the Roman Catholic Danger', which in October 1949 urged the opening of an Action Fund to oppose the spread of Catholicism. Presumably the D.R.C. is mainly concerned about the possibility of losing its Coloured and African members,[76] as it is difficult to imagine that many Afrikaners would change their denomination.

The Congregational Union of South Africa is a predominantly Coloured church, with three Non-Europeans (two Coloured, one African), out of seven Moderators. In 1946, the highest office, that of Chairman, was held by a Coloured minister, the Rev. C. Z. Hendrickse. The old connection of this Church with the great defender of Coloured rights in the nineteenth century, the London Missionary Society, and the high degree of local autonomy possessed by each congregation, are undoubtedly reasons for continued Coloured adherence to this Church.

Coloured and European ministers are trained separately, though their qualifications must be the same (matriculation or its equivalent). Stipends depend upon the arrangements made by each congregation. Congregations are apparently racially separate for the most part,[77] but there is full inter-racial co-operation 'in all courts of the Church', to quote a European minister.[78]

The old German missionary societies (Berlin, Rhenish and Moravian), which did so much for Coloured advancement in the nineteenth century, have shifted their main activities to other parts of Africa. Nevertheless, they still maintain schools and congregations amongst the Coloured people.[79] Most of their members are Coloured, as one would expect from the field of their original work.

The Moravian Church has many Coloured ministers, trained at separate seminaries but paid equal stipends. Several are said to occupy high office in the Church. The few Europeans who attend services are separately seated. The Church is opposed to *apartheid* and advocates the Christian unity of all races.[80]

The Berlin Missionary Society has some Coloured ministers, four in charge of congregations. There is no separate seating, although it is said that Europeans tend to sit apart. There are some separate church buildings in larger towns, and a separate catechism. There is reported to be very little co-operation between Europeans and Non-Europeans in church associations.

The Methodist Church, to which in 1946 belonged nearly 10 per cent of all Christian Coloureds, is strongly opposed to the colour-bar. At its conference in November 1950 it endorsed a declaration on racial policy in Southern Africa issued by the Methodist Church of Great Britain, declaring that all who wish to worship God should be welcome in any church; that while not advocating a general racial admixture it could not allow that such mixed marriages were contrary to any law of God, nor that they should be penalised by any law of man; that it was opposed to any system excluding Non-Europeans as such from the general franchise; advocating a large development of Non-European education, and adopting the motto put forward by the Christian Council of South Africa: 'Not *Apartheid*, but *Eendrag*' (Not Segregation but Unity through Team Work).[81]

Mixed racial congregations are not formally forbidden, but on the whole church-goers of different ethnic groups attend churches in their own areas. At Synods and Conferences Communion is administered to all irrespective of race. Church activities are for the most part conducted by parallel organisations, between which there is, however, considerable co-operation. There are nine Coloured ministers out of a total of over 500. They are trained at the Non-European College of Fort Hare, or extra-collegiately. The training is the same as for Europeans, as is the minimum academic qualification (Junior Certificate). Stipends differ quite considerably, being £375 for Europeans, £225 for Coloureds and £180 for Africans; these figures include cost of living allowances. So far the highest office attained by Non-European ministers is that of Circuit Superintendent, although there is no formal ban on their achieving the highest office.

The Presbyterian Church, most of whose Non-European work is done amongst Africans, officially subscribes to the 'Not *Apartheid* but *Eendrag*' principle. Nevertheless, one of its Moderators, the Rev. D. A. Diederich, gave a notable illustration of the way in which Christianity may take on local colour by a public declaration of his enthusiastic support for *apartheid*, because it was in keeping with Christian principles and was the only way the Coloured people could come into their own as a race.[82]

The Salvation Army may be classified as a religious or a welfare organisation, but will be included here. Cape membership is said to be approximately half-Coloured, half-European. Local units have no official colour-bar, but are usually more or less European or Coloured, a division which roughly corresponds to residential distribution.

An official said that a very obvious Coloured who wanted to join up in a European area might be given the suggestion that he should join nearer his own residence. Coloured corps had so far had European officers, as it was thought that Coloureds preferred this. A policy of training Coloured officers was now being introduced. Hospitals had to be segregated, in order to conform to provincial requirements.

This brief account of the practice and policy of the major Christian denominations shows the difficulty which even the least segregationist churches have in combating the general attitudes of their white congregations. At a high level, church leaders constantly urge the need for a more Christian attitude, and condemn retrogressive and oppressive measures such as are being applied to-day,[83] but the majority of white church-goers have still to be convinced that the 'brotherhood of man' includes non-whites.

*   *   *   *   *

Other social and cultural associations, particularly those with overseas connections, have also been compelled to adapt their attitudes to local *mores*. In some local organisations, however, there is no problem for the organisers, as membership is restricted to Europeans. This is true of all Afrikaans-speaking associations, with the exception of the Students' Christian Association of South Africa, which appears to be predominantly Afrikaans-speaking, but has Coloured and African members and officials.

Several overseas associations have avoided direct conflict with local race-attitudes by setting up separate and parallel organisations for the various ethnic groups, the European organisation usually being the first and senior. Amongst them are the Y.M.C.A., Boy Scouts Association and the South African Legion of the British Empire Service League. In the latter the Coloured[84] section is subsidised from National Headquarters. Coloured members pay the same subscription (5s. per annum), while Africans pay less. Coloured members in need attend the same central office or their own branch office and receive the same aid as Europeans. The Coloured branches have a Coloured National Chairman who attends the annual Congress.[85] Inter-racial relations appear to be cordial.[86]

All four sections within the Boy Scouts Association are officially autonomous, but the European section is called the parent body, and does the clerical work for all sections. Despite the lack of an official colour-bar Non-Europeans are not represented on the South African Scout Council, which decides all relations with overseas scout organisations.[87] When joint rallies are held, the sections are marshalled separately.[88]

A Coloured scouter said that some Coloured scouters in the Cape had recently resigned because of the parent body's *apartheid* policy. The Coloured section had originally refused the European offer to run its secretarial work because it was felt to be a step back (more recently it has accepted this assistance). He also declared that inter-section relations were cordial only at higher levels, while a European boy scout would not even salute a Coloured one in the street.

A similar separatist tendency is said to be evident in the small Coloured association of the Y.M.C.A., another association which has no official colour-bar, but which has separate clubs for Europeans and Non-Europeans. In this case, however, a Non-European (African) sits on the National Council, and an African was amongst the delegates who represented the South African Y.M.C.A. at a World Conference in Edinburgh.

The Girl Guides' Association, unlike the Scouts and Y.M.C.A., is affiliated to the British and not merely to the international body. Officially it has no colour-bar, but Coloured and African Guides have their own companies with leaders of their own group. Higher ranks, however, have so far been held by Europeans. Before 1936, similar Coloured and other Non-European organisations had their applications for affiliation rejected four times. In 1936 they were allowed in as a separate Wayfarers' Branch, and in 1945 on an equal footing.[89]

Here again, relations at higher levels appear to be cordial. The Guide Movement is said to be the object of some official suspicion, as it organised an All-African Conference in Johannesburg in early 1948, which was attended by 100 visiting guides of all races and colours. The problems involved in arranging accommodation, feeding and transport for the visitors were very great, and a number of un-pleasant incidents occurred on buses, in cafés and at the airport.

In general, even those associations which have no formal colour-bar tend to be predominantly or entirely European at high levels. This may of course be due to Non-European apathy or distrust,[90] and to the comparative lack of able and qualified Non-Europeans who would be willing to serve on such bodies, as much as to covert European prejudice or paternalism.[91]

Such considerations would appear to apply to the S.A. Institute of Race Relations, one of the most unprejudiced of all European-initiated associations,[92] to the various Joint Councils and Civil Rights Leagues, the Springbok Legion (a left-wing ex-servicemen's organisation), the National Council of Women,[93] the Penal Reform League, and the National War Memorial Health Fund. Some of these have one or more Non-Europeans on their national councils, but all remain predomi-nantly European in leadership and composition.[94]

An organisation with a reversed colour-bar (excluding Europeans but also other Non-Europeans) is the Eoan Group, a Cape Town cultural organisation founded in 1934 by an Englishwoman; this trains Coloured children only in elocution, acting, ballet, and singing, and also gives general character-training and instruction in hygiene. The Principal and most teachers are now Coloured.

*   *   *   *   *

The inter-racial social contacts involved in associational life remain artificial, in face of the overpowering social colour-bar which prevails in South Africa. Inter-racial meetings are held in buildings which will permit them (usually belonging to churches, the 'mixed' universities, or such municipalities as Cape Town). Tea is sometimes drunk at these meetings, and a Non-European may be offered a lift home, but there social mingling ends in the majority of cases.[95] European officials sometimes attend Non-European public functions. In Cape Town and other large cities various prominent Europeans in official positions even attend formal or semi-formal receptions given by the members of the Coloured or other Non-European communities,[96] though such actions are deplored by various sections of the white population.[97]

Where informal social relations are concerned, it should be emphasised that even in the absence of a colour-bar comparatively few Coloured people would have the entrée to white upper or even middle-class society on purely class grounds. Amongst the urban skilled artisans of Cape Town, however, who meet at work on a more or less equal basis regardless of colour, there seems in the past to have been considerable social intercourse. Several informants recollect playing with white neighbours' children when young, and attending mixed gatherings in the homes of white families, who, they emphasised, were definitely not Poor Whites (although they may have been 'pass-for-whites' or recent immigrants—S.P.). It was stated that this type of social intercourse had largely ceased, and there was now little neighbourliness between white and Coloured neighbours in 'mixed' streets.[98]

With such exceptions, inter-racial etiquette has long crystallised into a pattern which fully upholds the social structure. The best instance of this is probably to be found in the differing usages evolved in the Afrikaans language for Europeans and Non-Europeans.

In direct speech Coloureds and other Non-Europeans are customarily addressed in the second person singular (*jy*), or, if in a group, in the corresponding second person plural (*julle*).[99] They are not, except in the case of some privileged old family retainers, expected to use the same forms in return, but the third person singular, with a title.

In the old days, slaves were called *Pay*[100] or *Jong* and had to address their master as *Seur*, while hired Hottentot servants expected to have their non-slave status recognised by being called *Hotnot* or *Booi* (Boy), and addressed their masters as *Baas*.[101] At a later period, Coloured servants were expected to address their master and mistress as *Baas* and *Nooi*, with the corresponding diminutives for the sons and daughters of the house.

In return, whites called respected old Coloured servants *Outa* and *Aia* as a prefix to their Christian names,[102] and made their children do the same. Although the intention was courteous, the use of these two terms has come to be regarded as a badge of servitude by almost all Coloureds.[103] The corresponding terms used by whites amongst

K

themselves, and reflected in internal Coloured usage, are[104] *Oupa* and *Ouma*.[105]

In addressing or referring to other whites whom they do not know well, Afrikaners use the titles *Meneer*, *Mevrou* and *Mejuffrouw*, for 'Mr.', 'Mrs.', and 'Miss' respectively. It is one of the biggest grievances of urban Coloureds who have achieved some status within their own community that comparatively few Afrikaners will accord them these titles. Low-class whites are said to ignore all titles, but better-educated ones will sometimes use such titles as 'Reverend', 'Doctor' and so on, wherever it is possible.[106]

The Afrikaans language has a series of descriptive terms which apply to Coloured as distinct from whites. For instance, while *seun* (or the more common diminutive *seuntjie*) denotes a white boy, *jong* refers to a Coloured man, a young Coloured boy being *kleinjong* or *klonkie*. Similarly, *meid* refers to a Coloured woman of any age, while *meisie* refers to a white girl.[107] Only whites are 'men' and 'women' to most South African whites, whether English- or Afrikaans-speaking. Coloured farm labourers, collectively, are *volk* (people) or sometimes *skepsels* (creatures).

The term '*Hotnot*' is now generally hated and regarded as insulting by Coloured people. One of the most resented actions of the Nationalist Government was a Minister's reference to the Non-European groups as *Hotnots, Kaffers en Koelies*.[108] In polite and educated speech, Cape whites use *Bruinmense* (Brown people), but this term is rapidly being supplanted by *Kleurlinge* (Coloureds), probably under English influence.[109]

English-speaking people in South Africa have not evolved such a wealth of differential terms. A similar paternalistic tendency to regard Non-Europeans as childish and immature as a group is shown in the common use of the terms 'boy' and 'girl', when speaking of most Coloured people. Nevertheless, the predominantly urban English-speaking South Africans, who are less imbued with the old rural status-hierarchy, find it less difficult to address educated Coloured people as Mr., Mrs., or Miss.[110] Nor does English provide any such derogatory term as '*Hotnot*', 'Coloured' being the only word now in general use.[111] It is for such reasons that many Coloured people now prefer to use English in their contact with whites.[112]

Differential modes of behaviour are firmly established, particularly in rural areas. It is extremely rare for a white person to shake hands with a Coloured, even when the latter occupies a high status within his own community. White men rarely make way for a Coloured woman, remove their hats or stand up at her approach, although a rigid protocol is enforced on Coloured people in the presence of whites.[113]

The treatment of Coloured people in casual contacts, in the streets, on the highway,[114] in public buildings, in shops and elsewhere, has been mentioned incidentally in other chapters. Some Coloured informants have stated that in Cape Town, where in general inter-racial contacts run more smoothly than elsewhere in the Union, unpleasant incidents are more frequent now than a decade or more ago.[115] They attribute this to the increasing numbers of 'low-class' rural Afrikaners in the City, as shop-assistants, clerks in public offices, and police officers.[116] Like the petty frustrations of spatial *apartheid* in transport, the increasing expression of colour-prejudice and fear by members of the dominant group in everyday contacts serves to exacerbate the effects of the greater discriminations in the political and economic spheres.[117]

The conventional patterns of casual contact do show some signs of modification in the urban areas, as a result of overseas influences, industrialisation and the slow rise of an educated Coloured group. The traditional pattern of social contacts between white and Coloured remains, however, the master-servant relationship, which does not preclude close proximity and even affection so long as the status difference is maintained.[118]

*   *   *   *   *

The great aversion felt by almost all white South Africans to the idea of social intercourse on equal terms is intensified in the case of sexual intercourse, legal or otherwise, which is thought to be the inevitable end of 'social equality'.[119] Behind this assumption lies the implied belief that whites of both sexes, but particularly men, do in fact find Coloured people sexually attractive if sanctions are relaxed. The presence of nearly one million Coloured people, 'no mean miscegenatory feat', as one white South African put it, provides considerable support for this belief.[120]

At first sight, it seems paradoxical that popular demand for legal sanctions against mixed marriages and casual sexual intercourse should have increased while the number of mixed marriages between Europeans and Coloureds has decreased absolutely, despite the increasing size of both groups (see Appendix V[121]).

Until the middle of 1949, Coloured people in the Cape and the Free State were free to cohabit with or marry whom they chose.[122] In Natal there were provisions for mixed marriages but a ban on illicit intercourse between a white woman and a Coloured person (i.e., any Hottentot, Coolie, Bushman, Lascar or Kaffir). In the Transvaal there were separate provisions for white persons marrying white persons, and for Coloured persons marrying Coloured persons, but none for mixed marriages. Such couples usually crossed the border into Natal or the Cape to get married. There were also severe penalties for 'unlawful carnal intercourse' between white women and any 'native' (Africans, Coloureds, Asiatics, American Negroes, St. Helenans).[123]

The earlier legislation concerning illicit intercourse laid most stress on the relations between white women and non-white men. The 1927 Immorality Act, however, indicated a change and general hardening of white attitudes, by prohibiting all illicit intercourse between Europeans and Africans. Attempts were made in 1927, 1936 and 1937 to pass legislation prohibiting mixed marriages throughout the Union,[124] but this was finally done only in 1949. The provisions of the present Act forbid all marriages between Europeans and Non-Europeans. A companion Immorality Amendment Bill, to extend the provisions of the 1927 Act to all Non-Europeans, was dropped in 1949 but was brought up again and passed in the 1950 session.[125]

Various European individuals and organisations protested, and the United Party opposition put up a lively fight against the Mixed Marriages Bill. All such opposition was, however, vitiated by the necessity for opponents to declare their belief in the undesirability of mixed marriages. The Churches, with the exception of the D.R.C., were in a stronger position in that they could declare that mixed marriages were not 'contrary to the law of God', however 'inexpedient' and 'unhappy in their results' they might be.[126]

After the two measures became law, their enforcement produced a number of hardships and abuses. Under the Mixed Marriages Act the determination of an applicant's race is left initially to the marriage officer.[127] In a case where a Roman Catholic priest was found guilty by a magistrate of performing a marriage between a European man and a 'slightly Coloured' woman whose associations were all with Europeans, but three of whose four grand-parents were registered at birth as Coloured, the judge upheld the priest's appeal on the grounds that both the woman and her mother clearly consorted with Europeans and were accepted as Europeans.[128]

Other hardships involve widows and widowers whose partners were of another race, and who may wish to remarry a person of that race in order to provide for the future of the children.[129] The Act also penalises the poor, as wealthy couples can establish a domicile elsewhere and return to South Africa, when their marriage will be legally recognised.

It is, however, in the administration of the Immorality Amendment Act that most abuses have arisen. The chronological sequence of the two Acts made it impossible for couples living together as man and wife to regularise their position, unless they had sufficient presence of mind to beat the ban before the Mixed Marriages Act was gazetted. A number of pathetic old couples were haled before the courts, sentenced, and ordered to separate, and considerable public indignation was aroused, before the Attorney-General's office announced that there would be no further prosecutions of 'aged' couples who had lived together 'for a long time'. These instructions are, however, vague, the decision being left to public prosecutors, and lack the force of law which they would have had if embodied in an amendment to the Act.[130]

The Act is also said to have provided a fruitful field for blackmailers,[131] and to have encouraged white prostitution by driving Coloured girls off the streets in all but Coloured areas.[132] Magistrates have been accused of discriminating between Europeans and Non-Europeans when giving sentence under this Act, and a perusal of the many cases reported suggests that this is so,[133] although allowance must be made for the cases in which the male accused is a foreign seaman, not always conversant with the law.[134] Other anomalies have arisen under this Act. On one occasion a European police constable who had had intercourse with a Coloured woman without her consent successfully appealed against his conviction under the Immorality Act, on the grounds that the woman had not consented.[135] Moreover, girls who were formerly protected by the Girls' and Mentally Defective Women's Protection Act from being charged with crimes may now be charged and sentenced under the Immorality Act.[136]

The difficulty of determining ethnic affiliation in border-line cases sometimes leads to unpleasant and humiliating incidents in the courts. On one occasion a woman charged with living with a European man was asked by her counsel to pull up the sleeve of her dress, so that the magistrate might see the whiteness of her skin. The magistrate also asked her to take her hat off so that he might examine her features. The couple were subsequently found not guilty and discharged.[137] In another case a man living with a Coloured woman, both of whom were charged under the Act, submitted that he was a Coloured and not a European. He had previously bought liquor as a European and was registered as a European voter. The couple had lived together for ten years and had three children. The magistrate is reported to have said: 'If he wants to be a Coloured man, however, he must be branded once and for all as such.'[138]

*   *   *   *   *

A complex of discriminatory patterns in all spheres has been built up over the centuries to justify the perpetuation of an original economic domination in which the dominated groups happened to be distinguished not only by their culture but by their colour. In the course of time, and with the increased acculturation of the Coloured group, the stress has shifted from the economic to the social sphere,[139] until to-day Nationalist speakers can argue that economic *apartheid* is essential because contacts at work lead to social intercourse and intermarriage. Social segregation has in fact become an end in itself, and it would be social and political suicide for any white to advocate 'social equality'. It is in this sphere too that the least differentiation is made between Coloureds and Africans by the white in-group. All non-white groups represent an equal threat to white race 'purity', the Coloureds even more than the Africans, since it is with them that most sexual intercourse occurs, and through them that 'black blood' might seep into the white group.[140]

PART THREE
THE PRESENT SITUATION

CHAPTER EIGHT

THE CAPE COLOURED PEOPLE—
INTERNAL STRUCTURE

No man can live to himself in this world, and none of you will make much headway against the stupendous opposition you have to face if he detaches himself from his fellows . . . The lowest black or Coloured man is part of us . . . That unfortunate should be given a helping hand. Some of us may hold our heads aloft in pure ether, but the common farm labourer, the hooligans of the city slums, are our people.[1]

ATERIAL for a detailed anthropological study of even one section of the Cape Coloured People is not available. In this chapter it is proposed merely to indicate the extent to which the patterns of differentiation and discrimination described have helped to produce, condition and perpetuate a separate Coloured group. We shall try to outline the structural framework of this group and the internal sources of satisfaction available to group members, and to examine the possible bases of group solidarity.

In attempting to describe the social structure of a large and heterogeneous group of this type, existing within the framework of a larger society in which all formal, legal, political and economic control is vested, one is faced with a more complicated task than is the anthropologist who studies an isolated primitive tribe.[2] The Coloured group consists to-day of a series of sub-groups, lacking common ethnic, cultural and historical antecedents.

The processes of detribalisation and acculturation of these groups have long been completed, but as the Coloured group is divided economically and geographically into scattered rural and concentrated urban units, these processes have differed both in kind and in degree. It is thus difficult to establish any sort of social norm.

It must be stressed that the ensuing account of the structure of the Coloured group is only a series of hypotheses for further study. The illustrations given are not the product of statistical methods; they are simply the result of preliminary observation, which it is hoped may provide the sign-posts for further field-work. We shall consider the

146

basic social units amongst the Coloured group in the following order: kinship groups, local units (household, neighbourhood), voluntary associations, social classes and the community.

The family or kinship patterns amongst the Coloured People in general do not strike the European observer with the same sense of strangeness as do, for instance, Bantu African systems. The danger is in fact that one may take their similarity for granted in all points without adequate examination.

As we have emphasised throughout this study, the Cape Coloured people are now essentially European in culture. But for the Cape Malay[3] and one other type, it seems doubtful whether any of the kinship-patterns encountered amongst Cape Coloured people can be traced to influences other than those which operate for white South Africans in the same geographical and economic environment.[4]

Thus, in the urban areas, the major social groupings of the Coloured People are not those of a simple, small-scale society, but the complex inter-relations of extended families, associations and social classes found in contemporary European urban society. In this, kinship-structure plays a far less important part, and certain functions of the kin-group, such as education, health and recreation, are increasingly taken over by the various associations and the State. In the more static and isolated rural situation, kinship-groupings have more importance, but exist in conjunction with a class-hierarchy[5] which has land-ownership and stock-ownership as its chief determinants for both European and Coloured groups.

While we cannot hope to find any single kinship pattern within so heterogeneous and dispersed a group, it is, however, possible to discern certain main types of family or kinship-group, associated with varying economic and social factors, and in particular with occupation, economic and social status, and rural or urban residence.

An attempt was made to study these kinship forms by applying the criteria evolved by social anthropologists for simpler societies.[6] While they provided pegs on which to hang an initial analysis, their inadequacy to provide a full description of more complex groupings soon became evident, as the following paragraphs show.

In general, the principle of descent, although formally patrilineal as in the case of white South Africans and Europeans generally, may often be temporarily matrilineal owing to the high incidence of illegitimate births (from 20–25 per cent in some areas). The principle of descent, however, varies quite haphazardly from generation to generation, according to the marital condition of the individual. Descent groups are bilateral,[7] as in contemporary white South African groups. There is a certain bias in favour of the paternal side amongst both white and Coloured farmers, which may be associated with the inheritance and working of land or stock, but no clear exclusion of maternal kinsfolk as in some Non-European patrilineal societies.

There are no fixed residence rules, and the residential group varies according to economic situation and personal wishes in each case. In most urban areas this haphazard diversity has been further intensified by an acute housing-shortage.

Marriage regulations follow the customary Christian monogamous pattern, except in the Cape Malay community. Theie seem to be no preferred marriages based on kinship relationships, as in primitive groups. The choice of a partner is usually based on individual attraction, although one may still expect to find a few arranged marriages between rural land-owning families. Incest rules are based on the Churches' forbidden degrees of consanguinity.

As far as terminology is concerned, the investigator's task is simplified by the fact that the Coloureds speak a European tongue. No variations from customary European usage have so far been noted; that is to say, all cousins are identified with one another, but distinguished from siblings,[8] while uncles and aunts on both the father's and the mother's side are not distinguished from one another.[9]

The criteria just enumerated are too definite and formalised to give an adequate picture of the fluid and heterogeneous kinship groupings found in any complex society. In a not dissimilar situation, Professor Franklin Frazier postulated four main family types amongst American Negroes: matriarchal, patriarchal, unstable and equalitarian.[10] This typology has been found very helpful in the South African context. For the first two it seemed better to substitute the less forceful terms 'matricentral' and 'patricentral', to denote the partner on whom falls the main stress of maintaining the family, both emotionally and economically. In the equalitarian and the unstable family, the stress falls on both partners, but the relationship is totally different in each case.

The family may be either a conjugal family or some form of extended family.[11] Such an extended family may include all or any living individuals within the bilateral vertical span, but in the collateral range is usually confined to siblings, and (if the latter are married), their families. The principles on which such family groupings are based seem to depend entirely on economic resources and personal inclination.[12]

Although the formation of family groupings is apparently so casual and changeable, there does, as has been said, seem to be a general association between certain types of family and certain economic, social and residential factors.

The patricentral family seems to be mainly associated with the senior male's ownership or tenancy of some form of property,[13] or with his possession of some economic skill or training. Preliminary observation suggests that the incidence of such families is greater amongst the professional classes, skilled artisans and farmers than it is amongst the labouring classes which constitute the bulk of the Coloured People. There seems to be a strong pattern of paternal authority and dominance in such families, the woman's authority being decreased by the absence of any compulsion on her to become a joint wage-earner.

Conversely, where the man possesses no skill or property, it may become necessary for the wife to go out to work.[14] In such families we find a decrease in the authority of the male,[15] lowered marital stability, and a weakening of family ties amongst the children due to the absence from home of both parents during working hours. This is the unstable family type, probably the most common amongst the Coloured People, and found amongst both the urban and the rural proletariat.

As we have said, both the unstable and the equalitarian family are characterised by a lack of any very marked authority on the paternal or maternal side. The significant distinction would appear to lie in the fact that the relationship between the two sexes is in the former case based on a negative acceptance of adverse circumstances, in the latter on positive partnership and aspiration. The equalitarian type of family, which is essentially a conjugal family, is so far found only amongst a few younger members of the urban professional classes.[16]

The unsatisfactory nature of the unstable family from the woman's point of view has helped to perpetuate and probably to increase the incidence of our last type, the matricentral family. This is the only pattern which finds little or no parellel in white kinship-groupings. It can be traced back to the days of slavery, in which, as elsewhere, slaves were torn away from their original kinship and social groupings, and the formation of new groupings in the new situation was made difficult if not impossible.

In the Cape Colony slaves were not permitted to marry until a decade or so before Emancipation. Permanent associations between male and female slaves were often discouraged except for breeding purposes, and little attempt was made to sell family units together, except in the case of mothers with young children. In such circumstances the mother-child bond was the only one with much chance of survival, although slaves had not the right to dispose of their children, and older children were sometimes sold away from their mothers.[17]

To-day the matricentral family type has probably a fairly high incidence in the Coloured group, particularly amongst the urban lower classes, but may even occur in the lower-middle class.[18] It is not of course confined to the descendants of slaves, many of whom are now to be found in the Coloured upper classes. Nevertheless, the family type which was forced on many slaves provided a pattern which has been adopted willingly by free women who have come to consider a husband as an economic liability rather than as an asset. In its pure form the matricentral family type consists only of a woman, her dependent children and possibly her mother. A common pattern is for the woman to send the child or children resulting from transient liaisons to live with her own mother or other female relative, while she supports the whole family from her earnings.[19] These, if she is a well-paid domestic servant, or a semi-skilled industrial worker, may be as high as or higher than those of a man. There are of course many marginal families in transition from the unstable to the matricentral type, with a permanent or temporary male as mate and father.

The incidence of illegitimacy amongst the Christian Coloureds in rural as well as urban areas is quite striking,[20] and does not seem to be confined to the lowest class. Undoubtedly it is not regarded as desirable amongst the professional and skilled artisan classes, but amongst the more respectable semi-skilled working class it apparently carries little moral stigma.[21] One may perhaps associate this general attitude to illegitimacy not only with economic considerations[22] but with the desire to 'get the blood white', which has until recently caused extra-marital sex-relations with Europeans to be regarded with considerable complacency by lower and lower-middle class Coloureds at least.[23]

In general the familial tie amongst the Coloured people appears to be strongest in the vertical parent-child or grandparent-grandchild relationship, and to a lesser degree the sibling link. The husband-wife relationship does not seem to have achieved the predominant position which it holds in American society, or certain sections of British society, except amongst some younger members of the small urban professional class (the equalitarian family type already described). This is the position despite the rarity of arranged marriages and the great rôle played by mutual attraction in the choice of a partner. It may be that, as with other working classes elsewhere, mutual attraction is soon lost in the exigencies of hard work and child-bearing.

In its relationship to the whole internal social structure, the Coloured family is not, and in most cases never was, a self-sufficient unit, except for a few land-owning groups. Even in the latter case, pressure on land and soil erosion have often made other sources of revenue essential.[24] With the immediate family unit dependent upon what it earns outside the extended family, one might expect to find the extended family pattern breaking down into a series of single-family units or conjugal families, particularly in the urban areas, where cramped housing facilities accentuate the process. Such single family units are of course encountered in great numbers, but there is still a tendency for married children (particularly from patricentral families) to settle in the same neighbourhood as their parents and to continue to live a highly integrated family life, helping their parents or being helped by them financially and otherwise.

Contacts are often maintained between rural and urban kinsfolk within the extended family range. Those from the rural areas may lodge with their urban kinsfolk when they come to the town to school or in search of work, and urban relatives may stay with their rural kinsfolk when ill or on holiday.

Undoubtedly there is an economic background to the continued strength of the family bond. However, the fact that this bond is accepted and upheld, not only by those who benefit from it but by those who lose in that they share out the gains of their own labour or enterprise,[25] suggests that the family is primarily the focus of other than purely economic drives. Voluntary associations have only a limited range, while community bonds are tenuous and uneven. The family is therefore for most Coloureds the only social unit which can give them any sense of stability and a feeling of 'belonging' in a society where their status is so uncertain.

In country districts there is still a closer coincidence between the kinship-unit and the local unit than there is in the towns.[26] The household consists usually of a simple family or extended family, while in some reserves[27] a large proportion of persons in the larger local unit are descended in the male line from the original occupier or occupiers.[28] In the urban areas, minimum local units may vary in composition, according to the accommodation available, from the extended family, the immediate family, the family with a lodger or lodgers (who may or may not be relatives), to the tenement type of unit with its heterogeneous and often unrelated collection of residents.[29]

Turning to larger local units, we find little of the uniform structure that is characteristic of many primitive peoples. Where political,[30] legal and economic institutions are largely imposed from outside, the only major function left for a local unit is to provide some social satisfaction for those individuals who compose it. In some villages[31] and smaller towns with a relatively stable population, there appears to be a certain feeling of 'community' which may take the form of joint action of some kind.[32] Such action is, however, often centred round the church or the school or, more accurately, round the minister or the teacher, and should more properly come under the heading of 'voluntary associations'. In the country, the growth of stable communities is further hindered by the fact that many Coloured people work and live on isolated farms, and that they tend to be migratory within a limited area.[33] A few more stable communities with leaders who are invested with certain local powers are to be found in the mission station and reserves, and in such units as the former 'Republic' of the Bastards of Rehoboth.

It has been suggested that the rural extended family in such areas still constitutes a nucleus for those members who have to work away from home. Such a neighbourhood unit too may have some appeal, as the unskilled Coloured worker finds little to replace it at his place of work, whether in a city or on a European farm.[34] There his inferior status is constantly brought home to him, while in his own community, where usually the only European is the missionary, he may have standing and perhaps even authority.

Even in these instances, however, it is probable that only the official ban on alienation of land to Europeans has prevented the break-up of these self-contained communities, as happened in the case of the Griquas.[35]

The voluntary associations play a similar or larger rôle in urban areas, where neighbourhood ties and loyalties tend to be as weak as they are in most European urban societies. Factors which accentuate this lack of community feeling are the strong class-distinctions amongst the Coloureds themselves, the constant flux of residents and the fact that several residential areas in Cape Town at least have a racially mixed population, so that Coloured and poorer white families often live interspersed in the same street and even house in a contiguity that does not necessarily involve intimate social contacts.

In the large cities, however, some community feeling seems to exist in the longer-settled areas which house the better-off permanent residents; as ratepayers[36] these have some say in municipal administration, and in areas where they predominate may elect a Coloured member to represent them on the City Council. There may be something in the nature of semi-permanent larger local groups in the poverty-stricken communities living out on the quasi-rural Cape Flats. Amongst the great shifting mass of transient unskilled workers who inhabit the urban slums, it is doubtful whether there can be anything in the nature of a larger unit than the family, immediate or extended.

*   *   *   *   *

Before passing on to discuss the Coloured community as such, we must consider the association, a type of social unit which cuts right across kinship and local ties.[37] Most of the great South African political and economic associations are in European hands. There are, however, other small-scale associations which have arisen spontaneously within the Coloured group.

A major function of these Coloured associations is to fill the social void left by the European monopoly of political, legal and economic organisation, and by the rigid social exclusion enforced by the dominant group. This void is deepened by the monotonous and uninteresting nature of the work done perforce by most Coloured people, the weakening of family ties, the inadequacy of the husband-wife relationship, so that each sex is thrown back on itself for distraction and interest, and the widening of horizons consequent upon increasing education, urbanisation and the often unconscious desire to duplicate European *mores* even if participation is denied.[38]

The number and diversity of associations amongst the Coloured people appears to correspond to the degree of education, urbanisation, leisure and economic position. In the simpler rural communities, the family has more importance and associations are few, though increasing in number as isolation wanes and wants increase. Amongst isolated rural families working on farms there is little opportunity for associations outside the family. In urban slums only simple associations seem to prevail, of the type classified as primary or face-to-face groups by MacIver.[39] He cites as examples the play group, the group of friends, the gossip group, the partnership, and the gang, all of which are characterised by spontaneous assembly.

All or some of these play a fairly large part in the tenuous social life of the majority of Coloureds. For the majority associations remain simple, spontaneous and fluctuating. Except for religious associations, the larger, more permanent associations, with their specialised aims, appear to be mainly confined to the professional and skilled classes.

In Part II we have referred in passing to various types of association which have arisen amongst the Coloured people as a reaction against their exclusion from European organisations. Here we shall give a further account of such associations, classified under the headings of the various ends, social, political and economic, which they serve.

The various 'social' associations may be sub-divided under the following headings: social intercourse, recreation, culture, welfare, and religion. These are not necessarily mutually exclusive, and sometimes overlap.

In the sphere of social intercourse, the types of face-to-face association already noted play a very large part in Coloured social life wherever spatial contiguity permits. Extreme gregariousness is a notable trait amongst the Coloured people in general. It takes the form, often still on a family basis, of lively gossip groups amongst the women, noisy play groups amongst the children, informal congregations amongst the men, in the city barbers' shops, for the purpose of drinking and gambling, or (amongst the upper and middled-classes) of sport, whether active or spectator.

Other associations of this nature are those between young men and women past the age of puberty, for dancing, cinema-going, picnicking and sexual intercourse. Such inter-sexual associations are more restricted by upper-class families, whose *mores* approximate closely to those of the corresponding European groups, and who do not regard premarital promiscuity with the same leniency as do lower-class Coloureds.

Amongst socially-maladjusted young people, 'skolly'[40] gangs tend to emerge. An experienced social worker recently described the genesis and *mores* of such gangs:

'Amongst all these people the same traits are to be observed: a mode of dress easily identifiable from the usual normal form, but displaying certain common characteristics with members of the gang, idle daylight hours spent lounging in public places, a disinclination to accept regular work or discipline, a malevolent and suspicious scowl habitually on the face, congregation after dark in groups under leadership of the strongest, and organised acts of violence. The background of almost every confirmed skolly is one of filthy slum or *pondokkie* (shack) housing; perpetual neglect and hunger while an infant because both parents are working; the gnawing pain of veld sores, septic wounds and rotting teeth all his life; no supervision over his schooling so that he never passed anything higher than standard three or four; continued idleness while a youngster because there was nobody to make him go to school or work; filthy streets or playgrounds because the house is locked while parents are away at work; illiterate, drunken and often demoralised parents.'[41]

These Coloured gangs do not seem to be primarily economic in function.[42] The peculiar and highly noticeable dress affected by gang members,[43] the attempts to attract general attention and admiration, the strong gang loyalty, and the large proportion of time devoted to other than economic pursuits (i.e., promenading, gambling, drinking, cinema-going and inter-gang warfare or other acts of violence without the motive of gain),[44] would all appear to place these associations in the same category as social clubs in the better-adjusted sections of the community.[45]

In urban slum areas, membership of a skolly-gang is almost unavoidable for boys[46] in the lower-lower class, and even attract some from the upper-lower group, particularly those who despite ability are unable for financial or other reasons to continue with their education or to gain entry to the skilled trades.[47] Once through their teens, most members of these junior gangs graduate into ordinary life as unskilled workers. A few, however, often the most able, proceed to a life of crime, either on their own or as members of adult crime-gangs. These do not appear to be on a scale comparable with the Rand gangs, which are sometimes organised by whites and have cars, armouries and capital at their disposal.

Of at least one of the skolly-gangs, called the 'Globe Gang' and, like 'Jack the Ripper' in London, credited with being omnipresent by law-abiding Cape Town Coloureds, some informants have suggested that it is at times used for political purposes by certain European interests. It was said that the Globe Gang had consistently attempted to break up the meetings of one political group, while those held by the opposing group went unscathed.[48] In any case, the Globe and other 'corner boy' gangs are a powerful force in Coloured life in Cape Town, and terrorise not only their own areas but those in which live the more prosperous artisans, thanks to the inadequate policing of predominantly Coloured districts.

Economic limitations have probably impeded the development of clubs designed purely for social intercourse amongst urban Coloured communities. Even clubs with a specialised recreational purpose seem to be as yet restricted to the upper and middled-classes. We are here referring to purely Coloured clubs, not to the various boys' and girls' clubs and associations which are run by European individuals or organisations amongst all sections of the Coloured community.

Coloured recreational clubs are the answer to European social exclusiveness, and are usually connected with some sport. From small local beginnings, clubs connected with the major sports have achieved national organisations, to which all local Coloured clubs are affiliated.[49] The minimum requirements of equipment, training and leisure still confine these activities for the most part to better-off individuals.[50]

The rigid colour bar applied by Europeans in sport has produced a certain definite reaction on the part of Coloured sportsmen.[51] For instance, in Chapter VII we described how in most sports the European association has pre-empted affiliation to the international organisation and thereby won the right to represent South Africa. This was countered in the case of table tennis, as the International Table Tennis Federation refused to recognise the South African (European) Association on the grounds that it practises discrimination against Non-Europeans. The South African Table Tennis Union (composed of Non-Europeans, but expressing its willingness to have members of all colours and races) therefore applied for membership of the international organisation, and was in February 1949 recognised as the controlling body of table tennis in South Africa.[52] It is feared by the Europeans,[53] and hoped by the Non-Europeans, that this may create a precedent for other sports, and open a breach in the sports colour bar.

In the intellectual sphere, many educated Coloureds seem to feel that their leisure is better devoted to political work than to cultural pursuits of a more academic nature. Both the New Era Fellowship (membership of which is not officially restricted to Coloureds or Non-Europeans) and the Cape Literary and Debating Society tend to discuss political subjects. There are probably many informal study groups and reading circles, about which, however, no information is available. Dramatics, dancing, art and music seem to centre around the schools and churches, although a Coloured amateur orchestra (the Spes Bona), with a membership of about forty, has been in existence since 1917.

While there are a number of recreational clubs unconnected with purely intellectual or sporting pursuits (such as mountain clubs, domino clubs, garden clubs), in existence amongst the urban middle classes, the initiation and sometimes even the running of welfare clubs, youth organisations, sewing circles and so on amongst the poorer Coloureds is still often left to European individuals and organisations. Many observers have commented on the prevailing aloofness of more fortunately placed members of the Coloured group, although in recent years an increasing number have come forward to help the poorer majority.

The purely Coloured associations best known to the outside world are the Cape Town 'coon troupes'. These are associations of men and boys, who come together every New Year for the 'Coon Carnivals'.

L

The Carnivals themselves began only in about 1902, and the various troupes were first organised into boards in 1910. The coon troupes, however, are older, and their origin is not precisely known. A Cape chronicler of 1823[54] writes of bands parading the streets at the New Year,[55] and it was apparently the slave owners' custom to allow their slaves a holiday at New Year, perhaps on the lines of the Roman *Saturnalia*. The *Saturnalia* analogy is supported by the fact that the authorities permit much greater license to Coloured performers and audiences than at any other time.[56] The mass of urban Coloureds feel that this is 'their day', and possibly the authorities recognise the psychological need for this much-harassed group to let off steam at least once a year.[57]

The Carnivals are held on different showgrounds in Cape Town, each under its own Carnival Board, which gives a large number of prizes to the best troupes and soloists. Each troupe[58] meets regularly for months beforehand to assemble its costumes[59] and prepare its repertoire, the whole procedure being shrouded in secrecy until Carnival-time.

For three or four days in the New Year (when commercial establishments are traditionally closed) the troupes march to[60] and perform at the show-grounds before large, mostly Coloured audiences,[61] with the Mayor and Mayoress of Cape Town and other European officials in the box. The performances are somewhat ragged to European ears and eyes, but immensely enthusiastic and rhythmic to the point of auto-intoxication on the part of the performers, who march, strum and sing for hours under a blazing sun with no apparent fatigue.[62]

The coon troupe seems to be the association *par excellence* of lower-class Coloureds who participate in few if any other associations, except the churches. While it retains its popularity with this group, it is increasingly attacked by upper and upper-middle class Coloureds. The two main grounds for objection seem to be that the performances give a wrong impression of the Coloured people and their potentialities to European and overseas witnesses,[63] and that the troupes exert a bad influence on younger members.[64] Moreover, those who are proud of their white associations probably do not like the association with 'coons'.

On the other hand, the Coloured thousands who throng to it seem blissfully unaware of any such interpretation and their attitude to the 'Kentucky Minstrel' aspect appears to be that of the average European. That is to say, they accept face-blacking as a convention and dress up as 'darkies' without apparently considering that their own brown skin tone could in any way be identified with the pitch-black of the 'coon'.

Although members of the Coloured upper classes tend to frown on the 'coons', membership of these troupes appears to have a certain status value amongst the more settled urban working-class.[65] The fact that a fairly expensive costume must be provided by each member annually is a limiting factor. The regular meetings throughout the year provide an important social outlet, and it is hinted that some troupes fulfil certain political functions, by organising Coloured voters at election-times. It can in any case be said that any person or group seeking to organise the Coloured community for political purposes would probably seek to do so through associations already existing for other purposes, such as the coon troupes, the burial and other welfare societies, perhaps the lodges, or even the skolly-gangs.

Another type of recreational association which has been in existence for over fifty years is the 'Christmas string band' or 'choir'.[66] These choirs play probably as important a part in Coloured urban lower-middle class life as do the coons amongst the lower classes.[67] In Cape Town alone they are organised into five unions. Members march in parade on Christmas Eve and Sundays until the end of each January, and hold inter-choir competitions at the show grounds on Sundays in aid of charity. Unlike the coons, the bands march instead of dancing along, wear dignified uniforms, play Christmas carols and hymns, and each carries a banner embroidered with Nativity scenes. The religious emphasis is very strong, although the churches do not sponsor any of the choirs. The majority of the members in any one choir usually belong to the same church. While coons usually have no other outlets or interests, choir members tend to belong to other religious and recreational associations.

The lodges are said to play a very important part in Coloured life, particularly amongst the skilled artisan and commercial classes. It is difficult to know whether their purpose should be classified as welfare, recreational or economic, as they now partake of all three, like similar lodges elsewhere. Orders and lodges in certain parts of Europe and the United States have also in the past had a strong political significance.[68]

The major orders are the Independent Order of Oddfellows, the Independent Order of Foresters, the Ancient Order of Free Gardeners (Scotland), the Mechanic and Fidelity Lodge, the Independent Order of True Templars (I.O.T.T.),[69] and the Order of Free Gardeners (Africa).[70] A reliable informant estimated their total membership at about one-tenth of the Coloured population, a very high figure which would mean that their influence extends far down beyond the *bourgeoisie* into the ranks of the semi-skilled and even unskilled workers.[71]

The same informant stressed that the major function of the lodges is to act as benefit societies for members and their families in case of sickness and death.[72] They maintain cordial relationships with the various Christian denominations, with the exception of the Roman Catholic Church. There are no Moslem members. The lodges have been long established[73] in the major towns, but are now being extended to the country towns and villages.

Burial and other benefit societies play a very important rôle in Coloured life amongst the lower income groups, who form the bulk of the community. The fear of a pauper's burial seems to be a common phenomenon amongst the respectable and churchgoing working-class in many countries.[74] Such societies arose amongst the Cape Coloured in an attempt to help families living on a bare subsistence level to face the crises of illness and death amongst wage-earners and dependants. In the absence of an adequate state system of social security, the societies still meet a definite need. They are sometimes run in conjunction with the local church, although one large burial society[75] is run by a political group, the African People's Organisation.

No further reference will be made here to the various welfare and religious associations which, although they operate amongst the Coloured people, are branches of larger European associations, and have Europeans in the controlling posts. We have distinguished such organisations from the associations evolved by the Coloured community *per se*, although the former have of course become part of Coloured social life, and have undoubtedly played their part in making the Coloured person feel his cultural kinship with the European, thereby helping to delay the growth of any real and separate community feeling. As we tried to show in Chapter VII, however, there has usually come a point where Coloured people felt ready to share in the administration, and the Europeans were unable to abandon their attitude of benevolent paternalism or to yield any real share of authority to the people whom they still subconsciously considered as inferior.

At present there are some signs of a move away from the general Coloured tendency to accept immediate inferiority of status and European leadership but to press for equality and integration, and to condemn all attempts at *apartheid*. This is particularly noticeable in the sphere of religious associations. Christianity has played a great part in the evolution of the Coloured community, and still has a great hold over the majority of its members.[76] Despite the differentiation practised by the various Churches, there has so far been little evidence of the trend so characteristic amongst African Christians—the formation of hundreds of small autonomous African Churches.[77] There are a few Coloured Churches, which, unlike the more flamboyant African Churches, tend to retain European dogma and ritual unchanged, while ridding themselves of all European leadership or authority.

One such Church is the *Volkskerk van Afrika* (People's Church of Africa), established in 1922 by the Rev. J. J. H. Forbes, a Coloured minister who started in the Wesleyan Church, then moved to the Congregational Union. The *Volkskerk* has a membership of over 3,000. Although it began with the professed desire to 'perpetuate the good feeling that existed between the Dutch, English and Coloured in the early days of the Cape',[78] the founder took as the theme for his 1950 pastoral the need for unity amongst the Coloured races of South

Africa.[79] A more recent splinter-church (predominantly Coloured in membership but with no official colour-bar) is the South African Calvinist Protestant Church, whose original nucleus was the former Dutch Reformed Mission congregation of Crawford, Cape Town. Eighty per cent of its members broke away from the parent-body under their pastor, the Rev. I. D. Morkel, in October 1950,[80] following a long series of incidents in which the latter figured as a critic of *apartheid* and the 'bad boy' of the D.R.M.C. This Church has already grown to six branches, with four ministers and over 2,000 members, despite the lack of funds and buildings and the fact that the Church has not yet been registered, so that its ministers are not recognised as marriage officers. In addition, it is said that seceding members of D.R.M.C. congregations have been threatened by European D.R.C. ministers and members with loss of employment unless they remain within the Mission Church.[81] Dogma remains Calvinist in the new Church; as its founder explained: 'The Coloured people are essentially conservatives. You cannot make too many changes. If you change the Church, you must keep the dogma.'

The present tendency amongst Coloured church members to reject European direction is now said to be swelling the ranks of the Congregational Union. In the Union this is a predominantly Coloured Church, and its decentralised organisation is particularly suited to the growing Coloured demand for local autonomy.

Political associations, which are usually the nucleus of an organised protest movement, have also been influenced amongst the Coloured people by the Europeanising tendencies of the upper and middle classes, which still contain the only individuals with education, leisure and the necessary economic status to enable them to play an active part in politics. Those Coloured men who qualified for the franchise in the old Cape Province voted 'European' instead of forming their own parties and putting up their own candidates. Theoretically, they might have joined with African voters to form a united Non-European party and a powerful pressure group. However, Coloured voters in the past seem to have felt, and been encouraged to feel, that their interests were similar to, if not the same as, those of the Europeans, and equally threatened by the 'blanket-Kaffir'.[82]

Just before Union, however, some Coloured leaders decided that their interests were not fully safeguarded by the European political parties. In 1902 the Cape Malay, Dr. Abdurahman, founded the African Political Organisation (later the African People's Organisation or A.P.O.).[83] This organisation had a hundred branches all over South Africa by the time of Union in 1909. It advocated the extension of the franchise to Coloureds outside the Cape, and usually backed the British connection and the South African Party. In the 1920s a rival party, called the African National Bond (A.N.B.), was formed. This organisation supported the Hertzog policy of complete segregation for the African, but second-grade status for the Cape Coloured, next to the white man.[84] Both the A.P.O. and the A.N.B., entirely Coloured in membership despite their names, looked to one or the other European party for leadership and assistance.[85] They apparently found support amongst skilled artisans and small business-men, who wished to protect their own vested interests.

In the 1920s, it was still possible and indeed necessary for both major European parties to woo the Coloured vote with promises of preferential treatment. The general intensification of white colour-prejudice since then and the removal of the African from the general political arena have, however, had their effect in producing Coloured disillusionment with the European connection,[86] and a consequent stiffening of separate political consciousness and organised protest. Coloured leaders seem always to have felt, however, that a purely Coloured political movement would not be sufficiently strong. The various political associations which have from time to time been formed amongst the Coloured People, and which are so far largely confined to the upper and middle classes, may be classified under two main divisions: those which seek unity with the Europeans on a cultural basis, and those which seek unity with other Non-Europeans on a colour basis.[87] The latter is a more recent development, and has probably arisen as a result of the narrowing gap between the various Non-European groups as acculturation proceeds, and also as a reaction to the European rejection of Coloured attempts to achieve integration or political and economic equality, and the increasing tendency to class all Non-Europeans together.[88]

The history of Coloured political parties, like those of other ethnic groups in South Africa, has been characterised by violent cleavage, dissension and realignment.[89] At present Coloured political groups are divided as described above. The origins of the present cleavage may be traced back to the institution of the Coloured Advisory Council in 1943. Coloured radicals thereupon formed an Anti-C.A.D. or C.A.C. Committee, dominated at the time by Trotskyists, and unleashed within the politically-conscious sections of the Coloured group a bitter civil war which shows no signs of dying down.[90]

Since 1944, therefore, the Europeanising group, often aligned with the United Party, has been the Coloured People's National Union (C.P.N.U.), with its weekly, the *Sun*, and its teachers' association, the Teachers' Educational and Professional Association (T.E.P.A.). The movement which advocates Non-European unity is the Non-European Unity Movement (N.E.U.M.).[91] Amongst the Coloured community it is backed by the Anti-C.A.D. Committee,[92] the Trains Apartheid Committee,[93] the 'purged' African People's Organisation (A.P.O.),[94] the Coloured People's Congress (Transvaal), and the 'purged' Teachers' League of South Africa (T.L.S.A.).[95] Its newspaper is the weekly *Torch*, which is said to have a circulation of 10,000.

The C.P.N.U. seems to draw considerable support from skilled artisans, business men, ministers and some of the teachers, particularly the older ones. In general its members have a certain vested interest in the *status quo*.[96] On the other hand, the radical group apparently consists mainly of the younger professionals and more highly-qualified teachers in undenominational schools. It is definitely a movement of younger intellectuals, who are probably in revolt against their own older generation as well as against increasing discrimination from outside.[97]

It is difficult to assess relative numerical strength. The C.P.N.U. claims 48,000 members, the T.E.P.A. over 1,000. On the other hand the T.L.S.A. claims 1,500 members for itself, and about 500 for the T.E.P.A. No figures could be obtained for the A.P.O.

The C.P.N.U. suffered a bad set-back early in 1950, when the utter futility of attempting to modify Nationalist policy towards the Coloured group became evident, and all but four members[98] of the Coloured Advisory Council, which consisted mainly of C.P.N.U. supporters, resigned *en bloc*. Immediately after these resignations the C.P.N.U. convened a general Coloured protest meeting against *apartheid*, to which all Coloured representative bodies were invited. The various radical groups, however, held aloof, and in fact accentuated their attacks on the C.P.N.U. In October 1950, the C.P.N.U. initiated a National Convention Co-ordinating Committee, which drew up a memorandum which was presented to Mr. N. C. Havenga, Acting Prime Minister; he, as a lieutenant of the late General Hertzog, was thought to be somewhat more vulnerable to emotional appeals referring to the white man's honour and pledged word than other members of the Cabinet. The radical group again held aloof, and the appeal to Mr. Havenga proved fruitless.

In early 1951, moderates and ex-Communists came together to form a Franchise Action Council,[99] which claimed the support of the National Convention Co-ordinating Committee, the African People's Organisation (in reality it had the support only of some Transvaal branches), the African National Congress (led by ex-members of the Native Representative Council), and the South African Indian Congress. This FR.A.C. organised a mass demonstration against the proposed franchise legislation in Cape Town in March 1951.[100] The Council's cohesiveness, however, became even more open to doubt when the minority of moderate C.P.N.U. members associated with it declared their opposition to the one-day protest strike which was organised by the FR.A.C. on 7th May, 1951.[101]

The Non-European Unity Movement successfully predicted that FR.A.C. attempts to prevent the passage of the Franchise Bill by petitions, demonstrations and strikes would fail, and that thereafter less would be heard from this group. It has itself, whether through political cunning or impotence, continued to pursue a Brer Rabbit policy, reiterating its programme of non-collaboration in all spheres.[102]

It is difficult to evaluate the relative influence of these two political trends amongst the Coloured people. The Coloured municipal councillors in the Cape Peninsula seem to be divided about equally between the C.P.N.U. and Anti-C.A.D., which gives some indication of the views of the comparatively small number of Coloured ratepayers. The radical group has possibly gained more supporters as a result of the failure of the FR.A.C. to achieve its ends in the 1951 session.

Coloured economic associations are not so completely divorced from South Africa's major economic institutions as are Coloured political groups. As we have seen, some Cape trade unions are either all or mainly Coloured, even to the extent of having Coloured executive committees. These Coloured unions are, however, small in size and represent the minority interests of the small group of urban skilled and semi-skilled workers. They have, therefore, a vested interest in the *status quo* and cannot truly be said to represent or further the economic interests of the Coloured community as a whole.[103] In addition, they are usually not independent, but belong to trade union groups under white leadership.

The main autonomous economic associations found within the Coloured community apart from the burial and benefit societies already described are co-operative and building societies.[104] In view of the poverty, illiteracy, lack of skill and wide dispersal of the Coloured people, it is not surprising that such associations are few and on a fairly small scale.[105] Recently impetus has been provided by the lack of openings in European trade and commerce for educated Coloured individuals and by the challenge of the minor invasion of Indian storekeepers, who cater largely to a Non-European clientèle. Perhaps the gradual rise of community feeling under the pressure of European discrimination is also playing its part. As far as could be ascertained, there are four such co-operatives at present, one in Athlone, Cape Town, opened in May, 1948, the others in Upington, Mamre and Steinkopf.

We have said that associations are playing a considerable and increasing part in the life of the Coloured people. So far, however, the scope of organised associations has been mainly restricted to the urban Coloured population, and especially to the *bourgeoisie*,[106] whose economic status and *mores* have long kept them apart from the vast majority of Coloured people, and close to the European community. Under the increasing pressure of discrimination against the Coloureds as a group, however, the political associations have the opportunity of extending their influence to the Coloured masses, both urban and rural, whose only associations at present are the primary ones of informal encounters and the bottle-store or canteen.

*　　*　　*　　*　　*

Throughout this study the terms 'Cape Coloured People', 'Coloured group', and 'Coloured community' have been used somewhat loosely in the same context. It remains to be determined, however, how far the Cape Coloured group does in fact form a community in the sociological sense, or how far it is a loose nexus of smaller communities, or a hierarchy of classes based on economic, cultural and even racial distinctions.

The general marks of a community seem to be the conscious sharing, not of particular interests, as in associations, but of the basic conditions of a communal life, within a definite territorial area.[107] This does not necessarily mean that the group in question is the only occupant of that area. On the other hand, a group occupying a single area need not necessarily be a community. For instance, we should not at present speak of the South African community or even the Cape Town or Wynberg[108] community. We should, however, speak of the Cape Town Malay community or the South African Jewish community. Although all Non-European ethnic groups in South Africa are more or less scattered and acculturated, it seems possible to consider them as potential if not actual communities.

In the case of the Cape Coloured People, there is a powerful geographical focus for them in the Cape Province, and, since the development of modern communications, in Cape Town itself. That this has some unifying influence is shown in the name Cape Coloured People, or even, simply, Cape People. On the other hand, their differing origins and the bases of internal class status are powerful factors against internal cohesion or subjective community of 'interests, sentiments and behaviour'.[109] Before considering the centripetal and centrifugal forces which act on the Coloured group as a whole, we should therefore give a brief outline of its internal class structure.

Europeans in South Africa as a whole are barely conscious of the existence of social classes within the Coloured group. In their conception of the general class structure, the rôle of the Coloured group is to remain an urban or rural proletariat, at the bottom of the pyramid.[110] The Coloured class structure has not perhaps so large an upper or middle class proportionately as the Negro structure in the States, nor are its economic status-determinants so high.[111] Nevertheless, class-stratification does exist, and some Coloured informants have claimed, almost with pride, that their group recognises more class-distinctions than do South African whites amongst themselves.

Earlier in this chapter we have often found it necessary to refer to class distinctions when discussing family and associational groups. A great deal more study would be necessary to determine the gradation and relative size of such classes, and here we can only indicate what seem to be the major determinants of the class distinctions that have arisen. These determinants are: education, occupation, property, appearance, birth and ethnic origins, in one combination or another, with the major emphasis on the first two.

The economic basis of class differentiation differs from town to country. In the urban areas it is usually the possession of a skilled trade or profession,[112] in the rural areas the possession of land. In the towns, a certain amount of education is essential for the acquisition of a skill, and of course much more so of a profession, and the gaining of a secondary or higher education is largely dependent upon the parents' financial resources. In the absence of great wealth education is more important as a status-determinant in the Coloured community than amongst white South Africans.[113]

In the country, too, the educational determinant is assuming more importance, particularly with the decline of the well-to-do Coloured farmer,[114] and the gradual breakdown of the rural class-stratification based on birth and ownership of land. It is the teachers, and sometimes the Coloured ministers, who are now coming to be the spokesmen if not the leaders of rural Coloured communities in the larger Coloured group.[115] The former rural status-hierarchy on the reserves and mission stations consisted of registered occupiers or '*Burgers*', most of them the male descendants of the original settlers, *Bywoners* (usually immigrants, many of them sons-in-law of *Burgers*), and 'servants' or labourers.[116] Here status is clearly based on descent as well as on the ownership of land, and the structure bears strong relationship to the Boer system from which it is largely derived.

Where ethnic determinants are concerned, the Coloured group appear to have taken their race prejudices over from the Europeans and even to have accentuated them.[117] Amongst the middle classes at least, lightness of colour is still prized.[118] Apart from any symbolic value, 'light' colour has so far had the very real advantage of enabling its owner to 'pass' and enjoy the privileges of the white group, the supreme instance of upward social mobility for a Coloured person.

Overt references to the European connection and 'white blood' are not made by the upper and upper-middle class racial leaders who are seeking unity with other Non-Europeans.[119] On the contrary, those who are light enough to 'pass' in casual encounters often force the persons involved to treat them as Non-Europeans.[120] The more conservative Coloured leaders, however, are far more more openly conscious of their white ancestry,[121] to the extent that their political opponents accuse them of favouring a policy whereby the lighter and more Europeanised Coloureds should be absorbed into the white community (as so many have already been), while the remainder should be absorbed into the African group.[122]

Amongst the urban middle-class, lightness of colour and the absence of 'Hottentot' traits such as pepper-corn hair[123] and flat noses, or Negroid traits such as prognathism and crinkly hair,[124] seem to be highly prized and to confer status. Dark colour is excusable on the grounds of Malay or Indian ancestry.[125] In the Western Cape and urban districts, fairness is to some extent negated by the presence of 'Hottentot' traits, so that the regular-featured, dark-skinned, straight-haired Malay may have a higher status amongst other Coloured people, despite his lack of 'white blood', than the Hottentot-white hybrid with his broad, flat nose, tightly-curled, rusty-coloured hair,[126] and yellow, freckled skin.

Amongst the rural Coloureds, Malay and Asiatic strains are rare, so that lightness of colour becomes the major determinant, particularly in areas of contact with Bantu peoples.[127] This is well exemplified in the Buys clan,[128] which for so many years tried 'to get the blood white'. Amongst the Rehoboth Bastards, Professor Marais quotes Fischer[129] on the class structure:

'I was not able to determine whether, in the days of their white ancestors, the van Wyks, Moutons, Beukeses, Koopmans or Diergaarts were more prominent or respected people than the Vries, Engelbrecht, Orlams or Vrey families, but to-day at any rate, the first-mentioned call themselves the "good", the "old" families and are almost all well-to-do . . . some of them even wealthy.'

Marais continues:

'These families were more European in appearance than the others, no doubt owing to the fact that "Europeans were more easily attracted towards marriage with their daughters." They had inter-married a great deal and formed a closed group.[130] "A man of the lower classes could never marry a girl of the higher class." The lower classes consisted of the poorer people, most of whom lived in miserable huts in the more remote parts of the reserve, and some of whom had married Hottentot women.'[131]

The lower economic classes still seem to coincide roughly with the ethnic types regarded as least desirable. A reason for this is suggested by the passage above. The wealthier families, which value whiteness, have taken steps to assure its perpetuation by closing their group to the infiltration of darker blood. In the lower class there are probably large numbers of Coloured people with little or no white admixture, the product of slave-Hottentot crosses, or more recently of Coloured-Bantu crosses. Allowance should also be made for the effect of sunburn on a dark or sallow skin, particularly in the case of labourers who are exposed to the elements for long periods. On the other hand, upper and middle-class people are less exposed to such a process in their normal way of life, while some individuals, especially women, actively avoid it.

A further reason for the considerable correlation between light colour[132] and/or Caucasoid traits and superior economic status has already been touched upon in our account of the historical origins of the Coloured People. The Asiatic slaves were culturally and technologically superior to the African slaves and most slaves considered themselves and were considered superior to the indigenous Hottentots.[133] The mixed-breeds had greater cultural and economic contacts with their white owners and progenitors, while the frontier Bastards were given lands and status by authority in return for guarding the frontier against Bushmen, Hottentots or Bantu.

All these factors gave the light-coloured[134] and Caucasoid-featured an economic start on the rest of the Coloured group, which they have to a large extent maintained till now. The Indians and some Bantu are, however, beginning to challenge their lead on the rest of the Non-European community.

At present there seems to be a growing hostility amongst Coloured people of all classes to the continued acceptance of lightness and Caucasoid traits as a determinant of superior class-status within the group.[135] The conservative political leaders are accused of guarding the interests only of those with such traits, while in the lower economic classes 'keeping oneself proud like a white' has come to be a potent source of resentment.[136]

The movement towards unity with other coloured groups has, however, not yet succeeded in eradicating the long-standing cultural and economic dependence of the Coloured man on the white. Nor is there much chance of setting up a counter-focus, such as the Garvey movement, with its emphasis on past African glories and pride in blackness, gave to a considerable part of the American Negro masses in the early 1920's.[137] Many Coloured people, of the middle class at least, still seem to feel that they have even less to expect from possible African dominance than from the present European ruling-class, which contains many persons of Coloured origin who have 'passed', only outnumbers them by two to one, and has so far accorded them a formal status above that of the African.

To sum up, then, status within the Coloured group is largely determined by educational and occupational criteria, which are for the most part found to coincide roughly with certain ethnic traits indicating a Caucasoid strain.[138] Because of their continued desirability, these ethnic traits tend to be self-perpetuating within the upper and middle classes.[139] It is not known to what extent lower-class persons who have entered the upper or middle class by reason of economic or educational achievements seek to consolidate their new status by marrying 'light', nor to what extent Coloured men from the different classes marry 'lighter'. Detailed investigations should also be conducted amongst upper and middle-class Coloured families, who speak of themselves and are spoken of as 'select' or 'good' families, to ascertain on what other determinants this judgment is based. It may be that after Emancipation the 'Free Blacks' and 'Free Malays' drew a sharp line between their own group and the slaves who were freed only by the Emancipation Act, a distinction which is perpetuated, perhaps unwittingly, by families descended from the former group.[140]

In addition to the major determinants on which class affiliation is based, there are also certain indices which are associated with membership of a particular class, but which do not determine such membership. Such indices in the Coloured group are speech, manners in the wider sense, membership of certain associations,[141] social display, dress and material possessions.

It seems probable that, as in the corresponding classes of white South Africans, literacy, good vocabulary and diction are indices of upper, and to a lesser extent, of upper-middle class status. A knowledge of the English language is also an index of higher class amongst the habitually Afrikaans-speaking Coloured group.[142] Manners and *mores* vary considerably amongst the different classes, particularly where attitudes to sex are concerned.[143] Courtesy and respect for people who are older, more educated or have a higher social status (including of course whites), seem to be characteristic of all classes but the lowest and the younger section of the professional upper class.

The indices of social display, dress and material possessions, such as furniture, radiograms and kitchen equipment, are more characteristic of the middle classes, and particularly of the precariously situated lower-middle class, than they are of the upper and lower classes. They are probably the means by which members of the lower-middle class demonstrate their rise or distance from the upper-lower class,[144] and their aspirations towards upward social mobility within their class and beyond.[145] Members of the upper-lower class, being usually unable to afford such material display, demonstrate their distance from the anti-social lower-lower class by keeping their persons and dwellings impeccably clean and their way of life 'respectable'.[146] In both classes money which can ill be spared may be spent on prestige purchases such as extra pairs of shoes, small household articles,[147] seeds and plants in the case of the upper-lower class, furniture and elaborate clothes[148] on the hire-purchase system in the lower-middle class. Even upper-middle class families will indulge in prestige-spending on social functions such as weddings or coming-of-age parties, on a scale far beyond their means.[149]

Any attempt at a quantitative presentation of the socio-economic class structure of the Coloured group could at present be made only tentatively on the basis of the Union occupational and industrial censuses. By far the greater number of Coloured people fall into the lower class. This consists of the unskilled labourers of the town and the landless proletariat of the country. Members of this class are poorly-educated, or, more frequently, illiterate.[150] They are the successors not so much of the slaves as of the mainly Hottentot servants and the Hottentot-slave hybrids. Their group is now being augmented by Bantu-Coloured hybrids.

The lower class may be subdivided into two major sections, one (the upper-lower) which accepts the social structure into which it is born without overt and permanent revolt,[151] the other which has become detached from and sunk below its place in the structure, often as a result of moving from a rural to an urban environment. This is the lower-lower class, *les bas fonds*, the anti-social, the habitual criminals, skollies, vagrants, drunkards, drug-addicts, beggars and unemployables. It is almost impossible to estimate how the lower class is subdivided between these two groups. The statistics for drunkenness and crimes of violence give us no clue, since most lower-class Coloureds carry a knife, while many Coloured even of the lower-middle class drink to excess.

The determinants of class affiliation within the white and Coloured groups are not identical, although the class-*mores* of the latter group are modelled upon those of the corresponding European classes,[152] whether rural or urban. We are arbitrarily lowering the economic criteria of status within the Coloured group in order to get a truer appreciation of internal class-structure.[153] If we accepted South African European economic and occupational criteria, we would have to class almost all Coloured people as lower class, and only a few on the fringes of the middle class. Within the Coloured group, however, a person employed as a domestic servant often belongs to the lower-middle class, while a woman factory-worker may belong to the upper-middle class, depending upon the status of their own family, their wages, and in the former case, the class-status of the European employer.[154]

The middle class we again subdivide into upper and lower-middle. In the lower-middle class we should place most skilled artisans and all semi-skilled urban workers with their families whose combined wage brings their household expenditure above the bare minimum necessary to maintain existence, and allows the family to participate in associations; the corresponding European family would be only upper-lower. In the rural context, we should possibly place farm tenants and *bywoners* (i.e., landless persons owning cattle) in this class. Such lower-middle class persons may be on their way up or down. The status of this group is a precarious one by reason of its economic bases, which can be destroyed by unemployment, ill-health, or the requirements of a large family.[155]

In the upper-middle class we should rank the few proprietors and managers of businesses, most teachers, nurses, clerks, civil servants, some farm-owners, and possibly some urban skilled artisans.[156] This class, particularly in the urban areas, has considerable stability and permanence. Status appears to inhere in families rather than individuals, some of whom may fail to achieve the necessary economic or occupational qualifications, while male members may marry below their class, without necessarily losing their class status, although their descendants may do so.[157]

The most prosperous farmers should perhaps be ranked in the infinitesimal upper class,[158] in which we must also put the few professional persons whom the Coloured community has so far produced,[159] and the most highly-qualified teachers.[160] The distinction between the upper-middle and upper classes, and the extent to which these two classes have hitherto been depleted by the 'passing' of light-skinned members, need to be worked out with much greater precision in the field, and the whole class structure given above is outlined only tentatively, as a basis for further investigation.

It should be emphasised that, irrespective of the manner of its classification, the actual existence of this somewhat complex and rigid[161] class structure within the Coloured group is a result of the colour-barrier (or as Myrdal would call it, the caste order). Without this almost complete segregation the Coloured professional would have been forced to meet white competition in the open,[162] and to acquire individual status within an open-class structure in which the whites, starting far up the scale, would for a while at least have retained the major opportunities and advantages.

We have now described the attributes which confer status within the Coloured group, and indicated the class-stratification which exists. It remains to decide to what extent the Cape Coloured People constitute a 'community', or whether they are simply a heterogeneous collection of groups and sub-communities[163] of diverse origins lumped together for administrative purposes by the dominant white group. The mere fact that such diverse groups have for over a century been treated alike administratively would of course have assisted integration to some extent.

A community provides not one but several foci for its members. Does the Coloured group have such internal foci? We have mentioned the territorial focus of the Cape, and more particularly of Cape Town. But what basic conditions of a common life are shared by the Cape Coloured People, such as are shared by, for instance, the Balobedu or the ! (this represents a click) Kung Bushmen? They lack a separate political, legal and economic structure, or even a proportionate share in the administration of this structure within the larger group.

In the political field, Coloured leaders have usually looked to one or another outside group, rarely appealed to a purely Coloured ethos. In the economic sphere, the skilled-artisan class has in the past felt that its interests tie up rather with those of European skilled artisans than with those of the great mass of unskilled and unprotected Coloured and Non-European workers. The Coloured lower classes, on the other hand, have increasingly come to share their poverty and restrictions with other Non-Europeans. Only in the social sphere do we find a focus of community, the result of the complete social colour-bar imposed by the dominant group. Even here the feeling of community is weakened by sharp class divisions.

Nevertheless, administrative distinctions, the constant pressure from outside, and the increasing burden of differentiation and discrimination are having their effect in producing a feeling of at least political community,[164] nebulous as yet but undoubtedly on the increase.[165] This growth of community feeling is further helped by the extension of the voluntary associations, most of which are exclusively Coloured, to classes which formerly took no part in their activities.

Operating against a purely Coloured community sentiment are the lack of any wider group-myths or traditions,[166] or of any common ethnic origin, and the desire of many of the group's leaders for integration with, or acceptance by, the white community, and of others for a wider community with the non-white groups. The first desire is now waning, while the latter is gaining in power, although it is hindered in the upper and middle classes by the wide differences in culture and *mores* between the various coloured groups. It might be still further impeded by the continuation of the 'divide and rule' policy, with a distinct status and privileges for each ethnic group, but the present trend of administration seems to be designed to produce as great a community feeling as possible amongst all non-whites.[167]

CHAPTER NINE

THE CAPE COLOURED PEOPLE WITHIN
THE LARGER STRUCTURE

National, religious, geographic, linguistic and cultural groups do not neces-sarily coincide with racial groups; and the cultural traits of such groups have no demonstrated genetical connection with racial traits . . . the myth of 'race' has created an enormous amount of human and social damage . . . it still prevents the normal development of millions of human beings and deprives civilisation of the effective co-operation of productive minds.[1]

SOCIAL status, whether of a group or an individual, has two aspects; it is both self-assigned, and assigned by the larger society in which one lives. Full social stability is attained only when these two aspects of status approximately coincide, so that the individual or sub-group accepts the status ascribed to him or it by the society, and the determinants on which this ascription is based.

The larger South African society is in fact equivalent to the white community, which has been and still is in a position to secure its own dominant position within the general social structure, and to ascribe status to other groups according to the determinants considered to serve its own interests best. As far as the Cape Coloured group is concerned, the status ascribed to it by the European ruling group and the determinants on which this assumption has been based have shown considerable variations.

In the early contact-situation the status assigned to such Hottentots as were sufficiently integrated with the European society was apparently based on religious and cultural criteria. The Hottentots were both pagan and primitive, and their status in European eyes was therefore extremely low.

For a considerable time, even after the introduction of slaves, bap-tism continued to confer a status which was equal in theory and often in practice.[2] Even here, however, the element of birth began to intrude, in the tendency to differentiate as regards the right to baptism between children of mixed slave-European parentage, and those whose parents were both slaves and unbelievers.[3] Although the emphasis may initially have been on the Christianity of the European, it was to shift more

M   171

and more on to the essential Europeanness, and later the whiteness, of the Christian.[4]

With the change from entrepôt to settlement, and the introduction of coloured, Non-European slaves, economic factors began to undermine the Christian-heathen stratification,[5] and to set up in its place an economic and social hierarchy based, naturally enough, on colour, because those in the lowest status-groups were persons clearly differentiated by this trait.[6] This colour-bar did not at once take on the full rigidity which it later developed,[7] and religious determinants retained sufficient force through the eighteenth century to prevent slave-owners from making any great attempt to convert their slaves to Christianity, for fear of the latter claiming their freedom.[8] In 1792 the question was referred to the Cape Town Church Council. This body pointed out that neither secular nor state law explicitly forbade the retention of baptised persons in slavery, that local custom strongly supported the practice, and that such a stipulation would obstruct the progress of Christianity if introduced.[9]

The idea of creating a buffer-group of half-breeds who were to be baptised, trained in useful occupations, freed and given land, was envisaged by the High Commissioner, H. A. van Rheede, who visited the Cape in 1685.[10] He considered that such a group, owing everything to the Dutch East India Company, would make excellent subjects.[11]

Both the Dutch and the British authorities at the Cape seem often to have dallied with this idea, to the extent of using Bastards and other mixed-breeds as troops[12] and settlers of frontier lands. Even at this early stage, however, it was rendered impracticable by the European colonists, who have always preferred to see the racial situation as a simple dichotomy between in-group and out-group, whether Christian and non-Christian, freeman and slave, European and Non-European[13] or white and non-white.[14]

It is difficult to trace the precise development of European attitudes from the original situation, whereby social status was allocated on religious and cultural criteria (the two being considered to coincide), to the position which has obtained since Union, whereby status in the larger society is completely determined by colour. The transition may have been virtually complete by the end of the eighteenth century,[15] although culture was revived as a status-determinant in the Cape after the middle of the nineteenth century, when the Cape social structure began to take in Bantu in large numbers. At this stage and until the 1920s the Coloureds were formally ranked on the side of European culture.

The status-hierarchy which evolved in the settled Western Cape and more particularly in Cape Town was until recently never entirely rigid. The lowest economic class coincided to a great extent with colour distinctions, as it still does. Individual persons of colour with suitable religious, economic and cultural qualifications were, however, at first accorded equal status and even accepted into the European group. Europeans, many of them of part-coloured descent, Free Blacks, free Malays, prize Negroes, half-caste slaves, full-blooded slaves and slave-Hottentot apprentices all lived at close quarters in a society whose complex stratifications still linger in the Cape Town of to-day, where it is often impossible to determine on visual evidence who is ranked sociologically as a European and who is not.[16]

The frontier-situation was, however, simplified by the fact that the Non-Europeans (whether Hottentots, Bushmen or later Bantu) encountered by the frontier-Boer were all 'heathen', of a less advanced culture and clearly distinguished in skin-colour and other physical traits.[17] Owing to the Boer habit of ignoring what these Non-Europeans had considered their rights to the use of land and springs, the latter were for the most part hostile. They were, moreover, often greatly superior in numbers.

The fear and even hatred of the Non-European which still play as great a part in South African race-attitudes to-day were built up less in the settled environs of Cape Town,[18] or as a result of contact with the Hottentots, than during the incessant Bushman campaigns along the expanding frontier in the eighteenth century. This fear was greatly intensified by the nineteenth-century Kaffir wars in the Western Cape and beyond, as the Voortrekkers made their way north in the face of the advancing Bantu.

In such circumstances, there was no room for the development of any complex status-hierarchy. Then as now, in the interests of self-preservation, the Boers closed their community,[19] not even admitting the Bastards who were their kinsmen. Racial, cultural and religious criteria were by now completely linked, and Non-Europeans were not apparently considered by many Boers to be fit vessels to receive Christianity.

In the Boer Republic which they founded after leaving the Cape, there was to be no equality between whites and people of colour in Church or State.[20] The 'white blood' which had strayed into black channels was regarded as thereby contaminated,[21] and must be rejected and considered as lost. The colour-line was to be drawn once and for all, and thereafter the blood was to be kept pure.[22] There was to be one marriage law for the whites and another for the non-whites, and no provisions for inter-marriage.

This uncompromising belief in the fundamental inferiority of Non-Europeans was not restricted to the Voortrekkers. It was held, in perhaps a less aggressive form, by many if not most Europeans in the Cape, particularly outside Cape Town.[23] The initial impetus which gave rise to 'Cape liberalism' was mainly provided by the British philanthropic movement in the early part of the nineteenth century, working through the missionary societies and their sympathisers in the colonial administration.[24]

Those British and Dutch settlers who remained in the Cape were at least willing to accept the new legislation which conferred equal legal status on Hottentots and slaves, if not to extend their acceptance to the humanitarian principles which underlay the legislation. It was probably easier for them to accept formal equality of status, because in fact the Coloured people as a whole were economically and culturally on a lower level, and fell automatically into the lowest class. It was only later, when some Coloured individuals achieved educational, economic and cultural parity, that the question of equal social status arose in an acute form.

It has been suggested earlier that after the granting of self-government to the Cape in 1853 'Cape liberalism' as an indigenous growth did not always triumph over other local attitudes. Undoubtedly it was more difficult for politicians dependent upon local support to legislate boldly for racial equality than it had been for the Colonial administration in Whitehall. The arrival upon the Cape scene of large numbers of 'uncivilised' Bantu further intensified colour-attitudes.

Moreover, while the Coloured people had equal political and legal status, the *laissez-faire* economic doctrines of the last half of the nineteenth century, and the moderation of missionary efforts, weakened their chances of achieving any comparable economic status, which might have helped to tilt the horizontal colour-bar. By the end of the century the Coloured people had done little to convert their formally equal status into a real equality. Politically they were not united.[25] Economically the vast majority remained an urban or rural proletariat, divided from the few Coloured urban artisans by a class feeling almost as powerful as the colour-bar.

Nevertheless, by the time of Union, a certain tradition of mildness and tolerance in colour questions still prevailed at the Cape,[26] and particularly in Cape Town. There was in existence a rough division of labour, based largely but not entirely on colour lines, which entailed the minimum of friction.[27] Except in the Western Cape, farming was almost entirely in the hands of Afrikaans-speaking Europeans, being the only occupation (except for the professions) considered fit for a white man.

Trade and commerce were largely the preserve of the English-speaking South African. Skilled artisan work in the towns had since slave days been monopolised by Coloured people. The European artisans who had arrived more recently did not at first adopt local prejudices to a very great extent, so that here the different ethnic groups worked together fairly amicably. Unskilled labour was entirely in the hands of the Coloured people, except in the Eastern Province, into which even cheaper African labour was successfully infiltrating.

Had the Cape situation been left to itself, it seems possible that as a result of the high degree of cultural identity between Coloureds and

Europeans, and the considerable extent of existing racial intermixture, a fluid situation would have arisen, with the majority of Coloured people remaining in the lower economic strata for a considerable time, while a minority would have risen to economic and possibly social parity with the Europeans. On the other hand, some Europeans (and the Cape produced a large percentage of the Poor Whites) might have sunk to the lowest economic level and thereby lost their superior social status,[28] assuming that the Cape authorities did not protect them with a 'white labour policy' on a similar scale to that administered by the Union Government.

All this is, however, mere conjecture. Union was accomplished and Cape liberalism compromised. Since then the attitudes of the Northern Republics and Natal have increasingly directed political developments in South Africa, aided by a resurgent Afrikaner nationalism in the Cape itself, with its intellectual centre at Stellenbosch only thirty-five miles from Cape Town.

The great influx of Poor Whites into the towns after Union brought a new menace to the few urban Coloureds who had achieved some economic status as skilled artisans and craftsmen. To whites conditioned to the idea that all non-whites were inferior to them in status, it seemed intolerable that Coloured men should enjoy the economic status of skilled workers while white men did 'Kaffir work'. The first generation of urban Poor Whites were perhaps irreclaimable, but the second could be trained and assisted to a more fitting economic status.

The Africans suffered much more than the Coloured people as a result of the 'civilised' or 'white labour policy'. Nevertheless, the correlation of the terms 'white' and 'civilised' left the onus on the Coloured person to prove that he was 'civilised', while the 'civilisation' of the white was taken for granted.

Thus since Union in South Africa, or for the last forty years, there has been a growing insistence from the European group that colour and inferior status be equated. This has occurred side by side with, and perhaps as a result of, the increasing demand by Coloured and African individuals for an equal status on the grounds of achievement. The European is now being confronted with the situation that, given reasonable opportunities, some Non-Europeans are capable of achieving equal status.

Such a development, however, does not fit into the European's ideal scheme and must therefore be rejected. Any attempt to improve the conditions or status of the Non-European is construed as a threat not only to white supremacy but to continued white existence in South Africa.[29]

The origins of white race-attitudes in South Africa may be traced historically to motives of a primarily economic nature, in the widest sense of a struggle for labour, land and self-preservation. After three centuries these motives have, however, become blurred and complicated by the introduction of social and religious sanctions,[30] of value-judgments as to the 'good' and 'bad' qualities of 'blood', and of distorted scientific theories. Above all, the attitudes have become sanctioned by time and habit.[31] Only a small minority of white South Africans ever consciously analyse or question the major premises on which the dominance of their ethnic group is based; the conditioning to this end from early childhood is too all-embracing and effective.

The average white in South Africa never encounters Non-Europeans except as servants and inferiors.[32] As a child, he soon notices that Non-European children do not have the same material privileges as himself, and that association with them is discouraged and usually forbidden by his own group. It becomes or is made clear to him that such material inferiority and the prohibition of association is to be associated with the most noticeable trait of the Non-European, his dark skin.

If, as an adult, any doubts enter his mind they are usually dispelled by some form of rationalisation, as a second line of defence. Subconsciously the doubter is seeking for considerations which will resolve his doubts, and enable him to continue to accept the *status quo*. The preservation of the existing situation is, or seems to be, entirely to his advantage. He finds such pretexts for its continued acceptance in the observably inferior character traits of many Non-Europeans, the backwardness of the indigenous cultures in general, the results of comparative intelligence tests carried out in a European context, and so on.

Having successfully rationalised the existing social order, the doubter may quiet any remaining pangs of conscience by contributing his time or money to some welfare organisation.[33] This is socially acceptable to most members of the white group, including those who have never consciously queried the colour-hierarchy, provided that the organisation concerned works within the existing social framework. Non-Europeans may be fed, healed and taught such approved social habits as honesty, industry, self-discipline, thrift, cleanliness, sobriety and respect for their betters, and may also in the process learn that many Europeans are well-disposed to them.

Where do the Coloured people fit into this situation? The answer is that they, and particularly the urban educated class, have no place in the simple situation of white in-group and black out-group. Like the free black burghers of the seventeenth and early eighteenth centuries, they do not conform to the stereotype of the inferior, alien, uncultured black.[34] Physically, they may not always be immediately recognisable as members of the out-group.

In addition, their inheritance of 'white blood' logically entitles them to some consideration from those who uphold its superiority, thereby creating an intermediate situation intolerable to the believers in a simple white-black dichotomy.[35] Moreover, the strong religious and social emphasis imposed on racial purity may well have engendered in the native-born European a feeling of responsibility and guilt for the 'sins' of his forefathers,[36] or even a suspicion that 'colour' may lurk within his own family, which again is more likely to evoke hostility than a favourable response.[37]

A result is that many European South Africans to-day have evolved a stereotype of the Cape Coloured which is definitely less favourable than that which they have of the African,[38] particularly of the tribal African. Such sentiments as: 'The Coloured may be more intelligent than the Native, but at least the latter is honest',[39] and 'the Coloured is the product of everything that's worst in the parent groups, while the pure tribal Native is a real gentleman',[40] are common currency amongst South African whites.[41]

These two statements are really based on the myth[42] of the mental, moral and physical inferiority of the mixed-breed as such, which may be described as the myth of the 'bad blood'.[43] Implicit in the final statement is the belief that culture and race are, or should be, coterminous. The African living in his tribal culture and environment is in his proper place, the detribalised African has strayed from his proper place, but may be reclaimed by implementing the policy of *apartheid*, but the Cape Coloured, that member of a 'marooned community',[44] is doubly in error, for he has lost any vestiges of cultures other than the European[45] and is also a racial hybrid.

This is part of the mythology which has become common currency amongst most European South Africans, because it supports the existing colour-hierarchy and does away with the need for individual thinking on the subject. The modern myths are based mainly on erroneous or distorted scientific theories.[46] They are more sophisticated than the eighteenth and nineteenth century myths, which were largely based on the Old Testament. Myths of the latter type, however, still have a considerable currency amongst South African Calvinists.[47]

All such myths, though reflecting the spirit of the times, perform the same function, which is to justify and uphold white supremacy, and to prevent the adulteration and disappearance of the white group. They are so much a part of the cultural background of white South Africa that they usually lurk implicit in the thought, speech and writing of many South African Europeans with avowedly humanitarian and liberal attitudes. Particularly is this true of the myth of the 'bad blood' and that of miscegenation between persons of different colours as contrary to the natural order. These myths are sometimes expressed in quasi-biological rather than social terms and are often projected on to their object, who is represented as accepting them.[48] They are well illustrated in the following passages:

'The true key to the Half-caste's position lay in the past, as it still lies to-day, in the fact that he is not at harmony within himself. He alone of all living creatures despises his own blood . . . Of that divine contentment with his own inalienable personality which lies at the root of all the heroic and half the social virtues, the Half-caste can know little. If it were possible for him with red-hot pincers to draw out every ounce of flesh that was black man's and leave only the white, in most cases he would do it. That race which would accept him he despises; and the race he aspires to refuses him . . .'[49]

A similar reflection of current myths occurs in the work of Sarah Gertrude Millin:

'Although the Coloured man vociferates sometimes that his heart is as white as the white man's, that he does not consider himself anyone's inferior, his attitude is a mere pathetic bluff. It is this very heart he speaks of, the spirit within him that is not white. However he may have proved himself in war to be not deficient in physical courage, it is as if the darkness of his skin descends also on his soul when it finds itself pitted against a white man. And how should it be otherwise? Consider his ancestry. In his veins runs, on one side, the blood of slaves; on the other side, the blood of the careless, the selfish, the stupid, the vicious. Consider his life—unwanted by the world, born into ostracism. When, poor betrayed being, shall pride and hope and courage come to him?'

'. . . But that the Cape man is a civilised being must be firmly insisted upon. He is more civilised than the European peasant, more civilised than the South African backwoodsman or the poor white . . . And yet the less civilised white peasant of Europe is to this extent the Coloured man's superior: the blood in him is stronger for advancement. Given the opportunity, the descendants of serfs may become a Tchekov. But the child of colour, unless his colour is attenuated to the verge of vanishing point, does not seem to have it in him to rise.'[50]

The reverse side of the myth of 'bad blood' is the myth of 'pure blood'. Both the European and the Bantu groups in South Africa are supposed to be 'pure',[51] despite the Coloured admixture which has filtered into the former, and the Arab and Hottentot strains often clearly visible in the latter. The fact that the scientific basis of the myth can so often be disproved does not, however, affect its sociological importance or validity.[52]

This myth has the additional advantage of being acceptable to the Bantu, as it favourably contrasts them with the mixed bloods. On the other hand, the myth of the superiority of 'white blood', extended to the Coloured, enables the latter to feel superior to the African because of his share of it.

It is impossible here to do more than mention a few of the various colour myths prevalent amongst white South Africans.[53] One of the most common is that of the 'coloured baby'.[54] This is widespread and finds adherents even amongst people who would reject the 'pure blood' and 'different species' myths as unscientific, and who would regard the appearance of a little dark stranger in a supposedly white family only as socially undesirable and embarrassing.[55]

Another myth is the 'white woman' myth. This is comparable to that of 'Southern Womanhood',[56] but first impressions suggest certain variations in degree, if not in kind.[57] The concept is possibly invested with less flamboyantly chivalrous trappings[58] by the South African European. This may be attributable to the different social environment, and the absence of a plantation-aristocracy, in which women become decorative, languid and aloof.

The concept is, nevertheless, an integral part of European mythology in South Africa.[59] A white woman who married a Coloured man lost status to a far greater degree than a white man who married a Coloured woman.[60] The woman lost membership of her ethnic group, while the man might succeed in having his wife accepted as a European. It is considered almost unthinkable by whites that a white woman should have casual sexual relations with a Coloured man,[61] while the converse is admitted as an unpleasant reality.[62]

The only type of sex relationship between white women and Coloured men which the white group is able to accept is one based on force, i.e., rape of the white woman by the Coloured man. This does not offend its ideal concept of 'white womanhood' and enables it to mete out exemplary punishment to the offender. The sharply differentiated sentences passed on Non-European men found guilty of raping women of different ethnic groups have already been mentioned. As in murder cases a Non-European life is cheap, so, in cases of rape, little value is set on Non-European virtue. On the other hand, a Coloured man's punishment for soiling the virtue of a white woman may be as great as if he had taken her life.

The general tendency of South African whites to reduce all racial problems to sexual terms[63] requires a great deal more investigation of both a sociological and a psychological nature than can be undertaken here.[64] In South Africa, where Non-Europeans outnumber Europeans by nearly five to one, the 'purity' and even identity of the white group appear more immediately threatened than they can possibly do in the United States. Nevertheless, this sex preoccupation should on the sociological level be regarded, not as an end in itself, but rather as a traditional means of perpetuating a status-hierarchy based originally on different cultural and economic achievements, which fortuitously coincided with contrasting physical traits.[65] Further explanation of the intense and indeed excessive emotions aroused in Europeans to-day at the very idea of inter-racial sex-relations should probably be sought not on the sociological but on the psychological level.[66]

White South African mythology concerning Non-Europeans also contains a series of stereotypes. These stereotypes aim at establishing the antithesis between the bad or inferior qualities of the black out-group and the good or superior qualities of the white in-group.[67] The black man is often held to be stupid, unreliable, uncivilised, lazy, ungrateful, dirty, lascivious, violent, callous and superstitious.[68] The unfavourable aspect seems to be stressed more highly in the case of detribalised urban workers or farmhands who have had some schooling.

In the case of the tribal African, this is less evident and emphasis falls rather on his inferiority. Within his status-limits he may even be allowed such favourable qualities as do not affect his inferior status. He may be represented as brave, carefree, straightforward, good-humoured, childlike,[69] enduring, religious, hospitable, fond of children and docile. Certain other traits of a childlike nature, such as naïveté, love of bright colours, singing and dancing, tendency to malapropisms and other evidences of a poorly-digested schooling, are also attributed to him.

The stereotypes applied to Coloureds do not seem to differ greatly in kind,[70] although the unfavourable aspects are probably stressed more sharply.[71] Reference has already been made to the frequent comparisons drawn between the dumb but honest African and the intelligent but dishonest Coloured.

In the country districts, and in Afrikaans fiction, one still encounters the preferred type, the respectful and respectable old Coloured servants, Outa and Aia, who correspond to the 'folk negro' of the old South.[72] This stereotype is, however, being superseded by others, which suggest the worst effects of acculturation, such as drunkenness,[73] irresponsi-bility,[74] laziness,[75] lack of group loyalty,[76] dirtiness,[77] dishonesty and criminality. Statistics often support the latter stereotypes, but the South African white who cites them to support his stereotype rarely mentions the greater willingness of the police to arrest, and of courts to convict, Non-Europeans. He also ignores the causal factors of ignorance, poverty, frustration, insecurity, ill-health and bad housing which usually prevail in groups with a high crime-rate. The European prefers to attribute the high crime-figures to the innate viciousness of the mixed-breed. The current stereotype is continually reinforced by reports of individual cases[78] in which the main emphasis is placed on assaults,[79] gang-warfare, rape,[80] and cruelty to animals.[81]

It seems likely that the unfavourable stereotype of the Coloured as compared with the African may be associated with the closer cultural and ethnic approximation of the former to the dominant group, and the consequent need for the European to justify his continued exclusion of the Coloured man from political, economic and social equality. For both groups, the preferred stereotype is one which stresses lower-class traits,[82] the exceptions being ignored, or represented as cheeky, comical and third-rate imitations.

*   *   *   *   *

There are several major ways in which the members of a minority group can respond to the imposition of a status-hierarchy by a dominant group. These behavioural responses will be classified under the following heads: acceptance (or submission), avoidance (or escape), and aggression (or resistance).[83] The nature of the response made depends upon such factors as personality-type, social conditioning, class affiliation and a conscious appreciation of the system of rewards and penalties by which the dominant group enforces its status-patterns. It is proposed merely to indicate the most important responses, which may have some bearing upon our final discussion of possible developments and trends in the South African status-hierarchy.

In the initial South African contact-situations, broadly speaking, the slaves (perforce) and Western Cape Hottentots adopted the first response of acceptance, the Bushmen, Nama and Koranna Hottentots (and some Bastard communities) the second of avoidance or escape, and the Bantu that of resistance or aggression. At present, most Non-Europeans in South Africa have little choice other than to accept the inferior status assigned to them by the European group. At times, individuals or groups can practise avoidance, where geographical isolation, social separation or material independence makes this possible. Under present conditions, aggression is expressed covertly, flaring into overt life only on rare occasions.[84]

These responses are not mutually exclusive and shade over into one another.[85] Apparent acceptance may be tinged with covert aggression, while deflected aggression may partake of avoidance. Both avoidance and all but total aggression seem to be alternate ways of meeting the sense of frustration generated in individuals who have ceased to accept the status-situation unconsciously. It is therefore difficult to define the exact conceptual boundaries of these responses.

The most complete form of acceptance of or accommodation to the status-hierarchy is found amongst rural Coloureds of all classes,[86] and particularly amongst the labouring class. This group, which is largely of Hottentot origin, with white and slave admixture, is sociologically akin to the 'folk Negro' of the rural South. The strength of the *vis inertiae* in perpetuating the status-hierarchy has already been stressed from the European side. It applies equally well in the case of illiterate, isolated Coloured groups or communities, where there is little opportunity for the entry of new social ideas.[87]

While discontent with the general situation amongst this group usually takes the behavioural form of apathy or fatalism, unconscious compensation or outlets are often sought in non-institutionalised behaviour such as emotionality, drinking, *dagga*-smoking, gambling and intra-group violence. Such behavioural modes are more or less acceptable to the dominant group in so far as they do not harm the latter. These escape-mechanisms will be described under the heading of avoidance, as they seem to be an unconscious attempt to evade or escape unconditional acceptance of the existing system.

The majority of the Cape Coloured People probably still accept their own status in the social structure to a greater or lesser degree. Complete and unthinking acceptance is, however, decreasing with increased mobility, the spread of education and democratic ideas, and the hardening of colour prejudice amongst white South Africans.[88]

There is, however, a considerable degree of conscious acceptance, particularly amongst Coloured people of the urban upper-middle and upper classes. Up to the present time the gains accruing to these classes by reason of acceptance of the status-hierarchy have probably been greater than the losses; such gains for instance as the 'vested interest' of some Coloured business and professional men in the system of segregation.

In the political sphere this response has taken the form of 'collaboration' with the white group and an acceptance of intermediate political status, provided there was no attempt by the Europeans to rank all Non-Europeans on the same status-level.[89] In the social sphere, it is manifested in the acceptance of colour-gradations.[90] Until recently, such acceptance has been facilitated by the existence of a common culture, and the somewhat ambiguous European policy which, although allocating the Coloured group lower status, nevertheless gave it a status superior to that of the Africans, and, in many respects, to that of the Indians.

Acceptance of the status-system is often associated with avoidance of certain of its implications. This response of avoidance may, however, be carried to the extreme length of physical withdrawal, as in the historical (though unsuccessful) cases of the Nama Hottentots and the various Griqua and Bastard communities, which trekked away from the European settlements to form frontier-colonies on their own. Other cases of avoidance occurred after the setting-up of mission stations, to which Hottentot labourers and freed slaves flocked in thousands, thereby escaping the full impact of the economic system.

At the present time avoidance takes somewhat different forms. Complete avoidance is possible for a comparatively few wealthy or talented individuals,[91] who leave the country, either for temporary educational purposes or permanently.[92]

Another type of response which can perhaps be classed as avoidance is the act of 'passing', 'trying for white' or 'playing white', as it is known amongst the Coloured people. This enabled the individual concerned to evade the implications of the colour-hierarchy almost as much as if he were to leave the country. He does not, however, escape the internal tensions consequent upon the necessary severing of all family ties and the constant apprehension, at least in the first and second 'passing' generation, of discovery and 'demotion'.

Until recently, however, these internal tensions do not seem to have been as severe as in similar cases in the American South.[93] This was probably due to the widespread incidence of 'passing' in the Cape urban areas,[94] and the willingness of whites to take fellow-whites at their face value.[95] Moreover, many whites will hesitate to accuse a person unknown to them of being Coloured, as such a charge, if unfounded, has been held as defamatory by the courts.[96]

In South Africa a colour probe is not generally carried back beyond the grandparents, appearance and/or associations being the most important considerations. On the not infrequent occasions when a child of an accepted European family of several generations' standing shows apparent colour admixture, the general tendency is to overlook this 'lapse' and to continue to accept both family and child.[97]

There are degrees of 'passing'. Some individuals pass over completely into the white group, breaking all Coloured ties so that their descendants may be in ignorance of their Coloured ancestry.[98] To facilitate the process, they often move to another town or province. Cape Coloureds who might not 'pass' so easily in the Cape often move to the urban areas of the Transvaal, particularly to Johannesburg, where the local Coloured people may not know them, and where the European eye is used to the unequivocal darkness and Negroid features of the African, and is not so quick to note the subtler indications of colour.[99] Others are said to 'pass' only in order to avoid the institutional restrictions placed on them by their membership of the Coloured group. These individuals may in their private social life maintain a considerable degree of connection with the Coloured community. I have heard of several such cases in Cape Town. They often originate when the individual's parents succeed in placing the lightest child or children in a European school,[100] whence they proceed to apprenticeship and 'European' jobs. It is then a matter for the individual to decide whether he will maintain or break completely with his Coloured connections.

There is a further type of casual or intermittent 'passing'. This occurs when the individual, without any intention to 'pass', is treated as white by private persons or officials in contact-situations. For instance, employees on the Cape Suburban Line have, since the introduction of *apartheid* for first-class passengers in 1948, been attempting to persuade all Europeans to use the compartments marked '*slegs Blankes*'—'Europeans Only'. Light Coloured people are sometimes asked to move into the European sections, and some of them do so. A series of such incidents may of course incline the individual concerned to 'pass' in earnest and permanently, the material inducements to do so being so great.

The attitudes of Cape Coloured people to those who have 'passed' give an index of their own response to the existing structure. 'Passing' occurs mainly in the middle and upper classes, whose members alone are economically and culturally qualified to enter the European group.[101] Many Coloureds in these classes, whose acceptance of

European colour-attitudes has already been mentioned,[102] tend to regard 'passing' with approval, to protect those relations and friends who have 'passed' by a conspiracy of silence,[103] and even to feel some pride in the possession of 'European' relatives, though they may not have any further contact with them. This approbation of 'passing' sometimes appears to contain an element of covert aggression, a feeling of 'putting something over' on the superior whites, by making them accept Coloured individuals as their equals.[104]

Amongst a small but growing number of upper-class people there seems, however, to be a feeling that 'passing' is both an indignity, because it is an acceptance of inferior status, and a betrayal of the Coloured group;[105] it is felt that those who can 'pass' should remain to work for their own people. This trend is comparable to the much more intense attitude amongst American Negroes. Community feelings and 'race pride' are, however, much more developed amongst the latter, so that there is more positive pressure upon and inducement for a Negro who could 'pass' to remain within his group. It is said that many persons who remain Negroes in the United States are so 'white' as to provoke disbelief in their race even on the part of Southern whites.[106]

In the Cape, on the other hand, very few instances of individuals who could pass as white and yet remain in the Coloured group have been encountered by the writer.[107] This is a purely personal impression, and it is quite possible that many more such persons do exist. The impression gained from my own observation was, however, that most of those who could 'pass' still did so,[108] and that dubious cases were much more frequent in the officially 'white' population.

With the growth of community feeling, group disapproval of 'passing' would probably have grown, and its incidence decreased, even without such legislative checks as the Mixed Marriages Act and Population Register. Myrdal has listed possible reasons, other than the fear of group disapprobation, which may operate to prevent 'passing' in the United States.[109] They include: (a) race or group pride and a missionary zeal to work for the group's betterment; (b) a constant feeling of strain and apprehension of discovery in white company; (c) the difficulty of attaining a status as high as one would hold in the Negro community against the far greater competition in the white community, and the lower prestige consequent upon the attainment of even a high professional position in the white community; (d) the pleasanter and fuller social life in the Negro community; (e) sheer inertia, and disinclination to make the careful plans and take the great decision involved.

All these factors have probably had a certain influence on the Cape Coloured group. In future the incidence of 'passing' will also be drastically checked by the proposed nation-wide introduction of registration-cards, on which the individual's ethnic origin will be recorded. One can foresee a lively trade in forged identity cards, but even so would-be 'passers' will be deterred, not only by such informal consequences of discovery as loss of desirable jobs or transfer to Coloured schools, but by legal sanctions against such offences as false declaration.

In these circumstances it is probable that a process will occur in South Africa similar to that which has already occurred in the American South. There the light-skinned and usually culturally superior mulattoes were long ago rejected by the white group to which they aspired. They found sufficient compensation for their rejection in leadership and high status within the Negro group, and consciously furthered the growth of group feeling and pride. The Cape Coloured are now being rejected by the European group in the same way, and there are already signs of a similar development,[110] with some Coloured leaders thinking not in terms of Coloured community but of Non-European unity.

'Passing' and leaving the country are avoidance-mechanisms for those whose appearance or financial standing enables them to take these ways out. For those who remain within the Coloured group there are various modes of avoidance, usually correlated with class affiliation. Members of the upper and middle classes who wish to avoid unpleasant casual contacts with Europeans may do so by using private means of locomotion and by avoiding contact-situations generally. Another clear form of avoidance shown mainly by members of the upper and middle classes is in their preference (already mentioned) for the English language-medium when speaking to Europeans, although they may speak Afrikaans amongst themselves.

The upper and middle classes have, generally speaking, built up a fairly adequate social life within the group, which compensates many of them for their exclusion from European social life and facilities. This is not true of the lower class, who, sometimes unconsciously, sometimes perforce, accept their position in the status-hierarchy even more unreservedly.

For them avoidance often takes the usually unconscious form of the only ways of escape open to them—excessive drinking,[111] *dagga*-smoking,[112] gambling (fah-fee, dice, etc.), magic and the bioscope (cinema).[113] The two former often produce aggressive behaviour which provides a fairly satisfactory but socially-disapproved outlet for internal tension and frustration.

Coloured people of the lower-middle and lower classes are said to resort very frequently to magical practices and the use of charms. Such resort to magical practices provides an outlet for aggressive impulses directed against the dominant out-group, which may be interpreted as an attempt to control by supernatural means adverse circumstances which have remained unaffected by human agencies.

Educated informants were inclined to deny the continued high incidence of such practices, which would to them have the same sort of derogatory significance for the group as the 'coon carnivals'.[114] Nevertheless, they do persist, and the most expert practitioners are stated to be the Cape Malay '*doekums*'. Some middle-class Coloureds, particularly women, have recourse to fortune-tellers or clairvoyants, who may be European, Coloured or Indian, while lower-class Coloureds who live in close contact with African groups are said to resort to Bantu magic and its practitioners.

Another very important kind of avoidance is concerned with interracial sexual relations. The formal and customary sanctions applied by Europeans in the event of such infringements are not perhaps of so drastic a nature as lynch-law in the Southern States.[115] They are, nevertheless, always present as a threat and deterrent in the background.

Amongst the lower classes the usual response to this particular situation is probably one of unthinking acceptance,[116] particularly in the rural areas where there are comparatively few whites of the corresponding class, and opportunites for contact are few.[117] Middle and upper-class Coloureds must on the other hand adopt a more conscious avoidance response. In all classes, the greater degree of avoidance occurs between Coloured men and white women.[118] Until 1949 Europeans tended, though decreasingly, to look with more leniency on sex relations, particularly extra-marital relations, between white men and Coloured women. Coloured women who did not desire such encounters had to avoid situations which might have encouraged them.[119]

There is one further response commonly made by Coloured people to whites which is best classified as a form of avoidance. The white community has established a colour-hierarchy, and has emphatically banned social contacts and 'social equality'. The Coloured group has accommodated itself to this social colour-bar and sought compensations in its own internal social life. In contacts with whites there is a certain restraint and artificiality. Coloured people feel that the whites think of them as inferiors and are not genuinely interested in them as individuals: they therefore put on a courteous avoidance-mask which is immediately dropped when they meet another Coloured person.[120] This is the duality of rôles which is described by Dollard as the 'Dr. Jekyll and Mr. Hyde' aspect of the American Negro.[121]

The response of aggression is probably more widespread amongst the 'docile' Cape Coloured people than would appear on the surface.[122] As Dollard puts it: 'The normal human response to frustration is aggression against the frustrating object'.[123] The Cape Coloured people are in the same position as the Negroes in the Southern States. They can rarely if ever display overt aggression, and must respond to the status-situation with at least formal acceptance.

There are, however, a number of covert ways in which aggression can find an outlet which will not provoke white counter-aggression.[124] In addition, impulses of overt aggression can be deflected on to less dangerous objects, such as the in-group or other Non-European groups.

Alternatively, they can be transposed into legal and political channels which are officially sanctioned.

A major form of covert and often unconscious aggression current amongst the lower classes is expressed in waste of time and materials at work. The rewards of good work and the chances of promotion are so few that there is no incentive to work hard. Idleness and inefficiency are both cause and effect of the European stereotype of the Coloured worker.

Often this type of aggression is further extended to petty thieving of material by workmen and of food by domestics. Such petty thieving is, within limits, apparently expected and even tolerated by many employers. Newcomers to the Union are warned by acquaintances to lock up all food and drink, as otherwise they must expect it to disappear. On the other hand, plate, clothes and so on are not accepted 'squeeze', and their disappearance is usually followed by dismissal or a summons to the police.

Akin to this sort of aggression, which might be termed economic sabotage, is the habit of leaving jobs at short notice, or failing to turn up on the appointed day after agreeing to start a new job. The unreliability of Coloured workers in this and other ways is a favourite stereotype amongst Europeans, but it does not appear to be entirely without foundation at least in so far as domestic workers are concerned.

Another mode of covert aggression, manifested by those Coloureds who are in continual close contact with Europeans, takes the form of malicious discussion of European individuals or groups[125] and the formation of stereotypes about them, often derived from European stereotypes. Thus, one discussion with a lower middle-class Cape Town woman produced the opinions that the 'Dutch' were unkind, coarse and cruel, while the Jews were '*slim*' (cunning) and 'out to do one'.[126]

An extension of this verbalised aggression[127] is to be found in the frequent references by Coloured people amongst themselves to the presence of Coloured blood in highly-placed Europeans, particularly those who are regarded as the enemies of the Coloured group.[128] This verbalised aggression took overt form in January 1950, when Mr. J. H. Rhoda, until then a member of the Coloured Advisory Council, said in a press interview that there were many people 'masquerading in high places as Europeans', and that if the Government persisted in their *apartheid* policy, a list of them would be produced.[129]

Amongst the upper and middle classes, aggressive impulses are sometimes canalised into determined efforts to raise the individual's economic and social status above the level conventionally allotted to all Coloureds by the European group as a whole. Such efforts are regarded as provocation or aggression by many, though not all, Europeans, particularly when increased prosperity takes the outward form of good clothes, a new car and so on.[130]

Higher education, professional qualifications, and outward signs of

N

prosperity do not conform to the conventional European stereotype of the Coloured person.[131] Even a skilled artisan who does his job efficiently but shows some sign of independent decision may be called 'cheeky' and 'above himself'.[132] This form of aggression is not, however, as common amongst Cape Coloureds as amongst South African Indians, who seem much more determined to raise their individual status.

Direct overt aggression by Coloureds against Europeans is infrequent (more so than African aggression) and usually takes the form of individual outbursts of violence.[133] White pedestrians or drivers are sometimes attacked or beaten up in the poorest Coloured districts. Coloured thieves surprised while robbing a house often resort to violence in order to escape. In such cases as the latter, however, the main motive is theft,[134] the violence merely a concomitant. Nevertheless, many Coloured of the urban lower class carry knives, coshes or razor blades, which they use freely amongst themselves, so that the temptation to fight their way out of any compromising situation must be considerable.

Individual aggression without a further motive also occurs in cases of rape or lesser sexual assaults by Coloured men against white women or girls.[135] Rape is, as Dollard points out in the American context, 'the most intensely hostile act a Negro can perform within the purview of Southern regional culture'.[136] The fear and expectation of such sexual assaults are very intense amongst South African whites,[137] and produce the severest possible counter-measures.[138]

As in the Southern States, it is possible that Coloured men who commit sexual assaults are motivated, consciously or unconsciously, by a desire to get even with the whites in the person of their womenfolk, a desire aggravated by resentment of the more frequent miscegenation between white men and Coloured women.

In addition, Coloureds who have been conditioned to feel a certain superiority to other Non-Europeans because of their share of 'white blood' may sometimes feel an unrecognised desire to possess the idealised, forbidden 'white woman' for prestige purposes. All these impulses and aggressions might be liberated by a chance encounter between one or more Coloureds, often under the influence of drink or even *dagga*, with a white woman or girl in a lonely place.

Occasionally, direct aggression may take the form of non-sexual assaults against individual whites, from motives of revenge against individuals, particular groups, or the white group in general. Because of their more directly hostile attitudes and frequent brutality, lower-class whites, especially those in official or semi-official positions, such as police officers, bus conductors[139] and so on, are the main targets for such overt attacks, which occur most frequently in crowded Non-European urban areas where the assailants are amongst their own people and can more easily escape arrest.[140]

Overt aggression of a violent nature is usually confined to the lower classes. The urban upper and upper-middle classes have evolved modes of overt aggression within the legal framework of South African society. These can be subdivided under the headings of legal, political and economic aggression. No instance of overt social aggression, such as attempts to gain entrance to European homes, hotels, clubs and places of entertainment by Coloured people too dark to pass, have so far been encountered.[141] Such incidents may have occurred, but upper and middle-class Coloureds seem less concerned with obtaining 'social equality' than with augmenting their rights and status in other spheres.[142]

Legal aggression takes the form of bringing cases to test various discriminatory local regulations in relation to the enabling statute. Such test cases are sometimes won, but the ultimate effect may be to effect an extension of the statute to cover the loop-hole.[143]

The Carelse case referred to in Chapter VI was an example of another type of aggression through legal channels. Not only did Mr. Carelse take his white assailants to court, an action regarded as a breach of race etiquette, as the second beating by unknown Europeans showed, but when the magistrate exonerated one of the accused he took the case up on appeal to a higher court and won it. As a consequence he had to leave the neighbourhood and cover his tracks, a sequel which might deter all but a very few individuals from following his example. A further deterrent is the financial aspect, and the growing belief that it is useless to expect complete impartiality in European courts.

Direct political aggression appears in the formation of parties with a platform of equal rights for all, such as the Anti-C.A.D., the former National Liberation League and Non-European United Front,[144] the Unity Movement, the former Communist Party, and the Franchise Action Council (only the former being confined to Coloureds).

In 1948 the Trains Apartheid Resistance Committee provided a visible demonstration of formalised group aggression with a series of public protest meetings, and a single deliberate though non-violent flouting of the new regulation by several hundred Coloured passengers. This type of aggression was not continued, but Mr. A. E. Abdurahman, who instigated the breaking of the new rule, fought his conviction through to the Appeal Court with ultimate success.[145]

This kind of group political aggression, through orderly mass meetings and demonstrations, has so far not been employed very effectively by the Coloured people. This may be attributed to a combination of such factors as the lack of any profound community feeling, the continued acceptance of the *status quo* by many Coloured individuals,[146] and the fear of white sanctions.

A good deal of verbalised political aggression finds an outlet in the Coloured press. Theoretically, this press is available to all ethnic groups, but it is doubtful whether one in a thousand Europeans has ever laid eyes on a Coloured publication. Such verbalised aggression has therefore the advantage of being apparently overt, while avoiding any major repercussions. The *Torch* in particular is filled with attacks on the 'white fascists' and 'Herrenvolk', and rather spiteful and belittling remarks about prominent white personalities which must afford considerable satisfaction to both writers and readers, without producing any immediate adverse consequences.

Overt aggression in the economic sphere can take the form of workers' action in the form of strikes or go-slow movements, or can be initiated by consumers in the form of boycotts. So far effective aggression of this type has, as we have shown, been prevented by the lack of community feeling amongst organised skilled workers, by the low purchasing power of Coloured consumers and by the lack of effective organisation within the Coloured or Non-European groups.

Finally, overt aggression may be deflected from its original object on to some less dangerous person or group (thus becoming covert), or it may be expressed in verbal or behavioural forms to friendly Europeans, usually from countries outside South Africa.[147] Only a few Coloured persons have such an opportunity, however, and the main objectives of this deflected aggression are the other Non-European groups or the Coloured in-group itself.

Both these responses are encouraged by Europeans who regard the 'divide and rule' policy as one of their best weapons. The Cape Coloured people have on the whole been allowed to believe that their mixed blood and their long European cultural association put them on a much higher level than the primitive, unacculturated African.[148] They have suffered from the economic competition of the African worker,[149] and have smarted under the racial arrogance of Africans who have also taken over the white preoccupation with pure blood.[150]

The deflection of aggression on to the African group has been facilitated by the status-hierarchy, in which discrimination has so far fallen much more heavily on the African than on the Coloured. The European tendency[151] in many spheres to group Coloureds and Africans together, in hospitals, clinics, transport, and often prisons, while it has brought about a certain political *rapprochement*, has also proved an added irritant to Coloured people who are more concerned with immediate material aspects. Many Coloureds of the middle classes in particular object to being classified with Africans, the reasons adduced being similar to those given by Europeans for desiring spatial segregation between themselves and Non-Europeans, such as the difference in standards of living and behaviour.[152]

Amongst the lower classes, there may be less cause for resentment on this score, particularly towards detribalised urbanised Africans. On the other hand, the official policy of differential treatment has so far given even the lowest Coloured a certain superiority of status over the African, which he is naturally unwilling to relinquish.[153] The venting of aggression by Non-Europeans within their own group rather than on Europeans may to some extent be encouraged by the markedly lighter sentences passed on such offenders by the courts.

The Indian group is not a very considerable target for Coloured aggression. There are few Indians in the Cape, where they are officially accorded the same status as the Coloureds, and many Indian men marry Coloured women, or Malays in the case of Moslems. The Cape Coloured people on the whole do not seem to feel the same resentment against Indian store-keepers as Africans are alleged to feel in Natal.

Nevertheless, during the visit of Pakistani and Indian delegations to Cape Town in February 1950 for round table talks with the South African Government, the Coloured Press displayed a tone of some hostility and resentment against the South African Indian community, which has tended to remain rather aloof from unified Non-European protest movements.[154]

The greatest deflection of Coloured aggression is probably that aimed towards the in-group itself. In the American context this type of deflection has been defined by Dollard as a negative form of Sumner's proposition: 'The relationship of comradeship and peace in the we-group and that of hostility and war towards others-groups are correlative to each other.'[155] Dollard also stresses the strong social and economic dependence of the Negro upon the white group, which make it difficult for the former to establish the latter as an out-group.[156] This proposition would carry even more weight in the case of the Cape Coloured, whose status as a permanent and inferior out-group has not been so long nor finally established, and for whom the European group is similarly not a cultural out-group.

A great deal of internal aggression within the Coloured group takes the form of unpremeditated, almost haphazard violence. As has been said, many lower-class Coloureds carry knives, coshes, bicycle chains or razor-blades. The prevalent escape mechanisms of drink, *dagga* and gambling may provoke rather than substitute for aggression.[157] Violence often occurs as a routine evening pastime between rival skolly-gangs, or is directed against more solid members of the community. The social distance and occasional hostility between the Coloured middle and lower classes has already been described. Middle-class Coloureds provide a safer[158] outlet for violence than the Europeans whom they are accused of 'aping'.

The *mores* of Coloured family life in the lower and even lower-middle classes seem to include a great deal of violence, from parents towards their children, and husbands towards their wives. This may be a further outlet for covert aggression. Wife-beating after the week-end visit to the canteen, bottle-store, or shebeen is apparently as well established as it was, we are told, amongst the British working-class in the last century. It is apparently accepted in much the same spirit, as a normal concomitant of married life and preferable to indifference.

Amongst the upper and upper-middle classes violence is frowned upon and internal aggression takes the form of internal dissensions and political controversy. The animosity shown by the rival parties towards each other sometimes appears more intense than the hostility shown towards out-groups. In the case of the radical leaders, their 'collaborationist' opponents undoubtedly serve as a substitute target for aggression against the European group, while for middle-class and upper-lower-class Coloureds the Cape Malay sub-community, which is in some ways a cultural out-group, is often the object of latent hostility.[159]

In this study we have tried to show the evolution of a status-hierarchy designed to further the interests of a dominant group, and based successively on religious, cultural and colour criteria. We have indicated the gradual breakdown of customary sanctions, and the increasingly formalised measures adopted by the dominant group to preserve the colour-hierarchy in the face of changing economic and social conditions; these measures have lately taken the form of attempting to impose a rigid, caste-like system, in which colour distinctions will again be qualified by differences in cultural levels.[160] Finally, an attempt has been made to show the increasing rejection by the more advanced sections of one subordinate group of the status ascribed to their group on grounds of colour alone, coupled with demands for higher status within the larger society on the grounds of cultural and economic achievements.

These demands are not yet backed by sufficient strength or unity to force any concessions out of the dominant group. Nevertheless, the growing colour-prejudice felt by the dominant group,[161] and the increasingly aggressive counter-measures with which it is trying to reinforce its status, are in turn driving all subordinate groups to unite against it. In the South African situation, the dominant in-group has taken its stand firmly on colour and not culture, with the result that the Coloured group, which is neither culturally nor racially marginal, is nevertheless being forced into a position of leadership amongst the dominated out-groups.

From the detailed description of various forms of differentiation and discrimination given in Part II, it seems fairly clear that there has since Union been a growing tendency amongst all whites to adopt the simple black-white dichotomy of the Northern provinces, both in custom and in legislation.[162] Such preferential provisions as are still made for Coloureds in the Cape are a survival of the 'old Cape liberal tradition', or a concession to the small political strength which they have until now possessed. The frequent promises of vertical development 'in their own areas' which are made to each group by the apostles of *apartheid* mean in practice only that these groups must accept subordination in European areas, and may be interpreted as a continuation of 'divide and rule' methods.

On almost every page of this study has fallen the great shadow of the African community, nearly 8,500,000 strong. It is between this group and the whites that the real issue lies. In an amalgamative situation the Coloured people would have become the bridge, in a colonial situation the buffer middle-class. In the nineteenth century Cape there were some traces of these situations, and there were few Africans, so that the gradations of colour and culture were numerous and gradual instead of being sharply dichotomised. In the bipartite[163] situation that prevails in South Africa to-day, however, the status ascribed to the Coloured group must inevitably decline.[164]

On their side, politically-conscious Coloureds are not prepared to continue to accept their present status in the larger society, much less to submit to a lower status. The same consideration applies to the acculturated sections of the African and Indian groups. Acculturation has brought and will continue to bring these sections and groups closer together. As unity and resistance spread, as they must ultimately do despite such obstacles as geographical separation, inter-group prejudice, envy, poverty and ignorance, it is difficult to see how a violent upheaval of the social structure can be avoided unless the dominant group reverts to a cultural basis for its status-hierarchy.[165]

Such a development may seem quite improbable seen against the background of the European attitudes described in this chapter and earlier. European attitudes are not, however, monolithic, but show certain variations which may have dynamic possibilities. Most important perhaps are the attitudes which appear to lie dormant[166] at the back of modern industrial and commercial development in South Africa, which has demonstrated that a man's skill does not depend on his colour, and that a coloured man's money, if he has enough of it, is as good as a white man's money.

With increasing overseas contacts, there is also a growing liberalism, as yet confined to a comparative few, but indigenous and less paternalistic than the philanthropy of the nineteenth century. Whether such attitudes can break down the barriers of fear and hatred in the white group before irrevocable hostility is aroused in the non-white groups is, however, a question that only time can answer.[167] A third possibility, which may at present seem far-fetched, is that if certain white sub-groups are threatened or persecuted too far, the unity of the white group may be broken, and these dispossessed whites may look for allies amongst the non-white peoples.[168]

NOTES

NOTES

CHAPTER I—THE APPROACH

1. Myrdal, pp. x–xi.
2. The same pattern is to be found in C. S. Johnson's *Patterns of Segregation*.
3. Colour attitudes have not, of course, always been entirely uniform throughout the Union, but will be found to differ in intensity rather than in kind at present.
4. Although this was the expressed hope of Cape politicians at the time of Union (*v.* Ch. III, p. 34). Since then the position has been reversed, and the comparatively liberal structure of the old Cape Colony undermined by Union legislation.
5. MacIver (1), pp. 5–11.
6. See Louis Wirth; *The Problem of Minority Groups*, p. 349, in *The Science of Man in the World Crisis*, ed. Lynton. See also Cox, pp. 368–9, on the denial of civic pride to coloured peoples in what he calls the 'bipartite situation'.
7. By way of contrast, South African Non-Europeans who visit or live in Britain are, subject to the usual regulations, entitled to the full franchise as British subjects, although the majority are denied any form of franchise in their own country.
8. Stonequist, pp. 22–3.
9. There has, of course, been European-Bantu miscegenation, the product of which is classed as 'Coloured', but not specifically 'Cape Coloured'.
10. Even now Bantu penetration into the Cape Coloured stronghold of the Western Cape and Cape Peninsula is slowed by the operation of the Native (Urban Areas) Consolidation Act (No. 25 of 1945)—see *Race Relations Handbook*, pp. 232–42.
11. 'Racial' problems are, of course, concerned less with biological fact than with what individuals and groups conceive to be biological fact. And so, in South Africa, there is a growing number of Europeans, usually recent arrivals, who are unaware of the historical background of the Cape Coloured people, and regard them as 'biologically' or 'racially' marginal because they happen to be intermediate in colour.
12. As acculturation proceeds amongst the Bantu, these cultural differences will of course diminish.
13. Marais, pp. 281 and 283.
14. There have, however, always been small upper-class groups which are biologically and culturally marginal between their own Coloured group and the Europeans (see Ch. VIII).
15. A frequently-encountered charge against South African liberals is that they are a 'Fifth Column' within the ranks of 'White South Africa' (cf. Hoernle (1), preface, p. vii).
16. *v.* MacIver (2), p. 114.
17. *v.* Cox, Part I, *passim*.
18. Cox, pp. 431–2.
19. For instance, Myrdal, Allison Davis, John Dollard (but see E. Franklin Frazier (1), p. 673, n. 15 for a comment on this.)
20. *v.* Cox, p. 82 *et seq.*
21. If complete political, economic and social *apartheid* were to be applied in

South Africa for some generations, the system might come to resemble a true caste-system, as the reclassification of individuals into their appropriate colour-group which now takes place every generation would be prevented by the rigid operation of the Population Registration Act (see *Institute of Race Relations Memorandum*, R.R. 45/50, Dar., 29th March, 1950, p. 3).

22. MacIver defines a social class as 'any portion of a community which is marked off from the rest, not by limitations arising out of language, locality, function, or specialisation, but primarily by social status. Such a subjective factor involved also as a rule, objective differences, income levels, occupational distinctions, distinctions of birth, race, culture, and so forth, within the society . . .' But, he points out: '. . . the concept of class loses its sociological significance if it is *defined* by any purely objective criterion, such as income level or occupational function. Class does not unite people and separate them from others unless they feel their unity or separation . . . There is no social group whose members do not share some sentiment of what they have in common, and what we cannot, without destroying the very meaning of the term, make class an exception to this rule.' (MacIver (1), p. 167.)

23. 'Only the racial barrier of colour completely resists the triumphant claim of wealth to be at length the chief determinant of class, and this defeat is less decisive because of the general poverty of the coloured people.' (MacIver (1), p. 171.)

24. Cf. Louis Wirth. 'The Problem of Minority Groups', from *The Science of Man in the World Crisis*, p. 353.

25. 'The practical efforts of the marginal man to solve his own problem lead him consciously or unconsciously to change the situation itself, as nationalist, conciliator, interpreter, reformer or teacher. In these rôles he inevitably promotes acculturation.' (Stonequist, p. 221.)

26. Dominant groups usually contain a certain number of individuals who do not fully accept the bases of the existing status-hierarchy. In such areas as South Africa and the American South, the irreconcilability of the colour-bar with the 'European' or 'American' ideals whose operation is still largely restricted to the dominant group cannot fail to strike objective observers. Cf. Cox, p. 434.

27. E.g., the '*asimilado*' of Portuguese East Africa, and the '*élite*' and '*evolué*' of the French and Belgian colonial empires.

28. 'What constitutes the race problem is not the fixed character of the relations, but their dynamic character. There would be no race problem if the Negro group uniformly accepted the status assumed for it.' (Johnson, *Growing Up in the Black Belt*, p. 276, quoted by Myrdal, p. 1,189.)

29. Professor MacMillan, writing over twenty years ago, recommended a closer study of the Cape colour problem, for this purpose ((1), p. 25).

30. August 1948 to November 1949, and January–February 1951.

31. Even here, I was unable, owing to an insufficient mastery of the language, to examine the Afrikaans sources in the same detail as I did the English language literature. The major reference books are however listed in the bibliography, in the hope that others may be able to make greater use of them. A further difficulty was the absence of up-to-date official statistics, most departmental reports being at least three years out of date. In many cases, later figures could be obtained by visits to the departments concerned, but time and distance often made such visits impossible, and written requests were not always answered in detail. Moreover, Dr. Malan has stated that 'receiving information from a government office is not a right but a privilege'. (*Cape Times* second editorial, 21st May, 1951.) Nevertheless, the great majority of government officials approached for information have been courteous and helpful, notably those in the Bureau of Census and Statistics.

32. As an Englishwoman, who therefore came more into contact with English-speaking South Africans, and was occasionally exposed to the hostility of individual Afrikaners in a country where the Anglo-Boer War is still a very live issue, I had to guard against a tendency to make the Afrikaner the villain of the piece. As a

liberal, believing in the principle of common humanity, and accepting cultural rather than racial divisions and affiliations, I sometimes found it difficult to maintain an objective approach to problems on a happy solution of which depends the future of all Europeans in South Africa.

33. The main danger was that in looking for evidences of colour-prejudice, I tended to become more colour-conscious than the people whose reactions I was trying to study, and to interpret all actions and attitudes from this viewpoint without further analysis, forgetting that behaviour in such a situation is usually the result of habit rather than of logical thinking.

34. Cf. Dollard, pp. 7–12, for an account of similar difficulties encountered in 'Southerntown'.

35. This 'unwritten law' is now supported by the Mixed Marriages Act of 1949 and the Immorality Amendment Act of 1950. (See Ch. VII.)

36. Cf. Dollard, p. 8.

37. See Ch. IX, p. 58, for a more detailed discussion of this, and other evidences of aggressive behaviour.

CHAPTER II—THE CAPE COLOURED PEOPLE

1. General J. B. M. Hertzog, in a speech at Smithfield, 13th November, 1925.

2. The main sources of information are the census reports and the official records of births, marriages and deaths. In the case of Coloureds, the latter are now said to be more or less complete; in the case of Africans they cover only urban areas. Censuses were quinquennial for the European population and decennial for Non-Europeans from 1911 to 1946. The Coloured groups and other Non-Europeans were omitted from the 1931 Census on the grounds of economy, which accounts for the fifteen years' gap between 1921 and 1936. Only a few preliminary figures are as yet available for 1946, fewer still for 1951, which enumerated all ethnic groups.

3. In the 1951 Census the Cape Malays, who had previously been included in this group, were enumerated as a separate ethnic group. Broadly speaking, the three Non-European groups are geographically based, although large-scale infiltration has occurred. The Cape Coloureds are mainly found in the Western Cape, Africans in the Eastern Cape, Zululand, the Protectorates and the Transvaal, and Indians in Natal.

4. See Appendix D for the racial composition of the total Coloured group, based on voluntary returns.

5. The Griquas, now of Griqualand East, are the best-known of these communities. Outside the Cape there are the Rehoboth Bastards in South-West Africa, the Buys Clan of the Northern Transvaal and the Dunn Family of Natal. The two latter are Euro-Bantu in origin and do not use the name 'Bastard', although they too pride themselves on their white antecedents. These and other past 'mixed' communities merit more detailed study than it has been possible to give them within the scope of this work, owing primarily to their geographical isolation (Rehoboth is over 700 miles north of Cape Town, and Kokstad (E. Griqualand) 650 miles north-east ; Rehoboth and Kokstad are over 850 miles apart, while the Zoutpansberg, where the Buys Clan lives, is nearly 1,000 miles north-east of Cape Town, about 250 miles north-east of Johannesburg and separated from Rehoboth by over 750 trackless and waterless miles, consisting mainly of the Kalahari Desert). Mention of these groups is thus necessarily confined to references where these occur in the literature. A list of the principal works giving a detailed account of their origins and history is given in n. 44 of this chapter, and a brief reference to class and family groupings will be found in Ch. VIII, n. 11, on p. 165.

6. See Appendix A. The drop from 8.8 per cent to 7.9 per cent between 1911 and 1921 is attributed in part to the influenza epidemic of 1918, which fell more severely on the Coloureds than on any other group (see *Race Relations Handbook*, p. 25), in part possibly to a high incidence of 'passing' into the white group (see Ch. IX,

n. 93). Since then the proportion has risen again, due to a decreasing death rate, and possibly a decreasing incidence of 'passing'. The percentage increase for each ethnic group between the 1946 and 1951 Censuses was: Europeans—9.1 per cent; Coloureds (and Malays)—16.7 per cent; Asiatics—25.8 per cent; Africans—7.4 per cent.

7. See Appendix B.

8. In 1946 Cape Town (including Wynberg) had nearly 37 per cent of the whole urban Coloured population of the Union, and the Coloureds constituted 43 per cent of the Cape Town total population (all races). By 1951 this figure had risen to 46.35 per cent (Cape Malays being included in both cases), and the Coloured group outnumbered the European group for the first time.

9. In 1937 T. S. Shannon estimated that the Coloured urban population was increasing in the small and large urban areas rather than in the intermediate ones, and that only 50 per cent of the Coloured urban population was in the large areas. (S. A. J. Econ. No. 5, 1937.) This article re-analysed the official figures by reckoning 'urban areas' as areas with over 2,000 European inhabitants, instead of areas possessing any form of local government under any law, as laid down by the 1918 Act. The figure of 50 per cent arrived at in the article has probably increased greatly since 1937.

10. See Appendix C.

11. See Appendix E.

12. See Appendix F and Ch. VII, pp. 131–7.

13. See Appendix H for these. As long ago as 1937, the Cape Coloured Commission commented on the inadequacy of the Union's vital registration system, and pointed out that reliable figures were available only in the large urban centres, some of which distinguished only between Europeans and Non-Europeans. It is noticeable in such publications as the *Union Year Book* (e.g., No. 23 of 1946) that in comparisons with other countries vital statistics are given for Europeans only, which compare very favourably with those of other members of the Commonwealth, and of such countries as Sweden, Denmark and Holland. For instance, South Africa is shown as having the lowest death-rate of thirty-six countries, with Egypt in the 36th place. This would certainly not be the case if the total population were adequately registered and included as a single entity.

14. The whole system of classification is somewhat arbitrary. Most of those classified as 'Europeans' and 'Asiatics' have never been to Europe or Asia, but are as much 'natives' as the Africans who are classified as 'Natives'. At times it has been found necessary to accord certain nations a status within the Union hierarchy, for trade or other reasons. Thus Japanese and Syrians are classed as Europeans (see circular issued by the Minister of the Interior on the 15th March, 1928), while Chinese, Siamese and Egyptians are not, exceptions being made for accredited diplomats. Chinese status has suffered since the Communist régime began; Dr. Dönges announced on the 9th November, 1950, that Chinese would be classed as Non-Europeans for the Group Areas Act. The Afrikaner is more logical than the English-speaking person in calling Europeans: '*Blankes*' ('whites') and Non-Europeans: '*Nie-Blankes*'. In Afrikans, however, the term '*Afrikaner*' is reserved primarily for Afrikaans-speaking Europeans, while the Africans are '*Naturelle*' (natives). In English, 'Non-European' is customarily spelt with a small initial 'n' by all but European liberals and Non-Europeans themselves, but this usage is regarded as discriminatory by the latter, and I have kept it only where it actually occurs in quotations.

15. Further details of this Act may be found on p. 44.

16. The 1805 Census gave 29,545 slaves, 20,006 'Hottentots' (including Bastards and Bushmen); the 1821 Census gave 35,698 slaves and 28,635 'Hottentots' (Marais, p. 31, n. 1).

17. A few hundred West African slaves were landed during the time of the first Governor, van Riebeeck, but the experiment was not repeated (*v. ibid.*, p. 1).

18. *Ibid.*, p. 2.

19. Professor G. P. Lestrade of Cape Town University (Marais, p. 1, n. 2).

20. No more were brought in after 1767, while supplies of African slaves continued until the abolition of the slave trade in 1807.

21. Such as the famous Sheikh Joseph, whose burial place at Faure, Western Cape, has become a holy place for the Cape Malays.

22. Even a casual observation of the red-fezzed Malays of Cape Town bears out this point. Caucasoid, Mongoloid and Negroid traits are all in evidence, and the skin-colour may vary as much as it does for the Christian Coloureds. Only 'Hottentot' traits are rare amongst the Malays. In the eighteenth and early nineteenth centuries Islam seems to have spread widely through the slave population despite official attempts to combat it. Professor Marais quotes the Commissioners of Enquiry in the 1820s as authority for a total of 1,325 Moslem slaves, and continues: 'It is doubtful whether the Christian slaves totalled one-tenth of this number. Mohammedanism did more to bridge the gulf between the slave and the free-born than did the Christianity of most Christians in the Cape Colony' (*op. cit.*, p. 172-3).

23. See Schapera, *The Khoisan Peoples of South Africa*, Routledge, London, 1930, *passim.*

24. Marais (pp. 13-14) disputes Theal's view that they were incapable of improvement, and refers to a missionary's statement that under supervision the Bushmen between the Orange and Vaal rivers had become quite considerable pastoralists by 1820.

25. See Marais, pp. 17-19 for the considerable numbers of Bushmen killed or taken prisoner in the late eighteenth century, and for contemporary allegations of enslavement of Bushmen children. See also Engelbrecht for the Koranna practice of taking in Bushmen children (p. 70).

26. Marais, p. 24.

27. Professor MacMillan quotes an anonymous missionary's comment in 1848: 'I have not seen a pure Hottentot since I have been in the Colony; some are scarcely distinguishable from white men, others, by connection with the slaves or Kaffirs, have darkened their skins, but I cannot say deteriorated their character, as almost any remove from the pure Hottentot must be an improvement' (p. 273). For the mingling of Bastards, Hottentots, Bushmen and Bantu beyond the Orange River in the nineteenth century, see Engelbrecht, pp. 65-79.

28. Professor I. D. MacCrone quotes Theal's estimate of the origin of the 1,000 permanent colonists in 1691 as over two-thirds Dutch, about one-sixth French, a very small fraction Swedish, Danish and Belgian, and one-seventh German (MacCrone, p. 7, n. 1). Later an increasing British element was introduced until to-day the English-speaking South Africans constitute 44 per cent of the total white population. The German group was also strengthened at various times during the nineteenth century.

29. Cf. a similar situation in Brazil described in Freyre's *The Masters and the Slaves*, p. 298.

30. These seamen have become the scapegoat for the past sins of all whites in South Africa in contemporary Nationalist mythology (cf. Dr. Dönges, Minister of the Interior, reported in *Hansard*, 19th May, 1949, col. 6165, and Mr. S. F. Papenfus, Member for Harrismith, reported in Hansard, 2nd March, 1950, col. 2251-2.

31. See V. de Kock, p. 114.

32. See Appendix V.

33. See Marais, p. 9, n. 5: 'Cases are also known of colonists marrying slave women. The children of such marriages were classed as Europeans. Deherain, 217; Colenbrander, 20/105.' Professor MacCrone (p. 42) points out that many of these early mixed marriages were with Bengali slave women, in whose case aesthetic objections were not likely to be strong. Marriage between European men and freed slaves of full colour was prohibited by the High Commissioner H. A. van Rheede

in 1685, but Europeans were still allowed to marry half-breed slaves following their emancipation. An early Governor, Simon van der Stel, was of mixed blood through his mother, Monica da Costa. For the attractiveness and light skin of some slave women see V. de Kock, pp. 115–16. For the numbers of such marriages amongst the old German settlers, see Hoge.

34. In such cases the European partner was usually the man. A reason sometimes advanced for such marriages from the man's point of view was that Coloured women made better housewives, and did not expect a maid to do the housework. I heard of about ten such cases from Coloured members of the women's families. The European branch of the family would naturally make no such admission.

35. See Advocate George Findlay's pamphlet on 'Miscegenation' for an attempt to estimate the number of Coloured persons who have passed into the European group. According to his calculations the number of escapes was between 500,000 and 733,000 for the whole period from 1652 to the early 1930s (or between one-quarter and one-third of the entire European population).

36. See p. 36.

37. '. . . children, the progeny of Europeans and slaves of whom twelve were then at school, were to be taught, and particular care to be taken that they were not alienated, so as to remain in constant slavery, but that they might in due time enjoy the freedom to which, in the right of the father, they were born.' (Moodie, quoted by MacCrone, p. 76.) See also MacCrone, p. 76, n. 1.

38. At this stage the dichotomy was still between Christian and non-Christian, rather than between European and non-European.

39. MacCrone, p. 45.

40. In 1950, the first year of its operation, the following numbers of people were prosecuted and convicted under the Immorality Amendment Act within the various racial groups (excluding Africans, who were already covered by the 1927 Act).

	Europeans		Coloureds		Asiatics	
	male	female	male	female	male	female
Prosecuted	83	12	8	85	5	4
Convicted	58	8	6	58	2	0

41. See speeches by Mr. A. G. Barlow and Mr. J. J. Fouche reported in *Hansard*, 25th May, 1949, cols. 6458, 6461–4, 6471–8, also *British Africa Review*, March, 1951, p. 18.

42. MacCrone, pp. 43–4. The marriage was probably intended to cement a political alliance; Eva herself was not, it would seem, a very savoury character, in later years at least.

43. MacMillan, p. 92. See also Mi. s. 18.

44. For these and other European descriptions of the 'race of greasy Hottentoos' see MacCrone, pp. 46–9. The term 'Hotnot' is regarded as highly offensive by respectable Coloured people to-day.

45. See Edwards, p. 20.

46. Engelbrecht, p. 30. See also Marais, pp. 10–12, and Stuart Cloete's novel *Watch for the Dawn*, which deals with Frederick Bezuidenhout, who had such a 'wife', and whose violent death while resisting arrest by a Hottentot detachment under a European officer in 1815 precipitated the Slagter's Nek Rebellion.

47. The term 'Bastard' is commonly confined to a white-Hottentot cross. Although to European ears it would have a somewhat derogatory connotation, the Bastards themselves bore it proudly, as perpetuating the memory of the 'white blood' that flowed in their veins. For a detailed account of their origins, history and decline from burghers of independent republics into a landless rural proletariat see Marais, Ch. II and III; S. J. Halford on the Griquas, and E. Fischer on the Rehoboth Bastards, also *Coloured Mission Stations and Reserves Report*, according to which

the Griquas of E. Griqualand had only nine farms left in 1947, having sold in all 483,366 morgen of land (s. 98).

48. By 1823 there were said to be 5,000 Bastards living along the Orange River and organised into several groups.

49. In the pastoral district of Graaff-Reinet the average Boer family is said to have employed five Hottentots to every two slaves at the end of the eighteenth century (Marais, pp. 8 and 13).

50. See M., p. 22, s. 84–5, for an account of Cape Coloureds, Griquas and Bantu-European hybrids living together in the Transkeian Territories. No doubt there are social distinctions based on origin within this community.

51. There were 262 Coloured-African marriages in 1925, 6 per cent of all Coloured marriages and 2.2 per cent of all African marriages. The corresponding figures for 1946 were: 630 marriages, 7.5 per cent of all Coloured marriages and 2.9 per cent of all African marriages. The percentage increase over the intervening years has been small but consistent. It was higher in 1942–5 (figures taken from Sofer, Table 15). It would be interesting to know whether the comparatively low rate of increase of the African group, 7.4 per cent between the 1946 and 1951 censuses (see Appendix A) indicates a loss of members to the Coloured group, in addition to denoting a high African mortality rate.

52. Two informants claimed that some Coloured lower-class women prefer an African husband, because he is a hard worker, a steady wage-earner and less prone to hard drinking than the Coloured men of the same wage-group. From the African's point of view, there are not sufficient women of his own group to go round outside the Reserves, while he may see some material advantage for his children, in that their Coloured status will entitle them to better schooling, and other privileges not available to Africans. While the African affects to despise the mixed-breed Coloured, it is possible that some of the more Europeanised have sufficiently absorbed prevalent European colour prejudices to regard the acquisition of a light-coloured wife as desirable. This is a matter for further inquiry.

53. In an M.A. Thesis (London, 1949) by Cyril Sofer, on 'Some Recent Trends in the Status History of the Coloured People in South Africa.'

54. European public opinion, always highly susceptible to the threat of a 'coffee-coloured South Africa', is fully aware of this leak of 'black blood' into the lower economic strata of the Coloured group, It is feared that such 'black blood' will eventually seep up to the white group through miscegenation (see speech by Mr. S. E. Warren, reported in *Hansard*, 25th May, 1949, col. 6484). This fear found formal expression in the Mixed Marriages Act of 1949 and the Immorality Amendment Act of 1950, which forbid marriages and sexual relations between Europeans and Coloureds, though not between Coloureds and Africans.

55. We have in footnote 52 suggested some reasons for such marriages. The majority of these marriages occur between Coloured women and African men. In 1946, 349 Coloured females married African men, 281 Coloured males married African females. The percentage of Coloured male-African female marriages to the total of Coloured-African out-marriages was therefore 44.6 per cent. This percentage has shown a steady increase from the 1925 percentage of 28.6. Perhaps a study of more detailed statistics giving the area in which the marriages occur and the economic status of the contracting parties might suggest some reasons for this increase. (Figures taken from Cyril Sofer, Table 17.)

56. In 1946 there were 102 Coloured-Asiatic marriages; this was 1.2 per cent of all Coloured marriages and 6.1 per cent of all Asiatic marriages. Since 1925 the respective percentages have shown a slight consistent increase; in that year they were 1.1 per cent and 4.3 per cent respectively. Of the 1,004 marriages between Coloureds and Asiatics in the period 1937–46, 875 (or 87.2 per cent) were between Coloured females and Asiatic males. (Figures from Cyril Sofer, Table 12.)

57. The same Coloured informant who had married a Malay, and subsequently divorced him, often declared that she would like a good Indian husband who would

o

give her enough housekeeping money, and not force her to go out as a charwoman to pay the rent, as her first husband had done, while he spent his wages on gambling. (In this case his behaviour did not conform to that of the ideal Malay type—S.P.) She added that Indians did not waste their money on drink like so many Christian Coloured men.

58. See supra, pp. 164–6, for an account of Coloured physical types as correlated with social class. See also G. F. van Wyk: *A Preliminary Account of the Physical Anthropology of the Cape Coloured People* (*Males*), from *Annals of the University of Stellenbosch*, Vol. XVII, sec. A, No. 2 (Sept., 1939), Nasionale Pers, Beperk, Cape Town, and J. A. Keen: 'Craniometric Study of the Cape Coloured Population', in Transactions of the Royal Society of South Africa, vol. XXXIII, Part I (1951), pp. 29–51.

59. These consisted of several thousands of freed slaves, Prize Negroes (Africans taken from slave-ships captured by British cruisers, and freed in Cape Town after serving as apprentices to local burghers), and the descendants of criminals or political prisoners and their retinues from the East, originally sentenced by the Dutch East India Company. Most of them were Moslems, who lived in Cape Town and formed 'a large portion of the lower class of Tradesmen, Fishermen, and Mechanics'. (Marais, pp. 161–2.) Their position was in some ways similar to that of the Free Negroes in some southern cities of the United States.

60. Van Riebeeck, who held a very low opinion of the Hottentot character, nevertheless included in his first proclamation the proviso: '. . . and should anyone ill treat, beat or push a native—whether he be right or wrong—he shall in the presence of the latter receive fifty lashes, so that the natives may be made to understand that the deed has been against our will, and that we desire to associate with them in all friendliness and kindliness . . .' *Edicts issued by the Commander, Jan van Riebeeck and Council from 9th April*, 1652, *to 14th October*, 1652, pp. 120 foll. quoted by MacCrone, p. 19. See also *ibid.*, pp. 17–18. Fore present-day attitudes, see *ibid.* Ch. IV *passim.*

61. As attested by van Riebeeck in a dispatch quoted by MacCrone, p. 24.

62. MacCrone (p. 30) quotes Theal on the quality of the early freed men, who were recruited from the servants of the Company, which had 'a most disagreeable name in Europe , while its servants were often enticed from the 'unwary and vagabonds of all nations . As Theal comments: 'it is not surprising that such men . . . in general made very unruly and improvident citizens', and probably they were not greatly concerned with the maintenance of cordial relations with the Hottentots.

63. Dispatch from the Council of India, 13th December, 1658, quoted by MacCrone, p. 32. Cf. also the passage from Theal, *op. cit.*, p. 33.

64. Slavery at the Cape was part of a largely subsistence-economy, unlike the intensive plantation systems found in the West Indies, the Southern States of North America and elsewhere. There were roughly the same number of slaves as there were Europeans who numbered approximately 40,000 in 1833. Some emancipated slaves returned to their native lands; their life as slaves at the Cape is said to have been easier than slavery elsewhere. (V. de Kock, pp. 199 and 217–18.)

65. Cf. Marais, pp. 112 and 120.

66. Professor MacMillan cites a case in which the Company cancelled a grant of land on the ground of the prior occupational rights of one 'Wild-Schut, a Hottentot captain on the outskirts of Stellenbosch' (*op. cit.*, p. 35). On the same page he states that the Company regarded the Hottentots as an independent people, outside the Colony and beyond its laws, which seems not entirely consistent with the instance quoted. Professor Marais (*op. cit.*, p. 111) denies that they were 'outside the law' in this way, and cites further instances and instructions to prove it. Nevertheless, whatever their formal position, the Hottentots were undoubtedly regarded by the colonists as outcast nomads, with a status lower even than the slaves, and were probably treated accordingly wherever the central authority was unable to enforce its writ.

67. Landdrost Maynier was accused of preferring the 'Heathens before the Christians'; (Theal (b) III, p. 308, quoted by Marais, pp. 112–13). The wording used shows that the 'Christian-heathen' antithesis had not yet entirely passed into the 'white-black' formula (*v.* Ch. IX).

68. Marais, *Maynier and the First Boer Republic*, p. 105–6.

69. See also Marais, pp. 131–4.

70. See Marais, pp. 116–19; cf. also MacMillan, Ch. XIII.

71. Caledon's law of 1809. Marais quotes Theal as saying that this law saved the Hottentots from utter destruction (p. 122).

72. Cradock's law of 1812.

73. Somerset's decree of 1819.

74. See Marais, p. 120–1, for the transition to the new type of 'colour-blind' justice, and for an account of the Black Circuit of 1812, which is still remembered in many quarters as an example of unjustified interference by missionaries and officials with colonists.

75. See the case quoted by Edwards, p. 27.

76. Cf. the Black Codes of the American South for similar legislation, though in a different historical context (Johnson, p. 158 f.).

77. Marais, pp. 124–5.

78. Marais, p. 129; MacMillan, p. 164.

79. From 1824 Report of Commissioners of Inquiry on Police System quoted by Marais, p. 127, n. 2.

80. Professor W. M. MacMillan quotes an abortive Vagrant Law of 1834 as a perfect illustration of the Hottentots' traditional mode of subsistence and the white colonists' attitude to it: 'The searching for and the digging for roots or fruits, the natural produce of the earth, or wild honey, or the searching for, taking and killing any game, or any other wild animal, of what kind soever, on any ground not being the property of the person so doing', or 'not having previously obtained permission', shall not be deemed to be 'lawful employment by which any person can honestly earn the means of subsistence.' The official members of the Legislative Council opposed and disallowed this measure on the ground that the Hottentots had been deprived of their natural means of subsistence without compensation, and without being taught any other way of life (Marais, p. 34).

81. See *The Blessed Missionaries* by Dr. Edwin Smith for an account of missionary work as it influenced the fate not only of Hottentots and Bastards but later of Bantu in the Eastern Cape and Natal.

82. At this time the Hottentots there still lived in their old manner, spoke their own language and possessed some cattle. Fifty years later, they owned fewer cattle, could all speak Dutch and some had worked for the Boers. (Marais, p. 135.)

83. Marais, pp. 135–7.

84. *v.* Marais, pp. 135–40 for the early history of Genadendal.

85. *v.* Marais, pp. 145–51.

86. For an illustration of this process, see Engelbrecht, p. 12.

87. *v.* MacMillan, p. 154.

88. *v.* Marais, 149–53.

89. 'And whereas by usage and custom of this Colony, Hottentots and other free persons of colour have been subjected to certain restraints as to their residence, mode of life, and employment, and to certain compulsory services to which others of His Majesty's subjects are not liable: Be it therefore enacted, that from and after the passing of this Ordinance, no Hottentot or other free person of colour, lawfully residing in this Colony, shall be subject to any compulsory service to which other of His Majesty's subjects therein are not liable, nor to any hindrance, molestation, fine, imprisonment, or punishment of any kind whatsoever, under the pretence that such person has been guilty of vagrancy or any other offence, unless after trial in due course of law; any custom or usage to the contrary in anywise notwithstanding.' (Ordinance 50/1828 (Cape), clause 2, quoted by MacMillan, p. 211, n. 1.)

90. See Chapter III, pp. 33–4.

91. Dr. John Philip's comment was: 'The real object was to have the Hottentots again in the farmers' power on what terms they might please to hold them . . . Arbitrary control, when indulged, becomes one of the strongest passions in the human mind and the last species of authority which men are disposed to part with.' (MacMillan, pp. 223–4.)

92. Even the Governor, Sir Lowrie Cole, shared their sentiments (MacMillan, p. 234).

93. Despite the State's rejection of this Draft Law in 1834, the attitude of many colonists was such that several veld cornets took action on the Draft alone (Mac-Millan, p. 244), causing considerable hardship to the Hottentots concerned. Some of the offending officials were suspended by the Governor.

94. *v.* MacMillan, pp. 224–32.

95. *v.* Marais, p. 185.

96. See Marais, pp. 162–78, for a detailed account of slavery in the Cape; also V. de Kock and Edwards *passim.*

97. Marais, pp. 166–7; Edwards, p. 15.

98. Professor MacMillan considers that the rebellion of some discontented 'Hottentots' from the Kat River Settlement and Theopolis, who joined the Kaffirs again the Europeans in the 1851 war, was 'disastrous for the future of the Coloured People, by causing the missionary institutions to be accused of fomenting rebellion, and therefore blighting their economic and social work amongst the rural Coloureds'. (pp. 279–87.)

99. The first three sections of Retief's manifesto (the classic statement of Trekker grievances) protest against the prevalence of vagrancy, against slave regulations, and against losses by emancipation and by 'the continual system of plunder endured from Caffres and other coloured classes'. He ended '. . . whilst we will take care that no one shall be held in a state of slavery it is our determination to maintain such regulations as may suppress crime and preserve proper relations between master and servant'. (MacMillan, p. 245.) See also *ibid.,* p. 81 and MacCrone, p. 126.

100. See Marais, p. 160.

101. It should be noted that they also took with them a considerable number of coloured servants, whose contribution to the success of the Trek is rarely mentioned; their present-day representatives were not even invited to attend the Voortrekker Celebrations in late 1949.

102. Rustenburg Grondwet of 1858.

103. See MacCrone, p. 267 f., for summarised answers to a questionnaire answered by European students on the aspects of historical contacts between Black and White which had most impressed them. Many of the replies stressed hostile, antagonistic and warlike relations.

104. One might draw a parallel between their situation and that of the free black burghers of the eighteenth-century Cape, whose status necessarily suffered because of the existence of a large coloured slave group, and the increasing tendency of Europeans to associate colour with inferior status. (See MacCrone, pp. 71–3.)

CHAPTER III—POLITICS

1. H. J. Laski: *Grammar of Politics,* p. 27. He continues: 'The limitation in the number of those upon whom social good is conferred, whose personality that is to say finds satisfaction in the working of political institutions, has always meant in the end an assault upon the foundations of the state by those excluded from a share in benefits.' The applicability of the proposition contained in the final sentence to the South African situation will be considered in the concluding chapter. (Cf. also passage from *The Negro Citizen* by Du Bois, quoted in Myrdal, p. 1,332, n. 11) and the following extract from Resolution 1a of the Non-European Unity Move-

ment Conference held in April, 1951: 'The disabilities of the Non-European oppressed flow directly from the lack of political rights, and the struggle for the Franchise . . . is the pivot of the struggle for the National Liberation of the oppressed people of South Africa.' (Quoted in the *Torch*, 10th April, 1951.)

2. Cf. Myrdal, p. 442, for the use of this parallel by American exponents of the pro-slavery doctrine. While the Cape society might have been likened to Athens, the Boer Republics had more in common with Sparta.

3. Point Eight of the United Party statement of policy announced by General Smuts in November, 1949 reads as follows: 'In pursuance of its policy of national unity the United Party will encourage the cultural development of the South African people. Both racial constituents (i.e., the English and Afrikaans-speaking groups—S.P.) of our nation will be assisted to lead a full life, finding expression in varied cultural activities in a spirit of healthy co-operation, as equal contributors to a broader and richer South African culture.' (*Cape Times*, 10th November, 1949.)

4. The major end pursued by all European parties with the exception of the Communist Party (now dissolved), is that of preserving 'a white South Africa'. Differences of policy occur mainly in connection with the means adopted to secure this end.

5. Cf. the one-party system in the American South, which produces a similar effect: 'The South votes for men—Democratic men—but rarely ever for issues, unless the issue is defined in black and white.' (Ralph Bunche, quoted by Myrdal, p. 483.) The importance of politicians rather than policies in South Africa is also probably to be considered as a survival of a frontier society.

6. 'Coloured' is here used in its widest sense, as including all Non-Europeans.

7. Cape Flats (a constituency in the poorer, semi-rural part of Cape Town) has 25.7 per cent of Coloured voters. The present United Party Member, Captain R. J. du Toit, who was elected in 1948, has been noticeably active in Coloured interests in the House, an activity which is sometimes effectively discounted by Nationalist accusations that he is a second-class member, dependent on 'Hotnot' votes. See the *Hansard* reports of the exchange between Captain du Toit and a Nationalist M.P., Mr. Serfontein, on Wednesday, 30th March, 1949, and the charge made by Mr. H. T. van G. Bekker, Nationalist M.P. for Kimberley District, against Mr. H. F. Oppenheimer (U.P., Kimberley City), on 4th May, 1949. Such imputations make good reading amongst the more race-conscious whites. Even the M.P.s concerned do not usually parry the charge by saying that a Coloured vote is as good as a European vote, but rather seek to prove that their majority would be sufficient on white votes alone.

8. Cf. *Race Relations Handbook*, p. 524, and the following passage: 'Every five years we have to decide which members of the slave-owning group will have the opportunity to pass oppressive laws against us. Whatever party we have helped to put in power, it has shown itself to be against us, the United Party no less than the Nationalist Party.' (Mr. I. Tabata, speaking at the Anti-C.A.D. Conference, 29–30th May, 1948, Cape Town—Report of Proceedings, p. 22.) For the views and policy of this radical Coloured group, see Ch. VIII, pp. 160–2.

9. Even before Union, this group of voters seems always to have been singled out as the Coloured or Non-European 'Vote', it being conceived that colour rather than economic or other interests are the main dividing factor in politics as elsewhere in South African society. In such circumstances, one might have expected Coloured voters to group together increasingly as the racial pressure increased, in an endeavour to make the most of their limited political power. For further discussion of Coloured voting-blocs and alleged corruption, see Ch. VIII, n. 85.

10. Such constituencies were: Hottentots Holland, Port Elizabeth District, Vasco and Caledon (won by the U.P. with small majorities in 1948 (general election) and 1949 (provincial election), Paarl and Bredasdorp (narrowly won by Nationalists in 1948 and narrowly lost in 1949); see Thompson, pp. 45–62.

11. This lack of adequate representation of Coloured minority interests in a

hardening race-situation was used somewhat speciously by Nationalist leaders as a reason for their proposed segregation of the Coloured vote. See the remarks of Dr. Dönges, Minister of the Interior, at the 1949 Cape Nationalist Party Conference, reported in the *Cape Times* of 29th September, 1949. It is noteworthy that in the campaigning for the bye-election in the Cape farming district of Ceres in April, 1951, under the shadow of the Separate Representation of Voters Bill, neither side dared openly to canvass the 600 Coloured voters, lest they lose more than that number of white votes by so doing. In 1948 there was a Nationalist majority of 1,952 (see *Cape Times*, 11th April, 1951, and 14th April, 1951); this majority was increased to 2,418 in 1951, so that the Coloured voters could not have gained the seat for the United Party.

12. Since the Citizenship Act of 1949, a 'South African national'.

13. This is restricted to wage or salary, not to an income of any other kind. The consequence is that some fairly wealthy Coloured building contractors who work on their own account, live wherever they are working and have no permanent house, are ineligible for the franchise, while their employees may qualify. These qualifications remain valid for Coloured males wishing to be registered on the new separate roll.

14. May, p. 142.

15. Section 7. For the proceedings which led up to this removal, see *The Cape Native Franchise* by Professor Eric Walker, published by the Continuation Committee of the National Conference on the Native Bills, Cape Town, 1936. Even this separate franchise has been threatened with extinction by members of the present Government, a threat which has not inspired Coloured people with great confidence in the future and stability of their coming separate representation.

16. The Secretary of State, Lord Newcastle, said: '. . . It is exceedingly undesirable that the franchise should be so restricted as to leave those of the coloured classes who in point of intelligence are qualified for the exercise of political power practically unrepresented. It is the earnest desire of Her Majesty's Government that all her subjects at the Cape without distinction of class or colour should be united by one bond of loyalty and a common interest and we believe that the exercise of political rights enjoyed by all alike will prove one of the best methods of attaining this object.' (*British Parl. Papers*, (1636) of 1853, p, 25.) The British Government of to-day is adopting a similar attitude in other African territories, and is facing similar opposition from white settlers bent on obtaining a greater say in territorial affairs.

17. Franchise and Ballot Act No. 9 of 1892 (Cape); Glen Grey Act, 1894 (Cape).

18. It should be noted that these qualifications also excluded considerable numbers of poor and illiterate Europeans. The situation is comparable to that obtaining in the American South as a result of the poll-tax provisions (see Myrdal, p. 1,318).

19. This right remained theoretical in the half century before Union. On one occasion only, in 1893, did it seem possible that a Coloured man, in this case a Malay called Ahmed Effendi, might be nominated. It further appeared likely that he would be elected by the Malay voters, 'under the system which allowed each voter in the Cape Town electoral division, which returned four members, to give four votes to one candidate. It was largely to prevent this that cumulative voting, which in any case was an anomaly, being confined to the Cape division, was abolished by Act No. 16 of 1893. Ahmed Effendi was not nominated in the insuing election.' (Thompson, p. 7, s. 14, who cites also Eybers, p. 30, J. H. Hofmeyr, *The Life of Jan Hendrik Hofmeyr* (Cape Town, 1913) p. 451, and James Rose-Innes, *Autobiography* (Oxford, 1949) p. 100.) Oliver Walker quotes a Nationalist member from the Orange Free State as saying on 31st March, 1946: 'If Mr. Hofmeyr ever succeeds in bringing Indians and coloured persons into the House as members of Parliament, I should be given a machine-gun, and they will be brought down as fast as they come in . . .' (*Kaffirs are Lively*, p. 106.)

20. By agreeing not to count Coloured voters in the delimitation of constituencies,

the Cape Province delegates lost parliamentary seats *vis-à-vis* the other provinces. Coloured voters are counted in the delimitation of constituencies within the province, once the distribution of seats between provinces has been made. In 1948 the average number of voters to each representative by province was: Cape—10,225; Natal—8,726; Transvaal—9,490; Orange Free State—9,371. (*Union Year Book No. 24, 1948, p. 102.*) In 1950 six seats were given to 23,934 South-West African white voters, an average of about 4,000 per seat.

21. Bearing in mind that this National Convention met only a few years after the Anglo-Boer War, one might find a parallel between the attitude of compromise and concession shown by the Cape representatives and the British Government in 1909 in the face of the uncompromising colour-attitudes evinced by the Northern provinces, and the American North's condonation of Southern violations of the Constitution, in its attempt to heal the wounds of the Civil War.

22. Even while Coloureds still appear on the common roll, they were not permitted to mingle with white voters in the House of Assembly. In a recent session the Speaker said that *apartheid* or separation had been applied form any years in the House of Assembly building. '. . . A room adjoining the entrance to the House and before the entrance to the Lobby is reached was set aside for Coloured and Native visitors of members . . . A separate bay next to the public gallery was provided exclusively for Native and Coloured visitors to the House, which makes it impossible for these persons to mix with Europeans, and special instructions were given that as soon as this space was taken up, no more Coloureds or Natives should be admitted and allowed to stand in the passages of the House or in the gallery, as Europeans are often allowed to do, as this would result in Europeans and non-Europeans mixing. The article alleged further that Europeans and non-Europeans made communal use of the public convenience. This is emphatically denied by the officials in charge . . . and if it had been brought to their notice, they would have seen to it that it did not happen as the convenience referred to is for Europeans only.' (*Hansard,* 2nd February, 1948, p. 503.) In addition, the Catering Committee of Parliament insists that no Non-European, even of diplomatic standing, may be entertained in the House unless he has first been sponsored by a Cabinet Minister. The *Rand Daily Mail* and *Star* of 23rd February, 1951 reported that a Senator was 'on the carpet' for a breach of these rules when he entertained the Chinese Consul-General.

23. Clause 35(i). Even an abstention would therefore count as a vote against any amendment. It would seem that this provision for a two-thirds majority was intended to safeguard the Cape African and Coloured franchise for·all time— (*v.* Walton, p. 156). By 1936, however, the necessary majority had been found to do away with the franchise for Africans. In the case of the Coloured franchise, the present Speaker gave a ruling which permitted the Government to proceed with its abolition on a bare majority (see *Hansard,* 11th April, 1951, and S.A. press of that and succeeding days). In 1950 this legislation was postponed to the 1951 session because the Nationalist Government's 'bare majority' depended upon the nine votes of Mr. Havenga's Afrikaner Party. Mr. Havenga, while not disagreeing in principle with the removal of Coloured voters from the common roll, had, until late 1950, after the Nationalist majority was reinforced by six South-West African seats in the House of Assembly, some scruples about proceeding on a bare majority. On the party-political manoeuvrings which led to the Malan-Havenga statement of 13th October, 1950, see Senator E. H. Brookes in the *Forum* of 3rd November, 1950, and *Sunday Times,* 15th October, 1950.

24. However, a Cape representative named Maasdorp told the Convention that 'the views expressed by the delegates from the Cape so far were not the views held by all the electors there and it was open to question whether they were the views of the majority. Among farmers in the Cape there was a strong feeling against the Franchise for Natives and Coloured men, and some years ago the Cape raised the qualification with the special intention of preventing the spread of evil.' (Walton, pp. 140–1.) An amendment to prevent the Cape Non-European franchise being

entrenched by the 'two-thirds majority' provision was put forward by Mr. Smyth of 'British' Natal, and defeated by twenty-four votes to six, five of the latter being Natal delegates, the sixth General de la Rey of the Transvaal (*ibid.*, p. 155).

25. Amongst those who did not share the prevailing optimism or willingness to compromise with their principles was W. P. Schreiner, whose views contrast strikingly with the official utterances of responsible politicians to-day. He wrote: 'It is idle, to my mind, to think of building anything permanent in South Africa by the mere goodwill of ourselves, the European-descended minority . . . We shall, if we deserve it, remain dominant. But it must be a dominance in a free country, where career is open to talent and to civilised men, with no discrimination or distinction upon such grounds as colour or race.' When the draft South Africa Act was published, Schreiner called its provisions for Non-European political rights 'a blot on the Constitution', and wrote: 'We (in the Cape) are in the position of trustees, and the rights of the coloured people should not be bartered away for any benefits which the Europeans may get . . . So serious is the vista of the future that I would stand out of Union rather than give up the trust . . . Union without honour is the greatest danger any nation can incur.' Schreiner carried the battle for Coloured rights to London, but again failed to carry his case (cf. Walker, pp. 11–15).

26. See Appendix J.

27. The definition of a woman was a woman who is wholly of European parentage, extraction or descent. This was amended by Act 41 of 1931 to read: 'a white woman'. (C., s. 1,152.) The latter distinction is in keeping with the general Union practice of deciding ethnic affiliation mainly from appearance, particularly with regard to the Coloured people.

28. As it still was, all Non-Europeans being included. In this instance one great minority group (women) was given rights at the expense of another (the Non-Europeans). Myrdal has some pertinent observations on the similarities between the Negro problem and the problem of women's rights in Appendix 5, p. 1,073. W. P. Schreiner also pointed out the connection in a speech on woman's suffrage in 1912: 'I class the discrimination on the ground of sex with the fearful discrimination against humanity on the ground of race or colour. I say to you that the solution is on the basis of a sound qualification. There lies safety . . . South Africa has the opportunity of showing in what true democracy consists, the maintenance of the glorious principle of equality of opportunity.' (Walker, E. A. (1), pp. 14–15.)

29. *Hansard*, 2nd March, 1928, col. 1650. In May, 1929, he was reported in *Die Burger* as advocating the extension of the Coloured franchise through the country (Thompson, p. 26). The occasion was a meeting in support of a Nationalist parliamentary candidate at Stellenbosch, which has a considerable Coloured vote. On the same occasion, a photograph was taken of this candidate, Mr. Bruckner de Villiers, who won the seat, being chaired through the streets by some of his Coloured supporters, an occurrence which would be unthinkable to-day (see reproduction in 'Rand Mail' of 14th May, 1951). See also the letter written by Dr. Malan in 1923 to Dr. Abdurahman, then leader of the major Coloured organisation (the A.P.O.), quoted by Captain R. J. du Toit, M.P. (*Hansard*, 23rd March, 1949, col, 2657.)

30. See Thompson, pp. 21–2 for these points from General Hertzog's Smithfield speech of 13th November, 1925, which also included a statement that it was 'high time that his (the Coloured man's) right to vote in Parliamentary elections be admitted by the Northern Provinces.' This pamphlet also gives details of the two Coloured Persons' Rights Bills containing provisions to extend this franchise which were introduced by Hertzog in 1926 and 1929. By the time the Cape Coloured Commission appointed in 1934 had produced its report, the urgency of taking any further steps to extend the Cape Coloured franchise had apparently passed. Nothing further was done, despite the Commission's unanimous representation that the 'franchise privileges held by the Coloured people in the Cape Province be extended to include the Coloured people resident in the other three provinces who

hold the necessary qualifications.' (C., s. 830.) By 1949, attitudes had shifted so greatly that Dr. Malan was able to argue that 'if it was right to retain the Coloured vote in the Cape, then it would be right to extend it to the northern provinces as well. Such reasoning, he felt, made complete logic of his proposal to disfranchise the Coloured people in the Cape.' (Quoted in an editorial in the *Cape Times*, 7th November, 1949.)

31. Phrase used by General Hertzog in a joint session on 20th February, 1929, and quoted by Thompson, p. 22.

32. Only to recur with redoubled urgency in recent years amongst non-Nationalists (see editorial in the *Star* of 16th October, 1950, headed 'A Million New Enemies' —the implication in the wording is that other non-Europeans are already enemies, and letter to the *Natal Daily News* quoted in the *Forum*, 23rd March, 1951.)

33. In 1929 the Coloured and African voters together represented 19.8 per cent of the total vote, and the Coloureds alone approximately 13 per cent. By 1931 the Non-European vote was only 9.9 per cent of the total vote. See Appendix J for detailed figures. The fear of a Coloured-African *rapprochement* has now revived in an extra-parliamentary context.

34. This Nationalist-S.A.P. party came to be known briefly as the United Party.

35. Thompson, p. 28. The fourteen-point Nationalist programme announced then differs very little from that with which the Nationalist Party won the 1948 Election, and which it is now putting into practice.

36. The most important sections of this speech are given in the *Cape Times* editorial of 22nd March, 1949, and by Thompson, p. 29.

37. That the intensification of Nationalist hostility to the Coloured vote was to be correlated with the fact that almost all Coloured people now vote for the United Party was suggested by a speech made by Mr. Eric Louw, the present Minister for Economic Affairs, at Mayfair, on Saturday, 13th August, 1949. (See report in *Cape Times* of 15th August, 1949.) See *Cape Argus*, 12th February, 1951, for an estimate of the probable loss to the United Party following the removal of Coloured voters.

38. An instance of this type of inquiry was published in the *Cape Times* of 29th October, 1949, in an interview with the son of the woman questioned. His mother was first visited by a young man from 'the party offices', who asked her 'defamatory questions about her parentage with the greatest audacity. My mother was badly taken aback, but she told him that she was a descendant of the Voortrekkers, that she belonged to the Dutch Reformed Church (*v.* Ch. VII), and that her grandfather was a Minister in that Church. The man replied that lots of people were members of the Dutch Reformed Church who were actually Coloured.' The party organiser then sent in the mother's name to the Electoral Office for further investigation, and a tactful inspector called shortly afterwards, but was satisfied that the family was European. The account continued: 'But my mother has been terribly upset . . . and I have had to get the doctor in. I have found that some dark-skinned people who live not far from me have had the same performance. In the case of a friend of mine, an official from the Electoral Office went to the factory in which he works to interview him about his parentage. I also know of two Dutch Reformed Church ministers in Cape Town who have been asked whether they are Europeans as shown on the voters' roll.'

39. The following report suggests that such endeavours can backfire: 'Mr. J. W. Mushet, M.P. for Vasco (United Party), said that one canvasser in the Parow-Vasco area, who apparently did not know his district well, had caused commotion by alleging that some fervent Nationalist voters were Coloured women.' (*Cape Times*, 26th September, 1949.)

40. In some cases, private persons, usually connected with a political party, apparently represented themselves as Electoral Office inspectors when calling at the houses of voters. In October, 1949, Cape Peninsula inspectors were issued with letters of identification bearing their photograph and signed by the Chief Electoral

Officer of Cape Town, in order to check this abuse. (*Cape Times*, 26th October, 1949.)

41. Cf. *Rand Daily Mail*, 26th October, 1949. This report also stated that about 1,000 Peninsula voters classified as European had so far had their racial status questioned, and 115 had been ruled to be Non-Europeans. (I was unable to obtain any official figures then or later by direct application to the appropriate authorities.) A Coloured teacher told me that this questioning about neighbours had already produced some unpleasant consequences. Certain Coloured people who had been 'passing', but were now unmasked, had been informing on neighbours in a similar situation, 'out of sour grapes', as he said.

42. 'Inspectors are questioning thirty to forty voters a day in their homes. Many are called in for further interrogation at the Cape Town Electoral Office. Persons who appear to be European have been officially re-classified as non-Europeans on the strength of entries in official documents concerning their parents. This had led to apparently white persons discovering that there has been mixed blood in their families. The consequences to family and neighbourhood relations, to the children's schooling, and even to the breadwinners' employment, are described as grave.' (*Cape Times*, 26th October, 1949.)

43. The forthcoming Population Registration scheme is designed to prevent such inter-group mobility.

44. Mr. A. Bloomberg (U.P.) reported in the *Cape Times* of 29th October, 1949.

45. This ruling was greeted with editorial approval even by the liberally-minded *Cape Times*, which concluded: 'We trust therefore that the laudable attempt to arrive at accurate voters' rolls will now be pursued with a large proportion of common-sense decisions based on appearance and habits, and fewer embarrassing probes into ancestry.' (4th November, 1949.)

46. As early as 1926, when General Hertzog's first Coloured Person's Rights Bill was drafted, Dr. Abdurahman criticised it as a deliberate fraud, saying: 'We do not want to sell the Natives' rights, or to be bribed by the Government to leave the Native in the lurch.' (*Cape Times*, 17th June, 1926.) Later that month, he spoke against the Colour Bar Act in Johannesburg. On the other hand, the African National Bond, a Coloured organisation which supported the Nationalists, was at the same period trying to dissociate the Coloured community from the Africans in all spheres. (See request of a Transvaal deputation to the Minister of Lands, Mr. P. G. N. Grobler, to request the Administrator of the Transvaal to make provision for the segregation of Coloured people from Natives, reported in the *Cape Times*, 16th April, 1926.) On 29th May, 1943, Dr. Abdurahman's judgment was reiterated by Dr. G. N. Gool, Chairman of the Anti-C.A.D. Conference: 'We knew that immediately after the African it would be our turn. Yet we did nothing to assist the African in his hour of need. We lived and fed on illusions and promises, and, like ostriches, buried our heads in the sand, in the vain hope that the storm would not touch us.' (*Report of Proceedings*, p. 2.)

47 Now, however, the proposed Coloured Representatives will probably join with existing Native Representatives in the House of Assembly to form a minority group It was the Nationalist Government's intention to abolish this Native representation, in the Assembly at least, and the Native Representative Council, but the former has been reprieved for the moment, in order that the proposed Coloured representation and Council may not seem too empty an alternative. The N.R.C. was actually called late in 1950 in order to support the explanation that Coloured voters were getting a worth-while exchange for their former vote on the common roll. Unfortunately for the Government the N.R.C. meetings proved a failure and broke up (see *Forum*, 15th December, 1950, *Cape Times* of 17th February, 1951 and 2nd March, 1951); it was then abolished altogether by the Bantu Authorities Act (No. 68 of 1951).

48. See Thompson, p. 43, for the statement that there has apparently been an absolute decrease in the number of registered Coloured voters since June, 1949.

A member of the Non-European Unity Movement told me that, quite apart from this association's policy of boycotting elections, he and many of his friends (of the urban upper class) were not willing to submit to the registration procedure, which he described as a 'nauseating process', and had never registered as voters, although they could qualify as such. Another Coloured leader of different political beliefs, himself a registered voter, told me that he estimated that there were over 100,000 potential Coloured registered voters in the Cape, but that the registration procedure and other forms of coercion acted as powerful deterrents. This may be an optimistic estimate, but the actual figure of under 50,000 seems a low one in relation to the total of about 200,000 Coloured men of 21 years and over in the Cape Province (186,423 in the 1946 Census). Other deterrents include the prospect of losing some hours' or a day's work, and consequently of pay. Employers are often unwilling to grant such leave-of-absence, and some Coloureds claim that they have been deliberately kept waiting at the police station, and sometimes even told to return the next day. It is obviously difficult to check such stories, but the feeling that discrimination exists is undoubtedly present. The terms of the 1951 Separate Representation Act, outlined later in this chapter, will probably be the greatest deterring factor of all.

49. Under the Act applicants are required to write only their name and address on the form, while the remainder of the questions (1 and 5–15 on the special form) may be filled in by someone else. The same informants stated that some police officials have required applicants to write all kinds of sentences, and have dismissed their applications if they were unable to do so. On the other hand, a certain Goosen Richards of Paarl was in May, 1949, found not guilty by a Magistrate's Court of contravening the Electoral Act, under six counts which alleged that Richards had assisted with the false registration of two Coloured men as voters. Richards apparently wrote out the name and address and other particulars required on a separate piece of paper, and the others copied them out on the form. In his judgment, Mr. van der Riet said that he found it difficult to see how visual assistance could be considered 'any stronger than mental assistance. That this loophole had lent itself to undesirable practices could not be denied, but he was forced to the view that without proof of physical aid, the charges must fail.' (*Cape Argus*, 6th May, 1949.)

50. That large numbers of Coloured voters did not trouble to do so is suggested by the drop in the total Coloured vote from 54,134 in 1945 to 39,110 in 1947 (See Appendix J).

51. Speaking for the British Labour Party in this debate, Keir Hardie prophetically disagreed with these sanguine remarks.

52. Speaking at an A.P.O. social at the Strand in December, 1926, Dr. A. Abdurahman said: 'There was a hand that kept back the oppressor. That hand has now been removed and the oppressor is now free to do with us just what he likes.' (Reported in *Cape Times*, 15th December, 1926.)

53. See *Star* editorial of 9th November, 1950, and *Forum* of 19th November, 1950. The Opposition took the unusual, though unsuccessful, step of proposing a rival nominee for the Speakership.

54. For the legal issues involved, see: the Speaker's ruling (*Hansard*, 11th April, 1951); Cowen—'The Entrenched Sections of the South Africa Act,' May—*The South African Constitution*, Chs. I and XVIII; Crown law advisers by Dr. Malan (*Hansard*, 25th January, 1949); speech by Mr. J. G. N. Strauss (*Hansard*, 8th March, 1951); *Cape Times* of 18th January, 1951; *Star* of 18th–20th December, 1950; and reports of case hearings and judgments. After the Act was passed, four Cape Coloured voters brought a case to test its validity. On 17th April, 1951, Dr. Malan told Parliament that if the Courts declared this legislation invalid they would be assuming powers belonging only to the legislature and undermining Parliament's authority. He made an apparent reference to the 1897 case in which the Transvaal Chief Justice, Sir John Kotze, found a Volksraad resolution invalid according to the provisions of the Grondwet. President Kruger threatened the High Court and

dismissed Sir John a year later. In March, 1952, the Appeal Court declared the Voters' Act invalid, whereupon the Government rushed through an Act setting up a High Court of Parliament with power to review this decision. The four Coloured voters brought a further case contending that this Act too was invalid on the same grounds. In August 1952, the Cape Supreme Court upheld this contention; two days earlier the High Court of Parliament (boycotted by all but Nationalist members) had set aside the Appeal Court's decision in the first case. The Government registered an appeal to the Appellate Division against the Cape Supreme Court's decision. If this appeal were rejected, and the Government nevertheless persisted in its attitude, the subsequent conflict of jurisdictions would present public servants and citizens with a grave dilemma.

55. The United Party had two major reasons for defending the 'entrenched clauses': one was the danger of losing several Cape seats if Coloured voters were removed to a separate list; the other was the possible threat to the English language as an equal official language with Dutch or Afrikaans, the parity of the two languages having been similarly entrenched by the South Africa Act. The latter consideration was particularly important in English-speaking Natal.

56. The former operated mainly through written protests (see manifesto signed by 150 leading citizens—*Cape Times*, 14th February, 1951), and a mass petition signed by about 100,000 registered voters and organised by the Civic Rights Leagues throughout the Union (for text see *Cape Times* of 17th April, 1951). Nearly half these signatures came from the Transvaal; the Cape Town response was surprisingly poor (9,000 signatures). The moderate Coloureds of the National Convention Co-ordinating Committee joined with the Civic Rights League of Cape Town to open a 'Defend the Franchise' Fund (*Cape Times*, 11th January, 1951), but also associated themselves with the extremists of the Franchise Action Committee, whose methods were mass demonstrations and token strikes (see Ch. VIII). In May, 1951, groups of European ex-servicemen, prominent amongst whom were Group-Captain A. G. ('Sailor') Malan and a Boer veteran of the South African War, Commandant and ex-Senator A. J. de la Rey, formed War Veterans' Action Committees in Johannesburg, Cape Town and other major cities and towns. A torchlight procession was held in Johannesburg on 4th May, 1951, and a 'steel commando' of war-time jeeps from Johannesburg, joined by convoys from other centres, entered Cape Town on the night of 28th May bearing resolutions condemning the attack on the Constitution, and were received by a crowd estimated at about 50,000 or the largest yet seen in Cape Town. After the meeting, a disorderly minority, mainly Coloured, amongst the crowd, began to taunt and throw missiles at the police. The police stood up to this treatment patiently for a while, but when ordered to clear the area closest to Parliament, charged the crowds indiscriminately with batons, with the result that about 160 people (seventeen of them policemen and many others innocent bystanders, both Europeans and Coloureds, including a white St. John Ambulance nurse) are said to have been injured. Nationalist leaders accused this group, now generally known as the Torch Commando, and the United Party of inciting a 'mob' of '*skollies*' against the police, but have so far refused to institute a formal inquiry into the riots. See Cape press of 29th May and subsequent weeks and the Assembly debates on the clash reported in *Hansard* of 29th May, 1951, pp. 7912–8024, and 20th June, 1951, pp. 10120–176.

57. The Council of the Institute of Race Relations, at its annual meeting in January, 1950, did pass a resolution opposing the proposed removal of the Coloured voter from the common roll, on the grounds that it would be a backward step, would be unjust to the Coloured people and would harm the prestige of the Union. The Council further recommended that the franchise should be extended to the Cape Coloured in the other Provinces. (Report in *Cape Times*, 21st January, 1950.) See also letter in the *Sunday Times* of 4th March, 1951, headlined 'The Slogan Should Be Not Defend Coloured Vote; But Extend It.' On the other hand, the Transvaal Civil Rights League on 9th December, 1950, passed a resolution to defend

the *status quo* as regards the Coloured franchise. Some speakers from the floor suggested a more positive programme, but the general feeling was that this would frighten away various organisations which might otherwise give support. On April, 1951, for the first time in the forty years' history of the House of Assembly, a member moved that the franchise be eventually extended to all Non-European adults, male and female. This provoked Nationalist mirth. The mover was Mrs. Margaret Ballinger, a Native Representative. Her amendment fell away. (*Hansard*, 17th April, 1951, col. 4641.)

58. In 1944 the Coloured Advisory Council (for which see pp. 121–4) asked the Smuts Government to extend the franchise to the Northern provinces, and was told that this was 'not practical politics'. (C.A.C., 1944–5, p. 13, E (b).)

59. No. 46 of 1951. The original title of the Bill (the 'Representation of non-Europeans Bill') as published in the *Government Gazette* on 13th February, 1951, was amended, presumably to avoid the charge of partiality in relation to a particular group.

60. *Hansard*, 17th April, 1951, col. 4590. He added that this was not the first legislation which constituted such a relative diminution, and that the Coloureds were now losing only 'the power to turn the scales between the Europeans in their constituencies.'

61. *Hansard*, 8th May, 1951, col. 6162–4. The Minister added, in apparent reference to the Native and future Coloured Representatives: 'I say that if people come here imbued with . . . certain ideological ideas of equality and if they consider that they are thereby serving the interests of the non-Europeans, then they are making a big mistake.'

62. C.s. 1,110.

63. C.s. 1.065. At the end of 1950 the Natal electorate comprised 148,568 Europeans and 1,180 Non-Europeans. There were 6,539 Coloured men of 21 years and over in Natal in 1946.

64. C.s. 1,067. About 6,000 or roughly 50 per cent of Mauritians in Natal are registered as Europeans (*Cape Times*, 13th February, 1951). As no special provision is made by the Act to cover such cases, it seems that this right will now be taken away; and each Mauritian will be classed as European or Non-European, according to his appearance and associations.

65. Chapter XXXIV of the *Law Book* laid down in Article 10 that: 'Coloured persons who, according to this ordinance, have acquired or already possess immovable property shall never be regarded as Burghers, but like Burghers shall be liable to render military service or to provide goods for commando service if lawfully requested by the competent persons.' (C.s. 1,077.)

66. Another instance of the common tendency amongst South African whites to equate 'the people' with their own group. See also report of Mr. Swart, Minister of Justice, speaking at a Nationalist *Strydag* at Winburg, where he said that to the Nationalist the 'Nation' consists only of whites. (*Torch*, 31st July, 1950.)

67. A section of Law 4 of 1890 gives one more illustration of the unequivocal attitude of the Voortrekkers towards Non-Europeans which is most influential in South Africa to-day: 'Persons of colour, bastards, persons of openly bad behaviour and unrehabilitated bankrupts are not eligible for either Volksraad.' (Cited in C.s. 1,086.)

68. Acts 42/1925 and 22/1929. This arrangement was confirmed in 1950, when the territory gained the right to send representatives to the Union Parliament. The Rev. Z. R. Mahabane, President of the N.E.U.M., commented: 'The White people of . . . an erstwhile enemy territory have recently been admitted into the legislative Councils of the Union . . . while the children of South Africa, the Non-White sons and daughters of the soil, are treated as "undesirable foreigners", "unwanted *uitlanders*" . . . in their *vaderland*, and disqualified from all the rights, privileges and responsibilities of citizenship in the land, for the territorial integrity

of which the blood of their kith and kin has been shed from time to time.' (*Torch*, 6th March, 1951.)

69. Dr. Abdurahman and Mr. Dolley.

70. The City of Johannesburg, however, has a Non-European Affairs Department, which concerns itself with Coloured and Indian as well as with African problems.

71. Over recent years there has been a tendency for separate Coloured Ratepayers' Associations to emerge; their programmes suggest that they do not always agree that the Coloured residents' needs receive the same attention as do those of Europeans. See also statement by Councillor I. Ospovat (*Cape Times*, 6th April, 1951).

72. Ordinance 10 of 1912 and amending ordinances; see also Act No. 36 of 1919.

73. The importance of the municipal franchise in making the Coloured man feel himself a 'citizen', not an 'outcast', and in conferring a more satisfactory social and economic status was drawn by contrasting Cape Town and Johannesburg conditions in a speech made by Mrs. McBride at a meeting on 'Coloured Affairs' convened by the Johannesburg Branch of the National Council of Women in November, 1950.

74. There are about 30,000 Coloured voters in this area, but no figures are available for municipal voters, women being also eligible in the latter case. In 1949, there were five Non-Europeans (including one woman) and forty Europeans on the City Council, a proportion which may, as was suggested in a *Cape Argus* article on 8th August, 1949, roughly represent the respective voting strength. The article prophesied that despite their silence about local representation the Nationalists would hardly be likely to leave this state of affairs as it is. In the last provincial elections more than one rural audience was told to beware of the fate of Cape Town, where the City Council had been 'swamped' by Non-Europeans. At present there are six Non-Europeans on the Cape Town City Council, one Malay in Simonstown, and a Coloured man and a Malay in Goodwood.

75. A decision in the case of Kramer *v.* Port Elizabeth Revision Court (30th November, 1943) held that weekly tenants of municipal housing schemes do not qualify for the municipal franchise, as they are not liable to pay rates. This loss of the municipal vote is a source of bitterness amongst many Coloured tenants of housing-schemes, bitterness which is usually directed against the municipality concerned.

76. In remoter districts ignorance, apathy and European prejudice may operate to deprive Coloured who would otherwise qualify from registering as municipal or divisional council voters. See C.A.C. Report, 1943/4, p. 24 (4) for the ignorance of Coloured smallholders in the Blinkwater district.

77. According to Section 11 (3) of the same Ordinance, a European who cohabits with a coloured woman is liable to disfranchisement. I was unable to ascertain how many Europeans, if any, had lost their franchise in this way.

78. C.A.C. Report, 1944–5, p. 13, E (a).

79. Ordinance No. 11 of 1925, s. 13.

80. C.A.C., 1943–4, p. 1, s. 2. Members received a subsistence allowance, the Chairman £90 p.a., and the Secretary £60, plus his grade salary as an employee of the Social Welfare Department.

81. For further details of this resentment see Ch. VIII (pp. 38–41).

82. The correctness of such an assumption was proved in March, 1951, with the institution of the new Sub-Department of Coloured Affairs.

83. 'Where there is a section of the population which does not enjoy full franchise rights, special means must be found by which the interests of that section of the population must be guarded. This is possible only when the Government is able to keep in close touch with the opinion and needs of the Coloured people, and it is in this respect that the C.A.C. is fulfilling a definite need. It is for the same reason

that one particular Department of State (Department of Social Welfare) is acting as the watch-dog of Coloured interests.' (C.A.C. 1945–6, p. 16, Ch. 8.)

84. As no reports of C.A.C. activities after 1946–7 are available, it is hard to say whether the Council's difficulties increased under the new régime.

85. The resolution read: 'Since this Council finds itself unable to carry out its function of advising the Government on matters affecting the welfare of the Coloured people, as the Prime Minister refuses to see a deputation of the C.A.C. on the question of the Government's policy of *apartheid* unless that deputation is prepared to discuss only the manner in which *apartheid* is to be applied, and will offer no protest against it, and since this Council recognises the fact that the proposed scheme of *apartheid* as enunciated by the Government . . . is in direct conflict with the wishes and aspirations of the Coloured people . . . this Council forthwith resigns.' (*The Sun*, 12th January, 1950.)

86. Their resignation, and subsequent appeal for Coloured unity, did not soften the hearts of their Coloured opponents. An Anti-C.A.D. commentator wrote unkindly: 'For seven long years this species of humanity, political outcasts and un-touchables, has lived apart from the true aspirations of the Coloured people, and now, therefore, their so-called 'revolt' against *apartheid* impresses nobody. There appears to be no particular virtue in doing now what they should have done seven years ago . . . Let us keep away from the carriers who imagine they have been disinfected, but still carry the germs of dissension and collaboration around with them.' (The *Torch*, 16th January, 1950, p. 6.)

87. As will be seen in Ch. V, further discrimination is made as regards salaries, pensions and so on.

88. 'Every Coloured group of races . . . will be segregated, not only as regards the place of dwelling or the neighbourhood dwelt in by them, but also with regard to spheres of work. The members of such groups can, however, be allowed to enter white territory, under lawful control, for the increase of working power and also for the necessary increase of their own incomes. (*a*) To each of such segregated race groups of Coloured subjects of the Republic, self-government will be granted within their own territory, under the central management of the general Government of the country in accordance with the fitness of the group for the carrying out of such self-government, for which they will have to be systematically trained.' (Draft Constitution of the Republic, as authorised by Dr. D. F. Malan for publication in *Die Transvaler*, 23rd January, 1942, and republished in translation by *The British Africa Monthly* in a special supplement, July, 1948.) See *The Forum*, 23rd June, 1949, for an article showing how the Nationalist Government's record of work follows this Constitution. In late 1950 Dr. Malan issued a somewhat ambiguous disavowal of this document. (See *Rand Daily Mail*, 4th October, 1950, and editorial comment, 5th October, 1950.)

89. At the 1949 Cape Nationalist Party Congress, Dr. Donges declared that Coloured people would staff post offices in their own areas, and that steps had already been taken to train them (*Cape Times*, 29th September, 1949.) Early in 1950, however, the Postmaster-General said that little headway had yet been made with these plans, as the Public Service Commission had not yet fixed a salary-scale— once this was done, the Department would recruit about six men, and training would begin. (*The Sun*, 3rd February, 1950.) For the over-all number of Europeans and Non-Europeans employed in various government departments, see *Union Year Book* No. 24, 1948, pp. 81–2.)

90. The new Afrikaans dictionary defines *apartheid* as follows: 'A political (*staatkundige*) policy direction in South Africa founded on the broad principles of (*a*) differentiation, in accordance with differences of race and/or colour and/or standard of civilisation, in contrast to assimilation, (*b*) the maintenance and perpetua-tion of the identity of the different colour groups constituting the population, and the separate development of these groups according to habits (*aard*), trading and aptitude, in contrast to integration.'

91. See editorial and statement by Dr. J. S. Moroka, *Cape Times*, 8th February, 1951. In 1950 (following an embarrassing call from the Dutch Reformed Church for the implementation of complete territorial *apartheid* despite the great sacrifices which this would demand from the white group), Dr. Malan admitted that complete *apartheid* was not practical politics, and that his own modified programme would take many years to accomplish (*Cape Times*, 7th April, 1950). At the 1951 Conference of the South African Bureau of Racial Affairs (S.A.B.R.A.), set up in 1949 to counter the 'liberalistic' Institute of Race Relation, speakers questioned the practicability of *apartheid*, while approving of it in theory. (See *Star*, 12th January, 1951.) A year earlier they had accepted the total territorial segregation plan rejected by the Minister of Native Affairs in the House of Assembly on 7th September, 1948 (See *Cape Times* editorial, 14th February, 1950).

92. Hoernlé, p. 168.

93. That this is so is strongly suggested by the care taken to define the two groups: Clause 1 (iii) ' "Coloured person' means a person who is not a white person or a native' (xv) " 'White person" means a person who in appearance obviously is, or who is generally accepted as a white person, but does not include a person who although in appearance obviously a white person, is generally accepted as a coloured person.' (A.B. 26–'50.) General Smuts, attacking the Bill on 9th May, 1950, in the House of Assembly also stressed this point. See also *The Sun*, 24th March, 1950, p. 4, for a Coloured comment. Note the use of 'White' instead of 'European' in the English version, a new and logical development.

94. It will be based on the 1951 Census returns, with decisions in dubious cases devolving on untrained, temporary census enumerators. Objections will be decided by a Board of three, presided over by a judge or magistrate (active or retired). From this Board's decision an appeal may be made within thirty days to the provincial division of the Supreme Court and therefrom to the Appellate Division (an expensive procedure). Objections to the classification of other persons must be accompanied by a deposit of £10, to be forfeited if the Board rejects the objection. It was estimated that the extra cost of establishing the Register would be £165,000, and its annual maintenance £115,000 (*Hansard*, 8th March, 1950, col. 2511).

95. The *Torch* (6th March, 1951) called these documents 'a passport for the White, and a pass for every Black person', showing that it does not accept the Nationalist argument that the Act is not discriminatory because its provisions are theoretically identical for Europeans and Non-Europeans. In opposing the passage of the Act, the United Party attempted to arouse indignation amongst Europeans by pointing out that white women would have to carry 'passes' while their African maidservants did not. 'This Bill is aimed at insulting the European population, and at making White Kaffirs of the Europeans. It is a White Kaffir Act. The White man and the White woman will have to carry a pass.' (Mr. Sarel Tighy, U.P. member for Johannesburg (West), reported in Hansard, 9th March, 1950, col. 2685.)

96. See Ch. VI C.

97. Mr. Schoeman, Minister of Labour, was reported by S.A.P.A. on 7th March, 1949, as saying that he did not think that Non-Europeans would be allowed to attend conferences overseas so long as there was a Nationalist Government in South Africa. Shortly afterwards the Minister of the Interior withdrew the passport of the secretary of the Coloured branch of the Garment Workers' Union, who was to have represented the Transvaal Council of Non-European Unions at the W.F.T.U. meeting in Milan (*Cape Times*, 8th June, 1949.) See Ch. VII for a similar ban on foreign Non-European delegates desiring to attend conferences in the Union.

98. *Race Relations Handbook*, p. 37.

99. Delay was reported in the case of the Coloured tennis player, David Samaai (*The Sun*, 8th April, 1949). Since then, however, passport regulations have been tightened up for all racial groups, and passports are only issued for a period of one year. Certain Europeans, prominent in race relations and social welfare work, have found it difficult to get passports. Recently the Indian Government offered

six scholarships to Non-European students from the Union, one of whom was a Coloured doctor. He and two others were refused passports to India, although he was subsequently granted one to enable him to go to England. (*Cape Times*, 21st November, 1950.)

100. The 1947 Annual Report of the Department of Justice gave the number of licences issued to Coloureds and Europeans respectively under the Arms and Ammunition Act as thirty-four and around 70,000. There are also restrictions on the possession of knives for all races, although many Coloureds of the skolly class seem to carry these illegally.

101. Many Coloured people believe that the Nationalist desire to deprive them of existing rights is intensified by the past readiness of the Coloured community to join the British side in any conflict, whether in South Africa or overseas. Speaking at a meeting called by the Paarl Apartheid Resistance Committee, Mr G. Richards said it was ironical 'That the Coloured people, who had fought in two wars for democracy, should now lose their vote at the hands of the Nationalists who had opposed participation in those wars and were now out to take revenge.' (*Cape Times*, 21st October, 1949.)

102. Marais, p. 96.

103. See Marais, p. 131, who also gives a more detailed account of earlier Coloured military history.

104. Marais, p. 134. Cf. Pierson, p. 170.

105. *v. Race Relations Handbook*, pp. 534–55, for a fairly full account of the Non-European record in both Great Wars. See also A. Desmore, *With the Cape Corps in South Africa*.

106. *Cape Times*, 19th April, 1949.

107. 'Many more would have volunteered had it not been for the outcry from the farming areas that recruitment was reducing the supply of Coloured labour. The government accordingly closed certain areas to recruitment, much to the disappointment of keen young men.' (*Race Relations Handbook*, p. 541.) This attitude on the part of many farmers resulted in Coloured labourers enlisting without their employers' permission, with the result that the latter repudiated responsibility when it came to compulsory reinstatement in their work.

108. *Hansard*, 24th February, 1950, cols. 1921–2. *Ibid.*, 22nd January, 1942, cols. 233–4 and 239.

109. Several informants, both European and Coloured, have suggested that Non-European prisoners-of-war received worse treatment at German and Italian hands than did European South Africans.

110. Formal relations between European and Non-European servicemen were laid down in a gazetted amendment to the National Emergency regulations, which laid it down that Non-European N.C.O.s held their rank in the Non-European Army Services only and might not exercise any command or authority over European members of the Forces. European personnel might, however, exercise command over Non-European personnel by virtue of superior rank, or because of having been placed in command of such Non-European personnel. In the event of an emergency, the senior European N.C.O. or private should be deemed to have been placed in command of the Non-European personnel, irrespective of rank (reported in *Rand Daily Mail*, 26th January, 1942). In April, 1946, the Coloured Advisory Council unsuccessfully requested that the Cape Corps be made a permanent unit with Coloured officers; it added that the Coloured man was not interested in having his officers saluted by white ranks (reported in *Rand Daily Mail* of 4th April, 1946). It has not been possible to examine informal relations between Europeans and Non-Europeans in the S.A. Forces, or the extent to which European officers differentiated racially in their treatment of other ranks. That an increased cordiality between ethnic groups arose in some cases is suggested by the activities of the Springbok Legion and the more conservative and non-political South African Legion of the B.E.S.L. (*v.* p. 137.) At the 1949 conference in Port Elizabeth, the National Execu-

P

tive expressed its grave concern at the 'possibility of the voting rights of Coloured ex-servicemen being altered to their disadvantage', and agreed that: 'every endeavour would be made by the South African Legion to guard these rights of Coloured ex-servicemen who came forward in a time of great national emergency to volunteer and serve their country.' (*Cape Times*, 28th April, 1949.) On the other hand, some Europeans have complained to me of the 'cheeky' attitude acquired by Coloured soldiers in Egypt and Italy, especially when they found that they could have as many white women as they wanted. See also complaints against some local demobilisation committees' treatment of Coloured applicants. (S.A. Coloured Ex-Servicemen's Legion, B.E.S.L., report of interview with General Brink, 8th April, 1947.)

111. *Race Relations Handbook*, p. 539.

112. For instance, after 1943, a European (non-artisan) Corporal received a basic daily rate of 8s., a Coloured, Malay or Indian Corporal 4s. and an African Corporal without dependents 2s. 9d. Married allowances were: Europeans (all other ranks) 5s. 3d. for a wife only, 2s. for the first child and 1s. for each additional child; Coloureds (wife only) 3s. 6d., with 1s. for the first child and no allowance for any others; Africans 9d. for any and all dependents, and no additional allowance. See *Race Relations Handbook*, pp. 546–7 for full details; also *Year Book* No. 24, pp. 228–30 for military pensions.

113. On 17th April, 1949, the *Government Gazette* announced the disbanding of the Cape Coloured Corps as a unit of the S.A. Permanent Force. A comment by Mr. George Golding, a member and ex-chairman of the C.A.C., was reported in the *Cape Times* of 19th April, 1949: 'I have no doubt that if the present Government is ever faced with war it will find it impossible to do without the combatant services of the Coloured people, who, if called on, will respond loyally and readily.' The decision, however, aroused great bitterness amongst Coloured ex-servicemen, and the offer to raise 100,000 Non-European troops in South Africa for service in Korea, which was made by the former Director of Non-European Army Services, Brigadier E. Stubbs, and forwarded to Washington in mid-July, 1950, aroused no great enthusiasm. (See the *Torch*, 24th July, 1950, and 25th September, 1950, the *Sun*, 21st July, 1950 and letter in the *Cape Argus* of 4th September 1950.)

114. Cf. *Cape Times* editorial, 24th March, 1949.

115. 'If the Government had not yet introduced complete *apartheid* the people must not be discouraged. It would come: then there would be no more rubbing of shoulders with the Coloured *boetie* of the South African Party at elections. "I am convinced", said Dr. van Nierop (Nationalist M.P. for Mossel Bay), "that God has sent Dr. Malan to save White South Africa, and the Englishman will live to thank God and Dr. Malan for having saved the White race in South Africa." ' (*Cape Times*, 30th January, 1950.)

116. In a speech at Vredefort on 3rd July, 1949 (*Cape Times*, 4th July, 1949). These have now become the most derogatory and offensive terms that can be applied to Coloureds, Africans and Indians in South Africa. Four months later another member of the Government, Mr. J. G. Strydom, Minister of Lands, said at Potgietersrust that a vote for General Smuts would mean 'digging the grave of our people. The Coolies and Coloureds will once more have the vote and we shall again be British subjects.' (*Cape Times*, 14th November, 1949.) See also the report of similar language used at the Cape Nationalist Party Congress in September, 1950. (*Cape Times*, 29th September, 1949).

117. 'Congress requests the Government to see to it that Seretse Khama and his wife will be refused entry to any part of the Union,' 'The revision of their (i.e., non-Europeans') wages in the Public Service to bring them into conformity with what farmers can afford to pay . . . That the pension scheme for non-Europeans should be thoroughly investigated, and thereafter restricted . . .' 'That every district's kaffirs remain employed in their own district' . . . 'Separate telephone booths for Europeans and non-Europeans . . .' 'The wage of Native labourers

on the Railways at £7 a month is too high and takes Native labour from the farms'
. . . 'Stronger action against Natives and Coloureds using foul language on railway
stations' . . . 'That no non-European medical practitioners should be allowed
to attend European patients' . . . 'The provision of legislation preventing Natives
or Coloureds from driving European-owned motor vehicles' . . . 'That Natives
should be prohibited from owning dogs.' (*Rand Daily Mail*, 5th September,
1949.)

118. The Transvaal Nationalist Party also refused to accept Jewish members
until 1951, when this ban was officially lifted.

119. Several European informants have told me that this type of language is
frequently used in speeches to country audiences. On 15th December, 1949, *Die
Burger* in a leading article spoke of the 'Party whose hope to govern was dependent
on the untutored Coloured masses.'

120. Despite the fact that the Nationalists are said to have received some Coloured
votes in the 1948 Election and even to be quietly canvassing the Coloured voters in
the Ceres bye-election (*Cape Times*, 18th April, 1951). The late Mr. J. H. Hofmeyr
was often accused of being a 'Kaffir-*boetie*' (negrophile), and was presented to
Nationalist audiences and readers as the crypto-Communist bogey-man who
advocated social equality between all races in South Africa. The *Forum* of 23rd
July, 1949 (pp. 18–19) described the methods used by Nationalist canvassers at
Vrededorp, a Johannesburg mixed lower-class residential suburb, with many
lower-grade public employees. Such voters were told that it was a shame that persons
doing such important work should have to live next to 'Kaffirs' and 'Coolies', while
a bricklayer just laid off would be told: 'Now the U.P. wants to give building work
to Kaffirs—imagine what unemployment that would cause.'

121. March 1st, 1949. The article ended with the 'shocking' news that two Nationalist officials had found a white, English-speaking woman sitting at one desk in this
office with a Coloured man seated at another in the same room.

122. Sir de Villiers Graaff, U.P. member for Hottentots Holland, where Coloured
voters form nearly 14 per cent of the electorate, said in East London that 'he did not
think there was any doubt that we have enough in common to find a national all-
party policy and to lift this matter out of party politics. The U.P. could not agree on
political *apartheid*, but if it disregarded this aspect there was much on which they
might find common ground.' (*Star*, 24th February, 1950.) Cf. 'We do not believe
in equal rights, but in reasonable segregation . . .' (Major Piet van der Byl, M.P.,
reported in *Rand Mail*, 25th September, 1950); 'We must retain the good will of the
Coloured population and encourage the immigration of another couple of million
Europeans' (Dr. L. Steenkamp, M.P., reported in *Sunday Times*, 10th December,
1950); 'The security of White leadership in South Africa . . .' (Mr. J. G. N. Strauss,
Leader of the Opposition, reported in *Rand Daily Mail*, 22nd November, 1950.)

123. In March 1949, the Transvaal Senator J. M. van H. Brink was expelled from
the U.P., and subsequently resigned from the Senate. In a statement, the former
Senator said he had told the United Party caucus that, *inter alia*, 'as a European
and a South African he could not oppose the proposed legislation of the Government
to establish a separate voters' roll for the Coloured voters and to abolish the present
Natives' representation.' He claimed that it was U.P. policy and not his views which
had changed. (*Cape Times*, 29th March, 1949.) In late December 1950, on the other
hand, the U.P. Vigilance Committee requested Mr. Hugh Parker, M.P.C., a Native
Representative candidate for the Senate, to resign because he had in his manifesto
supported 'equal rights and franchise for all races irrespective of colour', and
direct representation of Africans and Non-Europeans in Parliament and provincial
and municipal councils. (*Star*, 28th December, 1950.)

124. 'During the debate . . . Mr. Strydom, Minister of Lands, stated again that
the United Party stood for equality between Europeans and non-Europeans . . .
Dr. Jonker (U.P.) offered to resign his seat . . . if Mr. Strydom would prove that
any responsible U.P. leader or any official statement of policy issued by the U.P.,

had ever advocated equality between Europeans and non-Europeans. Needless to say the Minister did not accept this challenge.' (Letter from U.P. supporter, *Cape Times*, 8th February, 1950.) Some weeks earlier the Minister of Justice claimed that the defeated U.P. candidate in the Harrismith bye-election had said he was in favour of separate rolls for Coloureds. (*Hansard*, 25th January, 1950, col, 105.)

125. From statement on 'The Native and Coloured Peoples' Policy of the United Party', as available at U.P. branches in 1951; also quoted in *Cape Argus* of 2nd October, 1948.

126. During the Provincial Elections in 1949 I volunteered to drive electors to the polling station in one of the Cape Town constituencies. In the party headquarters I was asked whether I would object to driving Coloured supporters. While on our rounds, the European party official who accompanied me said 'I hope they send us after Europeans next time.' A Cape Nationalist comment on such situations was: 'On Election day they (the Coloureds) become great gentlemen who ride to the poll in the glittering cars of the U.P. . . . but after the little cross is drawn . . . they sink into the grinding mass of a brown proletariat . . . the highest bidder got their vote and the Nationalist Party lagged behind because, to its honour, it was not prepared to play the political game of the Sap politicians.' (*Die Burger*, 18th October, 1950, quoted in *British Africa Review*, December, 1950, p. 14.)

127. Officially, the basic requirement for membership is that applicants are competent to be registered as voters in connection with Parliamentary and Provincial Elections (Constitution of the United S.A. National Party as amended and adopted at the Union Congress, Bloemfontein, 6th December, 1944). A United Party organiser told me that the committees were 'for election purposes mainly, and under European supervision.'

128. The only inter-racial party which, until its dissolution in 1950, admitted Non-Europeans to full membership, and which advocated immediate and absolute political equality, was the Communist Party, which had some success amongst Coloured people for this reason. Members of all races, including Europeans, sat on its National Executive. The Afrikaner Party had little following in the Cape, and is now amalgamated with the Nationalist Party. The Labour Party, whose members are mainly Northern urban workers, has gradually evolved a more liberal policy towards unskilled non-European labour, and opposed the proposed Non-European Franchise Bill in its entirety. In April, 1949, the formation was rumoured of a new and progressive political party to be called the Libertas Party. The report in the *Rand Daily Mail* of 25th April, 1949, stressed that the projected party 'would not consider social equality between European and non-European'. No more has been heard of the proposal to date. A well-known liberal, Senator E. H. Brookes, wrote in *Forum*: 'Ultimately Liberalism is bound to stand for the common voters' roll, a roll on which non-Europeans reaching a proper civilisation test, which may be set at a high level, may appear as full and equal voters for the same candidates and in the same constituencies. Few, if any, liberals would stand for the immediate enfranchisement of masses of illiterate voters . . . But increased community representation, even by men of the same colour as the voters, is not, in true Liberal theory, however possible as a transition stage, a real solution.' (19th January, 1951.) The Torch Commando, which is not strictly a political party, has increasingly stressed that it is a European group, though Coloureds may join a separate section.

129. For an attempt to separate the question of Coloured rights from the overall colour problem see Keppel-Jones' exposition of his federal scheme in *Friends or Foes*, particularly pp. 55–62.

130. Cf. Myrdal, p. 446.

131. The present situation in Southern Rhodesia follows the same pattern. The value of property to be occupied by a voter is to be increased to £500, and his annual earnings must be £240 or over. The Prime Minister recently said that the cash earnings stipulation was 'purely a temporary measure designed to retain the common roll, but also to ensure that no undue number of Natives got on to it', and that other than

property qualifications would have to be introduced at some future date. (*Cape Times*, 13th February, 1951.) In March 1951, Mr. R. S. Brooke, U.P. Member for Mowbray, Cape, suggested that there might be a case for raising the educational and property qualifications for Coloured voters. (*Forum*, 30th March, 1951.)

132. Colour prejudice would appear to be strongest amongst the poorer and less educated white classes, in South Africa as in the American South. There may be a connection between the extension of universal adult franchise to the Cape in 1931 and the intensification of effective colour prejudice in this Province in recent years.

133. With the rise of an increasing class of Europeanised Africans, the continued presence of Coloured voters on the common roll provides an opening for the demand of similar rights for similarly qualified Africans, a process which, once readmitted, might ultimately result in the outnumbering of European voters.

134. Writing in 1927, before the full effects of Union could be felt in this sphere, Professor MacMillan was able to say of the Coloured People what can no longer be said to-day: 'Such measure of freedom as they have enjoyed is, however, justified by its fruits . . . Their "problem" is in a measure "solved".' (p. 287.)

135. '. . . It seems to be a fact that Negroes can feel sure that, unless this country undergoes a veritable revolution, their right to vote will remain unquestioned in the North, independent of any increase due to continued migration from the South. Without any doubt, this is one of the strategic protections of the Negro people in American society . . . The Northern vote might become the instrument by which the Negroes can increasingly use the machinery of federal legislation and adminis-tration to tear down the walls of discrimination.' (Myrdal, p. 440.) In the United States, the liberal creed is the federal one, that of the larger society, and it is on the offensive against sectional prejudices. In South Africa the half-hearted liberalism of a section is on the defensive against the illiberalism of the larger society. 'One by one the kindly happy traditions between the races which we in the Cape Province have known for a hundred years are gradually being destroyed by a new force let loose in this country.' (Mr. S. F. Waterson, M.P., reported in *Rand Daily Mail*, 25th October, 1950.)

136. '. . . European paramountcy, from its very nature, is irreconcilable with the full extension of democratic franchise rights to the non-Europeans who con-stitute the vast majority of our inhabitants, simply and most undemocratically, because they do constitute the overwhelming majority of our population.' (From a letter to the *Cape Times*, 8th April, 1949, written by Dr. W. J. van Zijl.)

137. The 1950 Dutch Reformed Church Congress, which accepted total *apartheid* as the only solution, realised the consequences of admitting Non-Europeans to European areas: 'We cannot expect . . . that they will be satisfied to leave their economic, political and social interests in the hands of others. They will fight for a say in national affairs, and in this struggle they will seek support from various quarters, even outside our country.' (Quoted in the *Star*, 28th November, 1950, in Article II of *A Plan for South Africa*.) See also *Cape Times* editorial (24th March, 1949) the speech by Mr. W. Traub in the report of a symposium held by the Insti-tute of Race Relations (*Cape Times*, 20th January, 1950, and Joshi, p. 7).

138. As Coloured people, unlike tribal Africans, have no separate political institutions of their own, political *apartheid* cannot even be said to provide them with an opportunity to 'develop along their own lines', as the Nationalist Party likes to claim. In the modern world, however, a discriminatory attitude based solely on such criteria as skin-colour is increasingly harder to maintain. Those who hold it are therefore at pains to justify their attitude by adducing other and cultural inferiority, such as ignorance and irresponsibility (*v.* pp. 176 and 179–80). As these cultural differences disappear, the dominant group is logically faced with the alter-natives either of modifying its attitude or abandoning its beliefs. A third alternative, adopted by many white South Africans, is to refuse to think the problem out

to its logical conclusion at all, but to hope that the *status quo* will somehow be perpetuated.

CHAPTER IV—THE LAW AND ITS ADMINISTRATION

1. Wille, *Principles of South African Law* (2nd edition, 1945) Section 2, pp. 6–8. See also below, n. 6, which qualifies this.

2. 'Nevertheless, although "class" legislation became taboo in 1828, laws passed after that date continued to bear testimony to the presence in the Cape Colony of large masses of backward people. In this sense "class" legislation, in fact, if not in form, continued to find its way on to the Colonial statute-book . . . When all has been said, however, the fact that Colonial legislation remained, as a general rule, non-discriminatory in form is immensely important. It represents the homage that successive generations of colonists, often in spite of themselves, continued to pay to the departed spirits of the philanthropists. From the point of view of practical politics it was a real safeguard of the interests of both Coloured people and Bantu in that it made the Legislature chary of passing oppressive laws which might be applied to Europeans as well as non-Europeans.' (Marais, p. 158.)

3. C.s. 955–8. The post-Union liquor laws have continued this differentiation.

4. Brookes, p. 93. The reference is to the Native Administration Act of that year, which gave the Governor-General summary and extra-judicial powers. See also provisions of the Native Laws Amendment Bill before Parliament in 1951.

5. C.s. 1,021–3. For details of such legislation up to 1936, see C.s. 968 f., and for later legislation see other chapters of this study, particularly those dealing with political and economic discrimination. In many cases, the legislation has not contained specific reference to the Coloured people. Certain Provincial measures differentiating against Coloured people are still extant in the Orange Free State and Transvaal. Coloureds are not now subject to 'pass laws', which were, however, only repealed for them universally in 1923. (Act No. 21/1923, s. 28.)

6. 'The supreme legislature is not bound by this restriction (i.e., that of partiality) for the Courts can no more question the validity of its laws on the grounds of partiality than they can on the ground of unreasonableness. Throughout South Africa there exists a social chasm between the European and non-European races which has had its effect on legislation . . . our statute books simply teem with laws establishing differential treatment as between European or "white" persons, and non-Europeans or coloured persons, in almost every department of life . . . What is known as the "colour-bar" is deeply entrenched in the laws of the Union.' (Wille, pp. 6–8.)

7. The comparative paucity (until recently) of laws specifically concerned with the Coloured people as compared with Africans may be ascribed to the fact that they have exerted some slight political power by their presence on the common roll.

8. See Reports of Select Committee on Delegated Legislation (S.C. 8–'48, S.C. 17–'48 and S.C. 8–'49) for a general discussion of the growth of this tendency, though not with specific reference to Native legislation. Other instances of legislation designed, *inter alia*, to enforce the officially-approved relationship between white and non-white, in which great powers are delegated to the administration, are: the Riotous Assemblies Act (No. 27 of 1914, as amended by Act No. 19 of 1930), for an instance of the operation of which see Du Plessis *v*. Minister of Justice, 1950 (3) S.A.L.R. 579 (W.O.D.); the Suppression of Communism Act (No. 44 of 1950); and the Suppression of Communism Amendment Act of 1951, the action of which is retrospective, with no appeal to the courts for the person involved.

9. Members of the public often take this law into their own hands, or constitute themselves its officers. Before the mass demonstration called by the Franchise Action Council in Cape Town in March 1951, the Minister of Justice issued a warning to the public to leave the maintenance of law and order altogether in the hands of the police. (*Cape Times*, 7th March, 1951.) See also below, n. 11.

10. '. . . There is in South Africa a deeply rooted tendency to regard law not only as the primary but as the sole agency of social control. This is a fundamental illusion. In no form of society are the laws respected by the common man unless there are also other social forces at work which encourage him to respect the force of law. In our own European societies these other forces obviously include the home, the family, the school, the neighbourhood, the suburb, as well as the church, the professional or vocational body to which a man belongs, and, not least, the desire to advance in power or wealth since in an acquisitive society none of us is really free from this incentive.' ('Crime and the Community'.) The deterioration in administration consequent upon such a limited view of social control methods is perhaps shown in the rise in the number of prosecutions per 1,000 population from forty-six in 1912 to ninety-six in 1949, and the increase in the percentage of undetected serious crime from 9.53 per cent in 1940 to 17.89 per cent in 1949 (the latter perhaps partly due to the inclusion after 1948 of certain offences not previously so classified). Figures taken from S.A. Police Report for 1949.

11. A Coloured informant wrote to me: 'Lynching does not exist in South Africa in the same sense in which it occurs in the States. Here they cut the ceremonials, mistake you for a baboon or a burglar and settle all with a bullet. A "mean white" mob would never gather outside a county jail to pull out a nigger to lynch him. The police will pulp the fellow, anyway.' See also Ch. IX, n. 115.

12. In early colonial times the officers of the law had at their disposal a number of 'Caffres', mostly Indian exiles, who were employed to arrest suspected persons, and to assist with the scourging of sentenced offenders of all colours. In 1780 the Governor remarked on the undesirability of having Cape burghers and other white men arrested by these black 'Caffres', and the Fiscal was allotted four European constables. (V. de Kock, pp. 147 and 168.)

13. Under the terms of the Police Act, No. 14 of 1912, s. 8, the Governor-General may, in case of war or other emergency, employ the Force to assist in the defence of the Union anywhere in South Africa. This necessitates a certain amount of military training for European recruits. The Police Commission of Enquiry emphasised the vast difference between the duties and responsibilities of a soldier and those of a policeman (s. 61), and recommended that the period devoted to such military subjects be diminished and more time spent on the technicalities of police work proper. (s. 62—see also s. 60.)

14. P. s. 37; *Star*, 7th December, 1950.

15. 'The average Southern policeman is a promoted poor white with a legal sanction to use a weapon. His social heritage has taught him to despise the Negroes and he has had little education which could have changed him.' (Myrdal, p. 540-1.) Cf. also Johnson, p. 32. It must be admitted that the training of the South African policeman compares very favourably with that of his U.S. colleague. In addition, the dependence of the latter upon direct political support, particularly in the higher ranks, constitutes another factor making for injustice which is not present to such an extent in a professional police force.

16. 'The general relationship of white to non-white in South Africa determines very largely the fate of Coloured persons under arrest. Manhandling and forcible arrest of Coloured persons are not unheard of. In these cases the attitude of the white constable seems to be that of a white individual towards "just another Coloured criminal". It is recommended that handcuffs should be used only in cases where the arrested person is violent . . .' (C.A.C. 45/6, p. 17.) See also the cases of Detective Samuel Botha (*Cape Times*, 4th June, 1949); Police Constable H. J. Swiggelaar (*Cape Argus*, 16th May, 1949); two unknown policemen in Wale Street incident (*Cape Times*, 17th May, 1949). See S.A. Coloured Ex-Servicemen's legion, B.E.S.L.; Report of Interview with Commissioner of Police at Pretoria, 8th April, 1947 (p. 3) for complaints of police treatment of ex-volunteers in Namaqualand. See the *Cape Times* and *Cape Argus* of 15th June, 1950, photograph in *Die Burger* of 16th June, 1950, and correspondence columns of ensuing days (especially letter from Mr.

Stanley Uys in *Cape Times* of 16th June, 1950), for independent eye-witness accounts of incidents during police baton charge against crowd of 500 Coloured men and women demonstrating outside Parliament on evening of 14th June, 1950, against Suppression of Communism Bill. Nothing has as yet been heard of the police inquiry instituted as a result.

17. L.s. 120–1. It should be remembered that the Lansdown Commission Report, like all other official reports, reflects the attitudes and bias of a section of the European community, however much they may strive for objectivity. In these circumstances, their findings must be regarded as an under-statement rather than the reverse. See also Cape press of 29th May, 1951, and subsequent days, and *Hansard*, 29th May, 1951, pp. 7912–8024 and 20th June, 1951, pp. 10,120–75, for a discussion of police methods during the Cape Town riot on the night of 28th May, 1951, following the Torch Commando parade.

18. This difficulty was experienced to a far greater extent by me, as I lacked the facilities available to the Commissioners. I was informed of many such cases but was unable to verify them, although the mere telling suggested the existence of a widespread belief in and expectation of police brutality amongst all Coloured classes. On the few occasions when I had first-hand experience of police treatment of Coloureds, the treatment was not such as would be meted out to Europeans. It improved after my intervention and protests.

19. On 3rd November, 1947, a statement by Major-General R. J. Palmer, then Commissioner of the South African Police, was published by the *Rand Daily Mail*, which stated that it was 'the policy of the police to deal drastically with members of the Force who commit unprovoked assaults on any members of the community, irrespective of colour, race or creed, and in the past, apart from prosecution before the courts, dismissal from the Force had followed.' The provisions of Police Standing Order No. 339 also deal with this.

20. European acceptance of police attitudes to Non-Europeans is well illustrated by the following recent cutting from a Cape paper (unfortunately undated). The episode described was cited as an instance not of police irregularities but as a good joke: 'Did the detective give you the usual warning when he arrested you?' the prosecutor inquired of Japie, who was in the dock. 'Ja, Baas,' said Japie at once. 'And what did he tell you?' 'He said: "Come along with me now or I'll break your b—— neck." '

21. A number of Coloured people have complained to me that they do not get adequate police protection in predominantly Non-European residential areas. It is said that several Coloured districts in Cape Town are terrorised by gangs, especially at week-ends, and that neither white nor Coloured police dare to intervene except on motorised raids. One informant spoke of the 'pick-up vans which terrorise the Coloured districts especially when the pubs close', and the arming of white policemen in Non-European districts only at first. Now firearms are carried by foot police on all urban beats.

22. With the exception of a few individuals in the Cape Town Traffic Police, which is a municipal force in which no such discrimination is made. Several Coloured traffic police direct traffic in and around Cape Town, and are entitled to deal with European traffic offenders. In practice, they seem to be more courteous and less anxious to report or reprimand Europeans than their white colleagues. Many members of the European public, particularly from outside Cape Town, resent their authority most bitterly. See also Hoernle, p. 6, n. 1, for the remark of Mr. Strydom in May 1939 that, if the authorities did not give orders that Native Railway Police were no longer empowered to arrest white men, he advised Europeans confronted with such a possibility to resist arrest with force.

23. One lower-middle class Coloured woman said that Coloured police were 'as bad as the whites' in their treatment of the public; when I attended a Coloured political meeting in early 1951, I heard the Coloured C.I.D. men who were present called 'Nationalist stooges'. This hatred or dislike of the Coloured policeman is

probably deflected from its real object, the white policeman (see Ch. IX, pp. 190–1).

24. 'It stands to the credit of the Coloured police, that they have earned from their superior officers the highest praise; that they have proved themselves honest, diligent and capable; that in spite of the poor wages they have not fallen victims to bribery and corruption, and that they have not injured the reputation of their community, when it is considered that these men earn less than African unskilled labourers . . . The State would remove a blot from its records, the sooner it introduces a civilised salary scale for their Coloured police.' (C.A.C. 1944–5, p. 44.) See S.A. Coloured Ex-Servicemen's Legion B.E.S.L. Report of Interview with Commissioner of Police at Pretoria, 8th April, 1947 (p. 1), for complaints about booklet entitled *Career for Non-European Members of the S.A. Police*, which held out a 'notch for notch' wage scale for ex-volunteers which had led the Legion to recommend ex-volunteers to enlist; the wage scale had not been adhered to, and the Commissioner admitted that its mention in the booklet was a mistake, and the Government would not allow it.

25. Despite recommendations in P. sections 33 and 53. The present policy is, however, to take Standard IV as a minimum.

26. Both the 1926 and 1937 Police Inquiry Commissions commented upon the absence of systematic training for Non-European constables, and recommended the institution of a simple course of instruction at each police divisional headquarters. They did not consider drill or physical training necessary in such cases, and did not press for the institution of a systematic training scheme, 'for financial and other reasons'. (s. 68.) The Public Service Inquiry Commission of 1946 did, however, recommend the latter for Africans; a training institution was set up at Umtata in the same year, with what are said to be 'encouraging results'. In 1946 a training depot for Coloured policemen was started in Wynberg, Cape, and later depots in Auckland Park, Johannesburg, and at other district headquarters.

27. The authorised establishment and actual strength (figures in brackets) on 31st December, 1949, were: constables 602 (475); Second Class Sergeants 55 (29); First Class Sergeants 16 (13). Even this small establishment was still considerably under strength, making a logical application of *apartheid* principles to the policing of Coloured areas impossible. Nor was the top non-commissioned rank of Head Constable open to Coloured men, despite the proposal of the Centlivres Report. (Part III, s. 57.) (Establishment figures from Annual Report of the Commissioner of the S.A. Police, 1949, p. 1.)

28. Comment by a Coloured teacher: 'Coloured people—like most people—don't like being arrested by anybody, white or black. In any case, Africans are *deliberately* used in Coloured ghettoes and Coloureds in African ghettoes, and there is always trouble.'

29. 'Quite recently a native policeman in Beaufort West treated a Coloured person very harshly, which incident ended in the court. It is requested that respectable Coloured men be recruited for the police force, and that they be given adequate training, and definitely more training than non-European policemen are receiving at present.' (C.A.C. 1944–5, p. 21.) See pp. 164–70 and 190–1 for middle-class Coloured attitudes towards Africans.

30. Cl/VI, s. 650–6.

31. The belief that Coloured people who can look to a white (usually an employer) for protection will receive better treatment at the hands of the police was encountered on several occasions. Cf. Myrdal, p. 551 for leniency shown in Southern courts to Negroes for whom whites appear as character witnesses.

32. See P.s. 274 *et seq.* The Report goes on to say that this attitude does not characterise the relations between the police and the Indian and Coloured communities (s. 305). This may have been true in 1937, but it is not the writer's impression of the present situation. The increasing tendency to consider all Non-Europeans as a single group would in any case militate against such a distinction.

33. Nevertheless, a curious incident occurred recently in Cape Town, which

suggests that officials at a fairly high level in the police force take a somewhat comprehensive view of this force's duties. The Rev. I. D. Morkel, a Coloured minister in Cape Town, in July 1949 claimed that hundreds of Coloured people were coming into the Cape Peninsula from the country districts as ' "refugees" from *apartheid* persecution and ill treatment.' *Die Burger* (Cape Nationalist daily) stated that his allegations amounted to a serious accusation against the administration of the law, an accusation which demanded the 'immediate attention of the highest police authority.' The same day two detectives visited Mr. Morkel's house, after the latter had received two telephone calls from the *Burger* asking whether the police had yet arrived. The same thing happened next day, when the police were actually in the house. The *Cape Times* asked editorially: 'How did the police come to be used to support a Nationalist newspaper's political argument? How did the *Burger* know that the police were going to call on Mr. Morkel? Would not such a visit, at that time and in the particular circumstances, necessarily amount to a form of pressure?' (quotation and account taken from *Cape Times*, 22nd August, 1949).

34. A Coloured teacher of radical views who read this chapter will not agree to this proposition. He comments: 'This is Institute of Race Relations bunk. The police force is undivided in its attitude to non-Whites, and no non-White expects anything but brutality from the police. In Britain the *Daily Worker* can carry an advert for police recruits. Depraved as it is, the *Guardian* (former S.A. Communist organ) dare not; nor even the *Sun* (pro. C.A.C.).'

35. Many Coloured people interviewed believed that the police tend to arrest Non-Europeans on flimsier evidence than they would Europeans. It is difficult to get precise evidence of such cases.

36. Except in Natal, where there is a Native High Court to try Africans, all courts try all races, and the cases are taken as they come, Coloured, Africans and Europeans mixed up on the same list. Non-European and European accused are kept in separate cells below the court while awaiting trial, but if charged jointly stand together in the dock. See *Hansard*, 26th April, 1950, cols. 5120 and 5123–4 for an extension of *apartheid* in the court-room.

37. This limitation is nowhere laid down, but the difficulties which face Coloured people in the civil service and legal profession make it impossible for them to reach the Bench. Most Europeans in South Africa find the idea of a non-white person in high office unacceptable, repugnant or ludicrous. Halford (p. 109) cites the instance of Sir Harry Escombe in the middle of the nineteenth century being fined £5 in Griqualand East for contempt of court because he had called the Griqua magistrate 'that ugly chimpanzee'.

38. One European legal expert of 'liberal' views commented on this passage: 'Few would doubt that the belief (in magisterial prejudice) is well-founded. The question is whether the superior courts are in reality less prone to bias.'

39. In one case personally attended by the writer and members of the accused's family, the latter afterwards commented with some surprise on the fairness and patience displayed by the magistrate.

40. 'The system which, with the rarest exceptions, limits the magisterial bench to persons whose only earlier acquaintance with criminal law and procedure was obtained through their tenancy of the office of Public Prosecutor, leads all too frequently to a bias on the Bench and consequently to a serious injustice to accused persons. In addition, the poor salaries which occupants of even the higher magisterial posts receive have naturally led to the appointment of persons of lesser qualifications for their important tasks than is essential. It has further led to the failure on the part of very many such officials to carry out their duties.' . . . 'After nearly thirty years of practice, I would be hard put to it to compile a list of a dozen magistrates who carried out their duties in a manner which was entirely unbiased.' (Extract from a Memorandum submitted to the Lansdown Commission by the Johannesburg Bar Council.)

41. South African magistrates have also a great volume of administrative work,

and in the country districts this is often their primary task. Such country magistrates, while not directly dependent on local political support as is the lower judiciary in the United States, are unlikely to be able to resist strong local feelings, by virtue of their very proximity. Such local feelings, if directed against the magistrate, may also result in a demand for his removal. One rather cynical young advocate said that this procedure could be reversed on occasion; if a magistrate wished to be transferred from some undesirable post he had only to give a few light sentences to Non-Europeans convicted of stock-theft, and local indignation would result in a rapid transfer.

42. It should be emphasised that in South Africa a magistrate is not a lawyer by qualifications or status. The required qualification is the civil service lower law examination, which does not demand any wider study of the sociological background of the rules of law.

43. *Race Relations Handbook*, p. 61.

44. In this context, the following incident has extra point: 'When a Coloured man appeared before Mr. L. Haneman at Caledon Square yesterday on a charge of assault with intent to do grievous bodily harm, the complainant and another witness said that they did not know the accused, and denied that he was responsible for the assault . . . the man was acquitted for lack of evidence.' (*Cape Times*, 24th March, 1949.)

45. See also Appendix M.

46. Most members of the Bench were appointed under earlier governments, but there have already been some Nationalist appointments, not all of which can be said to lack a 'political' tinge. This process will, of course, continue, and as the list of colour-bar legislation grows, the area of judicial impartiality will of necessity be limited.

47. L.s. 289.

48. 'An accused has a legal right to subpoena witnesses through official channels at State expense, if he can show that they are necessary to his defence, and that he is unable to pay the charges involved. Accused persons are not told of this right unless they ask for information. Many do not get to know about it and the majority have not the assurance to avail themselves of the right. In gaol, and cut off from his witnesses, he does not know whether he can depend on them. In court he may find that they are hostile, or afraid to take up a stand, as they see it, against the police.' (H. J. Simons, *Race Relations Handbook*, p. 70.)

49. 'If the magistrate refuses bail, or fixes it at too high a figure, the accused has the right of appeal to the Supreme Court. In practice, magistrates seldom grant bail unless the police consent, and they usually oppose in cases against a Non-European, on the assumption that any Non-European is likely to abscond, or because they hope to obtain disclosures from the accused by persistent questioning. In any event, the majority of Non-Europeans charged with an offence are ignorant of their right to ask for bail, or cannot find sureties for the amount fixed, and have neither the knowledge nor the means to appeal against a refusal by a magistrate.' (Dr. H. J. Simons, *ibid.*, p. 72.)

50. See the recommendations of the Lansdown Commission, p. 83 (5) and (6), and the Cape Coloured Commission, s. 111.

51. 'Where an accused person is undefended he frequently elects to make an unsworn statement from the dock instead of giving evidence. In that way he escapes cross-examination but is likely to find that what he says is disregarded, for it has been held that it does not amount to evidence to be weighed against the evidence of the Crown witnesses . . . Cases on review sometimes suggest that the importance of the election that accused is called upon to make has not been fully brought home to him; it might be a good thing if a statutory form were read over to the accused at the close of the Crown case in all trials where he has pleaded not guilty, in which the differences between unsworn statements and evidence would be briefly but clearly explained.' (Mr. Justice O. D. Schreiner, *Crime and the Community*, p. 7.)

52. Except in large urban centres, the prosecutor is often the police officer who has laid the charge, and, Dr. Simons says, 'his reputation as a prosecutor depends on the number of convictions he obtains.' (*Race Relations Handbook*, p. 71.)

53. L. s. 308.

54. *Crime and the Community*, p. 5, and C. sections 114–5.

55. See P.s. 239 and 290 for references to pressure put on arrested persons during questioning by detectives, and advice given to plead guilty and to escape with a lighter sentence.

56. L. s. 222.

57. L. s. 226.

58. For a further discussion of these, and an account of their inception and present constitution, see L. pp. 33–8.

59. The Institute is no longer wholly responsible for these Bureaux, which are controlled by committees on which are represented various government and provincial departments, municipal councils, the local Bar and Side Bar, Social Services Association, magistrates, the Institute itself, and so on.

60. 'The argument for an independent organisation rather than direct Government control is supported by the finding of a Royal Commission in England appointed in 1929 . . . one of the main reasons given being that the relationship between attorney and client would be destroyed if the applicant had to deal with a Government official. It is claimed that this argument is of considerable force in South Africa, for it is said that the Coloured and Native sections are sensitive to and suspicious of officialdom, and would not have the necessary confidence in Government legal aid officials . . . they would always suspect collusion between a State defender and the prosecutor.' (L. s. 259.) In 1950 the Cape Town Legal Aid Bureau handled cases for 163 Europeans, 712 Coloureds and 338 Africans.

61. Probably the number barely runs into double figures.

62. A jury is normally composed of nine men, of whom seven must agree on the verdict. Women may apply for inclusion on the jurors' roll, but are not automatically included. These rolls being based on voters' lists, it could in theory happen in the Cape that Coloured voters would be called for jury service. In practice, however, the sheriff who draws up the roll does not include their names. In the nineteenth century, Coloured jurors did at times serve on juries in remote country districts (Eric Walker (3) p. 142, quoting Lord de Villiers in 1879). For the position in the American South, cf. Myrdal, p. 149.

63. Act 31 of 1917, s. 216. As early as 1827 a Cape Commission of Inquiry found it necessary to recommend that 'for the present' Hottentots and Bastards should have the option of being tried by a Judge sitting without a Jury, in order that they might be afforded protection 'against the prejudiced and sometimes hostile feelings of those (Europeans) who may from circumstances form the Juries or constitute a large majority of them.' But 'the Commissioners' recommendations were disregarded. The Charters of Justice of 1827 and 1832 which introduced the Jury system into the Cape Colony made no distinction between its inhabitants on the ground of colour or race and directed that all serious criminal cases should be tried before one or more Judges and a Jury. Juries predominantly or entirely European were called upon to deal with cases in which one of the parties was European and the other Coloured or Bantu, with the result that serious miscarriages of justice occurred from time to time.' (Marais, p. 159.) Cf. also MacMillan, p. 191.

64. L. s. 358.

65. Dr. H. J. Simons (*op. cit.*) quotes a comment by the Hon. P. S. Twentyman-Jones (from the *Cape Argus*, 20th September, 1946). 'The person who does not exercise the choice accorded him by law is the guilty individual who hopes to avoid conviction either by complicating the issue and so confusing the inexperienced jurymen, or by appealing to that element of prejudice which unfortunately often comes into play and which is founded on race, creed, or colour.' Dr. Simons con-

tinues: 'Indeed, a European accused of an offence involving injury to a Non-European will invariably prefer a jury trial.' No detailed figures are available for 1948–50 to show the number of such trials, the verdicts passed in each case, or the races involved. See statement by Minister of Justice (*Hansard*, 7th February, 1951, col. 723–4).

66. No. 31 of 1917, s. 216 (1). See s. 216 (2) for the mode of selecting assessors, also objections by Mrs. Bertha Solomon, M.P. (*Hansard*, 26th April, 1950, col. 108).

67. But cf. Myrdal, p. 524.

68. See Schreiner, *Crime and the Community*, p. 3.

69. See Marais (p. 173) for the differentiation between slave and European evidence. No such official differentiation of course exists now, but its practical incidence is often sufficient to deter Coloured people from bringing cases against Europeans who have injured them. Cf. Myrdal, p. 550.

70. See *Crime and the Community*, p. 8, for an account of the harsh operation of the indeterminate sentence in relation to Non-European prisoners.

71. Under sections 359/360 of Act 31 of 1917.

72. *v.* Appendix M.

73.   TABLE A

(Persons charged with Murder, 1941–4, including convictions for Culpable Homicide or a less serious crime.)

Accused	Deceased	Prosecutions	Convictions	
			Number	Per cent of Prosecutions
European	European	40 (32)	16 (14)	40.0 (43.8)
African	European	99 (82)	50 (32)	50.5 (39.0)
Coloured	European	26 (12)	12 (3)	46.1 (25.0)
European	Non-European	37 (24)	5 (8)	13.5 (33.3)
African	Non-European	3,042 ⎱ (2,441)	952 ⎱ (652)	28.0 ⎱ (26.7)
Coloured	Non-European	248 ⎰	77 ⎰	31.0 ⎰

Taken from *Race Relations Handbook*, p. 99 (compiled from statistics provided by the Director of Census and Statistics). The figures in brackets are those for the two years 1949–50, during which period the discrepancies were not so high.

74. It will be noticed that the data supplied by the Census and Statistics Department were fully classified according to the race of the accused, but were only classified into the basic divisions of European and Non-European for the victim.

75. Cf. Myrdal, p. 526.

76. For the widespread European belief that Non-Europeans themselves hold their own lives more cheaply, see L.s. 460.

77. On 7th November, 1949, however, the Executive Council confirmed the death sentence on one Holzhausen, a miner who was convicted of the murder of an African girl employee, who was pregnant. Sentence was carried out the same day.

78. Dr. Simons cites further statistics to show that death sentences are somewhat more frequently commuted in the case of Europeans than of Non-Europeans, suggesting a racial bias on the part of the executive. (*Race Relations Handbook*, Table XVII, pp. 98–9.)

79. In 1949, out of forty-seven cases reported of European males raping Non-European females, twenty led to prosecutions, and there were only eleven convictions. Corresponding figures for Non-European males accused of raping European females were: fifty-four reported, forty-two prosecuted, thirty convicted,

80. See Appendix M for some comparative sentences. At a recent National Conference of the *Sustersbond* (a women's organisation) of the *Gereformeerde Kerk*, a demand was raised for public executions of Non-Europeans as a deterrent to crime (*Forum*, 20th April, 1951).

81.   TABLE B

(Showing the numbers and percentages of prisoners admitted to major gaols with and without option of a fine, between 1st January, 1945, and 30th June, 1946.)

Males					
Europeans		Coloureds and Indians		Africans	
With Option	Without	With Option	Without	With Option	Without
2,564	1,416	15,511	2,290	77,252	16,162
64.44%	35.56%	87.14%	12.88%	82.69%	17.31%

Total: 115,195

The corresponding figures for females were:
Europeans, 252 (77.78%) and 72 (22.22%).
Coloureds and Indians, 2,758 (87.83%) and 382 (12.17%).
Africans, 13,829 (90.63%) and 1,429 (9.37%).

Total: 18,722.

Taken from L. p. 79. No later figures could be obtained from the department concerned.

82. It is commonly held by Europeans that Non-Europeans do not regard imprisonment as a stigma in the way that the European does. In the case of most Africans, this may have an element of truth, in that the enormous mass of petty statutory offences make it difficult for the most law-abiding to avoid such contact with the law at some time in his life. 'The criminal sanction has been so widely applied to what are, to the Native, trivial misdemeanous that conviction and imprisonment carry no social stigma.' (Dr. Ellen Hellmann, *Rooiyard*, p. 76.) The Coloured community has, however, no separate legal institutions, and has not until recently been harassed by many discriminatory statutes. There are large numbers of respectable, law-abiding Coloured people to whom imprisonment comes as a definite social stigma, and who deplore the lawlessness of the lower sections of their own people as tending to give the whole community a bad name with other ethnic groups. As statutory discrimination increases, one can, however, detect evidences of growing disregard for the law, as being increasingly alien to the interests of any group but the dominant one.

83. A Coloured informant who is usually fairly reliable told the writer of an incident which occurred in 1948. Her husband was arrested for drunkenness, and taken to Cape Town's Roeland Street Gaol. Next day he was sentenced to a fortnight's imprisonment or a fine. He was given no facilities for getting in touch with his family, and his wife was for three days unable to get any information as to his whereabouts, although she went to the gaol every day. She finally managed to see the Superintendent and pay the fine. In the meantime her husband had, she claimed, been compelled to work three days of his sentence on a farm at Strandfontein. When instructions were given for his release, he was allowed to go, but no transport was provided, so that he had to walk from Strandfontein to Lansdown (about eight miles) at the end of a working day.

84. 1948 figure: 'Whether the object of imprisonment is punitive or reformative, it is obvious that nothing much can be done in less than six months. Even if we take

three months as the limit, it is obvious that in over 80 per cent of the cases the sentences can serve no useful purpose either to the State or the prisoner, but on the contrary merely remove from petty offenders any fear of gaol that they may previously have had and often enable them to get a first-class knowledge of criminal conduct of which they might otherwise have remained ignorant.' (Hoal Report on the Elliott Committee investigation in 1942 into crime on the Witwatersrand and in Pretoria, quoted in C.s. 109.)

85. A recent examination of the records of hundreds of long-term prisoners showed that the vast majority were recidivists with a number of previous convictions who 'almost invariably had started their criminal careers with a petty offence . . . leading to a sentence of a small fine with the alternative of a short term of imprisonment . . . There is high probability that, had the case been otherwise dealt with at the commencement of the series, recidivism and ultimately serious crime might have been prevented.' (L.s. 535.) Of 174,595 admissions (all races) to prison in 1948, 107,214 (or 61.4 per cent) were for periods of one month or less. (1948 Report of the Director of Prisons.)

86. A South African argument for the retention of corporal punishment is cited in L. s. 484.

87. A prominent Western Cape wine farmer told me that he adopted this method; his labourers preferred it to a court case and dismissal, although many of them knew they could have him charged under the Masters' and Servants' Act. Other viewpoints were assembled by the *Cape Argus* (22nd July, 1949): A magistrate: 'Lashes . . . solitary confinement and spare diet are the things the non-European criminal fears most. The *skollie* with a knife is a coward at heart and cannot take physical punishment, while a prison sentence has no stigma for him and is no deterrent. Often he is better fed and clothed in gaol than out of it.' (The latter observation is often made by South Africans. It is intended as an attack on the prison system for 'pampering' non-European prisoners, but its makers usually fail to realise that it is still more an attack on the social and economic conditions which make prison seem preferable to some.) A Cape lawyer: 'In my opinion talk of the so-called deterrent sentence, at any rate as far as the Coloured criminal is concerned, is sheer nonsense. Nothing deters the Coloured criminal for the simple reason that he commits his crime in the fond hope that he is not going to be caught . . . Our problem should not be imposing the punishment to fit the crime, but imposing the punishment to fit the criminal. Rehabilitation, however disheartening, should be the constant aim.' For the firm measures used by the early colonial authorities against slave-owners who so took the law into their own hands, see V. de Kock, pp. 52–7. For the 'Black Circuit' of the early nineteenth century, see Marais, p. 121.

88. L.s. 495. The Commission did, however, recommend the abolition of the cat (still in use in 1948), and laid down limitations as to whipping (s. 496, 498).

89. L.s. 496. In early December, 1950, the Union and Belgium abstained when the U.N. General Assembly voted to abolish corporal punishment in all Trust territories. (*Rand Daily Mail*, 4th December, 1950.)

90. In 1949, 67 Europeans, 705 Coloureds and 4,911 Africans were convicted of stocktheft. 168, 866 and 6,619 respectively were prosecuted. (1949 Report of Commissioner of S.A. Police.)

91. L.s. 497.

92. Taken from Dr. H. J. Simons, *Race Relations Handbook*, p. 98, Table XVI (based on the Annual Reports of the Director of Prisons). 1948 figures added from 1948 Annual Report.

93. The Lansdown Report comments on the zeal of some magistrates in exercising their powers to order whippings under Section 92(3) of Act 32 of 1944. 'Emotional reactions to human wickedness should be absent from the minds of those charged with the serious and solemn duty of sitting in judgment upon their fellow men,

and the only consideration in passing sentence should be whether the form of penalty selected is likely to be deterrent and corrective.' (s. 494.)

94. Under the Magistrate's Court Act No. 32 of 1944, s. 92.

95. The argument that spare diet would have a deterrent effect on Africans or more impoverished Coloureds and Europeans, 'to whom, generally, the urge for food is a strong mental and physical factor,' was considered by the Commission to be outweighed by 'the undesirability of the State, whose function in respect of its prisoners is to rehabilitate them in mind and keep or make them fit in body, adopting measures which must militate against the latter of these two purposes and will, in all probability, impede the former.' (L. s. 510–11.)

96. See L. s. 406.

97. L. s. 503.

98. Industrial schools and reformatories are administered by the Department of Education, places of safety by the Department of Social Welfare.

99. An instance of this indifference—figures for the sentences imposed on children of sixteen years or under are available only for Europeans. (L. s. 389.) Nor are police attitudes even to innocent juveniles always what they should be, to judge by the following complaint. 'The practice of members of the C.I.D. of fetching juveniles from school and transporting them to the charge office in open vehicles (usually motor bicycles) is to be deprecated. Cases are known where even witnesses are so fetched. This leads to a slur being cast on the individual about to tender information and also on the institution where he receives his education. Juveniles could as easily be contacted at their homes.' (C.A.C. 45/6, p. 17.)

100. And also, in the view of members of the C.A.C., on the absence of legal representation: 'No juvenile should be brought to trial unrepresented by an attorney or other legal agent. This is especially important when the complainant is a European. The acute feeling prevailing between European and Coloured tends to make such a complainant unremitting in his quest for retribution when he believes that he has suffered by an act alleged to have been committed against him by a Coloured youth. Thorough cross-examination by a legal representative of both the complainant and the accused in such cases is absolutely essential to offset this tendency.' (C.A.C. 45/6, p. 18.)

101. L. s. 172—See ibid., Ch. III and Appendices F. and G, also 1945 Report of the Department of Social Welfare, showing how inadequate accommodation of all types was then for children of all races, particularly for Coloureds and Africans. In that year 10,802 of the 77,604 persons of all races under 21 (i.e., juveniles and juvenile adults), convicted in the courts, were in prisons, not hospitals or reformatories. In 1950, 8,572 Europeans, 82,308 Africans, 18,560 Coloureds and 2,458 Asiatics under 21 (i.e., in the categories of juveniles (16 years and under) and juvenile adults (17–20 years)) were convicted in the courts. Of these, the following numbers were in prison: 474 Europeans; 10,180 Africans; 2,657 Coloureds; and 47 Asiatics.

102. 1947 Report of Department of Social Welfare, pp. 19 and 21. In June, 1949, the following accommodation was available for children in need of care: (1) State places of safety: Europeans—202; Non-Europeans—250; (2) certified institutions: Europeans—6,590; Coloureds—2,781; Asiatics—62; Africans—710; (3) uncertified institutions: Europeans—3,071; Coloureds—384; Asiatics—335; Africans—124; mixed Non-European—270; (4) certified hostels: Europeans—613; Coloureds and Asiatics—60; Asiatics—20; Africans—300; mixed Non-European—48; (5) industrial schools: Europeans—1,984; Coloureds only—76. Several state institutions for children have recently been established (see Ch. IV, n. 107). For the situation in 1945 see L. Ch. III and Appendices F. and G.

103. L. s. 171. In June, 1949, the following reformatory accommodation was occupied and available:

	Accommodation available		Enrolment	
	M.	F.	M.	F.
European				
Constantia	180	—	214	—
Durbanville	—	48	—	38
Non-European				
Diepkloof				
African	530	—	590	—
Eshowe				
(i) African ⎱		110	—	(i) 51
(ii) Coloured ⎰				(ii) 40
Porter				
(i) Asiatic ⎱	700	—	(i) 25	
(ii) Coloured ⎰			(ii) 665	

104. L. s. 164–5.
105. As racial discrimination grows, there is an increasing tendency for inflammatory and unsubstantiated rumours to spread and gain credence in the Coloured community. An instance of this was the story repeated to me by a Coloured minister and a school teacher about a Coloured boy from the Eastern Cape who had his feet slit in order to prevent him running away from a reformatory after he had made one attempt.
106. At Eshowe in Zululand (L. s. 131.) A reformatory with accommodation for thirty Coloured girls was opened at Simonstown in the Cape Peninsula on 27th May, 1950.
107. C.A.C. 1944–5, p. 14. See also Annual Reports of Ministry of Social Welfare for 1945 and 1947. Thirty-one Coloured children were apprenticed under this system between 1st November, 1949 and 30th October, 1950. Four such institutions have now been established, with accommodation for 275 Coloured and 100 African children.
108. Part IV, pp. 90 et seq.
109. See L., Appendix R. The overcrowding is not so marked in accommodation for women prisoners, where it exists at all. In the men's sections it is mainly due to the presence of large numbers of short-term prisoners, many of whom would never have been serving a sentence but for economic reasons, as we have seen earlier. 112,116 persons of all races served prison sentences in 1945–6 because they could not pay fines. Such overcrowding makes the effective segregation of short-term prisoners from serious offenders the more difficult. During and after the war, the position deteriorated; in the period 1939–46, while the average daily prison population increased by some 7,000, additional accommodation was provided for only some 700 persons; further accommodation for 1,800 was provided between 1946 and mid-1951, but the average daily prison population rose from 22,850.2 to 28,266.4 persons of all races and both sexes. A small percentage of non-European male prisoners would presumably be serving as convict labour outside the main penal institutions.
110. The extent to which attitudes have changed is illustrated by the sentence passed in 1728 on a European woman convicted of aiding and abetting in the theft of wreckage; she was to be placed in the slave lodge, and to labour at the public works with the female slaves. (V. de Kock, p. 37.)
111. Act No. 13 of 1911, s. 19 (1) reads: 'In any convict prison or gaol (b) as far as possible white and coloured convicts and prisoners shall be confined in separate parts thereof, and in such a manner as to prevent white convicts or prisoners from being in view of coloured convicts or prisoners . . .' Superior status is to be

Q

preserved even behind the bars, and the sight of white fellow-prisoners might break down the myth of the superior white man.

112. The Lansdown Report recognises this distinction in its proposals for classification of prisoners, by laying down that whereas Europeans *must* be located apart from Coloured persons and Africans, Coloured persons *should* be kept apart from Africans, wherever their number justifies this course. (s. 767.)

113. The early colonial authorities apparently held that criminals, of whatever race, forfeited any superior status. In 1712 convicts on Robben Island were issued with the same rations as the slaves. (V. de Kock, p. 40.) The Cape was for a long time a convict station and Europeans were sent there too. In 1794 it was suggested that European exiles should at least be separated from Hottentots and slaves. (*ibid.*, p. 192.)

114. C.A.C. 44/5, p. 34.

115. According to information kindly supplied by the Director of Prisons, African, Coloured and Asiatic males are issued with the following clothing: A moleskin cap, a white duck jumper, a red flannel shirt, a red-and-white striped worsted jersey, moleskin breeches, boots or veldskoens, and socks or stockings to Coloureds and Asiatics, sandals to Africans who are accustomed to wear boots, or as ordered by the Medical Officer, hats to Coloureds and Asiatics, but only to Africans on the Medical Officer's order, and crash towels.

Non-European female prisoners are issued with: A grey flannelette skirt, brown wincey blouse, red-and-white striped worsted jersey, brown wincey skirt, handkerchief, apron, red cotton doek (head-scarf), comb, towel, safety pins and veldskoens, stockings and garters to Coloureds and Asiatics, but to Africans on special order only.

The same garb is issued to all types of prisoners, including those serving short terms. Despite the provision for the issue of footwear to Coloured male prisoners, I have myself seen some barefoot Coloured prisoners in the Cape Peninsula (whether this was their own choice could not be ascertained), and a complaint was made on this score in a C.A.C. report (1945–6, p. 18).

116. The average floor space available to each prisoner is 6ft. by 3 ft. (L. s. 615.)

117. L. s. 632.

118. L. s. 620 and 622; C. s. 593.

119. L. s. 626.

120. See recommendations (as yet unimplemented) in L. s. 628 and 633.

121. A high-ranking European civil servant formerly connected with the prison service said that the Coloured diet was not adequate for a middle-class Coloured person. Coloured prisoners are frequently given a choice between their own and the African diet scale. Those from country districts, whose normal diet usually approximates to that of the African, tend to choose the latter scale which gives a bulkier diet. In so doing they may be classified as Africans for other prison purposes. This practice gives rise to the frequent complaints that Coloured people are being treated as Africans, put under African warders and so on. See L. Appendix S for the various diets. New and approved diets are to be introduced in 1952.

122. These short-term scales were made deliberately unattractive in conformity with strictly deterrent ideas of dealing with short-term offenders. Their abolition was a temporary measure, pending a report by expert dieticians. The long-term diets were also improved by the addition of a greater sugar allowance. Those for Non-Europeans are said to be deficient in first-class protein, calcium, fats and certain vitamins. (L. s. 650.) The projected new diet-scales have not so far been introduced for financial reasons. To bring the fat allowance up to the amount suggested would apparently have made serious inroads on the Union's total fats supply.

123. 'Mr. C. G. Volschenk (acting gaoler at the time) told the *Paarl Post* representative that in his opinion many of the Coloured prisoners lived in comparative "luxury". Quite a few of them normally stayed in holes along the banks of the Berg River and slept under bags, and they had to scratch around for whatever food they could find. Where had they ever enjoyed such comforts as regular and plenty

of food every day, sleeping under three blankets in the winter, and in a shelter which admitted no blasting wind or gushes of rain water? One might almost say that they are doing well for themselves in the Paarl Gaol.'' (*Paarl Post*, 29th August, 1947, feature article on Paarl's Hof Street Gaol, built in 1942.)

124. I was also told by a European prison official that some pregnant Coloured and African women get themselves arrested on a minor charge just before their confinement is due, simply to have it in the prison hospital, which provides better conditions than they would otherwise get. After the baby is born, they pay their fines and walk out. The baby is not penalised as the birth-certificate does not explicitly mention the place of birth as prison. See similar statement by Minister of Justice (*Hansard*, 26th April, 1950, col. 5157).

125. A study of L. Appendix S will suggest that if the meagre diets there provided for the Non-European are an improvement on their normal diets as free men, the stress should fall rather on augmenting the latter than decreasing the former.

126. 'The idea still to some extent persists that the only purpose of prison is punishment, and many unconstructive forms of labour are still performed in prisons and gaols.' (L. s. 820. *v*. also s. 824.)

127. The Lansdown Commission urged the necessity not only of making up deficiencies in general and vocational education, but also of transforming anti-social into socially-cooperative persons. (L. s. 821.) The attitudes of lower-grade prison-officers are, however, not always such as to inspire social co-operativeness in their charges.

128. 12,000 volumes (L. s. 829).

129. L. s. 831.

130. L. s. 835.

131. The Commission recommended (s. 843) that some Coloureds and Africans should be trained in modern methods of agriculture on prison farms.

132. L. s. 875.

133. Economic differentiation was maintained by the Lansdown Commission in recommending an increase to 25s. for Europeans, 15s. for Non-Europeans, and an extension of the ex-gratia payment to prisoners eligible for the earned gratuity, but with a limit on the total discharge payment of £5 for a European and £3 for a Non-European. (L. pp. 128–9.) It is usually claimed that a European has more difficulty in finding work after serving a prison sentence, so perhaps this larger limit might be considered necessary in order to tide him over the intervening period. On the other hand, the Coloured has usually a larger family to support, and fewer financial resources.

134. *v*. L. s. 882 (c). The sight of white prisoners doing 'Kaffir work' would probably outrage European susceptibilities; worse still, it might undermine white prestige in the eyes of Non-Europeans. There is a further discriminatory aspect to this provision, in that, intentionally or not, it serves to create or maintain a stereotype of Non-European criminality. (See MacCrone, pp. 261–2 and C.A.C. Report, 1945–6, p. 18.)

135. A total of about 4,000 prisoners per day to all types of work (L. s. 883.) See also L. s. 897–9 and 907 for an account of the special arrangement formerly prevailing in the Western Cape with six Constantia farmers, who supplied food and accommodation and had members of their families or European overseers sworn in as special warders to relieve the single regular warder in charge of each party.

136. L. s. 913.

137. The *Cape Times* of 3rd September, 1949, gave details of a private company, the Leslie Farmers' Association Labour Supply Company, which had just built a gaol which was opened personally by the Minister of Justice, Mr. Swart. The Company had fifty shareholders, who bought their shares at £40 each, and hired convict labour in proportion to their shares. This was the fifth gaol of this type in the Bethal district. At the opening ceremony Mr. Swart announced his intention of continuing the policy of providing convict labour for the farmers.

138. L. s. 1,105(c). See also *Penal Reform League of S.A.*, Newsletter No. 11, October, 1949, and *Race Relations Survey*, 1949–50, p. 45.

139. Prison Regulations 400–408.

140. This is extended to Christmas privileges. On Christmas Day, 1950, Europeans each received a pound of fruit cake, Coloureds one pint of coffee with sugar. (*Cape Times*, 15th December, 1950.)

141. Prison Regulations 400–408.

142. The Lansdown Commission recommended the extension of this privilege: '. . . to all male prisoners of all races serving sentences of six months and upwards. In the case of male non-smokers and women it is recommended that these be granted an issue of sugar, sweets or jam.' (s. 936.)

143. L. s. 941.

144. A high-ranking civil servant connected with the Prison Service said that there would be 'hell to pay in Parliament' if one asked for 'luxuries' for Non-Europeans.

145. L. s. 968–71. See modifications suggested by the Commission. (s. 999.)

146. In addition to the penal staff, reformatory work and after-care are entrusted to Social Welfare Officers under the Social Welfare Department. The approved establishment in April 1947 was 203, little enough for the enormous prison population. Only 150 posts had been filled, while not one of the eight lowest grade Temporary Coloured S.W.O. posts had been filled (L. Appendix W). For the position in 1948 and 1949 see Report of the Departmental Inquiry into the Training and Employment of Social Workers. (U.G. 13/1950.)

147. The Lansdown Commission found it necessary to remind prison officers that 'the prisoner has not been sent to prison for punishment; but that his punishment consists of his having suffered the obloquy of conviction and in the deprivation of his liberty'. (s. 640.) It also found that the overcrowding, understaffing and existence of no less than fifty-five regulations and thirty specific offences 'have resulted in almost completely nullifying the policy of assistance to and reformation of prisoners contemplated by the Act.' (s. 639.) On the question of mishandling of prisoners, one high prison official wrote to me: 'There are very few assaults on prisoners . . . All prisoners are at liberty to complain to the Superintendent daily if so mishandled and you can believe me they are not backward in coming forward. Their complaints are then properly investigated and 90 per cent are found to be frivolous.' Another wrote that it was very difficult to obtain reliable evidence, and it was all tainted. He added that in all cases of congregations of people, such as the army, navy or boarding schools, complaints are fewer than they should be for fear of later victimisation.

148. 'On the point of the treatment of prisoners, I spoke to a young European prisoner in the prison's antiquated workshop. He seemed a typical army type and I asked the superintendent and others to move out of hearing while I spoke to him. I asked: "Do they kick you about here?" Answer: "No. They are all right." "What about the Coloured prisoners? Do they kick them about?" Answer: "Yes. I mean they shout at them. That's all. But they do shout at them all right." ' (*Sunday Express*, 15th June, 1947. Feature by Terence Clarkson on Roeland Street Gaol.)

149. *v.* L. s. 641.

150. The Lansdown Report recognised the ill-will thus featured in its recommendation that: 'Whenever the number of Asiatic, Coloured or Native prisoners justifies the expenditure, Non-European warders of these classes should be engaged, and that whenever practicable, Asiatic and Coloured prisoners should not be members of gangs placed under Native warders.' (s. 728.)

151. An indication of the extent to which attitudes have changed is provided in a passage written by Mr. J. de Villiers Roos in the *Union Year Book* for 1910–16. Although the practices referred to had clearly occasioned sufficient European protest to make their discontinuation necessary, they had nevertheless existed in the Cape before Union: 'The detention of Europeans and Natives in the same wards

is now forbidden. The guarding of European prisoners by Coloured warders has now been discontinued . . .'

152. The Lansdown Report recommended that such a qualification be introduced, up to the level of Standard VI for Coloured warders and Standard IV for Africans, followed by the introduction of higher posts and a rise in salary-scales (s. 729).

153. For actual and proposed pay-scales see Cl. IV, Annexure F.

154. See *Torch* editorial of 29th May, 1950. Cf. Myrdal, p. 525 for a similar development in the Southern States.

155. 'The Union of South Africa has more discriminatory racial laws and customs than any other country in the British Commonwealth; or, for that matter, in the civilized world. The fact that some of these laws or customs may be considered necessary in the interests of the natives themselves makes it all the more imperative that the administration of justice should be based on full recognition of the absolute equality of human rights . . . May I conclude with an extract from a latter written to me by Professor Hoernlé : ". . . The Rhodesian judge who said that 'a judge could not go too far in advance of public opinion'—white public opinion, for native opinion does not matter for white justice—merely expressed what the Nazis, under the name Rassenrecht, have elevated to the dignity of a legal principle. Incidentally the Russians, too, use the Courts to maintain both the orthodoxy of doctrine and the social order set up by the Communist revolution, while we use, or tend to use, the courts in order to maintain what I call our 'racial caste society'." ' (From 'In South Africa To-day', by Charles Don, published in *The National Review*, February, 1947.

156. This point was made by the dissenting judge, Mr. A. J. A. Gardiner, in the case of Minister of Posts and Telegraphs *v.* Rasool (A.D. 1934, pp. 167–92.) Cf. also the following passage: '. . . The liberals, lawyers and other rose-water addicts who wax poetical about the "rule of law", might be interested to know that in District Six for years past we have been accustomed to refer to police thugs as "*Die Law*". With their truncheons, size nine revolvers and pick-up cars, they have represented the blindfolded goddess of Justice for many years now. With the state of legislation in this country, they have been worthy ambassadors.' (*Torch*, 26th June, 1950.)

CHAPTER V—ECONOMIC LIFE

1. Dr. John Philip, quoted by MacMillan, p. 178.

2. Unlike the white English convicts sold into bondage in the New World colonies, there appear to have been no European slaves or bondmen in the Cape Colony, although there were some exiled white convicts.

3. See *Cape Times* report (18th December, 1950) of All-African Convention, and Mr. I. B. Tabatha's discussion of 'White Citizens and Black Serfs'.

4. Lord Olivier (p. 9) quotes the Dutch East India Company's representative, van Imhoff, as commenting in 1716: 'Having imported slaves . . . every common or ordinary European becomes a gentleman, and prefers to be served rather than to serve. We have in addition the fact that the majority of the farmers are not farmers in the real sense of the word, but plantation owners, and many of them consider it a shame to work with their own hands.' It is worthy of note that the 1820 settlement was based on a white labour economy, slave-owning being forbidden to the settlers by the British Government. (Edwards, p. 67.)

5. See Marais, p. 129.

6. See MacMillan, p. 169.

7. MacMillan, p. 178, mentions shops set up at Bethelsdorp and Theopolis in 1821.

8. MacMillan, pp. 284–6.

9. At this time the immigration was not so much into the Western Cape and Peninsula as into the Eastern and North-Eastern areas, e.g., increases between 1921–36:—East London—18,583; Albany, 6,532; Alexandria, 5,769; Glen Grey,

20,537; Kimberley, 5,501; Kuruman, 7,413; Mafeking, 9,518; Port Elizabeth, 20,855; Queenstown, 6,027. In the late thirties, however, and still more during and after the war, Africans began to pour into the Western Cape and Peninsula. In Paarl their number rose from 474 in 1936 to 2,628 in 1946, and in Worcester from 375 to 2,881. In Cape Town itself, there were 14,160 Africans in 1936, 34,408 in 1946, and 50,000 in 1950.

10. The solicitude shown to 'Poor Whites' by the South African authorities during the nineteen-twenties and early thirties may seem excessive to an outsider when it is considered in relation to the far more widespread and continued poverty of millions of 'Poor Blacks'. The Poor Whites, however, whatever else they lacked, had votes, and, more important still, their plight constituted an ultimate threat to the privileged status which the European community had assigned to itself since the beginning. This status is described in the findings of the Carnegie Poor White Commission: 'The term "Poor White" itself implies that traditionally the European nhabitants have a higher standard of living. The criterion of a "European standard of living" depends on the views commonly accepted in the white community. An increase of the average welfare of the Europeans (especially if accompanied by an improvement of the standard of living among a part of the non-European races) is sufficient to make the position of the less prosperous Europeans appear relatively unfavourable.' (Ca/Joint Findings, par. 61.)

11. 'Bricklaying, plastering, painting and decorating, engine-cleaning (the first step towards employment as a locomotive driver) and such other trade work now done by Europeans were considered fit for Coloured men and overseas workers, but not for the colonial born, who, if not belonging to the professional classes, perhaps not unnaturally preferred a more adventurous career such as transport-riding.' (Ca/III, p. 54.)

12. The Carnegie Poor White Report estimated the number of Poor Whites just before the 1930–1 depression at between 220,000 and 300,000 (Ca/III, p. vii). The Industrial and Agricultural Requirements Commission of 1941 held that 400,000 Europeans were poorly educated, underfed and badly housed (not all would necessarily be regarded as 'Poor Whites').

13. As we have seen earlier, the Hottentots, due to their dispersal, restrictions on mobility, and their imperfect knowledge of the market, had hardly been in a position to influence the level of their remuneration. An example of this tendency of some white South Africans to invert cause and effect is found in the Carnegie Report's Joint Findings, par. 62. For the 1938 ratio of skilled to unskilled wages in the Union and elsewhere see Social and Economic Planning Council, Report No. 13, p. 30.

14. '. . . this attitude even in the Poor White is purely a habit and not inborn, as is evidenced by the fact that the white man to-day, when circumstances demand it, will do any kind of work and is not adverse to, or incapable of, doing manual work if the stimulus is specific enough.' (Ca/III, p. 22.)

15. 'Often, however, the term is not applied to manual work as such, but rather manual work done for a master and for a wage . . . Sometimes Europeans apply the expression 'Kaffir work' to their labour if the wages paid them are more or less the same as those which natives would receive, or if the wages are lower than those they consider due to a European.' (Ca/II, p. 56.)

16. 'Should . . . the poor white be beaten in the competition for work he is far from taking this as proof that the native has become his superior, or even his equal. On the contrary, he views the outcome as a further injustice which the European government of the country should not permit.' (Ca/II, p. 57.)

17. 'The great majority of poor whites are still imbued with the conviction of their superiority over the Non-Europeans. This feeling has played an important part in preventing miscegenation between the poor white and the Non-European, especially the native . . . It does occur between the Coloured (rather than the native) people and a small minority of poor whites, namely, those who are also in other respects of an inferior type. Long-continued economic equality of poor whites

and the great mass of Non-Europeans, and propinquity of their dwellings, tend to bring them to social equality. This impairs the tradition which counteracts miscegenation, and the social line of colour division is noticeably weakening.' (Ca. Findings, paras. 66–7.) It is of course a myth that only 'poor whites' cohabit with non-whites, but one which serves to bolster up ideas of 'white purity'. Such myths are more fully discussed on pp. 176–8.

18. Ca/III, pp. 62–3, and Findings, paras. 65–7. The particular horror felt by whites for this process, and the demand for official action to counteract it, reflect the need to maintain the physical and psychological integrity of the white group, in order to uphold its superior status and privileges. See also Brookes, p. 29.

19. The East and North Cape Province provided an unduly large proportion of Poor Whites, possibly because the process of rural impoverishment had been going on rather longer there than in the more recently settled Northern Provinces.

20. Cf. Brookes p. 6 and MacMillan p. 24.

21. This officially came into existence after a circular issued from the Prime Minister's Office on 31st October, 1924. Civilised labour was defined as 'the labour rendered by persons whose standard of living conforms to the standard generally recognised as tolerable from the usual European standpoint. Uncivilised labour is to be regarded as the labour rendered by persons whose aim is restricted to the bare requirements of the necessities of life as understood among barbarous and undeveloped peoples.' It was laid down as a matter of definite policy that civilised labour should, wherever practicable, be substituted in all public employment for uncivilised. The Government hoped by this policy to set an example to private employers. Further measures taken by the Government to induce private industry to follow its example will be described later in this Chapter.

22. 'It is clear from the wording of the . . . circular that the distinction aimed at is not determined by the nature of the work but the class of person who performs it. In a memorandum submitted to the Commission the Labour Department stated that the term 'civilised labour' was interpreted as including Coloured persons; that the distinctions between the classes of labour referred to in the circular depended solely on the standard of living defined. In order to emphasise this point, it was stated that it had been held by the Department that Natives could be included as civilised . . .' (C. s. 165–6.)

23. Evidence given at Port Elizabeth showed that the policy was there interpreted on the barest minimum living wage, though this was not laid down anywhere; on this basis most of the Coloured people in the town would, it was said, be classed as uncivilised. The Town Council at Port Elizabeth submitted that the term was understood to apply to the employment of white labour. The Trades and Labour Council of Johannesburg stated that the phrase was interpreted to mean the employment of White Labour by the displacement of Natives and Coloured, especially Natives. (C. s. 171–7.) The Cape Coloured Commission minority report called on the Government to issue instructions 'explaining explicitly that the term "civilised" labour has no reference to any particular race or colour.'

24. Dr. A. Abdurahman of the A.P.O. saw this very clearly, and opposed the Colour Bar Act. In April 1926, an A.P.O. delegation called on Mr. C. W. Malan, Minister of Railways, to protest against the displacing of one section of the community in order to find work for another (the civilised labour policy). The delegation pointed out that Coloured men taken on at the Cape Town docks were receiving the same pay as the Africans whom they had displaced, although the organisation had understood that these Coloured men would be paid a wage which would enable them to live a civilised life. In reply, Mr. Malan asked when and where he had ever said that Coloured and white would be treated alike on the railways. There was a difference of civilisation between the two, and therefore they could not expect him to pay the same wages to the Coloured as to the white man. (*Cape Times*, 16th April, 1926.)

25. A future danger of the policy of providing sheltered work for poor whites

was foreseen by the Carnegie Commissioners: 'It is insufficient if the state merely provides the European with employment without at the same time taking measures to ensure that those who are assisted in this way are spurred on to greater personal efforts and to improving their efficiency . . . A policy of protection by reservation of work for the European should be treated as merely a measure of transition for a period during which the poor white is given the opportunity to adapt himself to new conditions in South Africa. It will be disastrous for the poor white himself if any protection given him is of such a nature that it results finally in impairing his ability to compete with the non-European on the lavour market.' Such 'sheltering', was an expensive affair; the replacement of 1,361 'uncivilised labourers' had cost £73,508 by 31st March, 1926 (Cl/V, p. 49).

26. The Public Service Act contains no formal colour bar.

27. *Race Relations Handbook*, p. 122. On 31st March, 1948, there were 87,174 Europeans regularly employed by the railways, 18,816 salaried, the remainder not, and 46,420 Non-Europeans. In addition, there were 10,891 Europeans and 43,220 Non-Europeans employed on casual labour.

28. C. s. 216–8.

29. According to a memorandum submitted by the S.A.R. Administration in 1937 (*v.* C. Appendix 12, p. 272). There were 192 Coloured 'graded' employees left from pre-Union days in April 1935, according to the same source. In 1947 there were only forty-one such employees (*Hansard*, 24th March, 1950, 3,617.)

30. The position in the 1930s was described in the same memorandum: 'It is an invariable rule that Europeans must not be called upon to work in mixed gangs, and, as far as is practicable, Coloured labourers are not mixed with Natives. This race-consciousness is still more sharply pronounced amongst the graded staff: Europeans resent taking instructions from, or working in harness with, Coloured staff . . . Neither by status nor regulation is the appointment of a person of mixed blood to a graded post prohibited; the fact that the Service as a whole is organised on the basis of a European graded staff originates primarily from the existing social order . . . the policy of the Department is to regard the various grades . . . as open only to Europeans . . . Any modification of the existing policy can be achieved only at the expense of the European section.' (C. p. 273.)

31. Cf. C. Appendix 12 for 1937 wage-scales, and *Race Relations Handbook* for 1943 figures. Even then, despite the rise in the cost of living due to the war, 72 per cent of the 8,138 Coloured unskilled labourers were receiving between 25s. and 36s. per week, while 73 per cent of the 15,301 unskilled European labourers were receiving from 49s. to 54s. per week. In the 1930s a Minister of Railways said in the House, in reply to a request for better wages for Non-European workers: 'The principle is perfectly simple. It is not the function of the Railway Department to assist in raising the general standard of wages—we are not concerned with it—we pay no better nor worse wages than are paid by most other employers.' (Quoted by Bishop S. W. Lavis: *Christianity in Industry*, Cape Town, 1949, p. 5.) It proved impossible to get more up-to-date figures of wages and numbers employed from the S.A.R. Administration.

32. In July 1946, no Non-Europeans were employed in the administrative, clerical, professional or technical divisions—249 Coloureds were employed in the general division, of whom all but twenty were employed in the Post Offlce. In the S.A. Police there were 334 Coloureds, and 21 Coloureds in the Prisons Department. (Cl. V., p. 42.) See also *Year Book* No. 24, pp. 81–2 for 1947–8 figures, and *Hansard*, 13th April, 1941, col. 4424 for the considerable shortage of European civil servants.

33. Cl/V, p. 297. The recommendation requested that 'departments of state explore the possibilities of an increased employment of Coloured persons, also in graded positions, particularly in branches of work serving the Coloured people.'

34. Including the S.W. Africa Administration. In this territory, 'the loss of S.W. Africa by the German Empire robbed hundreds of Coloured men of permanent employment. Before the war large numbers of Coloured men and even women were

used in development work there, but since the taking over of the mandate by the Union Government that avenue of employment has ceased to exist. This influx was the direct cause of starting the relief works. Unskilled Europeans were replacing Coloured men on one side and the Natives were replacing them on the other, and so eventually they were forced on to relief works.' (Mr. P. F. Heeger, speaking at the First National Coloured-European Conference, 1933.)

35. Cl/V, p. 41. The attitudes of certain white civil servants of differing grades to an educated Coloured colleague in a responsible position were demonstrated to me during two visits to the Government office where he worked. On the first occasion, I asked the white doorman to direct me to Mr. A's office. He looked amazed, asked if I was sure I had the right name, and showed me in to a large room containing three white minor officials. One of them agreed to fetch A, omitting the prefix 'Mr'. When Mr. A arrived, he explained that I was collecting information for a thesis and asked if he might take me to a small adjacent room. The white official looked at me, and said, 'Well, if the lady doesn't mind.' On the second occasion I was shown into the same office, and confronted by a white official who announced himself to be the head of that section. He demanded somewhat abruptly: 'What do you want with A? He has no right to be giving out information. We don't like Europeans coming to Coloureds. Anything you want to know, ask me.'

36. Cl/V, p. 42.

37. No. 21 of 1945, quoted in Cl/V, Annexure 'C'.

38. The circular emphasised: (1) that no section of the population would be displaced to their detriment; and (2) that no situation would arise in which Coloureds would be placed in positions of authority over Europeans in the public service, 'as no beneficial results will follow on such a course.'

39. C.A.C., 1946/7, Appendices A–C. This total of 671 appointments comprised 93 artisans, 69 clerical and other allied services, 38 teachers, 269 policemen, 35 hospital and health services and 147 semi-skilled occupations. The plum of these appointments was that of Coloured Industrial Inspector at a salary scale of £300 × £20 = £440. Four new Employment Officers were also appointed by the Ministry of Labour at salaries of £12–£15 per month, and additional employment bureaux were established. See recommendation of Social and Economic Planning Council, Report No. 13, p. 47. The first Annual Report of the new Sub-Department for Coloured Affairs (due in early 1952) will, it is said, contain full details of the present employment of Coloured people in the Civil Service.

40. See Siegfried, 'African Journey' (Cape, 1950), p. 66. Some departments were dissatisfied and re-engaged Africans (*Race Relations Survey*, 1949–50, p. 61).

41. *Cape Times*, 5th January, 1951.

42. Hansard, 1st March, 1951, cols. 2,178–9 and 2,187. On 5th March, 1951, the *Star* carried a report of the severe wastage of European staff on the S.A. Railways (10,000 a year since 1948, now risen to 1,500 a month). The S.A.R. was said to be needing 5,000 men in the clerical grades, 500 artisans and 1,000 apprentices (all these avenues are closed to Non-Europeans, with the exception of some artisan jobs).

43. *Forum*, 24th November, 1950.

44. The totals of employees of all races in government service and private establishments in 1944–5 (see Industrial Census for that year) were respectively 57,259 and 431,402.

45. The Industrial Census divides the figures as follows: (*a*) average wages for all public and private establishments, and (*b*) for private establishments only. They are: Coloured—(*a*) £149; (*b*) £150; Africans (*a*) £91; (*b*) £92; Asiatic—(*a*) and (*b*) £145. On the other hand, the figures for Europeans are (*a*) £341; (*b*) £339. (1944–5 Industrial Census, Table 15.)

46. Out of about 860 employees in the Provincial Building, approximately sixty are Coloured.

47. This includes the seven municipal districts, but in practice administers the Peninsula area outside the Municipality. The policy of the Paarl Municipality is

similar to that of the Cape Provincial Administration except that no Coloured messengers are employed. Here the lowest European wage-scale is 8s. per day plus 19s. 9d. weekly c.o.l.a.; the lowest Coloured scale is 5s. 3d. per day plus 11s. 6d. weekly c.o.l.a. In Kimberley the position is similar, except that Coloured messengers are employed, and Coloured employees on the fixed establishment roll may contribute to the Joint Pension Fund on the same conditions as Europeans. The lowest Coloured wage-scale is 26s. per week.

48. Mrs. Z. Gool has since 1949 been Chairman of the Health and Housing Committee.

49. Amended by Act No. 37 of 1944.

50. Amended by Act No. 36 of 1937. The Industrial Conciliation Act was far more discriminatory towards Africans, as most of them were not included under its definition of an 'employee'.

51. Amended by Act No. 44 of 1937.

52. M. H. de Kock, *Economic Development in S.A.* (King, 1936), p. 89, and C.p. 38.

53. It provided for 'the registration and regulation of trade unions and employers' organisations, for the prevention and settlement of disputes between employers and employees, for the regulation of conditions of employment by agreement and arbitration, for the control of private registry offices, etc.'

54. There is need for a more specific examination into the working of various industrial councils, as it affects the interests of Coloured labour, and even of Coloured employers. In a memorandum to the Industrial Legislation Commission in 1949, Senator W. C. Ballinger, Secretary of the Society for the Friends of Africa, wrote that it is doubtful whether more than half a dozen such councils have Non-European members.

55. The 1944–5 Industrial Census gave the figures for European and Coloured working proprietors as 6,345 and 172 respectively.

56. 'In many instances representatives of independent councils and of trade unions admitted that they are not catering for the interests and needs of the less privileged labour groups.' (I. para. 113); cf. *Race Relations Handbook*, Ch. XII, p. 145: 'Pressure from the European trade union may, moreover, result in an industrial council agreement fixing wage rates applicable to all workers so high relative to their efficiency that Non-Europeans with lower standards of productivity will not be employed.'

57. The position is accentuated by the fact that a Coloured trade union representative may not get an equally sympathetic hearing from government officials and representatives of colour-bar trade unions. A high official of a Western Cape trade union told me in September 1949 that he would not advise any union to send a Coloured executive to deal with officials of the present government. He declared that officials had usually been more reasonable under the former government. See also *Cape Times* of 25th May, 1949, for the Nationalist Parliamentary Labour Group's refusal to see a T.L.C. deputation, on the grounds that one member was a Non-European.

58. C. s. 304. On 31st January, 1950 (*Hansard*, col. 396) the Minister of Labour said that he had refused to publish certain industrial agreements containing 'closed shop' provisions when the union (*a*) required members to subscribe to a political party, or (*b*) had a membership of mixed races.

59. I. s. 229.

60. I. s. 124. In fact, the original division was not maintained, and the same industry may be governed as to its wages by industrial council or wage board determinations in different areas.

61. Dr. Sheila van der Horst, *Race Relations Handbook*, p. 149.

62. 1948 Report of Department of Labour, pp. 26 and 31.

63. Such 'undercutting' has been advocated in the interests of Coloured workers themselves, notably by Professor W. H. Hutt of the University of Cape Town. (See his article in *The Cape Coloured People To-day*.) When Professor Hutt put for-

ward this theory at the First National Coloured-European Conference, Mr. P. F. Heeger did not agree that this would benefit the Coloured worker. 'I am definitely of the opinion that the removal of the minimum wage in industry and the return to the old standard of free labour and former sweating conditions will only result in a general lowering of the standard of living. The Coloured man will undercut the European, the one Coloured man will undercut the other, the Native with his accepted lower standard of living will undercut the lot. This latter fact is definitely true as it is only in the unskilled field of labour where there is no fixed minimum where the Native is displacing the Coloured man, simply because he is able to work for a much lower wage.' In the late '30s, it was possible for Coloured artisans to undercut European competitors in the smaller towns, where wage-fixing legislation did not apply. (D'Ewes, 'South Africa's Special Area'—article in *Nineteenth Century* (1938), Vol. CXXIV, pp. 300–13.)

64. The Industrial Census of 1944–5 gave the total number of employees of all races in industry as 431,402.

65. More highly paid than skilled work in most Western European countries at that time, while the disparity between wages for skilled and unskilled work have always been striking as compared to the figures for other countries. See I., Ch. II; Board of Trade Report on Manufacturing Industries (1948); and 1948 Report of the Department of Labour (pp. 33–45) for some recent wage determinations.

66. See I, p. 154, where the possibility of a misuse of the Wage Act is mentioned.

67. These two acts were described by Professor Hutt in his article in *The Cape Coloured People To-day* as 'disguised but oppressive racial legislation'. See this article for a more detailed discussion of the problem.

68. C. s. 310. Nevertheless, it is claimed that some employers found ways to evade the acts. For instance, a furniture-factory might require a Non-European employee to sign a declaration saying he had borrowed a certain sum of money, and that he agreed to repay it in monthly instalments of so much. (G. H. Calpin, 'The "Near Whites" of South Africa'—article in *Nineteenth Century* (1938), Vol. CXXIV, pp. 113–22.)

69. The effect of the increased numbers of European women in industry upon the position of Coloured male workers in the last decades is touched upon by Dr. H. J. Simons in *The Cape Coloured People To-day*, pp. 26–7, as a matter meriting further investigation. See also *Race Relations Survey* (1949–50), p. 62, for the adverse effects of juvenile labour on adult male employment in Johannesburg.

70. C. s. 338–46.

71. I. s. 239.

72. See Dr. H. J. Simons' article in *The Cape Coloured People To-day*. The writer pointed out that the influx of Europeans into the urban areas in the period 1921–36 was paralleled by an even larger influx of rural Coloureds, but that the percentage ratio of Coloureds engaged in industry had nevertheless tended to remain static or to decline during this period of rapid industrial development. Dr. Simons also showed that between 1924 and 1937 Coloured female workers suffered most from European competition (but the 1944–5 Industrial Census figures suggest that this lost ground has been more than made up). Coloured males had, on the other hand, suffered more from African than from European competition during that period. For the post-war period, see 1948 Report of the Department of Labour, p. 5.

73. The European percentage has dropped considerably, while the African one has increased.

74. See Dr. Albert Hertzog's complaint of Coloured infiltration into white skilled artisans' jobs during the war (*Hansard*, 9th February, 1951, col. 941). A considerable number of Coloured men were, however, also absent on war service, their jobs, if semi- or unskilled, being filled by Africans; this naturally had an adverse effect on Coloured employment in the post-war period.

75. See Professor Hutt, *The Cape Coloured People To-day*, pp. 12–13.

76. In 1927 Professor A. Leslie quoted the opinion of a number of trades unionists

and employers that the Coloured man would have disappeared from the skilled unions within fifteen years. (*J. Econ. Soc. S.A.*, Vol. III, Pt. II, No. 6, pp. 53–4, 1927.) On the other hand, the following figures were provided by the Department of Labour for the distribution of skilled artisans in certain trades in the Western Cape in 1947:

	European	Coloured
Furniture manufacturing	434	581
Clothing industry (cutters)	139	74
Bespoke tailoring (cutters)	17	—
Baking and Confectionery	113	182
Building	1,700	2,300
Engineering	1,363	1,305

77. One aspect of this prejudice is shown in the policy of some manufacturers in advertising their goods as produced by white labour only (a bacon factory advertises its wares on cinema screens as 'manufactured by 100 per cent white labour under completely hygienic conditions'). See *The Cape Coloured People To-day*, p. 27. The Association of 'whiteness' and 'cleanliness' is interesting psychologically.

78. S.E.P.C. Report No. 13, pp. 42–3.

79. In six industries, with a total of 14,856 employees in various areas affected by wage determinations in 1948 (1948 Annual Report of Department of Labour, p. 43), the distribution of workers according to racial group in the various grades showed a certain upward mobility amongst Non-Europeans.

Race	European	Native	Asiatic	Coloured
Percentage of all employees	32.1	55.4	5.2	7.3
Percentage of all skilled employees	83.8	5.8	5.6	4.8
Percentage of all semi-skilled employees	33.8	34.2	20.8	11.2
Percentage of all unskilled employees	1.5	80.8	4.5	13.2

80. At one Cape garment factory only 30 out of 250 workers (all Coloured) are men (Weiss, p. 11).

81. See Ch. IX, pp. 176–8, for this and other 'myths' of race.

82. During the 1949–50 recession, the number of unemployed rose as follows:

	European			Coloured		
Quarter	Juveniles	Adult Males	Adult Females	Juveniles	Adult Males	Adult Females
January, 1949	517	3,396	1,085	500	3,441	1,444
April, 1949	176	3,425	1,152	463	4,677	1,807
July, 1949	247	5,005	1,342	552	6,395	2,767
October, 1949	233	5,529	1,480	539	7,508	3,353
January, 1950	1,358	6,002	2,006	688	7,309	3,422
April, 1950	593	5,607	2,310	562	6,938	3,111
July, 1950	323	4,443	2,174	483	6,608	2,459
October, 1950	124	3,433	1,399	310	5,216	1,824
January, 1951	747	3,363	1,277	433	4,174	1,650

These figures show a far higher proportion of unemployed Coloureds than Europeans, when one takes into account the numerical strength of the respective ethnic groups, their participation in industry (55,329 Coloureds and 133,518 Europeans of both sexes according to the 1944–5 Industrial Census), and the concentration of the Coloured labour force in one main area, as contrasted with the wide dispersal of European workers. At the time of the 1932 depression, Industrial Census figures showed a disproportionate drop in Coloured male employment immediately before the depression of 1932, from 16,322 (or 46 per cent of the total employed in industry) in 1929–30, to 13,175 (or 43 per cent) in 1932–3. European figures for the same years were 13,750 (38 per cent) and 13,477. In both cases men suffered more than women and the number of European women employed actually rose from 3,383 to 4,212.

83. See D'Ewes, op. cit. in this Chapter, n. 63, for the situation in 1938; *Cape Times*, 16th January, 1951, for African infiltration into Peninsula dairy industry; *ibid.*, 12th January, 1951, for African displacement of Coloured volunteers in Peninsula during the last war; *ibid.*, 3rd February, 1951, on the change-over from Coloured to African labour in the Cape Town docks, the Coloureds having moved into industry, with its better hours and continuity of employment; *ibid.*, 12th November, 1950, for substitution of African for Coloured labour in the wine-producing area of Bonnievale. On the other hand, see *Cape Argus* of 24th and 25th January, 1951, for the almost complete change-over from European to Coloured crews on the Union's sea-going, coasting and small craft. This may be curbed by the new Merchant Shipping Act No. 57 of 1951), which provides, *inter alia*, for separate messing, sleeping and recreational quarters on board Union ships. On the other hand, the Act may accelerate the change-over.

84. S.E.P.C. No. 13, p. 61.

85. In the year 1944–5 there were 172 Coloured working proprietors in the Union, and 94 'managers, accountants and clerical staff'. The remaining 58,709 Coloureds employed in all industries are listed as 'artisans and other industrial workers'. These figures include both sexes and are taken from the 28th Industrial Census (the latest available); unfortunately there is no further breakdown of the latter category which would enable one to state how many of these Coloureds are employed in a skilled capacity.

86. *Op. cit.*, s. 51(3) quoted in *Race Relations Handbook*, p. 153. A memorandum presented to the recent Industrial Legislation Commission by the Western Province Local Committee of the S.A. Trades and Labour Council on 23rd June, 1949, stated that inspectors, to whose discretion such matters were left, had allowed factories to provide unsatisfactory sanitary conveniences, change rooms, and rest and dining-rooms for Non-European employees.

87. The border-line between light Coloured and dark European is so indistinct in the Cape that a factory inspector would not easily detect this subterfuge. This practice may have lapsed in recent years, with the increasing number of discriminatory statutes; the Population Register should dispose of it entirely.

88. This possibility merits closer study. It was suggested to me by a conversation with a middle-class Coloured woman, who has worked in the same Cape Town cigarette factory for the last eight years. The workers are graded from 1 to 4, according to skill and wage. Mrs. P. was in Grade 3. She said that few Coloured girls ever got to Grade 1. Europeans were usually employed on the machines, Coloureds not. The ethnic groups worked in segregated workrooms.

89. See S.E.P.C. Report No. 13, pp. 101–4, and *Race Relations Handbook*, pp. 153–6, for this legislation.

90. See criticism of this amending Act in Memorandum from S.A. Institute of Race Relations (*Cape Argus*, 13th June, 1949).

91. Mr. B. J. Schoeman, Minister of Labour, speaking at the Cape Nationalist Party Congress (*Rand Daily Mail*, 5th October, 1950). See also Memorandum on Unemployment Registration submitted to the Department of Labour in early 1951 by the Western Province Local Committee of the Trades and Labour Council, outlining various complaints made by workers of all ethnic groups against the administration of relief.

92. See *Year Book* No. 24 of 1948, pp. 264–9, and 1948 Report of the Department of Labour, pp. 5–7.

93. On 31st December, 1948, 4,264 such voluntary arrangements were in force, including 35 for domestic servants, 16 for diamond diggers, 1,354 for persons earning over £750 p.a., and 2,859 for farm workers. The number of employers registered compulsorily was 76,000. (1948 Report of the Department of Labour, pp. 84–5.)

94. Such questions as the following were included: (1) (f) (a): 'Do you favour separate employers' and employees' organisations for Europeans, Coloureds and Asiatics respectively? (1) (9) (d): Would this tension (i.e., between European workers fearful of Native competition, and Native workers resentful of the colour bar) not be eased to the general benefit of the country, if European workers felt that in their own areas they were protected from the competition of non-Europeans? (1) (9) (e): Do you support or not the reservation of certain classes of work for Europeans and other classes of work for Natives, Coloureds, Asiatics and others: (2) (A) (c): Are you of the opinion that Natives, generally speaking, have reached a stage when the rank and file can benefit fully from the trade union movement? . . . (2) (A) (i): Can you generally say that Native trade unions are the result of spontaneous efforts of the workers, or did the union originate from organisations from outside? If the latter, which body was responsible for the organisation of the workers?'

95. See evidence (1) of Mr. Simon Roytowski, a spokesman for various Cape industrial councils (Cape Argus, 15th February, 1949), (2) of Mr. A. P. Jenner, then Cape Secretary of the S.A. Trades and Labour Council (Cape Times, 15th February, 1949), (3) of Mr. A. A. Miller, a former chairman of the Industrial Council for the Clothing Industry, who said to Dr. Botha: 'You are setting yourself up as counsel and judge' (Cape Argus, 15th February, 1949), and (4) of Miss N. Dick, Secretary of the African Textile Workers' Industrial Union (Cape Argus, 22nd June, 1949).

96. As will be evident from other sections of this study, this social separation is advocated by almost all whites in South Africa. This joining of social with economic separation or association by Dr. Botha therefore contained a pitfall, which was, however, avoided by his interlocutor.

97. Cape Argus, 11th February, 1949. This attitude is in striking contrast to that of the last Industrial Legislation Commission, which wrote: 'Social aspirations and politics should be in harmony with economic realities and should not be in conflict with the economic policy of encouraging the expansion of industry and employment and thereby of the national income, the source of all wage payments. That policy requires that everybody be employed in that capacity where he or she is as productive as possible. The full application of such a policy, therefore, runs counter to the idea of "colour bar" and "colour bar legislation" as well as uneconomic "white labour" policies.'

98. The S.A. Institute of Race Relations, in its recent evidence for the Industrial Legislation Commission (R.R. 52/49) quotes the Johannesburg Secretary of Apprenticeship Committees on the 1946 position: '. . . according to my records there are only three or four non-European apprentices in this area, and they are employed in the Leather and Jewellery trades.' (In 1950 Johannesburg employers complained of a great dearth of apprentices: Star, 4th December, 1950.) There were thirty-four Coloured apprentices registered at the Natal Technical College in 1950. I have been unable to obtain complete figures of Coloured and European apprentices over a period of years. The Apprenticeship Committees, which apparently have the only full records, do not record race on the cards. It might be possible, with permission of a Committee, to go through its hundreds of cards and conjecture the ethnic affiliation of the individual concerned from the school attended (as all education is segregated). This would have to be done in each area separately, and investigations would have to be extended over a period of years if a trend was to be indicated, always supposing the older records were still available. Such conjecture would not of course cover the cases of those who had 'passed' and might even lay the inquirer upon to charges of defamation.

99. See Appendix O. The engineering industry has been largely European from the beginning. Several informants have suggested that the Amalgamated Engineering Union has somewhat illiberal views on colour.

100. Usually Standard VI or VII. In the latter case the boy must attend a secondary school (which is not free, like primary schools) for one year. When the proposed transfer of Standard VI to the secondary schools goes through (see Ch. VIA), the shortage of secondary schools may create a further obstacle for Coloured boys. For an early protest by the Cape Malay Association against the discriminatory effects of the Apprenticeship Act, coupled with a demand for compulsory education to counteract these effects, see the *Cape Times* of 9th March, 1926.

101. E. s. 79; I. s. 728; Industrial and Agricultural Requirements Commission (U.G. 40/1941, s. 168); Social and Economic Planning Council Report No. 2, s. 107. See provisions of the Apprenticeship Amendment Act (No. 28 of 1951) and the Training of Artisans Act (No. 38 of 1951) which are designed to speed up the training of artisans. On 12th March, 1951, the Minister of Labour tabled a report in the Assembly, which stated that the Union was short of 10,356 skilled men. The engineering industry needed 3,000 men, the printing industry 800, the motor industry nearly 1,000 and the furniture industry 300.

102. See *Race Relations Handbook*, pp. 151–2, and *The Cape Coloured People To-day*, p. 29, for accounts of a 'back-door' to skilled artisan status in industries where there is no closed-shop agreement.

103. Dr. H. J. Simons (*The Cape Coloured People To-day*, p. 28) reports labour department and trade union officials as stating emphatically that apprenticeship committees are not influenced by colour prejudice in dealing with applications. Officially, the racial origin of an applicant is not shown on his card, but can be discovered by reference to his medical report, or from the name of the school attended. Various apprenticeship committees, which must all be equally representative of employers and employees, do have some Coloured members. This might serve as a partial safeguard against any prejudice that may exist. On the other hand, a Coloured union leader, Mr. E. A. Dean, writes: 'Occasions have arisen in which Coloured employers have been refused the right to indenture Coloured boys because the Apprenticeship Committee concerned found that the workshop did not provide all the facilities that were required (in their opinion), for the boy to receive an adequate training as a skilled artisan'. (Race Relations, '*Patterns of Segregation*', 1948, p. 45.) See also V. s. 1973, and C. s. 272–6. In the same article Mr. Dean estimated that about fifteen Europeans were then being apprenticed to every Coloured boy apprenticed in Cape Town, though the Coloured and European populations are roughly equal.

104. 'The difficulties a hard-working respectable Coloured father is experiencing in trying to find a job with some sort of future for his 17-year-old son have emphasised the lack of opportunities to-day for educated Coloured youths. The father is anxious for the boy to enter the printing trade, but, although there is no legal colour bar to this, the prejudice is so strong that openings are very few, and the Juvenile Employment Bureau said that he had no hope of getting in. Mr. S. V. Petersen, principal of the Athlone High School, said that one of his hardest problems was trying to find worth-while jobs for the senior boys and girls when they left. 'Everywhere', he said, 'they come up against the colour bar, not a legal one, just a tacit one. I have 260 pupils from Standards VII to IX. Of those who will leave this year, three, whose parents can afford it, are to study medicine, and a few will train as teachers; the rest I cannot help.' An official of the Apprenticeship Committee said that the printing, engineering and motor trades would take very few Coloured apprentices. The building and furniture trades would take a fair number, but it depended very much on the individual employer. One of the rare sources of better employment for Coloured youths is the City Council, but even there they cannot offer many opportunities. 'We try to do what we can for them', Mr. F. W. Solomon, chairman of the Staff Management Committee of the council said, 'but we, too, are often up

against prejudice. We have found, however, that almost always when we have given Coloured men responsible jobs, such as traffic policemen or skilled work in the Electricity Department, they have proved good reliable workers." (*Cape Argus*, 27th September, 1949.) A Coloured trade union leader wrote in 1946: 'My experience has shown that all other difficulties are negligible once an employer has agreed to engage a Coloured lad for apprenticeship.' (E. A. Dean, Race Relations, '*Patterns of Segregation*', 1948. See also Dr. H. J. Simons, *The Cape Coloured People To-day*, p. 28.)

105. See Professor W. J. Hutt, in *The Cape Coloured People To-day*, p. 16.

106. In an interview with Mr. E. A. Dean, the late Mr. Madeley, formerly a member of the Labour Party, then Minister of Labour in the United Party Government, is reported to have said that it would be impossible to indenture Coloured boys in Government workshops because the skilled workers would not train them, and all European artisans would probably stop work. (*Cape Coloured People To-day*, p. 44.)

107. For detailed accounts of black and white trade-unionism see Roux, *passim*, and *Race Relations Handbook*, Ch. VI.

108. See Lily Rabkin, 'Why Our Trade Unions are in Trouble', *Forum*, 17th September, 1949, p. 14. See also Lord Olivier, *Anatomy of African Misery* (1927), *passim*, and Report of Third Non-European Unity Movement Conference, January, 1945, p. 14.

109. Here we must mention that under existing legislation Africans are not allowed to join registered European trade unions, nor to have registered unions of their own (*Race Relations Handbook*, p. 166). Unregistered African trade unions do in fact exist and some are even affiliated to one of the European organisations (the S.A. Trades and Labour Council.) Compare and contrast the American situation (Myrdal, p. 476).

110. It should perhaps be pointed out here that while most Europeans in trade and industry are fairly well organised from a union point of view, only about one-eighth of distributive trade workers are organised, and about 50 per cent of the total of 800,000 European wage-earners. It is amongst Non-Europeans, however, that trade union organisation has the greatest gaps to fill.

111. See Roux, pp. 337–9. The C.F.L.U. was founded in 1913. In 1945 the rump of the C.F.L.U. formed itself into a local committee of the S.A.T.L.C.

112. Some years ago Mr. Stuart opposed the introduction of segregated facilities for European and Non-European students at the Cape Town Technical College. In a memorandum to the recent Industrial Legislation Commission, he wrote: 'The policy of the trade union movement, and the Cape, has at all times been, and still is, to make no discrimination whatsoever against any group of employees on the ground of race or colour. I can see no possible reason, or justification, for the view that wages and other conditions of employment should be made dependent on the colour or race of the worker and not on the nature of the work done. Nor can I support any policy which is designed to segregate the non-European worker from the European worker, and to compel the establishment of parallel trade unions within each individual industry. I am, of course, fully aware of the aim and purpose which motivate the policy of differentiation. But I am convinced that even on this basis, the proposed policy will not accomplish the aim which its advocates profess to have to safeguarding the interests of the European employee. On the contrary, I feel that it will have the very opposite effect. It should be borne in mind that in the Cape the non-European employees predominate in a number of large and important industries . . . Any policy designed to separate the Europeans from the non-European employees will not only completely undermine all uniformity and effective control in the industry, but will also have the effect of promoting competition of a most unhealthy and destructive nature between two racial groups of employees in the same industry. I can think of nothing more detrimental to the interests of all employees, more particularly the European employees.'

113. *v.* Lily Rabkin, *op. cit.*, p. 14.

114. H. J. Simons, *The Cape Coloured People To-day*, p. 32. Various informants told me that some W.P.F.L.U. unions are inactive; they are also said to lack the confidence of many members. (A. G. Weiss, pp. 26–7.) On the Witwatersrand area the garment workers, whose union is a member of the T.L.C., are paid 40 per cent more than those in the Western Cape, a difference which is proportionately far greater than the difference between the cost of living in the two areas.

115. Mr. R. Stuart, in the W.P.F.L.U. memorandum referred to in Note 108, estimated that 80 per cent of employees in the clothing and baking industries and 60 per cent of motor lorry drivers and workers in the biscuit-making industry were Non-Europeans in the Western Cape area.

116. See A. G. Weiss, pp. 26–7.

117. Affiliated unions have ranged from the Cape Explosive Industrial Workers (with a formal colour-bar) and the Pretoria Tram and Bus workers (now disaffiliated), who objected to sitting unsegregated at Council meetings with African trade unionists, to unregistered African unions such as the African Sweet Workers. See the *Torch* of 27th February, 1950, for an account of a stormy election for the secretaryship of one of the more active and progressive S.A.T.L.C. unions (Garment Workers' Union). This gives some indication of the conflicting forces involved.

118. The composition of the T.L.C. in mid-1949, just after its reforming was: nineteen European unions with a total membership of 31,861; fifty-two mixed unions, with a total membership of 110,770; two Non-European unions, membership 1,030; and two unions for Africans only with a membership of 1,132 (figures from Supplementary Memorandum presented to the Industrial Legislation Commission in 1949). A number of the 'mixed' unions have separate branches for Non-European and European members, particularly in the Northern provinces.

119. Cf. first memorandum presented to the Industrial Legislation Commission (1949), by the T.L.C. (before it was re-formed), p. 13. Non-Europeans now constitute 66 per cent of the total workers in industry, according to Dr. F. J. van Biljon, then Under-Secretary for Agriculture, speaking at annual S.A.B.R.A. Conference (*Star*, 12th January, 1951).

120. The hopes of more progressive members were summed up in the memorandum presented to the Industrial Legislation Commission by the Western Province Local Committee of the S.A.T.L.C. (dated 23rd June, 1949): (Replies—2(j)): 'European workers in general have the same prejudice as their fellows and strong political forces bolster and support any racial prejudice. It is considered that workers of their own accord would overcome race prejudices if left alone to decide their own policies. Emotional and purely personal attitudes are less important than economic needs.' Unfortunately, one must add that workers are not usually left to themselves, and that many, if not most, put racial prejudice ahead of working-class solidarity at present.

121. In 1947 five Pretoria unions went out. Then the Mine Workers' Union dropped out with 20,000 members, and several unions, including the Amalgamated Woodworkers, with a membership of 4,765, and the Engine Drivers' and Firemen's Association (3,277 members), decided not to reaffiliate when the Council was re-formed. The Typographical Union (11,000) went next, giving grounds of a political nature for this decision. This Union has a constitution which divides its members into three classes (A, B and C) according to skill. Class A members have a full vote, Class B members half a vote, Class C members a quarter of a vote. As most Coloured members are in Class C, their voting power is greatly diminished. It has been noted earlier that Coloured artisans are being ousted from the printing trade.

122. *v.* S.A.T.L.C. (1949) Constitution and Standing Orders S(a) ; article by Lily Rabkin in *Forum*, 10th September, 1949, p. 6 and *Rand Daily Mail*, 14th May, 1951, which reports the appointment of two non-T.L.C. delegates by the Government to attend the thirty-fourth session of the I.L.C.

R

123. *Forum*, 12th November, 1949. See the *Sunday Times* of 22nd April, 1951, for a more recent development in the same direction.

124. See appeal issued by T.L.C. National Executive to these thirteen unions (*Cape Times*, 3rd February, 1951).

125. *Forum*, 10th November, 1950. See also letter protesting against this interpretation from Mr. E. S. Sachs (*Forum*, 24th November, 1950), and *Rand Daily Mail*, 1st November, 1950. For abortive attempt to form a new co-ordinating body out of these unions see *Rand Daily Mail*, 4th November, 1950, and *Guardian*, 22nd March, 1951.

126. South African white workers tend to vote according to their ethnic rather than their class interests (see Brookes, p. 29). Some unions are formally linked to the small parliamentary Labour Party, but on the whole the principle of non-participation in party politics has been applied, until the recent drive of Nationalist agencies to infiltrate various trade unions. (See *Race Relations Handbook*, p. 169.)

127. Not all Afrikaans-speaking workers fall into this category. For instance, the majority of Mr. E. S. Sachs' militant garment-workers are recently urbanised Afrikaans-speaking women.

128. In August 1949 it represented thirteen affiliated unions and had a membership of over 30,000 (*Cape Argus*, 26th August, 1949).

129. *Cape Argus*, 26th August, 1949.

130. See *Forum*, 7th May, 1949, p. 8. Dr. Albert Hertzog, who is head of the Labour Department of the *Broederbond*, was in August 1950 elected to the Mineworkers' Union Executive. See comment in *Forward* (28th August, 1950); *Cape Times* (23rd August, 1950); *Pretoria News* (24th August, 1950); and *Die Transvaler* (28th August, 1950).

131. 'To the trade unionist with overseas experience, much of what appears to be inter-racial conflict is recognisable as a somewhat aggressive form of the familiar struggle between skilled, semi-skilled and unskilled workers, or between unions organised on a craft basis and those organised for all workers in a given industry.' (Simons, *Race Relations Handbook*, p. 168.)

132. See Dr. H. J. Simons, *The Cape Coloured People To-day*, p. 20.

133. E., p. 193, s. 142. See also I., p. 17, for comment on the high rates of skilled wages in South Africa as compared with other industrialised countries.

134. 'The majority of White South Africans to-day are working people earning small incomes as skilled artisans or semi-skilled operatives and having great difficulty in making both ends meet on wages which are not extravagantly high, and who often think that even this modest position is made insecure by the threat of non-European competition.' (*Star* editorial, 7th September, 1950.)

135. 1946 Census—the exact figure was 86,493, a considerable drop from the 1936 figure of 90,352 (43 per cent of the total). See Appendix G for the distribution according to occupation of men and women in the four ethnic groups in 1936 and 1946.

136. The 1936 census figures are given in the *Race Relations Handbook*, p. 114; those for 1946 were supplied in advance of publication by the Bureau of Census and Statistics. There were also 1,400 Coloured market gardeners in 1936; by 1946 the figure had dropped to 527.

137. There is no trade union organisation amongst Coloured farm-workers. Agriculture is excluded from the operation of the Wage, Industrial Conciliation, and Factories Acts. Workmen's compensation insurance is only compulsory in certain instances. There is no legislation laying down minimum wages or conditions of work. (*Race Relations Handbook*, p. 156.) In view of the number and political power of the white farmers with which both major political parties must reckon, thanks to the 15 per cent 'weighting' of country constituencies, one would not indeed expect any government to attempt the introduction of such legislation. The power of the white farmers has been demonstrated in such cases as the Smuts' administra-

tion's ban on Coloured recruiting in certain areas during the war following protests of labour shortage on farms (see Ch. III, n. 107), the recent extension of the principle of hiring out convict labour to private persons, and the direction of Coloureds receiving unemployment insurance benefits to farm labour. (Cf. 1948 Report of Department of Labour, p. 79, cases (e) and (f).)

138. Each province has a separate Masters' and Servants' Act. (See C., pp. 205–9.) In 1950 there were 20,673 prosecutions under these laws (*Hansard*, 6th February, 1951, col. 711). This figure would include domestic service contracts.

139. Latterly the administration has helped to increase the supply of farm labour by contracting prisoners out to private employers. Under the Unemployment Insurance Act, it has also been able to deprive lower-income workers of their benefits if they refuse any work offered, including farm work. As the Minister of Labour admitted, however, in a speech at Kimberley, 'most Coloured workers preferred doing without the allowance to accepting work on farms. He could not agree with critics who said that his department spent too much time protecting the conditions of Non-European workers.' (*Rand Daily Mail*, 5th October, 1950.)

140. '. . . The labourer's illiteracy and simplicity place him at an unfair advantage in his relations with his employers, for, being unable to write, his verbal notice to quit . . . may be ignored and he may find himself arrested for desertion of service and made a criminal.' (A criminal charge under the Masters' and Servants' Acts—S.P.) Bishop S. W. Lavis, speaking at First National Coloured-European Conference, 1933.

141. On the employer's side the Industrial Legistration Commission speaks of 'a tacit or explicit agreement among employers in a particular district or industry not to pay more than certain low rates of wages, (when) the only alternative for the workman to accepting their conditions is to seek employment further afield or in another industry. Such pressure is sometimes exercised by custom or public opinion. This is the case in South Africa with regard to Coloured labour, especially in the rural areas. People will not pay more for Coloured labour than a uniform low rate because that standard has crystallised as the existing practice. Those who "spoil the nigger" by paying more have to fear social ostracism.' (I. s. 117.)

142. Wage scales quoted by Professor Marais (p. 198) from the *Masters' and Servants' Blue Book* (Cape 1849) show that agricultural wages have not risen greatly over the last century. The following were monthly wages, food and lodging being provided in addition: Cape Town 12s. to 20s.; Stellenbosch 10s. to 15s.; Paarl 9s. to 18s.; Malmesbury 7s. 6d. to 15s.; Swellendam 10s. 6d. to 20s.; George 6s. to 15s.; Uitenhage (Hottentots, not Bantu) 5s. to 7s. 6d.; Albany (Hottentots) 12s. to 20s. For farm wages in the early 'twenties, see E., Ch. I, pp. 11–13.

143. See also C. s. 427, for the existence of a system whereby the labourer is given, instead of cash, written orders on a local shopkeeper with whom the employer has a credit account. The Commission found 'opportunities for abuse' in this system, which is reminiscent of 'debt peonage' in South America.

144. See *Race Relations Handbook*, pp. 126–7, for details of these.

145. A report prepared in 1949 by two missionary ministers who formed the 'Current Problems Commission' of the Oudtshoorn Circle of the Dutch Reformed Church stated that farmers are now allowing their labourers far less land for their own cultivation—a consequence of the present high prices for farm products. As one worker said: 'Where before I got a morgen or more ground to work, the baas now gives me only a couple of rows.' Another explained: 'I get a piece of virgin ground to clear and plant for myself, and as soon as it is just right it is taken away again and I must clear another piece.' (*Rapport en Bevindinge van die Aktuele Vraagstukke Commissie, Ring van Oudtshoorn—Herald*, George, 1949, p. 15.)

146. If the farmer provides the accommodation, it may be of fairly solid construction. I have seen quite good stone-built cottages on Western Province farms. More often than not, however, it seems that the farmer provides only a building

plot, or the labourer lives in the location. In either case, he puts up his own dwelling, which is usually made of boards, corrugated iron, old petrol tins, cardboard, mats and any other pieces of material which can possibly be pressed into use. Those who have seen these appalling hovels, either alongside an isolated farm, or sprouting out of the veld in huddled clusters at a decent distance from any small South African town or village, will no longer wonder at the perpetuation of Coloured rural misery, through generations of squalor, ignorance and drunkenness. See C. s. 624–33, and report by Mr. P. M. Sonn on the social and economic conditions of the Coloured people on the platteland, tabled at the twenty-fourth C.A.C. meeting held in October 1949.

147. Obviously such wages are insufficient for the maintenance of a family at even a very low level of existence. In consequence, all members of the family who are able work to add to the budget, either regularly or during the harvests. Even with these additions, the total income is pitifully low. The report referred to in footnote 145 *supra*, held an inquiry into the weekly incomes of nineteen families (comprising 102 persons), being a random group consisting of the front three rows in a women's audience. It was found that the average income for the 102 persons covered was 2s. 6½d. per week, of which a greatly disproportionate amount went on drink. An inquiry into the diet of seventy-eight pupils in a school in this area showed that the great majority lived on bread and coffee, with meat at week-ends only. Only about one-third had vegetables included in their diet. 'Conditions at this school were not an exception', added the report.

148. Since 1672 (Lq. s. 63). See also Marais, pp. 3, 8 and 117 for the Caledon proclamation of 1809 laying down that 'no wine, brandy, or other spirituous liquors shall be considered as necessaries of life, and consequently no allowance shall be made for the supply thereof to a Hottentot by his master during the period of his employment.' Professor Marais comments: 'This clause, of course, did not prevent farmers from supplying liquor to Hottentots as part of their "real wages" '. Under the 1951 Bill amending the Liquor Act (this Bill was held over to the 1952 session), a loophole has been left which would permit the extension of the tot system to the Transvaal and Natal.

149. Lq. 69–70.

150. Marais, p. 269.

151. C. s. 99.

152. Lq. s. 143.

153. Lq. s. 63. The manager of a small wine-farm told me that prior to his taking over the customary daily tot on the farm had been higher than the legal maximum, and that this was the case on other neighbouring farms. He had cut the tot, and raised wages, despite prophecies (which turned out to be incorrect) that he would lose his labourers. On the other hand, see *Cape Times* report (20th November, 1950) of labour conditions in Bonnievale.

154. Most wine-farmers firmly believe this, and resent any attempts on the part of other farmers to dispense with the tot in exchange for higher wages or better food and accommodation. An Afrikaans-speaking Western Province farmer told me of the resentment shown by his neighbours when he dispensed with the tot and paid higher cash wages ten years ago. He regarded his experiment as successful. However, see instance of a brickfields foreman, who was fined £100 or six months for illicit dealings in liquor, necessitated, he claimed, by the demands of his workmen, who preferred less pay and more liquor. (*Cape Times*, 28th February, 1951.)

155. In a letter to the *Cape Times* a Mrs. C. N. Koch wrote that there was 'a difference in the liver-cells of Coloureds and Europeans so that alcohol does not affect their livers as it would ours.' (13th December, 1949, p. 14.)

156. A Coloured garage-attendant told me that his brother, who works on a Stellenbosch wine-farm, asked his 'baas' for the cash equivalent of the tot (he wished to send his son to secondary school), but was told that he could 'work himself to death before he would see another penny'. The details of this story may

have been sharpened in the telling, but there is no reason to doubt the main outlines. The owner of a large wine-farm not ten miles from Cape Town, who handles his labour with the most benevolent paternalism, told me he would not be willing to pay a cash equivalent instead of the tot if any labourer asked for it.

157. Lq. s. 66.

158. See debate on a motion for the revision of the Liquor Act (*Hansard*, 15th March, 1949, col. 2094 f. and 2354 f.) and in particular the speech of Mr. S. E. Warren, Nationalist M.P. for Swellendam, who said: 'I can give my hon. friend 200 texts out of the Bible where the use of wine in the form of rations or otherwise is praised. There is no getting away from it. Even the Great Master made wine.'

159. Lq. s. 69.

160. Recently Canadian grape-growers and vintners protested against undercutting by imported wines produced by 'serf labour'. (*Cape Times*, 30th January, 1951.) See the following passage from a temperance organisation's publication: 'At a farmers' meeting in Bethlehem (O.F.S.) in 1911 it was stated amid loud applause that the only way of effectually dealing with the Coloured problem in this country, and of forcing labour on to the market, was to hinder the prosperity of the Native and Coloured population by facilitating the spread of intoxicating drink amongst them.' (*Jubilee Book, Western Grand Temple*, I.O.T.T., p. 29.)

161. The high cost of 'cheap' agricultural labour is suggested by the fact that in 1936 agriculture accounted for only 12.5 per cent of the national income, although it employed 33 per cent of the working population (64 per cent if casual labourers on the reserves and peasants are included).

162. Under the Cape Masters' and Servants' Ordinance, a servant may be sentenced to imprisonment with the option of a fine for refusing to obey an order (see instance reported in *Cape Times*, 3rd May, 1949).

163. Almost the only exceptions are white housekeepers in large houses and hotels, and white 'nannies'. Such employees are paid high wages and the social gulf which yawns between upper and lower servants in Europe is accentuated by the colour bar in South Africa. In urban areas in the Transvaal, Coloured nurses are sometimes employed, and the social gulf is between them and the African servants. One training establishment for Coloured nurses requires that its trainees should have a room inside the main building, instead of in the servants' out-quarters.

164. On my arrival in South Africa in 1948 I consulted several people as to the customary cash wage for a Coloured female domestic servant. Answers ranged from £3 10s. to £8 a month. A woman in my Cape Town suburb supplied the lowest figure of £3 10s., stated that it was customary in the neighbourhood and deplored the tendency of 'you English' to 'spoil the market' by overpaying.

165. The low cash wages paid by many small farmers must also be attributed to their own poverty and small cash income.

166. In Cape Town they rose by 33 per cent and 38 per cent for male and female servants respectively between 1940 and 1944. (*Race Relations Handbook*, p. 136.) For wages at the beginning of the last war, see 1941 Census, U.G. 46/1946.

167. The Divisional C.I.D. Officer was recently 'horrified' at the conditions in some Cape Town hotels, where, *inter alia*, he said, the Non-European staff slept in the hotel building. (*Star*, 6th December, 1950.) Non-European servants, whether or not they sleep in the main building, are excluded from the operation of householders' comprehensive insurance policies, as regards losses of their clothing and personal effects. The effects of European servants are covered when they live in the main building, or if their outside rooms are forcibly entered. This provision by insurance companies reflects the prevalent stereotype of Non-European dishonesty.

168. A South African woman of Scottish ancestry told me, however, that her grandmother would never allow Coloured servants to touch the beds. These had to be made by the children of the house. She added that this was a fairly common convention in the Cape in her childhood.

169. In our furnished flat in a well-to-do Cape Town suburb, the maid's room at the back originally contained one rickety iron bedstead with half the springs gone and no mattress, one battered dressing-table with the mirror broken, and one electric light bulb. There were no curtains, no power-point for heating, no chair, bedcovers or provision for hanging clothes. Protests to the landlord brought no immediate action, until a small bedroom suite from the house itself was moved in. This produced a protest that the suite was 'far too good for a servant', and suitable furnishings were bought.

170. This attempt to justify the perpetuation of discriminatory treatment of a group on the grounds of its present inferiority is found in all spheres of South African life. Such treatment, if continued, also helps to perpetuate the complained-of inferiority. A letter from a Cape Town domestic servant pointed this out: 'If they trusted their servants a bit more they might be more truthful and there might also be less thieving, but they show quite plainly that they don't. Better food, a decent wage and a little more interest in their staff would help a great deal.' (*Cape Argus*, 22nd June, 1949.)

171. See Appendix Q.

172. See *Cape Times* (18th February, 1949) for an account of an unusual Coloured family: the father was a minister, one daughter has a doctorate of physics and holds an Indian government research post, the other is a physician practising in Liberia, where her brother is an advocate. The second brother has an Oxford LL.D., and is director of the African Historical Research Association. On the other hand, the *Cape Times* of 29th March, 1951, reported the case of a Coloured teacher, the first to get a B. Comm. degree at Cape Town University, who was unable to find a firm of accountants to accept him as an articled clerk.

173. There are still no facilities for training Non-European dentists, and hospital training has only recently been opened to would-be Coloured doctors. The head-master of a Coloured school told me in early 1951 that there is one Coloured dentist practising at present, who was trained overseas, while two more are now studying in Britain. He also said that several Coloured doctors have European patients (often of the urban skilled artisan class), as well as those of their own group, and suggested that this might be a relic of former beliefs in the efficiency of Malay 'magic'. On the other hand, some Coloured informants have expressed a preference for white doctors, on the grounds that they are better trained and have greater access to hospital and other facilities. Europeans are said sometimes to patronise Coloured doctors when they are suffering from certain 'social diseases' which they wish to conceal from their own circle. Cf. Myrdal, p. 322.

174. There were none in 1946, although the informant quoted in note 173 said that a Coloured attorney could build up a lucrative practice, but had initial difficulty in becoming articled, although the Cape Law Society had no colour bar (the Johannesburg Law Society abolished its colour bar in late 1950). He said that a Coloured advocate would get no work, in view of the prejudice in the courts. In early 1950, a Coloured man, Mr. Isaac Volkwyn of Cape Town, was admitted as an attorney, the first non-European to qualify in eighteen years. (*Torch*, 13th February, 1950.)

175. There is no colour bar in the Medical, Dental and Pharmacy Act, but only one Coloured pharmacist was registered in 1950. All apprentices must be accepted by a retail chemist, and must attend prescribed courses, which are not held for Non-Europeans unless there are sufficient applications to warrant it. In November 1949, the Registrar of the S.A. Pharmacy Board did not know of the establishment of any such courses. The Pharmaceutical Society of Great Britain's Certificate is recognised under a reciprocal agreement.

176. These professions are part of the official classification. I have been unable to find any Coloured engineers, though one architect was listed in 1946.

177. In 1946, there were 3,075 Coloured men and 1,641 Coloured women listed occupationally under 'education', and eight male nurses, 93 female nurses and

234 midwives. Miss Stella Jacobs, the first Non-European woman to obtain the B.Sc. degree at the University of Cape Town (in Botany), also holds the B.Ed. degree and the M.Sc. (Education) from the University of Syracuse, New York City. Afterwards she returned to her former teaching post in a Uitenhage school. Europeans holding similar degrees would have the prospect of a university or government appointment. She has now been appointed to the staff of Hewat Training College in Cape Town, which until then had an all-white staff.

178. To the overseas visitor who has had the chance of comparing Cape Malay bands and the usual European dance bands in South Africa, it may seem strange that the former are not engaged more often at public dances. Amongst a small group of European 'literati' in the Western Cape there seems to be a growing interest in Coloured artistic performances, and good training work is being done by the Coloured Children's Art Centre in Chapel Street, Cape Town, and the Eoan Group (*v.* Ch. VII, p. 138). In 1950, Louis Maurice, a Coloured sculptor, had an exhibition in the Gallery of the S.A. Association of Arts, which also showed the work of a group of Coloured school children. Officials claimed that there was no discrimination against Non-European artists, but that would-be exhibitors had to submit specimen work to a board, which made its decision on the grounds of merit alone. The reason why there were so few Coloured exhibitors was the general inferiority of their work so far.

179. There are two Cape Coloured ballet dancers of considerable merit in Great Britain to-day. See *Cape Times* of 27th June, 1950, and 12th October, 1950 for reports of a painter and singer who have had overseas successes.

180. The only English-speaking writer of any considerable merit is Johannesburg-born Peter Abrahams, who now lives in Europe. His work includes: *Dark Testament, Song of the City, Mine Boy, A Black Man Speaks of Freedom* and *Wild Conquest.* S. V. Petersen's Afrikaans novel, *As die Son Ondergaan* and his verse are said to reach a high standard.

181. The only unified cultural group within the Coloured community, that of the Cape Malays, has produced no traceable creative literature. Some religious speculation in the Arabic language exists, and many translations into English and Afrikaans for teaching purposes. (See *Race Relations Handbook*, p. 618.)

182. Most Europeans would not be interested in the work of Coloured writers, who have therefore additional trouble in finding a South African publisher unless they are prepared to find money for publication. (See *Race Relations Handbook*, p. 616.)

183. One Cape newspaper only has a regular Coloured contributor, while the weekly *Forum* often prints articles by Non-European leaders.

184. Individual artisans and handymen who use no mechanical power and employ less than three persons are not included in this figure. There are probably a fair number of such small Coloured employers, for whom no figures are available.

185. These advance 1946 figures were kindly supplied by the Bureau of Census and Statistics. Corresponding 1936 figures were: 431 Coloured managers and proprietors; 47 book-keepers; 350 clerks; 6 typists; 1,318 shop assistants; 2,436 hawkers; 19 photographers; 7 stockbrokers; no quantity or land surveyors; no theatre lessees or managers; 103 hairdressers and beauty specialists; 3 keepers of hotels and licensed premises; and 39 owners of restaurants and cafés amongst the Coloured population. The increase in the succeeding ten years was therefore considerable, although the totals are still small in relation to the group.

186. C. s. 462. The Commission was unable to verify these charges; but see C.A.C. 1944–5, p. 24, for allegations that licences were refused to Coloureds in Calvinia, and the case of Jaffer *v.* Parow Village Management Board (1920 C.P.D. 270). See also the reply of the Mayor of Parow that applications for business licences could not be refused on grounds of colour, when European residents protested against the application of a Coloured man to open a shop in Tyger Valley (*Cape*

Times, 1st July, 1949); for a suggestion of discrimination in Kimberley see the *Torch* (6th November, 1950).

187. C. s. 474 and 968–77.

188. These clauses are found, not so much in older titles or older areas (e.g., Rondebosch, Wynberg, Newlands), as in almost all new estates, in which any owner can usually contest a transgression by any other. See also *Cape Times* (1st July, 1949) for a reference to similar servitudes in various Bellville areas, and the case of the Claremont property of Miss A. E. Cook, in which Mr. Justice Fagan struck out a personal restricting condition on the request of the owner. *(Cape Argus,* 3rd August, 1949.)

189. See pp. 120–2 for an account of the Group Areas Act of 1950, and its probable consequences.

190. In 1921, about 7,000 Coloured men in the urban areas possessed property; the 1936 Census showed that just over 9,000 dwellings (about 30 per cent of them two-roomed) in the Cape Province were owned by Coloureds. No later figures are available.

191. Marais, pp. 71–3, p. 101, p. 245.

192. C. s. 388.

193. See MacMillan, p. 176.

194. The estimated share of the national income received by the Coloured group in 1936 was £14,475,000, which represents £52 per occupied Coloured person and £18 *per capita;* constituting 8 per cent of the total population, they received 4 per cent of the total national income. See *Race Relations Handbook,* pp. 333–40 for detailed analysis of Coloured incomes based on the 1936 Census figures. The Social Security Committee estimated the average income per head of the European population at about £125 per annum, that of Coloureds at £25, and of Natives at £10. (U.G. 14/44, s. 12.)

195. See Myrdal, pp. 313–4, and Johnson, p. 296. The *Cape Times* of 16th November, 1950, reports an attempt by some commercial firms to sponsor coon troupes (see pp. 155–7) to advertise their goods, which was, however, banned by the Western Province Coloured Jubilee Carnival Board.

196. See Footnote 186 *supra,* and *The Sun,* 30th March, 1950, which suggests that one establishment in Cape Town advertising that it employs European labour only should be reminded that a large percentage of its clients are Non-Europeans.

197. The result of an informal Chamber of Commerce agreement. One manager said: 'If they want to try things on we usually say we haven't the right size. If they insist, we try to prevent Europeans from seeing the process.' (This does not, of course, apply to shops in predominantly Coloured areas.) For American parallels, see Johnson, pp. 65–6. In one large Johannesburg provision shop, all Non-Europeans are served at a separate counter in a separate room. In grocers' and greengrocers' shops, Non-European customers are often served by Non-European assistants, Europeans by Europeans.

198. See letter in *Cape Times* (27th October, 1949). It is customary to ask Non-European customers: 'What do you want, John?' (or 'Annie', according to sex). Another mode of address is simply 'Yes?' the customary 'Sir' or 'Madam' being omitted. (See *S.A. Food Trades Journal* quoted by *Cape Times* of 4th April, 1951.) Coloured customers are, however, usually served according to their order of arrival in commercial establishments in the main urban centres, and are not compelled to wait until all Europeans have been served. In the country this is not always so; see the *Star* of 2nd December, 1950, for an account of the situation at Pniel, a mission village not fifty miles from Cape Town.

199. A middle-class Coloured woman told me that she preferred to go to the best stores because 'you get a better class of white assistant there, who knows how to talk to a person properly'.

200. A Coloured teacher told me of an incident in a large Cape Town store which at Christmas 1949 had a special Toy Fair, with a notice 'For Europeans Only'

on it. He had just bought a fairly expensive toy in the department, and went over to the entrance of the Fair. The assistant pointed to the notice, so he called a senior employee and complained. The latter apologised, saying the prohibition was only to keep out undesirable characters, and told the girl to let him in. On the other hand, a motion before the 1949 Cape Nationalist Party Conference asked for separate entrances for Europeans and Non-Europeans in all business premises. (*Cape Argus*, 15th September, 1949.)

201. With the exception of Coloureds living in locations under the same conditions as Africans, who are liable to pay Native local and general tax, and (until Act 46/1946) of Coloureds in the O.F.S., who had to pay £1 annual poll-tax. For a U.S. comment cf. passage from Edgar H. Murphy quoted by Myrdal, p. 1,319; also *The Sun*, 31st March, 1950: 'The Coloured people must not allow themselves to be bluffed . . . about who pays for the upkeep of this country. This country is yours, even though at present the Nationalists play boss over it. You pay taxes, you suffer as a result of the high cost of living, and you must therefore have a say in the government of the country of your birth.'

202. Of Cape Town's total population of over 450,000 (about half of them of taxable age) only about 40,000, most of them European, paid income tax in 1947–8. (*Cape Argus*, 30th July, 1949.)

203. On the radio programmes, their interests seem not to be considered at all. In January 1950, the Cape Town Regional Director of the S.A.B.C. ordered an inquiry into allegations by an *Argus* correspondent of 'crude jibes at the Coloured people', and 'an exaggerated version of a young Coloured woman's reaction to *apartheid*' in a New Year's Eve broadcast of *Vrolikheid in die Koffiehuis*. The *Sun* reported on 13th January, 1950, that an artist concerned in the broadcast had been severely reprimanded.

204. There are long waiting-lists for telephones in most Union cities at present, but two Coloured informants felt that no discrimination was involved in the case of Coloured applicants in Cape Town at least.

205. In the year ended March 1949 there was a total decrease of £411,300 in the total issue of Savings Bank Certificates to £1,986,500, while money repaid to holders totalled £2,200,300, an increase of £242,600 over the previous year. A decrease of £573,419 was shown in the amount of Union Loan Certificates bought during 1949, while the balance of investments in them dropped from £31,720,113 in 1945 to £27,855,577 in 1949. There is unfortunately no way of estimating to what extent, if at all, Coloured contributors figured in these changes, or, if they did, were motivated by a desire to strike at the Government, or simply by financial need in what was a period of some economic stress. See *Cape Times* of 21st October, 1949 for unanimous resolution passed by a meeting of 800 people convened by the Paarl Apartheid Resistance Committee calling for savings to be withdrawn from the Post Office, Union Loan certificates to be cashed, wireless licences to be cancelled, and for a boycott of Nationalist firms, 'as a means of countering the threat to the Coloured vote and as a protest against the policy of *apartheid*.'

206. The South, taken by itself, presents certain parallels. 'As is often pointed out, the South as a region is competing against the North by its recourse to low-paid docile white and Negro labour. It has actually advertised this as an opportunity for outside capitalists . . . "the South remains largely a colonial economy", complains Vance, one of the region's outstanding social scientists.' (Myrdal, p. 221.) Cf. statement in *Union Year Book* 1941, p. 258: 'It is generally admitted that the prosperity of South African trade and industry depends to a very great extent on an adequate supply of relatively cheap, unskilled, non-European labour.'

207. For reasons of space, it is not possible to outline the legal and customary discrimination which meets Africans in the economic sphere. In almost every case, however, it is much greater.

208. Cf. Lord Olivier, pp. 166–7.

209. 'Discrimination against Negroes is thus rooted in this tradition of economic

exploitation. It is justified by . . . false racial beliefs . . . This depreciation of the Negro's potentialities is given a semblance of proof by the low standards of efficiency, reliability, ambition and morale actually displayed by the average Negro . . . Poverty itself breeds the conditions which perpetuate poverty.' (Myrdal, pp. 207–8.)

210. See statement of the Economic Affairs Committee of the Association of Chambers of Commerce (*Rand Daily Mail*, 7th May, 1951).

211. In the 1951 session the Nationalist Government passed a Native Building Workers Act, which may also strike a blow against the monopoly of the skilled white worker (despite its avowed aim of protecting the latter's status). It proposes to train African building workers for work in their own areas, pay them a lower wage than white artisans, and debar them from operating in European urban (but not rural) areas. Labour M.P.s have objected on the grounds that it would undermine European wages in these rural areas, and would create a large pool of skilled black labour uncontrolled by industrial legislation and unaffiliated to registered unions.

CHAPTER VI—SOCIAL SERVICES—A

1. U.N. Covenant of Human Rights, Article 26, s. 2 (accepted by South Africa only 'with reservations'. *Star*, 6th March, 1951).

2. In the Cape, as we have seen in Ch. III, literacy has so far been a political asset, in that it is one of the qualifications for a male Coloured voter. This consequence of Coloured education has recently been made the subject of attempts to whip up white fears of ultimate swamping by Coloured voters, unless the latter are removed from the common roll.

3. The beginnings of such a process are visible amongst the Coloured people in South Africa. It may be accentuated by the fact that almost the only economic field open to Coloured intellectuals is that of teaching, and they are therefore in a position to exert direct influence upon the ideas and attitudes of the coming generation.

4. 'Dr. E. C. Jansen (then Minister of Native Affairs, now Governor-General), speaking at a meeting at Wynberg last night, said the policy of *apartheid* meant that each section of the population of the Union should be given the opportunity of separate development. Education of Coloured and Native people would no longer consist of book learning. They would be taught how to work. We have no interest in educating people to wear a white collar alone, the Minister declared.' (*Cape Times*, 25th February, 1949.) See also C. Appendix 46 (9) and p. 320.

5. MacCrone, pp. 15–16.

6. There were, however, some exceptions, *v*. Marais, p. 129: 'At the beginning of 1796 a number of Boers for the first time told the missionaries that they considered the Genadendal Hottentots better servants than any they had yet employed.' This was probably as enlightened an attitude to Coloured education as one could expect of colonists at that time. Cf. this passage from a memorandum by the O.F.S. Department of Education: '. . . the Department is convinced that in time employers will realise that Coloureds who have only attended a primary school are more useful owing to the fact that they have been disciplined and because in general they will be in a position to perform work in a more intelligent manner than those who have not attended school at all.' (C. Appendix 46, p. 320.)

7. See Marais, p 137, for a further account.

8. Marais, p. 128, quoting from *Records* XXXV, p. 322.

9. In that year there were only twenty Dutch women and children altogether in the total population of 260 (C. Appendix 48, p. 326), so that a school for Europeans would have been superfluous.

10. In which there were at that time thirty-two male and twenty-six female half-caste children (C. Appendix 48). Except where otherwise stated, all facts and

figures in this historical account are taken from this source, contributed by H. P. Cruse. Cf. also V. de Kock, p. 100 *et seq.*

11. The lodge slaves, and consequently their school, had such a bad name that most European owners seem to have put financial interest ahead of colour prejudice, preferring the risk of close contact between their own children and their slaves to the possible lowering of their property's value as a result of acquired bad habits. Even in the more colour-conscious farming districts such as Stellenbosch and Paarl, a few 'free blacks' and even slave children were reported in the public schools as late as 1806 and after.

12. With this exception, education was mainly secular. Only eighty-six slaves passed the baptism tests between 1810 and 1824, despite the efforts of the South African Missionary Society, which began work among them in 1794. (See Marais, p. 168.)

13. Three of the principal societies concerned were German—the Moravian Church and the Berlin and Rhenish Missionary Societies (many of their missionaries were trained artisans). The only important British society in the early period was the London Missionary Society. For parallel missionary and educational work cf. the Jesuit schools in Paraguay and Uruguay.

14. There were of course more mission schools than institutions. By 1860 there were 123 such schools, with an enrolment of 14,265, while the 102 government and state-aided schools had 4,492 pupils. The enthusiasm which produced these enormous classes in the mission schools cannot have helped their efficiency.

15. For instance, tanning and shoemaking at Wupperthal (Rhenish); knife factory at Genadendal (Moravian Church); printing press at Bethelsdorp (L.M.S.); fruit drying at Amalienstein (Berlin Missionary Society). The introduction of modern large-scale production put an end to these small industries.

16. The great bulk of the children in mission schools were below Standard I, i.e., pre-primary, up to the time of Union. (A. W. Cook, *Race Relations Handbook*, p. 350.) Education in the public schools seems to have become increasingly superior to mission education towards the end of the nineteenth century.

17. Marais, p. 269.

18. This was emphasised strongly in a memorandum of 1839: 'At all times every government seminary will be accessible to every individual in the community.'

19. C. Appendix 48.

20. For the administrative device that made this possible see C. s. 860.

21. There were nearly 6,000 European school children in mission schools in 1883, under 550 in 1910 (Marais, p. 271). On the other hand, children from well-to-do 'mixed' families often seem to have been accepted at European schools. An informant told me of two instances at the school which he attended in the Western Cape before 1914.

22. In 1863 a government commission reported on the type of education there given: 'A great amount of information on Bible history and geography and of knowledge of the text of the Holy Scriptures is imparted. These exercises, with singing and repeating hymns, form the chief occupation of the day . . . Secular elementary instruction, of which the essential subjects are reading, writing and arithmetic, is seriously neglected.' (Marais, p. 270.) Naturally, such a syllabus does not apply at the present time.

23. Marais, p. 271.

24. See the discriminatory provisions of Act 43 of 1887, which introduced grants and pensions for meritorious teaching service. Pensions were calculated according to the meritorious service grant, which was available to all teachers in public schools, but in the case of mission schools only to principals. By this date quite a number of teachers in mission schools must have been Coloured, as several training-colleges, notably Genadendal, had been functioning since the second quarter of the nineteenth century. This was, therefore, the beginning of discriminatory treatment of Coloured teachers and Europeans teaching Coloured pupils.

25. Only state and state-aided education will be described. There are a few private schools for Coloureds, and a large number with excellent facilities for Europeans.

26. 'The applicant, being the father of two children by a coloured wife, obtained their admission into a public undenominational school in the school district of Keimoes, and paid the necessary fees. The parents of the other pupils of the school withdrew or threatened to withdraw their children if the applicant's children were allowed to remain, whereupon the School Committee refused to allow the children to continue their attendance, and tendered back the fees, which the applicant refused to accept. Compulsory education for children of European parentage was in force in the district, and there were two mission schools in the district where children of other than European parentage could attend. *Held*: that it was part of the policy of the Cape School Board Act of 1905 to promote the establishment of separate public undenominational schools for children of European parentage or extraction. *Held*: further, that the applicant's children were of other than European parentage or extraction, and consequently he was not entitled to an order compelling the School Committee to receive his children as pupils.' (Moller *v.* Keimoes School Committee, D.L. 3517/1911. A.D.644.) It is often at school that a child is first definitely classified as a Coloured or a European, a procedure which determines the whole course of his future.

27. The educational segregation of the three Non-European groups in South Africa has probably contributed greatly to the success of the 'divide and rule' policy. As European children from the moment they enter school become conscious of their own superiority to '*Hotnot*' children and 'piccanins', so the Coloured child, in his segregated schooling with its preferential provisions, tends to gain a sense of superiority to the African, who in turn feels superior on account of his 'pure blood'. These are valuable psychological outlets for groups otherwise condemned to an inferior status.

28. For a recent account of African education see *Race Relations Handbook*, Ch. XV. African education is financed on a different and lower basis (not *per caput* as for Europeans and Coloureds); the syllabus is different; teacher-training qualifications are lower; the proportion of teachers to pupils is lower; their salary scales are less, etc. For a general comparison of the number and type of schools, of teachers and of average emoluments, for each racial group, see Appendix S.

29. Secondary education is free up to the calendar year in which the pupil attains the age of 15. (Social and Economic Planning Council Report No. 13, p. 64.)

30. The De Villiers Commission estimated Coloured adult illiteracy at 70 per cent in 1946 (corresponding figures for Africans and Indians—80 per cent and 75 per cent). Compulsory education for European children was introduced in 1906. In 1950 it was imposed up to Standard VIII or 16 years, instead of the present Standard VII, to take effect in 1952. There have, however, been no prosecutions of parents failing to observe this compulsion, even in the case of Europeans.

31. The percentage of attendance to total enrolment is somewhat less than in the case of Europeans, though not as low as one might have expected (in 1947 Coloured attendance was 87 per cent, European 93.3 per cent and African 84.9 per cent). A frequent reason for such absenteeism is suggested by the following report of the Lamberts Bay School: '117 children attend school. The attendance . . . is bad; the principal stated that his roll decreased when the canning factory is busy (September–May), hence he desired compulsory education.' (C.A.C. Report, 1943–4, p. 18.)

32. These school boards have usually administered both Coloured and European education in the Cape, and have had some Coloured members (school boards being elected by parents on the municipal voters' roll). Under Ordinance No. 11/1945, however, provision was made for the establishment of Coloured Education Committees in districts where the board was unwilling to administer Coloured undenominational education. Such committees exist in Robertson and Worcester, and the

Mayor of Parow, Nationalist Whip Dr. P. J. van Nierop, recently called for the application of *apartheid* to school boards after the Administrator of the Cape had appointed a Coloured member to the Board. (See *Cape Times*, 20th February, 1951, 22nd February, 1951 and 14th March, 1951.) See also *Torch* (6th November, 1950) for Coloured opposition to a suggestion for a 'Co-ordinating Committee for Coloured Education' in Port Elizabeth.

33. Cradock (January 1947); Kimberley and Simonstown (July 1949).

34. 57,833 in 1925, 84,821 in 1935, 163,013 in 1947 (C. Ed. S.), and 189,897 in mid-1951 (figure supplied by the Cape Provincial Education Department). See forecast by the Administrator of the Cape that every Coloured child of school-going age would be in school within the next ten years if the tempo was maintained. (*Cape Times*, 16th November, 1950.) The Cape Educational Amendment Ordinance of 1950, which prohibits the employment of European children under the age of 16, does not apply to Coloured children.

35. V. s. 1941–2. This figure was also mentioned by an official of the Cape Provincial Administration as the approximate number of Coloured children of school age in the Cape who were getting no schooling at all. (*Cape Times*, 12th October, 1949.)

36. 'There are many excellent men managing schools to-day. It is no exaggeration to say that no Coloured man could or would do more than they; but this system is also open to abuse. Schools are established for the education of children. Is it fair that a manager should be able to threaten the principal of a school who found it impossible to give a school concert to raise funds for the Church that he would dismiss two teachers and 100 children unless money was raised in some way? Yet this actually happened less than three months ago.' (Mr. E. F. Doman, speaking at the first National Coloured-European Conference in 1933).

37. In the mid-thirties, the majority of managers who answered the Cape Coloured Commission's questionnaire on the aims of Coloured primary education thought that the main aims of Coloured primary education should be, in this order: religious and moral training, practical education with a vocational basis, training for citizenship, teaching the three R's thoroughly, and enabling pupils to earn a living. (C. s. 852, Q. 1.) See also Appendix R on Christian National Education.

38. Coloured school managers were asked by the Cape Coloured Commission whether they required their teachers to perform duties not directly connected with their school work. The Report states that in a large number of schools the Coloured teacher seemed to be regarded as a church worker who had to perform definite duties, especially on Sundays. For this reason, preference was given in appointments to members of the denomination concerned (s. 852).

39. The following case shows that their persons might also be threatened. In Calvinia, Cape, in August 1947, the Rev. Gerhardus Cornelius Uys, of the D.R.C. Mission Church, and Giljon Jacobus Krieling, principal of the D.R.C. Mission School, visited Mr. Joseph Johannes Carelse, a Coloured teacher at the English Mission School. The former carried a *sjambok*, and a flogging was administered to Mr. Carelse (for being 'cheeky', it is said). Mr. Carelse was awarded £110 damages plus costs against Uys in the local Magistrate's Court. The magistrate, however, held that Krieling had not participated in the assault. He also 'accepted Mr. Uys's evidence completely. The thrashing was a mere token one and was not intended to injure Carelse seriously.' Mr. Carelse subsequently appealed to the Appeal Court in Cape Town, which altered the magistrate's judgment and awarded Mr. Carelse £110 damages against Uys and Krieling, jointly and severally. (Taken from a report in the *Cape Argus*, 17th February, 1949.) Mr. Carelse is now said to be teaching at a Cape Town school under a different name, as he was no longer safe in Calvinia; he was again flogged by unknown assailants a few days after the first award of damages was made.

40. C. s. 852, Q. 15.

41. See the remarks of a school inspector quoted by Marais (pp. 273–4) '. . . it is

impossible under such a system to avoid sectarian and even unseemly competition . . . It is illogical . . . to deny to any particular church the right to operate in any particular neighbourhood if it can guarantee the minimum constituency required by the law. In crowded urban centres we have to be satisfied with the smaller schools and unsuitable buildings. A concentration of senior pupils is almost impossible because no church is willing to surrender its children at the stage of adolescence when the response to religious appeal is serious and lasting.'

42. The numbers of pupils being educated by the major churches in 1947 were: D.R.C.—36,145; Anglican—26,997; Congregational—16,646; R.C.—13,578; Methodist—12,804. The three old German missions (Berlin, Moravian and Rhenish) had 11,370 pupils between them, and there were 3,681 Moslem pupils. (C. Ed. S. 1947.)

43. The continued use of the term 'mission schools' is not unnaturally resented by Coloured people. Cf. Mr. E. F. Doman speaking at the first Coloured-European Conference held at Cape Town in 1933: 'Since our people are no longer heathen, may I suggest that the word "Mission" be substituted by "Church"?'

44. E.g., Steinkopf in Namaqualand, originally L.M.S. (1819), then Rhenish (1840), taken over by the Dutch Reformed Mission in 1934; Komaggas (Namaqualand) and Zoar in the Karroo, founded by the Berlin Missionary Society in 1817, taken over in 1895.

45. 7,992 pupils in 1934, 13,578 in 1947. (C. Ed. S. 1947.)

46. A section of Coloured teachers, mainly the better-qualified urban teachers at the few undenominational, secondary and high schools, takes the view that Non-European education is left in church hands to 'drug a people into submission' (i.e., the 'opium for the masses' argument). Cf. 'The Present Condition of Education in South Africa', by R. O. Dudley, in the *Educational Journal*, Vol. XXI, No. 2, August 1949. See also *Educational Journal*, Vol. XXII No. 1, July–August, 1950, p. 7.

47. C. s. 863, and *v.* the following passage: 'Let us take an example. A loan of £300 is raised. At 6 per cent the Provincial Council pays £18 per annum. In thirty-five years' time they will have paid £630 in interest; more than twice the value of the building. And still the payments will go on, and the building never becomes the property of the State . . . The 6 per cent system also intensifies the competition between the various denominations. There are many pseudo-shepherds who see in this scheme a fine opportunity of procuring a building for their services. There are many children crying out for admission to schools. A case is made out for the establishment of a school and a hall is erected—ostensibly as a school—in reality a church in which they may propagate their doctrines.' (Mr. E. F. Doman, speaking at the First National Coloured-European Conference, held in Cape Town in 1933.)

48. *Race Relations Handbook*, p. 357. See Johnson, pp. 12–25, for distribution of educational funds between White and Negro schools in the American South.

49. The proportionate outlay per head on Coloured and European education, while in 1947 still only in the ratio of approximately 2 : 5, has improved since 1937, when the ratio was under 2 : 7. (Expenditure on African education was less than 1 : 9 in relation to that on European education in 1937, by 1947 approximately 1 : 8.)

50. Coloured children usually have to wait a year or more past the normal age of entry before entering the pre-primary classes. (See Appendix U for comparative Coloured retardation.) The Cape Educational Report for 1947 records the introduction of double-shift classes in the De Vos Malan Coloured Primary School, Port Elizabeth, for pupils in the sub-standards (pre-primary) owing to the difficult building position (p. 24).

51. '. . . As the resources of the mission churches, provided as they are by poor Coloured people, are very limited, it can be readily understood that many extremely unsuitable buildings have been pressed into use as schools. Indeed the Committee on the Financial Resources of the Provinces (U.G. No. 9—1944) considered that

nearly 70 per cent of the accommodation, that is for about 100,000 children, would require to be replaced.' V. s. 1941. See C. s. 852 for the position in 1935. The building position has been further aggravated as a result of the war, particularly in the Cape and Transvaal (see Provincial Financial Resources Committee U.G. 9/44, s. 327–8). In 1946 the Cape voted £1 million to be spent at the rate of £100,000 p.a. on Coloured school buildings. The rise in building costs has made it impossible to build more than two to three Coloured schools a year on this basis, as a school in an urban area may cost from £40,000 to £50,000. In 1947 twelve new European and two new Coloured schools were built, and £985 was spent on the purchase of land for a Coloured primary school at Vasco, out of a total of £34,059 spent on land for all groups (C. Ed. R., 1947).

52. Following the institution of the course at the Wesley Training College, Salt River, in 1938, 128 male teachers in all had been trained by 1946. This was not even enough to meet the needs of the Cape Town schools. There were no trained women instructors, but one course was opened at Zonnebloem in 1948. As to gymnasia, there was at the same date a deficiency of 154 for even the larger European Schools, and no new requests had been considered since the beginning of the war (C. Ed. R. 1946, p. 69). An official of the Cape Education Department told me in early 1951 that this was still so.

53. 'While the old-established undenominational secondary and high schools have been able to offer courses of study which included woodwork, needlework and domestic science, the more recently established schools, owing to the impossibility of procuring essential equipment, have been obliged to offer courses of study which are purely academic.' (Cape Educational Report, 1947, p. 23.) A Coloured teacher in Cape Town stated that much schoolroom equipment was handed down from European schools, when the latter obtained more modern supplies.

54. In Johannesburg, certain book-sellers are said to apply under-the-counter measures based on pigmentation in the disposal of textbooks in short supply. One European woman told me of an African child who was quite unable to get the set books until she went into the shop where the child had been refused and bought them on his behalf. The child was the only one in his class to have the necessary books, and the teacher kept them locked up for him lest they be stolen. My informant said that his unofficial ban extended to all Non-European children. I asked whether it applied in the Cape, but she thought it less likely; so did a Cape Town Coloured secondary-school teacher whom I asked about it.

55. See C. s. 852 and 865, for the position in the mid-thirties. In 1948, the De Villiers Commission reported: '. . . although the State makes books available at half-price, the poverty of many parents is such that they cannot take advantage of this provision. The Commission is convinced that this position will only be put right by a state system of free books. It is recognised to-day that an essential part of the equipment of a school is a library, where the pupils will be able to find not only books of reference . . . but in the case of poor Coloured children whose homes are totally devoid of books of any description, even books to supplement the class readers in learning how to read. The provision of books for the school library by the State on a £1 for £1 basis fails in most cases to help Coloured schools, which are unable to raise their share in order to get a grant.' (s. 1945–6.) In 1945, 289 Coloured schools (out of 1,055) had libraries, with a total of 90,864 books. The corresponding European figures were: 1,384 schools (out of 1,507), with a total of 860,986 books. (C. Ed. R., 1941–5, p. 33.) See also *Educational Journal*, Vol. XXII, No. 4, November–December, 1950, 'The Library in the School,' by George Francis, p. 10.

56. All but well-to-do Europeans are poorly served by nursery schools in the Union. In 1947, ten such schools with an enrolment of 578 Coloured children were in receipt of grants from the administration (C. Ed. S. 1947, p. 127). At the beginning of 1951 there were over 300 applicants for thirty places at the Hyman Liberman Institute in Cape Town (*Cape Times* 2nd February, 1951). See De

Villiers Report, p. 278, s. 2117(3) for the recommendation that the State should accept responsibility for all organised pre-school education. See also article by R. O. Dudley in the *Educational Journal*, Vol. XXI, No. 2, August 1949, pp. 6–7 and annual reports of the Nursery School Association of South Africa. (P.O. Box 673, Pretoria.)

57. 'There is a tendency to have too many classes in the sub-standards, and to force all the pupils to spend a year in each class. Perhaps the worst case that has come to light is that of a Coloured school in a large town, where there were no less than five sub-standard classes, in each of which a pupil was forced to spend a year. Thus, a pupil who left school after seven years' attendance had to be content with a Standard II attainment only, whereas by proper organisation, he might have reached a considerably higher stage.' (*Race Relations Handbook*, p. 359.)

58. In 1947 in the Cape there were three special schools listed for Coloured children, six for Europeans. For the latter there were also 296 special classes for a total of 4,225 enrolled children, and 30 teachers giving special classes for 1,178 children whose speech or hearing were defective. No such classes were listed for Coloureds. (C. Ed. S. 1947.)

59. See pp. 99–100 for an account of Coloured teachers.

60. Only Coloured training institutions and schools under school boards are visited by school doctors. In his 1945 Report the Cape Superintendent-General of Education said that the scheme could not be extended until the present staff of inspectors and nurses was substantially increased. The De Villiers Report commented: 'It is a state of affairs crying out for improvement most urgently, since disease, particularly pulmonary, is rife, and crowded classrooms are the very places where it is spread.' (s. 1944.) The situation remains the same in 1951.

61. Partly counteracted by the State school feeding scheme. (See V. s. 1946 for the beneficial results of this.)

62. This is complicated by the fact that, like the British working class at the time of the Factory Acts, many Coloured parents, themselves uneducated, do not appreciate the value of education *per se*, irrespective of immediate economic gain, and prefer to put their children to work as soon as possible. A protest meeting was held in Cape Town when the City Council proposed to ban street trading by boys under 12 and girls under 14. It was said that the newspaper boys' earning in particular were relied upon to supplement a family's income, and that the ban would cause hardship. (*Cape Argus*, 1st September, 1950.)

63. For an account of apprenticeship, see pp. 76–7.

64. Social and Economic Planning Council Report No. 13, pp. 64–5. European boarding bursaries are £20 p.a. plus 52 per cent c.o.l.a., Coloured bursaries are £18 p.a. plus 52 per cent c.o.l.a.

65. Parents are sometimes helped by local efforts, and a few bursaries are provided by such associations as the Grand Lodge of Free Gardeners (Africa), which has recently established a university scholarship of £60 p.a., tenable for three years. The Combined Schools Association (Coloured) has in the ten years of its existence assisted thirty university students.

66. For the situation in Namaqualand see C.A.C. Report 1943–4, p. 15.

67. See *Educational Journal*, November–December, 1949, p. 2, and *Torch*, 3rd July, 1950.

68. See *Cape Times*, 26th June, 1950. In mid-1951, there were 1,050 Coloured students in training institutions, 5,474 receiving secondary education (Standards VII–IX), and 183,373 primary education. Comparative figures for the European group were: 1,109, 31,296, and 138,579 respectively.

69. Amongst the reasons given by school managers for the slow growth of farm schools were: the prejudice, antipathy and apathy of many European farmers, and the fact that the children were needed for work on the farms. (C. s. 852, Q. 31.) Even in 1947 there were only fifteen farm schools in the Cape, although it is probable that such schools would constitute the only chance of education for perhaps thou-

sands of children in the more remote country districts of the Cape. Cf. Johnson p. 21 for conditions on Negro farm schools in the cotton-growing areas.

70. 'Not only the importunity of the farmer who needs child labour, and in consequence does not encourage education, but extreme poverty leave their trail, in the necessity that children should work and become breadwinners at an age when the town Coloured child is receiving education.' (The Right Rev. S. W. Lavis, Coadjutor Bishop of Cape Town, speaking at the 1933 Coloured-European Conference.)

71. The special syllabus for Coloured schools was introduced in 1921. The Superintendent-General of the time described it as 'a cross between the primary syllabus for European schools and that for Native schools. While the Coloured people are rightly ambitious that their children should receive as good an education as possible, and while they resent a form of education ostensibly inferior to that provided for Europeans, it is nevertheless the fact that the education of Coloured children will prosper best with a curriculum specially adapted to their needs.' (Quoted in *Race Relations Handbook*, p. 359.) A new and apparently undifferentiated primary syllabus was announced in the *Education Gazette* of 2nd November, 1950, to be compulsory in all but African schools by 1953.

72. The simplified nature study course is accounted for by the fact that many of the children are town-dwellers, with little opportunity to get into the country.

73. C. s. 805–7.

74. For the ensuing account see *The Primary School Course*, Department of Public Education (Cape), 1946.

75. For instance, European children in Standards III and IV are taught about 'the non-European population and the missionaries', 'the aboriginal inhabitants of South Africa and their modes of living and habits', 'difficulties with the natives', and 'slavery as a world phenomenon and slavery in South Africa'. Coloured children in the same standards (unlike European children, Coloureds in Standards I and II have no history instruction), are simply taught thirty major events or dates in South African history and some elementary civics. In the latter, the European syllabus provides for the child to be taught his duties and privileges as a Union citizen, a proviso which is omitted from the simplified Coloured syllabus.

76. European children in Standards I–IV are taught about the activities of such South African types as sheep farmers; fruit farmers; mealie and grain farmers; sugar planters and forest workers. They are also taught about Native life, and how gold, coal and diamonds are obtained. Under the heading of 'Modern Conveniences' they learn about: lighting, heating, furniture, houses, cooking facilities and labour-saving devices in the home. Coloured children in Standards I and II are taught about life on different types of farms, about workers in mines, woodcutters and fishermen. The section on 'Modern Conveniences' is omitted in their syllabus.

77. In laundrywork European children are taught to wash 'small articles' such as mats and pillow-slips, Coloureds all types of washing. In domestic work proper, Europeans are taught to 'plan routine household work', to look after home invalids, to keep household accounts, pay bills and act as hostesses. Coloured children, on the other hand, learn general cleaning, how to lay a table and serve meals.

78. The Minister of Health, Dr. Karl Bremer, caused some indignation amongst white South Africans when he said in Parliament on 20th February, 1951: 'I will welcome the day when every girl from a less well-to-do family is put into service with a well-to-do family.' A correspondent signing herself '100 per cent Afrikaans Woman' wrote to the *Rand Daily Mail* on 23rd February, 1951: 'Had a statement like Dr. Bremer's come from a foreigner or an Englishman, a shout would have been raised about it . . . But from a man like Dr. Bremer it is unforgivable, because he knows that domestic service by Europeans is unknown and rightly considered *infra dig.* in this country.' (See also editorial comment of the same date.)

79. The following extract from a reading book used by both groups is said to be by no means unique: 'Look here, Caspar', said she half-angrily, 'You are a good deal too friendly with the "Hotnots". Why don't you look for work with the Town

s

Council? What sort of example are you for your children if you work for "Hotnots"? I should be ashamed if I were in your place, Caspar.' (*Te Last* by P. H. Venter, p. 7—Afrikaans reading book quoted by A. Hector in *Educational Journal*, November-December 1949, p. 4—the dialogue is between two Europeans.)

80. It would seem that the demand for secondary education is much greater than the supply. See the following passage describing the situation in Cape Town at the beginning of the 1950 school year: 'In Cape Town literally hundreds of pupils who had passed Standard VI last year were not able to gain admission to Standard VII . . . "Another High School in Cape Town is long over-due" said one irate parent whose children are still walking from school to another. "They have not even been placed on the waiting list for next year" . . . It means that the education of his children must now end and higher education and an apprenticeship would be right out of the question for them. His boys were only thirteen and fourteen and he wondered what they were supposed to do.' (*Torch*, 30th January, 1950.) The same situation arose at the end of 1950, and was finally met by the provision of four new secondary schools in temporary buildings. See the *Torch* of 12th December, 1950, the *Cape Argus* of 3rd February, 1951, and 6th February, 1951 and the *Cape Times* of 9th February, 1951, for various viewpoints in the recent controversy about the lack of Coloured secondary facilities in Cape Town.

81. 'Practically the only openings at present for pupils who matriculate are the teaching, and in the case of a very limited number, the medical profession. The Commission was informed that two-thirds of the male teacher-students drift into the training colleges for lack of any other occupation, and that many do not possess the necessary aptitude for teaching, and thus become "square pegs in round holes".' (V. s. 1,979.)

82. 'Why should they trouble to improve themselves if that is to bring no return? Why should they seek further education if the result of acquiring it is only to make them more vividly conscious of an impassable barrier to their advance?' (Professor W. H. Hutt, speaking at the First National Coloured-European Conference.) A Coloured viewpoint is put by R. O. Dudley in the *Educational Journal*, Vol. XXI, No. 2, August 1949, p. 7: 'In all Provinces, European, Coloured and Indian pupils use the same syllabuses and write the same examinations . . . Has, say, a Cape Junior Certificate earned by a Non-European boy as much value as the same Certificate in the hands of a European? Does it allow him free entry in the trades? Does it allow him to compete on equal footing with all-comers for a clerical job? When he mentions the name of the school where he was educated, supposing he has been mistaken for "white", what is the immediate reaction? We know the answer; society grudgingly allows its helots to be educated, then sets their education at nought.'

83. See C. s. 852, Questions 1, 2 and 4.

84. 'The aims of Coloured and European education should be identical.' (C. Appendix 45—Memorandum submitted by the Teachers' League of South Africa (Cape).)

85. C. Ed. R. 1946–7, p. 41. In 1950, according to information given by the Cape Education Department, 149 out of 263 Coloured matriculation (S.C.) candidates passed, as compared with the European average of 82 to 85 per cent. The best results were achieved by an Afrikaans-medium denominational school at Genadendal.

86. A particularly bad instance was noted by a Coloured committee, consisting of a minister and a doctor, which went to investigate famine conditions in Namaqualand in 1943: 'At one school the teacher showed us four cases of active Pulmonary Tuberculosis . . . All four children had high temperatures: Boy aged 12 years weighed 60 lb.; girl aged 10 years weighed 40 lb.; girl aged 11 years weighed 44 lb.; girl aged 14 years weighed 70 lb. These children were not isolated, they were attending school and were not receiving medical treatment. Cod-liver oil was issued irregularly, and several teachers complained that the supply had now ceased. Many

children in various schools stated that they never partook of breakfast and several had no supper. The average meal consisted of bread and tea with occasional stew. Green vegetables were unknown to them.' (C.A.C. Report, 1943–4, p. 14).

87. Cf. 'One means of limiting the effectiveness of education is the strategy of making education itself seen useless to Negroes. They are barred, by force if necessary, from opportunities which call for initiative in thinking, so that relatively their education tends to become a costly luxury deteriorating rapidly from non-use.' (Cox, p. 457.) Cf. the comparative intelligence test reported by the Cape Coloured Commission, which commented: 'The results do not go beyond showing that there is amongst the Coloured on the average, under present circumstances, a lower ability than amongst Europeans on the average to perform the types of mental operations tested.' Referring to the belief, repeatedly encountered, that there is some connection between scholastic ability and the amount of white blood present, the Commission stated, perhaps tongue in cheek: 'As far as is known, no investigation of a scientific nature . . . has as yet been carried out or published to test this statement.' (s. 897.) See also Social and Economic Planning Council Report No. 13, pp. 58–61.

88. C. s. 898–926.

89. 'There are still too few students who pass the Senior Certificate who are available for training as teachers. The Junior Certificate will therefore have to remain the entrance qualification for training schools for as long as the numbers taking the Senior Certificate remain low. One third-year course for the Coloured Primary Higher Teacher's Certificate at Kimberley had to be discontinued as there were insufficient students for this course.' (C. Ed. R. 1946–7, p. 42.) In 1947 the numbers of candidates who entered for the Senior Certificate Examination were: Europeans, 4,456; Coloured, 182; Africans, 187. These numbers constituted respectively 2.81 per cent, .11 per cent and .08 per cent of the total numbers of children of the three ethnic groups at school that year (*ibid.*, p. 41). N.B.—All Cape educational statistics include Indians (of whom there are not, however, very many) in the Coloured group.

90. C. Ed. S., 1947, pp. 31 and 123.

91. Like Europeans, Coloured secondary school teachers are trained by the Universities. An official of the Cape Education Department said that the system whereby some Coloured teachers work up by correspondence courses through the National Senior Certificate to an external B.A. in the University of South Africa is not entirely satisfactory. They are allowed to accumulate subjects, many of which have nothing to do with school work, and have never attended a lecture, or trained under a professor. The Department now stipulates that about half the subjects taken must be those used in school work if the qualification is to be recognised for teaching purposes.

92. 'The institutions thus find themselves in a position where their staffs have to be drawn wholly from the ranks of the Coloured teachers, and the supply of properly trained Coloured teachers is hardly adequate to provide for the needs of all the institutions. From reports which have come in it appears: i) that some of these teachers are not in possession of the required academic qualifications for the subjects they are required to teach; ii) that some of the graduate teachers in Training Institutions have had little training in subjects which are of practical value in such institutions; (iii) that the work done at some of the institutions is definitely weak.' (C. Ed. R. 1946–7, p. 10.)

93. For specialist Europeans, the following were available in 1947: Agricultural Nature Study (at one college); Art (one); Cookery and Housewifery (two); Infant School Teaching (five); Laundrywork (two); Physical Education (three). For Coloured teachers the specialised courses were as follows: Infant School (one); Music (two); Physical Education (two); Manual Training (one); Handwork (one); Art (one). (C. Ed. S. 1947.)

94. Neither was the position as regards specialised European teachers regarded

as satisfactory. It was stated in the 1946–7 Cape Educational Report (p. 6) that teachers could always be sure of posts after the initial two years' training, in view of the teacher shortage. In addition, the new salary scales were thought not to reflect the benefit of additional training sufficiently early in the teacher's professional life. The same reasons were said to hold good for Coloured teachers.

95. Hewat Training College in Cape Town, established in 1941. This is the only training college and the only undenominational institution; of the remainder, two are run by the Dutch Reformed Church (one was Rhenish until it was taken over recently), two by the Anglican Church, one each by the Roman Catholic, Methodist and Congregational Churches, while the last is inter-denominational. All these are training schools. Both the schools and Hewat Training College charges an annual fee of £6. The Junior Certificate is the entrance examination for the training schools, Senior Certificate for the college.

96. Figures taken from *Race Relations Handbook*, p. 362. Table VI. Despite this great increase, the number of Coloured teachers has barely kept up with the increased number of pupils. The same table also shows that the percentage of male teachers in the total rose from 44.2 per cent in 1930 to 62.6 per cent in 1946. This is attributed to the fact that few girls go beyond the primary standards, and those who do often find skilled or semi-skilled industrial work a more attractive economic proposition than teaching. Thus over the period 1946–48, only about 165 girls were admitted annually to teacher-training, whereas the annual intake should have been 340. (C. Ed. R. 1941–5, p. 35, and *ibid.*, 1947, p. 9.)

97. See Transvaal Education Report, 1944, p. 14.

98. The 'white mission school' legislation introduced by Dr. Muir provided for higher salary scales. The salary scales at the ordinary mission-schools, however, continued to apply to both Coloured and European teachers employed by them. A Coloured teacher can, of course, have the same or better qualifications than a European, without being entitled to an equal salary under the present system.

99. Education (Teachers' Salaries and Pensions) Ordinance (1944), amended by Education (Teachers' Salaries) Amendment Ordinance (No. 20 of 1946): 'It was ably pleaded . . . that the principle of "equal pay for equal work irrespective of colour or race" should be adopted. But the Committee as a whole felt that this principle was one of high public policy, to be decided upon by the Union Government; that, to judge by the differing rates, as between European and Coloured, recently fixed by the Union Government for the award of cost of living allowances to pensioners, the Union Government (then United Party, under General Smuts— S.P.) was not at present prepared to accept this principle . . . Even if the 70 per cent basis had been retained, the Coloured teachers would have shared proportionately in the benefits that have accrued to European teachers; the raising of the basis to 80 per cent has meant that relatively speaking the Coloured teachers have fared better than the European teachers have—and it is right that they should, since Coloured teachers' salaries have undoubtedly been too low in the past.' (C. Ed. R. 1941–5, p. 18.) In fact, as at the time of Union, the Cape was not prepared to make a determined stand for its former (at least theoretical) egalitarianism.

100. Some examples of the 1946 scales: (i) Coloured woman teacher, Scale I (primary assistants or principals of primary schools with less than twenty pupils enrolled), category (a) (Primary Teachers' Lower Certificate or other equivalent qualification)—minimum £144 rising by £16 per annum to a maximum of £320; (ii) Coloured male teacher, Scale 5 (principals of primary schools with 200–350 pupils, or of secondary schools with 20–50 pupils above Standard VI, category (c) (Primary Teachers' Higher Certificate, plus Senior Certificate plus the completion of at least half the requirements of a University degree, or Coloured Primary Teachers' Lower Certificate, plus a University degree)—minimum £320 rising by £20 per annum to £640 maximum; (iii) Coloured male teacher, Scale 11 (the highest scale—for principals of training colleges with triple classes in the first year of the course), category (f), (University degree plus successful completion of two years'

post-graduate training—the highest category)—minimum £810 rising by £40 to £930.

101. C. Ed. R., 1946, p. 20.

102. Quite a number of Cape Coloured primary schools exceed this figure, which is brought down by counting in the better-staffed high and secondary schools. For instance, in 1947 the Primary School at Beaufort West had fifty-three pupils and one teacher, the D.R.C. Mission Church at Fortuin in the Caledon district had fifty-one pupils and one teacher, the Anglican school at Nelspoort Sanatorium (for tubercular patients) had fifty-five pupils to one teacher, and the R.C. Mission School at Blaauwkopnedersetting near Kenhardt had ninety-nine pupils to two teachers. (Examples selected at random from the 1947 Cape Educational Statistics.) Staffing figures in the Provinces are apparently arrived at by dividing the total of pupils by the number of teachers, without taking into account the number on leave, employed on part-time clerical or other non-scholastic work, or unqualified to teach all forms or subjects.

103. Information supplied by the Cape Provincial Education Department in March 1951. To start a farm school, a minimum of five European pupils or ten Coloured pupils is required.

104. For example, the T.L.S.A. memorandum (Appendix 45, C.) refers to complaints of poor food and accommodation from teachers going to the country. In addition, it claims that managers often neglect to take an interest in the personal welfare of young teachers. Cf. C.A.C. 1943-4, p. 15. 'One disappointment was the scarcity of female teachers in the schools—in Namaqualand we could see that low wages and the absence of suitable living conditions and the lack of social amenities were most largely responsible.' Cf. Peter Abrahams' novel *The Path of Thunder*, *passim*.

105. In the Transvaal and Natal Coloured teachers are forbidden to belong to political organisations or to participate in political activities.

106. The Johannesburg Coloured representatives complained that, while Coloured teachers might use the Education Department's library in Pretoria, a colour-bar clause had been inserted in the constitution of the Johannesburg Public Library when the latter was taken over by the Municipality a few years before. (C. Appendix 47.)

107. This is in sharp contrast to the relations said to have prevailed in the Transvaal at the time of the Cape Coloured Commission's inquiry. See the memorandum of the Johannesburg Joint Temporary Committee of Coloured Organisations: 'The psychological effect which the European teacher has upon the Coloured child is detrimental to his race consciousness and pride. He generally regards the Coloured child as inferior and adopts a superior attitude. European teachers in Coloured schools also look down upon the Coloured teacher, his qualifications are regarded as of no value and his opinion on matters affecting the progress and well-being of the school is disregarded . . . In mixed schools (i.e., where there are teachers of both ethnic groups), Coloured teachers have to use the same latrines as the children, while European teachers only use the staff latrines. Some European principals do not hold staff meetings . . .' (C. Appendix 47.) The latest available figures (December 1948) showed that forty of the ninety-six principals of Coloured and Indian schools in the Transvaal were European, as were sixteen of the twenty-five vice-principals and 127 of the 538 teachers.

108. The S.A.O.U. in April 1950 opposed an S.A.T.A. proposal that European and Non-European teachers should be placed on a single register, as this would mean that Non-Europeans would have a share in exercising discipline over Europeans.

109. The T.L.S.A. is the more radical group, which through its organ, the *Educational Journal*, conducts a serial battle with the Cape Education Department, often on the principle that any measure emanating from the latter must be bad. T.L.S.A. members claim that although their qualifications are often better, T.E.P.A. members are usually chosen for good posts, such as the headmasterships of

Coloured schools built recently. In view of the uncompromisingly critical attitude adopted by the T.L.S.A., it would not be altogether surprising if this were so.

110. An article by A. C. Jordan in the *Educational Journal*, November–December 1949, p. 12, describes conditions on an O.F.S. farm school: 'The farmer had the power to call at the school any time, and demand an explanation why the pupils were being taught such things as reading and arithmetic and English; the farmer could decide any time to pick out any boy from any class, and send him an hour ahead of him to open all the gates on the road leading to town, wait at the last gate until the farmer's "express" car had passed through, and then close all the gates on his return journey, probably at about 2.30 p.m., just when the school was breaking up; the farmer could decide any day that instead of "book-learning" the whole school should go and work in one of his fields, with the teacher as "baas-boy"; the farmer could at any time induce the Inspector to remove a teacher for being "cheeky", i.e., for refusing to address him as "baas", or for speaking English, or for dressing well and never handling a spade "like the other native boys"; there were cases where teachers' wives were compelled to live apart from their husbands, because once they joined them on the farms, the farmers forced them to do menial work in the *huis*; certain farm schools were so badly equipped that the teachers used the class-room doors as blackboards, e.g., the inside face of the door for Standard I work, and the outside face for Standard II, which meant that the Standard II class must be outside the classroom.'

111. In 1950, except for Natal, where only the 1949 figures were available, the number of Coloured and European children attending school (exclusive of private schools) in the three Northern provinces was as follows:

| | Natal | | Transvaal | | O.F.S. | |
	Primary	Secondary	Primary	Secondary	Primary	Secondary
European	32,961	5,912	162,286	48,091	37,585	8,166
Coloured	6,063	228	10,799	1,147	2,673	17

112. Social and Economic Planning Council Report No. 13, p. 64, Table VIII.

113. The De Villiers Report commented on the inadequate vocational facilities at present open to Coloured children (s. 1,967), spoke of the need to establish technical schools in the larger centres and recommended the setting up of a separate Non-European vocational training institution in the Western Province. Such training would counterbalance the discriminatory effect of the present rigid apprenticeship regulations, and produce more skilled workers to meet the growing demand of modern mass-production industry. (See V. s. 1,968 and 1,980–1.)

114. V. p. 10.

115. Including continuation classes (138 Coloured pupils in 1949), and education from Standard IV at the following state-aided vocational schools: Sacred Heart Convent, Aliwal North, C.P. (girls): R.C. Mission School, Flagstaff, C.P. (girls): St. Joseph's Trades School, Aliwal North, C.P. (boys): Holy Rosary Mission, Cradock, C.P. (girls): St. James' Home, Schauder Township, Port Elizabeth, C.P. (girls): Kirkwood Domestic Science School, Kirkwood, C.P. (girls): St. Columcille's Domestic Science School, Uitenhage (girls): St. Thomas' Coloured High School, Port Elizabeth, C.P. (boys and girls): Midland Trades School for Coloureds, Graaff-Reinet, C.P. (boys): and Immaculata Secondary Vocational School, Clare Road, Wittebome, C.P. (boys and girls). These had a total average enrolment of 508 Coloured pupils in 1949 (information supplied by Union Department of Education). As may be seen, a considerable proportion are Roman Catholic. For details of the number of Coloured and European ex-volunteers trained under the C.O.T.T. scheme see *Union Year Book* No. 24, 1948, pp. 267–8.

116. Agricultural courses only at the Non-European University at Fort Hare (there were six Non-European students taking this course in 1946).

117. '. . . vocational education in all the provinces until 1925 had its origin largely in the depressed economic condition and poverty of a large selection of the European population. Its object was the social rehabilitation of the poor white youth of the country, the majority of whom left school at the end, and many even before the end, of the primary school, ill-equipped for life.' (V. s. 55.) It is instructive to compare the official solicitude towards 'poor white youth' with their indifference to the fact that the majority of Coloured children also leave school well before the end of the primary stage, even more ill-equipped for life, except that unskilled labour is regarded as their natural destiny.

118. V. s. 46.

119. V. s. 77–8.

120. In 1946, 1,372 European pupils were taking book-keeping and commercial arithmetic, 1,389 shorthand and typewriting, 226 woodwork and metalwork, 636 domestic science and 426 needlework (*ibid.*, s. 103).

121. V. s. 733–68.

122. V. s. 786.

123. The nature of the threat to the universities is referred to in the resolution on 'academic freedom' passed in 1949 by the Assembly of the National Union of South African Students (N.U.S.A.S.): 'This Assembly considers that university education in South Africa must remain free from State interference and from party-political differences; of the very essence of this freedom are the rights: (*a*) to determine who shall enter a university, (*b*) to determine in what manner classes will be organised within the university, including classes for groups of students of varying racial origin, (*c*) to appoint members of the academic staff without reference to governmental authorities, and (*d*) to conduct its courses as it sees fit, and not in accordance with any state-imposed system of thought and philosophy. That . . . the Assembly views with great concern the statements of the Rt. Hon. the Prime Minister and of the Hon. the Minister for Education that the system of *apartheid* is to be introduced into higher education and interprets these pronouncements as being directly prejudical to the freedom of the Universities and their rights as defined under (*a*) and (*b*) above.' (Res. 57, 1949.) At the Transvaal Nationalist Party Conference in 1949, one resolution was moved asking the Government to cease entirely its assistance to non-*apartheid* universities. (*Rand Daily Mail*, 5th September, 1949.)

124. 'At one of these (Opposition-controlled) universities, the student body, N.U.S.A.S., advocates equality amongst the races and does not recognise any social colour-bar. In the lecture rooms, on the sports fields, and socially, Blacks and Whites mix freely.' (Mr. J. G. Strydom, Minister of Lands, addressing Transvaal Nationalist Youth 10th Annual Congress (1949), and reported by S.A. Press Association.) This description is hardly applicable to Cape Town University, as we shall show later. As for N.U.S.A.S., there was no Non-European on the National Executive before 1951, when an Indian student, Mr. N. G. Moodley, of Durban University, was elected Treasurer and Director of Relief. No Non-European student has so far been a member of the National Executive, and the organisation has always made it quite clear that while advocating complete educational equality it had never advocated social equality. 'With regard to local functions at constituent centres, N.U.S.A.S. accepts the prevailing practice of the Students' Representative Councils at these centres. On a national level, N.U.S.A.S. recognises the right of all members to participate in all functions at its national gatherings. Therefore N.U.S.A.S. will refrain from organising any social function which might embarrass any of its members, e.g., it does not hold dances, but it may hold an official tea-party.' (N.U.S.A.S., Principles and Policy, 1949, s. 1. 155, p. 3.)

125. With this affiliation Rhodes will assume a 'parallel' structure, and move from the first into the third category of universities. In theory, there has since 1948 been a regulation empowering the Council, on the Senate's recommendation, to

consider applications for admittance to courses in Grahamstown (i.e., European courses) from Non-European students, where such courses are not available at Fort Hare, such students being required to live in approved lodgings. In fact only one such student had been admitted (to an Honours B.Sc. course in Physics) by 1951.

126. *Race Relations Pamphlet*, Vol. XV, Nos. 1–2, 1948 (pp. 60–6).

127. 'It is a condition of appointment that staff members in Durban are expected to lecture also to Non-Europeans. This naturally means the duplication of lectures, and a considerable increase in staff, which cost quite a lot.' (*ibid.*, p. 62.) Not all subjects are available to Non-European students as yet. Absent from the list are— Mathematics, Engineering, Art and the natural sciences. Medical courses became available in 1951, when well over a hundred Non-Europeans applied for about forty places.

128. On this point Dr. Malherbe adds: '. . . they can have direct access to the Principal, without having to go through a European Students' Representative Council, where they may be in a hopeless minority, and where it is possible that they may not be very sympathetically treated.' (*ibid.*, pp. 62–3.) He justifies his own experiment in the following words: 'To those blind worshippers of abstract principles, the Natal experiment may seem mere capitulation to the existing social order whatever its weaknesses may be, or a pandering to the prejudices of a section of our European population . . . But one cannot change the sentiments of a whole people overnight . . . One must temper one's idealism with a certain amount of realism . . .' (*ibid.*, pp. 64–5.)

129. In the United States only three Negro colleges (Howard, Fisk and North Carolina Negro Universities) are recognised by the American Association of Universities and Colleges (out of twenty public and sixteen private colleges). Cf. also Frazier (1), pp. 484–5.

130. For an expression of such resentment by Coloured students at Cape Town, see the following passage: 'One of the people concerned in the organising of the Annual Varsity Rag in aid of hospitals, approached a few Non-European students and asked whether they would take collection-boxes on Saturday. The students asked him why he was suddenly so "friendly" and "liberal", and why he seemed to want to include them in that holy ritual, the Rag. "Oh", came the reply, "Non-Europeans don't seem to want to put money into the collection-boxes nowadays, especially if whites are collecting. So, if you fellows collect then Coloured people will probably give to Coloured students, and Africans to African students." The reply of the students . . . is unprintable.' (*Torch*, 3rd April, 1950.)

131. Nevertheless, this cannot always shield the Non-European student from snubs in the purely academic sphere. For instance, a science lecturer who had recently arrived from England wished to give his students a practical demonstration, which entailed a visit to a nearby Afrikaans-medium agricultural college. One of the students was Coloured, and on arrival at the college, a member of the latter's staff asked the science lecturer not to bring this student along as he could not answer for the students or the staff if they should see a Coloured man in such a situation. My informant also said that he had arranged seating accommodation in cars alphabetically, so that one Coloured male student would have been in a car with white women students. 'That, however, was quickly re-arranged', but without overt unpleasantness.

132. An indication of various student attitudes was given by a third-year anthropology student, who said there was a 'minor *Broederbond*' at the University and linked this up with the recent statement by Mr. Schoeman, Minister of Labour, forecasting Nationalist counter-activity to 'liberal' attitudes in the mixed Universities. She said it was 'awkward' to talk to Non-Europeans even of the same sex, as there was always a feeling of being watched. On one occasion she got an Afrikaans-speaking student in a Paul Jones at a University 'hop', who, on learning that she was doing anthropology, burst out that she must be one of these 'damned Com-

munists' who wanted equality for the Blacks. On the other hand, an American post-graduate student spoke of attending a party given by European students at which Coloured students were present. He said, however, that most Coloured students avoided such social contacts, particularly mixed parties. A Coloured student acquaintance of his, good-looking and able to pass for white, always refused to go along to mixed parties, though he would meet European men in cafés in town.

133. Coloured alumni of U.C.T. speak of an occasion, over fifteen years ago, when an English member of the staff took a Coloured girl student to a university dance; his white students are said to have boycotted his lectures for a week in protest. The story is also told of a Coloured man who tried to join the Dramatic Society in the late 'thirties but was told: 'We're not doing Othello this year.' A common view was: 'If we step out of line or break the "gentlemen's agreement", we're made to feel that we are only there on tolerance.'

134. See Hoernlé, p. 125, and *Cape Standard* of 22nd February, 1937. Although the South African College was founded as a 'colour-blind' institution in 1827, the first Non-European student (an English-Xhosa half-caste) was admitted only in 1910.

135. One hundred and five in 1950, none taking a higher degree, as compared with 3,723 Europeans. The small number of Coloured university students is due not only to the lack of professional openings after graduation, but to the comparatively high fees for tuition. There were thirty-four Coloured students at Fort Hare in 1950, 111 taking external courses with the University of South Africa, sixteen at Witwatersrand University, and a few more at Durban and overseas.

136. A white student who went to a 1949 U.C.T. students' debate attended, she estimated, by about 3,000, on the question of continued affiliation to N.U.S.A.S., as this student organisation permitted the affiliation of Non-European student bodies, told me that feelings ran high, and that a Coloured student who attempted to speak was 'howled down'. The vote to continue affiliation was lost by ten votes, but reversed at a subsequent S.R.C. meeting. In 1950 a Coloured student was elected to the S.R.C., backed by a united Non-European vote, and the votes of a number of whites. There was apparently some trouble over a reception, which S.R.C. members attend *ex officio*. Nationalist S.R.C. members threatened a boycott if the Coloured student were asked.

137. Non-European medical students may not treat or see European patients, nor may they attend post-mortems on European corpses. A sardonic joke current in Cape Town Coloured circles concerned a Coloured student who was turned away from an operation on a European girl. He left without demur, but said to a nurse on the way out: 'I don't know why they make so much fuss. After all, she's my sister!' At the University of the Witwatersrand, Non-European candidates are not accepted for the Faculty of Dentistry nor for the B.A. degree in Fine Arts. The other Faculties, Arts, Science, Medicine, Engineering, Commerce, Law and Architecture, are open to them.

138. Cf. the recommendation of the Cape Coloured Commission (s. 949) that a separate Coloured college should be set up, affiliated to a university and possibly providing openings on its staff. To this Dr. Abdurahman (the only Coloured representative on the Commission) dissented on the grounds that it was a retrograde suggestion. In July, 1949, it was announced that the Union Department of Education was investigating the possibility of establishing a university in Cape Town exclusively for Coloured people. (*Cape Times*, 30th July, 1949.)

139. On 16th February, 1950, at a conference of Students' Representative Councils attended by representatives from Stellenbosch, Rhodes, Maritzburg, Durban, Pretoria and Potchefstroom, it was agreed without dissent to support the principle of separate facilities for Non-European students, such as exist at the University of Natal at present. The *status quo* at the mixed universities was accepted as 'temporary and regrettable'. The Universities of the Witwatersrand and Cape Town declined to send official delegates (*Cape Times*, 17th February, 1950). There is, however, a branch of the Junior Nationalist Party, the *Jeugbond*, at Cape Town,

though not yet at the Witwatersrand. This infiltration is the result of official directives to establish branches in the 'liberal' universities. As early as 1938 a body called the *Skakelkomitee van Kultuurvereenigings* sent a memorandum to the Cape Town Principal proposing university segregation. (*Cape Standard*, 12th April, 1938.) See *Forum* (4th May, 1951) for an outline of the relations between the different student bodies and organisations.

140. 'It is obvious that the Nationalists want to institute an educational system that will turn out good robot-controlled Coloured serfs. The aim is not to train people to think for themselves, but rather to stunt their intellect and to fit them for the jobs of cleaners and domestic servants.' (*The Sun*, 10th February, 1950, p. 1.)

141. Speaking at the 38th T.L.S.A. Conference (1950—p. 3 of Report) Mr. W. van Schoor said that Non-European education was a compromise between the demands of industrialists and that of the 'Boer Barons' for untrained, unskilled black labour.

142. The attitude of one Coloured teacher is given in the following passage: 'What then am I after? How do I view my job? Well here goes! I never really wanted to be a schoolteacher. Like so many of my colleagues, I was projected into this profession because the other doors were closed. At the present time I have the opportunity of getting out of it and earning more money in an equally "safe job". I have no intention of giving it up, for the simple reason that I think I am living a useful life as a teacher . . . As I view my task, my very first job is to encourage my students . . . to have a critical approach to everything. They live in a country where oppression has caused stagnation and where Herrenvolkism has a vested interest in their unquestioning acceptance of the *status quo* . . . when I speak of the "social responsiblity" placed upon them by their education, I mean that they have to help to change this country from a system of despotism into a real democracy.' (From an article by Noreen Appolis in the *Education Journal*, November–December 1949, pp. 13–14.)

CHAPTER VI—SOCIAL SERVICES—B

1. Miss Helen Keller, speaking of segregated services for white and non-white sufferers, on her recent visit to the Union. (*Star*, 30th March, 1951.)

2. U.G. 30/1944. Cf. also *Race Relations Handbook*, Ch. XVI, by George Gale; *Union Year Book*, No. 24/1948, Ch. IV; and Report No. 13 of the Social and Economic Planning Council, Ch. 8.

3. The 1921 Census Report pointed out that the European group would have shown a steady decline in relation to the rest of the population, but for the great influenza epidemic of 1918, in which about half a million Non-Europeans died, but only 10,000 Europeans (Pt. I, pp. vi–vii, 22). Cf. also Alexander Campbell, *South Africa—What Now?* (Stewart—Cape Town, 1947), p. 108. On the whole problem of health and social welfare services for a group whose decrease is desired by members of the dominant group, cf. Myrdal, pp. 161–75.

4. With the exception of mental health, which is promoted through education and through the aid of child guidance and psychopathic clinics. The latter facilities are available in Cape Town and other large urban areas, where their activities serve to demonstrate the inadequacy of curative facilities for Non-Europeans. (See Annual Report of Cape Mental Health Society for the period April 1st, 1949, to March 31st, 1950.)

5. *Race Relations Review*, 4th Quarter, 1939, Vol. VI, No. 4, pp. 14–15. For some comparative vital statistics and detailed death-rates in the Union and larger towns see Appendix H.

6. Vaccination is compulsory for all under the Public Health Act, and is carried out free by district surgeons all over the country. In the remoter areas, however, some Non-Europeans manage to escape notice. (*Year Book* No. 24, p. 154.)

7. Non-personal preventive health services are primarily the responsibility of

the local authorities (under the Public Health Act of 1919), over whom the provincial authorities exercise financial and other control, while the central Department of Public Health exercises inspectoral and advisory powers over them. These local authorities, which do not cover all rural areas of the Union, are too financially weak, except in the urban areas, to provide much in the way of public health services. (*Race Relations Handbook*, pp. 393–4.)

8. S.E.P.C. Report, No. 13, p. 92, and *Race Relations Handbook*, pp. 402–3. Cf. also *Cape Times* of 20th July, 1949, for report on the new health and social service centre at Retreat.

9. The number of maternity homes of all types available for Europeans and Non-Europeans respectively in 1946 was 151 and 10. (*Year Book*, No. 24, pp. 178–9.)

10. Particularly in rural areas, where the Department pays a direct subsidy to a small number of district nurses and midwives, to encourage them to practise in areas where they could not otherwise make a living.

11. See Gluckman Report, pp. 89 and 134–5.

12. Cape Town operates over twenty combined maternity and child welfare clinics, most of them for Non-Europeans (*Cape Times*, 12th April, 1949).

13. See Gluckman Report, pp. 45–6, and later Annual Reports of the four Provincial Education Departments. In 1948, 33,497 European and 2,101 Coloured children were examined in Cape provincial schools.

14. Cape Town provides free mass radiography at its T.B. clinics, which have segregated hours of attendance for Europeans and Non-Europeans. Such screening is compulsory for all municipal employees. It also operates free V.D. clinics. The Council subsidises a Care Committee for T.B. patients, which accommodates about sixty Coloured children who are T.B. contacts in a day nursery.

15. See Report of conditions in Windermere, *Cape Times*, 6th January, 1951.

16. Cf. *Cape Times* of 9th November, 1949, for F.O.S.A., a much smaller association which, operating on the 'help your neighbour' principle, recruits helpers as Friends of the Sick, to visit T.B. sufferers and their families. These Friends are first given lectures on hygiene, the causes and incidence of tuberculosis, and on disability aids and grants. Many are Coloured factory-workers and do their visiting in their spare time.

17. See the *Sun* of 7th April, 1950, for the formation of such a new group by former members of a Cape Town division of the St. John Ambulance Brigade.

18. *Race Relations Handbook*, p. 399, and G. Ch. XVII.

19. The few doctors who customarily practise in these areas are grossly overworked, while others who are called upon in an emergency may hesitate to enter certain unsavoury areas where they are not known. (Cf. *Cape Times* report of the death of a premature baby in District Six, 3rd May, 1951.)

20. At the time of the Gluckman Report there was one doctor to every 900 in Greater Cape Town, but only to every 8,430 in the Hay-Barkly West-Herbert area (*op. cit.*, p. 86). The average in 1948 seems to have been in the neighbourhood of one doctor to every 2,500 of population (5,220 medical practitioners and 806 specialists). The shortage of dentists was even more acute (854 in 1948). The 1948 figures are taken from *Year Book* No. 24, p. 170. In the *South African Medical Journal* of 12th May, 1951, Dr. C. M. Grundlingh complained of an over-production of medical men, but his main argument was based on Johannesburg figures.

21. In 1948, there were 408 district surgeons in all, of whom only forty-one were whole-time officers (*Year Book* No. 24, p. 143).

22. By 1946 there were eighty-two such societies, with a total membership of all races of 43,110 (*Year Book* No. 24, p. 204).

23. *Race Relations Handbook*, p. 400.

24. Such detached services are subsidised at 100 per cent of approved net cost by the Union Government.

25. For the historical background to this development see G. Ch. XIV.

26. G. p. 64, s. 37.

27. Of whom about 3 million were tribalised Africans, many of them not 'hospital-minded'. European and Non-European patients have long been segregated, either in separate wards or separate buildings. In Non-European hospitals, Coloured and Asiatic patients are usually segregated from Africans in different wards, with nurses of their own or the White group to attend to them. According to information given by the Union Department of Health, no standard rates of expenditure have been laid down for hospital buildings and equipment for patients of different racial groups, but costs of Non-European hospitals tend to be lower, though not markedly so. This is borne out by eye-witness impressions of Non-European hospital accommodation, which usually seems more simple and austere than that provided for Europeans. In Port Elizabeth, however, two official visitors reported to the Hospital Board that for the purposes of Non-Europeans the newly-built Livingstone Hospital was 'palatial' and 'much too elaborate', apparently on the grounds that it provided too great a contrast with their ordinary living conditions. (*Cape Times*, 26th July, 1951.)

28. See *Year Book* No. 24, pp. 178–80 for hospital statistics. 3,568 beds of the meagre provision for Non-Europeans, in this case mostly for Africans, were provided by the seventy-eight private mission hospitals operating in 1946, many of them in areas such as the reserves where no hospitalisation would otherwise be available. The ratio of beds to population aimed at 'in all civilised countries' for general medical and surgical cases is 1 : 200. This has almost been achieved for the European group. The Hospital Survey Committee (U.G. 25/1927, pp. 1–2) recommended a non-European ratio of 1 : 700 outside the Western Cape area. Both ratios were passed in Natal by 1941, but nowhere else. Provincial ratios were as follows: Cape—European, 1 : 255—Non-European, 1 : 894; Natal—European, 1 : 111—Non-European, 1 : 625; O.F.S.—European, 1 : 256—Non-European, 1 : 1,319; Transvaal—European, 1 : 217—Non-European, 1 : 920. In 1941, the Gluckman Commission calculated that the Cape Province required nearly 4,000 additional beds to make up a ratio of 1 : 200 for Coloured (and Asiatic) patients, and 899 more beds to meet similar ratio for Europeans (G. p. 68.) There has, however, been great progress in improving the ratio over recent decades (see S.E.P.C. Report, No. 13, p. 90, for comparative provincial figures). For U.S. figures see Frazier (1), pp. 586–8.

29. 1,299 beds for Europeans, 2,340 beds for Non-Europeans in 1946.

30. *Cape Times*, 29th January, 1951. In the year 1949–50, 380 Non-European children under the age of 2 died of diarrhoea and enteritis in Cape Town. This was nearly 10 per cent of all Non-European deaths (Preliminary Annual Report of the Medical Officer of Health).

31. Four thousand sick persons were turned away from six Cape Peninsula hospitals during nine months of 1949, while Groote Schuur had a waiting list for the orthopaedic section alone of 700, over half of them Non-European. Cf. also *Cape Times* of 29th January, 1951, and 9th February, 1951.

32. See *Race Relations Handbook*, pp. 405–6, for details of free hospitalisation arrangements in the four provinces. In general, nearly all Non-Europeans, being in the lower-income groups, get free hospitalisation.

33. At the end of 1945 the accommodation for Europeans was overcrowded by 17.4 per cent and for Non-Europeans by 42 per cent; in addition it was admitted that at least 200 Europeans and 700 Non-Europeans who should have been in institutions were at large, unable to obtain admission (S.E.P.C. Report, No. 13, p. 91). At Valkenburg hospital (all races) then there were one-third more patients than could be accommodated comfortably, with a waiting list of 170, mainly Coloured men. (*Cape Times*, 15th October, 1949.)

34. *Year Book* No. 24, pp. 159–62.

35. See *Cape Times* of 19th November, 1949.

36. *Year Book* No. 24, pp. 149–51. The total was made up of seventy-five Europeans, seventy-six Coloured and eight Asiatics. Another 3,000 or so persons were known and discharged cases of arrested leprosy.

37. While the European death-rate from tuberculosis is 32.5 per 100,000, and thus comparable with that of other civilised countries, the Coloured rate is 500, that for Asiatics 250 (attributable to their higher standard of living), while the available death-rate for urbanised Africans in the larger towns is over 800 per 100,000. (*Year Book* No. 24, p. 155.) See Appendix H for detailed urban death-rates.

38. *Ibid.*, p. 154.

39. *Race Relations Handbook*, pp. 404–5. This also lists the major T.B. hospitals operated by all authorities. In 1947 there were 1,000 beds for Europeans, over 3,000 for Non-Europeans. More have since been provided but a shortage of nurses is holding up large-scale developments (cf. *Cape Times*, 13th June, 1949).

40. According to information supplied by the Union Department of Education, there were available in mid-1951 in all categories of hospitals (i.e., Government, local, mission, etc.) the following beds: For Europeans—1,114, Asiatics only—300, Coloureds only—233, Africans only—887, mixed Non-European—3,995.

41. *Cape Times*, 11th September, 1950; article by John Dronsfield on 'Fighting T.B. among Cape's Non-Europeans'. A new sanatorium which will ultimately accommodate 500 patients was opened on 8th May, 1951 in Cape Town.

42. *Race Relations Handbook*, p. 406.

43. They do not, however, give anything like a full picture. No separate figures are available for Coloureds. About this one disease statistics relating to Africans are more reliable than for Europeans, as routine examinations are conducted at pass offices and mines. A former Venereal Diseases Officer for the Union estimated the incidence among urban Africans at 25–30 per cent, much of it latent. Surveys carried out in a rural and an urban area amongst African school children showed an incidence of just over 23 per cent in both cases (G. p. 96, s. 18).

44. Cf. G. p. 97. The Commissioners also pointed out that health services in the Union are not organised on a national basis, are not in conformity with the modern conception of health, and are not available to all sections of the population; they recommended the creation of a free and unified national health service in respect of all except promotive aspects of health; to be in operation by 1955 at an annual cost of £20.5 million, well over half of this sum to be provided by an annual tax of 4 per cent on all incomes over £240. (See G. Parts III, IV and V, and *Year Book* No. 24, pp. 139–43.)

45. G. pp. 26–7, s. 1.

46. Occupational therapy is available only at the larger general hospitals, mental and T.B. hospitals. We have already commented on the deficiencies of all vocational training for Coloured people in Ch. V. In 1948, only four occupational therapists were registered for the whole Union. (*Year Book* No. 24, p. 170.)

47. Mention has already been made of the C.O.T.T. schemes available to all ex-servicemen. In addition, sheltered employment had been made available to 1,056 Europeans and 772 Non-Europeans by 31st March, 1949; there is one Coloured settlement for married, unfit ex-volunteers and civilians at Kraaifontein near Bellville, Western Cape, with twenty-six families with a total of 151 individuals in residence; and a settlement (said to be for all races) at Eersterivier near Cape Town (1937–49 Report of the Department of Social Welfare, Ch. VII.) See this Report, p. 102, s. 4 for a report of the Coloured Vocational Training Corps for ex-soldiers. This was closed down in the middle of 1949, after more than 500 trainees had passed through it. The European Corps, which had trained over 300 persons by the end of 1948, was in October 1949 made available to civilian applicants.

48. For instance, the State pays out over £300,000 annually on blind pensions (*Year Book* No. 24, pp. 220 and 222), £39,324 of it on Coloured blind, but only about £3,000 per annum on prevention (*Cape Times* of 20th February, 1951, article by H. H. Kelly) and a further £50,000 to registered societies for augmentation of blind persons' wages, maintenance costs, salaries and capital expenditure (Report of the Department of Social Welfare, 1937–49, p. 111).

49. The total may be much larger, as not all blind Africans are aware that by

registering they can get a state pension. See also Dr. P. H. Boshoff, 'Blindness and Diseases of the Eye in South Africa,' *S.A. Medical Journal*, 12th May, 1945; in this article the incidence of blindness amongst different ethnic groups is estimated as follows (per 100,000): Europeans 81.06; Coloured 127.74; Africans 400; (in the N.W. Cape, W. and N. Transvaal the figures for Africans are worse, being between 1,000 and 2,000 blind per 100,000 sighted and partially sighted). For somewhat different figures, higher in the case of Europeans and Coloureds, lower for Africans, see Report of the S.A. National Conference on the Post-War Planning of Social Welfare Work, 25th–27th September, 1944 (published by the Union Government, 1945), pp. 175–80. This also contains a suggested welfare programme for the blind. Much of this blindness would be preventable if medical facilities were available, but continues to spread unchecked. The Order of St. John is building an Ophthalmic Hospital at Orlando, Johannesburg; this will be the first of its kind in the Union, which at present also has no ophthalmological post-graduate school. The hospital will serve all races; its Non-European sections will be staffed by Non-European nurses, except for a small European supervisory staff, and possibly by Non-European doctors, when available.

50. Figures from Report of the Department of Social Welfare, 1937–49, pp. 111–2.

51. Only 200 blind Europeans and three Africans are at work on the open labour market. (*Cape Times* article of 20th February, 1951.) Unfortunately no figures were given for Coloured blind.

52. See *Year Book* No. 24, pp. 351 and 354 for details.

53. By 1951 special training was available for 500 European and 540 Non-European deaf children (*Cape Times* of 19th April, 1951, reporting the Secretary of Education).

54. On the care of epileptics, see *Race Relations Handbook*, p. 427; *Year Book* No. 24, pp. 219, 227, 351–4; Post-War Planning of Social Welfare Work Report, pp. 90, 173, 203–6, 226; Department of Social Welfare Report, 1937–49, pp. 102–3.

55. Orthopaedic training courses are not available for Non-European nurses in South Africa, but the Cape Cripple Care Association recently gave a bursary of £100 each to a Coloured sister and staff-nurse to study in England.

56. For details of cripple care in the Union see *Year Book* No. 24, pp. 223–7.

57. Coloured and other Non-European medical students were first allowed to qualify at the University of Cape Town in 1938. In that year, too, the training of Coloured nurses was begun. Wentworth Medical School for Non-Europeans was opened in 1951 as part of the University of Natal.

58. The European director of a large Non-European hospital in the Transvaal told me that the medical staff consisted only of Europeans, 'as we can't have European nurses taking orders from Non-European doctors'. The staff were strictly segregated into ethnic groups, Non-European nurses and European doctors not being allowed to participate in sports together, or to mix socially, the former 'not being ready for it yet'.

59. During the 1950 session the Minister of Health introduced a Nursing Amendment Bill which, *inter alia*, tried to introduce a colour bar into the Board of the S.A. Nursing Association, and into the S.A. Nursing Council. There had been no official demand for this from European nurses, and the Council asked that the Bill be postponed, pointing out that despite the disparity in wages, all nurses paid the same subscription, and were compelled to belong to the Association by the 1944 Nursing Act, which contained no colour bar, while the Western Province Branch of the S.A. Nursing Association passed a resolution condemning the proposed amendment. The Bill was dropped for the 1950 session. (*A Survey of Race Relations, 1949–50,* pp. 35–6; *Hansard*, 30th March, 1950, col. 4008 f; and *Torch*, 13th February, 1950.)

60. *Race Relations Handbook*, p. 409.

61. *Year Book* No. 24, p. 170.

62. *Cape Times*, 30th January, 1951.

63. See *Race Relations Handbook* for 1947 figures, no later ones being available. Salaries vary according to the province. See also Cl/IV, Annexure D, for actual and recommended scales a year earlier. By way of example, the salary offered for a qualified Coloured midwife as a district nurse in the Worcester district (W. Cape), was £72 × 6 — £120 per annum, plus £80 cash allowance and cost-of-living (*Torch*, 9th January, 1950), while a Non-European staff nurse in the Cape got £96 × 6 — £120 plus free board, quarters, laundry and uniform, in 1947.

64. There are facilities at the Somerset Hospital in Cape Town for training twelve Coloured male nurses at a time, but only two men have so far enrolled. The course takes three and a half years, and is on the same level as that prescribed for European male nurses, but the Coloured salary is lower.

65. The 'social security' services, as generally understood, are only a part of social welfare. In its widest interpretation, social welfare involves adequate health services, housing, and educational, cultural and recreational facilities for all groups in the community, and is also concerned with enabling each individual to develop his full potentialities and capacity for the benefit of the society in which he lives. (Cf. MacIver (2), p. 331 f.)

66. For further details see: (1) The Conference on the Social Survey, University of Cape Town, February 1942. (2) Report No. 1 of the Social and Economic Planning Council U.G. No. 9, 1943. (3) Report by the Committee on Social Security (U.G. No. 14, 1944). (4) Report No. 2 by the Social and Economic Planning Council (U.G. No. 14, 1944). (5) Report by the Select Committee on Social Security (S.C. 10, 1944). (6) Report of the Chairman of the Inter-Departmental Committee on Social Security (B. 6061/26/9/44). (7) The Government White Paper: Memorandum on the Government's proposals concerning some aspects of Social Security (1945).

67. An old age pension arrangement for Indians (on a much lower scale than for Coloureds) was introduced in 1935. In 1944 Indians were granted approximately the same old age pension rights as Coloured, while Africans were also admitted to the scheme.

68. In his 1951 Budget speech, the Minister of Finance forecast considerable increases in the free income allowed to pensioners, plus a bonus on the pension itself. The maximum pensions are for persons living in cities. Pensioners in towns and rural areas get lower amounts. From *Hansard* (6th February, 1951, col, 705–8) we learn that the average pension paid out to pensioners of each ethnic group and the number of such pensioners in 1950 was as follows: Europeans—(69,772)—£62 5s.; Coloureds —(36,098)—£24 17s.; Indians—(5,258)—£23; Africans—(197,170)—£6 4s. The figures for old age pensions given in the *Race Relations Handbook*, p. 424, do not tally with the *Year Book* figures.

69. There are no provisions for war veterans' pensions for Africans, but *ex gratia* allowances are made on the same rates as old age pensions. As at December 1948, 2,300 Africans received such allowances, averaging £7 each (*Year Book* No. 24, p. 222).

70. *Year Book* No. 24 p. 230. See also *Race Relations Handbook*, p. 424.

71. European average, £106 13s.; Coloured and Indian average, £26 13s. (Hansard, 6th February, 1951, cols. 705–8.)

72. Europeans—£64 6s.; Coloured—£25 14s.; Indians—£23 11s.; Africans— £6 9s. (*Hansard, ibid.*)

73. *Cape Times*, 23rd July, 1949.

74. *Race Relations Handbook*, p. 425.

75. This possibly accounts for the somewhat higher average blind pensions paid in the case of the three Non-European groups in 1951: (Coloured—£29; Indians— £27 1s.; Africans—£6 17s.). The European average was, however, slightly lower (£61 5s.)—*Hansard, op. cit.* Blind pensions were increased early in 1951, by £1 a month for Europeans as from 1st April, by 10s. a month for Coloureds and Indians, and 5s. a month for Africans; the rises for the Non-European groups were

to come into effect three months after the European rise. (*Sun*, 11th May, 1951.)
76. Paras. 26 and 147.

77. A minimum parental income was stipulated in order to ensure that people did not relinquish remunerative work, while persons who are able to work but are employed receive £1 less for every £1 by which their income is lower than a certain minimum (£60 per annum for Europeans in cities, £57 for Coloureds). 1937–49 Report of the Department of Social Welfare, pp. 69–71. According to *Year Book* No. 24 (p. 209), the minimum for Coloureds is £51, not £57.

78. Two other forms of social security confined to 'workers' under the definition of the Industrial Conciliation Act are described in Ch. V; they are unemployment insurance and workmen's compensation.

79. A reason given for this discontinuation was the great number of Indian applications, of which many 'had to be treated with the greatest care.' (1937–49 Report of the Department of Social Welfare, p. 69.)

80. *Ibid.* This is a fine example of the blatant inequality of the Union's social services.

81. See Edna Parlo, '*A Contribution to the Study of Family Allowances in Cape Town*' (unpublished thesis in the University of Cape Town Library).

82. 87.29 per cent. All but three Coloured families were from the Cape, and 738 of the European families; of the total of 943 European families 87.17 per cent were rural. (See 1937–49 Report of the Department of Social Welfare, pp. 68–71, on family allowances generally.)

83. It was in this year that a separate Department of Social Welfare was first established, with an initial budget of £650,138, which by 1949–50 had risen to £4,672,000. Prior to that the various social security allowances were administered by other departments.

84. See 1937–49 Report of the Department of Social Welfare, pp. 71–7, for details of maintenance grants.

85. They were higher for abnormal children.

86. More recently, however, the Child Life Protection Society in Cape Town complained about the increasing difficulty of finding Coloured foster-parents (see the sharp editorial comment on the disparity in this and all other allowances in the *Sun* of 16th March, 1951).

87. The ration scales are generally recognised as 'not sufficient for minimum subsistence' (*Race Relations Handbook*, p. 431).

88. Revised Memorandum on Poor Relief, issued by the Department of Social Welfare in 1945.

89. For instance, physical disabilities and mental disorders were responsible for pauperism in the case of 55.3 per cent of all beneficiaries dealt with in Cape Town in 1947. 20 per cent of all cases were actually the result of tuberculosis (1947 Report of the Cape Town General Board of Aid, p. 13).

90. '*Poverty and Poor Relief*' (Report Series No. 4, December 1943, issued by the Cape Co-ordinating Council of Social Welfare Organisations), p. 24.

91. *Race Relations Handbook*, p. 432.

92. In 1946–7 there were 12,463 beds for Europeans and 3,871 beds for Non-Europeans in 209 charitable institutions. (*Year Book* No. 24, p. 199.)

93. On the social aspects of housing see also Report (Series No. 7) issued in August 1945 by the Cape Co-ordinating Council of Social Welfare Organisations.

94. Butter is sold at reduced prices in urban centres to needy Europeans and Coloureds (Indians and Africans are excluded from this scheme). For further details of all these social welfare services see *Year Book* No. 24, Ch. V, *Race Relations Handbook*, Ch. XVII, and 1937–49 Report of the Department of Social Welfare, *passim*.

95. On the status of the social worker in the Union, see Post-War Planning of Social Welfare Work Report, pp. 116–21. This emphasises the sense of frustration induced by the palliative nature of most social welfare services, and the subordinate

level of the work which qualified social scientists are usually given. See also Report of the Departmental Inquiry into the Training and Employment of Social Workers (U.G. 13/1950) and the Institute of Race Relations' evidence before this Committee (R.R. 133/48).

96. In recent years many European voluntary workers have, however, come forward to work amongst Non-Europeans, particularly in the large cities. Only a decade ago, however, Professor Batson commented upon the unpopularity of such work amongst Cape Town Europeans ('The Social Services: Discrimination and Counter-Action', *Race Relations*, 2nd Quarter, 1940, vol. VII, No. 2). Even to-day, many avoid it, perhaps because of the inconvenience and even hazard involved in visiting unsavoury areas, particularly at night.

97. U.G. 15/1940, p. 20.

98. *Race Relations Handbook*, p. 439. According to *Year Book* No. 24 (p. 189) there are now 2,500 private welfare organisations, not including the social welfare committees in the various churches. State aid through grants to institutions was lower for the Non-European groups because there were fewer institutions.

99. Even here, there has been constant opposition from many whites, on the grounds that non-whites are being 'pampered', 'pauperised', or turned into 'won't-works' living in idleness on their allowances (see Report of the Commission appointed to investigate the operation of the Unemployment Insurance Act of 1946, tabled on 15th March, 1949).

CHAPTER VI—SOCIAL SERVICES—C

1. U.S. Department of Justice brief to the Supreme Court quoted by S.A.P.A. U.P. and reported in the *Cape Times*, 8th October, 1949.

2. Act 29/1909, Act 30/1930, Act 7/1946, Act 12/1949—The last extended the provisions to the rest of the Union where Coloured mission stations and reserves had formerly been administered by the Department of Native Affairs. See also *Race Relations Handbook*, p 553, and M. p. 10. There had been previous unsuccessful attempts to enforce general compulsory residential segregation. In 1938 the Cape Provincial Administration prepared a draft ordinance providing for spatial segregation of Coloured people, which was opposed unanimously by the Cape Town City Council, and provoked a large-scale demonstration in Cape Town, organised by the left-wing National Liberation League (Roux, p. 365). About the same time, the Nationalist Party made Coloured segregation a main plank in their election platform and the Fusion ministry (U.P.) adopted a milder segregation scheme based on the local option plan, which would 'peg the present position'. The latter again provoked a large Coloured protest meeting in Cape Town which ended in violence. (Walker, *A History of South Africa*, pp. 639–40.)

3. On the subject of Coloured housing and living conditions in Cape Town generally, see the *Cape Town Social Survey, passim*, and *The Cape Coloured People To-day*, p. 33. The general pattern of Coloured housing in Cape Town, Johannesburg and other major cities is that of other working-class and lower-income groups in European cities. It is the pattern of rapid urbanisation, of the decline of merchant-class residential suburbs into over-crowded slums, of industrial development and the consequent eviction of the central slum-dwellers, of the growth of shanty-towns on the outskirts of the urban areas to house those evicted slum-dwellers, of the influx of newly-urbanised groups, and so on. The problem is not in essence one of colour, but is accentuated by the fact that the group most in need of housing is deprived of political power by reason of its pigmentation, and is consequently less able to demand alleviation of the conditions in which it lives. The shortage of housing is universal in South Africa's urban areas, and naturally presses most harshly on the under-privileged non-white groups. In Cape Town, over 9,000 Coloured families, or 45,000–50,000 persons, were waiting for homes in February 1951 (*Cape Argus*, 8th February, 1951). In Johannesburg, where four-fifths of the Coloured population of about

T

32,000 are estimated to be living in slums (*Race Relations News*, October, 1950), over 700 Coloured (including some Indian) families were estimated to be facing ejection in early 1951 as a result of industrial development (*Star*, 9th March, 1951).

4. Such clauses are the product of growing white race-prejudice, with its economic consequence that property values are reduced whenever Non-Europeans move into an area. See letter headed 'Coloured Penetration' in the *Cape Times* of 14th July, 1949.

5. *Die Burger* on 14th September, 1949, published a letter from a Mr. Cyrus Smith in which the writer gave an account of the mixed residential areas, whites living in the same house as Coloureds and children playing together, mixed marriages and in general corrupting influences. The letter ended by quoting the words of 'a white mother': 'I am an Afrikaner mother who loves her children. It was my ideal to give them all something that would make them feel proud of their national life. Here I live amongst these Coloureds in the same flats. Everywhere around me and my children is poverty, equality, dissipation, drunkenness, fighting and cursing. What is going to become of my children? May God hear my prayers. May God rescue our people.' Non-European enclaves in European areas are now generally known as 'black spots'.

6. 'From the bitter experience of conditions when they (Europeans, Coloureds and Africans) lived side by side we decided they would be happier and better citizens if they lived apart and we therefore decided to allot a separate locality to each race. This process of natural separation proved a great success in every respect.' (Councillor A. Schauder, J.P., *The Evolution and Development of Municipal Housing Schemes in Port Elizabeth*, p. 3—address reprinted by the Port Elizabeth City Council Housing Committee.) When the United Party proposed its 'voluntary colour segregation policy' in March 1939, however, as a counter to determined Nationalist propaganda demanding the abolition of the Coloured franchise and a ban on the employment of Coloureds in industry and commerce, thousands of Coloured people in Cape Town reacted by marching on Parliament in a mass demonstration which was finally broken up by the police with some violence (see daily press of 28th March, 1939).

7. For methods of financing such schemes see Annual Reports of the National Housing and Planning Commission. A correspondent in *Die Vaderland* of 18th August, 1950, complained that town councils were giving more consideration to the housing of Non-Europeans than to the needs of less-privileged whites.

8. See Annual Reviews of Council Activities issued by the Mayor of Cape Town for new housing projects.

9. Annual Report of the Medical Officer of Health, Municipality of Kimberley, for the year ended 30th June, 1950, pp. 76–7.

10. See report of a meeting in the Gleemoor Town Hall, Cape, on 12th October, 1950 (*Torch*, 23rd October, 1950); also *Rand Daily Mail* (11th December, 1950) for the views of a Johannesburg Coloured organisation.

11. The enabling statute is Act 25/1945.

12. See the Location Regulations of the Municipality of Graaff-Reinet, approved by the Cape Provincial Administration on 24th November, 1949. *Inter Alia* registered holders are forbidden to have visitors or lodgers other than their wives and families without the Superintendent's written permission, may lose their permits if they are out of work for more than one month, or work outside the area of the Council's jurisdiction for more than one month, may not convene or address public meetings within the location without giving the Superintendent twenty-four hours' notice, nor collect money for other than church purposes without such notice, may not keep dogs nor hawk any merchandise or produce other than milk without a permit, etc.

13. See C. s. 969. Such restrictions here and elsewhere do not apply to Coloureds or other Non-European domestic servants living on their employer's property. Nor

apparently is there any suggestion that intensified residential *apartheid* should apply in such cases.

14. C. s. 976.

15. See C. s. 968. There was a further restriction in these two provinces on land-ownership by Coloured women married (by European law or Asiatic rites) to Asiatics, who were included in the definition of 'Asiatics' under the terms of the Asiatic Land Tenure Amendment Act (No. 53 of 1949). In the Group Areas Act (No. 41 of 1950), Coloured women married to or cohabiting with Africans are included in the African group for the purposes of this Act. The Governor-General is also empowered to single out ethnic, linguistic, cultural or other groups from amongst the African or Coloured groups for the purposes of this Act, though it is not specifically stated, unless by implication in s. 3 (4), that Coloured women married to or cohabiting with men belonging to such a group will be treated as members of this group under the Act.

16. And possibly under the terms of Ordinance 11/1926, which empowered municipalities and village councils to assign segregated areas to different racial groups (*Race Relations Circular*, RR. 234/49).

17. According to the housing survey of Johannesburg's Western Areas completed early in 1950, the proposed transfer of the Non-European population elsewhere would necessitate finding accommodation for 16,154 African families and nearly 2,000 Indian, Coloured and Chinese families. To move the Coloureds alone two new townships would have to be built, one sub-economic of about 804 homes, the other economic of about 471 homes (*Star*, 14th March, 1951).

18. Figures from the *Rand Daily Mail* (9th November, 1950). Other details supplied by the Director of the Municipal Department for Non-European Affairs, Mr. L. I. Venables, in November, 1949.

19. Protea is a Coloured home-ownership township fifteen miles from the city centre, developed by private enterprise over the last few years. It has 3,200 residential plots, on which owners may erect their own houses of a minimum value of £400. (For further details see the *Star*, 4th October, 1948 and the *Industrial Review* of November 1950.)

20. Following a series of proclamations in the *Government Gazette Extraordinary* on that date.

21. On 29th August, 1949, the *Cape Argus* gave the view of various officials and estate agents that to implement the Bill in the Cape Peninsula alone would involve a mass movement of about 200,000 people, at immense cost.

22. E.g., the Sidwell European Ratepayers' Association in Port Elizabeth (*Guardian*, 22nd March, 1951).

23. 'Ostensibly not discriminatory, the Bill in fact is grossly so. The administration could assign to Non-Europeans an area adequate, and more than adequate, for their needs; or it could assign an area that would be quite inadequate. Everything, therefore, would depend on the way in which the measures were administrated—ultimately therefore on the kind of political issue involved and the nature of the influence at work. In this case the issue arises out of a clash of interests between racial groups—a clash provoked to a large extent by legislation such as this—and the influences that will make themselves most felt are those of the European group. It cannot be doubted that the administration would lean heavily towards the white group. Exemplified here is the axiom that in an oligarchy the subordinate groups stand to gain more from free competition than from State control, which is why State control is instituted.' (*Race Relations Memorandum*, 67/50.) See this Memorandum for a more detailed analysis of the Act, and also *Race Relations Survey*, 1949–50, pp. 26–8. The Act is already said to be causing divisions not only between white and non-white, but between various sections of the non-white group, for separate areas are to be assigned to Coloureds, Malays, Indians, various African tribes and even Chinese, and some property-owners seem to be concerned more with their own immediate advantage than with considerations of political unity. (*Torch*, 24th April, 1951.)

24. For reasons of economy, however, all telephone booths other than those in central post offices and railway stations continue to be used by members of all ethnic groups, despite frequent protests from Europeans about this practice. (See statement by the Postmaster-General in the *Star* of 7th April, 1951.)

25. See the *Cape Times* of 11th October, 1949, for an account of the introduction of *apartheid* in the main Cape Town G.P.O. A correspondent to the *Cape Times* on 17th October, 1949, asked: 'Could anything have been designed to produce more pin-pricks for the Coloured people without any tangible advantages to anyone?'

26. Although many were so indifferent to the provisions made for their benefit that several officials were kept busy in the main G.P.O. moving Europeans from Non-European telephone booths, seats and queues.

27. *Cape Times*, 16th November, 1949.

28. See *Torch* (9th January, 1950, p. 6) for recommendation by the Mayor of Goodwood, and *Cape Times* (20th October, 1949) for recommendation of the Stellenbosch Civic Association for segregated counters for non-white ratepayers.

29. *Sunday Times* (1st April, 1951). As the estimated cost of this hall is only £3,500, the facilities which it provides will presumably be separate but not equal. A similar segregated hall is already in existence at Somerset East.

30. In Cape Town, the *Groote Kerk* Building, which houses private organisations and firms, many of them Afrikaans-speaking, has one lift for all races and one 'for Europeans only'.

31. They do not, however, always escape the bad manners and abuse of some white road-users, who apparently feel that they should have priority by virtue of pigmentation. White traffic policemen, too, are not always scrupulously objective in their duties; it is apparently natural to assume that the non-white is at fault in any accident or breach of the road code.

32. Certain sections of the Coloured middle class resent being classed with Africans in this way. See C.A.C. Reports, *passim*. The following passage, which describes conditions in S.W. Africa, is typical: 'The practice on these trains is to provide one coach for non-Europeans, and it does not really matter what class ticket a passenger holds . . . with the result that people who pay a second-class fare for the sake of comfort, convenience and privacy are often bundled up in a compartment with raw natives who hold third-class tickets. Not anywhere *en route*, nor on the train, is there any refreshment to be had for Coloured passengers; except at Keetmanshoop where a Coloured person may purchase a cup of coffee or tea at the refreshment room if he is prepared to stand at the door (for he dare not enter), until all the Europeans have been served, when (if he chances to catch the eye of the proprietor), a native boy is sent out to him to collect his receptacle and fill it with tea or coffee as he may require. So humiliating is this practice that some of us whose misfortune it often is to travel by this train, have received sufficient of the Grace of God, not to thirst until the journey ends. On the Usakos–Tsumeb narrow gauge line second-class accommodation is provided or refused to Coloured persons according to the whim or will of local officials and there is no redress. This statement may seem sweeping but we are prepared to substantiate it with facts from personal experience.' (C.A.C. 1945–6, p. 29.)

33. With the exception of internal lines in the Transvaal, where there is no third-class accommodation for whites (Hoernlé, p. 31, n. 1). A somewhat humiliating distinction is made in the issue of railway concessions to Non-European public servants (including teachers). According to the regulations Non-Europeans may be issued with third-class tickets only, but if they are neatly dressed, they may now be granted second-class berths anywhere in the Cape (*Torch*, 6th February, 1950).

34. See question asked by Senator Brookes in the House on 15th February, 1949.

35. See report of train accident on Kroonstad–Bethlehem line in *Rand Daily Mail*, 11th December, 1950.

36. In other words, Europeans who can afford to keep up their superior status by travelling first-class are given the choice of travelling in separate compartments,

but the few who cannot afford to travel other than second or third class must travel with Non-Europeans. In fact, almost all Europeans can afford first-class fares over this short distance, although some travel in the first-class non-segregated compartments, usually as an anti-*apartheid* gesture or because they are less crowded during rush hours, as only middle and upper-class Coloureds use them regularly. (See correspondence in *Cape Times* of 10th January, 1951, 24th January, 1951 and *Cape Argus* of 4th December, 1950.) Lower middle-class Coloureds travel second-class and lower-class Coloureds and Africans travel third-class. Occasionally, an apparent European is visible in a second-class compartment. The authorities are said to regard the provision of segregated accommodation in the other classes as unnecessary because of the lack of effective demand.

37. *Race Relations Survey* 1949–50, p. 35. See also p. 189.

38. Under Act 22/1917. Separate benches on platforms are also provided, and the competence of the Administration to do this was upheld in the case of Rex v. Herman, 1937, A.D. 168. In May 1950, a Coloured woman teacher was found guilty and admonished for having leant against a bench marked 'Europeans only' and for having refused to give her name and address to the police (*Torch*, 6th May, 1950).

39. '. . . *Apartheid* is a declaration of war on a section of the taxpayers, with threats of worse to come. Small wonder then that we resent it . . . The non-Europeans consider themselves co-partners in the Railways, which are the property of the taxpayer.' (Letter from 'Distinctly Coloured' in *Cape Argus*, 8th September, 1948.)

40. Motor Transportation Act No. 39/1930 as amended in 1932 and 1941.

41. With the exception of the S.A. Railway buses, on which *apartheid* was introduced on 30th January, 1950, Non-Europeans now sit at the back of single-decker buses, or in a portion of the upper deck of double-decker buses. That the interests of Coloured and other Non-European passengers are not given equal weight was shown when the old railway buses to Hermanus were replaced by luxury coaches for Europeans only. Coloureds travelling to their families in Hermanus at week-ends were compelled to take a round-about route by bus and train which took over double the time of the direct route, and left them with only one night at their homes instead of two nights and a day.

42. In a case heard before Mr. Justice Pittman at the Port Elizabeth Circuit Court in October 1938, three European women teachers testified that they walked half a mile to school rather than travel in 'all-class' buses. One said she objected to travelling with Non-Europeans on account of the plague outbreak and for 'sanitary reasons'. Mr. Justice Pittman: 'You mean the smell, I suppose?'—'Yes'.

43. Information supplied by the municipalities concerned.

44. *Cape Argus*, 15th October, 1949.

45. In late 1950, the Johannesburg Municipality was compelled to raise road transport fares. Unofficial suggestions were made that a rise in fares might be avoided if certain sections of buses and trams were set aside for Non-Europeans instead of operating separate transport. The white public's response was, however, highly unfavourable, many people declaring their readiness to pay higher fares rather than have Non-Europeans on the same vehicles (see *Rand Daily Mail* of 6th October, 1950, 10th October, 1950, and 26th October, 1950, and *Star* of 14th October, 1950).

46. See the remarks of the President of the Road Passenger Transport Association of S.A., at the 14th Annual Conference held in late March 1950.

47. Cf. *Cape Times*, 6th February, 1951, and *Cape Argus*, 5th February, 1951, and 6th February, 1951.

48. For municipal and private objections to taxi *apartheid* in (*a*) Port Elizabeth and (*b*) Cape Town, see the *Cape Times* of 25th November, 1949, 14th February, 1951 and 27th April, 1951.

49. This only affects the state-owned South African Airways, which operate all

internal air-routes and one to the U.K. Foreign-owned lines such as B.O.A.C., Pan-American and K.L.M. apply no colour-discriminatory measures to passengers in their planes.

50. For these instructions see *Rand Daily Mail* of 6th December, 1950, and 7th January, 1951. A letter of protest in the *Star* of 18th January, 1951, commented: 'The S.A.A. is a Government organisation and, unless this incredible instruction is repudiated, the Government must bear the responsibility for its issue and implications. It is bad enough that all Union non-Europeans should be officially branded unclean pariahs in the land of their birth. But since the S.A.A. operates an international air service, this instruction also implies that all non-Europeans, irrespective of class or country, are of necessity physically filthy compared to Europeans; so much so, in fact, that the ordinary processes of washing knives and forks or laundering linen are inadequate to remove the traces of their contamination. It is an unforgivable insult that such an instruction should ever have been issued, and it deserves action under the law relating to the incitement of racial tension.'

51. When I travelled from Cape Town to Southampton in October, 1949, there was a certain amount of feeling about a large and noisy troupe of fair-ground gypsies in the third-class. A Coloured teacher was, however, very popular, and served on the Sports Committee. It was noticeable, however, that he avoided dances, and other mixed social events.

52. For the superiority of European cemeteries, see Hoernlé, p. 31.

53. Acceding to a request for separate hearses from the local *Handelskamer* (Chamber of Commerce), an official of the Klerksdorp Town Council said that it was 'unhealthy and unpleasant to contemplate that a hearse which carried the corpse of a Native to the cemetery might be used the next day to convey the corpse of a European'. (*Cape Argus*, 15th October, 1949.) The *Argus* in a leader two days later described this attitude as *departheid* and asked whimsically: 'Will St. Peter provide separate counters for applicants for immortality?'

54. 'Stand back!' shouted a policeman brusquely to a group of Non-Europeans at General Smuts' funeral in Johannesburg. 'It's O.K., big boy', retorted a Coloured man with a touch of sorrow and resentment, 'to-day it is the *Oubaas*, to-morrow Dr. Malan, the day after you and I; and remember, it's a one-way street, and there will be no *apartheid* signs'. (*Race Relations News*, November 1950.) Long ago, Dr. Abdurahman said: 'The Dutch *predikants*' aim is to make the Coloured man travel in a different compartment on his journey to heaven, where there will be no colour question, and where He who sits on the right hand of His Father is not of "European descent".' (At the 9th A.P.O. Conference, on 1st January, 1912, reported in the *Cape Standard*.)

CHAPTER VII—SOCIAL LIFE AND RELATIONSHIPS

1. Schweizer, *On the Edge of the Primeval Forest*, Ch. VII, quoted by MacMillan, p. 69.

2. See Myrdal, pp. 60–7, for a discussion of the 'rank order of discriminations' amongst Southern whites, which also places most stress on the sexual and social barrier. See also Ch. IX, n. 142.

3. In former times there were two theatres at least, the Opera House and the Tivoli, which did not exclude non-whites. (*The Sun*, 24th February, 1950.)

4. See *Cape Times*, 30th August, 1949, 22nd October, 1949, *passim. Cape Argus*, 20th September, 1949—15th October, 1949. *Die Burger*, 28th September, 1949 and the *Torch*, 27th February, 1950.

5. This measure was applied to all cultural associations in receipt of adult education grants from the Department of Education. Most were forced to accept the condition, as they would not have been in a position to carry on financially without the grant. An exception was the University of Cape Town Ballet Club. See *Cape*

Times of 21st and 28th April, 1951, for the Cape Town Adult Education Council's decision to dissolve itself after the official refusal to renew the grant to the Cape Town Institute of Citizenship, and for a statement of the new policy.

6. *Torch*, 27th November, 1950; *Cape Times*, 8th November, 1950. Some months later it was claimed that the Repertory Society had lost many European members and was financially in the doldrums as a result of the colour-bar (*Guardian*, 22nd March, 1951).

7. *Cape Times*, 11th November, 1950, and 21st November, 1950. The proposed site was Hanover Street, the main thoroughfare of the central Coloured 'District Six'.

8. *Cape Times*, 10th November, 1950, and *Torch*, 27th November, 1950.

9. 'These people may only appear as amusing servants; and they will be acted by white people with blackened faces. In radio dramatic scripts, African parts may not be taken over by the skilled African broadcasters, since it is not permissible for them to be in the same studio as Whites . . . For some strange reason, dark-skinned faces are allowed in picture galleries, in spite of the shocking thought that the artist—often a woman—may have sat alone in the studio with the model . . . South Africa cannot have both art and a colour-bar . . . In this land we have material for the grandest art yet produced . . . But the colour-bar shuts it off and we are bidden to trifle with the pallid themes of middle-class conventionality'. (Letter from Mrs. J. Hertslet in *Cape Times*, 27th September, 1949.) See also letter from 'Harriet' in the *Cape Times*, 22nd February, 1951. In March, 1951, the white U.S. athlete Fortune Gordien was cast for the small part of the Negro butler in a Cape Town production of Lilian Hellman's *The Little Foxes*. (*Cape Times*, 7th March, 1951.) During the visit of the Italian Opera Company to the Union in early 1951 a correspondent to the *Rand Daily Mail* objected to the theme of *Madame Butterfly* on the grounds that it portrays sympathetically the sexual relationship between an Asiatic woman and a white man. (4th May, 1951.)

10. The board of film censors issues four classes of certificates: *A* for general exhibition; *B* for Europeans only; *C* for Europeans and Non-Europeans, including Africans (presumably *A* does not include Africans); *D* is for pictures which are not to be shown to certain other classes, e.g., children and all Africans, these two classes being sometimes grouped. Apparently films are not withheld from Coloured persons in the same way. The board is empowered to ban any film which 'depicts in an offensive manner', *inter alia*, nude human figures, passionate love scenes, scenes representing antagonistic relations of capital and labour, the drug traffic, scenes of juvenile crime, scenes of the technique of crime, of brutal fighting, of drunkenness and brawling, pugilistic encounters between Europeans and Non-Europeans, inter-mingling of Europeans and Non-Europeans. (L. s. pp. 16–17.) The film *Pinkie*, which deals with a 'pass for white' girl in the Southern States, was, however, shown recently to European audiences, possibly because the heroine finally renounces her white Northern doctor and goes back to work amongst her own people. The Customs Department has also the power to prohibit or restrict the importation of undesirable literature along the same lines, or the Department of the Interior may ban it. (L. s. 113.)

11. However, Mr. Brink, Nationalist M.P., for Christiana, spoke in the House about the 'unpleasant' position in the Art Gallery, Museum and Library in Cape Town, saying that few Europeans go because they are usually crowded out by Coloureds. He asked for separate hours of attendance (*Hansard*, 7th February, 1951, col. 825). The figures of attendance do not support this allegation.

12. In 1950, 67,986 Europeans and 31,247 Non-Europeans (including many school-children) visited the Gallery. The latter figure suggests that a large number of Coloureds are ready to take advantage of any available cultural facilities. An official said that 200 to 250 Coloureds visited the Gallery for every one African visitor.

13. Plans for a cafeteria in the basement have been held up for some time; an

official said that they could hardly refuse to serve Non-Europeans if such a cafeteria were opened, and difficulties would therefore arise.

14. When I visited the Pretoria Museum in early 1949, Non-Europeans were definitely excluded on Sunday afternoons (the only free time for many). In October 1949, however, a municipal official wrote in reply to a questionnaire that the museum was open to Non-Europeans at all times.

15. In early February 1950 the Cape Town Council refused to accept the Provincial scheme by 16 votes to 12 (*Torch*, 6th February, 1950).

16. No. 21 of 1935. As a result of the judgment in the case of Rex *v.* Carelse (1943 C.P.D. 242, 251) the regulations at the Strand were found *ultra vires* as being partial and unequal. Meanwhile an amendment to the regulations had been gazetted, so that the restrictions remained.

17. See *Torch*, 21st August, 1950.

18. Every season, the Cape papers publish a number of letters from white visitors, often from the North, protesting against the behaviour of Coloureds, usually fishermen, on that part of Muizenberg beach which is now used mostly by Europeans. On Muizenberg beach further customary segregation has arisen between sections of the European community, to the point where different parts of the beach have actually been referred to in the local press as 'Jewish' and 'Christian Beach'. The former is the main beach in front of the Pavilion and huts, while the latter has no facilities other than a vast car-park. Segregation is almost total, and will probably remain so despite the official move to rename the beaches 'First', 'Second', and so on, following a protest by the South African Jewish Board of Deputies.

19. See Report of C.P.N.U. deputation's visit to the Cape Divisional Council to ask for better camping and bathing facilities (*Cape Argus*, 23rd January, 1949).

20. The Municipality of Parys (O.F.S.) has erected a board at the entrance to a bathing-enclosure on the Vaal River which reads: 'Non-Europeans and Dogs Not Allowed.' A great many white South Africans were highly indignant when informed by their press that hotels in India were now putting up notices: 'Dogs and South Africans Not Admitted.' Citing these instances Julius Lewin wrote: 'The one difference is that in India South Africans are foreigners: in this country Non-Europeans are citizens of the Union.' (*Forum*, 25th December, 1948, p. 14.)

21. In the middle of the eighteenth century slaves were prohibited from entering the Gardens except when accompanying their owners or in charge of children. (V. de Kock, p. 98.) The latter exception still holds good in Johannesburg parks for Non-European servants.

22. On the shortage of Non-European recreational facilities in Johannesburg, see *Race Relations News*, November 1950, pp. 115–18.

23. Although it is stated that fenced parks are sometimes closed to Non-Europeans at night. In October 1950, however, the Council adopted a draft bye-law enabling it to set apart recreation grounds reserved exclusively for persons of various racial groups. (*Star*, 10th October, 1950.)

24. The greater part of the information on municipal recreational facilities was obtained from the departments concerned.

25. Bars, which are reserved for men only in South Africa, also apply strict segregation. Bottle-stores usually have a separate counter for Coloureds, who must in any case comply with certain provisions of the Liquor Act which do not apply to Europeans. The Cape Town group of Alcoholics Anonymous, an international organisation which aims at rehabilitating habitual drunkards, observes no formal colour-bar at its meetings and has had a few Coloured visitors, but only one success amongst this group so far. A small Coloured group is now being formed under white supervision, the separation being said to be at their own request.

26. Exceptions are apparently made in the case of such eminent persons as the Aga Khan and his family, who have on occasions visited Cape Town's Moslem community. According to my informant, they had the best suite at the best European hotel. One of the best hotels in Johannesburg is also said to accept distinguished

Non-European foreigners, and a well-known correspondent told me that he had on more than one occasion dined in this hotel's restaurant in a mixed party of Europeans and Non-Europeans of both sexes without any unpleasantness.

27. A Cape Town woman told me that she used to meet a well-known Coloured woman teacher there for tea some years ago, but I have never seen any Coloured people there myself.

28. A Non-European hotel, the first of its kind in South Africa, was opened in Cape Town in 1949. In a few Cape towns, private guest-houses are run by Coloureds.

29. Intercollegiate athletic contacts are reported between Rhodes University, an entirely European institution, and the affiliated Non-European College at Fort Hare, between which a general spirit of friendly co-operation is said to exist (*Race Relations Handbook*, p. 699). From another source I heard that cricket and other games in which 'it is possible to maintain social distance' are played, but not, of course, football.

30. Cape Malays are still credited by many Europeans with special magical powers. See reference to Coloured doctors in Chapter V, n. 173, and to Malay magic on p. 186.

31. At least one writer finds this belief unacceptable. (George Orwell, *Shooting an Elephant and other Essays*, Secker and Warburg, 1950, pp. 193–4.)

32. From my own observation of pre-kindergarten children playing in various Cape Town suburbs, ranging from Wynberg (middle-class Coloured and upper-lower-class white), to Muizenberg (Jewish middle-class), and even Constantia (upper-class white), I noticed that white and Coloured children (servants' children in the two latter areas) sometimes participated, usually, as far as could be judged, on equal terms, in the games. The 'little master and mistress' attitude which is said to colour such relationships in a rural area seemed to be lacking, and not to be insisted upon by the European parents concerned. On the other hand, little, if any, mingling of this kind was observable amongst older children. In one case a small Jewish boy who had played quite amicably with the Coloured servant's little girl until he went to school was heard shouting '*Hotnot*' experimentally at both mother and daughter. The sequel was perhaps not entirely typical, in that the Coloured maid slapped him hard, for which she was not rebuked by her employer.

33. It is, however, quite in order for Non-Europeans to perform before a mixed audience. A notable example is the famous Pretoria institution of semi-gladiatorial Sunday mass-fights between gangs of young male Africans, held under armed police supervision and attended by Europeans of both sexes. The primitive savagery displayed at these fights is of course not disturbing to European stereotypes concerning the inferior and barbarous African. A Coloured informant also told me that about 75 per cent of the audiences at Coloured and African fights in Cape Town were Europeans.

34. A joke was current in Cape Town to the effect that it was illogical not to ask the New Zealanders to drop their nickname of 'All Blacks'.

35. Non-European South Africans who are outstanding sportsmen are eligible as British subjects to represent the U.K.; e.g., Mr. R. Eland, Coloured weight-lifter, who represented Britain in the 1948 Olympic Games (*Cape Times*, 30th January, 1951). An informant claimed, with what accuracy I have been unable to determine, that light-coloured individuals who excel at sports have been encouraged to 'pass' at schools, universities and clubs in order that they might be included in European teams.

36. See letters in the *Rand Daily Mail* on 5th and 13th July, 1951, and leader on 9th July. In the latter letter a Coloured man is quoted as saying: 'I fought for my King and Country. But my country *wil my nie he nie* (does not want me). Therefore I booed my country to-day.' For the somewhat different position as regards international table tennis, see p. 155.

37. Attempts made to ascertain the whereabouts and addresses of Coloured sports associations in the Western Cape, unlisted in the telephone directory, from

secretaries of European associations, met with complete failure. A Coloured informant claimed, however, that informal Sunday tennis and cricket had been played and that Europeans used Coloured cricketers for nets practice at Newlands. Coloured boxers are also used as sparring-partners by whites (*Torch*, 2nd October, 1950), although the formation of a Commonwealth Boxing Board of Control is said to be held up by the (European) S.A. Board, which, according to an editorial in the magazine *Fight* (October, 1950), has threatened to withdraw from any such body should the latter insist on 'mixed' fights. (*Torch*, 13th November, 1950.)

38. The poorer facilities for sports and recreation available in Coloured schools and residential districts constitute a further discrimination. In addition, complaints are often made in the Coloured press about discrimination in the provision of municipal sports facilities. For instance, Coloured athletes who hired Green Point Track on Thursday evenings were forbidden to use the showers. Moreover, European footballers were said to be monopolising the ground, although Coloureds were not admitted at all when Europeans had hired the ground. (*Sun*, 6th April, 1949.) See also *Torch* of 17th April, 1950, and 29th May, 1950, for protests by Coloured soccer and cycling associations. On 26th April, 1951, the City Council adopted a recommendation that the track should be handed over to the Coloured community when the new stadium and fields on Green Point Common had been completed, thus accepting the principle of separate sports facilities.

39. An unpleasantness occurred some years ago at Newlands Ground in Cape Town when the referee's brother was refused entrance to the European seats on the grounds that he was a Coloured man. The Western Province Rugby Union is said to have opened the enclosure to all races after this incident (Minister of the Interior, speaking in the House of Assembly, *Hansard*, 25th May, 1949, col. 6492).

40. This was the case in Durban until early 1950, when the Turf Club announced that it would no longer issue permits to Indians and Coloureds for entry into the gold ring. Henceforward the silver ring was to be known as the Non-European enclosure, while Africans would be restricted to the Native ring. Pamphlets were distributed in the city urging a Non-European boycott of the races, but apparently without result (*Cape Times*, 13th February, 1950).

41. Membership of the Kenilworth Turf Club, and thus entrée to the Members' Enclosure, is restricted to Europeans. In the Union, unlike other African territories, jockeys are all European, although stableboys are always Non-Europeans.

42. *Torch*, 2nd October, 1950.

43. Myrdal, pp. 10–11.

44. An increase of .1 per cent over the 1936 Census figures.

45. See also the article by Jordan K. Ngubane: 'Death-Blow to Mission Work of D.R.C.?' in *Forum*, 24th November, 1950, and the break-away of the Crawford Mission Church congregation under the Reverend I. D. Morkel in September 1950 (described on p. 159). In the *Sunday Times* of 17th October, 1950, it is suggested that some Coloured former D.R.C. members have become Moslems and many more have joined the Roman Catholic Church.

46. Successive Year Books contain membership statistics supplied by some of the Churches, which in no case approximate to the census figures. The main Dutch Reformed Church (*Nederduitsch Gereformeerde Kerk*) gave the following figures for its European and Mission Churches (the latter including both African and Coloured members in the ratio of approximately 1 : 2).

| | EUROPEANS | | NON-EUROPEANS | |
	Members	Adherents	Members	Adherents
1944–5	512,700	892,125	127,350	356,820
1947–8	558,154	949,960	136,097	362,907

These figures were taken from *Year Books* Nos. 23 and 24 (Ch. V) respectively;

the 1947-8 figures show the following percentage rise over those for 1944-5:—European members—8.7 per cent; European adherents—6.5 per cent; Mission Church members—6.9 per cent; Mission Church adherents—1.7 per cent. See Appendix F for the religious affiliations of the major ethnic groups, as given in the 1936 and 1946 Census returns.

47. The Congregational Union's own statistics show a rise from 54,412 to 55,431 Coloured members and adherents between 1944-5 and 1947-8 (57,701 in 1950-1). These figures are far lower than the 1946 Census total of 99,771 Coloureds who declared themselves Congregationalists. An official of the Union was unable to offer any explanation of this considerable discrepancy, which is found in the statistics for other churches too.

48. Over 80 per cent of Coloured schoolchildren in the Cape still attend denominational schools (C. Ed. S. 1947).

49. In 1934 the Congregational church schools in the Cape had 3,915 enrolled pupils, which had increased by 1947 to 16,646 pupils. The corresponding figures for the Roman Catholic schools were: 7,989 pupils in 1934, and 13,578 pupils in 1947. This suggests a tremendous intensification of work by these churches. It is, however, paralleled by the D.R.C. figures, which were 16,521 and 36,145 respectively for 1934 and 1947, which brought the D.R.C. above the Anglicans in the educational field. The latter increase, however, may be accounted for by the fact that many isolated areas have only one school, which is likely to be the school run by the predominant European denomination, usually the D.R.C., in rural areas outside the 'English' Eastern Cape. (Figures from C. and C. Ed. S. 1947.)

50. More properly, one should speak of the Dutch Reformed Churches: (1) the *Nederduitsch Gereformeerde Kerk* ; (2) the *Gereformeerde Kerk van Suid-Afrika*; (3) the *Nederduitsch Hervormde Kerk*. Their members in 1946 numbered 48.47 per cent, 2.94 per cent and 2.88 per cent respectively of the white population. For details of these Churches see *Year Book* No. 24, 1948, pp. 244-6.

51. See the ban on Coloured equality in 'Church and State' in the Transvaal Republic referred to on p. 41, the Christian National Education programme (Appendix U), and the *Draft Constitution of the Republic*, Article 2: 'The Republic is grounded on a Christian-National foundation, and therefore acknowledges, as the standard for the Government of the State, in the first place, the principles of justice of the Holy Scriptures . . .'

52. See Marais pp. 168-70 for an account of this period. He quotes an example from van der Kemp of a D.R.C. deacon of Graaff-Reinet who in 1801 refused to allow a female slave to be baptised 'lest her pride should grow insupportable by her admission among the Christians'.

53. The latest developments towards complete *apartheid* between Non-Europeans is the establishment of the D.R.C., for Africans (*Nederduitsch Gereformeerde Bantoekerk*), the first congregation having been instituted in the Cape Province in November 1950 (*Die Burger*, 24th November, 1950).

54. Only about five of the 352 D.R.M.C. ministers are Coloured. They are trained separately and the educational qualification required of them is lower.

55. In 1949 a D.R.M.C. minister wrote to me to say that the idea of separate catechisms, hymn-books and prayer-books has been mooted in recent years, but that only the hymn-book and women's guild prayer-book are already in use. The Youth Brigades are completely separate and never hold joint rallies. The same informant claimed that Coloured Brigades are forbidden to march or hold public meetings in some platteland towns, and are therefore breaking up.

56. C. 1,172.

57. White or European domination has often been justified on Biblical grounds, the African aborigines being considered as doomed to perpetual servitude as the accursed descendants of Canaan or Ham. President Kruger is reported to have shouted at a deputation of Indians: 'You are the descendants of Ishmael and therefore from your very birth you are bound to slavery. As you are the descendants of

Esau and Ishmael, we cannot admit you to rights placing you on an equality with ourselves.' (Roux, p. 110.) The ban on mixed marriages is also justified by reference to Jehovah's injunction to the Israelites, while the Afrikaners are seen as 'God's chosen' with a mission to the heathen. See also the *Draft Constitution of the Republic*, Article 1.

58. See a series of articles by Dr. B. B. Keet, of the Stellenbosch Theological Seminary, published in *Die Kerkbode* in November-December 1949 on 'The Bible and Apartheid', in which the writer contended that *apartheid* cannot be justified on Biblical grounds. See also a letter from the Rev. P. S. Latsky of Cape Town published in *Die Kerkbode* and quoted in the *Cape Times* of 7th April, 1950.)

59. In Chapter IV, n. 33, it was described how police called on Mr. Morkel following publication of his statement in the *Cape Times* in August, 1949. In addition, the D.R.C. organ *Die Kerkbode* criticised his action, and stated: 'Mr. Morkel is one of the first-fruits of our attempt to train Coloured ministers for the mission church, a development from which, alack, we expected much. But if these men do not understand the responsibility of their position, and become handymen of malicious propaganda against our policy, then it will certainly be very necessary to review this entire undertaking.' (*Cape Times*, 25th August, 1949.)

60. On 14th October, 1949, just before the D.R.C. Synod met, a meeting to protest against *apartheid* was held by representatives of Western Cape Churches with Non-European members. This 'united front' originated with the D.R.M.C. Wynberg Ring and included the A.M.E. (American Methodist Episcopal Church), the Volkskerk, the Moravian, Rhenish and Methodist Churches. It is an interesting development which may forecast certain changes in Coloured religious groupings.

61. *Cape Times*, 22nd October, 1949. On the same occasion Professor A. C. van Wyk, who is attached to the institute for training Coloured missionaries, was reported as saying that it was 'impossible to make Europeans of them'.

62. *Cape Times*, 16th November, 1949. The statement also cited a list of scriptural grounds for the Church's concept of differences between the races, including Gen. 15: 18-21; Amos 9: 7; Acts 17: 26; Mat. 4: 8 and 15; Acts 2: 9–11; Rev. 5: 9.

63. See *Rand Daily Mail* leader, 16th January, 1951, and address by Dr. N. Diederichs, M.P. before the Cape Town Institute of Citizenship, reported in *Cape Times* of 13th April, 1951. Cf. Ch. III, n. 89.

64. See the *Star*, 26th March, 1951, and 12th April, 1951, and *Rand Daily Mail*, 13th April, 1951.]

65. Cf. Roux, pp. 37–8.

66. Coloured ministers are ordained, but are mainly confined to Coloured areas and are not considered mature enough for the higher offices. They are, however, trained in the same institutions and paid the same stipends as Europeans.

67. '. . . the Church has not in practice always been faithful to her own principles and has allowed herself to be infected by racial prejudices in the world around her.' (Concluding paragraph is resolution condemning racial inequality passed by the Anglican Synod in Cape Town—reported in the *Star*, 27th November, 1950.) Speaking at a meeting on civil rights in November 1950, an Anglican priest said that some Christians misuse and misunderstand Christianity and that it sometimes is easier to co-operate with people who do not call themselves Christians. See also the letter by the Archbishop of Cape Town, Dr. G. H. Clayton, in the Cape Town Diocesan magazine (*Rand Daily Mail*, 25th October, 1950: 'For us who live in this country it is a great thing to belong to a religious body that has world-wide affiliations. Nothing but disaster can come from the religion of a country being an expression of the national spirit of that country. It is our business to preach the faith to the people of South Africa, not to preach the faith of the people of South Africa.'

68. In the country, and urban segregated areas, there are often separate churches, as much because of convenience and proximity as by deliberate intention.

69. One parish-priest in a mainly Coloured urban area told me that he refused

communion to a European who protested against sharing the cup with Coloureds, and was upheld in this action by his Bishop.

70. See account in Cape press of 27th and 28th November, 1950. In an interview, the Coadjutor Bishop of Cape Town said that even if some Europeans were to leave the Church as a result of its colour-policy, this policy would not be altered. Everywhere the rule must be observed that no confirmed member of the Church, whatever his race, might be excluded from any Anglican congregation, while all Anglicans should be ready to accept the ministration of every Anglican priest, of whatever race he might be (*Star*, 28th November, 1950). On the same day the Minister of Economic Affairs criticised the Synod resolutions as 'hypocritical', on the grounds that the exclusive Anglican private schools did not admit Coloured children (*Star*, 29th November, 1950). These schools are not controlled by the diocesan organisation, but by their own trusts and governing boards, on which, however, some Anglican ministers sit.

71. In a statement condemning the proposed change in Coloured political rights, the Catholic Guild of Cape Town said that if the assertion that the Coloured people have an identical culture with the white people is maintained, it follows that their rights should be identical and that certain injustices should be removed. (*Rand Daily Mail*, 23rd October, 1950.)

72. On 5th November, 1949, the *Cape Times* published a letter from a Mr. E. Edward on the subject of Catholic colour-attitudes: 'Catholic congregations have never segregated. Coloured, Native and White choir boys serve the priest at Mass together. A heart-warming gesture in my own parish church is the unwritten reservation of the front pews for children of all races. As it happens, Coloured children predominate. At the Heathfield Parish Fête last Saturday, no sign of the colour-bar existed. It might never have been heard of. Lunches and teas were served on the Monastary stoep to all races. Children of every shade queued together for pony rides. While not presuming to claim that all South African Catholics have as broad-minded and Christian an attitude to the Coloured races as the teaching of their Church enjoins, at least that teaching shines forth in a country but dimly lighted in this respect by other denominations.'

73. A large number of Africans have, however, been ordained all over Africa. In Uganda there is an African Bishop with white priests serving under him.

74. But see the case of the Roman Catholic priest who married a European to a 'slightly coloured woman' (p. 142).

75. Segregated education being in force in state-aided schools, there could be no inter-racial schools or groups in these even if a particular organisation were not opposed to it.

76. One recent Coloured convert from Calvinism to Roman Catholicism in a poor Cape Town district told me: 'The priest is the only one who is not too proud to come and see us in our *pondokkie*' (shack).

77. One Moderator, writing in the *Rand Daily Mail* of 29th October, 1949, said he had conducted many special inter-racial services all over the Union, and had 'yet to hear of any Non-European being excluded from one of our European churches or vice versa.'

78. Many Non-European Congregational churches were originally established in areas which are now predominantly European, and are therefore threatened under the Group Areas Act; if it is applied to them, they will have to vacate their premises without compensation. (*Star*, 16th October, 1950.)

79. In 1947 the Moravians had 5,602 enrolled pupils, the Rhenish 2,442 and the Berlin Society 3,326.

80. Information regarding the Moravian Church and Berlin Missionary Society was given in the form of answers to a written questionnaire. No information could be obtained from the Rhenish Society authorities despite two written requests.

81. Following the Methodist Conference in Johannesburg in late 1950, the

Nationalist press was roused to bitter denunciations of what it described as 'the church of the liberalists' whose 'political parsons' (as *Die Transvaler* called them) have perpetuated the 'pestilential tradition' of Philip and van der Kemp, and 'see the world through the unchangeable spectacles of prejudice, based on the outworn philanthropism of 150 years ago'. The same paper, however, failed to denounce 'politicking' by parsons when the Federal Mission Council of the D.R.C. met in Pretoria on 9th–11th November to discuss co-operation between Church and State towards the independent development of the various ethnic groups.

82. See *Cape Times* of 27th September, 1949, 29th September, 1949 and *Cape Argus* of 26th September, 1949. For the official rebuttal of Dr. Diederich's views by the Clerk of the General Assembly of the Presbyterian Church, see *Cape Times*, 30th September, 1949.

83. See Reports of the Rosettenville Conference of 1949, and other reports and statements of the Christian Council of South Africa, to which belong most of the principal Christian Churches in the Union, with the exception of the D.R.C., the Roman Catholic Church and the small Protestant Church of England, not to be confused with the (Anglican) Church of the Province of South Africa. This Church of England in South Africa was in October/November, 1950 one of the moving spirits behind a conference called in Pretoria by the Protestant Association of South Africa. This conference afforded an example of the growth of intolerance and prejudice in the field of religion as well as of colour-relations by proposing a general anti-Catholic front amongst Protestants and a ban on the immigration of Roman Catholics. The Methodist, Presbyterian, Congregational, Baptist and Anglican Churches subsequently repudiated all association with these resolutions (*Rand Daily Mail*, 2nd November, 1950).

84. The Coloured section was originally the Cape Corps Association, which affiliated to the B.E.S.L. in 1945.

85. However, a European represents Coloured ex-servicemen on the National Committee.

86. We have already cited the protest made by the B.E.S.L. against the proposed transfer of Coloured voters to a separate roll (see Ch. III, n. 110).

87. The Constitution contains the following passage on race-relations: 'Here then is the true conception of the inter-relation of colour. Complete uniformity in ideals, absolute equality in the paths of knowledge and culture, equal opportunities for those who strive, equal admiration for those who achieve; in matters social and racial a separate path, each pursuing his own race purity and race pride, equality in things spiritual, agreed divergence in the physical and material. And whereas it is recognised that it is not possible in South Africa to form one Association embodying the principle of the International Scout Movement, which provides that there shall be no distinction of race, each of the sections of the Movement within the Union will be self-contained, self-governing and entirely separate from the other, save as hereinafter set forth.'

88. There were 2,288 Coloured Scouts, 15,496 European scouts, 1,062 Indians and 13,376 Pathfinders (African) at the end of 1950. Coloured membership is largely confined to urban areas. Since 1948, Coloured membership had risen by 221, European by 666, while Indian and African numbers had dropped by 500 and 4,155 respectively.

89. In the case of Brownies, the name was changed to Sunbeams for Non-European children. 'It might have been thought offensive', said a European guider.

90. For instance, the Institute of Race Relations has over the last few years experienced the gradual withdrawal of Coloured interest and co-operation, not only from the Institute itself but from the Europeans in general. (Senator E. Brookes, reported in *Cape Times*, 17th February, 1951.)

91. In addition, such associations must often have dealings with officialdom, whose attitudes make it difficult to use Non-Europeans in such contacts. For instance, the Minister of Native Affairs, when asked by the S.A. Institute of Race

Relations to receive a deputation, said that he would prefer to interview the European and Non-European delegates separately.

92. An Afrikaans-speaking race-relations organisation (S.A.B.R.A.) was started in Stellenbosch in 1949, presumably to counter the monopoly possessed by the S.A.I.R.R. Its first monthly publication contained an article (the only one in English) titled 'Apartheid—The Only Solution', and this tone has been retained, although some speakers at its 1950 Annual Conference demonstrated the impracticability of the concept in modern conditions.

93. In practice the membership policy of the N.C.W., which is affiliated to the colour-blind International Council of Women, and which claims to speak for South African women of all races, varies from branch to branch. A few, including the Cape Town branch, have a handful of individual Non-European members (the annual subscription of one guinea being possibly an obstacle); a number of branches have affiliated Non-European societies, whose representatives attend meetings. The N.C.W. passed a strong protest against the removal of Coloured voters from the common roll, and has in general adopted a liberal though not equalitarian attitude towards Non-European problems.

94. For a fuller account of inter-racial co-operation in various associations see *Race Relations Handbook*, Ch. XXXII. Such co-operation is not of course favoured by supporters of *apartheid*. Cultural associations within the Union have been penalised by the Government threat to withdraw adult education grants if they permit mixed audiences. (See protest by National Council of Women, *Cape Times*, 14th December, 1950 and 29th December, 1950.) In 1950 the Government declared its intention to refuse entry to coloured delegates to a proposed International Student Service Conference, and the Joint Medical Associations planned for 1951; the latter was subsequently called off by the B.M.A. (see *Rand Daily Mail* of 13th December, 1950 and *Cape Times* of 20th December, 1950). The Synodal Committee of the Transvaal D.R.C. also decided not to receive a mixed delegation from the World Council of Churches which was desirous of visiting South Africa (*Star*, 26th October, 1950).

95. It is only fair to say that social relations with other Europeans encountered in such work are often equally superficial, on account of intra-group social distinctions. In the case of non-whites, however, the social avoidance is usually based on colour and not class differences.

96. See Myrdal p. 608 for white attitudes towards eating with Negroes in the American South.

97. On polling-day at Vrededorp (a poor mixed European-Coloured Johannesburg district) in the August 1949 bye-election, Nationalists outside the polling-booth are reported to have displayed photographs showing a European woman and an African man having tea together, as a warning to voters of what would happen to South Africa if they voted for the United Party. (*Rand Daily Mail*, 18th August, 1949.) After the 1949 Commonwealth Conference in London, the Nationalist press dealt with photographs showing Dr. and Mrs. Malan with Indian, Pakistani or Ceylonese delegates either by excising the latter or not publishing the photographs. When the photographs were published in the English-speaking press, a Mr. H. A. Willemse of Durban wrote to the *Natal Mercury*: 'The alleged radio picture you published on Friday, 22nd April, of Mr. Malan standing next to an Indian and Mrs. Malan seated next to Mr. Attlee on the same bench with an Indian woman must be a lie. Our Premier and Mrs. Malan would never deign to mix socially with Indians. I am sure that if you inquired into the origin of the picture, you will find that it has been deliberately fabricated by some malicious anti-South Africa propaganda-maker who wishes to besmirch our Premier and Mrs. Malan in the eyes of their people.' (*Forum*, 7th May, 1949.)

98. In more intellectual circles, and amongst students, some social mingling occurs, and Non-European diplomats or visiting celebrities are often excepted from the general social bar. A difficulty sometimes encountered is the attitude of local

Non-European servants, who accept the colour-bar completely and regard the presence of Non-European guests as lowering the status of their European employer.

99. Similar usages were or are still to be found in some European languages (e.g., French and Polish), probably as survivals of the estate structure. In Afrikaans, as in most other European languages, the second person singular is also used as a mark of intimacy between equals, and it is very common, particularly amongst rural Afrikaners, who often use it even to strange whites. It is not yet considered respectful for children to use it to their parents or older people. The formal 'u' (you) is still regarded as sophisticated usage, confined to urban and high-level official dealings.

100. Victor de Kock (p. 50) translates *Paaij* (or *Pay*) as 'good old man'.

101. Liechtenstein, quoted by MacCrone, p. 120, n. 2. This word has entered deeply into Coloured sensibilities, to the extent that a Coloured who is considered to be collaborating overmuch with the white group is now dubbed by his more militant fellow-Coloureds a *Ja-Baas* (U.S. equivalent, an 'Uncle Tom'). See *Torch* leader of 2nd August, 1950. The most recent urban usage is *Meneer* and *Miesies*.

102. Literally 'old papa' and 'nurse'.

103. See a letter from Mr. Booker Lakey published in the *Cape Times* in August 1949: 'The prevalent use of the words *outa* and *aia* and *hotnot* become part and parcel of the training of young white children, and no Coloured man or woman . . . dare raise the slightest form of protest.' For a similar resentment by U.S. Negroes of the term 'uncle', see Johnson, p. 305.

104. Coloureds of the upper and middle classes use all the courtesy forms and titles reserved by whites for whites when talking among themselves. One word, however, is difficult to take over; that is the Afrikaans version of 'gentleman'—*'witman'* (white man). The evolution of this word shows just how far colour and not culture has come to be the principal status-determinant in South Africa.

105. The English-speaking *Cape Times*, however, printed an article on the hundredth birthday of a Coloured woman, Mrs. Georgina Less, in which she was referred to as *'Ouma* Less'. The different usages may prove an embarrassment in border-line cases, as the following passage from a 'letter to the Editor' shows: 'Years ago a young woman, in a very responsible Government position in the country where everybody uses the courtesy titles of *Niggie* (niece) and *Oomie* (uncle), was confronted by a man of very dark complexion. He extended his hand in greeting her, "*More, Niggie*". She was in two minds whether to shake hands or not: and then she took his hand, but said, "*Ekskuus Meneer, ek is Juffrou X, en ek wil nie 'Niggie' by almal genoem word nie.*" The proprietor of the business premises in which her little office was situated was present at the time, and when the man left, considerably embarrassed, said, "Miss X, you made a nasty *faux pas*. He is a member of one of South Africa's most prominent families." Just imagine her own embarrassment and horror at her mistake.' (*Rand Daily Mail*, 2nd December, 1950.) Afrikaans-speaking speakers at public meetings of Coloured people do commonly address their audiences in the mass as *Meneer die Voorsitter, Dames en Here* (Mr. Chairman, Ladies and Gentlemen).

106. This is true of the American race situation also. An Afrikaans-speaking lecturer at Cape Town University told me that, while he made no distinctions in addressing Non-European students, he had to make a conscious effort to overcome the strangeness of addressing Coloured men as *Meneer*, owing to his upbringing on a farm where such a thing was unheard-of.

107. But see MacCrone p. 42 f. for honorific terms applied to *baptised* Coloured women in the early settlement period.

108. *'Hotnot'* is still a common appellation in the country, and the acting chairman of the Cape Nationalist Party had to call an elderly delegate to order at the 1950 Congress for using it (*Rand Daily Mail*, 5th October, 1950). Some of the older generation of rural Coloureds apparently refer to themselves as *'Hotnots'*, reflecting

local white usage. This has had one adverse effect, as those declaring themselves to be '*Hotnots*' when applying for a pension get the lower rate payable to the aboriginal Hottentot (C.A.C. 1945–6, p. 40).

109. Coloureds also use these terms when speaking of their own group.

110. I do not suggest that most English people do so, simply that the language lacks such a wealth of traditional differentiating patterns. Exceptions are frequent, even in official interviews and correspondence, as the following instance suggests: 'When people receive letters from the Groote Schuur Hospital, they are amazed to find just the plain Christian and surname and address on the envelope, without any Mr., Mrs. or Miss in front of the name. There is also no salutation to the actual letter—no Dear Sir, or Sir,—but just—"Here is a . . ." If this is not discourtesy, then what is? I wonder if Europeans receive letters addressed in this manner?' (*Sun*, 5th March, 1950.) The rudeness of some white hospital nurses is almost proverbial amongst Coloured people. Miss Mary Attlee, who has worked among the Coloured people for forty years, was recently reported as saying to a Presbyterian congregation in London: 'I say it with shame, but the way the Europeans, both the British and, especially, the Afrikaans-speaking people address the Coloured people made me very unhappy . . . I regret to say that it is so-called Christians who are at fault in this matter . . .' (*Star*, 29th November, 1950.) On the other hand, I was told by the Editor of a Cape Town paper: 'The —— has a very strict rule about referring to Non-Europeans in print. We use "Mr., Mrs. and Miss" in precisely the same way as we do for Europeans. In court and crime reporting, these prefixes are not used for either Europeans or Non-Europeans. I think that this is a general convention in English newspapers.' Of latter months, this paper has tended to avoid mentioning the race of individuals in the news, other than in the crime reports.

111. I should perhaps qualify this by saying that in fifteen months' stay in the Cape I never heard another word used, although I was told that 'Cape' or 'Capie' was sometimes used until recently. In the absence of a derogatory term such as '*Hotnot*', the English word 'Coloured' can, in certain contexts, assume a more derogatory significance than the somewhat formal and colourless Afrikaans '*Kleurling*'. I have, however, heard some English people refer to Indians as 'coolies' and Africans as 'blacks', 'niggers', 'coons' or 'kaffirs'. Most, however, refer to the African by the official term of 'Native'. The use of the preferred term 'African' is very limited amongst whites, while some Coloureds do not use it either (on this point see Jordan K. Ngubane's article 'Africans or Natives?'—*Forum*, 30th September, 1950, and letter in the *Torch* of 17th April, 1951). In polite Afrikaans an African is a '*Naturel*' (Native), the word '*Afrikaner*' being pre-empted for Afrikaans-speaking whites (or extended sometimes to all white South Africans); '*Afrikaan*' is apparently too similar to be used for Africans, and one Nationalist paper wrote that 'the name African would imply that the Natives were the only racial group with a permanent habitat and permanent rights in Africa.' (*Die Burger*, quoted by *Forum* of 16th March, 1951.)

112. See letter from 'South African' in *Rand Daily Mail*, 3rd March, 1951.

113. In a Courtesy Week speech at the Cape Town Rotary Club lunch, Sir Herbert Stanley, a former Governor of Ceylon, said that European men should be prepared to give up their seats to Coloured women in buses; the test of courtesy was politeness to social inferiors and to people of other races (*Rand Daily Mail*, 7th March, 1951). The *Rand Daily Mail* commented approvingly on this speech in an editorial (8th March, 1951), but *Die Transvaler* of the same date characterised it as nonsense and 'courtesy run wild', adding: 'non-Europeans in the same bus as Europeans are as out of place as in the same sitting-room. Anyone who advances such ideas wrecks the better race relations which he intends to further.'

114. One correspondent to the press has suggested that the high accident rate in the Union is partly due to racialism (*Rand Daily Mail*, 17th October, 1950). See also report of a Durban parking incident (*Star*, 18th October, 1950), and letter

U

in the *Star* of 7th March, 1951. On highway etiquette between Black and White in the United States cf. Johnson, p. 126.

115. See *Rand Daily Mail* (19th September, 1949), for a letter describing the haphazard stoning of Coloured children by a hired motor-bus full of young European men on the Main Reef Road near Johannesburg. See also a letter from Mr. A. P. Kriel, a Nationalist supporter, in *Die Burger* (quoted by *Forum*, 24th November, 1950), suggesting that it should be made a punishable offence to insult Non-Europeans and that many who think themselves 'good Afrikaners' are doing more to further Communism by such behaviour than are the local Communists. Until recently, as Hoernlé points out, the technique of domination was not synonymous with ill-treatment or inhumanity in personal relations (*op. cit.*, p. 49).

116. It was further stated that policemen in such areas as Parow and Wynberg sometimes 'chase Coloured people off the pavement'. In the Transvaal Republic Africans were forbidden to walk on the pavements, while in 'British' East London no Non-Europeans were allowed to use the side-walks as late as 1929 (Roux, pp. 122–3).

117. See the plea for a Union-wide campaign for 'racial courtesy' made by the Rev. S. B. Sudbury, acting Chairman of the Cape District of the Methodist Church (*Race Relations News*, October 1950). See also a letter from a Coloured correspondent expressing surprise and pleasure at the courtesy of a white fellow-traveller on the Cape Suburban Railways: 'It is the simple "do ye unto one another" little act which, if multiplied in our daily lives, will make this country a happier place to live in.' (*Cape Times*, 2nd December, 1950.)

118. See the House of Assembly debate referred to in the following footnote. The same speaker declared: 'There is only one policy to follow if you wish to preserve the colour instinct and remain a European race in South Africa, and that is we should follow the policy of separation between the races so far as it is a question of equality, not where he is your servant; and to carry out that policy consistently in any field of life.'

119. Myrdal regards the demand for 'no social equality' as psychologically dominant to the aversion to 'inter-marriage', which he considers to be an irrational escape on the part of the whites from voicing an open demand for difference in social status between the two groups for its own sake (p. 591). This proposition may be applicable to the South African situation, but the fact that the whites are so heavily outnumbered in the latter situation does seem to give their fears of 'a coffee-coloured South Africa' a more rational basis. A typical example of such reasoning was given by Mr. J. G. Strydom in the House of Assembly in 1947: 'The European race in South Africa can only remain a European race if it preserves its feeling against colour. Once it loses that feeling, as in the way it is absent in most European countries which have had no experience of the coloured problem and who have had no coloured people, South Africa cannot remain a white man's country; . . . if we lose our colour feeling and the non-Europeans are developed and civilised we must become a coloured nation. Then it would be quite useless to speak about white civilisation and the Christian white civilisation—it will then be a fantasy. Then it will drive you to the logical conclusion, and it will happen that in the Assembly and in the Provincial Councils and in the Town Councils you will get intermingling, and that coloureds can travel with you in the same compartment and eat with you in the same dining-room and at the same tables; and eventually you will have no objection to living with them if they are decent and civilised.' (Oliver Walker, pp. 110–11.) Cf. also the use made of the Seretse Khama marriage to condemn mixed social functions in the Union by Dr. Malan at Standerton (*Argus* editorial, 29th August, 1949).

120. In the House of Assembly, 25th May, 1949, Mr. S. E. Warren (Nationalist) is reported as saying that if a line were drawn between Europeans and Coloureds and some Coloureds fell on the European side, that was of no consequence, 'but what we are afraid of is the ten and a half million'. (*Cape Argus*, 25th May, 1949.)

For the incidence of mixed marriages in the early period see Hoge, *Personalia of the Germans at the Cape*, and De Villiers' *Geschlachtsregister*. For attempts to prevent race-mixture in the eighteenth century see Dr. P. J. v. d. Merwe, Ch. VI, s. 6. In the House of Assembly, Colonel Pilkington-Jordan referred to the famous old Cape families with Coloured blood (*Hansard*, 24th May, 1949, col. 6433), while two upper-class white women brought up in the Cape told me that there were certain families or branches of old families whom they as children were told to avoid as playmates for this reason.

121. This may not necessarily mean that the actual number of such marriages was diminishing, as a considerable number of Coloured persons were probably able to register as Europeans for the purposes of the marriage ceremony. The decline in officially-registered mixed marriages was, however, probably the result of intensified colour-prejudice amongst whites, of which the demand for legal sanctions was a product, while its causes are to be sought elsewhere. The possibility of the partners to a mixed marriage living happily amidst the intensified prejudices and hostility of both groups have diminished considerably in recent years (see *Cape Argus*, 16th June, 1949, for such an unhappy mixed marriage in Port Elizabeth). *Die Transvaler* seized upon the proposed divorce between Rita Hayworth and the Aly Khan as an illustration of the impossibility of wiping out the 'natural and immemorial barriers between East and West' (2nd May, 1951).

122. Prior to the 1927 Immorality Act the only ban in these provinces was on voluntary sexual intercourse between a white woman and an aboriginal native for gain. See Mi. Chs. IV and V for this legislation.

123. For the various Provincial laws see Mi. Chs. IV–V. This Commission, which sat just before the war, recommended legislation against mixed marriages on the Transvaal model, and severe penalties for illicit intercourse, which it regarded as the main source of miscegenation. One commissioner proposed the increased immigration of 'numbers of young European women of good type', as there were in 1936 17,686 more adult European males than females in the Union (p. 39), but deprecated legislation on the subject.

124. On 26th January, 1926, an article in the *Rand Daily Mail* contained the following passage: 'He (the European) is being sapped at the root and is sinking into the yellow flood. Nothing can stay that decline except a legal division of the whole population into two separate groups and the absolute prohibition of miscegenation.'

125. Act No. 55/1949 and Act No. 12/1950. Comparisons have been drawn between these measures and the anti-Jewish Nüremburg Laws (*Torch* leader, 10th April, 1950). In May 1951, the Natal Native Medical Council (a witch-doctors' group) asked that the Act be extended to offences between Indians and Africans.

126. See statement issued in Cape Town by representatives of the Anglican, Roman Catholic, Methodist, Presbyterian, Congregational and Baptist Churches, and the Salvation Army, published in the *Cape Times* of 7th May, 1949. The Dutch Reformed Church did not associate itself with this protest, and has lost no occasion of condemning mixed marriages and of advocating legal preventive measures (see proceedings of D.R.C. Synod, sitting in Cape Town in October 1949). In the last half of the nineteenth century, however, the Rev. P. E. Faure of the D.R.C., Wynberg, seems to have found the idea of a mixed marriage less offensive than that of continued concubinage; it was he who urged and conducted the marriage between Harry Gray, later Lord Stamford, and Martha Williams, the latter's Coloured servant, in December 1880. The son born to the pair before their marriage (who but for this inversion of birth and legitimation would have inherited the title) attended a European church school in Claremont, where he was known as the 'Black Earl' (Lawrence G. Green, 'Coloured Cape Town', article in *The Outspan*, 17th November, 1950).

127. I have been told that certain clergymen avoid this harsh responsibility by advising a couple of doubtful race to apply for a special licence, thereby putting the onus on the civil authorities.

128. *Cape Argus*, 31st August, 1950. The judge also quoted the cases of Ex Parte Larsen (1936 N.P.D., *Prentis Hall Weekly Legal Service*, 1936, Vol. II, K. 79) and Ex Parte Kinnear (1921, C.P.D. 737) to support the view that a 'slight mixture' does not make a Non-European. During the discussion the Cape Attorney-General said that '6½ per cent of Coloured blood' would be sufficient to make a person a Non-European. See the case reported in the *Star* of 29th May, 1951, in which appearance was held to be the determining factor, although the woman had only one Coloured grandparent.

129. See motion by Senator Brookes reported in the *Star* of 23rd February, 1951.

130. See *Star*, 27th October, 1950, and 11th December, 1950, and *Cape Times*, 11th December, 1950. In one such case a 65-year old European man and a 70-year-old Coloured woman were arrested at 1.45 a.m., after a policeman had looked through their bedroom window. The woman had looked after the man for two years as he was ill and poor. They were given a suspended sentence but told they must separate (*Cape Argus*, 2nd September, 1950). In another case of a young couple (the Coloured wife being 19), who had been living together for three years, had one child and were expecting another, the girl was taken to the police station at 2 a.m., twelve days before her baby was due. She was given a suspended sentence on condition that she separated from her man. The magistrate, Mr. J. A. N. Beyers, said: 'You have not been together so long that you cannot separate.' (*Star*, 6th December, 1950 and 26th December, 1950.)

131. *Star*, 15th December, 1950 (letter from John Tunstall).

132. *Sunday Times*, 5th November, 1950. It is also said to cause irritation to couples enjoying the evening air in parked cars, from policemen intent on determining whether the Act is being infringed (*Cape Times*, 14th December, 1950).

133. *Cape Times*, 6th December, 1950. See also *Die Burger* of 10th August, 1950, for an explanation and a justification of such discrimination in the case of Non-European women 'of a particular type', to whom a prison sentence does not make much difference.

134. Though a circular of 'Advice to Visiting Seamen', issued by the National Advisory Council for the Welfare of Merchant Seamen in Union Ports, is now handed to the officers of each ship in Union Harbours, in which clause 7 reads as follows: 'Premises, particularly in the Coloured and Indian quarters of this city, to which contact men, pimps or taxi-drivers, hansom-cabs and rickshas may take you for liquor or women are to be avoided; you are liable to be drugged, assaulted and robbed in these places. SEXUAL INTERCOURSE *between whites and non-whites is a serious criminal offence in South Africa.* MARRIAGE between whites and non-whites is prohibited by law.'

135. *Star*, 4th December, 1950. The Judge-President commented: 'I can only say that he was extraordinarily fortunate that he was not charged with rape.'

136. In one such case the man got four months' hard labour under the Girls and Mentally Defective Women's Protection Act, while the girl (aged 15) was convicted under the Immorality Act and sent to a reformatory for four years (*Cape Argus*, 31st January, 1951).

137. *Star*, 24th November, 1950.

138. *Cape Argus*, 11th September, 1950, *Torch*; 21st August, 1950 and 18th September, 1950. At the second hearing the magistrate apologised for using the word 'brand'. The couple were acquitted.

139. 'The extent to which the economic interests of the dominant class in this country have moulded our current moral code and the emotional attitude of society at large is immense. Fundamental in it is the horror of miscegenation, which is deliberately or unconsciously exploited as a basis for imposing restrictions on Non-European competition. That this is so has been strikingly proved to me by the fact that more than once when I have been pleading for economic freedom in the labour market I have encountered the irrelevant charge: "You want a coffee-coloured South Africa". (Professor W. J. Hutt, speaking at the First National Coloured-

European Conference, 1933.) Douglas Reed quotes the Afrikaner from Standerton who said: "We won't have Hofmeyr. He wants mixed marriages and five pounds a week for the Kaffir." ' (*Somewhere South of Suez*, p. 157.)

140. Between 1925 and 1946 the number of Coloured-African marriages (probably not a complete figure as the reserves are not included) rose from 262 to 630, or from 6 per cent to 7.5 per cent of all Coloured marriages. This was less than the 1943 figure of 653 or 9.2 per cent of all Coloured marriages (Sofer, Table 15). Cf. also Mr. A. Steyn, Nationalist member for Kroonstad, speaking in the Mixed Marriages Bill debate on 19th May, 1949, Hansard, col. 6,190; and the *Cape Times*, 15th January, 1951 (*Peninsula Native Problem*, III) on Coloured prostitution in African shanty-towns in the Peninsula.

CHAPTER VIII—THE CAPE COLOURED PEOPLE—INTERNAL STRUCTURE

1. Dr. A. E. Abdurahman, speaking at the 10th Annual A.P.O. Conference in 1913.

2. The mission-station communities, with their small numbers, local self-government, comparative absence of other ethnic groups, geographical isolation and cultural continuity, are the nearest approach to the traditional anthropological field to be found amongst the Coloured People.

3. A number of Cape Malays still practise polygamy, though not to the extent of more than two wives, so far as I could ascertain. All subsequent observations in this chapter relate to the Christian Coloured group, unless otherwise qualified.

4. For instance, the semi-patriarchal type of family still prevalent among Coloured farm-owners is more likely to be related to the fact of such ownership and its economic and social consequences than to be a survival of the old Hottentot patriarchal structure, which was based on communal property, not on individual land tenure, and was swept away by the eighteenth century. On the other hand, the rural Afrikaners from whom the Coloured landowners derived so much of their culture have a similar type of patriarchal family, evolved during the nomadic, pastoral phase of their trek away from the Western Cape. Cf. Frazier (1), pp. 13–14.

5. The social classes to which I am referring are those which exist within the Coloured group, which are described later in this chapter. They are similar to those found within the white group, though the emphasis placed on some status-determinants varies in degree. Unlike the white class-structure, the Coloured hierarchy consists as yet of an infinitesimal upper class, a very small middle class and an enormous lower class.

6. The six criteria here applied constitute a modified version of those enumerated by Professor G. P. Murdock in his work on 'Social Structure'. They were put forward by Dr. Edmund Leach as a basis for written work and discussion at a seminar on 'Kinship Structure' held at the London School of Economics in 1950.

7. That is to say, an individual is affiliated to some members of both his father's and his mother's kin-groups, usually those who are his own nearest genealogical kinsmen (Murdock, p. 44–6 and 56 f.).

8. Murdock's 'Eskimo' type.

9. Lowie's 'lineal' type. The tendency of rural Afrikaans-speaking whites and Coloureds to extend classificatory terms such as 'uncle' and 'aunt', 'niece' and 'nephew', to unrelated persons considered to be their social equals within their own ethnic group should be noted here for further investigation. President Kruger was known as *Oom Paul*, while Mrs. Smuts is often referred to even in the English-speaking press as *Ouma* (grandmother).

10. Frazier (2), pp. xi–xii.

11. Perhaps the best known of these extended families are the Buys Clan of the Zoutpansberg (Northern Transvaal), the other the Dunn family on the Tugela River, Natal, neither of which are, however, typically Cape Coloured. The Buys

Clan or 'tribe', as it is sometimes called officially, consists of descendants of the Boer Coenrad Buys and his various African and Coloured wives. A 1945 survey estimated the population at between 250 and 300, of whom about one-fifth were apparently regarded as 'non-Buyses' by the rest, on the grounds that they had married Africans instead of trying to 'get the blood white'. By 1944, however, it was reported that this severity had been relaxed to the extent of recognising the children of a Buys man and an African woman, but not those of a Buys woman and an African man. (1944 Report of Messrs. Honck and Yeld, cited in M., p. 35.) The formal emphasis on the importance of patrilineal descent is interesting. The Dunn family also originated in the last century, with a British settler who gained the status of a Zulu chief (confirmed by Sir Garnet Wolseley in 1879), and lived in the African way with a considerable number of African wives and one Malay wife. At his death he left one Cape Malay and twenty-two African wives and seventy-nine children. There are now about 220 of his descendants living in the Reserve. Seventeen Europeans have again married into the family. In cases where European men have married Dunn girls, there seems to be no opposition from the Dunns to their acceptance and to their acquiring plots through their wife's rights. (See M., pp. 28–35.) This desire to 'get the blood white' seems often to cut across normal Coloured family structure and *mores*, as will be seen when we come to discuss mixed marriages and 'passing'.

12. Many rural Coloured family units are of the extended type, with a vertical range of three generations, and a horizontal one which may include some of the collateral and affinal relations. A landless son-in-law may live with his wife's parents, and the family group may also include the children of a son or of a daughter working in the town. (See also M., p. 4.)

13. On the reserves and mission stations land is usually occupied by the male descendant of a registered occupier. The latter may, however, be female in the absence of a male claimant (M., s. 32).

14. See Weiss, p. 24, in which it is stated that nine-tenths of the women in that particular factory regard their job as a means to implement the family income. Not all of course are married.

15. In rural areas, this process is often accentuated by the necessity for the landless labourer or even at times the smallholder to look for work away from home or to pasture his cattle far afield (M., p. 49), and this may cause authority in the family to shift to the woman.

16. Such equality in the home is not entirely reflected in public life, where the Coloured woman has no vote, and shares with her white sisters the various disabilities laid on women by Roman-Dutch law. In this connection it may be noted that, in families where the parents are legally married, the father seems to be formally deferred to, although the wife or mother may be, in the lower-middle classes at least, an equal wage-earner, and a more stable element in the family.

17. On this subject generally see C., s. 66–7, Marais, p., 171, MacMillan, p. 76, V. de Kock, pp. 114 and 205, and cf. Myrdal, p. 931, and Freire, p. 456, for the U.S. and Brazilian situations.

18. Cf. Weiss, pp. 109–10 and 130–2.

19. One might expect the frequent absence of the mother in her capacity as wage-earner (often the major wage-earner) to weaken the mother-child tie. This would, however, appear to be partly compensated for by the fact that she is the household provider and therefore the centre of stability and cohesion, while her rôle as mother is filled during her absence by female members of her own family.

20. Illegitimacy rates for a number of urban and rural areas have been found to range between 20 per cent and 35 per cent, about ten times more than corresponding European rates (see Appendix H for some urban statistics). In one rural Cape area (Oudtshoorn) the report of the D.R.C. Ring mentioned elsewhere cites the baptismal registers to show that up to 20 per cent of children baptised during the previous year were illegitimate (*Cape Times*, 13th September, 1949). See also C.,

s. 68–72, for the estimate that between 30 per cent and 40 per cent of all Coloured births are illegitimate.

21. This chapter was written before I read Mrs. Weiss' thesis on *The Cape Coloured Woman*. On this point and others where a reference is made to her work, I was glad to find that her detailed observation of a small cross-section of industrial workers and my own more superficial impressions of the wider situation had produced similar findings or hypotheses. Mrs. Weiss deals with differing class attitudes to extra-marital pregnancy in pp. 44–5; she states that it is rare and regarded as a disaster in the upper class, occurs more frequently in the middle class (when the girl usually 'gets a hiding' and is forced to marry the man). In the respectable lower class it is mainly deplored because earning power is lost, and marriage may not ensue; in the 'outcast' class it is regarded as normal but stupid.

22. The economic reasoning behind this attitude was expressed to the writer as follows by Mr. A. J. H. Goodwin of the University of Cape Town: 'If I have a baby and am not married, I can sue the father for alimony and the police collect. If I marry him, he can throw up his job, and provided that he is not working I have to support him. If he is working I sue for support and have trouble in my home.' The economic situation is further accentuated by the fact that there is usually a greater field of available employment for Coloured women than there is for Coloured men, particularly at times of financial crisis. An unascertained part of the illegitimacy disclosed in available statistics is the product not of transient affairs but of semi-permanent unions, which are accepted by many Coloured people as equivalent to formal marriages.

23. Cf. Regina Neser: *Kinders van Ismaël*, pp. 14–16.

24. 'It has now become apparent that, for years, very few Coloureds in these localities have been able to earn their living solely by cultivating their land. Most of them have to supplement their income by occasionally working away from home. The elders remain at home while the children work on the farms and in the cities and send money home. Those engaged in outside employment do not take their families with them.' (M., p. 6, s. 33.) The last two observations suggest that the rural extended family still remains a very real nucleus for its members, at least as far as the Coloured population on the reserves and mission-stations are concerned.

25. It is sometimes suggested that one reason for the absence of a considerable Coloured well-to-do commercial class is the general toleration of needy relatives, who swarm around any member of the immediate family who has prospered, even to the extent of coming to live with him. Cf. an observer's comment in 1890 on the 'communistic form of life' prevailing at the mission institutions, quoted by Marais, pp. 81–2.

26. See M., s. 28.

27. The number of Coloureds living on the mission stations and reserves was 27,299 in 1946 (M., p. 65). The total rural population was about 360,000 in the same year (preliminary census figures). A large number of the 333,000 not living on mission stations or reserves belong to the landless rural proletariat; they hire their labour by the day or week, and are unlikely to be able to maintain a very stable family life or relationships.

28. 'According to general tradition a father who is a registered occupier retains his rights until his death, when they are transferred to his widow . . . Even if she remarries she still retains them, and after her death they are disposed in terms of the will. Usually they are bequeathed to a single heir who has to pay the others for their shares. The identity of the heir is known beforehand, and those who do not inherit apply to the Board for other rights. Although the land is registered in the name of one person only, it often happens that a father and his sons cultivate it jointly.' (M., s. 32.) 'Concordia has an interesting system which allows the youngest, who usually looks after his parents, to receive his father's rights and to compensate the others for any improvements.' (M., s. 161.)

29. See the Cape Town Social Survey for a detailed account of Coloured house-

holds in Cape Town. From a random sample of 834 households, it was estimated that, of the total number of Coloured households in Cape Town (about 25,000 in 1939), 53 per cent had an income below the Poverty Datum Line (a purely 'physical' standard of health and decency). Only 4,000 of the total enjoyed what was classified as an 'adequate' income, while some 5,000 existed on an income even insufficient to purchase half the minimum essentials for health and decency. The percentage of European households below the Poverty Datum Line was estimated from preliminary calculations as 6 per cent. (Social Survey 4 C.T., p. 2 and p. 7.) In these tenements lives what Bishop Lavis, speaking at the First National Coloured-European Conference in 1933, called 'that crowning horror of civilisation, the "one room" family' (he estimated that about 60,000 Coloureds were so living at that period). He continued: 'That one room is the scene for a whole family, parents, children, and sometimes friends and relations—of all the circumstances of daily life. That one room is the kitchen, bathroom, dining-room, sitting-room, bedroom, and the scene of birth and death for its unfortunate inhabitants.'

30. In Zuurbraak, near Swellendam, local political government was recently handed over to the Coloured community by the London Missionary Society. The local inhabitants are said to be so apathetic about self-government that 'the magistrate has to hunt around for people willing to serve on the Board'. (M., s. 54.) There may be several reasons for this apathy, such as internal class and colour dissensions, the struggle to earn a bare living which leaves no time for other activities, ignorance of the implications and methods of self-government, or a growing disinclination to co-operate with the European authorities.

31. A good example of such a small-town community bound together by the bonds of long settlement and a common economic livelihood is the Coloured fishing community at Hout Bay in the Cape Peninsula.

32. Such as the Coloured Vigilance Committees recently set up by many Coloured sub-communities in the Western Cape. Nevertheless, the lack in many rural areas of a desire to co-operate in general communal activities, such as ploughing, improving land and so on, is stressed in M., p. 81.

33. 'In the Cotton Belt one does not find rural communities similar to the old Russian *mir* or an Irish village community, where deeply rooted customs and traditions govern the relations of life. Nor does one find rural Negro communities like those in Haiti, where a landowning peasantry has preserved over five or more generations a cultural heritage embodying many elements of African culture. At its worst, the rural Negro community, within its dependence upon the exigencies of a capitalistic agriculture and the dominant white community shows . . . the degradation of the impoverished country Negro.' (Frazier (1), p 214.)

34. The Commissioners reported with some asperity on the labour difficulties caused by Coloured attachment to the land: 'At all the places visited . . . time, labour, and manpower are wasted. The Coloureds leave their work in order to go home and plough their lands. These lands are very small and miserable, the means employed to cultivate them ineffective and the individual's knowledge nil, and for this precarious existence they give up their jobs. But 'scratching in the ground is in their blood, whether or not they profit by it.' (M., s. 37.) The suggestion in the last sentence, that agriculture, however inefficient, has become part of the *mores* of the rural Coloured, is incidentally a tribute to the generations of missionaries who laboured to convert the original Hottentots from pasturalism to agriculture.

35. See Marais, Chs. II and III, and Halford, p. 120 f., for an account of this process in Griqua and Bastard areas.

36. Several Cape Town wards have active Coloured Ratepayers' Associations, e.g., Athlone, Crawford, Wynberg.

37. See McIver (1), p. 9. A worker at one Coloured community centre in Cape Town's District Six described the activities of the large number of associations which made their headquarters at the centre, but spoke of the tendency to remain in watertight compartments and not mingle or co-operate in wider activities. The

free film show once a month and the Christmas parties are the main co-ordinating force. The tentative growth of some community spirit is, however, shown in the increasing amount of food and books, etc. contributed to the club, and the prestige attached to membership of the centre.

38. *Die wite menschen maken zoo* (the Europeans do it like this) was a phrase often on the lips of Adam Kok III, Paramount Chief of the Griquas, though not always in an elevated context. (Halford, p. 147.)

39. MacIver (1), p. 236.

40. The meaning of '*skolly*' (Afrikaans—*skollie*) is given in the Afrikaans dictionaries as street-arab, ragamuffin. It is generally applied in the plural to groups or gangs of youths or young men, usually from the depressed urban classes, who band together for various anti-social purposes, which often involve the use of violence against the public, the police and other gangs The corresponding African gangs are called *tsotsis* or *amalaitas*.

41. Article by Dr. O. D. Wollheim, Warden and Manager of the Cape Flats Distress Association, titled 'What is the Cure for Cape Coloured Skollydom?' and published in the *Cape Times*, 10th September, 1949.

42. *Pace* MacIver, who classes gangs under associations representing economic interests, a classification probably applicable in the American context.

43 'Our Cape Coloured skollies usually wear caps back to front, or with the peaks turned up or sideways or some other unusual form of headgear; their trousers are often "half-mast", and their jackets, shirts or belts display emblems of various kinds.' (Dr. O. D. Wollheim, *ibid.*)

44. See report of a fight between the 'Killers' and the 'Globe Gang' which ended in the Magistrate's Court. (*Cape Argus*, 26th January, 1951.)

45 The activities of better-adjusted individuals in their clubs are naturally not anti-social in this way, although the *mores* here outlined are not altogether uncharacteristic of certain robust social clubs which existed in the days of pass degrees at various British Universities.

46. There are apparently no corresponding gangs for girls of the same class, unlike the American teen-age girl gangs which are affiliated to the boys' gangs. Coloured girls may go on the streets, but prostitution is not organised on a large scale in Cape Town. Overt brothels are not legally sanctioned, but some private houses perform this function covertly.

47. See remarks made by Bishop S. W. Lavis and Miss M. Lockyer, the Warden, at the annual meeting of the House of Youth, Salt River (*Cape Times*, 22nd April, 1949). The increasing number and scope of boys' clubs is said to have caused a decrease in skolly-gang fights and crime in recent times (*Cape Times*, 17th April, 1951).

48. Quite independently a Johannesburg informant told me that such notorious adult tribal gangs as the 'Russians' and the 'Japanese', which roam the Johannesburg African townships at week-ends, are sometimes manipulated for political ends in the same way. See also *Hansard*, 18th April, 1951, p. 4785.

49. European exclusiveness in the sporting field is mirrored in the existence of separate sports clubs and associations for Africans, Coloureds and Indians, although the latter, unlike the former, do sometimes organise inter-racial meetings (an appeal for closer inter-racial co-operation in cricket was made in the *Sun* of 13th April, 1951). The Coloureds have a nation-wide organisation in boxing, rugby and soccer, cricket and lawn-tennis. Swimming, hockey and athletics are organised locally but have not yet achieved national associations.

50. As we have shown in Chs. VIa and VII, the sporting and recreational facilities provided for Non-Europeans do not come up to the European standard, while schools are hardly equipped for sports. Moreover, the Coloured community is too poor to provide its own facilities on a large scale.

51. See also article in the *Sun* (13th April, 1951) appealing to Coloured football fans to fight *apartheid* by patronising their own teams, and ceasing to 'swell the

coffers of white unions', and *Torch* (17th April, 1941) for a similar move by soccer players.

52. As a result of this, the projected visit of the British players Barna and Bergmann to South Africa in 1949 had to be cancelled; the question of their accommodation and entertainment would have been 'awkward', as a Coloured official of the association put it. *Die Burger* (Cape Nationalist Daily) thought the matter worth a two-column spread on the front page, headed *Sportveldtog teen Blanken* (Sports Campaign against Europeans). Bergmann subsequently disobeyed the British body's order, and came to the Union on his own to play matches with European players, for which he was suspended. In March 1950, the chairman of the European Table Tennis Union, Mr. W. Crumley, was reported as saying in an English paper that his Union had no colour-bar but a 'social bar', peculiar to South Africa, but not understood outside. (*Sun*, 17th March, 1950.)

53. A prominent South African athletic authority, discussing a suggestion that Non-European sports organisers might now try to have this ruling extended to other sports, said that if this was done every sport connected with the Olympic Games would be affected. The table-tennis move, he said, might be the 'thin end of the wedge.' (*Cape Times*, 18th June, 1949.)

54. At some later date in the nineteenth century the Kentucky 'darky minstrel' tradition was introduced, with blackened faces and strumming banjoes. This was possibly due to contacts with the Southern States (one of the best-known Coloured songs 'Alibama' originated with the visit of the Southern ship *Alabama* to Table Bay during the Civil War, despite the fact that it represented the slave-owning side and might therefore have been expected to be unpopular with the recently enfranchised Cape slaves). Another theory attributes the 'coon' type to a Cape Town baker, Mr. C. J. Cole, who in 1894 dressed his employees up as American minstrels to advertise his bakery (*Cape Times*, 28th December, 1949). It is also claimed that at that period the private clubs (Afrikaans: *Klops*) which welcomed in the New Year were not exclusively Coloured in membership (see *Cape Times*, 4th January, 1951, for report of an interview with Mr. David Stevens, a Scottish building contractor, said to be the only white coon captain to-day).

55. Most of the foregoing information was published in an article in the *Cape Times* of 28th December, 1949. See *Picture Post* of 7th August, 1948, for photographs.

56. 'The police do give us a lot of privileges at New Year. It is the only sport we can indulge in to our hearts' delight and we look forward to it' (David Peterson, leader of the Spes Bona Coons, quoted in the *Cape Times Magazine*, 20th January, 1951).

57. In 1949 I saw an extremely drunken 'skolly' followed by an admiring group of gang members, making his way round the grandstand with a half-empty bottle in his hand. The white policeman on duty paid no attention until he got too near the Mayor's box; then a Coloured police officer was sent to remove him, and a lively and good-humoured chase followed, ending in the skolly's escape into the crowd. The matter would not have been handled so tolerantly on an ordinary day.

58. Characteristic troupe-names are: 'The Panamanian Crooning Minstrels', 'The United Broadway Serenaders', 'The Loyal Ex-Volunteer Darkies' (wearing waistcoats made of Union Jacks), 'The Liberty Philadelphia Minstrels', 'The Zonk Swingtown Minstrels'. Each troupe may have anything between 150 and 300 performers.

59. The troupes are not organised on the age-group principle, at least as far as the carnival itself is concerned. Grown men, youths and tiny boys participate in this, but no women or girls (until 1950, when one troupe had a 5-year-old 'drum majorette'). Each man or boy must buy his own costume every year. It normally consists of a silk shirt, big bow tie, white tennis shoes, top hat or cloth cap covered with silk, and silk jacket and trousers, all in the troupe's colours. The total cost may be anything from £2 10s. to £12, no small sum to a Coloured working family. The total

cost of organising both shows in 1949–50 was £26,000. The troupes are drawn mainly from the upper-lower class, with a smaller lower-lower element. Captains may come from the lower-middle class, as they have to exert considerable authority and possibly to advance the money for their troupes' costumes until the final instalments are paid by individual members (see *Cape Times*, 4th January, 1951).

60. Those Coloureds who cannot afford show-ground prices are thus enabled to see the troupes on their traditional lines of march. Rural families often come in for the day and picnic along the streets of District Six and Woodstock.

61. There is no segregated seating at these affairs, but Europeans wishing to attend are charged approximately double.

62. The songs and dance music are now largely American, but prizes are still offered for the traditional Cape *liedjies* (old or topical songs in Afrikaans) and *moppies* (comic songs). *Liedjies* are very popular amongst white South Africans, and a correspondent to *Die Burger* once asked angrily why 'good Afrikaners' should sing these 'slave songs'.

63. 'At Green Point a well-dressed Coloured man said. "This is not wholly typical of the Cape Coloured People. In a way it is just a safety valve, for there are many among us with noble aspirations and a real desire to better ourselves".' *Sun*, 6th January, 1950.) The left-wing *Torch* did not report the 1949–50 Carnival at all, but sardonically called the later ceremonial opening of Parliament the 'whites' coon carnival'. After the 1950–1 Carnival two rival coon boards took their carnivals travelling round the Union, and one even planned a visit to London later in the year. The carnivals played to large mixed audiences everywhere except in Kimberley, where the local Coloured community boycotted the show, on the grounds that there were separate performances for Europeans and Non-Europeans and that the show was 'degrading and disgusting and not representative of the Coloured People.' Boycott posters and pamphlets also claimed that the show was Government-sponsored, and that the forthcoming tour abroad was intended to ridicule and belittle the Coloured People to overseas audiences in order to justify the Government's *apartheid* and franchise policy (*Cape Times*, 5th February, 1951, and 6th February, 1951).

64. In early 1951 (see *Cape Times*, 2nd February, 1951) the principal of a large Coloured primary school announced that he was opposed to his pupils being members of coon troupes during the holidays and would discourage such children from joining the school, as they got into bad company and bad habits at carnival time. He claimed that juvenile coons at his school were ostracised by the other children; another principal, however, said that his children were inclined to hero-worship the coons, a tendency which he strongly discouraged (*Cape Times*, 5th February, 1951). See also letter in *Cape Times* of 6th February, 1951, deploring the influence of coons on school children, and report in *Cape Times* of 23rd March, 1951, of a large-scale 'coon' brawl in Paarl.

65. It seems likely that some troupes have greater prestige value than others, and membership is therefore more desirable. The total number of troupes varies from year to year, but is in the neighbourhood of fifty. Total membership may be anything from 10,000 to 20,000, but the Municipal Traffic Department sets a limit to the number of those allowed to parade through the streets at New Year.

66. Known colloquially amongst the Coloured people as 'choirs', although its members do not sing. Instruments are violins, banjoes, mandolins, guitars and saxophones. Another type of New Year choir, in this instance genuine, are the Malay choirs, which wear more expensive and less garish costumes than the coons (costing from £12 to £30), perform more sedately at a separate ground or in the City Hall, and are said by the coons to 'think themselves better than the rest' (many are of the artisan class). Dr. I. D. Duplessis, an authority on the Cape Malays, estimated that there are about fifty such choirs, with an average membership of forty. In the case of the younger members, he said that although there is no decline in the number of competitions or competitors, younger members tend to be the less sophisticated

type of Malay. In a recent statement to the press, the Chairman of the Cape Malay Choir Board, Mr. E. Schroeder, estimated that this Board, which is the largest organised group of choirs in the Malay Community, has an active membership of more than 3,000 (*Cape Times*, 9th March, 1951).

67. I am indebted to Mr. George Manuel for all information on the Christmas string bands. Of their class affiliation he writes: 'Choir members are drawn chiefly from the artisan and the factory worker class. Emphasis is on the social standing of would-be members. Not each and every one is accepted . . . The choirs have a strict code of conduct and soberness is essential.' The choirs have received little or no publicity in the European press in South Africa, unlike the flamboyant and 'picturesque' coons. In 1938 considerable indignation was aroused amongst them by a report in a Cape Town European paper in which a choir leader was referred to as a coon leader (see *Cape Standard* of 4th January, 1938).

68. Cf. Frazier (1), pp. 374–5: 'The secret society welded the Negroes together in a sacred brotherhood for mutual and common loyalty in a hostile white world. In fact it was charged by the whites that the lodge meetings were "often plotting places where groups of Negroes devise plans and encourage thoughts against the white man." Although the Negro enjoyed a freedom of expression in the lodge that he did not have outside, there is no evidence that the lodge was a place where plots were formed against the whites.' This is not a close parallel with the Coloured position, as the latter have not until recently felt the full and uncompromising hostility of the whites. Nor do the lodges appear to have the wide membership and power amongst the Coloured community that they do amongst American Negroes.

69. The I.O.T.T. is the only lodge about which detailed information has come to hand. It is primarily a temperance organisation, with (according to a recent year-book), 20,000 Coloured and African adult members and 30,000 juvenile members. A number of Europeans, including the Cape politician W. P. Schreiner, brother to Olive Schreiner, have occupied prominent offices in the I.O.T.T., and the present Right Worthy Templar is Mr. J. W. Mushet, M.P.

70. The first three are said to have mixed membership, but with separate lodges except in the Order of Free Gardeners (Scottish), and 'it is common for Coloured members of certain lodges to visit European lodges and vice versa', according to the informant quoted elsewhere. In the early 1930's, the Provincial Grand Master of one world-wide order with mixed membership was a Coloured man. The I.O.T.T. has a very large African membership, but some other lodges or orders do not encourage African membership and even have a definite understanding to exclude them. Most lodges have male members only, but the I.O.T.T. has members of both sexes.

71. On the other hand, another informant estimated the total numerical strength at 30,000 to 40,000, a considerably lower figure.

72. They may also fulfil wider welfare functions. For instance, the Grand Lodge of Free Gardeners (Africa) provides high school bursaries for deserving Coloured children, and has now established a university scholarship (£60 p.a. for three years).

73. For example, the Order of Free Gardeners has been in existence for over eighty years, the Mechanic and Fidelity Lodge for seventy-five years. The I.O.T.T. and the Mechanic and Fidelity Lodge have no connection with European lodges, but were founded independently.

74. See the *Cape Times* of 11th March, 1950 (article by George Manuel) and cf.: 'from the beginning the burial societies have been more popular than the societies providing "sickness benefits". However destitute of worldly goods the rural Negro has been, he has often borne his lot patiently as long as he was consoled by the prospect that he would be "put away right", i.e., given a decent burial.' (Frazier (1), p. 376.) Coloured payments now average about 2s. per month per family (excluding married children or those over 21).

75. The A.P.O. Society has a membership of about 3,500 families. An official said that the members came from the poorer sections of the community; higher-

income groups tend to take out policies in the large, European-owned insurance companies.

76. Mrs. A. G. Weiss makes the point that religion and religious activities give Coloured women in particular a deep satisfaction and assurance denied to them in their daily life (p. 130).

77. In 1918 there were seventy-six secessionist religious bodies in the Union, 320 by 1938 and nearly 1,350 by 1950 (only eighty-one officially recognised). The enormous number of such sects was to some extent paralleled by the number of European missionary bodies in South Africa (eleven in 1850, forty-four in 1938). (Figures from *Race Relations Handbook*, Ch. XXIII, except for those for 1950, which were given to the press by the Under-Secretary for Native Affairs, Mr. F. Rodseth (*Star*, 20th February, 1950).)

78. Report of Foundation Address in the *Silver Jubilee Celebrations* booklet, p. 2.

79. *Volkskerk van Afrika*—Twenty-eighth Anniversary Report, p. 64.

80. 'The policy of unending trusteeship is no longer acceptable to us and, as we claim to have reached maturity, we feel capable of managing our own Church affairs.' (Quoted from the manifesto sent by the seceding members of the Crawford congregation to the governing body of the D.R.M.C.—*Rand Daily Mail*, 6th October, 1950. See also *Star*, 17th October, 1950.)

81. Such a statement is very difficult to check, but seems likely in view of the hold exerted by the D.R.C. on its members in every sphere. It in any case reflects the current hostility and fear felt by many Coloured people towards the D.R.C.

82. The 'divide and rule' policy has until recently been highly effective in preventing Non-European unity. In addition, many Coloureds had reached a standard of living and culture which, though low and precarious, was superior to that of the incoming Africans, and saw their achievements endangered by the latter.

83. See Marais, pp. 275–80, for this period.

84. *Cape Times*, 20th February, 1926.

85. The fact that the Coloured minority has no chance of securing the election of its own representatives has caused voters to give their support to the white party which promises them most at election time, even though such promises may not be fully carried out. 'In these circumstances, it is not surprising that individual voters and some leaders have attempted to use their franchise in order to derive temporary and personal benefit, and not to advance the interests of the community. Coloured organisations have been developed whose main purposes it is to enable the leaders to bargain with candidates and parties for the Coloured vote; the political "bosses", big and small, can offer as many votes as each commands to the highest bidder. The practice undoubtedly exists. It involves not only Coloured political organisations, but a variety of other societies such as churches, clubs, and burial societies, and it extends to municipal as well as parliamentary and provincial council elections.' (*Race Relations Handbook*, p. 524.) See also B. K. Long, pp. 129–30, and Thompson, pp. 46–9.

86. 'The political influence of the Cape Coloured voters is stated to have had a significant part in causing the Europeans to class them on their side. If this policy continues one may expect an increase in racial admixture between the whites and the mixed bloods. On the other hand, if the policy is reversed, mixed bloods may eventually be driven over to associate themselves with and assume the leadership of the increasing mass of detribalised and race-conscious blacks.' This fairly accurate forecast was made in 1937 by Stonequist (p. 24). In Chapter IX we shall be discussing some Coloured-African attitudes which may hamper such unity and undermine such leadership.

87. In more general terms, we may divide protest movements in a minority group into those which accept the existing social structure but protest against the status ascribed to themselves (in this case the Europeanising group), and those which protest against the whole framework of the existing society (the advocates of Non-

European unity). Marginal groups, whether they are socially, culturally or racially marginal, rarely proceed to the second and more radical type of protest until their bid for better conditions and higher status within the existing framework has been finally rejected. In such circumstances, they may turn away from the dominant group which has rejected them, and place themselves at the head of the dominated group, if the latter is willing to accept them. Probably the best instance of this process is to be found in the history of the assumption of Negro leadership by the mulattoes of the American South. Even here, however, the major Negro protest organisations seem not to reject the American way of life, but to demand full participation for their own group in it.

88. This development was envisaged long ago by Dr. A. Abdurahman, in his presidential address at the 9th Annual A.P.O. Conference in Johannesburg: 'If the Europeans persist in their policy of repression, there will one day arise a solid mass of Black and Coloured humanity whose demands will be irresistible.' Cf. *Rand Daily Mail* editorial of 2nd March, 1951.

89. An excellent account of Coloured political life and trends is given by René de Villiers in *Race Relations Handbook*, Ch. XXI. See also Roux, pp. 362–7.

90. The position after the setting up of the C.A.C. in April 1943 is described by a Coloured journalist: 'The fight was on. It was a bitter fight with no quarter asked and none given. It was carried into all spheres of communal life—football clubs, cricket clubs, tennis clubs, cultural clubs, societies, churches, and even into domestic life. Fathers and sons, brother and brother became avowed enemies. Never before had the Coloured community experienced the like.' (Article by Mr. A. C. Scholtz in *Cape Times*, 8th July, 1949.) Instead of being directed entirely against the dominant Europeans, Coloured protests against their situation have been partly deflected on to intra-group rivalry.

91. In theory it advocates total unity, expressly stating that those Europeans who subscribe to the Ten-Point Programme will be welcomed. This programme is: (I) The Franchise, i.e., the right of every man and woman over the age of 21 to elect and be elected to Parliament, Provincial Council and all other Divisional and Municipal Councils. (II) Compulsory, free and uniform education for all children up to the age of 16, with free meals, free books and school equipment for the needy. (III) Inviolability of person, of one's house and privacy. (IV) Freedom of speech, press, meetings and association. (V) Freedom of movement and occupation. (VI) Full equality of rights for all citizens without distinction of race, colour and sex. (VII) Revision of the land question in accordance with the above. (VIII) Revision of the civil and criminal code in accordance with the above. (IX) Revision of the system of taxation in accordance with the above. (X) Revision of the labour legislation and its application to the mines. (Taken from Third Non-European Unity Movement Report, 1945, p. 34.) As even the most liberal South African white would find it hard to agree to the immediate implementation of Points I and VI, and all white politicians belonging to any existing South African party would be committing political suicide if they attempted to advocate these points or even Points II, IV, VII and X, it is not surprising that the movement is one of Non-European unity in name and in practice. The All-African Convention (A.A.C.) is the major African political organisation in the Unity Movement, while Indian organisations have been rather aloof. See Roux, p. 29 f. for the National Liberation League, a leftist protest movement of the late thirties.

92. This committee has consistently advocated boycotting of elections, advising Coloured voters in the 1948 General and 1949 Provincial Elections to go to the polls and write across their forms: 'Full democratic rights.'

93. Founded in 1949 to combat the introduction of partial segregation on Cape Town suburban trains. Most of its leaders are the same as those of the Anti-C.A.D. See also p. 189.

94. The A.P.O., after the death of Dr. Abdurahman, passed into the hands of what its present leaders call 'collaborationists' (i.e., those Coloured leaders who

disliked and feared the African connection, and saw the best hope of Coloured progress in co-operation with the Europeans, even if it meant endless compromise. At the 1944 Conference, however, the Anti-C.A.D. 'captured' it, and since then most Cape branches have pursued the anti-collaborationist policy. More or less the same developments occurred in the T.L.S.A. In the Transvaal, however, the A.P.O., although its Life President, Mr. A. P. Dickenson, is a politician of the old Abdurahman school (see *Torch*, 24th April, 1950), is said to contain both moderate and pro-Communist elements, and it has come out in support of the inter-racial Franchise Action Council, which represents a combination of similar elements in the Cape. So have elements of the Natal A.P.O. (*Sun*, 27th April, 1950). The former A.P.O. Chairman, Mr. S. M. Rahim, who resigned in mid-May 1951, also backed the activities of this committee without the approval of his Executive, but his presence has enabled the committee's promoters to claim A.P.O. support. At its Conference in April 1950 the A.P.O. altered its constitution so as to allow all Non-Europeans to join.

95. The T.L.S.A. was in March 1950 informed by the Cape Education Department that no further communications from it would be accepted until the T.L.S.A. was prepared to restrict its activities to education alone. On the other hand, the *Torch* announced a week later that T.E.P.A. membership dues would in future be collected by the Education Department, thus making T.E.P.A. members into its 'stooges'.

96. See Joshi, p. 33, for the Non-European groups which have such an interest in the *status quo*.

97. Each group claims to speak on behalf of the Coloured people, and their major energy, particularly in the case of the Anti-C.A.D. movement, has so far been devoted to fighting each other. In 1949, Mr. G. J. Golding, headmaster of Upper Ashley St. Primary School, Cape Town, editor of the *Sun*, a member and ex-Chairman of the C.A.C., sued the *Torch* for £4,500 damages for defamation. After a trial which lasted several days and cost a great deal, the plaintiff was awarded damages of £150 and costs. The articles to which exception was taken called Mr. Golding a Quisling and a traitor to his people, implied that he drew rents from slum property, and spent his time playing tennis and smoking cigars. A cartoon was also said to have portrayed him as a pig—a serious matter for a leader in a community containing Moslem voters, as was brought out in the evidence. More than once during the trial, however, the judge protested that the court was apparently being used as a political forum (see *Cape Argus* and *Times* for the period 8th–16th June, 1949, and *Cape Argus*, 11th August, 1949, also *Sun*, *Torch* and *Guardian* for these dates).

98. At least one of these four members represented a small group of Transvaal Coloureds who support the Nationalist Party. This group, the *Transvaalse Kleurling Volksbond* (Transvaal Coloured People's Association), has little significance or popular support, but its utterances are at times useful to the Nationalist Government. For instance, Dr. Dönges was enabled to claim during his visit to U.N.O. that he had Coloured support for the Group Areas Act, having received a deputation from the *Bond* before he left (*Torch*, 19th December, 1950). One of the *Bond's* leaders is a Mr. Fredericks, one of the four C.A.C. members who did not resign. Of him the *Torch* wrote: 'A supporter of Christian-National Education, Fredericks is reported to have said that the Coloured people, as a distinct race, must remain apart from the Europeans, Africans and Indians, because they had a separate culture. "The Coons prove this," he said. And if the Coloured people united with the other Non-Europeans, this great feature of their culture would sink lower and lower, and a part of the better-class Coloureds would go over to the whites.' (16th January, 1950.) See also *Guardian* (22nd March, 1951). See the *Torch* of 19th December, 1950, for information about a group of Stellenbosch Coloureds called the *Moedertaalstryders* (Fighters for the Mother-Tongue), whose professed aim is to foster Afrikaans in Coloured schools. In May 1951, a small Coloured Syndicate in Kingwilliamstown (E. Cape) sent a deputation to the Prime Minister to offer its support for *apartheid* (*Cape Times* of 26th May, 1951).

99. See *Rand Daily Mail*, 1st March, 1951, and 5th March, 1951. Their political opponents suggested that a major reason for this *rapprochement* was to be found in the political advantages which might accrue to both sides. (*Torch*, 16th January, 1950, 30th October, 1950, and 13th March, 1951). Similar uneasy *ententes* between Communists and Conservatives or Nationalists may be traced amongst other non-white groups in the Union and elsewhere in Africa.

100. For varying reports on the success of this demonstration, see the *Rand Daily Mail*, *Cape Times*, *Die Burger*, of 9th March, 1951, and the *Torch* of 13th March, 1951, and *Sun* of 16th March, 1951.

101. *Cape Times*, 2nd April, 1951. The motion was, however, carried by 133 to 11 votes. The strike was supported by perhaps 50 per cent of Coloured organised workers in many Cape districts, by some Africans and by many Coloured school children. There was no violence. (*Rand Daily Mail*, 8th May, 1951.)

102. See Report of 1951 National Anti-C.A.D. Conference. (*Cape Times*, 6th January, 1951.) The N.E.U.M. is also calling for an eventual boycotting of the elections at which the new Coloured Representatives are to be elected when the Act goes through, on the grounds that if all Coloured voters stay away from the polls the Act will be unworkable. As the N.E.U.M. is unlikely to command the allegiance of all voters, the effect of such a boycott will merely be to ensure the election of candidates backed by other groups.

103. See *Torch*, 10th April, 1950.

104. An instance of an informal self-help association is the old-established system of *Kanalawerk* (whence Kanaladorp—the old name for Cape Town's District Six). *Kanala* is said to be a Malay word for 'please' and *Kanalawerk* is work done to please a friend. It is an old custom among Coloured and Malay artisans at the Cape to help one another to build their homes at week-ends, the only recompense being the knowledge that similar help will be forthcoming in their own need. (See Lawrence E. Green, *Coloured Cape Town* in the *Outspan*, 17th November, 1950, and editorial in the *Cape Times* of 14th November, 1950, commenting on an industrial agreement which would have the effect of stopping this custom.) See also *Cape Standard* of 29th March, 1938, on the various Coloured newspapers which have existed at different times.

105. The Cape Town A.P.O. Terminating Building Society (five years old) had in March 1950 a total figure for share subscriptions of about £26,500. The People's Mutual Terminating Building Society (thirty-one years) has a total of about £23,000. Both are said to have European subscribers. In the case of the former, one such subscriber is said to have withdrawn as a consequence of the present tendency in legislation, giving this as the reason.

106. An obituary notice in the *Sun* of 27th January, 1950 (p. 8), gives a fairly typical outline of the associational life of an upper-middle-class building contractor of Parow (near Cape Town). He was a foundation member of the local Anglican Church, church officer and warden for over forty-seven years (the funeral service was conducted by the (European) Coadjutor Bishop of Cape Town). The dead man had also been President of the Ramblers Rugby Football Club, a foundation member of the Parow Sports Board of Control, a former Captain of the Church Lads' Brigade, and active in his Trades Union and the Red Cross.

107. MacIver, p. 8 f. Cf. also Max Weber, *The Theory of Social and Economic Organisation*, p. 126, para. 4.

108. A Cape Town suburb with a large white and Coloured population.

109. Warner and Lunt, p. 16.

110. Compare and contrast the unified class structure of Brazil: 'In the Brazilian rural society of the colonial period Oliveira Vianna identifies three distinct social stratas: the predominantly white *senhores* of the upper rank, the predominantly mixed-blood free artisans, *rendeiros* and petty officials of the middle tier, and the predominantly black slaves of the lower stratum. The duration of this particular

organisation was, however, brief. As the colour line bent further under pressure of the rising mulatto, certain of the more able or more successful mixed-bloods broke through into the upper tiers.' (Pierson, pp. 164–5.) In the pre-Union Cape, the Coloured problem was essentially a class problem, intensified by colour differences. Since Union it has increasingly become a race problem.

111. For class-stratification within the American Negro group see Johnson, pp. 231–6; Myrdal, pp. 1,129 and 1,382; Frazier (1) pp. 286–7. For Coloured internal class-structure see C., s. 42–55 and Weiss *passim*.

112. We have commented before on the lack of Coloured commercial and business enterprise.

113. Cf. Myrdal, pp. 77 and 694, for a parallel situation amongst American Negroes. Amongst Coloureds this has developed only since 1920, according to a speaker (Mr. A. L. Charles) at the first National Coloured-European Conference in Cape Town, 1933.

114. 'Teachers have no rights in these localities (Reserves), unless they are descendants and registered occupiers. It is, however, worth noting that four of the five members of the C.A.C. which your committee interviewed during its tour are teachers.' (M., p. 4, s. 22–3.)

115. 'Perhaps this intellectual class (the teachers) contributed much towards rousing the so-called race-consciousness of the Coloureds. Practically everywhere the teachers are the leaders of societies which have come into being in these places and actively interest themselves in Church matters.' (M., s. 22.)

116. M., p. 4.

117. 'The American order of colour caste has even more directly stamped the Negro class system by including relative whiteness as one of the main factors determining status within the Negro community.' (Myrdal, p. 696 f.)

118. A Cape Town girl of the lower-middle class who brought her second baby along to my house said: 'See how fair she is—isn't it lucky?' (Cf. Millin (1), p. 193.) The mother herself was not very light. The father was darker, but her maternal grandfather had been a German settler, a fact which was frequently mentioned, apparently with the intention of impressing the family's status on the hearers. Of a friend of hers, whose father was white, she said: 'She's such a nice woman—not at all proud although her father was white.' A helper at the Cape Town child Life Protection Society told me that prospective adoptive parents often want to have a lighter child (although the society discourages this preference, and tries to place dark children with dark families, and so on).

119. These are the people who have struggled up to the same intellectual and cultural level as the educated European, only to find themselves rejected on grounds not of ability but of colour.

120. See *Torch* of 22nd May, 1950, and *Cape Times* of 24th December, 1949 (Man on the Spot's column), for two such instances.

121. Two such Coloured leaders took pains to point out to the writer, while being interviewed on quite different subjects, that at least one of their grandparents was white.

122. This view has probably been held though not expressed publicly in so many words by several major white politicians, as one method of solving the Coloured problem. These light-coloured upper or upper-middle-class Coloureds are of course racially marginal between their own group and the white group, in a way in which the Coloured group as a whole is not. It would therefore be only natural for them to strive for integration with the white group, with its high status and greater material advantages.

123. A Coloured woman who was employed as a cook in Muizenberg, a Cape Peninsula seaside resort, used to complain that she had no one to whom to talk in the neighbourhood. It was suggested that she might make friends with the Coloured servant in the flat below, but she said contemptuously that the latter was a 'Bushman girl'. Asked to expand this statement she said that the girl had 'pepper-corn hair'

x

(her own words) and was a low class of girl. A song recently current amongst lower-class Coloureds began with the words: '*Hi-bop, ree-bop*; *hi-bop, reebop* ; *Boesman-meid met haar peper-korrel kopf.*' (Bushman girl, with her pepper-corn head.)

124. The *Sun* often carries a small advertisement offering a hair-straightener, but there seem to be fewer such products or skin-bleaches here than amongst American Negroes (but see *Cape Times* report on Coloured beauty shops, 10th May, 1951).

125. Malays and such Indians (usually Christians or Moslem) as enter the group often rank high in the Coloured group on cultural and economic grounds. The aboriginal Hottentot had a skin that was not dark but a light yellow-brown, and the prevalent brown skin of the Cape Coloured person is often darker than that of the pure Hottentot, probably due to the Negroid slave admixture. Amongst the Bastards and other rural Coloureds, the fear of 'darkness' is probably now related to Bantu infiltration.

126. Coloured children with this ancestry often have golden blond hair, which, however, darkens to the familiar rusty-brown. A few instances of brilliant red hair have also been seen, combined with brown or grey-green eyes and freckles, and 'Hottentot' features.

127. See Marais, p. 96, n. 3, on the difficulty experienced by members of the Carnegie Poor White Commission in distinguishing between Poor Whites and impoverished Bastards. It was finally solved when they realised that the Bastards always called them *Baas*.

128. M., p. 34, s. 138.

129. Marais, pp. 103–4.

130. Marais adds (*ibid.*): 'The Rehoboth burgher has a pride in his white blood which makes him glory in the fact that he is "not native but a Bastard". As such he holds himself excused from "Kaffir work", which may easily be stretched to include all labour with the hands. Fischer mentions as an example of this harmful racial pride the fact that the well-to-do (who are also the whiter) families speak contemptuously of the rest of the community as "*half-natjies*" (half-breeds).' From these extracts it can be seen to what extent white race-attitudes have been taken over and preserved by a rural Coloured group. Following the introduction of spatial *apartheid* in post offices, stations, etc., the Rehoboth burghers asked that it be abolished in their Reserve, as it meant that they had to share the Non-European counter with Natives. If this were not done, they demanded that all Europeans should be compelled to leave the Reserve. The S.W.A. Administration granted this request (*Cape Times*, 30th November, 1950, and 30th January, 1951). On the Rehobothers see also *Die Huisgenoot* (27th October, 1950).

131. 'In addition to these classes amongst the Bastards themselves, there were in 1925 about 2,500 natives, mainly Hottentot, Herero or Bergdamara, living amongst them as servants of the well-to-do, or rent-paying squatters. These the Bastards called their *volk* (people) or *bywoners*, in the Boer manner.' (Marais, pp. 102–3.)

132. We have already stressed that dark colour is acceptable in the case of Malays or Indians, other status-determinants being equal. It is interesting to note too that when units of the U.S. Navy visited Cape Town in 1949 the Negro members of the crew, many of them very dark, were entertained by local middle-class Coloured people with every semblance of hospitality and friendliness. Such American Negroes as reach South Africa seem to be accepted as of equal status by Coloured people because of their educational and economic achievements, general acculturation and admixture of white blood.

133. Marais quotes Cape Government Publication No. 60 (pp. 5, 15) of 1890 for a comment on the inhabitants of the Namaqualand stations: 'amongst whom there was a sprinkling of the descendants of slaves . . . the latter being decidedly a superior race in the matter of industry and thrift' (p. 75, n. 4).

134. It is possible that some employers prefer light Coloureds for certain work.

Advertisements for 'high-class waitress, slightly coloured', appear not infrequently in the Cape Town press. Light Coloured women seem to expect higher wages as domestic servants on this ground alone, but some white employers think them 'touchy' and 'cheeky' and prefer to employ dark Coloured or African women. There is a certain ambiguity about European attitudes to degrees of colour.

135. Cf. Davis Gardner and Davis (p. 235), quoted by Myrdal, n. 15 to Ch. 32, pp. 1,382–3.

136. In June 1949, a light Coloured woman of the lower-middle class told me how she ran into a group of 'skolly-boys' while walking in her dance dress from the bus-stop to a dance at the Tafelberg Hotel. The youths accused her of 'dressing-up', trying to 'play white', and threatened to 'cut' (i.e., use their knives on) her.

137. See Myrdal, pp. 746–9.

138. This includes proto-Malay and Indian strains.

139. Myrdal, p. 698.

140. This would correspond to the exclusive attitude of the free mulattoes of the Southern States (cf. Frazier (1), pp. 59–81, and Myrdal, pp. 695–9). I was unable to verify this hypothesis from the few upper and upper-middle-class individuals whom I questioned. Some professed ignorance and disinterest, while others denied that 'good' families have any slave ancestry, an unlikely statement but one which precluded further questioning. The great majority of these families probably have one or more white grandparents or great-grandparents, but their other ancestry must certainly have included at least one slave or freedwoman.

141. Membership of a particular religious sect does not, however, have the same class connotation as in Britain, where the distinction between 'church' and 'chapel' is still firmly drawn. On the eagerness of upper and lower-middle-class Coloured women to take part in committee work, see Weiss, pp. 36 and 41.

142. I am indebted to Dr. K. L. Little, lately of the London School of Economics and now of Edinburgh University, for this suggestion, which, on further inquiry after my return to the Cape, I found to be correct. One teacher said that those Coloureds who cannot speak English are regarded as barbarians. The fact that primary education is given in the home language (in this case usually Afrikaans), so that only those who proceed to secondary schools would learn grammatical English, is probably a contributory factor to the importance of English as a status-determinant.

143. See my earlier section on family structure (pp. 148–50), and Weiss, pp. 44–5.

144. 'If one remembers that the *Lebensraum* in which the Coloured have to live, their "Life chances" as Weber calls it, are very limited, and have to fit into a pattern moulded by European usages, one will realise that one of the few ways Coloured families can express their social status is by possessing and displaying expensive furniture. To possess a piano, radiogram, a chesterfield suite is not a sign of inane spending, but the outer expression of the social standing of a family, it is a symbol —a question of prestige.' (Weiss, p. 79.)

145. On the upward social striving of lower-middle-class Coloured women see Weiss, p. 41.

146. A housing manager told me how even in a sub-economic housing scheme class-distinctions or intra-class gradations would be drawn within a few months, so that certain streets would become desirable, others to be avoided.

147. I remember a former primary-school teacher, who had 'married beneath her', and lived in a one-roomed shack with a shiftless, drunken husband and nine children ranging from a baby-in-arms to a thirteen-year-old. Often there was no food in the house, but there was always money for school-books, shoes, soap and disinfectant, and it was surrounded by an attractive little garden.

148. The prestige value of clothes was recently demonstrated by certain principals of Coloured schools who insisted on school uniforms in order to raise the standing of their schools, thereby causing considerable distress amongst poorer pupils. (*Cape Times*, 24th March, 1951.)

149. Cf. Weiss, p. 103.

150. They are not always poorly educated from choice, but from lack of higher educational facilities or sufficient financial resources to make use of such facilities. The recent extension of secondary school education, combined with the narrowing of economic opportunities, is likely to produce increasing numbers of comparatively well-educated people who will fall into this economic class through necessity. It has been suggested that the increase of 'skollydom' amongst Coloured youths is partly due to the increased numbers of such economically frustrated persons.

151. Cf. Myrdal quoting C. S. Johnson, *The Shadow of the Black Belt*: 'The "folk" Negro has a low degree of assimilation to modern American standards but has, nevertheless, some measure of family organisation and internal group cohesion' (p. 702).

152. Coloured class-mores and class-indices are even more similar to those evolved in the complex class-stratification of Great Britain. The South African white class-structure tails away at the bottom, as most whites who would elsewhere be labourers are in the foreman class. There is, however, a corresponding white 'skolly' class.

153. If the colour-barrier were raised, and the Coloured group left to find its own economic and cultural level in relation to the South African European community, each Coloured class would be lowered by one peg or more. Coloured upper-middle-class persons would not at present be able to compete on equal terms with the European upper-middle class, but would find themselves level with the lower-middle class. Moreover, the order of evaluation in the European and Coloured class-systems is somewhat different, and the latter could not be integrated into the former as it exists at present, even a peg or more lower. Such groups as the teachers and nurses would lose in status, as the European class-system places less emphasis on education and occupation than on wealth and property.

154. Cf. servants'-hall snobbery in nineteenth-century England.

155. Cf. Weiss, pp. 41 and 96.

156. In the case of urban skilled artisans, their social class would probably depend on other than occupational or economic determinants (for instance on membership of a 'good' family) and this particular occupational class would therefore be split between the two social classes. This point requires verification in the field.

157. In both the upper and the middle classes, a family's status is determined by the man's and not by the woman's position. The woman may, however, do much to consolidate and maintain this status.

158. There are certain difficulties in integrating rural groups into an open-class system of this type. In the rural context, social status is still largely determined by ownership of land or livestock, and it is difficult to evaluate the relative social status of, say, a Rehoboth patriarch and a Cape Town secondary school-teacher with an overseas degree. Probably each, when in his own environment, would regard the other as belonging to a lower class. To the teacher the Burgher would lack education, while to the Burgher the teacher would be landless.

159. Such 'select' families usually establish an hereditary professional tradition. The *Cape Times* of 22nd February, 1951, described the Hendrikse family, which had produced teachers and professional men for a century. The same article mentioned one other such family, and also a third which provides a clear instance of upward social mobility through economic status-determinants. This is the case of a Cape Town builder whose children are, respectively, a doctor, dentist and the principal of a girls' primary school.

160. As we pointed out in Ch. V, teaching is the only profession at present open to Coloured men on a large scale. The status of a teacher is therefore higher in the Coloured community than amongst Europeans, and most Coloured leaders of to-day are teachers.

161. Inter-class mobility seems to be less frequent than in the South African white group. The supreme example of upward social mobility in the Coloured

group is, however, not between classes, but the act of 'passing' into the white group.

162. '. . . it is known that the C.A.C. men were always ready to accept the opportunity to become the exploiters of their own people in segregated areas where sole business rights would be reserved for Coloureds only.' (*Torch* editorial, 30th January, 1950.)

163. The most important of these local sub-communities is the Cape Malay or Moslem community of over 62,000 persons (1951 Census figure), the great majority domiciled within the Greater Cape Town area. The internal structure of this community would require a separate study, as it remains largely a closed group, in which status is based on religious criteria, which coincide with economic ones. Its members belong mainly to the skilled artisan class. Their religion gives them a sense of assurance and a feeling of community lacking in the Christian Coloureds. Unlike the latter, Malays do not feel themselves inferior because they are not white, nor do they copy European ways nor attempt to 'pass' into the European group. Because Islam is a 'male' religion, in which women have little status, Malay women tend to be uneducated and lacking in initiative compared with Christian Coloured women of the same class; they are often looked down on by the latter. On the other hand, Malay men have equal or higher prestige in relation to Coloured men of the same class, and a Coloured woman of the lower-middle class who marries a Malay and becomes a Moslem does not lose 'caste' in either group (on relations between Coloured and Malay industrial workers see Weiss, *passim*). The Malay group has contributed several prominent Coloured leaders, notably the late Dr. A. Abdurahman, his son, Mr. 'Sonny' Abdurahman, and his daughter, Mrs. Z. Gool. There has always been some small Malay political association to collaborate with white advocates of 'segregation' or *apartheid*, perhaps because this group has no desire for integration with the whites, and no great sympathy with 'Pan-Africanism'.

164. See *Torch* of 23rd October, 1950 (paragraph headed 'Just Three Questions'), for an identification of the 'Coloured man' as one who subscribes to certain political beliefs, which is strongly reminiscent of the Nationalist tendency to identify 'good Afrikaner' with 'Nationalist'.

165. See Louis Wirth, *When Peoples Meet*, pp. 468–9, on the growth of minority consciousness and group solidarity under external pressure.

166. Speaking at the Coloured-European Conference in 1933, Professor Hutt said: 'Group consciousness exists among them, yet it is in a most rudimentary form. They have a loyalty to one another which one feels is little more than a reflex of a rebellious hostility to the white.' These remarks still apply. To-day, the 'rebellious hostility to the white' has intensified to the point when it may provide a genuine focus of group unity. Intra-group loyalty is sometimes evident in refusals to bring charges against other members of the group which would involve them in dealings with the law, or to give information which might be disadvantageous to them. (Cf. *Cape Times* of 11th March, 1950, on the code of loyalty in District Six.)

167. Despite the advocation by some Nationalist theorists of the desirability of encouraging a feeling of distinctness and racial pride in all ethnic groups (see *Die Vaterland*'s comment on the C.A.C. resignations, 11th January, 1950, and speech by the Vice-Chairman of the Griqualand West branch of the T.L.S.A. in Kimberley): 'It is high time that our young people wrote their own plays, glorifying their own people. Let us instil pride into the minds of our youth.' (*Torch*, 17th July, 1950.)

CHAPTER IX—THE CAPE COLOURED PEOPLE WITHIN THE LARGER STRUCTURE

1. Unesco Statement on Race Problems (Paris—1950)—from paragraphs 6 and 14.

2. See MacCrone, pp. 141–2. The Company freed its own slaves on condition that they had reached a certain age, had been baptised and spoke Dutch fluently (V. de Kock, pp. 209–10).

3. See V. de Kock, p. 111. Professor MacCrone cites (p. 45) the attitude of a visiting clergyman in 1666 who protested publicly against the proposed baptism of the child of an unbaptised slave woman. This particular protest was probably made on religious grounds, but it is easy to see how the attitude could spread to laymen (many of them slave-owners with much to lose from such emancipation) in a society where all unbelievers were economically and culturally inferior, and distinguished by quite obvious physical characteristics.

4. As one South African writer put it bitterly: 'Jan van Riebeeck . . . made the initial error in 1652, according to a leading Afrikaans writer, of assuming "that conversion to Christianity made acceptable human beings out of the aborigines". For 300 years since, white South Africa has been engaged in disproving this distasteful theory'. (Adamastor—*White Man Boss*, p. 50.)

5. Nevertheless the Fiscal still used this dichotomy in the mid-1750's when complaining of slaves who were so indulged by their owners that their behaviour towards Christians was becoming intolerable (V. de Kock, p. 48).

6. 'When colour differences coincide with differences in cultural levels, then colour becomes symbolic and each individual is automatically classified by the uniform he wears.' (E. B. Reuter—*The Mulatto in the United States*, pp. 99–100, quoted by Myrdal, p. 98.)

7. MacCrone gives several examples of the comparative freedom and familiarity of contacts between free white and coloured persons at that time, but foreshadows the inevitable development: 'The presence of a large number of black slaves within a community in which white slave-owners predominated was fatal to the prospect of a free black or Coloured population, since they would only tend to fall, and could never hope to rise in the social scale' (pp. 71–3).

8. As many did in earlier days (see MacCrone, p. 46). For an instance of non-baptism see V. de Kock, p. 199–200.

9. MacCrone, pp. 134–5. The disposal of slaves professing the Christian religion had been checked by an order of 1770 to the effect that they were not to be sold or otherwise alienated (V. de Kock, p. 112 and p. 213). See also the case of Jacobus Elisa Joannes Capitein, a negro slave who studied theology at Leiden and became a Christian minister. He wrote a dissertation to prove that slavery was not in conflict with Christian doctrines and even suggested that a few worthless whites should be enslaved as well (V. de Kock, p. 15).

10. *Ibid.*, pp. 77–8.

11. Cf. the 'Ruling Class Situation' described by Oliver Cox as typical of the British West Indies and (until recently) the Dutch East Indies: 'The white man's principal need is not a home but a satisfied and exploitable people to develop the resources of the country. This ruling class adopts a policy of "co-operation"; and, other things being equal, favours are distributed to the mixed-bloods on the basis of their apparent degrees of whiteness.' (Cox, pp. 350–3.)

12. In the frontier districts a certain intermediate status seems also to have been accorded locally and temporarily to the Bastards. They often remained in close contact with their white kinsmen, in the rôle of trusted and superior servants. They were allowed the use of horses and arms, and did not have to carry passes, all European prerogatives. Nevertheless, they were never fully accepted by the Boers, and, in the early days at least, many of them were not baptised. Even after the great missionary movement brought Christianity to them, however, in the early nineteenth century, their subsequent and notable devotion to religion (see Marais, p. 107) made them no more acceptable to the Boers. The status amongst the Boers was a precarious one, and depended upon their 'knowing their place', while their very existence was a threat to a status-hierarchy increasingly based on colour.

13. It is perhaps significant that the English translation of *Blankes* is 'Europeans' not 'Whites'. It perhaps reflects a fundamental difference of outlook between the two sections of the dominant group. (See letter on this distinction from Dr. R. J.

Jordan in the *Cape Times* of 2nd April, 1949), and: 'South Africa is two nations. There is a white nation and a black nation' (Mr. J. G. Strydom, Minister of Lands, speaking at Mafeking, *Rand Daily Mail*, 7th May, 1951).

14. An up-to-date statement of this dichotomy is given in the following passage: '. . . when national registration has been completed all their objection will evaporate because there will then be a clear line between European and non-European and if a person then falls within the European community even if his colour is not all that we desire he remains in the community in which he is registered.' (Mr. H. S. Erasmus, M.P. for Boshof-Hoopstad, speaking on 24th May, 1949. *Hansard*, col. 6411.)

15. Cf. MacCrone, p. 125. At this stage, however, the Cape was still used as a convict-station for Europeans from other Dutch East India Company territories, and no segregated gaol accommodation was yet provided. Victor de Kock quotes a plea from such incarcerated exiles in which the Christian-heathen and freeman-slave antitheses are still paramount: 'Never in Africa has it happened that Europeans had to live in chains for so long a time, nor found themselves mingled with heathens who not only are guilty of the most unprecedented crimes but are also born slaves . . . it is a shame and a blot on Christians that we should be mixed with them and treated in such a brutal manner.' It would seem that the thirty-two men concerned were subsequently separated from the Hottentot and slave prisoners (pp. 192–3), but see also *ibid.*, p. 219, for hardening European attitudes towards the slave class and the Free Blacks, who were accused of dirtiness and indolence.

16. 'You need only walk into the streets of Cape Town and this Peninsula to see that it is practically impossible to draw a line . . . ; the gradations are so gradual and large and so infinite that really there is no line . . .' (Field Marshal Smuts, reported in *Hansard*, 19th May, 1949, col. 6177.)

17. Many of the Boers were probably not particularly Nordic in appearance, particularly those with Huguenot blood, most of them from Provence. On the other hand, the Bantu are rarely a true black, and the Xhosa, who were first encountered, were often considerably lighter, due to their absorption of the easternmost Hottentot tribes. The 'Free Blacks' of the Cape probably ranged from *café-au-lait* to chocolate, according to provenance. Nevertheless, as MacCrone says: 'Though the skin colour in the one case is actually a kind of "distressed" pink, and in the other case a brown or dark-brown hue, the *Tendenz zur Pragnänz* will admit no intermediate shades to qualify its absolute opposition of the two skin-colours. Thought as well as action in the moral sphere involves less effort when everything can be recognised as right or wrong, good or bad. In the same way, when all men can be divided into the white or the black, the sheep or the goats, the social adjustments required to deal with them become a matter of simple conditioning.' (p. 291.)

18. Although there seem to have been recurrent threats of slave escapes and revolts even here, which may have contributed to the general fear complex (cf. V. de Kock, Ch. IV).

19. A characteristic modern Afrikaner view of this process is provided in the following quotation: '. . . The Voortrekkers of that time, who in difficult circumstances and surrounded by a lower civilisation, by a different culture, did not become the prey of what was the fate of so many other white communities, where they as a small band separated from their motherland were encircled by black hordes.' (Dr. Dönges, Minister of the Interior, speaking in the House of Assembly; *Hansard*, 19th May, 1949, col. 6167). The reference to 'other white communities' is obscure, but may allude to Latin colonising groups, whose objections to miscegenation were fewer.

20. Even in the north this did not preclude cordial and even affectionate relations between master and servant, so long as the latter kept his place. In recent years, urbanisation and industrialisation have been rapidly undermining this relationship, and exacerbating contacts between white and non-white.

21. See Marais, p. 282.

22. Cf. the attitude of the Boers to other European peoples whose views on

colour differ from their own. An extreme statement of such an attitude occurs in the following extract from a letter to *Die Transvaler* on 26th May, 1949: 'As a race-conscious person proud of the Germanic blood which flows in my veins, I note that in *Die Transvaler* the term "white" has been used on two occasions when the Portuguese have been spoken of. Let it be realised once and for all what "white" means, and let us be so proud of the word that we always use it correctly. "White" can only used be when the Germanic race is spoken of.' (Quoted in the *British African Monthly*, 4th July, 1949). The blood is also kept pure by extending colour-attitudes to coloured races outside South Africa, which accounts for the strange treatment of Non-European diplomats, transit passengers and so on.

23. Most Boers living in the isolated rural districts of the North Cape, and many who were not so far afield, tended to look north to the Transvaal or Free State for their ideology.

24. Notably Andries Stockenstrom, for whose career see Marais and MacMillan, *passim*.

25. This lack of specifically Coloured political activity may have been due to a feeling of sufficient integration into the European community amongst those Coloured people who were politically conscious and qualified to vote. This may also account for their failure to improve their economic status. Cf. the situation of the Brazilian mulatto, as contrasted with that of the American Negro (Pierson, p. 176).

26. That it was no longer a militant tradition was shown in the capitulation of the Cape delegates over the question of Non-European political rights at the Union discussions (see p. 34).

27. At this time, it should be remembered, an African was a rarity in the West Cape. An informant told me that when he was at school in Wellington just before the First World War the boys would crowd to look if one passed by.

28. 'A rich Negro is a white man, and a poor white man is a Negro.' (Pierson, p. 348.) Cf. also, 'Although it is true that dark colour, as we have seen, is ordinarily identified with lower status and white colour with upper-class position, rising in class tends to take a man out of even the colour category. For instance, a white Bahian remarked of an upper-class mulatto, "I would hesitate to call him a *pardo* although he plainly is one; some of his friends might overhear me." For use in such cases, *moreno* is the term *mais ĕlĕgante*.' (*Ibid.*, p. 219.)

29. The status-determinants laid down by the dominant group have thus always been adapted to maintain its interests and to keep the in-group small and the out-group large. As Christianity spread amongst the out-group, the determinant ceased to be religious affiliation and became a cultural one. With the increase of acculturation, the determinant came to be one of colour, a more satisfactory one in that it could not be acquired.

30. 'God willed different races, and therefore any race-mixture or breeding across the colour-line is an offence against God's will.' (Dr. J. G. Strydom, Secretary of the Free State D.R.M.C., from an essay in *Koers en die Krisis*, Vol. III, quoted by Joshi, p. 292.) Somewhat surprisingly, the Christian-heathen antithesis still crops up, though always subordinated to the white-black division. See the following extract from a speech given at an Institute of Citizenship Meeting by the Rev. B. J. Engelbrecht of the *Nederduits Hervomde Kerk van Africa*: 'In its relation with non-European groups . . . (the) whole question was not one of Western civilisation against the Bantu, or White against Black, but of Christianity against heathendom . . . The Church's decision on segregation and mixed marriages was not made as discrimination against race and colour, but against heathendom.' (*Star*, 31st October, 1950.) In view of the fact that almost all Coloured people are Christians, it is difficult to accept the last statement.

31. 'The rôle of habit in fostering group prejudice has never received that degree of attention which its importance deserves in a study of the psychological factors that underlie such prejudice.' (MacCrone, p. 284.)

32. 'Our complex of fears starts in early childhood because we are what I call a "nanny society". Nearly every child in South Africa has a nanny, a black one. So you get this constant splitting of the mother figure, because the child naturally develops an affection for its nanny. The child grows up with this affection until it realises that it is wrong—that is, according to our code. It must deny this feeling, and to achieve this it becomes more critical of the Black people than it need ever have been. The child has to fight its love for the black nanny, which is an emotionally charged love, meaningful in the family situation. It implies sexual attitudes, as all mother love does, so it becomes something evil and the child has to reject it. This is one very important reason why we go to such extremes of hate.' (Practising psychologist, quoted by *Forum* Science Correspondent, 15th December, 1950.)

33. The social situation in South Africa, and the attitude of a large number of upper and upper-middle-class whites, is in many respects similar to that prevailing in England in the generation following the Poor Law Act of 1834. The major difference is, of course, that in South Africa low economic and social status is almost totally identified with colour, and not with cultural traits as in the estates.

34. Cf. MacCrone, pp. 291–2.

35. The difficulty experienced by White South Africans brought up in the white-black situation in adjusting to an intermediate group was brought vividly home to me a few months after our arrival in the Cape. A Johannesburg friend who had not visited the Cape before came to stay. She congratulated me upon my excellent Coloured maid, but added: 'I wouldn't like to have Coloured people around myself. They seem to me neither one thing nor the other and I wouldn't know how to treat them.' I made a note of this particular incident before reading a similar passage in Professor MacCrone's book (p. 292).

36. A projection of such a feeling on to the group which is really its object is perhaps to be found in Sarah Gertrude Millin's novel *God's Stepchildren*, which is the story of a Bastard family sprung from a European missionary and a Hottentot woman. Despite the liberal sympathies of the author, certain race attitudes, such as the belief in the 'badness' of the mixed blood, are implicit throughout the book. At the end, the great-great-grandson, a minister who is about 18 per cent Coloured, but the legal son of a white land-owner and English-educated, suddenly feels the 'call of the blood', sends his English wife and child back to England, and decides to work amongst his 'own brown people' to expiate their sin and sorrow. Such heart-searchings do not seem to afflict most of the Coloureds who 'pass' and where they do are largely based on misplaced biological fears.

37. '. . . The careless aversion the pure white man has for the native is, in the case of the half-caste, intensified by secret, unconscious fear, and the nearness to danger.' (Millin (2), p. 237. Cf. also Adamastor, p. 160.)

38. It may be of interest here to recall the results of a social distance questionnaire carried out by Professor MacCrone in 1934 amongst 205 English-speaking South Africans, 100 Afrikaans-speaking South Africans and 111 Jews, all first-year students at the Witwatersrand University, 120 Afrikaans-speaking South Africans from Potchefstroom University College and 96 English-speaking South Africans from Rhodes University College, Grahamstown (the only Cape centre). In all cases returns showed a greater intolerance and lesser tolerance of Cape Coloureds than of Africans. In the Cape group, the general level of intolerance was somewhat lower and the level of tolerance somewhat higher for Coloured groups, compared with those of English-speaking South Africans in the Transvaal. The same was true of Afrikaans-speaking South Africans at the 'liberal' English-speaking University in Johannesburg as compared with their colleagues at Potchefstroom. The Jewish group were slightly less intolerant and more tolerant as regards Non-Europeans than the English-speaking Cape group, and also than their English-speaking and Afrikaans-speaking fellow students at the Witwatersrand. A further noticeable feature was the close correlation between low tolerance and high intolerance of the Portuguese and the Coloured groups, particularly amongst the Afrikaans-speaking groups, the

Portuguese being actually regarded with an attitude of greater intolerance than the African by the Potchefstroom group. (MacCrone, Ch. XI.)

39. For an illustration of the European stereotype of the Coloured person, and the latter's reaction to it, see letter published in the *Forum* (4th February, 1950, p. 13).

40. For a more literary statement of a similar antithesis cf.: '. . . even the Bantu, till we have utterly broken him under the wheels of our civilisation, grows up with a solid matrix about him, which inevitably results in a social training from which the Half-caste is excluded . . . His tribe may be broken up, but he still feels himself an integral part of a great people, up to whose standard he is bound to live, and in whose eyes, as in his own, he is one of the goodliest and completest creatures of God's earth. Until we have robbed him entirely of this sense of racial unity and of racial self-respect he is not morally on the same footing as the Half-caste.' (Olive Schreiner, *Thoughts on South Africa*, pp. 126–71, quoted by Stonequist, pp.21–2.)

41. This is so even in the Cape, where there has recently been a comparatively large influx of British settlers of the wealthier type. Some have come to South Africa after long military or civil service in India, and have readily projected their attitudes towards Anglo-Indians on to the Cape Coloureds. Their former admiration for the Indian warrior-castes seems to have been transferred to the tribal African and in particular the Zulu. This preference is shared by many South Africans and even by the authorities, who employ Zulus as prison-warders and boss-boys in authority over other Non-Europeans.

42. Myth—i.e., popular belief. Cf. Myrdal, Ch. 4, on the importance of these racial beliefs to justify and perpetuate the colour-hierarchy.

43. Cf. Kuper, p. 45, for the way in which Europeans in the British Protectorate of Swaziland buttress the myth of race by accusing Coloureds of being 'degenerate' and a 'mongrel race'. The myth is further supported by the contention that miscegenation occurs only between the 'dregs of society'. (Cf. Mr. Gay, U.P. member for Simonstown, *Hansard*, 2nd March, 1950, col. 2269, and Mr. J. G. du Toit, Nationalist M.P.C., at the D.R.C. Synod in Cape Town, 26th October, 1949.)

44. Kuper, *ibid*.

45. See Edgar H. Brookes, *The Colour Bar in South Africa*, Current History, July 1932, p. 429, quoted by Stonequist, p. 18.

46. I have not myself come across European South Africans who seriously maintain that the Negro and Caucasian races belong to different species. I have, however, been told by more than one informant that this convenient synthesis of religious and pseudo-scientific beliefs does linger in the minds of unsophisticated persons in the backveld. More typical of modern South African beliefs was the set of tests for Coloured blood outlined by Mr. W. H. Stuart, Native Representative for the Transkei, on 23rd May, 1949 (reported in *Hansard*, cols. 6348–50). They consisted of: the 'tell-tale mark under the nails'; the 'hair test' (only for Hottentot or Bantu blood, not valid for Indians and Malays); the 'eyelid' test, the eyelid being rather 'startlingly white'; 'certain medical tests which are final'—('there are signs in certain portions of the anatomy not to be discussed in public'); 'certain people should never part their hair; there is a slight touch of colour'; 'a matt surface' to the complexion, only observable in Europeans when they are ill and 'the shine goes out of their face', a shiny face being 'an emblem of utter fitness plus continuity of race. The Bantu pure has it as well as the European pure'. Cf. also a letter signed W.H.P.A. in the *Rand Daily Mail* of 7th December, 1950: 'The surest way of deciding is to examine the whites of the eyes, the outer edge of the lips and the bases of the finger nails. Should the eyes be bloodshot the little veins will show up distinctly *brown* and not red. The outer edges of the lips also show a brown (darker) than the lips. The base of the nails will also show brown and not white as with pure European blood.'

47. See the Report on the Biblical basis of *Apartheid* accepted by the D.R.C. Synod in April 1951. *Apartheid*, whether Biblically sanctioned or not, has in fact

become a potent myth amongst many South Africans, not all of Afrikaner stock. Its effect has been increased since the word *Apartheid* was substituted for the word 'Segregation' though this has about the same meaning. See Keppel-Jones, Ch. IV, and Presidential Address by the Rev. Z. R. Mahabane at the 7th Annual Conference of the N.E.U.M. reported in *Torch*, 3rd April, 1951. The obverse of this myth is the dictum that 'the maintenance of social separation is in accordance with the desires of . . . Coloureds' (U.P. statement of policy). Cf. Myrdal, p. 575.

48. In fact, the upper and middle-class Coloured do often accept the prevalent white myths and their own inferior status, as a result of social environment and conditioning. Whether this acceptance of the 'bad blood' and 'black taint' myth is so complete and shattering in its impact as Olive Schreiner and Sarah Gertrude Millin suggest is not so certain. There is usually a compensatory emotional outlet in attitudes towards the African.

49. Olive Schreiner, *Thoughts on South Africa*, pp. 126–7 (quoted by Stonequist, pp. 20–1).

50. Millin (2), pp. 245–7. In the last sentence, however, Mrs. Millin refers to a trait which has forced itself to the notice of many who have had dealings with the Cape Coloured. This trait can best be described as a combination of fecklessness and apathy, and an explanation of its widespread presence should be sought rather in terms of social conditioning and environment. We shall return to this point when we come to consider Coloured reactions to the rôle and status ascribed to them by the white group.

51. Cf. the 'Nordic' myth. However, it would seem that both 'black blood' and 'mixed blood' are 'bad' or 'inferior'. The Blood Transfusion Service in Cape Town has recently appealed for African and Coloured donors with some success. Blood so donated is not given to European patients, although European blood is sometimes given to Non-European patients. While patients do not usually inquire the source of the blood which they are given, some European donors have objected to the fact that their blood might be given to Non-Europeans, and have resigned as donors on this account.

52. Cf. Hoernlé, p. 41.

53. For instance, both Coloureds and Africans are alleged to have a different body odour from Europeans. During a discussion of group differences, several white South Africans told me that they could distinguish a Non-European in the dark by his smell alone, and that their dogs would attack a Non-European on scent alone. It was then suggested that any excessive odour might be due to dirty clothes, hard manual labour, dietary differences, the possession of a larger number of sweat glands, and a lack of washing facilities and soap. The informants, however, persisted in their claim that the odour was not simply greater but different, although they were unable to say what percentage of 'coloured blood' had to be present before the smell became different. Cf. the following passage: '(He) alleges that there are no Biblical grounds for *Apartheid*, but why did the Creator give them a different colour and smell? Isn't that *Apartheid*?' (Letter to *Die Volksblad*, 25th May, 1949.) Cf. also G. F. van Wyk, *op. cit.*, on the '*bouquet d'Afrique*' and 'smoky' Bushman smell; also Myrdal, p. 1,213, n. 8.

54. The 'coloured baby' myth has recently been given a novel twist. In an item headed 'No Test-Tube Babies—Danger of Coloured Blood', the *Torch* of 30th January, 1950, reports: 'The Mixed Marriages Act has given the racialists another headache. It is reported that members of the Dutch Reformed Church have approached the Government to ask it to ban 'test-tube babies'. There is the fear that there may be "coloured blood" hidden in the unnamed donor-fathers, and even though the "father" may appear to be "white", the "coloured blood" may make its presence felt in the new generation. As a counter-suggestion some have proposed that orphans be brought from Europe to be adopted by parents who desperately want a family.'

55. Cf. Edward M. East, *Heredity and Human Affairs*, p. 100, quoted by Myrdal,

p. 1,208–9: 'That there is still some scientific authority for their fears is suggested in the following passage: "The question as to whether passing will create *individual* cases of children with pronounced Negroid traits being born to ostensibly white parents is still a subject of controversy. It seems to be agreed by everyone that the offspring of two passable (or passed) mulattoes may have a darker skin than either of his parents. The controversy is around the question as to whether the offspring of a passed mulatto and pure-blooded white person can have a darker skin than either parent. Majority opinion amongst those who have looked into this question seems to be that it cannot happen . . . There is at least one biologist, however (Huxley, though with a later reservation), who takes the opposite view, and says the 'black baby' can happen, and occasionally does happen."'

56. 'There has long been a tendency towards idealisation of white women in the South, originally probably an upper-class pattern which has spread widely among the other classes. This ideal image is passionately and even violently defended, and the danger of soiling it is one of the threats which brings out the fullest hostility of Southern men, especially when the attacker is a Negro.' (Dollard, p. 136.)

57. On profounder differences of attitude on this subject between the Latin and the Anglo-Saxon groups, as correlated with different attitudes towards sex in general, see MacCrone, p. 298. In slave-owning Brazil there was a great tolerance of sexual intercourse between colonists and coloured women, while the upper-class white women had to conform to a rigid pattern of virtue. This pattern does not, however, seem to have arisen as a result of colonial slave-owning, but to have been derived from a Portuguese prototype. It would be interesting to inquire to what extent the 'purity of the home' was superseded as a slogan by 'the purity of the race (or blood)' in the Portuguese colonial context.

58. Cf. Dollard, p. 136, n. 4.

59. Cf. the incident where the Bastard Kleinhans helps the 15-year-old daughter of a white digger to look for her lost goat. Her father and two younger men ride up, and without more ado tie him up and whip him till he faints, then kick him, saying: 'That will teach you to speak to white girls, *verdomde Bastard*.' (Millin (1), pp. 95–7.)

60. Though see Mr. S. E. Warren's statement that in the country districts a European male who married a Coloured female was usually regarded as a Coloured (*Hansard*, 25th May, 1949, col. 6486).

61. See Mi., p. 14, on the subject of the 'white womanhood of South Africa', which had regarded miscegenation 'with abhorrence for 250 years'. For other expressions of the 'white woman' myth, see speeches by Mr. Sarel Tighy (*Hansard*, 9th March, 1950, col. 2687), and Mr. D. C. H. Uys (*Hansard*, 9th March, 1950, col. 2710); 'Stories from the Courts', *Star*, 29th November, 1950; editorial on the Pretoria Sunday Fights in the *Cape Argus*, 7th September, 1948; letter on women inebriates in *Rand Daily Mail* of 2nd November, 1950; letter on the indecent dress of schoolgirls playing basket-ball: 'Must we as parents agree that our daughters' legs must be ogled by whites and non-Europeans? . . . Mothers, we must pray warmly for our daughters, the future Afrikaans mothers' (letter to *Die Transvaler*, 12th September, 1950, quoted in *British Africa Review*, October, 1950); views on 'Bikini' swim-suits reported in *Sunday Times* of 8th October, 1950; letter signed 'Kathleen' in *Rand Daily Mail* of 14th December, 1950, asking for women police to 'teach some of the female drivers . . . a more decent way of entering and alighting from their cars: some are most disgustingly stupid, particularly in a city that is not wholly a white one', and letter in *Cape Times* of 19th January, 1951, criticising the presence of young women behind counters in Non-European bottle stores. Cf. also Mi., s. 62.

62. This subject is shrouded in reticence, except amongst Coloured people, who speak of it quite freely and possibly with some exaggeration. European men, usually of the lower class and mainly Afrikaans-speaking, were, until the passing of the two acts against miscegenation, said to make a habit of visiting Coloured dance-halls

in Cape Town, and I was told that white police were sometimes stationed there to remove them. Visiting ships' crews were said to frequent night-clubs and dives in the more unsavoury streets of the Coloured 'District Six' in the centre of Cape Town. A young business-man settled in Cape Town for several years spoke, apparently with intent to shock, of visiting a Coloured night-club with several friends because it was 'more amusing than the only European one'. A Coloured school-teacher referred bitterly to the Coloured 'housekeepers' kept, he claimed, by many European farmers and even ministers in the more remote country districts.

63. Best illustrated in the inevitable rejoinder to any proposals designed to promote Non-European education or social welfare, or generally to improve their economic lot: 'Do you want your sister (or daughter) to marry a Coloured (or Kaffir)?'

64. Readers are referred to MacCrone, pp. 229–305, Myrdal, pp. 589–92, Dollard, pp. 154–72, for detailed discussions of the psychological background of inter-racial sex-attitudes. Pierson suggests that is was only with the advent of the *Boerevrou*, or white woman, that Dutch attitudes to mixed blood changed (p. 323). In other words, the white woman saw her influence challenged, and took steps to protect her status and hold over the white man by upholding the myth of the 'white woman'.

65. Cf. Myrdal, pp. 590–1.

66. This study has not been primarily concerned with the effect of the racial situation upon the dominant group, a theme which is often neglected but nevertheless vital. Professor MacCrone has spoken about the compulsion to think and feel only in terms of dominating or being dominated (*Rand Daily Mail*, 19th March, 1951); this leads to fears of the 'black' and 'red' perils (see letter in *Rand Daily Mail* of 20th January, 1951, headed 'South Africa a Prison House, But who are the Prisoners?') and to intolerance even between the various European groups (particularly to anti-Semitism). The relatively absolute power which whites possess over non-whites is corrupting and demoralising; (cf. V. de Kock on the disastrous effects of slavery on the masters, p. 67); it produces arrogance, intolerance, hatred, fear, irresponsibility and inhumanity (see article in the *Forum* of 30th September, 1950: 'Are we Losing Our National Conscience?').

67. Kimball Young points out that such stereotypes enable the Negro to project his own difficulties or shortcomings on to the whites and their institutions. For instance, a sacking may be attributed not to the worker's incompetence but to the employer's race-prejudice (p. 277).

68. See MacCrone, pp. 258–79, for an account of such white stereotypes regarding Africans, and Myrdal, pp. 1,195–7, for varying stereotypes about the American Negro.

69. This concept is very common amongst white South Africans. In the political sphere it has produced the European 'guardian' and Non-European 'ward' concepts. A Nationalist M.P. from the North Cape once told me that I could naturally not understand the Coloured People as do those who have been born and brought up with them, and that the first thing to remember was that they were children, and could not be expected to behave in the same way as Europeans. See also Mr. Havenga's speech at the Voortrekker celebrations on 16th December, 1949 (reported in *Cape Times*, 17th December, 1949).

70. For general group stereotypes, cf. MacCrone, S.A. J. Sc., Vol. XXXIII, pp. 1,104–11, March 1937, *A Quantitative Study of Race Stereotypes*, and C., s. 852, Question 7.

71. That these stereotypes often correspond to existing facts is not denied. Here, however, we are concerned only with the way in which the stereotypes are used to help maintain the inferior status of an entire ethnic group. Cf. also Davis, p. 15 f., for sanctions for the subordination of Negroes.

72. Cf. *Stinkie*, by C. van der Spuy, pp. 167–8 (Afrikaans reading-book for Junior Certificate, 1949). Other 'good' stereotypes are implicit in the rather sentimental features occasionally published in English-speaking Cape Town papers, dealing

with the virtues of the Coloured people, their loyalty to each other, their attempts to live decently, their kindness to children and animals, their gaiety, and so on. All these stereotypes are balanced by exactly opposite stereotypes, sometimes implicit in other columns of the same issue. Cf. also Marais, p. 5, on the Afrikaner attitude to the Coloured man.

73. 'It was extremely difficult to find employment (in Johannesburg—S.P.) for Coloured men. The views of the employers were that they were not desirable employees because they were always drunk, their morals were low, they were less robust than Africans, and their presence among Africans always led to trouble.' (S.A. Institute of Race Relations Report, R.R. 114–50.)

74. One Mowbray housewife, speaking about a reference for a Coloured cook, said to me: 'You have to swallow your pride and accept what they're willing to do for you these days. They're a completely unscrupulous lot and will always let you down when it suits them. Those are our Cape Coloured people for you.' Since the war I have heard similar complaints about the London charwoman, but directed against an occupational, not an ethnic group.

75. Cf. letter from 'Ratepayer' in *Cape Argus* of 7th February, 1951.

76. The reasons for any lack of group loyalty or even feeling have been outlined in Chapters II and VIII. It is commented on frequently by whites and educated Coloureds alike. On the other hand, instances of Coloured co-operation in the face of white discrimination (such as refusals to give full evidence in court-cases, dragging strange drunks off the streets to avoid their arrest, etc.) are condemned as anti-social and attributed to Coloured 'slyness'.

77. An upper-class English-speaking woman from the Transvaal, now living in the Cape, told me that she did not go on the buses, because it meant sitting 'cheek by jowl' with Coloureds and Natives. She 'never knew what would jump on to her neck from such neighbours, and always felt like taking a bath when she got off.'

78. The English-language press often reports cases of European offences against Coloureds. This is less noticeable in the Nationalist Afrikaans-language press. All European papers report such Coloured offences as drunkenness, *dagga*-peddling and hooliganism. A regular feature in the *Cape Argus* reports the courts day-by-day. Through its column files a procession of Coloured stereotypes: Willy Marmalade *del gustes* and the *'bergie'* who camps out on the forested slopes of Table Mountain, Lizzie the 'Shebeen Queen', who appears behind the casks of cheap wine and brandy which she sells illegally to Africans, and pays her large fine with aplomb, Mustafa the *dagga*-runner whose fine is paid by a wealthy 'friend', Danie the chronic drunk, who has no cash or wealthy friends, so is led off to the cells . . .

79. ' "Crimes of violence will never be stamped out amongst Natives and Coloured persons, for it is in their nature to use the knife or stick", a senior police official said when interviewed yesterday.' (*Cape Times*, 20th August, 1949.) Cf. also remarks of Mr. Justice Steyn (*Cape Argus* of 6th February, 1951) and of the Chief Magistrate of Cape Town (*Cape Times* of 16th December, 1950), and protest from Mr. R. E. van der Ross, Editor, T.E.P.A. (*Cape Argus* of 1st June, 1949): ' . . . the idea prevails that the non-European is at heart a skolly, that nothing but violence can be expected of him, and that therefore he *must* be treated harshly, sometimes even before he is convicted of a crime.'

80. South African whites seem to regard sexual crimes committed by Coloureds against whites with as much disfavour as those committed by Africans. The stereotype is not born out by the 1949 figures, which show that forty-seven cases of European males raping Non-European females were reported, of which twenty were prosecuted and eleven convicted; fifty-two rapes of European females by Non-European males (who outnumber European males by approximately five to one) were reported, of which forty-two were prosecuted and thirty convicted (note the higher ratio of convictions to prosecutions and prosecutions to reported cases in the latter instance). Non-European males on the whole confined forceful sexual attentions to

Non-European females (762 reported cases). (From 1949 Report of the Commissioner of the South African Police, p. 10.)

81. See letters in *Cape Argus*, 17th August, 1949, *Cape Times*, 27th January, 1950 (and article in *Cape Times* of 28th January, 1950, rebutting 'generalised' allegations of Coloured cruelty to animals).

82. Such stereotypes are of course largely derived from the Coloured lower classes, with whom alone most whites have any considerable contacts. A series of such stereotypes are available in the *Cape Times* feature by the 'Man on the Spot', featured as 'To-day's Smile' (e.g., issues of 24th and 28th March, and 3rd and 5th April, 1951).

83. This analysis is to a considerable extent based on those used by Dollard, Chs. XII–XIV, Kimball Young, pp. 273–80 and Johnson, Chs. XI–XIV. Resistance in the initial contact-situation becomes aggression in the established status-hierarchy. It has been suggested to me that some of the instances of various types of behavioural response made by the Coloured group to the situation, particularly that of legalised aggression, go beyond the scope of the original psycho-analytical concepts of acceptance, avoidance and aggression. I am not qualified to determine whether this is so, and if I have been led astray into using the term 'aggression' in its wider and more popular sense. Nevertheless it seems to me that the classification remains valid as applied to the various types of behaviour, group or individual, into which the initial responses are translated.

84. There are few instances of overt aggression amongst the Coloured People since the Kat River Rising of 1851. The Bondelswart Hottentots of S.W. Africa, who had long fought German rule, in 1922 refused to pay a dog tax of £1 per dog, rising to £10 for five dogs owned. Their resistance was broken by the government of the mandatory power, South Africa, under General Smuts. He sent nearly 400 men with four machine-guns and two bombers. Over a hundred persons of all sexes and ages were killed and many more wounded. (Roux, pp. 149–50.)

85. Cf. Johnson, p. 263.

86. '. . . we find that the conditions under which the masses of the Coloured people have to live are so abject that they have become imbued with a feeling, having its roots in that resignation which springs from despair, that these conditions cannot or will not be improved and that as a consequence the retention of the good-will of their employers is greatly to be preferred to the futility and displeasure which in their minds might at once attend upon the free and open expression of their grievance.' (C., p. 242, Addendum by Dr. Abdurahman and Messrs. Buchanan and Fowler.)

87. 'A section of the lower classes of Coloured accepts the European without question as their superiors. This attitude reflects the whole history and the present position of the Cape Coloured people, taken as a group, in their relation to the European. It is the traditional attitude of servant to master, of those in an inferior position to those who have for generations been in a superior social or economic position, and on whom their lot is dependent.' (C., s. 29.) This attitude is now called the *Ja-Baas* attitude by resentful urban Coloureds. Cf. article 'On Prejudice' by J. C. Maurice, in the *Sun*, 30th March, 1951.

88. As always, the attitudes of the two groups are closely inter-connected; a change in one will evoke a different response in the other, and so on in a chain series of reactions. For instance, the prejudice of rural Poor Whites may spread to the white farmers, who will begin to treat their Coloured labour in a less paternalistic and more openly domineering way. The Coloured workers of the district, resenting this altered attitude and seeing certain white *baas*-es living on almost the same level as themselves, may become 'cheeky'. This 'cheekiness' may spread to workers on farms where the owners are still paternalistic. The latter will respond to the 'cheekiness' by a hardening of their own attitudes, and so the process will continue.

89. Cf. Guy B. Johnson, 'Personality in a White-Indian-Negro Community'

(*American Sociological Review*, Vol. 4, August 1939, pp. 516–23) on the Croatans of North Carolina.

90. By accepting the superiority of a white skin, the Coloured man automatically admits his own inferiority. Cf. article 'Has the Coloured Youth a Chance in Life?' in *Cape Standard* of 25th January, 1937, and the *Sun*, 16th March, 1951, p. 3. Cf. also the passage by E. B. Reuter quoted by Dollard, p. 68, n. 9.

91. Another form of complete escape available to all Coloureds is suicide, but available figures do not suggest that this avenue is used to any abnormal extent. Of 252 attempted suicide cases admitted to the Groote Schuur Hospital in Cape Town between January 1947 and May 1950, two were Africans, forty-six Coloured and 204 Europeans, women exceeding men in all racial groups. It was found that most Coloured people attempting suicide were young, while the attempt was more often than not a gesture to gain some end rather than a reasoned desire to die (from a preliminary report by the Department of Neurology and Psychology at this hospital published in the *S.A. Medical Journal*, 12th May, 1950). For statistics of successful suicides see annual reports of Medical Officers of Health in the larger urban areas.

92. A fair number of Cape Coloured people are resident in Britain. This number includes several writers, teachers, dancers, musicians and medical practitioners and at least one Coloured building contractor with a flourishing business. A South African European who is connected with a cultural organisation for Cape Coloured children and young people spoke of the difficulty of persuading talented Coloured girls and boys, whose overseas training the organisation financed, to return to the Union once it was completed. The contact with the much milder colour-prejudice prevalent in Britain (often not applicable in the case of light-coloured individuals) and, above all, the comparative lack of institutionalised economic, occupational and political discrimination, made it difficult for such persons to return to their South African status. The stream of wealthier Coloured *emigrés*, ribaldly nicknamed the 'Pilgrim Fathers' by some who remain in the Union, has increased recently. It is estimated that about 240 families left the Union in 1950, most to the U.K., but some for Australia, the American continent or other African territories (*Cape Times* of 5th February, 1951, 10th March, 1951 and 24th March, 1951). One white correspondent to the *Cape Times* suggested that a major motive for such departures was to 'marry a white wife', and proposed that Coloured families should be prevented from leaving the country (13th March, 1951).

93. Such tensions have greatly increased since the Prohibition of Mixed Marriages Act and the Nationalist Party's 'witch-hunt' in the Cape to discover 'Europeans' with recent Coloured admixture and get them disqualified as voters. In others, the persons unmasked denounced neighbours and relations who had 'passed'. A Coloured teacher described the attitude of such people as follows: 'Why should X get away with it when I haven't? He's a Coloured like me.' He did not approve of 'passing' and commented that they had got only what they deserved.

94. For various methods of estimating 'passing', and their efficacy, see Myrdal, pp. 1,207–8, and p. 129. In the Union, an attempt to establish a 'blood composition bridge' and to estimate the incidence of 'passing' was made by Advocate George Findlay in his pamphlet on 'Miscegenation', the calculations being based on the 1921 Census returns. He concluded that the line between Coloured and White was in fact the division between half-caste and quadroon-white, with over 500,000 'play-whites' in the officially white group. He pointed to the still noticeable lack of light-coloured persons in the Coloured group, and concluded that all who could pass did so. Once darkness and other 'native' traits were accepted in persons officially belonging to the 'European' group, the 'European' category was enlarged to accommodate an increasing number of escapes. Lawrence E. Green went so far as to define a 'Coloured person as one who had failed to pass as a White person'. (In his article on 'Coloured Cape Town' in the *Outspan* of 17th November, 1950.)

95. 'Although there is a good deal of romantic shuddering over hidden drops

of black blood, that is only conventional hypocrisy. If a person suspected of colour but not obviously dark, can pay his way in the coinage of success he may enter anywhere; he is not rejected socially or even matrimonially. Both past and future are taken on trust.' (S. G. Millin (2), p. 241.)

96. See Louw *v.* Kielblock, 1911, C.P.D. 209; Pitout v. Rosenstein, 1930, O.P.D., 117; Minister of Posts and Telegraphs *v.* Rasool, 1934, A.D. 167, at p. 188; Mi., s. 20. Cf. similar situation in the U.S.A. (Myrdal, p. 641.)

97. Captain du Toit (U.P. member for Cape Flats) gave the following instance of difficulties experienced by recruiting officers in the Cape during the war: 'One of these young men of about 18 or 19 came to the Castle and wanted to join up. The sergeant saw him and said: "No, I cannot take you; you must go to the Cape Corps (for Coloureds)." This boy went straight home and he came back in the afternoon with his parents . . . they wanted the sergeant charged for having insulted their son. I asked the parents if they were prepared to produce sworn affidavits to the effect that this boy was their own son because I must say that I myself would have sworn by everything that is holy that the boy was Coloured, because he had frizzy hair, very thick lips and a dark skin and, in fact, all the attributes of a lower-class Coloured person—or I won't say lower-class Coloured person but the type of Coloured person who is descended from a Hottentot or a Bushman . . . The medical officer found that this boy was Coloured and could not be accepted. I told the parents that I was in a very difficult position in accepting the boy but that if they could produce certain certificates to prove that he was a European child I would gladly accept him. They then produced his birth certificate; they produced two sisters of the boy, and these two girls were absolutely white. They produced a certificate from the Diocesan College at Rondebosch (an upper-class European school—S.P.) where the boy had been studying and by every other means showed that this boy was European. He was therefore accepted and sent north as a European.' (*Hansard*, 23rd May, 1949, col. 6355.)

98. These people are known amongst the Coloured community as *Quasis* (by the more sophisticated), or, more commonly, as *Venstertjies* (*venster* = window), because they are supposed to look into shop windows while their darker kin go by. In one such case, a Coloured woman who had 'passed' married an Afrikaner artisan in Cape Town. From time to time she would visit her Coloured sister, brother-in-law and their children. Her husband and children did not take part in these visits. Recently she became ill, and was taken to a European hospital. She sent a message to one of her Coloured nieces, of whom she was very fond, asking her to come and see her. The girl did not wish to go, not wanting to advertise the Coloured origins of her aunt to the hospital staff. Her mother, however, persuaded her to go, as the aunt was thought to be dying. When she got there, her European cousins were also there, but as she said afterwards, 'they stood on the other side of the bed and refused even to greet me'. Cf. also the account of a Coloured funeral in the correspondence column of the *Cape Times*, 31st May, 1949.

99. There is also the possibility of confusion with dark-skinned members of the local Portuguese communities on the Rand; this happened to a prominent Cape Coloured teacher who was being driven back to his host's home in Johannesburg by a European in late 1950. The teacher leaned out to ask the way from a white traffic-constable, who, seeing him in a car with an obvious European, had no doubt as to his Europeanness, and 'sirred' him most courteously. Cf. also *Hansard*, 24th May, 1949, col. 6456, for assertion by Mr. A. G. Barlow that Coloureds from the Cape were 'passing' in the Orange Free State, and marrying into 'good Free State families', and Kuper (p. 46) for the increasing tendency of light-skinned Coloureds to emigrate to the Union from Swaziland, where the community is too small to permit them to 'pass' successfully.

100. This is advisable, as otherwise the name of the school attended, or its locality, may serve to unmask the individual who has 'passed'. For an instance of 'passing' for economic reasons, see speech by Captain R. J. du Toit. *Hansard*, 10th March,

Y

1950, col. 2730 and for 'passing' in general, see speech by Mr. P. J. H. Luttig, *Hansard*, 13th March, 1950, col. 2855.

101. Possibly more women than men 'pass', the economic effort involved being less, since they have only to find a white husband, and to assume his status (cf. Dr. A. Jonker speaking in the Mixed Marriages Debate, *Hansard*, 19th May, 1949, col. 6186).

102. See p. 164.

103. Cf. *Cape Times* of 24th January, 1950, third Article on District Six.

104. Cf. Myrdal, p. 687, and Stonequist, p. 93.

105. 'Such accusations of "betrayal" by other members of the coloured upper and middle classes may be partly attributable to "private" envy, of which there is a great deal in a frustrated lower caste.' (Myrdal, p. 688.) Any hostility felt towards 'play-whites' by members of the lower class is even more likely to spring from envy, since few people in this class have the physical traits or cultural background and education to 'pass'. See C., s. 53, 61, 116–19 on 'passing' generally and Coloured attitudes to it in the mid-thirties; and letter from the Executive Committee of the Natal C.P.N.U. quoted by Mr. N. G. Eaton, expressing disapproval of 'passing'. (*Hansard*, 25th May, 1949, col. 6488–90.)

106. See Myrdal, pp. 683–4, n. C for some instances of this.

107. Instances have been encountered of persons who, seen in another context, such as London, Italy or Greece, would be regarded as Southern Europeans or Levantines. Only where 'Hottentot' traits are present, would it be easy to say of a swarthy person seen walking in a London street: 'That is a Cape Coloured.'

108. '. . . the absence of social agencies and amenities among Coloured people results in the secession to the White side of those who can be accepted as Europeans in order to obtain social advantages otherwise denied them. Coloured leaders complain that their community loses in this way the benefit of the social progress of some of the more highly endowed and progressive among their people. It is a rare occurrence to see, as a member of a deputation pleading for the rights of the Coloured people, anyone who can pass as European.' (Bishop Lavis, speaking at the First National Coloured-European Conference, 1933.)

109. *Op. cit.*, p. 686.

110. 'The Coloured people who because of their fair skins have been living just over the border have shown that blood is thicker than water, and are now coming back to their own, to swell the ranks of those who fight for true democracy.' (*Sun*, 16th March, 1951.) Elsewhere the article speaks of the new *rapprochement* between all Non-European groups; this, coming from the formerly moderate, aloof, pro-white, Coloured group, shows a great change in attitude over the last year or so.

111. A Coloured lower-middle class woman who had, after becoming pregnant, been forced by her father to marry a shiftless, unskilled urban worker, condoned her husband's continual drunkenness by saying: 'He says he can't bear to come each night and see how we live (seven children and two adults in a leaking, single-room zinc and iron hut condemned by the health authorities—S.P.), so he takes his pay and goes off to the canteen.' See also C., s. 84 and Lq., s. 43: '. . . Among a very large section of the Coloured people the week-end "drunk" is commonly regarded as the proper and eminently desirable reward for the labours and deprivals of the week—their one "little bit of heaven" as one clerical witness described it—and . . . this attitude is shared by the women.' The heavy addiction to drink of the Coloured masses is not only profitable to the producers of wine and spirits, but also serves to keep them backward, impoverished and apathetic to ideas of change or resistance, a fact which may or may not have occurred to European administrators.

112. See Appendix K for comparative figures for drunkenness and *dagga*-peddling or smoking. The Report of a recent Dagga Commission will be published in the near future. Giving evidence before the Commission, Dr. O. D. Wollheim, Warden of C.A.F.D.A., said: '*Dagga* is an anaesthetic which makes those who smoke it forget the filthy hovels in which they live, the fleas, the lice and the ticks.' He went

on to say that the effects of the moderate use of *dagga* were not so terrible as people thought. Its use evoked a spurious sense of self-confidence and well-being (*Star*, 25th September, 1950). On the other hand, the *Sunday Times* continued the building of stereotypes by reporting evidence given before the Commission on all night drink and dagga parties in Cape Town *shebeens*, at which Europeans and Non-Europeans 'mingle freely and strip off their clothes'. (24th December, 1950.) A further escape outlet for lower-class Coloureds is probably provided by sexual intercourse. An inquirer easily gets the impression that sexual adventures play a larger part in lower-class Coloured life than they do in that of other ethnic groups in South Africa, but there is no adequate evidence to support this impression, which may have been unconsciously absorbed from current European stereotypes in South Africa.

113. The types of films preferred by Coloured film-goers attest to their desire for escape: they like action and thrills (especially Tarzan), horrors, slap-stick, and horse-operas (cf. the *Cape Times*, Week-end Magazine, 29th October, 1949).

114. Another example of escape from the status-hierarchy, in this case temporary and permitted by the dominant group.

115. Lynching does not exist in South Africa to the same degree as it does in the Southern States. Amongst the reasons for this are the great numerical superiority of the Non-Europeans, their recent martial tradition, the fear-complex of so many Europeans and their greater certainty that the law provides sufficient sanctions to maintain the colour-hierarchy. Nevertheless, many white South Africans, particularly in rural areas, do take the law into their own hands, and administer punishments ranging from flogging to death. These acts are usually committed by individuals or small groups. The nearest approach to the mob-violence of the American South is probably the assembly of large numbers of armed white citizens to help the police during race riots (e.g., the Durban Riots and more recently the Witzieshoek Reserve disturbances).

116. But cf. the following incident which, although not typical, shows that covert aggression may take this form: 'Naked fishermen along the coast between Struisbaai and Cape Agulhas have caused several protests, according to reports reaching Bredasdorp. Mostly Coloured men, they are alleged to walk the beaches without any clothes on in front of European women and children. A warning has been issued to them, but they have ignored it and are alleged to have adopted an insolent attitude.' (*Sunday Times*, 1st April, 1951.)

117. Women visitors from Europe, particularly those who have visited the port-areas of Latin countries, are sometimes struck by the almost general absence of reaction to white women on the part of Non-European men encountered casually in the streets or public places and conveyances. This almost exaggerated impassivity should probably be attributed to a strong avoidance-mechanism, as in many cases Coloured men value light colour and general approximation to European appearance in their own women.

118. Middle and upper-class Coloured men whom I interviewed made no attempt to shake hands until I proffered my own, although hand-shaking is an important part of social *mores* in those sections of the Coloured group. They would also avoid simultaneous departure from the meeting-place (usually a public or semi-public building), which might have necessitated walking together through the streets for any distance. Coloured women were less reserved with a European of their own sex. In the Cape a Coloured assistant is usually called to carry sizable parcels purchased by Europeans to the waiting car or station; in my own case, the boy or man would invariably follow me at a distance of several paces, and look extremely embarrassed or disconcerted at any attempts at conversation. Dr. K. L. Little tells me that educated Negroes in the United States have come to regard as degrading the act of carrying parcels for somebody else, even as a gesture of courtesy, and to avoid it.

119. Cf. Dollard, p. 267. This avoidance was used with some sophistry by advocates

of the legislation against miscegenation, Coloured people being told that their womenfolk would no longer be subjected to the importunities of the worst type of white man.

120. Cf. Hoernlé, pp. 50–1. It should, however, be recorded that most Coloured individuals interviewed appeared to drop the mask almost completely as soon as they were convinced of my genuine interest. The fact that I was not South African but an outsider probably had a loosening effect on tongues, although there was still the tendency to tell me what it was thought I wanted to hear.

121. Dollard, p. 257. A curious form of avoidance was encountered in a press report of an elderly Coloured man of the upper-lower class who pretended to be illiterate when visited by inspectors, self-help society officials and so on, saying: 'In many matters it is not wise for a poor man to sign his name.' (*Cape Times*, 11th March, 1950.)

122. Frustration and incipient aggression is expressed in the following passage from a letter from an upper-middle-class Coloured informant, whose personal attitude towards Europeans is one of co-operation, written in January 1950: 'White South Africa brought us into this world. They have offered us their religion, their civilisation, their culture, and now, because we have proven ourselves to be true worthy South Africans, a credit to the country, we are to be despised, hated as if we were plague carriers or the like. There is a growing frustration among our people, which already makes us feel inclined to spurn the hand of European friendship. If there should be a further withdrawal of fundamental rights, it can only lead to bitter antagonism and strife.'

123. Dollard, p. 267.

124. Johnson defines overt aggression as intended to provoke a definite reaction on the part of the hostile attitude, while covert aggression gives vent to the hostility but avoids the reaction. He also points out that antagonism is often present in avoidance, but that in this the expression is controlled, while in hostility or aggression it is either unrestrained or deflected. (*Op. cit.*, p. 294.)

125. Gossip about individuals is most prevalent amongst domestic servants, who have more opportunity than other types of employee to see their employers off guard. The highly-coloured accounts of alleged drinking-bouts, sexual lapses or aberrations, peculiar personal habits and meanness of individual employers or their acquaintances which circulate in the kitchen quarters and via delivery boys or relatives and friends of the domestic concerned, would probably surprise many white South Africans, who tend to regard their Coloured servants as automata rather than individuals.

126. The stereotype of the 'English' as told me on this occasion was so favourable that it must be discounted as a courtesy to the interviewer! For other group stereotypes formulated by Coloured people about other ethnic groups in the Union see Kuper, p. 35, and MacCrone, *A Comparative Study of European and Non-European Differences in Race Preferences*, S.A.J. Sc., Vol. XXXV, pp. 412–16, December 1938. In this study of the preferences of a Coloured group of forty-seven people, the highest preference after their own group was for Englishmen, with Germans at the bottom of the list and Afrikaans-speaking South Africans under Portuguese and Indians, and just ahead of Natives and Jews. English-speaking South Africans, whether born in Britain or the Union, nevertheless put Cape Coloureds at the bottom of their list, below Indians, while the Afrikaans-speaking South Africans inverted this order. The Indian group preferred Englishmen and put Afrikaans-speaking South Africans at the bottom of their list, with Jews one above them.

127. Another instance of verbalised aggression was given me by a Coloured teacher, who said that he has often heard Coloured people say, as a European funeral passed by: 'There goes another white bastard!'

128. According to Findlay, those who have 'passed' (or their near descendants, if they are aware of their ancestry) and have risen to high place, carry with them the psychology of escape and tend to be the main emphasisers of the colour-bar: 'It

is surprising to note how frequently the discriminatory slogans of "White South Africa" and "Keeping the native people in their place" flourish in the mouths of those who in their own persons hardly exemplify their doctrine.' (p. 47.)

129. Reported in the *Cape Argus* of 5th January, 1950. On 30th January, 1950, a writer in the radical *Torch* stated that he personally knew two Members of Parliament, one member of the United Party and one Nationalist from the north, to have coloured blood. A recent letter received by me from a Coloured correspondent read: 'It is a well-known fact that hundreds and thousands of our men and women have been and are still serving in all branches of the armed forces in defence of this country. During the war they have served this country with distinction, some of them have become officers, some are still serving as such, some have been awarded medals for gallantry, etc. Amongst the very highest ranks of administration, etc., it has been found that there are men with Coloured blood in their veins. Quite recently a Coloured man turned out in all Test matches as a Springbok.'

130. I have on several occasions heard derogatory comments made in public places by lower-class Europeans about well-dressed Coloured people. Once, a white neighbour stopped my Coloured maid on her day off, and asked her where she got the money to buy such nice clothes. She further suggested that if her employer paid her such unusually high wages she should be saving up for a rainy day rather than putting it all 'on her back'.

131. At times the educated upper-class Coloured person makes use of his financial position to express covert aggression against the colour-bar. One such individual explained his methods: he gives large tips to white garage attendants (always accepted, he claims), speaks Oxford English to Afrikaners, and patronises English-speaking South Africans. The instances of Coloured courtesy and helpfulness to Europeans in distress (e.g., stranded motorists), which are so frequently reported in the correspondence columns of the Cape English-speaking press (e.g., *Cape Times* of 18th April, 1951) may perhaps be partly attributed to similar, if unconscious, impulses. By helping a European, a Coloured person steps outside the status-hierarchy and becomes an equal or even a superior for a few moments.

132. It has been suggested earlier in this study that most South African whites prefer their Non-European employees to be inefficient, stupid, lazy and pettily dishonest, according to the concept of inherent inferiority, than to show energy, intelligence, ambition and responsibility, which are the prerogative of the European, and therefore a threat to his privileged status if shown by others.

133. We are told that it was common for Malays to run '*amok*' in the early days of the Cape settlement, but this practice has long ceased. (V. de Kock, p. 195.)

134. Possibly crimes against property may in themselves be regarded as an instance of aggression, as may the fairly frequent activities of fire-bugs during the dry Cape summer, which often damage large areas of mountain and forest. (See *Cape Argus* of 31st January, 1951.)

135. On occasion it may also be expressed in insulting behaviour to a white who has put himself in a weak position where he is open to attack. In 1949, a middle-class white woman, obviously poor but scrupulously clean, neat, and dignified, came to my front door to sell some handwork, saying that she had lost her job and her daughter was in hospital. My own Coloured maid treated her with courtesy, but I watched her going to other houses later, and heard several Coloured servants treat her brusquely, while one slammed the door in her face. She had lost status by hawking goods from door to door in this way (although she went to the front door, not the back as a non-white would be expected to do), and had therefore put herself in a position where aggressive impulses could be vented. The frequent contemptuous references by upper and middle-class Coloureds to the Poor Whites are probably to be classed in the same category. (Cf. the Negro scorn for 'poor white trash'.)

136. Dollard, p. 295.

137. See the figures given in Ch. IX, n. 80; in studying these figures, one should also take into account the fact that some sexual encounters which would not be considered sexual assaults as between white men and Coloured women reach the courts as such when they occur between Coloured men and white women (the same consideration applies to other Non-Europeans). Since the passing of the Immorality Act, Coloured women have acquired a means of covert aggression of which some seem to have taken advantage. Cf. the case of two Europeans accused of soliciting two Coloured women in Cape Town, who immediately ran to a nearby police-van to report them. The men were finally acquitted, because the evidence against them rested on the unsupported word of the women, who were alleged to be prostitutes (*Cape Argus*, 12th December, 1950).

138. As has been noted in an earlier chapter, rape and murder are capital offences in South Africa, but no white man has ever been hanged for raping a Coloured or other Non-European woman.

139. A Coloured informant, asked to comment on a report of such an incident, deplored the behaviour of the skolly-gangs, but said that many bus-employees were of the poor white class and did not know how to treat Coloured people decently. She referred to instances where conductors enforced unofficial segregation, making all Coloured people go on to the top deck. Other types of unpleasant behaviour were for drivers with half-empty buses to ignore stops, even when theirs was the last scheduled bus, or for conductors to press the button for departure before Coloured people had properly embarked or disembarked. She herself had once had a bad fall from this cause, and it was harder still for old and crippled people. Sometimes conductors would even hit Coloured passengers. For the point of view of a Cape Town bus-conductor and a Rand ticket-examiner see the *Cape Argus* of 27th September, 1949, and *Rand Daily Mail* of 12th March, 1951, respectively.

140. Some urban areas, such as Cape Town's District Six, are said to be dangerous for any white between dusk and dawn. Even here, however, individual whites such as doctors, nurses and ministers, whose work takes them into such localities on foot, often recount how they are escorted safely out by a body-guard of one or more Coloureds, often belonging to skolly-gangs. In certain Johannesburg Non-European areas, even such visitors are said to be resented.

141. With the exception of one circus performance in a Cape Town suburb with a large Coloured population. Although there were only about thirty Europeans and a predominantly Coloured audience, there were separate ticket-booths and a large section of the tent was set aside for Europeans. The wife of one of Cape Town's Coloured councillors demanded to be served at the white booth, and ignored the segregated seating; others followed her example, despite efforts by the manager, staff, and finally the police, so that people at last sat just where they chose. (*Torch*, 1st May, 1950.)

142. Myrdal points out that the American Negro's 'rank order of discriminations' is the reverse of that of the white man, who ranks types of discrimination in the following order of importance: (1) miscegenation, (2) social equality, (3) spatial contacts, education, religion, (4) political rights, (5) legal and civic rights, (6) economic opportunities. However white South Africans might rearrange the other categories, it seems certain that they would also place the greatest stress on sexual and social barriers. Coloureds, on the other hand, are more concerned with the removal of economic, political and legal discrimination, and prominent individuals usually go out of their way to reassure the white group that they have no desire for 'social equality'. This attitude is brought out in the Addendum to the Cape Coloured Report by Dr. Abdurahman, Messrs. Buchanan and Fowler (C., p. 242).

143. As in the case of the Seashore Act referred to in Ch. VII, n. 16.

144. Some leaders of this group helped to organise the demonstration against the United Party Government's voluntary segregation policy in March 1939 (see Ch. VI c, n. 6).

145. The impulse of aggression behind such canalised political activities becomes

evident in the following Non-European analysis of the recent Newclare riots: 'The time has come for all to see that no Non-European in this country has a dog's chance against the guns of the military and the police. The senseless and useless tactics of flinging oneself against a curtain of bullets and swords which the ruling-class can put up cannot but lead to defeat, to greater frustration and needless loss of life, and victory for the oppressors . . . In our struggle for freedom we will time and time again be confronted with the problem of avoiding certain types of conflict which the very society which we oppose tries to force on us so that we may destroy our own forces in useless and directionless struggle . . . The fact that the widespread, deep and unfailing hatred for the oppression forced upon him has to issue in a blind, absolutely directionless and unplanned, wasteful and desperate upsurge of burning, looting, killing, anti-White action, is due to the gross failure of African politicians to provide correct political leadership . . . The hatred of oppression . . . will have to be canalised into political channels by honest political leadership.' (*Torch* editorial of 20th February, 1950.)

146. From time to time suggestions appear in the Coloured press that the Coloured People should adopt the methods so effectively employed by Mr. Gandhi in India. The moderate C.P.N.U. leader, Mr. George Golding, recently issued a statement to the press, stating that the Cape Coloured community should and would adopt the principle of 'no pay, no work' by participating in a token general stoppage of work throughout the Cape. This would, he claimed, paralyse industry, communications and agriculture, and demonstrate the vital rôle of the Coloured people in the Cape's economic life. Such a claim may not be without foundation, but the present question is whether there is sufficient organisation and community of feeling within the group to achieve such a united act of aggression.

147. Cf. Johnson, p. 310.

148. 'An attitude typical of many Cape Coloureds is that they are not only racially different from the Native, but that they are also superior to him. They feel that the white blood flowing in the veins of many of them, and their membership of a civilised society, place them above the Native as a member of an uncivilised, or at least semi-barbarous race, which is still vaguely feared as such, and is historically the enemy of the Cape Coloureds as of the Whites.' (C., s. 34.) See also C., s. 37–41, for other attitudes to the African, including the tendency for educated upper-class persons to make common cause politically while retaining social distance.

149. See C., s. 32.

150. Tengo Jabavu's attitude in the 1890s is described in the following passage: 'Whenever the Coloured people are mentioned in "*Imvo*" there are either references to bastardy, disparaging remarks, often only too well-founded, on the political ineptitude of the Coloured voters, or haughty advice tendered by one whose tremendous political experience and lofty principles were above reproach.' (Roux, p. 74.) The London *Daily Mail* of 4th July, 1949, reported an interview with an old Bamangwato headman, who said of the Cape Coloured: 'They used to be called by the proud name of Hottentot. They are just Coloureds now. God forbid that this fate should come to the Bamangwatos.' See also Stonequist, p. 20, and report of speech by the Minister of Native Affairs, Dr. H. F. Verwoerd, at Heidelberg (*Rand Daily Mail*, 28th October, 1950).

151. 'Cape Coloureds . . . often find this tendency extremely irritating, and the claim is sometimes voiced by them that they are, in reality, Coloured Europeans, and that the general term "non-European" should not be applied to them.' (C., s. 37.)

152. Instances of Coloured objections to this state of affairs: 'I observed last Monday, on Pinelands Station, that the waiting-room for Coloured women (1st and 2nd class) is now marked with an *Apartheid* brand: "For European women only." And now the result is that our Coloureds with 1st or 2nd class tickets have to mix up with the 3rd class travellers in the 3rd class waiting room, which is nearly packed with Natives.' (Extract from letter to the Editor of the *Sun*, 10th February, 1950,

p. 3.) Cf. also the complaint about S.W. African railway facilities in the C.A.C. Report, 1945–6, p. 29: 'On the Upington-Kakamas line conditions are equally bad. Not only is 2nd-class accommodation not provided for Coloured persons, but the 3rd-class accommodation is inadequate; and very often, Natives, Hottentots and Coloured persons are herded together.' Cf. also C., s. 35–6.

153. In the mid-1930s, the Cape Coloured Report referred to a 'weakening or absence of that feeling of difference and of superiority which tends in other cases to keep the two groups apart' (s. 39–40). On the other hand, about ten years later another Commission reported friction between Coloureds and Africans in the Transkei, and a recrudescence of a strong sense of separateness, due in part at least to the different pay and status of Coloureds in war service. (M., p. 25.)

154. Cf. the *Sun*, 10th February, 1950, and the *Torch*, 13th February, 1950.

155. Dollard, p. 28; see his Ch. XIII *passim*, also Kimball Young, p. 277.

156. 'The Coloured people have hardly any traditions. The history of the Coloured race has never been written from the Coloured point of view . . . We have been taught . . . of the great heroes of civilisation, all white people, and are staggered by the immensity of their genius. No wonder we feel that we belong to a insignificant race: that we are useless to ourselves or to our country except as humble workers who have no other status.' (*Cape Standard*, 25th January, 1937.)

157. The very high and increasing crime figures for the Coloured population (see Appendix N) may perhaps be regarded as an index of increasingly aggressive responses in this group, and of a decline in acceptance-responses.

158. Respectable Coloured town-dwellers complain that police protection in certain predominantly Coloured areas is either insufficient or totally absent. Moreover, it is said that offences against Coloured persons or property do not receive the same attention from the police as in the cases of Europeans, while in the event of convictions, the sentences are often not so heavy (*v.* Ch. IV *passim*).

159. Cf. A. G. Weiss (pp. 18–19) for an example of this in a clothing factory. I have encountered no instances of overt aggression or violence between Christians and Malays on those grounds, but they may well exist. See *Torch* of 8th May, 1951, for comment on official attempts to cause dissension between Coloureds and Malays.

160. Some Nationalist leaders seem to understand that colour by itself is not a sufficient determinant of status to permit of social stability, although it is doubtful whether the clock can now be put back to the days when colour and low cultural attainments or aspirations totally coincided, still less be held back there in perpetuity. It sometimes seems, however, that many white South Africans are quite unable to adjust to changing circumstances, although they suspect that to adhere to their present course of action means ultimate destruction. This 'death-wish' attitude was recently expressed by Sarah Gertrude Millin: 'Talk is useless. Africa is the black man's continent. In Africa the white man is a transient and embarrassed phenomenon.' Commenting on this, a writer in the *Star* said: 'This, too, is the private view of many Nationalists. The policy of *apartheid*, with its crudities and false reasoning, is to many of them a last ditch policy. They are prepared to go down fighting; but in their hearts they believe that they will go down in the end.' (27th November, 1950, *A Plan for South Africa*, Article 1.) Cf. also André Siegfried's comment on the pessimism of most South Africans, particularly about the future of their sons and grandsons, *African Journey* (Cape, 1950) (pp. 145–6).

161. 'Where status and the accompanying rôles are highly rigid and fixed in a caste system or in some other institutional arrangement making for segregation, prejudice, at least in the narrow and more proper sense, may not arise. Prejudice is really most striking when the strata of classes are changing, when one group is threatening another in its power and prestige.' (Kimball Young, p. 258.)

162. Cf. Hoernlé, pp. 146–7.

163. For an analysis of these and other racial situations, see Cox, Ch. 17.

164. A Nationalist outlined the desired solution of the Coloured problem as follows: 'We have the stratum of the Europeans: let me describe them as the top

stratum. We have the Coloured stratum in the broadest sense of the term; and we are getting now a very strong stratum of blacks, of Natives, and it has now become very clear to me in the visits I have made in the neighbourhood that as far as the Coloureds are concerned the suction towards the Natives is infinitely stronger than the force of the suction from above in the direction of the Europeans . . . The influx of Natives into the Cape industrial area . . . will eventually . . . simplify the matter of the dividing line between Europeans and non-Europeans.' (Mr. J. H. Steyn, member for Potchefstroom, speaking on 24th May, 1949 (*Hansard*, col. 6393).

165. See Hoernlé, p. 184.

166. Dormant, because other considerations still hold them in check. See Simons, *The Cape Coloured People To-day*, p. 20.

167. Cf. Myrdal on the practical importance for the resolving or easing of race-problems of the inverse relationship between the American Negro's and the white man's rank orders of discrimination, the Negro's major need being economic, while he places least emphasis on civil courtesies or inter-racial sex relations (p. 60 f.).

168. Cf. the predictions of Dr. Keppel-Jones in *When Smuts Goes*. The present defence of the Coloured franchise is dictated, not only by motives of political expediency, but by a feeling that 'What is being done to the Coloured People to-day might well happen to the English-speaking section, or the Jews, in the future.' (Mr. D. B. Molteno, speaking at a Protest Meeting called by the Cape Town Civil Rights League, 27th April, 1951, and reported in the *Sun*, 4th May, 1951.)

BIBLIOGRAPHY

BIBLIOGRAPHY

1. SOUTH AFRICA

(A) UNION GOVERNMENT PUBLICATIONS

C.   Report of the Commission on the Cape Coloured Population of the Union, U.G. 54/1937.

Ca.   Carnegie Commission Report on the Poor White Problem in South Africa, *Pro Ecclesia Drukkery* (S.A.), 1932.

C.A.C. Annual Reports of Coloured Advisory Council, 1943–47.

Cf.   Report of Committee of Inquiry into Cape Flats and Similarly-Affected Areas, U.G. 18/1943.

Cl.   Public Service Inquiry Commission Reports (Centlivres). (Appearing since early 1940s.)

E.   Economic and Wages Commission, U.G. 14/1926.

G.   Gluckman Commission Report on the National Health Services, U.G. 30/1944.

I.   Industrial Legislation Commission Report, U.G. 37/1935.

L.   Report of Penal and Prisons Reform Commission (Lansdown), U.G. 47/1947.

Lq.   Report of Cape Coloured Liquor Commission of Inquiry, U.G. 33/1945.

M.   Report of Inter-Departmental Committee on Coloured Mission Stations and Reserves, U.G. 33/1947.

Mi.   Report of the Commission on Mixed Marriages in South Africa, U.G. 30/1939.

P.   Report of the Police Commission of Inquiry, U.G. 50/1937.

V.   Report of the Commission on Technical and Vocational Education, (De Villiers), U.G. 65/1948.

Also Union Census Reports: 1904, 1911, 1921, 1936, 1946, 1951 ; Industrial Censuses: 1919 to the present time; *Union Year Book* No. 23 of 1946; Annual Reports of the Departments of Justice, Social Welfare, Education, the South African Police and Department of Prisons; Crime Statistics; Social and Economic Planning Council Reports (S.E.P.C. Reports); Report of the Departmental Committee of Inquiry into the Training and Employment of Social Welfare Workers (U.G. 13/1950), etc.

(*N.B.*—Where Reports are issued in more than one volume, this is indicated in the text by the Roman numeral immediately following the abbreviation, e.g., Ca/II.)

(B) PROVINCIAL AND MUNICIPAL PUBLICATIONS

C. Ed. R. Annual Reports of the Cape Educational Department.

C. Ed. S. Annual Statistics of the Cape Educational Department.

Also reports of the Transvaal, Natal and O.F.S. Educational Departments, and reports of various departments of the Cape Town Municipal and Cape Divisional Councils, etc., etc.

(C) INDIVIDUAL PUBLICATIONS

Abrahams, Peter, *The Path of Thunder*; Harper and Bros. (New York and London), 1948.

Blommaert, W., *Het Invoeren van de Slavernij aan die Kaap*; Archives Year Book of South African History, Vol. I, Pt. I, 1938.

Brookes, Edgar, *Colour Problems of South Africa*; Lovedale Press (S.A.), 1933.

Cowen, D. V., *Parliamentary Sovereignty and the Entrenched Clauses of the South Africa Act*; Juta (Cape Town), 1951.

Cruse, H. P., *Die Opheffing van die Kleurlingbevolking*; C.S.V. Boekhandel (S.A.), 1947.

De Kock, Victor, *Those in Bondage*; Allen and Unwin, 1950.

Du Plessis, I. D., *The Cape Malays*; Maskew Miller (Cape Town), 1944.

Edwards, Isobel E., *Towards Emancipation*; Cardiff University Press, 1942.

Engelbrecht, J. A., *The Korana*; Maskew Miller (Cape Town), 1936.

Findlay, G., *Miscegenation*; The Pretoria News and Printing Works, 1936.

Halford, S. J., *The Griquas of Griqualand*; Juta (Cape Town), 1950.

Hoernlé, R. F. A., *South African Native Policy and the Liberal Spirit*; Published on behalf of the Phelps-Stokes Fund of the University of Cape Town, 1939.

Hoge, J., Personalia of the Germans at the Cape, 1652–1806 ; *Archives Year Book for South African History*, 1946.

Jacobson, E., *The Cape Coloured* (Bibliography); University of Cape Town (photostatic reproduction), 1945.

Joshi, P. S., *The Tyranny of Colour*; printed by E. P. and Commercial Printing Co., Ltd., Durban.

Keppel-Jones, Arthur, *Friends or Foes*; Shuter and Shooter (Pietermaritzburg), 1950.

Kirk, J. H., 'A Comparison of Race Relations in South Africa and the Southern States'; *Social Forces* XIII (October 1934).

Kuper, Hilda, *The Uniform of Colour*; Johannesburg University Press, 1947.

Long, B. K., *In Smuts' Camp*; Oxford University Press, 1945.

MacCrone, I. D.,* (1) *Race Attitudes in South Africa*; Oxford University Press, 1937. (2) 'A Quantitative Study of Race Stereotypes'; *S.A. Journal of Science*, Vol. XXXIII, pp. 1,104–11, March, 1937. (3) 'A Comparative Study of European and Non-European Differences in Race Preferences'; *S.A. Journal of Science*, Vol. XXXV, pp. 412–16, December, 1938.

MacMillan, W. M.,* (1) *The Cape Colour Question*; Faber and Gwyer, 1927. (2) *Complex South Africa*; Faber and Faber, 1930.

Manuel, George, *The Coloured People* (Bibliography); University of Cape Town (typescript), 1943.

Marais, J. S.,* (1) *The Cape Coloured People*; Longmans, 1937. (2) *Maynier and the First Boer Republic*; Maskew Miller (Cape Town), 1944.

May, H. J., *The South African Constitution* (2nd Edition), Juta (Cape Town), 1949.

Millin, Sarah Gertrude, (1) *God's Stepchildren*; Constable, 1924. (2) *The South Africans*; Constable, 1926.
Olivier, Lord, *Anatomy of African Misery*; Hogarth Press, 1927.
Petersen, S. V., *As die Son Ondergaan*; *Unie-Volkspers Beperk.*, Cape Town, 1945.
Reed, Douglas, *Somewhere South of Suez*; Jonathan Cape, 1950.
Roux, Etienne, *Time Longer than Rope*; Gollancz, 1948.
Schapera, I., *The Khoisan Peoples of South Africa*; Routledge and Sons, 1930.
Schreiner, Olive, *Thoughts on South Africa*; Fisher Unwin, 1923.
Smith, Dr. Edwin, *The Blessed Missionaries*; Oxford University Press, 1950.
Sofer, Cyril, *Some Recent Trends in the Status History of the Coloured People of South Africa*; unpublished MS. thesis accepted by the University of London in 1949.
Theal, G. M., *The Yellow and Dark-Skinned People of Africa South of the Zambesi*; S. Sonnenschein & Co., 1910.
Thompson, L. M., *The Cape Coloured Franchise*; Institute of Race Relations New Africa Pamphlet, No. 20, 1949.
Van der Merwe, Dr. P. J., *Die Trekboer in die Geskiedenis van die Kaap-Kolonie* (1657–1842); *Nasionale Pers Beperk*, Cape Town, 1938.
Van Wyk, G. F., 'A Preliminary Account of the Physical Anthropology of the Cape Coloured People (Males)'; *Annals of the University of Stellenbosch*, Vol. XVII, Sec. A, No. 2 (September, 1939); *Nasionale Pers Beperk*, Cape Town.
Walker, Eric, A. (1) *The Cape Native Franchise*; (Cape Town), 1936. (2) *A History of South Africa*; Longmans, 1928. (3) *Lord de Villiers and His Times*; Constable, 1925.
Walker, Oliver, *Kaffirs are Lively*; Gollancz, 1948.
Walton, Sir Edgar, *The Inner History of the National Convention*: Longmans, 1912.
Weiss, A. G., *The Cape Coloured Woman—Within an Industrial Community and at Home*; M. Soc. Sc. Thesis, University of Cape Town, 1950.
Wille, G., *Principles of South African Law* (2nd Edition); Juta, Cape Town, 1945.
Ziervogel, C., *Brown South Africa*; Maskew Miller (Cape Town), Undated.
* Where no number is given after the names of their writers, the reference in each case is to (1).

(D) COLLECTIVE PUBLICATIONS

The Cape Coloured People To-day; Institute of Race Relations Publication (Johannesburg), 1942.
The Cape Town Social Survey; series of Reports and Studies issued by the Department of Social Science, University of Cape Town, since 1939 (including Report series of the Cape Co-ordinating Council).
Coming of Age; (Studies in South African Citizenship and Politics), Maskew Miller (Cape Town), 1930.
Crime and the Community; Institute of Race Relations Penal Reform Series, No. 3 (Johannesburg).
Findings of the National Convention, called at Cape Town on 4th–6th July, 1938, of Organisations concerned with the Welfare of the Coloured

People, to consider the Report of the 1937 Cape Coloured Commission.

Handbook on Race Relations in South Africa; edited by Ellen Hellman and published for the South African Institute of Race Relations by the Oxford University Press, 1949.

Report of the First National Coloured-European Conference convened in Cape Town on 26th–28th June, 1933, by the Cape Coloured and European Council and the South African Institute of Race Relations.

(E) PERIODICALS

S.A.J.Sc., *South African Journal of Science.*

S.A.J. Econ. (J. Ec. Soc. S.A.), *South African Journal of Economics.* The title was changed in the 1930s.

R.R. News, *Race Relations News*, published monthly by the Institute of Race Relations (I.R.R.).

The Forum, Johannesburg weekly (Liberal)—ceased publication in November, 1951.

The British Africa Monthly (now *The British Africa Review*—usually pro-United Party; strong advocate of British connection).

The Educational Journal. Cape Town monthly published by Coloured Radical Teachers' League of South Africa (T.L.S.A.).

Hansard (South Africa).

The Cape Times. Cape Town morning daily (independent, usually pro-United Party).

The Cape Argus. Cape Town evening daily (independent, usually pro-United Party).

The Rand Daily Mail. Johannesburg morning daily (independent, usually pro-United Party).

The Star. Johannesburg evening daily (independent, usually pro-United Party).

Die Suiderstem. Cape Town daily (United Party)—ceased publication 1950.

Die Burger. Cape Town daily (Nationalist).

The Sun. Cape Town Coloured weekly (organ of Conservative political group, the Coloured People's National Union, C.P.N.U.).

The Torch. Cape Town Non-European weekly (supports radical Unity Movement).

Pamphlets, brochures, etc., issued by the various political and other organisations.

2. UNITED STATES

Baker, Ray Stannard, *Following the Colour Line*; Doubleday, Page & Coy. (U.S.), 1908.

Cayton, H. R., and Drake, St. C., *Black Metropolis*; Cape (U.S.), 1946.

Davis, Allison and Others, *Deep South*; University of Chicago Press (U.S.), 1941.

Dollard, John, *Caste and Class in a Southern Town*; Harper and Brothers (U.S.), 1937.

Du Bois, W. E. B., *The Souls of Black Folk*; Constable (U.S.), 1905.

Frazier, E. Franklin, (1) *The Negro in the United States*; Macmillan (U.S.), 1949. (2) *The Negro Family in the United States*; University of Chicago Press (U.S.), 1939.

Johnson, Charles S., *Patterns of Negro Segregation*; Harper and Brothers, (U.S.), 1943.

Laski, H. J., *The American Democracy*; Allen and Unwin, 1949.

Moton, R. R., *What the Negro Thinks*; Doubleday, Doran (U.S.), 1932.

Myrdal, Gunnar, *An American Dilemma*; Harper and Brothers (U.S.), 1944.

3. OTHER COUNTRIES

(A) BRAZIL

Freyre, Gilberto, *The Masters and the Slaves*; Knopf (U.S.), 1946.

Pierson, Donald, *Negroes in Brazil*; University of Chicago Press (U.S.), 1942.

(B) UNITED KINGDOM

Little, K. L., *Negroes in Britain*; Kegan Paul, 1948.

4. GENERAL REFERENCE BOOKS

(A) INDIVIDUAL PUBLICATIONS

Burns, Sir Alan, *Colour Prejudice*; Allen and Unwin, 1948.

Cox, Oliver Cromwell, *Caste, Class and Race*; Doubleday (U.S.), 1948.

Dingwall, E. J., *Racial Pride and Prejudice*; Watts, 1946.

Dover, Cedric, *Half-Caste*; Secker and Warburg, 1937.

Linton, R., *The Study of Man*; Appleton-Century (U.S.), 1936.

MacIver, R. M., (1) *Society*; Rinehart (U.S.), 1937. (2) *The Web of Government*; Macmillan (U.S.), 1948.

Reuter, E. B., *Race Mixture*; McGraw Hill (U.S.), 1931.

Stonequist, E., *The Marginal Man*; Charles Scribner's Sons (U.S.), 1937.

Warner, W. Lloyd, and Lunt, Paul, *Social Life of a Modern Community*; Yale University Press (U.S.), 1941.

Young, Kimball, *Handbook of Social Psychology*; Kegan Paul, 1946.

(B) COLLECTIVE PUBLICATIONS

The Science of Man in the World Crisis (ed. Linton); Columbia University Press (U.S.), 1945.

The Study of Society; Kegan Paul, 1939.

When People Meet (ed. Locke and Stern); Hinds, Hayden and Eldredge (U.S.), 1946.

ABBREVIATIONS

Ch.—Chapter.
f.—and following pages.
n.—footnote.
p.—page.
s.—section or paragraph.

z

APPENDICES

APPENDICES

A. South African Population Figures and Percentages of each Group to Total, 1904–51.

B. Population of each Province by Race and Sex (1951), and increase over 1946 figures.

C. Distribution of Population by Race and Sex between Rural and Urban Areas, 1921–46.

D. Racial Composition of the Coloured Group by Provinces, 1936 (Percentages).

E. Home Language and Knowledge of the Official Languages amongst the Coloured Group by Province and Age, 1936 and 1946.

F. Distribution amongst the Major Religions and Denominations per Thousand of Population (1946).

G. Distribution according to Occupation of Persons gainfully occupied of 15 years and over (10 years and over in the case of Africans), 1946.

H. Vital Statistics and Others.

I. Some Definitions of a Coloured Person.

J. The Cape Province Common Roll Electorate, 1905–51.

K. Maximum and Minimum Salaries paid to Non-Commissioned Police Officers at Various Periods.

L. Percentage of Convictions to Prosecutions for Certain Serious Crimes, 1926–35.

M. Some Comparative Sentences.

N. Percentage of Wage-Earners by Race in all Industrial Establishments in the Western Cape, 1919–45.

O. Number of Apprentices at Cape Town Technical College, by Race, 1926–49.

P. Farm Wages.

Q. Occupational Groups in Cape Town, by Race, 1938–9.

R. Christian National Education.

S. Number and Type of Schools, Number of Teachers and Average Enrolments by Race in the Cape Province, 1949.

T. Expenditure on Education and Cost per Pupil in the Cape Province, by Race, 1937–49.

U. Median Age of Pupils in each Primary Standard by Race, 1949.

V. Annual Number of European-Coloured Marriages and Percentage involving Coloured Males, 1925–48.

APPENDIX A

SOUTH AFRICAN POPULATION FIGURES AND PERCENTAGES OF EACH GROUP TO TOTAL

Census Year	Total	European	Per cent	Coloured	Per cent	Asiatic	Per cent	African	Per cent
1904	5,175,824	1,116,806	21.6	445,228	8.6	122,734	2.4	3,491,056	67.4
1911	5,973,394	1,276,242	21.4	525,943	8.8	152,203	2.5	4,019,006	67.3
1921	6,928,580	1,519,488	21.9	545,548	7.9	165,731	2.4	4,697,813	67.8
1936	9,589,898	2,003,857	20.9	769,661	8.0	219,691	2.3	6,596,689	68.8
1946	11,391,949	2,372,690	20.7	928,484	8.0	285,260	2.6	7,805,515	68.7
1951	12,437,227	2,588,933	20.8	1,078,621*	8.7	358,738	2.9	8,410,935	67.6

(Taken from Union Census Reports, Race Relations Handbook, p. 9, Table III, and preliminary 1951 Census figures.)

APPENDIX B

1. POPULATION OF EACH PROVINCE BY RACE AND SEX, 1951

Province		European	Cape Coloured and Malay	Asiatic	African
Cape	m.	460,691	483,511	9,597	1,137,216
	f.	466,257	481,573	7,450	1,331,783
	t.	926,948	965,084	17,047	2,468,999
Natal	m.	134,568	14,865	152,902	863,997
	f.	136,129	14,954	145,304	914,271
	t.	270,697	30,399	298,206	1,778,268
Transvaal	m.	586,145	34,448	22,879	1,884,527
	f.	578,430	34,246	20,592	1,508,856
	t.	1,164,575	68,694	43,471	3,393,383
O.F.S.	m.	115,161	7,458	8	394,139
	f.	111,552	6,986	6	376,146
	t.	226,713	14,444	14	770,285
Union	m.	1,296,565	540,282	185,386	4,279,879
	f.	1,292,368	538,339	173,352	4,131,056
	t.	2,588,933	1,078,621	358,738	8,410,935

m. = male. f. = female. t. = total.

(This and the following table are taken from the First Preliminary Figures of 1951 Population Census, released by the Bureau of Census and Statistics on 20th August, 1951. It should be noted that the total Coloured population of the Cape is now larger than the European group, which exceeded it by over 40,000 in 1946.)

* Including 62,602 Malays, who were for the first time enumerated as a separate ethnic group.

2. INCREASE OVER 1946 FIGURES—NUMBER AND PERCENTAGES

Province	European	Cape Coloured and Malay	Asiatic	African
Cape	56,153 6.4	135,534 16.3	1,873 12.3	130,670 5.6
Natal	34,000 14.4	5,504 22.1	65.889 28.4	69,785 4.1
Transvaal	101,454 9.5	8,708 14.5	5,713 15.1	271,210 6.7
O.F.S.	24,636 12.2	391 2.8	3 27.3	107,355 16.2
Union	216,243 9.1	150,137 16.7	73,478 25.8	579,020 7.4

APPENDIX C

1. DISTRIBUTION BETWEEN RURAL AND URBAN AREAS, 1921–46

I. Urban Population

(a) Numbers Year	European	Coloured	Asiatic	African
1921	647,508	249,968	51,209	587,000
1936	1,307,386	414,907	145,596	1,141,642
1946	1,719,338	539,939	200,494	1,794,212

(b) Proportions of racial groups in urban areas, per cent

	European	Coloured	Asiatic	African
1921	58.78	45.62	30.90	12.50
1936	65.24	53.91	66.27	17.31
1946	72.46	58.15	70.28	22.99

(c) Increase per cent

	European	Coloured	Asiatic	African
1921–36	54.26	65.99	184.31	94.49
1936–46	31.51	30.13	37.71	57.16

II. Rural Population

(a) Numbers Year	European	Coloured	Asiatic	African
1921	671,980	295,580	114,522	4,110,813
1936	696,471	354,754	74,095	5,455,047
1946	653,352	388,545	84,766	6,011,380

(b) Proportions of rural groups in rural areas, per cent

Year	European	Coloured	Asiatic	African
1921	44.22	54.18	69.10	87.50
1936	34.76	48.09	33.73	82.69
1946	27.54	41.85	29.72	77.01

Table *II* continued.

(c) *Increase or decrease per cent*

1921–36	+3.64	+20.02	−35.3	+32.69
1936–46	−6.19	+ 9.53	+14.40	+10.19

2. DISTRIBUTION: URBAN AND RURAL AREAS BY RACE AND SEX, 1946

	URBAN			RURAL			
	Male	Female	Total	Male	Female	Total	Total
European	848,167	871,171	1,719,338	346,459	306,893	653,352	2,372,690
Coloured	258,468	281,471	539,939	207,317	181,228	388,545	928,484
Asiatic	105,488	95,006	200,494	43,588	41,178	84,766	285,260
African	1,097,486	591,567	1,689,053	2,899,671	3,243,191	6,142,862	7,831,915
All races	2,309,609	1,839,215	4,148,824	3,497,035	3,772,490	7,269,525	11,418,349

The figures in Table 1 are taken from the Union Census Reports; those in Table 2 were kindly supplied in late 1951 by the Bureau of Census and Statistics. The African figures do not altogether tally with those in Table 1, and presumably represent corrected totals.

APPENDIX D

RACIAL COMPOSITION OF THE COLOURED GROUP BY PROVINCES, 1936
(Percentages)

Race Branch	Cape	Transvaal	Natal	O.F.S.	Union
Cape Malay	4.54	4.74	2.30	1.34	4.43
Cape Coloured, Coloured	76.78	71.98	54.48	42.98	75.13
Bushmen	.60	3.00	.32	4.84	.85
Griqua	3.31	7.22	4.75	24.64	4.10
Hottentot	11.99	4.38	1.04	12.48	11.24
Koranna	.40	1.47	.05	7.28	.62
Namaqua	.49	.07	.01	.10	.44
St. Helenan	.26	.83	8.25	.29	.50
Swahili and Zanzibari	.05	.46	1.14	.14	.10
All other, including 'Mixed'	1.51	5.74	26.24	5.83	2.48
Unspecified	.07	.11	1.42	.08	.11
Total	100.00	100.00	100.00	100.00	100.00

Source: 1936 Population Census, Vol. 9, U.G. 12/42, p. 139. This detailed classification was dropped in later censuses. It was based on voluntary returns, but probably gives an approximate picture of the group's ethnic constituents. The census comment on this table pointed out that the 'Aborigines' (i.e., Bushmen, Hottentots, Koranna and Namaqua) were more important in the rural areas, and were probably more numerous in the North and North-West Cape. The Transvaal 'Bushmen' were concentrated in the south-west of the province, but few spoke Bushmen or Hottentot dialects. It is highly doubtful whether any of these 'aborigines' were unmixed with other stocks. The small number of St. Helenans are comparatively recent immigrants, drawn mainly to the South African coastal regions in search of work, and the same is probably true of the Swahili and Zanzibari group. The final category, 'All other, including "Mixed",' consists largely of Euro-Bantu crosses, most of them in Natal, where they form over one-quarter of the province's Coloured population.

APPENDIX E

1. HOME LANGUAGE OF COLOURED POPULATION (a) BY PROVINCE, (b) IN THE LARGER TOWNS—PERCENTAGES, 1946*

	English	Afrikaans	Other	Total
(a)				
Cape	7.3 (6.03)	91.5 (91.97)	1.2 (2.00)	100
Natal	67.1 (61.35)	24.6 (23.48)	8.3 (15.17)	100
Transvaal	15.5 (11.64)	80.4 (81.39)	4.1 (6.97)	100
O.F.S.	.6 (0.99)	98.0 (94.90)	1.4 (4.11)	100
Union	9.4 (7.62)	89.1 (89.69)	1.5 (2.69)	100
(b)				
Cape Town	21.07 (17.99)	77.26 (78.89)	1.67 (3.12)	100
Port Elizabeth	18.61 (17.44)	79.33 (79.61)	2.05 (2.95)	100
Durban	76.58 (71.22)	16.35 (19.17)	7.07 (9.61)	100
Johannesburg	24.92 (20.00)	71.40 (75.75)	3.68 (4.25)	100
Bloemfontein	2.18 (3.59)	96.21 (89.89)	1.61 (6.52)	100

2. KNOWLEDGE OF OFFICIAL LANGUAGES BY PROVINCE

	English and Afrikaans	English only	Afrikaans only	Neither	Total
Cape	34.65 (31.53)	1.70 (1.63)	63.50 (66.64)	0.15 (0.20)	100
Natal	35.59 (34.39)	55.59 (55.30)	6.14 (6.64)	2.67 (3.67)	100
Transvaal	66.05 (58.79)	4.09 (3.64)	29.08 (36.77)	0.78 (0.80)	100
O.F.S.	24.16 (17.14)	0.09 (1.12)	75.38 (81.34)	0.38 (0.40)	100
Union	36.54 (33.04)	3.27 (3.04)	59.93 (63.60)	0.26 (0.32)	100

3. AGE AND KNOWLEDGE OF OFFICIAL LANGUAGES

Age Group (Years)	English and Afrikaans	English only	Afrikaans only	Neither	Total
0– 6	13.5 (12.75)	5.71 (4.69)	80.1 (81.90)	0.6 (0.66)	100
7–14	(30.90)	(2.85)	(65.82)	(0.43)	100
15–24	(41.36)	(2.65)	(55.78)	(0.21)	100
25–34	(43.19)	(3.12)	(53.53)	(0.16)	100
35–44	42.6 (40.54)	2.6 (2.75)	54.5 (56.55)	0.2 (0.16)	100
45–54	(37.40)	(2.21)	(60.22)	(0.17)	100
55–64	(32.91)	(2.15)	(64.74)	(0.20)	100
65 +	(24.08)	(1.81)	(73.76)	(0.35)	100
Total	36.54 (33.03)	3.27 (3.04)	59.93 (63.61)	0.26 (0.32)	100
0–20	— (26.94)	— (3.41)	— (69.19)	— (0.46)	100
21 +	— (39.42)	— (2.65)	— (57.75)	— (0.18)	100

* In all tables, the figures in brackets are from the 1936 Census, Vols. IV, p. 122, and IX, p. xxviii. The 1946 figures in tables 1a and 3, which were kindly supplied by the Bureau of Census and Statistics, are available only to one decimal point, and in table 3 are still not available for detailed age groups; those in tables 1b and 2 were worked out by me from total figures supplied by the same source.

APPENDIX F

DISTRIBUTION ACCORDING TO MAIN RELIGIONS PER 1,000 OF POPULATION,
1936 AND 1946*

1. *Christian*	*European*	*Coloured*	*African*
Dutch Reformed			
(3 churches)	541.2 (542.8)	314.7 (292.0)	34.1 (23.4)
Anglican	161.5 (172.2)	200.1 (212.3)	70.6 (61.8)
Presbyterian	37.1 (41.1)	8.0 (8.0)	20.9 (16.4)
Congregational	5.5 (5.7)	107.5 (111.6)	14.4 (8.6)
Methodist	71.5 (70.7)	96.9 (105.6)	141.5 (120.6)
Lutheran	9.7 (12.9)	51.8 (77.3)	50.4 (46.6)
Roman Catholic	50.3 (46.1)	60.5 (46.9)	47.7 (35.3)
Greek	1.7 (1.7)	— —	— —
Baptist	9.9 (10.1)	4.0 (4.1)	9.0 (5.0)
Apostolic Mission	24.8 (15.9)	25.6 (15.8)	22.8 (2.0)
Native Separatist	— —	2.7 (11.1)	96.9 (165.3)
Total Christian†	937.1 (946.4)	900.1 (921.2)	526.3 (486.7)
2. *Non-Christian*			
Hebrew	43.6 (45.2)	— —	— —
Islam	— —	47.0 (45.6)	0.6 (0.2)
Pagan (Bantu and other)	— —	13.3 (23.0)	443.4 (503.9)
Total Non-Christian‡	57.1 (50.7)	86.1 (72.1)	456.2 (507.6)
3. *Unknown or Unspeci-fied*	5.8 (2.9)	13.8 (6.7)	17.5 (5.7)

* This table gives figures for the main religions only: those for Europeans are taken from the 1936 and advance 1946 Census figures given in *Year Book* No. 24, 1948, p. 244, which gives percentage figures for this group only for 1936 and 1946; the Coloured figures for 1936 are taken from the 1936 Census (Vol. VI, p. 88), while those for 1946 were worked out by me from the unpercentaged totals given in the *Year Book, ibid.* There are certain discrepancies between these advance figures and those later made available to me at the Bureau of Census and Statistics which I was unable to reconcile, the principal one being in the totals of Christian, Non-Christian and Unknown, which I worked out from the later figures as 913.2, 73.0 and 13.8 respectively. The 1936 African figures were worked out from the *Year Book* totals, and the 1946 figures (not given there) from totals supplied by the Bureau of Census and Statistics. Of the Asiatic group, figures for which are not here included, 628, 213 and 49 per 1,000 were Hindu, Moslem or Christian respectively in 1946 (the corresponding figures for 1936 being 727, 194 and 48). 1936 figures are given in brackets.

† Only the main denominational groupings are given here, so that in neither section will the separate ratios add up to the total.

‡ The division into Christian and Non-Christian, though still used in the reports, is perhaps somewhat misleading. A small but growing number of persons, particularly in the European and Coloured groups, professed belief in various sophisticated philosophies, or even non-belief in any religious dogma, while the number of persons with 'pagan' beliefs was definitely on the decrease.

APPENDIX G

DISTRIBUTION, ACCORDING TO OCCUPATION, OF PERSONS GAINFULLY OCCUPIED

15 years and over (10 years and over in case of Africans), 1946

MALE

	European 1936	European 1946	Coloured 1936	Coloured 1946	Asiatic 1936	Asiatic 1946	African 1936	African 1946
1. Agriculture and Livestock, Hunting, Fishing, Forestry	30.2	23.7	50.0	42.6	29.5	19.7	62.4	57.5
2. Mining, etc.	7.8	7.7	1.7	1.2	1.5	0.9	17.1	17.3
3. Manufacturing	10.7	14.7	10.7	15.9	15.3	25.1		6.2
(a) Food, Beverages, Tobacco	1.8	2.0	2.4	3.8	5.0	9.4		1.2
(b) Textiles, Clothing and Footwear, etc.	1.8	1.7	3.0	4.5	4.3	7.3		0.6
(c) Wood, Furniture	0.8	1.2	1.3	2.1	1.8	2.5		0.6
(d) Paper and Printing	0.9	1.1	0.5	0.7	0.8	1.3		0.1
(e) Leather and Rubber	0.3	0.4	0.5	0.7	0.5	0.6	} 9.1	0.1
(f) Chemicals and Mineral Fuels	0.7	0.9	0.3	0.5	0.6	1.0		0.5
(g) Non-Metallic Minerals	0.4	0.5	1.2	1.0	0.4	0.4		1.2
(h) Iron and Steel, Metal Products, Machinery, Vehicles, etc.	3.5	6.5	1.3	2.4	1.2	2.0		1.7
(i) Miscellaneous	0.5	0.4	0.2	0.2	0.7	0.6		0.2
4. Construction	6.5	7.3	10.3	11.6	1.9	2.7		3.0
5. Electricity, Gas and Water	0.4	0.8	0.2	0.4	0.1	0.1		0.2
6. Commerce	14.6	13.1	7.2	8.0	28.8	29.1	0.3	2.8
7. Transport and Communication	12.6	16.7	6.1	6.4	2.8	3.5	3·9	2.7
8. Services	17.2	16.0	13.8	13.9	20.1	18.9		10.3
(a) Government	11.5	8.5	6.0	5.2	5.2	3.5	} 1·5	2.4
(b) Community and Business	3.4	4.8	0.5	2.6	1.1	3.1		1.1
(c) Recreation	0.4	0.7	0.3	0.3	0.5	0.6	0.8	0.2
(d) Personal	1.9	2.0	7.0	5.8	13.3	11.7	4.9	6.6
Total	100.0	100.0	100.0	100.0	100.0	100.0	100.0	100.0

	European 1936	European 1946	Coloured 1936	Coloured 1946	Asiatic 1936	Asiatic 1946	African 1936	African 1946
Total number of Males Economically Active	609,975	701,312	209,034	246,892	62,613	73,135	2,303,071	2,661,930
Percentage Economically Active of Total Male Population of 15 years and over (10 years in the case of Africans)	87.1	84.8	93.1	91.9	90.7	88.4	96.0	89.6

FEMALE

	European 1936	European 1946	Coloured 1936	Coloured 1946	Asiatic 1936	Asiatic 1946	African 1936	African 1946
1. Agriculture and Livestock, Hunting, Fishing, Forestry	2.7	4.7	2.8	7.2	30.5	30.4		59.1
2. Mining, etc.	0.5	1.2	0.2	0.1	—	0.1		0.2
3. Manufacturing	22.0	18.5	8.0	16.4	8.3	19.5		0.4*
(a) Food, Beverages and Tobacco	3.3	3.0	2.4	5.0	2.4	5.5		0.1
(b) Textiles, Clothing and Footwear, etc.	14.0	8.6	4.5	9.4	4.6	12.2		0.2
(c) Wood, Furniture	0.2	0.3	0.1	0.2	0.8	0.4		—
(d) Paper and Printing	1.8	2.2	0.4	0.7	0.1	0.1		—
(e) Leather and Rubber	0.3	0.4	0.1	0.3	—	0.1		—
(f) Chemicals and Mineral Fuels	0.8	1.2	0.2	0.3	0.2	0.4		—
(g) Non-Metallic Minerals	0.1	0.2	—	—	0.1	0.1		—
(h) Iron and Steel, Metal Products, Machinery, Vehicles, etc.	0.8	2.2	0.1	0.3	—	0.1		—
(i) Miscellaneous	0.7	0.4	0.2	0.2	0.1	0.6		—
4. Construction	0.3	0.6	0.1	0.1	—	—	Differently classified in 1936	—
5. Electricity, Gas and Water	0.1	0.1	—	—	—	—		—
6. Commerce	26.2	29.3	1.0	1.6	20.2	19.8		0.1
7. Transport and Communication	3.0	5.7	0.1	0.1	0.1	0.3		—
8. Services	45.2	39.9	87.8	74.5	41.0	29.9		40.2
(a) Government	11.8	7.6	1.5	0.1	2.8	0.3		—
(b) Community and Business	16.7	22.7	0.8	3.7	2.3	7.6		1.2
(c) Recreation	0.6	0.9	—	0.1	0.2	0.2		—
(d) Personal	16.1	8.7	85.5	70.6	35.7	21.8		39.0
Total	100.0	100.0	100.0	100.0	100.0†	100.0		100.0

	European 1936	European 1946	Coloured 1936	Coloured 1946	Asiatic 1936	Asiatic 1946	African 1936	African 1946
Total number of Females Economically Active	131,710	186,869	72,766	102,008	3,713	6,034	1,919,324	2,181,649‡
Percentage Economically Active of Total Female Population of 15 years and over (10 years in the case of Africans)	19.4	22.7	33.0	38.3	7.3	8.7	82.4	75.5* (42.5)

(Taken from the Industrial Classification of the Economically Active Population, 1946 (Special Report No. 186—Preliminary Census Report).)

* The detailed official figures given for this section do not tally with the official total, possibly because the numbers of African women employed in other branches of manufacturing are too small to show in a percentage reckoning.

† The official statistics for the number of Asiatic women employed in 1936 in fact add up to 100.1.

‡ This figure includes an estimate of 1 million dependants on household duties. The percentage in brackets excludes this million.

APPENDIX H—VITAL

	Union[1]		Cape Town		Cape Division[2]		Port
	E	C	E	NE[4]	E	C	E
1. Birth Rate	(a) (1939) 25.2 (b) (1949) 26.3	(a) 46.3 (b) 48.4	17.35	45.56	(30.46)	(58.63)	30.49
2. Infantile Mortality Rate	(a) (1939) 40.5 (b) (1949) 40.1	(a) 158.8 (b) 147.9	29.59	101.47	30.76	121.28	38.78
3. Natural Increase or Survival Rate per 1,000	(a) (1939) 15.8 (b) (1949) 17.3	(a) 23.3 (b) 25.3	8.37	28.15	19.40	33.30	21.51
4. Expectation of Life	(a) (1937) m. 58.95 f. 63.06 (b) (1946-7) m. 63.78 f. 68.31	(a) m. 40.18 f. 40.86 (b) m. 41.70 f. 44.00	—	—	—	—	—
5. Illegitimate Births as percentage of total Births (or total Live Births)[5]	—	—	2.69	34.44	—	—	3.21
6. Masculinity Rate	(a) (1940) 105.41 (b) (1948) 104.2	(a) 102.41 (b) 100.8[6]	—	—	—	—	—
7. Death Rate per 1,000 of the Population	(a) (1939) 9.4 (b) (1949) 9.1	(a) 23.0 (b) 23.1	8.98	17.41	(11.06)	(25.33)	8.98
8. Deaths from T.B. (respiratory) per 1,000 of the Population	—	—	0.45	3.26[7]	—	—	0.58
9. Deaths from Bronchitis and Pneumonia per 1,000	—	—	0.37	1.94	—	—	0.68
10. Deaths from Syphilis per 1,000	—	—	0.05	0.29	—	—	0.02
11. Deaths from Cancer per 1,000	—	—	1.30	0.89	—	—	0.73
12. Deaths from Diarrhœa and Enteritis per 1,000[9]	—	—	0.09	1.74	—	—	0.24

[1] With the exception of the Union statistics, where specific dates are given, and unless otherwise stated, all municipal statistics are taken from the Reports of the various Medical Officers of Health for the year 1949–50. Figures given in brackets in these Reports were worked out by me from totals and estimated population figures given.

[2] The Cape Divisional Council is the local authority for the areas immediately outside the Cape Town municipal area; these areas include the municipalities of Durbanville, Bellville, Parow, Goodwood, Pinelands and Fish Hoek, and the Milnerton Local Board. The birth and death rates are calculated on the basis of the latest totals (1948) and the estimated population for the same year. No other figures could be supplied.

[3] Kimberley statistics are for the urban area only, except in the case of those for the European and Coloured illegitimate birth-rates, which include the rural

STATISTICS AND OTHERS

Elizabeth	East London		Kimberley[a]		Durban		Johannesburg	
C	E	C	E	C	E	C	E	C
48.85	26.21	42.73	24.68	52.09	20.04	51.25	24.55	46.15
162.57	39.53	188.03	49.04	129.14	28.74	73.06	31.90	95.51
24.29	15.71	11.34	13.58	25.00	10.98	37.20	16.44	27.96
—	—	—	—	—	—	—	—	—
32.99	1.62	34.62	2.94	33.43	1.82	24.20	2.70	20.14
—	—	—	—	—	—	—	—	—
24.56	10.50	32.69	11.11	27.09	9.06	14.04	8.11	18.19
5.47	0.35	9.50	(0.11)	(4.64)	0.26	2.18	0.37	4.89[s]
5.03	(0.59)	(7.67)	(1.05)	(5.18)	.35	1.48	0.31	1.85
0.13	(0.00)	(0.37)	(0.00)	(0.27)	0.00	0.32	0.08	0.41
0.57	(1.30)	(0.37)	(1.32)	(1.72)	1.32	0.70	1.18	0.85
3.70	(0.16)	(3.47)	(0.21)	(4.18)	0.08	1.25	0.09	1·93

area. The rural figures are in general less reliable and complete and are therefore omitted. The Coloured figures include the small Asiatic population.

[4] Although Cape Town gives no separate overall statistics for the Coloured group, the Non-European figures relate mainly to the Coloured group, as the vast majority of the 51,180 Africans in Cape Town at the time of the 1951 Census live in the location of Langa, for which separate figures are kept. According to the 1951 Census returns, Greater Cape Town had a population of 242,493 Europeans, 260,440 Coloureds and Malays, and 7,740 Asiatics. The African numbers have been kept down since 1946 by the restriction on the sale of railway tickets into the Western Cape area to Africans assured of work, and having a written authority from a Native Commissioner or Magistrate, under War Measure No. 81 of 1943.

[5] These statistics are specifically stated to be per mille *live* births in the case of Cape Town and Durban.

(For notes 6–9 see p. 360)

APPENDIX H

NUMBER OF PERSONS CONVICTED OF VARIOUS CRIMES (THOSE PREDOMINANT
IN THE COLOURED GROUP) BY RACE, 1947

	European	Coloured	African
Common Assault	3,846	5,136	30,107
Aggravated Assault	326	2,518	13,728
Cruelty to and Neglect of Children	539	1,074	—
Breach of the Peace	1,142	2,021	8,510
Riotous Behaviour	—	2,981	2,609
Common Theft	2,171	6,571	31,066
Housebreaking	585	2,366	7,371
Robbery with Violence	—	647	—
Livestock Theft	—	1,153	7,176
Dagga Laws	—	1,912	7,559
Gambling Laws	—	1,375	5,420
Drunkenness	12,192	33,138	34,243
Master and Servant Laws	—	1,727	16,784
Total Convictions for Serious Crimes	2,977	6,355	31,077
Total Convictions for Ser. Cr. per 10,000 pop.	12.3	67.2	39.1
Total Convictions for All Crimes	115,981	97,460	643,817
Total Convictions for All Crime per 10,000 pop.	478	1,030	810

(Taken from Office of Census and Statistics Special Report No. 178,
Crime Statistics, 1947. *N.B.*—Where gaps are left, detailed figures were not
listed amongst 'Predominant Offences'.)

---

[6] The 1948 figures were supplied in advance by the Bureau of Census and Statistics. In both 1940 and 1948 the Coloured masculinity rates at birth were very low compared with the European rates. Dr. H. Sonnabend has pointed out that this confirms that masculinity is lower where conditions of life are less favourable, and comments on the expectation of life figures (see *supra* on chart) that where mortality is high it is found that the difference between the sexes is not great. (*Race Relations Handbook*, p. 25.)

[7] The advance Cape Town figures for detailed causes of death (headings 8–12) were kindly supplied by the Medical Officer of Health. Those in the Non-European column are here specifically for the Coloured group.

[8] These figures include deaths at Rietfontein and Springkells Sanatoria.

[9] In the case of East London, the number of deaths from diarrhœa and enteritis were available only for the group under two years of age. In all areas this group provided the great majority of fatalities from this cause.

APPENDIX I

SOME DEFINITIONS OF 'A COLOURED PERSON'

The Cape Coloured Commission reported upon the confusion in existing definitions of 'a Coloured person': 'It is not surprising that the difficulty of distinguishing between "Coloured" and "European" should have given rise to litigation. In one case (Swart *versus* Pretoria Town Council, Transvaal Supreme Court, 1905) where the words to be interpreted were "white British subject", it was assumed that an admixture of Coloured blood was inconsistent with a claim to be considered "white" or of "European descent". It is obvious, however, that difficulties are bound to arise when the admixture of Coloured blood has taken place in the more distant past. In another case (Moller *versus* Keimoes School Committee and Another, Appellate Division, 1911) the emphasis is changed, and while it is stated that "children of European extraction" means children of purely European extraction, judgment is given to the effect that, "when once it is established that one of a man's nearer ancestors, whether male or female, was black like a Negro or yellow like a Bushman or Hottentot or Chinaman, he is regarded as being of other than European descent". In a further case (*Ex Parte* Kinnear, 1909) judgment was to the effect that 'this slight strain of Coloured blood (*sc.* 1/16) does not justify the classification of the applicant (*sc.* for being classified as a European in the voters' list) under "Mixed or other Coloured races", and that effect should be given to the greatly preponderating European blood.' (C. p. 8.)

The Pensions Act (No. 22 of 1928 as amended by Act No. 34 of 1931) gives the following definition: 'A Coloured person means any person who is neither white nor (a) a Turk or member of a race or tribe whose national ethnical home is Asia, nor (b) a member of an aboriginal race or tribe of Africa; nor (c) a Hottentot, Bushman or Koranna; nor (d) a person who is residing in a native location as defined in Section 19 of the Natives Taxation and Development Act, 1925 (Act No. 4 of 1925) under the same conditions as a native; nor (e) an American negro—and includes a member of the race or class commonly called Cape Malays and of the race or class commonly called Griqua.' (This definition is followed in the Disability Act of 1946— S.P.)

'In view of the borderline cases of different kinds, the term "Cape Coloured" as ordinarily used is not one with a strictly defined meaning, and this, as has been shown, also holds true of the term "Coloured". Official custom tends to limit the latter term to persons of colour other than Natives or Asiatics notwithstanding other usages to which reference has already been made. Thus Section 175 of the Liquor Act of 1928 defines a Coloured person as being a person who is neither a European, nor an Asiatic, nor a Native, but includes the class or race commonly known as the Cape Malay. A Coloured person, according to the Native Urban Areas Act, No. 21 of 1923, as amended, means any person of mixed European and Native descent, and includes any person belonging to the class known as the Cape Malay. Attempts at definition are largely in terms of exclusion, and in so far agree with the practice already referred to and followed, e.g., in census reports, which distinguish Europeans and non-Europeans, and among the latter, Natives, Asiatics, and "Mixed or other Coloured", who may, for practical purposes, be taken as being practically identical, numerically, with "Cape Coloured".' (C. p. 9.)

Three members of the Cape Coloured Commission (Drs. Wilcocks, de Villiers and Malan) attempted to set up a positive 'type definition' of a Cape Coloured person, which the other three members (Dr. Abdurahman and Messrs. Buchanan and Fowler) were unable to accept. (C. p. 10, paras. 13–15.) It ran as follows :

'A person living in the Union of South Africa, who does not belong to one of its aboriginal races, but in whom the presence of Coloured blood (especially due to descent from non-Europeans brought to the Cape in the seventeenth and eighteenth centuries or from aboriginal Hottentot stock, and with or without an admixture of white or Bantu blood), can be established with at least reasonable certainty (a) from a knowledge of the genealogy of the person during the last three or four generations; or/and (b) by ordinary direct recognition of characteristic physical features (such as colour of skin, nature of hair, and facial or bodily form), by an observer familiar with these characteristics.'

The present Nationalist Government, in applying its intensified *apartheid* policy, is attempting to set up a permanent classification of the major ethnic groups (White, Native, Asiatic, Malay and Coloured), based on the 1951 Census and perpetuated for all time to come in the projected Population Register. In the Population Registration Act (No. 30 of 1950), a 'white person' (note the substitution of 'white' for 'European' in the English version, which is increasingly evident in present-day South African usage) is defined as 'a person who in appearance obviously is, or who is generally accepted as, a white person', but not 'a person who, although in appearance obviously a white person, is generally accepted as a coloured person'. A 'native' is 'a person who in fact is or is generally accepted as a member of any aboriginal race or tribe of Africa' (and thus includes Bushman, Hottentot, Koranna and Namaqua). A 'coloured person' is defined as a person who is not a white person or a native, this definition again being based on the principle of exclusion.

The definition of groups in section 2 (1) of the Group Areas Act (No. 41 of 1950) follows this formula, but is enlarged to include in the 'native' and 'coloured' groups respectively 'any woman, to whichever race, tribe or class she may belong, between whom and a person who is . . . a member of a native (coloured) group, there exists a marriage or who cohabits with such a person.' It is not stated whether the woman could be reincluded in her former ethnic group in the event of divorce, separation or her husband's death. In the future it is not intended that such ambiguities should arise, between white and Coloured at least, as the Mixed Marriages Act of 1949 prohibits such unions. The operation of genetic selection will, however, after a generation or so, probably produce other anomalies in the shape of dark-skinned, fuzzy-haired individuals within the dominant 'white' group, and light-skinned, grey-eyed offspring in the 'coloured' group. The definition of a 'coloured' group given in this Act and the Population Registration Act includes Asiatics in the coloured group, unless these are specifically excepted and defined by the Governor-General for the purposes of either Act.

The Separate Representation of Voters Act (No. 46 of 1951), which places Coloured and Indian voters in the Cape on a separate roll, follows the definition of 'a white person' given in the Population Registration Act, but for 'a coloured person' substitutes the old Cape usage 'a non-European', defined for the purposes of this Act as 'a person who is not a white person and not a native for the purposes of the Representation of Natives Act, 1936.'

The primary aim of definitions has usually been to distinguish between white and Coloured persons, but similar ambiguities and difficulties have arisen in distinguishing between Coloured persons and Africans. Under the Native Taxation and Development Act (No. 41 of 1925), 'Native' means any member of an aboriginal race or tribe of Africa, but does not include a person of any degree of European descent, unless he is resident in a Native location. On the other hand, the Representation of Natives Act (No. 12 of 1936) enlarged the definition of a Native so as to include persons previously regarded as Coloured persons. This Act included in such definition any person, one of whose grandparents was a member of any aboriginal race or tribe of Africa, unless his parents were married according to European standards (as opposed to Native law and custom), or unless both (*a*) he is by general acceptance and repute a non-Native, and (*b*) his parents are or were by general acceptance non-Natives; also any person, not being a Native who (i) is desirous of being regarded as a Native for the purposes of the Act; or (ii) is by general acceptance and repute a Native; or (iii) follows in his ordinary or daily mode of life the habits of a Native; or (iv) uses one or other Native language as his customary and natural mode of expression; or (v) associates generally with Natives under Native conditions.

In this connection see the cases of Rex *v.* Willett (19 S.C. 168), Anderson *v.* Green (N.P.D., 1932, 241), Rex *v.* Parrott (16 S.C. 452), Witwatersrand S.C. Division case of Jacob Lesabeer Tsatsinyane (reported in *Cape Times* of 7th December, 1950).

APPENDIX J

THE CAPE PROVINCE COMMON ROLL ELECTORATE (ALL RACES), 1905–51*

Date	European Voters	Non-European Voters			Total Voters	Non-European Voters as Percentage of Total
		African	Coloured	Total		
1905	119,906	8,190	14,836	23,034	142,940	16.1
1909	121,336	6,637	14,394	21,031	142,367	14.8
						(1)
1921	156,501	14,282	26,790	41,072	197,573	20.8
1927	173,291	16,481	26,091	42,572	215,863	19.7
1929	167,184	15,780	25,618	41,398	208,582	19.8
						(2)
1931	352,658	12,271	26,378	38,649	391,307	9.9
						(3)
1933	369,182	10,776	25,005	35,781	404,963	8.8
1935	382,103	10,628	24,793	35,421	417,524	8.5
						(4)
1937	396,237	—	26,700	26,700	422,937	6.3
1939	411,005	—	29,839	29,839	440,844	6.8
1945	493,910	—	54,134	54,134	548,044	9.9
						(5)
Dec.31 1947	497,690	—	39,110	39,110	536,800	7.3
May26 1948	509,525	—	46,051	46,051	555,576	8.3
						(6)
Dec.31 1948	515,041	—	47,329	47,329	562,370	8.4
June30 1949	526,232	—	47,822	47,822	574,054	8.3
Dec.31 1950	514,883	—	47,098	47,098	561,981	8.4
						(7)
Sept. 1951	516,808	—	46,870	46,870	563,878	8.3

* Taken from Thompson, p. 55, with the exception of the final set of figures. N.B.—The 'Coloured' vote here includes the Cape 'Asiatic' voters, who would, however, constitute a very small percentage of the total number.

1. After Union the Coloured vote decreased in importance by the increase in the total electorate. (Union electorate not shown here.)

2. Women's Enfranchisement Act.

3. Cape European male franchise became universal. Introduction of right to challenge Coloured voters' qualifications.

4. African voters removed from common roll.

5. Introduction of compulsory registration for Europeans. New voters' list with compulsory registration and automatic transfer for Europeans only.

6. Tightening of Coloured registration procedure. This measure did not, however, have the desired effect.

7. Passing of Separate Representation of Voters Act; this seems to have had a somewhat discouraging effect upon Coloured registrations already.

APPENDIX K

Rank	Pre-1923†	1923†	1937	1946	Authorised Establishment 31.12.49
	£	£	£	£	
Constable					
European	173–318	150–282	150–335	200–400	9,050
Indian & Coloured	64–94	64–88	72–108	120–240	205/602
African	50–75	48–66	60–84	84–132	5,737
2nd Class Sergeant					
European	294–342	260–305	280–355	360–450	2,268
Indian & Coloured	100–112.	100–112	112–124	210–270	21/55
African	80–90	78–90	88–103	132–150	520
1st Class Sergeant					
European	337–389	300–350	320–395	450–500	915
Indian & Coloured	118–130	118–130	130–148	240–300	4/16
African	95–105	95–105	110–125	150–186	177
Head Constable					
European	379–441	340–400	365–505	500–600	363

APPENDIX L

1. *Murder*

Year	E.	C.	A.
1926	33.3	29.6	19.4
1927	5.3	33.3	23.2
1928	22.7	22.2	18.6
1929	Nil	15.6	16.1
1930	Nil	9.1	17.4
1931	19.1	30.4	21.8
1932	29.6	21.0	24.1
1933	Nil	17.4	24.2
1934	17.7	27.7	19.5
1935	25.0	26.1	22.8
1950	41.0	35.2	25.4

* Taken from *Race Relations Handbook*, p. 78, Table V. The figures are exclusive of non-pensionable allowances.

† The altered scales were applied to Europeans in 1923, but to Non-European police officers only in 1924.

‡ Percentages worked out for figures taken from the Union Crime Statistics for the period. Annual publication of crime statistics ceased after 1938, and has not so far been resumed. An abridged Special Report, No. 148 (roneoed), was issued for

2. *Attempted Murder*

Year	E.	C.	A.
1926	33.3	62.5	58.8
1927	27.8	35.7	62.5
1928	33.3	90.0	54.3
1929	50.0	72.1	60.4
1930	27.3	60.0	61.2
1931	46.4	55.0	53.3
1932	30.0	73.3	57.3
1933	55.5	50.0	55.3
1934	31.8	90.0	49.7
1935	29.0	64.7	56.4
1950	30.2	41.7	52.6

3. *Culpable Homicide*

Year	E.	C.	A.
1926	35.8	64.0	72.9
1927	29.4	72.0	61.9
1928	30.0	71.0	72.9
1929	31.8	66.6	78.8
1930	29.8	75.9	73.3
1931	36.9	62.1	75.1
1932	42.9	70.6	66.9
1933	45.9	75.0	72.7
1934	42.8	74.6	71.3
1935	42.2	75.4	75.9
1950	51.8	89.9	75.4

4. *Forgery*

Year	E.	C.	A.
1926	77.6	88.8	89.7
1927	81.5	88.1	87.1
1928	81.5	84.6	85.6
1929	81.8	95.0	85.4
1930	75.5	82.9	91.4
1931	81.8	80.3	87.8
1932	79.5	89.4	90.5
1933	74.2	86.4	88.3
1934	80.8	92.0	88.4
1935	73.1	89.4	89.3
1950	79.0	85.8	83.7

the year 1940, and a printed Special Report (No. 178) for 1947; these reports do not, however, contain such detailed statistics, the numbers of prosecutions are omitted and no figures are given under 'Fraud and False Pretences', while there is a single category for 'Housebreaking, over £20'.

The statistics given in the Annual Reports of the Commissioner of the South African Police are unsatisfactory for this particular purpose, as they either omit the race of those prosecuted, or simply distinguish between Europeans and Non-Europeans. The 1950 figures given separately at the end were kindly provided by the Bureau of Census and Statistics. It would be advisable to obtain similar figures for a number of successive recent years before concluding that trends in the earlier period have remained constant or altered.

5. *Fraud and False Pretences*

Year	E.	C.	A.
1926	65.9	84.0	71.5
1927	62.1	87.5	76.1
1928	64.1	86.7	74.3
1929	61.6	76.6	76.3
1930	66.0	80.1	73.3
1931	65.5	78.4	75.0
1932	65.8	84.4	76.0
1933	65.0	83.2	71.6
1934	64.6	86.3	77.7
1935	58.7	80.2	80.3
1950	61.8	85.0	69.6

6. *Housebreaking by Day*

Year	E.	C.	A.
1926	82.1	86.2	80.1
1927	75.8	88.0	77.8
1928	81.3	86.0	79.4
1929	76.0	82.7	78.5
1930	80.9	86.2	79.7
1931	74.4	87.3	81.5
1932	76.0	85.3	80.1
1933	74.3	87.1	81.6
1934	80.9	87.3	79.7
1935	76.8	86.2	81.4

7. *Housebreaking by Night*

Year	E.	C.	A.
1926	70.9	82.4	76.9
1927	76.2	79.9	78.0
1928	73.9	84.7	74.3
1929	79.7	79.7	74.4
1930	79.6	80.4	75.1
1931	81.2	80.0	74.7
1932	80.4	81.8	79.7
1933	81.8	81.6	77.7
1934	81.3	81.1	78.3
1935	79.6	79.9	79.0
1950*	72.6	81.6	71.9

N.B.—E.= Europeans, A.= Africans, C.= Coloured, exclusive of Asiatic, for which group no figures are given in these tables.

* Since the new classification of serious crime in 1948, all housebreaking figures are given together.

APPENDIX M

SOME COMPARATIVE SENTENCES

For raping a married European woman at Wellington (Cape), a Coloured brick-layer, John Pretorius (26), of Ceres, was sentenced in the Paarl Circuit Court yesterday to fifteen years' hard labour, the case being heard by Mr. Justice Ogilvie Thompson and two assessors. (From *Cape Argus*, 1st April, 1949.)

'Mr. Justice Herbstein at the Criminal Sessions to-day sentenced Hendrik Johannes Swiggelaar (20), a former constable, to two years' hard labour for raping a young Coloured woman in Assurance Lane, Cape Town, on the night of 25th February. The Crown evidence was that Swiggelaar, who was in uniform, entered a Non-European house in Buitengracht Street on the pretext of looking for a missing person. After searching the house he left, but returned about 2 a.m. and said the woman had to accompany him to the police station. He refused to allow a male member of the household to accompany them. On the way to the police station he was alleged to have assaulted her.' (*Cape Times*, 13th August, 1949.)

A Coloured man, Silert Rickert, and a Native, Bobbie Setsami, were sentenced to death by Mr. Justice E. M. de Beer in the Circuit Court at Ficksburg (O.F.S.) yesterday for raping a European spinster, a retired schoolteacher, at her home on 28th August last. The victim stated that she was unable to identify either of her attackers, but the accused were arrested six weeks later, after one of the most intensive police man-hunts in the history of the Free State. (From *Cape Argus*, early 1949.)

'At the Criminal Sessions, Cape Town, yesterday Willie Williams (30), Coloured, was sentenced to three years for assaulting and attempting to rape a European woman at Rosebank on 4th March.' (From *Cape Times*, 3rd April, 1949.)

For committing an indecent offence against a Coloured girl under 16 at Claremont on 8th February, James Philander (30), Coloured, was sentenced to one year. (From *Cape Times*, 3rd April, 1949.)

'Adam Meyers (41), a Coloured train attendant, was sentenced to three months' hard labour by Mr. H. B. Erlank at Caledon Square to-day for *crimen injuria*. Evidence was given that on a train travelling between Paarl and Wellington on 28th June Meyers entered a European woman's compartment, embraced her and kissed her. "This is a case which calls for cuts, only the law does not provide for them", said the magistrate.' (*Cape Times*, 12th July, 1949.)

'A non-European, Jacob Juries (23), was sentenced by Mr. Justice de Villiers in the Circuit Court here yesterday to nine months' hard labour and six cuts for raping a nine-year-old Coloured girl.' (*Cape Argus*, 24th September, 1949.)

'S. G. Allman (61), a European organist, of Hermanus (Cape), was found guilty by Mr. H. P. van Niekerk in the Magistrate's Court of committing immoral and indecent acts at Hawston, on Friday, with two Coloured girls, aged two and seven. Allman was sentenced to one month's hard labour suspended for a year.' (*Cape Argus*, 5th April, 1949.)

'Found guilty at the Criminal Sessions, Cape Town, yesterday, of culpable homicide, Christoffel Jacobus Etsebeth (25), a European farm foreman,

Retreat, was fined £25 or three months. It was alleged that on 28th July, on a farm near Steenberg, Etsebeth, who had been sworn in as a special warder to watch six prisoners who were pruning vines, hit and kicked one of them, Jacob Maclear (28), a Coloured man, rupturing his spleen. Maclear died in Somerset Hospital the following day after an operation. Evidence was given that on the day in question Maclear carried out his work in a careless and destructive manner. He was reprimanded and adopted an insolent and defiant attitude not only to Etsebeth but also to another warder. Mr. Justice de Villiers, who sat with the two assessors, described the case as a most unfortunate one. When Maclear became truculent Etsebeth lost his temper and hit him, injuring him more seriously than he intended.' (*Cape Argus*, 12th April, 1949.)

Jacob Coetzee (18), Coloured, was sentenced by Mr. Justice de Villiers, the Judge-President, at the Criminal Sessions in Cape Town, to five years' hard labour and eight cuts for fatally stabbing a European. Coetzee was found guilty of culpable homicide. He had 23 per cent of alcohol in his brain at the time. The judge told Coetzee: ' What you did was a dreadful thing. You were given no provocation. You had no business to carry a knife. You are lucky that you were not found guilty of murder with extenuating circumstances on the grounds of your youth, but you killed an elderly *white* (author's italics) person without any reason and you have to suffer for it.' (*Cape Argus*, 7th April, 1949.)

'A Bonnievale cartage contractor, Johannes Swanepoel, who, it was alleged, assaulted a Coloured man by pulling him off a cart, kicking and *sjambok*-ing him and later throwing him into a fire (the man subsequently died), was fined £20 or two months' imprisonment. He was allowed to pay the fine in monthly instalments of £5.' (Quoted by *Race Relations News* of July 1948, p. 75.)

Armien Hendricks (25), Coloured, was sentenced by Mr. I. Dekenah to two months and four cuts for robbing Johan von Sohen, European, of a packet of cigarettes. (*Cape Times*, 19th August, 1949.)

'Five young Europeans who beat up a Coloured man outside his home in Sydenham (P.E.) were convicted in the Magistrate's Court this week . . . Martens was fined £5 and the others £3.' (*Sunday Times*, 8th October, 1950.)

'In the Circuit Court (at Mossel Bay) . . . a Coloured man, Moos Matthee, was sentenced to ten years and twelve cuts with a cane for assault with intent to commit rape and robbery. He had attacked a young European woman on the George road a mile from the town . . . Sarah Julies, an 18-year-old Coloured woman, was sentenced to two years for the murder of her infant child . . . Koos September, a Coloured man of Riversdale, was sentenced to two years for the theft of £1 15s. . . .' (*Cape Times*, 6th March, 1951.)

Before Mr. Justice Steyn and a jury a European carpenter (Oswald Sauerman, aged 20) was acquitted at the Criminal Sessions of assault with attempt to commit murder. He was said to have shot Joseph Skippers, a 12-year-old Coloured boy, with a .22 revolver. Sauerman said a group of Coloured boys had been tormenting his younger brother, so he shot up the road to scare them and hit Skippers, who was returning home from a shop. (*Torch*, 17th October, 1950, p. 3.)

APPENDIX N

PERCENTAGE OF EACH RACE TO TOTAL EMPLOYED FOR (a) PRIVATE
INDUSTRY AND (b) ALL INDUSTRY INCLUDING GOVERNMENT ESTABLISHMENTS
IN THE WESTERN CAPE

Year	European		Coloured		Indian		African	
	a	b	a	b	a	b	a	b
1919–20*	36	36	64	64	64	64	64	64
1924–5	35	49†	50	40†	1	—	14	11†
1929–30	38	—	46	—	1	—	15	—
1934–5	44	48	44	41	—	—	12	11
1939–40	39	44	45	42	—	—	16	14
1944–5‡	29	33	48	46	—	—	23	21

(Taken from Union Industrial Censuses.)

* The 1919–20 figures show only totals for all establishments, and class all Non-Europeans together.

† In the 1924–5 figures (b) is for government establishments only. No figures are available for other than private establishments in 1929–30. It has therefore not been possible to establish full continuity over the earlier period.

‡ The 1945–6 figures (which are the latest available) show no change in these ratios.

APPENDIX O

NUMBER OF APPRENTICES AT CAPE TOWN TECHNICAL COLLEGE (BY RACE)

Trade*		1926†	1927	1928	1946‡	1949§
Engineer-ing‖	E	293	390	559	2,596	1,158 approx.
	C	3	10	15	25	25
Printing	E	84	92	103	204	200
	C	3	10	12	1	4
Building	E	214	282	404	575	470
	C	18	56	72	86	228
Furniture	E	143	235	215	not given	50
	C	207	231	295		83
Total	E	734	999	1,281	3,375	1,878
	C	231	307	394	112	340

E = European.
C = Coloured.

* Although officially speaking all apprentices should go through the Technical College, in practice some trades give training at the place of work, owing to lack of lecturers or low enrolments at the College (e.g., baking and confectionery). Thus these figures do not represent the full number of apprentices for the year. Full figures were unobtainable, as the normal source of such figures, the local Apprenticeship Committee, does not note down the apprentice's ethnic affiliation, this being expressly forbidden by the amended Act (No. 37) of 1944, Clause 5 (2) (*b*).

† Taken from Professor Leslie's article 'The Coloured Labour and Trades Unionism in Cape Town'. *J. Ec. Soc. S.A.*, Vol. III, Part II, No. 6, pp. 53–4 (1927).

‡ Taken from the chapter on Labour by Dr. Sheila van der Horst in *Race Relations Handbook*, p. 151. Her figures give the total attendance of students, which accounts for the somewhat higher numbers of Europeans. The Coloured figures are, however, substantially the same, as few Coloured students enrol for the trade courses unless they are already apprenticed, according to an official of the College.

§ Obtained by courtesy of the Technical College.

‖ In addition a certain number of Coloured engineering apprentices are trained at Simonstown Dockyard. The respective figures for 1946 and 1949 were 26 and 23. No Europeans are trained there.

APPENDIX P

FARM WAGES (PER ANNUM)

Type of Farming	Area	Year	Cash	Rations	Graz'g	Land	Other	Total
			£	£	£	£	£	£
Wheat	Caledon— ⎫	1938–39	27.0	23.0	—	—	(2.5)*	52.5
Wheat	Bredasdorp ⎬	1949–50	49.2	52.6	—	—	6.5	108.3
Wheat	Swellendam— ⎭ Riversdale	1938–39	20.9	22.5	—	—	—	43.4
Wheat	Malmesbury— ⎱	1938–39	16.9	26.0	—	—	(3.0)*	45.9
	Piquetberg ⎰	1949–50	28.1	50.8	—	—	6.5	85.4
Wheat	Malmesbury (Coastal)	1938–39	14.4	21.5	—	—	—	35.9
Mixed	N.-E. Orange Free State	1937–38	5.0	5.3	4.8	0.9	—	16.0
Citrus	Gamtoos	1938–39	12.0	6.0	—	—	—	18.0
Citrus	Fort Beaufort	1938–39	8.4	3.6	6.0	—	—	18.0
Citrus	Fish River	1938–39	8.4	4.8	—	—	—	13.2
Fresh Milk	Cape Town (peri-urban)	1943–44	79.37	9.83	—	—	1.02	90.22
Cattle Cream	N.-W. Cape	1944–45	11.35	10.69	0.4	0.0	1.8	24.25
Dairying Cheese ⎱	E. Griqualand	1944–45	10.91	11.56	0.71	1.05	0.17	23.4
Milk ⎰	Oudtshoorn and Cookhouse	1943–44	12.55	9.46	0.09	0.45	0.71	23.26
Cream	E. Province	1943–44	7.19	10.27	1.46	1.07	1.86	20.85
Poultry	Cape Western Province	1944–45	63.20	0.49	—	—	1.07	64.76

'The wide variations in amounts and form of wages are evident from the table. It will be seen that wages are highest near Cape Town and Johannesburg, and that wages in the Western Cape Province (on wheat and dairy farms) are considerably higher than in most other parts of the country, where cash wages of 10s. per month for an adult labourer are still frequent. The rations on farms vary considerably. Mealie meal (maize meal), usually 100 lb. (half a bag) per adult labourer per month, is the staple ration. Single men may be supplied with cooked mealie meal in place of the dry ration. Milk (usually skimmed milk) and meat may be supplied, but frequently these do not form part of the regular ration. Where meat is supplied it is seldom more often than weekly, and frequently it is only supplied intermittently. On farms in some areas a weekly ration of tobacco is given. Old clothes are also frequently given from time to time but do not form part of the regular ration. In some areas where improved transport has provided farmers with more outlets for their products, for example, fresh milk and cream, less milk may be supplied than previously. In the Western Province, where rations are supplied to Coloured labourers, these are usually more varied than those supplied to Africans.' (These figures and text are taken from *Race Relations Handbook*, pp. 125–6, with 1949–50 figures for the Caledon-Bredasdorp and Malmesbury-Piquetberg districts added from statistics kindly supplied by the Division of Economics and Markets.) No other later detailed wages are available; the average monthly cash wage paid out to 102,715 Non-European farm labourers in August 1947 was, however, just under £2 (*Year Book*, No. 24, p. 849).

---

* No figures are available in respect of the item 'Other' for the years 1938–9, but arbitrary estimates are given for these years.

APPENDIX Q

PERCENTAGE DISTRIBUTION OF COLOURED AND EUROPEAN MALE ADULTS
BETWEEN OCCUPATIONAL GROUPS, CAPE TOWN, 1938–9*

Occupational Group	Coloured	European
Professional	0 † ⎤	8 ⎤
Business	4 ⎬ 5	20 ⎬ 47
Clerical	1 ⎦	19 ⎦
Supervisory Clerical	1 ⎤	5 ⎤
Skilled Manual	12 ⎦ 13	17 ⎦ 22
Semi-Skilled Manual	26 ⎤	16 ⎤
Unskilled Manual	42 ⎦ 68	5 ⎦ 21
Non-Earners	8	10
Unemployed	6	1
	100	100

APPENDIX R

CHRISTIAN NATIONAL EDUCATION

Christian National Education is the educational policy put forward by the F.A.K. (*Federasie van Afrikaanse Kultuurvereniginge* or Federation of Afrikaans Cultural Associations), an organisation which has the backing of many important members of the Nationalist Party and present Government and whose major aims are the furthering of 'Afrikaner culture' in all its aspects. A recent pamphlet (*Christelik—Nasionale Onderwysbeleid*, published in Johannesburg in 1948) gives the major aims of this educational policy, which is to be 'a guiding principle in our cultural struggle', as follows: there is to be no truck with a mixture of languages, of cultures, or religions or of races (this refers not only to Non-Europeans but to English-speaking South Africans); education is to be 'Christian', i.e., 'based on Holy Scripture and expressed in the articles of Faith of our three Afrikaans Churches', and 'National', i.e., imbued with 'love for everything that is our own', with special reference to 'our country, our language, our history and our culture'; the schools envisaged are to be state schools.

* Taken from Official Report of the Social Survey Conference, Cape Town, 1941, p. 34. Unfortunately no later figures are available.

† The numbers of Coloured professional persons were too small to be shown at all in a percentage presentation of this type.

'Christian Education' is to be 'the key-subject' of the schools, and 'every subject must be taught in the light of the word of God, namely on the basis of the applicable principles of Scripture' (where this would lead historical and scientific inquiry provides a fertile field for conjecture); in civics, 'every schoolmaster must be moulded into a Christian and national citizen of our country'; in geography, 'every people and nation is attached to its own native soil, allotted to it by the Creator' (the South African Teachers' Association, a European body, comments that it 'can interpret the above quotation only as a desire to veil the facts of conquest with Divine sanction'); history 'must be taught in the light of God's revelation and must be viewed as the fulfilment of God's decreed plan for the world and the human race'; 'God . . . willed separate nations and peoples, and he gave to each separate nation and people its special vocation, task and gifts . . .'; Home, Church and School are the three moulding forces that should share responsibility for the education of the child; the Church 'must exercise supervision over the spirit and trend of education . . . must exercise disciplinary measures when the need arises, with reference to the doctrinal opinions and lives of the teachers as members of the Church'; the State's major educational function is apparently to 'assume the main share in defraying expenditure on schools.'

In the Universities the professors and lecturers must be convinced Christian and National scientists, and there must be no attempt to neutralise 'the fundamental opposites', such as man and animal, authority and freedom, the individual and society. To quote the S.A.T.A. again: 'The Association objects to the fundamentalist attitude seemingly expressed (in this paragraph) . . . it can but infer, for instance, that in the field of Biology, modern scientific teaching since Darwin would be banned in South African universities.'

Finally we have two short sections on Coloured and African Education respectively—(Articles XIV and XV). In keeping with the general principle of 'cultural *apartheid*', they are dealt with separately. The article on Coloured education contains several of the principles which we have already encountered in our historical outline. Coloured education must be regarded as part of the Afrikaner's vocation to Christianise the Non-European races; it must be based on 'Christian and National' principles, and thus make the Coloured man proof against 'his own heathen ideology and all sorts of foreign ideologies' (e.g., Communism); the Coloured child can be made race-conscious, 'if the principle of *apartheid* is strictly applied in teaching just as it is in his church life'; and the financing of Coloured education must be placed on such a basis that it is not provided at the cost of European education (this presumably means that the Coloured people should pay for their own education proportionately to the amount of taxes paid by them as a group).

(The English translation throughout is taken from *A Critical Commentary by the South African Teachers' Association, Cape Province, on Christian National Education,* issued in 1949 in Cape Town.)

APPENDIX S

NUMBER AND TYPE OF SCHOOLS, NUMBER OF TEACHERS, AND NUMBER OF ENROLMENTS IN THE CAPE PROVINCE, 1949[1]

Type of School	No. of Schools			No. of Teachers			No. of Average Enrolments		
	E.	C.	A.	E.	C.	A.	E.	C.	A.
Training	9	9	14	93	67[2]	121[3]	933	905	2,490
High	179	11	14	2 677	138[4]	141[5]	55,653	3,150	4,269
Agricultural	3	—	—	24	—	—	239	—	—
Secondary	60	7	37	476	76[6]	125[7]	10,775	378[8]	4,084
Primary	1,033	70	—	3,719	651[9]	73	96,061	22,558[10]	—
Mission	—	980	2,173	—	4,071[11]	5,611[12]	—	143,739	254,451
Farm	19	17	—	17	14[13]	—	141	309	—
Part-time	—	25	7	—	(68)[14]	(15)	—	1,137	456
Special	8	6	2	11(2)	2(4)[15]	(1)[16]	168	194	32
Industrial	—	—	—	—	—	—	—	—	720
Total	1,311	1,125	2,265	7,133[16]	5,108[16]	6,087	163,972	174,541	266,502

[1] Compiled from Cape Education Statistics (last quarter 1949)
[2] 44 of these are European teachers.
[3] 80 of these are European teachers.
[4] 25 of these are European teachers and 1 is African.
[5] 38 of these are European teachers.
[6] 18 of these are European teachers and 1 is African.
[7] 18 of these are European teachers.
[8] 1507 in Secondary Depts.
[9] 13 of these are European teachers.
[10] 664 in Higher Primary Depts.
[11] 111 of these are European teachers and 25 are African.
[12] 50 of these are European teachers and 8 are Coloured.
[13] 1 of these is a European teacher.
[14] The bracketed figures are the number of part-time teachers.
[15] All are European.
[16] These totals include 154 itinerant European teachers for European schools and 17 itinerant teachers for Coloured schools, of whom 4 are European, in addition to the part-time teachers shown in brackets.

APPENDIX T

THE EXPENDITURE ON EDUCATION AND THE COST PER PUPIL IN THE CAPE PROVINCE, 1937–49

Financial Year	Net Expenditure			Total	Net Cost per Enrolled Pupil		
	European	Coloured	African		European	Coloured	African
					£ s. d.	£ s. d.	£ s. d.
1937–8	2,857,283	541,842	373,614	3,772,739	18 6 4	5 0 5	1 18 11
1938–9	2,938,926	618,887	398,229	3,956,042	18 18 3	5 6 2	2 1 1
1939–40	2,995,183	656,371	399,487	4,051,041	19 2 5	5 7 8	2 0 6
1940–1	3,064,452	700,872	427,526	4,192,850	19 12 6	5 10 10	2 2 4
1941–2	3,119,097	752,363	473,227	4,334,687	20 2 10	5 16 5	2 6 0
1942–3	3,298,996	833,232	544,057	4,676,285	21 16 1	6 4 9	2 12 6
1943–4	3,451,565	942,285	657,903	5,051,753	22 10 9	7 4 2	3 1 11
1944–5	4,021,318	1,240,235	783,045	6,044,598	25 16 11	9 3 10	3 13 11
1945–6	4,556,062	1,639,582	862,490	7,058,134	29 3 1	10 10 10	3 12 1
1946–7	4,999,487	1,975,214	964,580	7,939,281	31 17 11	12 5 5	3 17 2
1947–8	5,366,389	2,195,571	1,422,976	8,984,936	33 16 7	13 3 2	5 9 10
1948–9	6,117,604	2,624,267	1,614,196	10,356,067	36 19 1	15 4 0	5 16 4

(Taken from C. Ed. R. 1947, p. 48, and C. Ed. R. 1949, p. 46, except for the figures of net expenditure for 1947–8 and 1948–9, which were kindly supplied by the Cape Educational Department. Over the period 1937 to end 1949, the average of enrolled pupils of different groups rose as follows: Europeans—155,988 to 163,972; Coloured—107,932 to 174,541; and Africans—191,913 to 266,502.)

APPENDIX U

MEDIAN AGE OF EUROPEAN, COLOURED AND NATIVE PUPILS IN EACH PRIMARY STANDARD ON 7TH JUNE, 1949

Standard	European	Coloured	Native
Sub-Standard A	6.70	7.78	8.81
Sub-Standard B	7.70	9.17	10.68
Standard I	8.71	10.28	11.87
Standard II	9.73	11.27	12.74
Standard III	10.74	12.25	13.68
Standard IV	11.76	13.04	14.53
Standard V	12.78	13.79	15.35
Standard VI	13.75	14.6	16.24

Taken from Cape Educational Report, 1949, p. 122, App. N.

APPENDIX V

COLOURED-EUROPEAN MARRIAGES AND PERCENTAGE INVOLVING COLOURED
MALES

*Annual number of marriages of Coloured males and females to
Europeans and percentage of these involving Coloured males, 1925–49.**

Year	Col. males to Eur. females	Col. females to Eur. males	Total	Percentage of Col. Male-Eur. Female marriages to total
1925	28	85	113	24.8
1926	15	66	81	18.5
1927	18	66	84	21.4
1928	12	76	88	13.6
1929	16	64	80	20.0
1930	15	60	75	20.0
1931	14	59	73	19.2
1932	7	63	70	10.0
1933	10	57	67	14.9
1934	13	47	60	21.7
1935	15	66	81	18.5
1936	16	44	60	26.7
1937	14	69	83	16.9
1938	23	61	84	27.4
1939	11	50	61	18.0
1940	16	83	99	17.6
1941	11	65	76	14.5
1942	7	100	107	6.5
1943	13	78	91	14.3
1944	14	72	86	19.4
1945	13	68	81	16.0
1946	14	52	66	21.21
1947	16	56	72	22.2
1948	13	62	75	17.3
1949	9	56	65	13.8

* The figures for 1925–46 are taken from C. S. Sofer, Table 10, p. 197. Those for
the subsequent three years, prior to the legal prohibition of such mixed marriages
in 1949, were supplied by the Union Bureau of Census and Statistics.

INDEX

A

Abdurahman, Dr. A., 159; 210, n. 29; 212, n. 46; 213, n. 52; 216, n. 69; 241, n. 24; 275, n. 138; 288, n.54; 303, n. 1; 312, nn. 88, 94; 319, n. 163; 329, n. 86; 336, n. 142; 362

Abdurahman, A. E., 123; 189; 319, n. 163

Abolition of Slave Trade, see also Slaves, 65; 201, n. 20

Abrahams, Peter, 257, n. 180; 271, n. 104

Acceptance (Behavioural response by Coloured people), 181–2; 329, nn. 83, 86, 87

Acculturation, 7–10; 146; 180; 193; 197, n. 12; 198, n. 25; 307, n. 38

Actors (Coloured and white), 127–8; 289, n. 9

Adamastor, 320, n. 4; 323, n. 37

Address, Modes of, 139–40; 243, n. 35; 258, n. 198

Adoption, 6; 315, n. 118

Adult education, see Education

Advocates, 55; 256, n. 174

African National Bond (A.N.B.), 47; 159–60; 212, n. 46

African National Congress (A.N.C.), 161

African People's Organisation (A.P.O.), 158–61; 210, n. 29; 213, n. 52; 241, n. 24; 288, n. 54; 303, n. 1; 310, n. 75; 312, n. 94; 314, n. 105

African Political Association, see African People's Association

Africans (see also 'Kaffir' and Bantu), (European attitudes to), 297, n. 97; 323, n. 37; 324, n. 41; (European stereotypes of), 177; 180; 291, n. 33; 327, n. 68; (gangs), 307, nn. 40, 48; (in churches), 135; 136; 293, n. 53; 295, nn. 72–3; (Boy Scouts), 296, n. 88; (Y.M.C.A.), 138; (Girl Guides), 138; (sport), 292, n. 40; 307, n. 49; (relations with Coloured group), 102; 182; 190–3; 203, n. 51; 212, n. 46; 227, n. 29; 286, n. 32; 303, n. 140; 310, n. 70; 311, nn. 86–7; 312, n. 88; 312, n. 91; 314, n. 101; 325, n. 48; 328, n. 73; 337, nn. 147–51; 338, nn. 152, 162; 361–3; (legal differen-

tiation), 50; 228, n. 36; 232, n. 82; 233, n. 90; 234, nn. 95, 101–2; 235, n. 103; 236, nn. 112, 115, 121; 238, nn. 150–1; (franchise), 33; 35; 208, n. 15; 209, n. 23; 223, n. 133; (labour force), 75; 82; 175; 241, nn. 22–4; 243, nn. 40, 45; 245, nn. 63, 72–4; 246, n. 79; 250, n. 109; 251, nn. 117–8; 260, n. 211; 311, n. 82; (infiltration into Cape Province), 66–7; 197, n. 10; 239, n. 9; 247, n. 83; 322, n. 27; (housing), 284, n. 6; 285, nn. 15–17, 23; (health and social welfare), 114–6; 278, nn. 27–33; 279, nn. 37, 39–40, 43; 280, nn. 49, 51, 53, 57, 58; 281, nn. 67–9, 72, 75; 282, n. 94; (in army), 220, n. 112; (economic discrimination), 259, n. 207; (taxes), 259, n. 201; (illiteracy), 262, n. 30; (education), 94; 98; 100; 102; 260, n. 4; 262, nn. 27–8; 264, n. 49; 267, n. 71; 274, n. 130; 374–6; (acculturation), 197, n. 12; (inadequate statistics), 199, n. 2; (geographical location), 199, n. 3; (film censorship for), 289, n. 10; (race preference tests), 334, n. 126; (alleged descent from Ham and Canaan), 293, n. 57; (trade unions), 79–81; 248, n. 94; (miscegenation), 20–1; 203, nn. 51–2, 55; 240, n. 17; 285, n. 15; 301, n. 124; 303, n. 140; 363; (in police), 227, nn. 26, 28, 29

Afrikaans Language, 200, n. 14; 313, n. 98; 317, n. 142; (as spoken by Cape Coloureds), 15; Appendix E; (preferred Coloured type in fiction), 180; (parity with English), 214, n. 55; (classificatory kinship terms), 303, n. 9; (usages when addressing or speaking of Non-Europeans), 139–40; 298, nn. 99–108; 299, nn. 110–11; (usages as employed by Rehoboth Bastards towards 'Natives'), 316, n. 131

Afrikaner Party (see also Havenga), 209, n. 23; 222, n. 128

Afrikaners (Afrikaans-speaking South Africans), see also Boers and Nationalists, 6; 19–20; 47; 51; 78; 130; 141; 174; 187; 198, n. 32; 200, n. 14; 207, n. 3; 274, n. 132; 284, n. 5; 299, n. 110; 300, n. 115; 303, n. 139;

378